HOW THEY MURDERED PRINCESS DIANA

The Shocking Truth

John Morgan

First published in Australia by Shining Bright Publishing

ISBN: 978-0-9923216-1-1

Cover: Princess Diana's ambulance stopped for five minutes just 500
yards short of the hospital entrance
The original source of the photographic material used is unknown
Artwork by Lana Morgan

John Morgan's Investigation Website:
www.princessdianadeaththeevidence.weebly.com

How They Murdered Princess Diana: The Shocking Truth

Is dedicated

To

Diana, Princess of Wales

And

Dodi Fayed

Killed in a mindless tragedy

The crash in the Alma Tunnel, Paris, at 12.23 a.m., 31 August 1997

And

To those few in their and Henri Paul's families

Who have had the courage to fight for the truth to come out

Who have been confronted with an unconscionable
travesty of justice

Known as the official investigations

That commenced in Paris immediately after the crash

That concluded at 4.33 p.m. on 7 April 2008 in London's
Royal Courts of Justice

The information in this book is based on around 5,000 pages of evidence and analysis in the *Diana Inquest* book series:

Part 1: Diana Inquest: **The Untold Story** (2009)

Covers pre-crash events in the Ritz Hotel, the final journey and what happened in the Alma Tunnel

Part 2: Diana Inquest: **How & Why Did Diana Die?** (2009)

Covers possible motives for assassination and post-crash medical treatment of Princess Diana – including deliberate mistreatment in the ambulance

Part 3: Diana Inquest: **The French Cover-Up** (2010)

Covers the fraudulent autopsies of the driver, Henri Paul, and the misconduct of the French investigation into the crash

Part 4: Diana Inquest: **The British Cover-Up** (2011)

Covers the post-death treatment of Princess Diana – including the embalmings and autopsies carried out in both France and the UK and the post-crash cover-up by UK authorities, including the Queen

Part 5: Diana Inquest: **Who Killed Princess Diana?** (2012)

Covers the involvement of MI6 and senior British royals in the assassinations of Princess Diana and Dodi Fayed

Part 6: Diana Inquest: **Corruption at Scotland Yard** (2013)

Exposes one of the biggest cover-ups in Scotland Yard history – it uncovers police corruption on a scale that should shock most members of the British public

Diana Inquest: **The Documents the Jury Never Saw** (2010)

Reproduces hundreds of key documents from within the British Operation Paget investigation – all documents that the inquest jury were prevented from seeing

Paris-London Connection: The Assassination of Princess Diana (2012)

A short, easy-to-read, fast-moving synopsis of the complete story of the events, including the lead-up, the crash and the ensuing cover-up – based on the *Diana Inquest* series

Other Books by John Morgan

Cover-Up of a Royal Murder: Hundreds of Errors in the Paget Report (2007)

Alan Power Exposed: Hundreds of Errors in "The Princess Diana Conspiracy" (2013)

Flying Free: A Journey from Fundamentalism to Freedom (2005)

John Morgan's Investigation Website:
www.princessdianadeaththeevidence.weebly.com

Contents

CONTENTS

CONTENTS

CONTENTS

CONTENTS

Acknowledgements

During the eight years of research for the *Diana Inquest* series I received invaluable support from many individuals.

This book could not have been written without that series.

No acknowledgements could start with anyone other than my wife, Lana – she has been a huge rock of strength amidst the madness of constant writing and progressing illness.

Lana – who identifies herself as the devil's advocate – has contributed immensely as a regular sounding board for ideas and analysis and has provided invaluable input into concepts and opinion during the development of the series.

On top of that, Lana has acted as artistic director with the principal role of designing the cover for each volume. She has also assisted with editing, thoroughly reading and re-reading manuscripts prior to publication.

Without Lana's support the series could never have been produced.

Paul Sparks, UK-based journalist and film producer, has been a consistent practical support right from the earliest beginnings of the books. Paul has provided invaluable help in filling the inevitable geographical void that is created as a result of the books being written in Australia – thousands of kilometres away from where the key events occurred. Right through the seven years since I typed the first words of Part 1 he has been willing to assist with anything I have asked. The volumes would have been a lesser work without Paul's long-term support.

I also am indebted to a forensic investigator in London, who commenced assembling an extensive archive with case notes on the Paris crash and its aftermath, within a week of the tragedy occurring. This person has constantly maintained and updated their records over the ensuing 17 years and has kindly passed on research information from that archive whenever I have requested it. They wish to remain anonymous.

As well, it is I'm sure evident to any reader of these books that the hundreds of documents from within the MPS Paget investigation that were passed onto me a few years ago have been a huge help in completing a thorough investigation of the crash and the resulting cover-up. I am very grateful to the people in the UK who threw caution to the wind and courageously provided me with that invaluable information. Without those documents virtually none of Part 4 could have been written. So, although the documents the jury never saw have lengthened this investigative project, it has more importantly filled in critical gaps in the jigsaw that would otherwise have been impossible to fit.

I am also indebted to a journalist who attended the inquest on every sitting day for six months. This person provided invaluable notes on what took place inside the courtroom. When those notes – which included assessments of body language and tone of voice – were looked at in the context of the court transcripts and evidence, it was made easier to build up a picture of what was actually occurring at the inquest.

There are other people in the UK who have assisted in sometimes critical ways, but wish or need to remain anonymous. To those people, who know who they are, I am extremely thankful for their assistance and they can hopefully appreciate that they have contributed towards establishing the historical record of what occurred in certainly one of the most significant assassinations of our time.

Then there are more individuals – mostly living outside of the UK – who have assisted in various ways and I wish to gratefully acknowledge their support: Belinda Frost, Jayne Dean, Richard Lancaster, Emmanuelle Quignon, Monica Hudson, Margaret Deters, Jos Deters, Rex Morgan, Sue Hindle, Anne Pledger, Tina Jones, Jon Oakton and Patty Saffran.

In specific reference to the knowledge now available regarding the activities of MI6, I wish to acknowledge the uncompromising courage of the late Peter Wright[a], Richard Tomlinson, David Shayler and Annie Machon. They have all been prepared to go public to address important issues that would otherwise have remained officially buried and hidden from our collective understanding.

---

[a] Peter Wright died in Australia in 1995, aged 78.

Preface

On 31 August 1997 Princess Diana and her lover Dodi Fayed died after their Mercedes crashed in Paris' Alma Tunnel.

Immediately following the deaths the French authorities set up an investigation into the circumstances of the crash. That inquiry was completed in 1999, with the finding that the accident was caused by the driver of the couple's car, Henri Paul, who was drunk and speeding.

In 2004 London's Scotland Yard opened up a second investigation into the crash, Operation Paget. After three years Paget reached a similar conclusion to the French – the deaths were caused by the driver, who was influenced by drink and speeding.

Following the completion of Operation Paget the British coroner, Lord Justice Scott Baker, commenced the inquests into the deaths at the Royal Courts of Justice. After hearing six months of evidence the jury concluded quite differently to the two police investigations. Their verdict was "unlawful killing, grossly negligent driving of the following vehicles and of the Mercedes".

The following vehicles were unidentified.

Why was the jury's verdict so different to the findings of the French and British police investigations?

Why has there been no effort by the British authorities to identify the following vehicles since the 2008 conclusion of the inquest?

This book will reveal that this crash was not an accident.

It was instead a staged operation carried out by some of the world's leading intelligence agencies at the behest of their governments and Britain's royal family.

The assassination of Diana Princess of Wales is one of the most outstanding crimes of the 20th century – the immense amount of planning, the sheer audacity of the operation in the heart of Paris, the massive scope of the ensuing inter-governmental cover-up.

This book reveals the hard evidence that exposes the crime – it shows the who, why and how of the shocking murder of the most loved princess of our time.

It exposes those who ran the operation and also those who gave the order. It uncovers the motives for the operation.

HOW THEY MURDERED PRINCESS DIANA

It reveals that Princess Diana survived the crash, but was later murdered by personnel in the ambulance on the way to the hospital.

This book is an abridgement of the six volumes of the *Diana Inquest* series – listed earlier. That series is the most detailed forensic assessment of the 1997 crash and its aftermath yet written.

How They Murdered Princess Diana is the most complete account of the deaths of Princess Diana and Dodi Fayed yet published in a single volume.

Guide for Readers

How They Murdered Princess Diana has drawn heavily on the information
– 7,000 pages of transcripts and other evidence – that is on the official inquest
website.

In 2011 a decision was made at the Royal Courts of Justice to close down
the official inquest website – which had been at www.scottbaker-
inquests.gov.uk

The inquest website can currently[a] be found in the UK National Archives:
http://webarchive.nationalarchives.gov.uk/20080521144222/http://www.scott
baker-inquests.gov.uk/

It can also be accessed using Google search with the words: "Diana
inquest transcripts".[b]

All quotes throughout this book have been fully referenced, and I
encourage readers to look up the website[c] for the full transcript of any
particular piece of witness evidence they need to view in its complete context.

This book also uses material from the 2010 book *Diana Inquest: The
Documents the Jury Never Saw* – often simply referred to as *The Documents*
book. Generally the page number references from that book have been shown
in the footnotes or endnotes in this volume.

Page numbers referenced to *The Documents* book relate to the UK edition.
Readers who have the US edition of *The Documents* book will be able to
locate the same excerpts within a few pages of the UK edition page number.

---

[a] In August 2014.

[b] The removal of the inquest website appears to be an attempt to cover up what has
occurred by making it more difficult for members of the public to find the inquest
transcripts. In this respect, it is significant that the RCJ failed to provide a redirection
to the National Archives site – and despite repeated requests, still refuses to do so. It
is also worth noting that the inquest transcripts can't be found by using the National
Archives search engine. This was the situation through much of 2011 and right
through to August 2014, when this book was written.

For those who find themselves unable to locate the official inquest transcripts or wish
to register a protest with the RCJ or the National Archives the phone numbers are:
Royal Courts of Justice: +44 (0) 20 7947 6655; National Archives: +44 (0) 20 8876
3444.

[c] Now at the National Archives site – see address above.

For example, if the UK edition quote is from page 300, it will appear before page 310 in the US edition.

Extensive witness lists shown at the start of Part 1 have not been included in this book due to lack of space.

I have deliberately included verbatim inquest testimony in this book – it reveals the words of the witnesses themselves as they describe what they saw or heard.

The inquest website[a] contains a large number of significant items of evidence: photos, documents, letters and so on. It is important to note that none of this evidence is stored in numerical or subject order – the easiest way to locate these items is by scrolling down the evidence list looking for the specific reference number you are seeking. The reference numbers, which usually begin with the prefix code "INQ", will often be found in the footnotes or endnotes in this book.

In addition, the website has several interesting and useful videos that are available for viewing by the public. These also are scattered through the evidence list and are prefixed with "TJS" except for the latest additions made on 21 May 2008.

Throughout this book underlining of words or phrases has been used as a means of emphasising certain points, unless otherwise stated.

WFJ (in brackets) is used throughout to show items of evidence that were **withheld from the inquest jury.**

Those readers wanting to see more information, evidence and analysis can access the *Diana Inquest* series volumes that are listed near the front of this book.

Books within the series are referred to in this current volume by Part number – e.g. "Part 1" is used instead of the name *Diana Inquest: The Untold Story.*

Timelines of Events are included throughout this book – these are a comprehensive chronological record of what occurred in the years leading up to the crash, during the weekend in Paris, in the Ritz Hotel on the night and also during the years since the deaths.

Not all events in the timelines are covered in the text of this book, but they help the reader to understand the full context surrounding what occurred. More detail is in the six-volume *Diana Inquest* series.

Word usage:

"Autopsy" and "post-mortem" are synonymous – "autopsy" is generally used in France, whereas "post-mortem" is generally used in the UK

KP = Kensington Palace, Diana's home

---

[a] Now at the National Archives – see address above.

Sapeurs-Pompiers = Paris Fire Service

BAC = Blood Alcohol Concentration

"Cours la Reine", "Cours Albert 1er", "Avenue de New York" and "Voie Georges Pompidou" are all names for the same riverside expressway that runs into the Alma Tunnel. The parallel service road is also known as "Cours Albert 1er"

Fulham Mortuary = Hammersmith and Fulham Mortuary

Imperial College = Charing Cross Hospital[a]

MI6 = SIS = Secret Intelligence Service

MI5 = SS = Security Service

The Operation Paget Inquiry Report into the Allegation of Conspiracy to Murder Diana, Princess of Wales and Emad El-Din Mohamed Abdel Moneim Fayed = Paget Report

Currency:

Monetary values have been shown in British pound sterling (£) or French francs (FF).

The following approximate 1997 exchange rates apply:

£1 = FF10
£1 = $US2
£1 = €1.50

John Morgan's Investigation Website:

www.princessdianadeaththeevidence.weebly.com

---

[a] Imperial College operates 5 hospitals in the area of West London, of which Charing Cross is one. Throughout this case the terms "Imperial College" and "Charing Cross Hospital" have been used interchangeably.

HOW THEY MURDERED PRINCESS DIANA

The Lawyers & Representation

Name[a]	Status	Representing
Ian Burnett	QC[b]	The Inquest
Ian Croxford	QC	President, Ritz Hotel
Tom de la Mare		President, Ritz Hotel
Henrietta Hill		Mohamed Al Fayed
Nicholas Hilliard		The Inquest
Richard Horwell	QC	Commissioner of Police
Jonathon Hough		The Inquest
Lee Hughes		The Inquest
Jeremy Johnson		SIS (MI6) & Foreign & Commonwealth Office
Richard Keen	QC	Henri Paul's Parents
Edmund Lawson	QC	Commissioner of Police
Jamie Lowther-Pinkerton		Princes William & Harry
Alison MacDonald		Mohamed Al Fayed
Duncan MacLeod		Commissioner of Police
Lady Sarah McCorquodale		Spencer Family
Michael Mansfield	QC	Mohamed Al Fayed
Martin Smith[c]		The Inquest
Robin Tam	QC	SIS (MI6) & Foreign & Commonwealth Office
Robert Weekes		Henri Paul's Parents

[a] Alphabetic Order
[b] Queen's Counsel
[c] Solicitor to the inquest

The Organisations

Abbreviation	Name	Definition or Function
BCA	Bureau Central des Accidents	Central Accident Bureau – French police
BJL	Hygeco or Bernard J. Lane	French embalming company – Subsidiary of PFG
	Brigade Criminelle	Department of French police dealing with murders, kidnappings and terrorism
BSC	British Security Coordination	North American branch of MI6 during WWII
CIA	Central Intelligence Agency	US Foreign Intelligence Service
DGSE	Direction Générale de la Sécurité	French Foreign Intelligence Service – French equivalent of MI6
DST	Directorate de Surveillance Territories	French Domestic Intelligence Service – French equivalent of MI5
	Elysée	Offices of the French Government
	Étoile Limousines	Provided chauffeured Mercedes to the Ritz as required
FBI	Federal Bureau of Investigation	Criminal investigative agency of the US Justice Department
FCO	Foreign & Commonwealth Office	UK Ministry of Foreign Affairs
FRU	Force Research Unit	British Military Intelligence Unit
GCHQ	Government Communications Headquarters	UK intelligence agency handling communications
IML	L'Institut Médico-Legal de Paris	Paris Institute of Forensic Medicine

Abbreviation	Name	Definition or Function
	Judicial Police	Department of French police dealing with judicial matters under direction of magistrates
LGC	Laboratory of the Government Chemist	Conducts chemical and DNA testing for the British Government
MI5	Security Service	British Domestic Intelligence Service
MI6 or SIS	Secret Intelligence Service	British Foreign Intelligence Service
MPS	Metropolitan Police Service	British Police – New Scotland Yard
NSA	National Security Agency	US Intelligence Service – handles communications
OCG	Organised Crime Group	MPS section dealing with terrorism, assassinations and organised crime
PFG	Pompes Funebres Generale	French Funeral Directors – Parent company of BJL
RG	Renseignements Généraux	Intelligence Gathering Arm of French Police – Equivalent to British "Special Branch"
SAMU	Service d'Aide Médicale d'Urgence	French Emergency Ambulance Service
	Sapeurs-Pompiers	Paris Fire Service
SB	Special Branch	Intelligence Arm of MPS[aa]

[a] In March 2004 the British government outlined the close connection between Special Branch and the intelligence agencies, MI5 and MI6: "Special Branch exists primarily to acquire intelligence.... In particular, Special Branches assist the Security Service [MI5] in carrying out its statutory duties under the Security Service Act 1989 – namely the protection of national security.... Special Branch also supports the work of the Secret Intelligence Service (SIS) [MI6] in carrying out its statutory duties in support of national security....

"All intelligence about terrorism obtained by Special Branch is provided to the Security Service.... The Security Service sets the priorities for the gathering of counter terrorist and other national security intelligence by Special Branch....": Guidelines on Special Branch Work in the United Kingdom, Home Office, Communication Directorate, March 2004, pp8-9.

Abbreviation	Name	Definition or Function
SIS	See MI6	
SMUR[b]	Service Mobile d'Urgence et de Réanimation	French Emergency Ambulance Service
SOE	Special Operations Executive	Conducted sabotage and resistance during WWII[c]
TRL	Transport Research Laboratory	British Government agency concerned with road safety and accidents
WAG	The Way Ahead Group	Policy discussion group of the royal family – Inner circle of family members and key advisers

---

Special Branch was closely involved in the actions by authorities to suppress the evidence relating to the MI6 involvement in the 1996 plot to assassinate Muammar Gaddafi – see Part 5 Chapter 1.

[a] In October 2006 Special Branch was merged with the Anti-Terrorist Branch forming Counter-Terrorism Command. According to the MPS website – in June 2011 – there are three commands under "Specialist Operations" – Protection, Counter-Terrorism and Security. "Intelligence" is one of four "strands" in the Counter-Terrorism Command. Sources: Sean O'Neill, Special Branch Absorbed into Counter-Terror Unit, *The Times*, 3 October 2006; www.met.police.uk/so/index.htm

[b] SMUR and SAMU are effectively the same organisation.

[c] After WWII the SOE was fused into MI6, becoming its Special Operations Branch.

The Paparazzi

The following table lists the paparazzi in the vicinity of the Ritz Hotel when the Mercedes S280 carrying Diana and Dodi departed at 12.18 a.m. on 31 August 1997. It also shows:

- whether they were present at Le Bourget airport when the couple's plane landed in Paris the previous day
- whether they were sighted in the Place de la Concorde at the same time as the Mercedes, a few minutes prior to the crash
- whether and when they were arrested by the French police.

Person	Vehicle	Le Bourget?	Place de la Concorde?	Arrested
Serge Arnal	Black Fiat Uno	No	Yes	In tunnel
Nikola Arsov	White BMW R100 GS M/bike	No	No	In tunnel
Serge Benhamou	Green Honda Scooter	No	Yes	Sep 5
Stéphane Cardinale	White Citroen AX	No	No	No
Fabrice Chassery	Dark Grey Peugeot 205	Yes	No	Sep 5
Stéphane Darmon	Blue Honda 650 M/bike	Yes	Yes	In tunnel
Dominique Dieppois	White Renault Super 5	No	No	No
Alain Guizard	Grey/blue Peugeot 205	Yes	Yes	No
Pierre Hounsfield	Black VW Golf	No	No	No
Jacques Langevin	Grey VW Golf	No	No	In tunnel
Christian Martinez	With Arnal	No	Yes	In tunnel

HOW THEY MURDERED PRINCESS DIANA

Person	Vehicle	Le Bourget?	Place de la Concorde?	Arrested
David Odekerken	Mitsubishi Pajero	Yes	Yes	Sep 5
Colm Pierce	No vehicle	No	No	No
Romuald Rat	With Darmon	Yes	Yes	In tunnel
Pierre Suu	Red BMW 750 M/bike	No	No	No
Jerko Tomic	With Suu	No	No	No
Laslo Veres	Black Piaggio Scooter	No	No	In tunnel

Timeline of Events

---

[a] Approximate date.
[b] Approximate date.
[c] Given to Morton through James Colthurst.
[d] There is conflict over when this first meeting occurred, but this is the most likely date – this is addressed in Part 5, Meeting Diana section of Chapter 1C.

HOW THEY MURDERED PRINCESS DIANA

Nov 24	Queen declares 1992 as her "annus horribilis" at the City of London's Guildhall
Nov 25	Charles requests a formal separation at Kensington Palace. Diana agrees to it [6]
Nov 27	Announcement that Queen is prepared to start paying tax [a]
Dec 9	Prime Minister announces the separation in Parliament

1993

Aug 14	Holiday with Diana, Rosa, Lucia and Beatriz to Bali and Moyo Island, Indonesia – organised by Rosa
Aug 19	Diana returns to London – early and on her own
Aug 24	Diana leaves London with William, Harry and other friends to holiday in Florida and the Bahamas
Nov	Ken Wharfe resigns as Diana's bodyguard after six years of service
Dec	Diana requests the removal of her police protection

1994

	Electronics and security expert, Grahame Harding, conducts a sweep of Diana's Kensington Palace residence – he finds a signal indicating an electronic device
Oct 18	Diana meets with the police and expresses concerns that she is under surveillance

1995

Oct	Relationship between Princess Diana and Hasnat Khan commences
	Diana pens a ten page note which includes an allegation that her husband Charles is planning to target her in an orchestrated car crash. She hands the note to her butler, Paul Burrell, for safe-keeping
Oct 30	Meeting between Diana and her lawyer Victor Mishcon – Diana says she fears a staged car crash
Oct 31	Mishcon writes up a note detailing the previous night's conversation with Diana
Nov 5	Diana records BBC *Panorama* interview with Martin Bashir
Nov 20	BBC *Panorama* broadcasts Diana interview by Bashir
Nov	Brakes fail while Diana is driving her Audi in London
Dec 10	Queen consults with PM John Major and the Archbishop of Canterbury about a potential Charles-Diana divorce [7]

---

[a] Article by Eugene Robinson in *Washington Post* on 27 November 1992 titled: "Elizabeth II Offers to Pay Taxes: Queen Trimming Family's Costs".

Dec 11	*Time* magazine quotes a "veteran royal watcher": "The Queen is disgusted with [Diana] and wishes she'd just go away" [8]
Dec 18	Diana receives a handwritten letter from the Queen, requesting her to divorce Charles [9]
Dec 19	Diana receives a letter from Charles, requesting a divorce [10a]

1996

Feb	MI6 is involved in an unsuccessful assassination attempt against Colonel Muammar Gaddafi, the leader of Libya
Mar 23	Diana's BMW is extensively damaged after being hit by a Fiat Uno whilst driving at night in London
Jun	MI6 and the CIA are both involved in an unsuccessful assassination plot against Saddam Hussein, leader of Iraq
Jul 15	Diana-Charles divorce decree nisi signed
Jul	Diana commences interest in the anti-landmine campaign
Aug 28	Divorce becomes absolute. Diana is removed from the royal family and is stripped of her HRH title
Sep 16	Way Ahead Group meeting held

1997

Jan 12	Diana commences four day anti-landmine trip to Angola
Jan 16	Diana returns from Angola
Jan 20	Way Ahead Group meeting held
Feb	Diana is warned to drop her anti-landmine campaign and is threatened with an "accident"
Mar 7	Diana secretly records the first of seven videos – 12 hours of footage – filmed by an ex-BBC cameraman throughout March. She talks openly about 17 years of mistreatment by the royals and reveals explosive information about the relationship between Prince Charles and his senior valet, Michael Fawcett
May	Allegation of theft from Harrods safety deposit boxes made against Mohamed Al Fayed by Tiny Rowland Scotland Yard's Jeffrey Rees is appointed SIO heading the safety deposit box investigation
May 1	Tony Blair's Labour Party sweeps to power in the UK
May 21	UK announces ban on the import, export, transfer and manufacture of landmines
Jun	Diana provides Simone Simmons with a copy of her "Profiting out of Misery" dossier on landmines, for safe-keeping

[a] The letters from the Queen and Charles both contained similar terminology: Paul Burrell, *A Royal Duty*, p222.

HOW THEY MURDERED PRINCESS DIANA

Jun 1	Rosa Monckton's daughter, Domenica Lawson's, 2nd birthday party
Jun 3	Royal gala performance of Swan Lake at the Royal Albert Hall – Mohamed Al Fayed invites Diana to holiday at his St Tropez residence
Jun 11	Diana writes note to Mohamed saying she and the boys are "greatly looking forward to" the St Tropez holiday Camilla Parker-Bowles involved in a serious car crash at Norton, Wiltshire
Jun 12	Diana makes major anti-landmine address to Royal Geographic Society, stating that she is on a personal anti-landmine crusade
Jun 13	Annick Cojean of *Le Monde* conducts Diana's final media interview – it is published in Paris just four days before the crash
Jun 25	Diana is forced to withdraw from attending a Landmines Eradication Group meeting in parliament
Jun 30	Rosa Monckton arranges to borrow a boat from "friends" to use on a Greek Island holiday cruise with Diana, set for mid-August
Jul 6	Diana's final meeting with Tony Blair at Chequers
Jul 8	Preparatory meeting for special July 23 Way Ahead Group meeting
Jul 9	David Davies[a] phones Robert Fellowes warning of police concerns about Diana's upcoming holiday to St Tropez
Jul 11	Diana, William and Harry travel to St Tropez for a 10 day holiday with the Al Fayed family
Jul 14	Dodi Fayed joins the St Tropez holiday
Jul 15	Diana tells the media: "You are going to get a big surprise with the next thing I do"
Jul 18	Camilla's 50th birthday party is held at Highgrove
Jul 20	Diana, William and Harry return to London from St Tropez *Mirror* article states that "Diana" is top of the agenda at the next WAG meeting
Jul 21-23	Diana and Dodi share significant periods of time including visits to Dodi's apartment and a private movie viewing [b]
Jul 23	Special Way Ahead Group meeting held
Jul 24-25	Diana visits her sister Sarah and stays for two nights
Jul 26-27	Diana visits Paris for two days with Dodi
Jul 29	Diana meets with Hasnat Khan[c] in Battersea Park
Jul 30	Diana breaks off her relationship with Hasnat at Kensington Palace

---

[a] Head of Royalty Protection.
[b] The detail of this is in Part 2, first Timeline of Events in Section One.
[c] Diana's previous boyfriend, a heart surgeon.

Jul 31	Diana and Dodi commence 7 day holiday cruise in the Mediterranean on the *Jonikal*
Aug 5	Diana and Dodi go ashore at Monte Carlo
Aug 6	Diana and Dodi return to London
Aug 7	*Daily Mirror* breaks story linking Diana and Dodi in a relationship
	Diana shares dinner with Dodi at his Park Lane apartment – she arrives home after 1 a.m.
Aug 8	Diana makes three day anti-landmine trip to Bosnia. She communicates with Dodi regularly by satellite mobile phone.
Aug 10	Diana returns to London from Bosnia
	"The Kiss" photo is published by the *Sunday Mirror*
	Diana and Dodi travel to Mohamed's Oxted estate. They stay overnight.
Aug 11	Diana and Dodi return to London from Oxted
Aug 12	Diana travels again with Dodi to Oxted, where they stay two nights
Aug 13	Diana and Dodi travel from Oxted by helicopter to see psychic counsellor Rita Rogers. They later return to Oxted.
	Diana gifts Dodi her father's cufflinks
Aug 14	Diana and Dodi return to London from Oxted. They share dinner at Dodi's apartment before attending a private pre-release screening of the movie *Air Force One.*
Aug 15	Start of 5 day Diana-Monckton Greek cruise
Aug 18	Phone call from Dodi to Frank Klein advises the couple will be coming to Paris end of August
	US President Clinton announces that the US will sign the treaty to ban landmines
Aug 20	Diana and Monckton return to London
Aug 21	Diana visits her local Anglican priest, Father Frank Gelli
	Diana visits her Chinese doctor – Dr Lily Hua Yu
Aug 22	Diana and Dodi commence a 9 day Mediterranean holiday aboard the *Jonikal*
	Palace press secretary Dickie Arbiter and other royal household members walk the projected funeral route for the Queen Mother's coffin – they discuss the funeral plans and agree on procedure[11a]

---

[a] This route and procedure was adopted for Princess Diana's funeral on September 1, the day following her death. As Arbiter says in his 2014 book, "it was helpful to have everything so fresh in our minds": *On Duty with the Queen*, pp173-4.

HOW THEY MURDERED PRINCESS DIANA

Aug 26	Senior MI6 officer – personal secretary to the chief – Richard Spearman arrives in Paris
Aug 27	*Le Monde* publishes an interview with Diana – on the royal family she says: "From the first day I joined that family, nothing could be done naturally anymore"
	Photographer James Andanson withdraws from following Diana three days before the cruise finishes – he returns home
Aug 28	Henri Paul passes medical examination to extend his pilot's licence
Aug 29	Henri Paul tells Philippe Dourneau that he will be driving the back-up car for the airport arrival
Aug 30[a]	Final Diana-Dodi cruise concludes
	Diana and Dodi leave Sardinia by Al Fayed jet and arrive at Paris' Le Bourget airport
Aug 31	Princess Diana and Dodi Fayed die after a 12.23 a.m. car crash in the Alma Tunnel, Paris
	Early edition *Mirror* article states that next week's WAG meeting will table an MI6 report on the Fayeds and will discuss the Harrods royal warrants
	French crash investigation begins
	Jeffrey Rees is appointed SIO in charge of the British crash investigation
	Police BCA investigators find debris in the Alma Tunnel belonging to the Mercedes S280 and another vehicle
	Completion of Form 13A showing autopsy samples taken during Henri Paul autopsy
Sep 1	Operation Paris set up with terms of reference: "Gathering evidence and facts on behalf of the coroners"
	Georges Dauzonne phones the police regarding his sighting of a zigzagging white Fiat Uno leaving the Alma Tunnel close to the time of the crash – he is told that his evidence is not relevant
	Official autopsy report for Henri Paul completed by Dominique Lecomte
	Completion of Form 12A showing autopsy samples taken from Henri Paul
9.44 a.m.	Police toxicologist Ivan Ricordel carries out first blood alcohol test
9.52 a.m.	Ricordel carries out second blood alcohol test
	Ricordel blood alcohol test reported – 1.87 g/L
11.38 a.m.	Public Prosecutor requests Gilbert Pépin by fax to test blood alcohol[12]

---

[a] Detailed Timelines of Events for August 30 and 31 appear later in the book.

	Pépin gets Blood Sample 2 picked up from the IML
1.19 p.m.	Pépin carries out blood alcohol test – 1.74 g/L
	Pépin reports his blood alcohol test result to the Public Prosecutor
3.37 p.m.	Pépin commences unauthorised toxicological testing, probably including carbon monoxide
	Press release from Paris Public Prosecutor's office announces Henri Paul was drunk at the wheel – 1.75 g/L
	Final edition of London's *Evening Standard* announces "Di's Driver 'Was Drunk'"
Sep 2	Simone Simmons destroys her copy of Diana's anti-landmine dossier
	Judge Hervé Stéphan is appointed examining magistrate of the French investigation
	Professor Peter Vanezis and John Macnamara arrive in Paris
	Vanezis suggests to the French investigation that an independent autopsy be conducted – this is refused
Sep 3	Search of Henri Paul's apartment uncovers one bottle of champagne and ¼ of a bottle of Martini
	Pépin receives request from Stéphan to carry out toxicological testing on the 1st autopsy samples and report by Sep 5
Sep 4	Nine 1st autopsy samples are collected from the IML by Pépin's technician
	Pépin officially conducts toxicology testing on Blood Sample 3
5.00 p.m.	2nd autopsy conducted at IML by Dr Jean-Pierre Campana in presence of Judge Stéphan – concludes at 5.45 p.m.
Sep 5	Suspected burglary at Big Pictures photo agency in London
	After 24 years' service James Andanson resigns from the Sygma agency and commences with Sipa
	Pépin carries out tests on the 2nd autopsy blood sample[a] – but not for carbon monoxide
	Vanezis returns to the UK, unaware of the 2nd autopsy
	Deadline for Pépin to report on 1st autopsy toxicological results is missed
Sep 6	Saturday
Sep 7	Sunday
Sep 8	Stéphan asks Lecomte to provide clear information regarding the sample source in the 1st autopsy

---

[a] Blood Sample 2 from the 2nd autopsy.

Sep 9	2nd police search of Henri's apartment "uncovers" 18 bottles containing alcohol
	Pépin officially carries out carbon monoxide testing on 2nd autopsy blood sample
	Lecomte report states that 1st autopsy blood samples came from the "left haemothorax[a] area"
	Pépin provides 1st autopsy toxicological report 4 days late
	Pépin report reveals carbon monoxide level on 1st autopsy blood is 20.7%
	Pépin provides 2nd autopsy toxicological report – this reveals a carbon monoxide level of 12.8%
Sep 10	Printed date on CDT[b] test analysis report
Sep 11	Stéphan orders Pépin and Véronique Dumestre-Toulet to conduct CDT testing
Sep 12	Police positively identify tail-light fragments as belonging to a Fiat Uno manufactured between May 1983 and September 1989
Sep 13	Saturday
Sep 14	Trevor Rees-Jones reveals to his parents that he was aware Henri had two alcoholic drinks
Sep 15	Posting of blood sample from Pépin to Dumestre-Toulet [c]
Sep 16	Kez Wingfield visits and speaks with Rees-Jones in hospital – apparently harmonising their evidence ahead of Rees-Jones' first police interview
10 a.m.	Dumestre-Toulet receives blood sample
Afternoon	CDT testing carried out – Dumestre-Toulet
Sep 17	Treaty banning landmines endorsed by 90 countries, including UK, in Oslo, Norway. USA pulls out after agreeing to join the ban on August 18
	French police announce they are looking for a second car that was involved in the Alma crash – a white Fiat Uno. The driver of the car has not come forward
	Diana's lawyer, Victor Mishcon, phones MPS Commissioner, Paul Condon to arrange a meeting
	CDT report signed by Pépin & Dumestre-Toulet
Sep 18	Mishcon delivers to Condon the 1995 meeting note – the Mishcon Note – revealing that Diana predicted her death by

---

[a] Chest cavity.
[b] Carbohydrate-Deficient Transferrin – CDT – testing can assist in determining the alcohol consumption habits of a person from whose body a blood sample is taken. In this case testing was conducted on one of the autopsy blood samples. CDT events are included in this timeline – CDT issues are addressed in Chapter 4 of Part 3.
[c] Some of the events listed relating to CDT testing do not appear to have actually occurred – this is covered in the CDT chapter of Part 3.

	staged car crash. Condon, and later John Stevens, lock the Mishcon Note in their office safe for the next six years
	Georges Dauzonne phones police after hearing of the media reports about the Fiat Uno
	Georges Dauzonne is interviewed by French police
Sep 19	French police interview Rees-Jones for the first time
	Sabine Dauzonne is interviewed by French police
	La Poste France item despatched from Paris – the docket is later signed as received by Dumestre-Toulet
Sep 20	Deadline for completion of CDT report
Sep 21	Sunday
Sep 23	CDT report received by the Clerk of the Court, Laurence Maire
Sep 26	Jeffrey Rees completes a report outlining his role in the investigation
Oct 9	Media reports that the Fiat Uno search has been narrowed to 300, based on tail light identification
Oct 14	David Laurent[a] is interviewed by French police
Nov 4	Police announce they are commencing a search of 40,000 Fiat Unos in the Paris region
Nov 7	French judges, lawyers and police express anger over the increasing cost of the investigation
Nov 12	Al Fayed experts discover high carbon monoxide level in a meeting with French lawyers
Nov 13	Four French police officers visit Le Van Thanh[b]
Dec	Rees informs Martine Monteil that Mohamed Al Fayed and some other Harrods staff could be arrested regarding the deposit box investigation
	Professors Oliver and Vanezis apply for a meeting with Lecomte and Pépin – this is declined
Dec 30	French police release to the media some details of the September 18 & 19 Dauzonne interviews but change their names to "François" and "Valerie"

1998

Jan 17	*Hello!* magazine publishes interview with the Dauzonnes
Jan 21	Dauzonnes are interviewed by Judge Stéphan
Jan 22	Rees completes a report recording his concerns over being appointed to head the British investigation into the Paris crash

---

[a] Laurent was a witness to the white Fiat Uno just before the crash.
[b] Parisian owner of a Fiat Uno at the time of the crash.

	British police advise French police about James Andanson[a]
Feb	Niall Mulvihill requests French help to conduct filming of the final journey route by British police
Feb 11	French police make initial phone contact with James Andanson, asking about the Fiat Uno and his movements – he says his alibi is he was in St Tropez
Feb 12	Andanson tells Commander Jean-Claude Mulès that his alibi is he was at home
Mar	Rees arrests Mohamed and five Harrods staff in connection with the safety box investigation. No charges were ever laid
Jun 19	Judge Stéphan appoints Lecomte and Pépin to investigate the high carbon monoxide levels[13]
Sep	Ricordel's alcohol-tested Blood Sample 1 is destroyed
Oct 16	Lecomte and Pépin publish report stating that the high carbon monoxide levels were produced from the Mercedes airbags at the time of the crash
Nov 17	Joint experts report refutes airbags as an explanation for the elevated carbon monoxide level

1999

Feb	UK experts make an application for a judicial "confrontation" with Lecomte and Pépin to discuss the elevated carbon monoxide – this is refused
Mar 1	UK ratifies treaty banning the import, export, transfer and manufacture of landmines
May 26	Right front door of the Mercedes S280 is destroyed in a fire
Sep 3	French investigation ends, concluding that the Alma crash was caused by a drunk driver, Henri Paul, who was also speeding

2000

	Lecomte destroys histologic liver sample
Jan 18	Police raid Burrell's home in Cheshire. They arrest him on suspicion of theft of items from Diana
Jan 19	Stevens takes over as MPS Commissioner from Condon Condon passes on control of the Mishcon Note – Stevens locks it away for a further four years
May 4	James Andanson is incinerated in a fire in his car in an area of secluded countryside about 400 km south of his home
Jun 6	Author Frédéric Dard dies following a lengthy illness

---

[a] White Fiat Uno owner at the time of the crash.

Jun 16	Sipa office in Paris is broken into – computers, disks and property belonging to James Andanson is stolen. No charges were laid
Aug	Set up of Operation Paget
Dec 20	Offer from experts to assist with DNA testing – this is declined

2002

Mar	Royal coroner John Burton resigns. He is replaced by Michael Burgess
Oct 14	Paul Burrell trial on theft begins in Courtroom No 1 of the Old Bailey
Nov 1	Collapse of Burrell trial after the Queen recalls information that indicates he is innocent
Nov 10	Simone Simmons goes public in the *Mail on Sunday* with details of nasty, vitriolic letters sent from Philip to Diana
Nov 23	Press release put out by Philip defending his letters to Diana
Nov 24	Rosa Monckton goes public in defence of Philip in her husband's paper, the *Sunday Telegraph*

2003

Oct 20	Publication of the Burrell Note in the *Daily Mirror* – handwritten by Diana, it accuses Prince Charles of planning her death in a car crash[a]
Oct 23	John Stevens, MPS Commissioner, seeks legal advice regarding disclosure of the Mishcon Note
Oct 27	Victor Mishcon phones John Stevens but he is unavailable
Oct 29	Mishcon again phones Stevens and again he is unavailable
Oct 30	Meeting at Scotland Yard between Mishcon, Stevens and David Veness. Agreement is made to disclose the Mishcon Note to the coroner
Nov 29	Lucia Flecha de Lima discusses her role in the Philip-Diana letters in an interview with Richard Kay in the *Daily Mail*
Dec 20	MPS interview Patrick Jephson in connection with the Mishcon Note
Dec 22	Mishcon Note is delivered by the police to the royal coroner, Michael Burgess

2004

Jan 6	British inquest into the deaths of Diana and Dodi opens

---

[a] The note published on October 20 was redacted and the naming of Prince Charles – "my husband" – didn't occur until January 2004.

Burgess requests the British police to conduct a full inquiry into the deaths

Burgess appoints MPS Commissioner John Stevens to be head of Operation Paget, the British inquiry

Inquest is adjourned while the police investigation proceeds

2005

Jan	Stevens resigns as MPS Commissioner but stays on as Head of Operation Paget
Feb 3	Judge Bellancourt[a] issues Commission Rogatoire for DNA testing to be carried out on Henri Paul's blood samples
Feb 10	French police visit ToxLab – they take Blood Sample 3 and the liver sample from the 1st autopsy
Mar 9	2nd autopsy Blood Sample 1 given to Operation Paget from the IML
	Professor Lecomte states to Paget that 1st autopsy blood sample source was "heart"
Mar 31	Professor Doutrempuich in Bordeaux reports DNA match from Blood Sample 3 1st autopsy to Gisèle Paul [b]
Apr 25	Dr Pascal in Nantes reports DNA match from Blood Sample 3 and liver 1st autopsy to Gisèle Paul
Dec	Professor de Mazancourt in Paris reports DNA match from Blood Sample 3 1st autopsy to Gisèle Paul

2006

Jan 27	Victor Mishcon dies at home, age 90, following a lengthy illness
	Publication of transcript of TV interview with John Stevens – Stevens states that the Paget investigation was more complex than anticipated
Jan 28	Burglary at John Stevens' office in Newcastle – two laptops and £750 cash is taken
Feb 5	Second burglary at Stevens' office complex – nothing stolen
Mar 1	David Forster arrested and charged with Stevens' burglary
Mar 22	Forster convicted and jailed over Stevens' burglary
May 31	Lecomte states to Paget that 1st autopsy blood sample source was "left haemothorax area"
Jul 22	Royal coroner Michael Burgess resigns from the case, citing a heavy workload
Sep 7	Appointment of Elizabeth Butler-Sloss as new coroner

---

[a] A French judge who has presided over separate proceedings that have taken place in the Court of Versailles.

  [b] Henri's mother.

Nov 8	Meeting at British Embassy in Paris between John Stevens and Henri Paul's parents. Stevens tells them: "Your son was not drunk"
Dec 14	British inquiry ends and the Paget Report is published. Stevens concludes that the crash was caused by the driver, Henri Paul, who had been drinking alcohol and was also speeding

2007

	Senior British police – Condon, Veness and Stevens – fabricate documentary evidence pertaining to the Mishcon Note ahead of the opening of the inquest into the deaths
Apr 24	Elizabeth Butler-Sloss resigns as coroner for the case, citing inexperience with the jury system
Jun	Scott Baker takes over as coroner
Oct 2	British inquest main hearings begin with an 11-person jury

2008

Apr 7	British inquest concludes with the jury's verdict that the crash was caused by "unlawful killing, grossly negligent driving of the following vehicles and of the Mercedes"
8	Worldwide media reports alter the wording of the verdict to read "paparazzi" instead of "following vehicles"
Jun	David Forster dies aged 30

2013

Aug 17	Scotland Yard announces it is "scoping" new information regarding the crash and "assessing its relevance and credibility" Media reports link this announcement to evidence that Soldier N – a former SAS soldier – had claimed that "it was [the SAS] who arranged Princess Diana's death and that has been covered up"
Dec 16	MPS release a report stating there is no substance to Soldier N's claims. The report fails to include the allegation, identities and roles of witnesses interviewed or the content of what witnesses told the police

HOW THEY MURDERED PRINCESS DIANA

1   The Watershed: 1992

Royally speaking, 1992 was a tumultuous year. In fact it was labelled by Queen Elizabeth II as her "annus horribilis".

That year will go down in history as the trigger for a long line of events that would finally seal Princess Diana's fate – death following a car crash in a Paris tunnel in late August 1997.

Squidgy then Morton: Enter Monckton

On New Year's Eve 1989 Diana Princess of Wales – who was at Sandringham House – spoke by telephone with her long-time close friend, James Gilbey. During that conversation Diana referred to her husband Prince Charles' family, the British royals: "Bloody hell, after all I've done for this fucking family". (WFJ) [a]

This phone call was electronically recorded by a device within Sandringham House and then four days later – on 4 January 1990 – it was re-broadcast. This re-transmission of the call – which later became known as Squidgygate – was picked up by two separate private ham operators, Cyril Reenan and Jean Norman, operating independently.

About six months later Princess Diana first met Lucia Flecha de Lima, the wife of the newly-arrived Brazilian ambassador.

Within weeks of that meeting Rosa Monckton – managing director of Tiffany's London – employed Lucia's daughter, Beatriz, and consequently met her mother around September 1990. The relationship between Lucia and Rosa developed during the following months. [bc]

---

[a] Evidence followed by **(WFJ) means that it was withheld from the jury** at the inquest.

[b] This is based on the available evidence, which is limited due to conflicts in the testimony of the two witnesses, Lucia and Rosa. See next footnote.

[c] Only two witnesses have ever been required to provide evidence on the development of the Diana-Lucia; Lucia-Rosa and Rosa-Diana relationships – they are Lucia and Rosa. The evidence of Beatriz, Lucia's daughter, has never been sought by the authorities. There are four primary official sources of evidence – Lucia's police

Then in March 1991 London-based journalist Andrew Morton wrote a particularly significant article in the *Sunday Times*. It was based on deliberately leaked material from Princess Diana, provided to Morton via her friend Dr James Colthurst. The article contained specific insider information regarding the situation within the Charles-Diana household.[14]

During the following month, April 1991, Lucia Flecha de Lima and her ambassador-husband, Paulo, accompanied Diana and Charles on an official visit to their homeland, Brazil. Lucia later told royal journalist, Richard Kay: "The first thing Diana said to me was: 'You are Lucia. I've been told we should become good friends.'" Lucia also told Kay that "a mutual friend suggested to me that I would be a 'good help' to Diana".[15] (WFJ)

After returning from Brazil the Diana-Lucia relationship blossomed. "Our friendship grew stronger and stronger", Lucia told the police in 2004.[16] (WFJ)

In May 1991 Morton wrote a second article for the *Times* again using information from Diana and this time about the "War of the Waleses" – difficulties in the Diana-Charles marriage.[17] (WFJ)

Then in July James Colthurst started conducting secret interviews at Kensington Palace with Princess Diana. Interview recordings were passed onto Andrew Morton via Colthurst, in preparation for an up-coming controversial book.[18] (WFJ)

Within months Diana was warned – through her private secretary Patrick Jephson – that the "men in grey suits" at Buckingham Palace knew about her involvement in Morton's book.[19] (WFJ)

Diana's activities were under constant surveillance.[a] There were now three events connected to Diana that could have raised alarm within the senior royal circle – first, the Squidgy recording[bc], second, the Morton articles and finally the secret Morton book.

---

statement, Rosa's police statement, Lucia's inquest testimony and Rosa's inquest testimony. There are major conflicts between all four accounts. Their evidence and the conflicts are fully addressed in Part 5, section on Meeting Diana in the Rosa Monckton chapter.

[a] See later Under Surveillance chapter.

[b] Although Squidgy wasn't made public until August 1992 (see below), there is evidence – heard at the inquest – pointing to possible involvement by GCHQ in the illegal recording of the conversation (see next footnote). Part 5 (Links to Intelligence Agencies section of Chapter 3) reveals that there is other evidence of connections between senior royals and British intelligence. There is a possibility then that if GCHQ recorded Squidgy they would pass on the transcript to the Queen.

[c] The Squidgygate evidence – including possible GCHQ involvement – is predominantly covered in the following transcripts on the inquest website: Robert Fellowes – 12 Feb 08; Patrick Jephson – 24 Jan 08; Ken Wharfe – 9 Jan 08; David Meynell – 4 Mar 08; David Veness – 15 Jan 08; John Adye – 28 Feb 08; Paul Condon – 16-17 Jan 08; Richard Dearlove – 20 Feb 08. Evidence references available on the website include: GCHQ denial press release – 14 Jan 93: INQ0060676;

Rosa Monckton's relationship with Lucia Flecha de Lima continued to develop. A detailed analysis of the conflicting evidence between the sole witnesses – Lucia and Rosa – indicates that later in 1991 Rosa sought to meet Diana with the help of Lucia.[a]

Rosa Monckton's relationship with Princess Diana is significant – because Rosa has close links to intelligence. At the inquest Rosa admitted that "somebody close to me is connected with ... MI6".[20] Rosa was referring to her brother, Anthony, who was an MI6 officer[b] – his cover was blown by a Belgrade newspaper in August 2004.[21] (WFJ) Anthony shows up in the official FCO Diplomatic List as the First Secretary Political in Zagreb in 1996 and the sole Counsellor in Belgrade[22] in 2001. (WFJ)

Other evidence reveals that Rosa's husband, Dominic Lawson, has operated as an MI6 agent. In 1998 ex-MI6 officer Richard Tomlinson alleged that Lawson, whilst editor of the *Spectator*, published articles by an MI6 officer under a false name. If this allegation was false, it should have been a simple matter for Lawson to prove that the articles were submitted by a legitimate journalist.[c] Dominic Lawson has failed to do this.

Hansard Reports – 14 Jan 93: INQ0060675, On GCHQ methods 18 Feb 93: INQ0060678 to 680, Mar 93: INQ0060682; Commissioner's 1992 Interception Report – INQ0060688-90; Squidgygate pre-investigation meeting – 21 Jan 93: INQ0060696, 698-9; Letter from Whitmore to Butler – 22 Jan 93: INQ0060700-1; Letter from Fellowes to Whitmore – 25 Jan 93: INQ0060702; Letter from Adye to Fellowes – 29 Jan 93: INQ0060703; Letter from Interception Tribunal to Adye – 2 Feb 93: INQ0061064; Letter from Adye to Interception Tribunal – 5 Feb 93: INQ0061065; Letter from Fellowes to Adye – 2 Mar 93: INQ0060704; Letter from Adye to Fellowes – 22 Mar 93: INQ0060727-8; Letter from Fellowes to Adye – 24 Mar 93: INQ0060729; Final Squidgygate meeting – 4 May 93: INQ0061066-7; Interception Act 1985: INQ0060736. Note that inquest evidence is not stored on the website in numerical or subject order – the easiest way to locate these evidence items is by scrolling down the evidence list looking for the specific reference number you are seeking.

[a] See Part 5, Rosa Monckton chapter, section on Meeting Diana.

[b] An officer, as opposed to an agent. Officers recruit and "handle" agents. Officers are permanently employed full-time. An agent will work for MI6 when needed, but is not normally full-time. Often an officer will be involved with planning a mission and the agents will carry it out.

[c] In 2001 the *Guardian* stated: "The articles were written from Sarajevo by a Kenneth Roberts, though the Spectator noted that the author's name had been changed at his request without revealing his true employer. The MI6 officer has since been publicly identified as Keith Craig." Ian Traynor & Richard Norton-Taylor, Editor "Provided Cover for Spies", The Guardian, 26 January 2001. Keith Craig appears on the MI6 internet list (explained in Part 5, section on MI6 Internet List in the MI6 in Paris chapter) and is also listed in the Diplomatic Service List 1996, p151. (WFJ)

Rosa Monckton has direct links to two MI6 employees – Anthony Monckton, her brother, and Dominic Lawson, her husband.

This makes any move by Rosa to create a relationship with Diana very significant – particularly in the aftermath of the three events mentioned above: the Squidgy recording; the Morton articles and the interviewing of Diana for Morton's book.

A few months after starting on the collaboration with Diana, around November 1991, Andrew Morton's office in central London was burgled – "files rifled through" he later wrote.[23] (WFJ) And during December Diana received a warning via her private secretary that the "men in grey suits" knew about her involvement with the book.

Meanwhile Rosa continued working on obtaining an introduction to Princess Diana. And in February 1992 – over a year after first meeting Lucia – she was successful. Lucia arranged for a luncheon for the threesome – Diana, Lucia, Rosa.

It will later be shown that Rosa was working as an MI6 agent throughout her dealings with Diana. This early-1992 luncheon was to be Rosa's personal introduction to Diana. But more importantly, this signified the beginning of over five years of intimate intelligence surveillance of Diana's activities and plans – by a person posing as a friend of the princess, Rosa Monckton.

The Book and the Aftermath

In the meantime Andrew Morton was working on his explosive book. It would contain frank revelations about the relationship between Prince Charles and Camilla Parker-Bowles, Diana's bulimia and her attempts at suicide. Publication was set for early summer, 1992.

It was unprecedented for a senior royal to be so publicly honest about their life.

Serialisation of the book – entitled *Diana: Her True Story* – commenced in London's *Sunday Times* on 7 June 1992.

The immediate effect was for Princess Diana to be ostracised by the other royals. Her butler, Paul Burrell, later wrote:

> **The princess went to Royal Ascot.... It was there [in the Royal box] that she was struck by the enormity of the damage that the book had caused. She felt the rest of the royal party ostracizing her, she said, and conversations were stilted, awkward and cold.... She saw that Andrew and [Prince Charles' mistress] Camilla Parker-Bowles were guests....[24] (WFJ)**

At the inquest Patrick Jephson[a] confirmed that following the Morton book the palace started "restricting [Diana's] use of the Queen's Flight and the

---

[a] Diana's private secretary.

Royal Train [and] ... downgrading ... the protocol due to her when visiting destinations at home or abroad".[25]

Precisely 11 days after the initial serialisation of the book, on June 18, Diana received a bombshell letter from her father-in-law, Prince Philip.

Her friend, Lucia Flecha de Lima, told the inquest that "she was quite upset about it".[26] Andrew Morton later wrote that Diana "was so alarmed ... that she ... asked [a friend] to recommend a solicitor to help draft a suitable reply".[27] (WFJ)

Diana ended up turning to Lucia for help. Lucia related to royal journalist Richard Kay what occurred during a November 2003 interview. Kay wrote:

> **The de Limas allowed [Diana] to use their home as a sanctuary.... It was there that she took the now infamous [1992] letters from Prince Philip[a] ... and there that [Diana] and Lucia would pour [sic] over her responses.[28b]** (WFJ)

Diana took three days to formulate her response and sent the reply on June 21. A short section towards the end of that letter appeared to set the tone for what turned into a series of ten letters – five from Philip and five replies from Diana.[c] Diana wrote:

> **I am very grateful to you for sending me such a heartfelt and honest letter and I hope you will read mine in the same spirit.[29]**

This could be interpreted to mean that Diana read that first letter – described as upsetting and alarming[d] – in a positive spirit: "I hope you will read mine in the same spirit". She appears to suggest that if she hadn't chosen to read the letter in that spirit, it could have been taken quite differently – in which case her sentiment may not have been "grateful", but something else.

Very short excerpts of nine of the letters were shown to the jury[e] – but nothing at all from the first Philip letter. It appears that there were no sentences in this first letter deemed viewable by the jury. It may not have

---

[a] There were five letters from Philip and five replies from Diana – commencing with Philip's initial letter on June 18 and concluding with Diana's final reply on 30 September 1992. The evidence surrounding these letters is addressed in detail in Part 5, Philip-Diana Letters section in the Rosa Monckton chapter.

[b] Lucia later changed her account of this – that is addressed later.

[c] The final reply from Diana was written on September 30, about 3½ months after the correspondence began.

[d] See above.

[e] The letters that were "shown" were very heavily redacted. They are reproduced on the inquest website: INQ0058912 to INQ0058961.

contained the niceties at the beginning and end that some of the later letters had – written after the receipt of Diana's initial generous reply.[a]

Despite the very small excerpts provided to the jury at the inquest and the revelation that the correspondence included discussion of issues in the Diana-Charles marriage, the true nature and contents of these letters from Philip has never been revealed.

Towards the end of this 3½ months of Philip-Diana correspondence, on 24 August 1992 *The Sun* newspaper published the full transcript of the 1989 Squidgygate phone call. The public was offered a hotline number they could call to hear it all for themselves.

Philip wrote a letter to Diana on September 28 to which she replied two days later on the 30th.

Philip never replied to that letter.

But just over a month later, in November 1992, the Queen set up the Way Ahead Group (WAG). This is a high-level committee co-chaired by the Queen and the Lord Chamberlain[30] which generally meets twice a year to discuss major issues facing the royal family.[b] Attendees include the senior royals – the Queen, Philip, their children, the private secretaries to the senior royals, the Lord Chamberlain, and the Keeper of the Privy Purse.[31cd]

Then on the 24th of that month the Queen declared 1992 to be her "annus horribilis".

The following day at Kensington Palace Charles requested a formal separation – agreed to by Diana.[32] (WFJ)

Exactly two weeks after that, on 9 December 1992, the official separation of Diana and Charles was announced in the British Parliament.

Seeds to a Tragedy

1992 was indeed a year of royal tumult and it did mark a watershed in relations between Diana and other senior royals, but the seeds for what occurred had been planted in previous years.

---

[a] In this light, it should be noted that the redactions on the letters from Philip to Diana were significantly heavier than those on the letters from Diana to Philip: a) the first letter (June 18) from Philip was completely withheld – all Diana's letters were shown; b) the beginning and end of all Diana's letters were shown. When it came to Philip's, only the beginning and end of one letter was shown – the July 7 one – and the beginning only, of the letters written on June 25, July 20 and September 28. Inquest website reference numbers to the letters are in the previous footnote.

[b] See later chapter on the Special WAG Meeting. The purpose and role of the WAG is also addressed in more detail in Part 5, Way Ahead Group section in The Royals chapter.

[c] It is possible that the Queen Mother attended the WAG meetings in 1997, but this was not declared at the inquest.

[d] Later evidence will indicate that the WAG played a key role in the events of 1997.

Years of mistreatment at the hands of senior royals, the long-term affair between Charles and Camilla and media and public pressure, had pushed Princess Diana to the point where she felt she could no longer bottle-up her feelings. She believed she had to reveal to the public some of the true nature of what was occurring in her life and her marriage.

This build-up of mounting pressure led to her 1991 decision to collaborate with Andrew Morton on the book.

Clearly this unprecedented move by Diana did not go down well with Philip and the Queen. And in fact it triggered what was apparently a ferocious letter from Philip to Diana.

After several months of correspondence – and the bad publicity surrounding the August release of Squidgygate – the Queen moved to set up the Way Ahead Group. There is little doubt that one of the main items on its first meeting's agenda could have been the handling of the aftermath of the Morton-Diana book.

The end result of this very public display of dirty royal linen – the Morton book – was the request for a formal separation between Charles and Diana.

That occurred quickly.

By the close of 1992 the British public had been made aware that the fairy tale was now over: the marriage between Prince Charles and his young Princess Diana was effectively finished.

And relations between Diana and the other senior royals were forever damaged – both in private and in public. Things could never return to where they had been in the earlier years of the marriage.

In retrospect, there were three major events that came to fruition in 1992 and would eventually have a key impact on the circumstances of the 1997 deaths of Diana and Dodi.

First was Diana's willingness to collaborate in the Morton book and its subsequent June 1992 publication.

Second, the Queen set up the Way Ahead Group to address major issues facing the royal family.

Third – and much less known about – was the recruitment by British intelligence of Rosa Monckton to become a friend of the princess. This was a direct result of concerns over Diana's words and behaviour – the Squidgy tapes; the 1991 Morton articles and the Diana-Morton literary collaboration.

Precisely how these three major events impacted on the build-up to the 1997 Paris crash will become clearer as this book develops.

At this stage this can be said:

By the conclusion of 1992 – the year of the Queen's annus horribilis – the public knew a great deal more about how things worked within the royal family; Diana had been removed from the royal inner sanctum; the Queen had set up a mechanism for dealing with any future problems – the WAG; and Rosa Monckton – MI6 agent – had worked her way into a friendship with Princess Diana.

"These were dangerous times. The knives were being sharpened for the Princess…."

-     Ken Wharfe – Diana's bodyguard, referring to 1992

2   Bali Holiday: 1993

On 14 August 1993 Princess Diana departed London heading for a holiday in first Bali and then later Moyo Island, Indonesia. She was accompanied by Rosa Monckton, Lucia Flecha de Lima and Lucia's daughter, Beatriz.

Diana returned to London around August 19, after about five days.

Then 2½ weeks later, on September 6, journalist Michelle Green wrote in the *People*:

> [Diana] flew to Bali ... for a five-day idyll – hiding away at two luxury Aman resorts.... [She slipped] out of London without attracting the attention of a single reporter.[33] (WFJ)

"Diana Wanted To Come Home"

Nothing was divulged by the participants about the Indonesian holiday for over ten years. Then in late November 2003 Lucia mentioned it during an interview with Richard Kay, published in the *Daily Mail*. Kay wrote:

> Once Diana, Lucia, her daughter Beatriz and Rosa Monckton travelled to the remote Indonesian island of Mojo [sic]. [Lucia said] 'After 12 hours, [Diana] wanted to come home. In the end, she came home alone.' [34] (WFJ)

Lucia went on to reveal much more when she submitted her police statement the following year:

> We had been scheduled to go for ten days but Princess Diana came back early. She was feeling very insecure at the time and had become very nervous about the press, Prince Charles and his courtiers. Princess Diana and I did argue and this was one such occasion. Rosa had gone to a lot of trouble to organise the trip and Princess Diana returned after three or four days. She would say, 'I'm not Beatriz. You can't treat me like that.' I would say, 'You're acting worse than Beatriz'.... Princess Diana and I had been to Paris together in May 1993 but that was completely different. She had been there as the Princess of Wales and she still had her Scotland Yard protection officers with her.[35] (WFJ)

This statement was not read at the inquest. Instead all the jury heard was a brief question – put to both Lucia and Rosa – just confirming that the holiday occurred.[36]

A key question – which the jury would not have been asking because all they heard was that this Indonesian trip occurred – is: Why did Diana want to come home after 12 hours?

Holiday Falsehoods

Lucia told the police: "We had been scheduled to go for ten days".

The holiday started on August 14, so that would mean it would conclude on August 24.

Green wrote in her September 1993 article: "On Aug 24 [Diana] swept Prince William, 11, and Prince Harry, 8, off to Florida to begin a 10-day vacation".[37] (WFJ) And Ken Wharfe, Diana's MPS bodyguard, revealed in his 2002 book that the Florida trip had been planned weeks earlier: "I advised Diana in my [2 August 1993] briefing memo that ... Disney ... has a VIP package which uses reserved routes".[38] (WFJ)

This indicates that Lucia's claim that the Bali holiday "had been scheduled to go for ten days" is false. It is evident that if Diana had stayed in Indonesia for 10 days, then she would have been too late to leave for the planned Florida-Bahamas holiday.

Lucia also provided the police with reasons for Diana's premature departure: "[Diana] was feeling very insecure at the time and had become very nervous about the press, Prince Charles and his courtiers."

Michelle Green however wrote that the group slipped "out of London without attracting the attention of a single reporter"; "was remarkably private"; "not one picture of her was snapped at either hideaway";[a] "[Diana's] presence caused barely a ripple".[39] (WFJ)

In support of this, there are absolutely no press reports of this holiday during the time it took place, and as Green says: "not one picture". Green's article was published retrospectively, on 6 September 1993[b] – about 19 days after Diana had returned to London.

There were no press snooping around Bali or Moyo Island.

Lucia Flecha de Lima has misled the police when she stated that Diana "had become very nervous about the press" as a reason why "Diana came back early".

In contrast, Green describes the press reaction to the Florida trip Diana embarked on just five days after her return from Bali – "Fleet Street [were] camped out in Orlando".[40] (WFJ)

And that was no accident.

Ken Wharfe, who organised that trip, stated in 2002: "It was clear that [Diana] had personally tipped [Richard] Kay off [about the Florida trip], and I

---

[a] Amanusa in Bali and Amanwana on Moyo Island.
[b] The article was published simultaneously in *Time* magazine and *People*.

was reasonably certain that [Kay] would have passed on the information, at her behest, to the rest of the royal rat pack."[41] (WFJ)

This behaviour by Diana – revealed by Wharfe and confirmed by Green – does not suggest a person that "had become very nervous about the press", as described by Lucia Flecha de Lima.

Lucia also says that Diana "was feeling very insecure at that time and had become very nervous about ... Prince Charles and his courtiers".

Ken Wharfe, who by 1993 had spent six years with the princess, says of that period: "For Diana, her sons always came first, and as the far-reaching implications of the dissolution of her marriage became clearer she began to focus on preparing them both, and William in particular, for what lay ahead."[42] (WFJ) And regarding Diana's own state of mind: "At last liberated from the shackles of her marriage,[a] [Diana] was a woman determined to enjoy herself after the years of frustration." [43] (WFJ)

Diana's concern with Charles at this time appears to focus on the battle over time spent with William and Harry. Green pointed out in her article that Diana was "unhappy about losing her sons to Charles for an 18-day vacation".[44] (WFJ)

But there is nothing outside of Lucia indicating that during this period Diana "was feeling very insecure" or that she was "nervous about ... Prince Charles and his courtiers" – instead the evidence reveals otherwise.

Lucia then pointed out to the police two differences between a Paris visit made three months earlier[b] and the Indonesia trip. Lucia said that in Paris "[Diana] had been there as the Princess of Wales" and she "still had her Scotland Yard protection officers with her".

Lucia used these points to show that the Paris trip was "completely different" to the Bali trip.

Ken Wharfe, who went as police protection on the Paris trip, has stated: "[Diana] was determined to go ... [to Paris] incognito.... We had use of a private jet and we flew undetected to Paris on a beautiful May afternoon." [45] (WFJ)

This indicates there was little difference in the publicity aspect of the two trips – there was none on the Paris trip and the lack of media articles on the Bali trip shows there was nil publicity there as well.[c] Both trips were low-key, "incognito" and didn't draw media attention. Neither visit was made official

---

[a] The formal separation had been announced in December 1992.

[b] In May 1993.

[c] Michelle Green wrote: "[Diana] flew to Bali ... without attracting the attention of a single reporter": Michelle Green, Ping-Pong Princes, People Magazine, 6 September 1993.

with Diana as "Princess of Wales" – as Lucia falsely described the Paris trip to the police.[a]

Lucia's other claim was that in Indonesia Diana did not have her "Scotland Yard protection officers with her".

Michelle Green however reported that the women were accompanied by "bodyguard Det. Sgt. Carol Quirk".[46] (WFJ) Diana's police protection wasn't removed until December 1993, four months after the Bali holiday.[b]

Lucia also said: "Princess Diana and I had been to Paris together" – indicating that Lucia and Diana went unaccompanied to Paris.

This is also false – Wharfe states that Hyatt Palumbo went. In fact, not only was she there, but Wharfe says: "Through Hyatt Palumbo ... we had use of [the] private jet" the group travelled in.[47] (WFJ)

In summary, Lucia Flecha de Lima provided several falsehoods in her formal Operation Paget statement. Firstly regarding the May 1993 Paris holiday:

- Lucia claimed that Diana was "there as the Princess of Wales" – she was not
- Lucia indicated they went alone – they were accompanied by Hyatt Palumbo and travelled in a jet organised by her

Then regarding the Bali holiday, Lucia also claimed:

- it had been scheduled to go for ten days – that couldn't be true
- there was no police protection – there was
- Diana left early because she was "very nervous about the press" – there were no press there
- Diana left early because she was "feeling very insecure ... and had become very nervous about ... Prince Charles and his courtiers" – Wharfe, who was with Diana on a daily basis, instead said she was now "liberated from the shackles of her marriage, [and] was a woman determined to enjoy herself".

Why This Cover-Up?

In the 2003 Kay interview Lucia had said: "After 12 hours, [Diana] wanted to come home" from Indonesia.[c]

And during the 2004 police interview Lucia divulged that "Rosa [Monckton] had gone to a lot of trouble to organise the trip".

---

[a] Wharfe points out in his book, regarding the Paris trip: "No one had any idea we were there, and I had taken the decision not to ask for any help from local police this time for fear of leaks to the press.": *Closely Guarded Secret*, p214.

[b] See following chapter.

[c] This is not in conflict with her police statement. The evidence indicates Diana wanted to come home after 12 hours, but didn't actually leave the holiday until four or five days had passed.

Questions arise.

Why does Lucia focus on the holiday in her police statement?[a] After all, this occurred four years before the Paris crash, so what bearing could it have on the deaths?

Why has Lucia apparently covered up the real reason Diana wanted to leave early?

Why did Rosa organise the Bali holiday?[b]

In March 1995 – just 19 months after the holiday – Lucia Flecha de Lima was interviewed extensively about her relationship with Diana, by Daphne Barak. There was no mention of this holiday at all in Barak's lengthy article.[48] It also doesn't figure in Wharfe's 2002 book, or Burrell's *A Royal Duty*, published in October 2003.

Then there is a brief mention of the holiday in the November 2003 Kay article, but Lucia's September 2004 police statement account is quite detailed.

The jury only heard two very brief references to this Indonesian holiday[c] – the police statements of Lucia and Rosa were not read out. There has also been no evidence sought from Lucia's daughter, Beatriz, or Det. Sgt. Carol Quirk, the bodyguard.

Evidence-Based Scenario

This dearth of available evidence makes it very difficult to establish what actually took place. Part of what follows includes speculation, but it is based on the known evidence.

What we do know is that the only account we have – Lucia's police statement – is littered with falsehoods.

It is shown later and in Part 5[d] that Lucia Flecha de Lima has covered for Rosa Monckton on other issues. It is possible that Lucia's lies in her police statement regarding this holiday could be to protect Rosa.

The general evidence from both Lucia and Rosa is that they were critical of Diana on similar issues – the way she was handling her marriage to Charles, the 1997 arrangement to holiday with Mohamed Al Fayed.[e]

During this 1993 period, the big issue was the Diana-Charles marriage – the separation had occurred the previous year, but there were still issues over

---

[a] We do not have Rosa's statement, but inquest lawyer Ian Burnett's questioning indicates that Rosa also included this holiday in her police statement: 13 Dec 07: 135.2.

[b] This is a question that also arises in connection with the final Rosa-Diana holiday which took place just two weeks before Diana died – see later.

[c] Lucia – 18 Dec 07: 93.21; Rosa – 13 Dec 07: 135.2.

[d] Rosa Monckton chapter in Part 5.

[e] This evidence is covered in the Rosa Monckton chapter of Part 5.

the children, and no doubt whether this was going to stay as a separation, or end in divorce. The prior year had seen the publication of Diana's view of her marriage in the Morton book, the publishing of the Squidgygate transcripts, the separation and the Queen announcing her "annus horribilis".

If the Establishment wanted pressure put on Diana to prevent a final termination of her marriage, then the ideally placed people to influence her were Rosa Monckton – who had MI6 connections – and the conservative-thinking Lucia Flecha de Lima – who was a close confidante.

Lucia has stated: "Rosa had gone to a lot of trouble to organise the trip". Was the trip also initiated by Rosa?

A possible scenario is that Rosa was asked by Establishment figures to either influence Diana or find out what she was thinking or planning regarding her marriage. Rosa may have organised the trip[a], but worked through Lucia to approach Diana with the idea. At that point Diana may have been more likely to go on a holiday with Lucia present, than with Rosa on her own.[b]

Lucia told Kay: "After 12 hours, [Diana] wanted to come home". Why?

There is then a possibility that Rosa was working to an agenda[c] during this Bali holiday that she organised.

Was Diana feeling pressure as a result of that? Such a scenario could have led to Diana wanting to leave after just 12 hours.

Maybe Rosa then backed off. Diana stayed for a few more days before leaving early, in order to be home ahead of the pre-planned trip with William and Harry to Florida.

Later evidence will indicate that Rosa Monckton worked for the British Establishment during her dealings with Princess Diana.

---

[a] Apparently with the help of Indonesian hotelier Adrian Zecha: Michelle Green, Ping-Pong Princes, People Magazine, 6 September 1993.
[b] There was also repeated witness evidence at the inquest that Diana would only rarely mix her friends with each other – she would keep them separate from one another. This is addressed in Part 2, Sharing of Information section in the Diana and Dodi Relationship chapter. The fact that Lucia and Rosa were both on this trip could be a reflection that Diana was wary of Rosa.
[c] Lucia described the Diana-Rosa relationship to the police: "Princess Diana thought maybe Rosa did have a hidden agenda" – confirmed at the inquest: 18 Dec 07: 131.11.

3 Under Surveillance: 1994

Four months after the Bali holiday, on 13 December 1993 Diana requested removal of her police protection.[a] This was the month following the resignation of Ken Wharfe, her bodyguard for six years.[49]

Detecting a Device

During 1994 Diana called in electronics and security expert, Grahame Harding, to conduct a sweep of her Kensington Palace apartment.

Harding told the police in 2006:

> **In order to allay her fears and to reassure her, I conducted a limited sweep of her premises using equipment that was not very sophisticated and would only locate the normal or basic type of listening devices.... Whilst conducting a sweep for listening devices my equipment detected an electronic signal, which indicated that a possible bugging device may have been present behind a wall in her bedroom. Princess Diana was present when I found this signal. I did not know what was on the other side of this wall and was not able to investigate further as I did not have access.... The next time I did a sweep of the area, which was a day or two later, the signal ... had gone. I did not tell anyone of my findings and do not know if Princess Diana looked into it further.... Had it been a sophisticated listening device, I would not have expected to find it.... I searched for electronic devices in the Princess' apartment at Kensington Palace on 3 or 4 occasions over a period of 5 or 6 weeks."** [50] **(WFJ)**

Under inquest cross-examination Harding revealed that the device was on the other side of one of the walls in Diana's bedroom – it was actually in Charles' room, which was locked and Diana apparently had not been given a key.[51]

If Harding found a device and showed it to Diana, then whoever was listening in would have been aware of that. Therefore it is common sense that

---

[a] Notes of her meeting with police on that day are on the inquest website: INQ0058863.

when Harding returns later, the device has been removed – "the signal … had gone". It is possible it had been replaced by something more sophisticated.

In his statement Harding says that the signal indicated it was a "possible bugging device", yet at the inquest he said to MPS lawyer, Richard Horwell: "I think that it was innocent".[52]

Harding fails to – and is not asked to – explain how a possible bugging device could be innocent.

Raising Concerns

On 18 October 1994, Princess Diana met with David Meynell, Head of Royalty Protection. During the meeting – which was at Diana's request and took place at Kensington Palace – Diana expressed concerns that she was under surveillance.

An excerpt from Meynell's report:

During the course of the conversation HRH bluntly asked me if her car had been bugged. I told her I would have it examined to establish that fact. She then said to me "Even when no one knows where I am going in my car there are people waiting for me at the other end." She again asked me if I had any knowledge of whether her vehicle was bugged. I informed her that we (the Police) had certainly not placed any form of device on her vehicle. She then told me that she knew her telephones were being tapped and that she was certain the same applied to her vehicle. She stated that she had proof that her phones were being tapped because she had "set traps on four occasions and she had got the necessary evidence". I told her that I should be allowed to deal with this matter. She stated that she was using her knowledge to her advantage - whilst she felt a great loss in not being able to use her telephones she had use of other devices and the fact she was not using her telephones would squeeze those people into different action. I explained to HRH that I had available a team of experts who were responsible for ensuring the integrity of Parliament, these were ordinary uniform officers and I could get them to do the necessary sweep of both vehicle and premises. Her response was to state that whilst she had a lot of enemies she had a lot of friends some in places of knowledge. She could not name them because they could lose their jobs but she had been told that without any doubt five people from an organisation had been assigned full time to "oversee" her activities, including listening to her private phone conversation and that from the same source she knew that two people from the same organisation performed a similar function in respect of Parliament. I told her this was a very serious matter in that it indicated that

SECRET

my team working in Parliament were not doing their job properly. She replied by stating that it was not a question of them not doing their job properly it was a question that they were against the experts in this field. I told her that I could get no comfort from the situation and again stated that the matter should be investigated. She stated that whilst she was certain of her ground she could not assist further without jeopardising the identities of her friends this she was not prepared to do.

My view is that today's meeting was basically to ask me whether I had placed some form of device on her vehicle.

D N Meynell

Figure 1

> Excerpt of David Meynell's report of his 18 October 1994 meeting with Princess Diana. The full three page report is reproduced in Part 2 (Figure 11) or can be viewed on the inquest website: INQ0058847 to INQ0058849.

Diana asked Meynell "if her car had been bugged". She said: "Even when no one knows where I am going in my car there are people waiting for me at the other end". Diana went on to say that "she knew her telephones were being tapped and ... she was certain the same applied to her vehicle".

Meynell stated in his report of the meeting: "I explained ... that I had available a team of experts who were responsible for ensuring the integrity of Parliament. These were ordinary uniform officers and I could get them to do the necessary sweep of both vehicle and premises."

Diana continued, saying she had some friends "in places of knowledge" and "she had been told that ... five people from an organisation had been assigned full-time to oversee her activities, including listening to her private phone conversation[s]" and "she knew that two people from the same organisation performed a similar function in respect of Parliament".[53]

In summary the personal surveillance concerns raised by Diana during the meeting were:

1) "she knew her telephones were being tapped"
2) "she was certain the same applied to her vehicle"
3) "five people from an organisation had been assigned full time to oversee her activities".

Police Lies

Did the police follow up on these concerns?

Meynell wrote up his report later in the day and discussed the issues with the Commissioner, Paul Condon. Three days later, on October 21, Condon briefed the Home Secretary.[54]

The way the inquest heard Condon and Meynell's testimony is important:
-       16-17 Jan 08: Condon is cross-examined
-       15 Feb 08: Meynell provides a statement for the inquest[55] – not seen by the jury
-       4 Mar 08: Meynell reads Michael Mansfield QC's 17 January 2008 cross-examination of Condon[56]
-       4 Mar 08: Later: Meynell is cross-examined by Mansfield.

In Meynell's February 2008 statement he said:

I offered Diana ... the opportunity to have a [POLSA][a] team of officers from the Palace of Westminster conduct a deep search of her apartments and vehicle in order to re-establish their security and to reassure the Princess.... This was clearly something she had not considered and [she] agreed to the search. The apartments and her car were searched with negative result by the team from the Palace of Westminster. I conveyed the result of this search to the Commissioner in an oral briefing. There was no written record kept.[57]

In summary, the events as Meynell stated it on 15 February 2008 were:
1)   Meynell offered the search of apartments and vehicle
2)   Diana accepted
3)   The search was conducted with a negative result
4)   Meynell conveyed this verbally to Condon
5)   "There was no written record kept".

Four weeks earlier at the inquest, in mid-January 2008, Commissioner Paul Condon had already stated:

We had experts who could have tested for any devices, but [Diana] was not prepared to assist us to do that.[58]

By mid-February Meynell's account under oath was the opposite of Condon's account under oath.

Then at the inquest on 4 March 2008, after Meynell had read Condon's testimony, he then stated:

[Diana] was quite adamant that she was not prepared to do anything further.[59]

This is a complete about-face in Meynell's account and when Mansfield confronted him on that, he stated: "I have obviously been very clumsy in my wording".[60]

Instead, what is obvious is that both accounts can't be right – Meynell, who was Deputy Assistant Commissioner of Police before retiring in 1995,

---

[a] Police Search Adviser.

has either lied under oath in his statement on February 15 or when he gave his evidence on March 4.

Under cross-examination, Meynell proceeded to state that he was mixed up with a sweep that he said occurred the previous year, in 1993:

> **Following the carpet incident[a] ... I asked fairly forcibly of the Princess that the premises would need to be re-swept and she quite reluctantly agreed.[61]**

Meynell went further:

> **I am quite adamant, sir, that I used a POLSA team from the Palace of Westminster to do the search.[62]**

The problem for the police is that there is absolutely no evidence of any sweeping done by the police on Diana's Kensington Palace apartments: a) Colin Trimming[b] stated: "I'm not aware of the results of those enquiries, if they were made. I'm not aware."[63] b) Patrick Jephson[c] confirmed that no one "appears to have reported back to [Diana]"[64]; and c) There is no written record of any sweep being conducted.

Meynell explained to Mansfield why there would be no written record:

> **I am saying to you that I had a verbal response from the Palace of Westminster after the sweep had been conducted to say that nothing untoward had been found, either in the premises, on the vehicle or, more importantly perhaps, on our mainframe.[65]**

When coroner, Scott Baker, pushes him on this, Meynell replies: "It may be that the Palace of Westminster made [a written record] at the time".[66] But then later, when Mansfield asks: "Did you write [a report]?" Meynell replied: "No." Mansfield: "Why not?" Meynell: "Because [the result] was a negative, sir."[67]

Meynell is not saying he can't remember. He is categorically making these statements: "I am quite adamant, sir"; "I am saying to you, sir"[68]; "I am saying to you that...."

On the official POLSA website[d], the procedure for the conduct of all searches – "main, routine and occasional" – is outlined.[e]

---

[a] Diana had privately arranged to have her premises swept for bugs. When the company arrived to do the job, they declared that they were carpet-layers. I have not covered this event but it is included in the inquest transcripts on the website.

[b] Prince Charles' police bodyguard.

[c] Diana's private secretary.

[d] This is what was available in 2009. The situation had changed by the time of writing this particular book, in early 2014 – see following footnote.

[e] This information was originally sourced during the writing of Part 2 in 2009. At that time the POLSA Job Specification was on the official UK website, albeit the URL for

The instructions include the following:
- "Read available reports ... to determine results of previous searches" at the same venue
- "Prepare a reconnaissance brief"
- "Produce written orders for the search operation"
- "Recording/documenting progress of search"
- "Maintain a search register"
- "Distribute search reports to the relevant agencies".

For every POLSA search there are at least 5 documents raised – whether the search is routine or not, and regardless of the results: much of the documentation is raised before the result is known. This is common sense, that POLSA would keep records of all searches.

David Meynell, who was in control of the POLSA team, has therefore lied again to the inquest by stating that no record would have been kept.

To Michael Mansfield, Meynell said: "I am saying to you, sir, if no damage is caused and nothing untoward is found, it would be part of their routine day."[69] But to police lawyer, Richard Horwell, he said: "This [POLSA team] was dedicated to the Houses of Parliament. That is why, as I say, it sticks in my memory because I was actually breaking new ground."[70]

So: "part of their routine day" or "I was actually breaking new ground" – these two statements are complete opposites.

Why is there no written record? I suggest the answer is: Because no sweep was ever carried out after the 18 October 1994 meeting (or in 1993).

Why was there no sweep? Mansfield may have answered this:

It was possible for security services to be involved in monitoring and you [Meynell] did not want to get involved in finding out whether there were any devices.[71]

Meynell and Condon both told the inquest that Diana didn't want a sweep, and that she refused to cooperate:

---

the actual role details was somewhat obscure: http://test2.kj-h.biz/html/job-specification.html At the time of writing (in early 2014) it appears that the UK website for POLSA now no longer exists, and the above Job Specification link has also been removed. POLSA is still referred to on the MPS website regarding the conduct of specialist searches. In 2011 an article outlining the role of POLSA in the conduct of searches was posted on the Police Oracle. This is an independent UK policing website. The article – which has similar content to what was on the POLSA website in 2009 – can be found at: http://www.policeoracle.com/news/SIO-Corner-Role-of-PolSA_40035.html
It is notable that in 2014 Canada has a dedicated POLSA website – www.polsa.ca – and the identical Job Specification details that were on the 2009 UK site appear there, under "Police Search". On the Home Page of the Canadian POLSA site it reads: "Bringing British expertise to Canadian Law Enforcement".

- Meynell: "She was quite adamant that she was not prepared to do anything further"[72] and "She declined to help in any way."[73]

- Condon: "We had experts who could have tested for any devices, but she was not prepared to assist us to do that";[74] "She was not prepared to assist us in any way"[75] and "At the end of the conversation she clearly refused to assist at all".[76]

The mystery about this is that according to the October 18 report, Diana said nothing of the sort.

When Mansfield asked Meynell: "Can you explain why the aide-memoire [report] does not make clear that the most important aspect of this is that the Princess was refusing to have a search?" all Meynell, the report's author, could say was "I really cannot answer that".[77]

The reason he can't answer it is because when Meynell asserts at the inquest that Diana was not at all cooperating, he has told another lie. If that had been the case, it would have been included in the "secret" report – but it is clearly not there.

When Mansfield suggested that Condon was lying about this as well, he responded aggressively: "I would say back to you that that is a complete nonsense".[78]

Later Mansfield tries again: "It does not say anything about 'I do not want you to search my premises or sweep them ...' does it?" Condon ridiculously replies: "No, nor does it say what she was going to do later in the day or a host of other things".[79]

Condon instead asserts: "This is not a note that was saying 'I said', 'She said', 'I said', 'She said', 'I said', 'She said'."[80]

If the reader has another look at the document, they will notice that it is a record of a conversation, in the third person. There are not many direct quotes, but the to-ing and fro-ing in the conversation is reported. Meynell uses the following phrases: "HRH bluntly asked me"; "I told her"; "She then said"; "She again asked"; "I informed her"; "She then told" – and so on.

The report is precisely what Condon is saying it isn't, except it is primarily in the third person.

Meynell concludes the report with the following words: "My view is that today's meeting was basically to ask me whether I placed some form of device on her vehicle."

As Mansfield states: "That [conclusion] doesn't appear to be reflected in the note".[81] The first 1½ pages of the report relate to issues other than surveillance and a glance over the surveillance concerns covered (listed earlier) reveals that other issues were dealt with.

A closer reading of the report reveals that Diana was asking whether Meynell had any knowledge regarding the bugging of her car.[a] Diana does not attribute the possible bugging to the police, and there is little doubt that if she had, Meynell would have made that clear in the report. What Diana did say was that five people from "an organisation" had her under surveillance – it is evident that she is not talking about the police. It's common sense that if Diana's car was bugged, that could have been carried out by the security services – and that appears to be implied from the term "an organisation". Mansfield suggested: "Her concerns were the security services, possibly even GCHQ" and momentarily accepted by Condon under pressure: "that is a reasonable interpretation of her comments".[82]

At the inquest Meynell insisted that Diana "asked me if I[b] had bugged her vehicle"[83] despite the report's description of the conversation clearly not including that.

The insistence by both Condon and Meynell that Diana was checking on whether the police were bugging her car – "the whole purpose of the meeting was to see if we were doing anything" (Condon)[84] – could be to distract attention away from the true focus of Diana's concerns: MI5, MI6 and GCHQ.

Scotland Yard's Disdain for Diana

What was the attitude of the police towards Diana during the post-separation period?

Jonathon Hough[c] asked Meynell: "Did you give [the POLSA team] any specific instructions arising out of this meeting [with Diana]?" To which Meynell confidently replied: "I did not, sir."[85]

The police had just been provided with three major concerns from the wife of the future King – telephone tapping, vehicle bugging and overall surveillance – and how did the police respond? They did nothing, and they appear happy to state that fact.

The theme of both Condon and Meynell's testimony was that Diana was bluffing and teasing – they both actually talk about "calling her bluff";[d] Condon says she was "teasing" or a "tease" six times in his full transcript,[e]

---

[a] Her precise statements, as attributed by Meynell were: "HRH asked me if her car had been bugged" and "She again asked me if I had any knowledge of whether her vehicle was bugged".
[b] At times he says "we" – the police – and at other times it is "I" – Meynell, presumably in his police role.
[c] Inquest lawyer.
[d] Condon: 17 Jan 08: 10.4 & 26.19. Meynell: 4 Mar 08: 53.2.
[e] 16 Jan 08: 164.14, 165.21; 17 Jan 08: 8.20, 10.8, 15.12, 17.11.

and refers to her being "mischievous" several times.[a] At one stage Condon states:

I say that our honest belief at the time was that this was one of those meetings where she was in a mischievous mood....[86]

The problem with this view is that the original report of the meeting does not reveal that – bluffing, teasing and mischief fail to receive a mention within it. Instead, Diana raises serious issues regarding her belief that she was under surveillance.

Having read the report several times, I believe Diana may have called this meeting to find out what the police position was, with regard to her surveillance by the intelligence agencies.[b] Diana comes across as a woman whose private life was under threat and she appears to be desperately trying to establish whether the police are in a position to help her – are they able to confirm to her whether her car is being bugged?

Diana already has established that her landline phone calls are under surveillance but she seems unsure about whether her car is bugged – but she wants to know: she is seeking information. Diana may have been trying to establish exactly where the police stood – were they on her side or not, with regard to the intelligence agencies?

The relevant inquest transcripts[c] help the reader to realise the true attitude the police had and still have towards Princess Diana.

The top police treated Diana with something between disdain and a joke. At one stage Mansfield asked Commissioner Condon: "You have all these epithets about 'mischievous' and so on. Is that really the real view you took of her?" Condon replied, "Yes" before checking himself after apparently realising what he had said.[87]

Why have Condon and Meynell told repeated lies under oath in their inquest evidence? The short answer is because they were placed in a position during the inquest where they had to hide the nature of what was really happening in their dealings with Princess Diana.

The disdain – even maybe contempt – that senior British police showed towards Diana in 1994 has carried through right to when they gave their evidence at the inquest. That is over a period of 14 years.

In life these senior officers completely failed to protect or support Princess Diana. In death these same people committed perjury to cover-up their failure towards her.

---

[a] 17 Jan 08: 10.10, 17.1, 17.12.
[b] When reading the report, one should bear in mind that it has not been written from Diana's viewpoint, but from that of Meynell – he was the author.
[c] Reproduced in Part 2, Police Issues section in the Surveillance chapter.

The full despicable role played by senior British police will become clearer as this story progresses.

Intelligence Documents

In 1998 the NSA[a] admitted that it had "1,349 documents … in connection with Lady Diana Frances Spencer".[88]

None of these have ever been released despite requests from relatives of those who lost loved ones in the Paris crash.

JoAnn Grube, NSA's Deputy Director of Policy, revealed that of the 1,349 documents, 1,167 were "foreign press articles" relating to Princess Diana.[89] That immediately raises the question: Why was the NSA collecting articles on Diana? And, if they are innocuous, why can't they be released?

None of the other 182 documents have ever been released. Grube wrote that of those only 39 were "NSA originated and controlled" – the others came from other agencies.[90] The reason Grube gave for the failure to release the NSA documents:

> **Their disclosure could reasonably be expected to cause exceptionally grave damage to national security.[91]**

Eight years later, in 2006, the NSA Director of Policy stated in a letter to Operation Paget that disclosure of the documents "could reasonably be expected to cause exceptionally grave damage to the national security of the United States by revealing intelligence sources and methods." [b]

What is contained in these documents? Why won't the US release them?

The point is that if Princess Diana simply died in a tragic accident, what has the NSA got to lose by releasing these documents to the next of kin of victims?

It is notable that whilst the US' NSA admits to having 1,349 documents, MI6 and MI5 have never admitted to having even one – yet they are the agencies most would expect to have an interest in Princess Diana.

At the inquest Richard Dearlove[c] denied there was any "eavesdropping, surveillance [or] bugging" of Diana or Dodi during the summer of their deaths.[92] Miss X, an MI6 administrator, confirmed that if either of them "had been of interest to the service, there would have been a card" for them in the MI6 system. She then stated: "There were no cards".[93]

Why does the NSA have 1,349 documents and MI6 has none?

---

[a] US National Security Agency.
[b] Letter from Lewis Giles dated 20 March 2006 – read out 13 Mar 08: 85.23.
[c] MI6 Director of Operations in 1997.

"She Was Being Followed"

One after another, witnesses spoke of belief[a] that Princess Diana was under surveillance:

- "[Diana] was always concerned about ... people watching her, listening to her"[94] – Richard Kay, journalist and friend
- "it was a reality that [Diana] just accepted ... that her phones were tapped and that she was being followed"[95] – Simone Simmons, friend and healer
- "on one occasion ... as she drove, she believed someone [who wanted to hurt her] was following in another vehicle"[b] – Roberto Devorik, friend and fashion designer
- "[Diana] felt her telephones were bugged and her house was bugged, and she seemed always very conscious ... that she was being watched"[96] – Raine Spencer, step-mother
- "[Diana spoke] about concerns that she was being recorded or bugged"[97] – Rosa Monckton, friend and MI6 agent
- "[Diana] feared about having her telephone bugged"[98] – Lucia Flecha de Lima, friend
- "[Diana] did mention that the phone lines were being monitored"[99] – Hasnat Khan, boyfriend
- "from [1989] on, [Diana] had a fear that she could possibly be listened into"[100] – Rodney Turner, friend and car dealer
- "[Diana] was concerned that ... people knew who she had called and who had called her on her phone"[101] – Grahame Harding, security consultant
- "[Diana] ... got a ... mobile phone that she thought couldn't be bugged"[102] – Maggie Rae, lawyer
- "[Diana's] actions were such ... that it was clear that [being monitored] was a concern to her"[103] – Michael Gibbins, private secretary
- "[Diana] believed that her apartments were being bugged"[104] – Sarah McCorquodale, sister
- "I was quite aware that [Diana's] communications might be monitored by the security services ... and I would quite often say to her that she must assume that her phone calls could be overheard"[105] – Patrick Jephson, private secretary

---

[a] Either belief by the witness or by Diana herself.
[b] Paget description of Devorik's statement - Paget Report, p119.

- "one of the police officers on royalty protection duty certainly had a list of calls purported to have been made from the Princess's phone"[106] – Patrick Jephson, private secretary
- "[Diana] believed that ... the services monitored everything [she] did"[107] – Paul Burrell, butler
- "[Diana] thought her mobile phones and the landline phones were all being listened to and recorded"[108] – Paul Burrell, butler
- "I believed that ... the services monitored everything [Diana] did"[109] – Paul Burrell, butler
- "[Diana] ... had this feeling that she was ... being listened to"[110] – Colin Trimming, husband's bodyguard
- "[Diana] asked me if certain people could [murder] her.... I assumed ... she was talking about security forces type people"[111] – Lee Sansum, bodyguard

The evidence of these 16 witnesses – Diana's friends, family and employees – supports Diana's position as recorded in Meynell's October 1994 report: she believed she was under surveillance. It also is further evidence that Paul Condon and David Meynell lied under oath when they insisted that Diana was bluffing and teasing over her surveillance concerns.

In 1994 Princess Diana was concerned about surveillance, but during the following year her concerns became even more personal, specific and sinister....

4   She Feared For Her Life: 1995

Between 1987 and 1995 several events occurred that could have given Princess Diana a genuine reason to fear for her safety.

First, in May 1987 her former bodyguard Barry Mannakee died in a suspicious road crash.

In July 1986, Colin Trimming or Prince Charles, or both, had perceived that an inappropriate relationship had developed between Mannakee and Princess Diana. Mannakee was immediately transferred to a different role and 10 months later he was dead.

The police investigation into the crash has never been released. Then 20 years later, at the inquest, lies were told regarding the circumstances of Mannakee's removal from proximity to Diana.[a]

In a 1993 video recording Diana said:

I think [Mannakee] was bumped off.[112b] (WFJ)

In 1989, two years after Mannakee's death, George Mountbatten[c] warned Diana's lover James Hewitt that he "should be very careful in his relationship with the Princess of Wales".[113] (WFJ) Hewitt also recounted to police that "around 1990 … he received threats…. They consisted of three telephone calls … each one telling him not to contact or see the Princess of Wales any longer." Hewitt told Paget that he discussed the threats with Diana.[114] (WFJ)

In August 1992 the Squidgygate tape was published and two years after that, in 1994, security expert Grahame Harding discovered an electronic signal behind Diana's bedroom wall at Kensington Palace.

Hasnat Khan – who commenced a relationship with Princess Diana around October 1995 – told Scotland Yard that he received "a lot of anonymous threats through the post". He added:

---

[a] This is addressed in Part 2, Barry Mannakee section in the Fears and Threats chapter.

[b] 1993 is an approximate date. This quote was included in a set of videos Diana recorded with her voice coach Peter Settelen, between September 1992 and December 1994: Paget Report, p132.

[c] Otherwise known as George Milford-Haven – a member of the royal family.

I have received envelopes containing cut-out pictures of me, together with a noose around my neck. This went on and on and ... I did mention it once to Diana.[115]

These events – the premature death of Mannakee, the threats to Hewitt, Squidgygate, Harding's discovery, Hasnat's death threats – could all have contributed to Princess Diana feeling, by 1995, that her life was under threat.

"They Wanted To Get Rid Of Her"

Many witnesses testified that they heard Princess Diana say she feared for her life:[a]

- "[Diana] said ...: 'I will finish like Mary, Queen of Scots, and be chopped. I am an inconvenience for them'"[116] – Roberto Devorik, friend and fashion designer
- "[Diana] said ... 'Prince Philip wants to see me dead'"[117] – Roberto Devorik, friend and fashion designer
- "[Diana] had said on many, many occasions that she was going to be bumped off"[118] – Simone Simmons, friend and healer
- "it was a pervasive belief in [Diana's] conversation [that] ... 'they' wanted to put her aside and get rid of her"[119] – Maggie Rae, lawyer
- "[Diana] expressed on more than one occasion ... fears that she might be killed"[120] – Sandra Davis, lawyer
- "Diana ... said that one of them had to go, Camilla or her"[121] – Hasnat Khan, lover
- referring to the assassination of Gianni Versace: "[Diana] said 'do you think they ... could do that to [me]'"[122] – Lee Sansum, bodyguard
- "[Diana] was quite obsessed by the idea of accidents ... primarily involving [herself]. She often mentioned helicopter crashes"[123] – Raine Spencer, step-mother
- "[Diana] told me that she knew Prince Philip/Prince Charles [wanted] to get rid of her"[124] – Mohamed Al Fayed, friend
- "Diana had told [Mohamed Al Fayed] that she would go up in a helicopter and never come down alive"[125] – John Macnamara, Harrods head of security
- "the Royal Family ... did not want [Diana] around anymore"[126] – Melissa Henning, Dodi's assistant.

These accounts reveal that Diana didn't keep her fears to herself – instead she communicated them to people she interacted with.

---

[a] Princess Diana's fears for her life commenced around October 1995 – this was close to the time her relationship with Hasnat Khan commenced and she also was making preparations for going on BBC's *Panorama* (see next chapter). The witness evidence below relates to Diana's communicated perceptions from 1995 through to her death in August 1997.

But the evidence is not just from Diana's conversations – there are also documents that reveal she feared for her life.

Burrell Note

During October 1995 – around the same time Diana's relationship with the Pakistani doctor, Hasnat Khan, commenced – she apparently felt it was necessary to put her fears to paper.

Princess Diana penned a note and passed it to her butler, Paul Burrell, for safe-keeping.[a] She wrote:

> **I am sitting here at my desk today in October, longing for someone to hug me and encourage me to keep strong and hold my head high – this particular phase of my life is the most dangerous – my husband is planning 'an accident' in my car, brake failure and serious head injury in order to make the path clear for Charles to marry Tiggy [Legge-Bourke]. Camilla is nothing but a decoy, so we are all....**
>
> **I have been battered, bruised and abused mentally by a system for 15 years now, but I feel no resentment, I carry no hatred, I am weary of the battles, but I will never surrender. I am strong inside and maybe that is a problem for my enemies.**
>
> **Thank you Charles, for putting me through such hell and for giving me the opportunity to learn from the cruel things you have done to me. I have gone forward fast and have cried more than anyone will ever know. The anguish nearly killed me, but my inner strength has never let me down, and my guides have taken such good care of me up there. Aren't I fortunate to have had their wings to protect me....[127]**

This note in Diana's own handwriting ran to ten pages[128] but the inquest jury was only shown one page – reproduced below.

---

[a] Paul Burrell has stated that this note was written by Diana in October 1996 (14 Jan 08: 93.20) but other evidence reveals that this is false – the true date was a year earlier, in October 1995. This issue is addressed in Part 2, Burrell Note section of the Fears and Threats chapter.

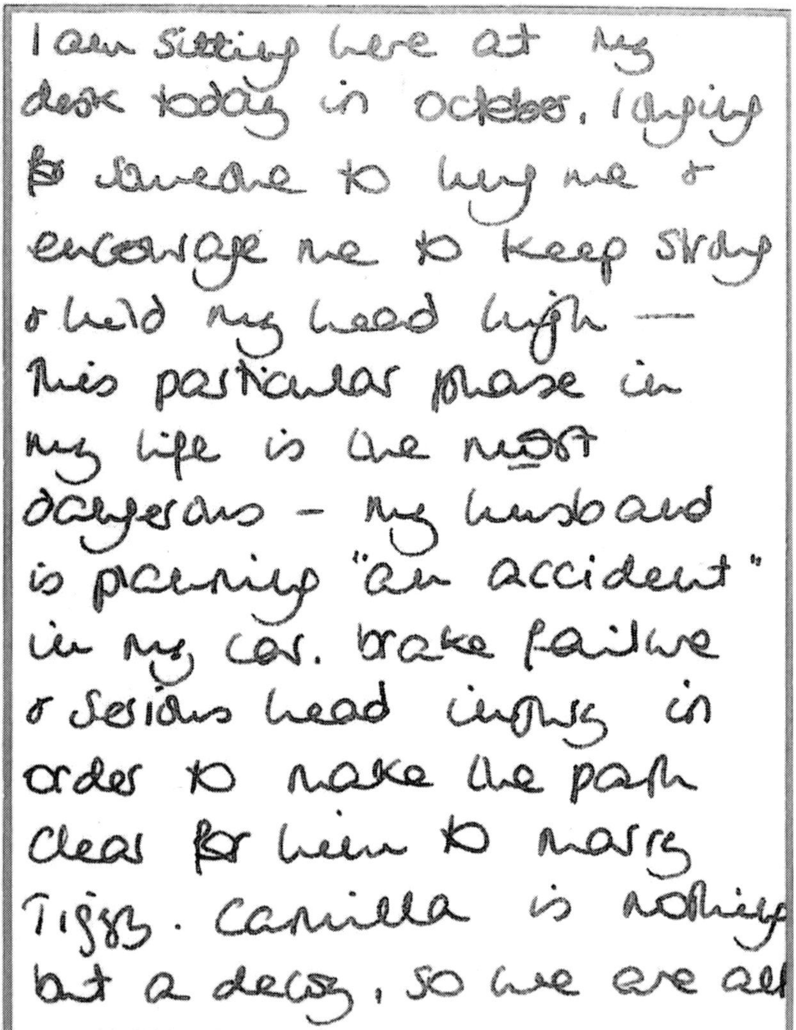

I am sitting here at my desk today in October, longing for someone to hug me & encourage me to keep strong & hold my head high — This particular phase in my life is the most dangerous — my husband is planning "an accident" in my car. brake failure & serious head injury in order to make the path clear for him to marry Tiggy. Camilla is nothing but a decoy, so we are all

Figure 2

The only page of Diana's October 1995 "Burrell Note" shown at the inquest. There were 9 other pages in this note that have never been made public.

Paul Burrell described the note as Diana's "insurance for the future".[129]
    Yet after Diana's death, the only insurance value the document could have, would be if it was made public. Effectively Diana was the owner of the

document[a], and after the crash the onus (out of loyalty to Diana's wishes) was on Burrell to make it public.

He waited six years and then finally divulged the contents of the note in a best-selling book: *A Royal Duty* published in 2003.

Mishcon Note

Late in the same month – October 1995 – Princess Diana met with her lawyer, Lord Victor Mishcon, at Kensington Palace.

During this meeting – at which others were also present[b] – Diana confided several concerns that had been passed onto her from "reliable sources". These included a fear of a car crash being orchestrated to "get rid of" her.

The next morning Victor Mishcon drew up a note[c] to outline Diana's fears. This key document later became known as the Mishcon Note.

Diana's concerns, as listed by Mishcon were:
-       the Queen would abdicate in April 1996 and Charles would become King
-       efforts would be made before April 1996 to get rid of Diana – or ensure serious head injury – in an orchestrated crash in her car by "brake failure or whatever", so she could at least be declared "mentally unbalanced"
-       Camilla was to be "put aside"
-       Tiggy Legge-Bourke had had an abortion.

Mishcon's initial reaction to the stated conspiracy was one of disbelief. But he immediately consulted Patrick Jephson who "said that he himself 'half believed' in the accuracy of what [Diana] had said as to the risks to her safety". Mishcon then said that he "would make [himself] available – day or night", if needed.

Some of the predicted events appear to have occurred – the brake failure in Diana's car;[d] a possible attempt to remove Camilla[ef] – whereas others clearly didn't – the Queen's abdication and Charles' ascension.

On 31 October 1995 Victor Mishcon wrote his note and arranged for it to be typed up – a copy appears below.

It would then remain locked in Mishcon's safe until after Diana died.[a]

---

[a] The document was a note – not a letter – as has been claimed by Burrell. See 14 Jan 08: 97.8 to 97.24 – even when challenged on this Burrell still refers to it as a "letter".
[b] Lawyers Sandra Davis and Maggie Rae and Patrick Jephson, Diana's private secretary.
[c] Reproduced below.
[d] See next chapter.
[e] See Part 6, Camilla Car Crash section of Chapter 2.
[f] It is also possible that Tiggy had an abortion – this is covered in Part 6, the Tiggy Legge-Bourke section of the Mishcon Note chapter.

HOW THEY MURDERED PRINCESS DIANA

31st October 1995

I attended on HRH at Kensington Palace yesterday 30 October at approximately 4 p.m. Sandra Davis & Maggie Rae of my office were also present as was Commander Jephson. Because of the serious statements made by HRH in the course of this meeting I decided unusually to write this entry and to give instructions that it should be securely held.

H.R.H. said that she had been informed by reliable sources whom she did not wish to reveal (they would speedily dry up if she broke her promise of confidentiality) that (a) The Queen would be abdicating in April and the Prince of Wales would then assume the throne and (b) efforts would be made if not to get rid of her (be it by some accident in her car such as pre-prepared brake failure or whatever) between now and then, then at least to see that she was so injured or damaged as to be declared "unbalanced". She was convinced that there was a conspiracy and that she and Camilla were to be "put aside". She had also been told that Miss Legge-Bourke had been operated on for an abortion and that she (HRH) would shortly be in receipt of "a certificate".

I told HRH that if she really believed her life or being was threatened, security measures including those relating to her car must be increased. I frankly however could not believe that what I was hearing was credible as to this alleged conspiracy and sought and obtained an opportunity of a private word with Commander Jephson who surprisingly said that he himself "half believed" in the accuracy of what HRH had said as to the risks to her safety. Reporting to or taking the police in to our confidence would be useless. I said that if anything further should arise on these matters I would make myself available - day or night.

HRH in answer to a question I put to her said that in her view the happiest solution for the future of the monarchy was for the Prince of Wales to abdicate in favour of Prince William and that without any malice whatsoever she wished to put that view forward in the interests of the Royal family and everyone. She was disappointed that the Prime Minister had not been to see her or got in touch with her for a very considerable time. I offered to pass this on to the Lord Chancellor on her behalf and did so later that afternoon in a private meeting I had with him. I told him no more.

VM

Figure 3

> Mishcon Note typed up following a meeting between Princess Diana and Victor Mishcon on 30 October 1995.

---

[a] Following the 1997 crash the way in which this key document was handled became extremely significant. This is addressed later.

5   Panorama and the Aftermath

On Sunday November 5, just six days after Princess Diana's meeting with Victor Mishcon, the BBC's Martin Bashir visited Kensington Palace. He conducted an in-depth interview with Diana and this was aired 15 days later on *Panorama*, 20 November 1995.

During the program Diana talked frankly and openly about her life and relationships, royal relationships and her failed marriage:[130]

- On her treatment by Charles and the royal family: "Anything good I ever did nobody ever said a thing. Never said, `Well done', or `Was it OK?' But if I tripped up, which invariably I did, because I was new at the game, a ton of bricks came down on me."

- On treatment by Charles' friends: "There's no better way to dismantle a personality than to isolate it"

- On Charles' relationship with Camilla: "There were three of us in this marriage, so it was a bit crowded."

- On supporting the 1992 Morton book: "I think I was so fed up with being seen as someone who was a basket-case, because I am a very strong person – and I know that causes complications in the system that I live in."

- On the post-separation situation: "People's agendas changed overnight. I was now separated wife of the Prince of Wales – I was a problem, I was a liability (seen as), and 'How are we going to deal with her? This hasn't happened before.'"

- On post-separation treatment by Charles and associates: "Visits abroad being blocked ... things that had come naturally my way being stopped, letters going, that got lost.... Everything changed after we separated, and life became very difficult then for me."

- On the publication of the Squidgygate tapes: "It was done to harm me in a serious manner, and that was the first time I'd experienced what it was like to be outside the net, so to speak, and not be in the family.... It was to make the public change their attitude towards me.... It was, you know, if we are going to divorce, my husband would hold more cards than I would."

- On her determination: "I'll fight to the end, because I believe that I have a role to fulfil, and I've got two children to bring up."

- On the enemy: "The enemy was my husband's department, because I always got more publicity. My work was more, was discussed much more than him."
- On her future role: "I'd like to be an ambassador for this country. I'd like to represent this country abroad.... I know that I can give love for a minute, for half an hour, for a day, for a month, but I can give – I'm very happy to do that, and I want to do that.... Let's now use the knowledge I've gathered to help other people in distress."
- On destroying the monarchy: "Why would I want to destroy something that is my children's future?"
- On being Queen: "I'd like to be a queen of people's hearts, in people's hearts, but I don't see myself being Queen of this country."
- On Charles being King: "I would think that the top job, as I call it, would bring enormous limitations to him, and I don't know whether he could adapt to that."

This extensive and frank interview aired throughout the United Kingdom, and then the world.

That same night, following *Panorama*, close friend of Prince Charles and Britain's Minister for the Armed Forces, Nicholas Soames, went on BBC's *Newsnight* and said:

Diana "really is [in] the advanced stages of paranoia".[131]

The next day Diana travelled to Buenos Aires with her Argentinian fashion designer friend, Roberto Devorik. She spoke to Prince William by phone, then told Devorik:

I am sure that Prince Philip is involved with the security services. After this, they are going to get rid of me.[132]

Philip did retaliate and was more vicious this time.

Letters From Philip

A new wave of letters ensued. And they were more hostile than 1992. Simone Simmons described them to the *Mail on Sunday* in 2002:

They "were the nastiest letters Diana had ever received. She had death threats which were worded nicer than [Philip's] letters. He called her a trollop and a harlot and said she was damaging the Royal Family."[133ab] (WFJ)

Paul Burrell also saw these vitriolic letters. In late 2002 he told the *Daily Mirror*: "Simone [Simmons] was the Princess's friend and confidante who

---

[a] In the media in 2002 and later at the inquest Rosa Monckton challenged Simmons' account of these letters. This is addressed later.

[b] Simmons indicated that "the letters stopped when Diana and Charles were getting divorced" – 28 Jan 08: 78.15.

was entrusted with her personal documentation. If she is revealing anything, that is solely her decision. I know the hurt these letters caused Diana. I cannot and will not get drawn into this."[134] (WFJ)

At the inquest Paget officer Jane Scotchbrook admitted that she had altered Simone Simmons' 2004 statement by leaving out certain "information ... about the nasty letters" from Philip.[135]

Scotchbrook was asked three times about this and on each occasion provided a completely different reason for the omission.

She told Michael Mansfield: "I didn't believe [the evidence left out] was relevant to the [murder] motive or to [any] motive [Philip] may have had".[136]

Next, Scotchbrook changes the reason to: Simmons "had actually asked for it not to be in the statement".[137]

This would immediately raise two questions: If Simmons didn't want it included in her statement, then: a) why did she tell the police in the first place? and b) why had she gone public with it in 2002? [a]

It is obvious that Simmons should have been questioned about Scotchbrook's account, but that never occurred.

Scotchbrook later introduced a third reason for suppressing the evidence: "I was just trying to protect people involved with that bit of information". It is ridiculous that Scotchbrook wasn't asked what she meant by that comment.

Prior to testifying in January 2008 to the London inquest, Simmons was warned not to mention these letters. She stated in a later interview that whilst waiting at the Royal Courts of Justice "somebody came in and said 'You're not allowed to mention the content of Prince Philip's letters.'"[138]

Miles Hunt-Davis, Philip's private secretary, only provided the inquest with the series of letters from 1992 between Philip and Diana.[b]

Mansfield asked Hunt-Davis if he had requested from Philip all of his correspondence with Diana. He replied: "To be honest, I cannot remember. It is a long time ago."[139]

Less than a minute later Hunt-Davis affirmed under oath that his letter request to Philip was "pretty recent"[140] – in fact, his statement outlining the request was dated 6 December 2007, exactly one week prior to his cross-examination.[141] In that statement Hunt-Davis also describes the request from the inquest for the correspondence[c] as "recent".[142]

Hunt-Davis' earlier sworn testimony that "it is a long time ago" was a lie.

---

[a] Following the premature closing of the Burrell trial, Simmons went public in the *Mail on Sunday* regarding Philip's vitriolic letters. See above. This is covered in detail in Part 5, Philip-Diana Letters section of Chapter 1C.

[b] By the time the jury got to see those letters they had been heavily redacted.

[c] That request occurred prior to Hunt-Davis requesting the letters from Philip.

In his statement Hunt-Davis said he only requested the letters written during "this period of their relationship". At the inquest he clarified that meant the period prior to the Diana-Charles separation in December 1992.[143]

Mansfield then asked: "Are you able to say to us today, hand on heart, that there is no other [Philip-Diana] correspondence?" Hunt-Davis answered: "I am not able to say so."[144]

Why did Hunt-Davis lie by saying it was a long time ago that he requested the letters when it had actually been recent? And why was he so reluctant to state which period of correspondence he had requested from Philip?

Hunt-Davis' failure to be open and honest regarding this adds credence to Simone Simmons' testimony – supported by Paul Burrell – describing the later vitriolic 1995-6 letters.

The tampering with Simmons' evidence, admitted by Jane Scotchbrook, raises very serious concerns of an attempt to suppress witness testimony regarding the true nature of Philip's later letters to Diana.

In light of that, the warning Simmons received at the Royal Courts of Justice confirms that the cover-up regarding these letters was a joint effort involving the police and the judiciary.

Seen together with actions in 2002 by both the Duke of Edinburgh and Rosa Monckton[a] to undermine Simone Simmons' credible public account, one realises the cover-up is both coordinated and widespread.

"Philip Wants To See Me Dead"

Other witnesses – despite not seeing the letters – perceived that there were issues in the Philip-Diana relationship. Following the *Panorama* interview – and the increasingly vitriolic letters from Philip – Diana became more vocal about her fears regarding the Duke of Edinburgh. [b]

Witnesses testified:[c]

- "[the Diana-Philip] relationship was a little tense or awkward"[145] – Susan Kassem, friend

- "[Diana] did not like the Duke of Edinburgh"[146] – Hasnat Khan, ex-lover October 1995 to July 1997

- "Did [Diana] like Philip? No."[147] (WFJ) – Alistair Campbell, Tony Blair's press secretary, conversation Diana, Blair and others, January 1997

- "[Diana] said ... 'Prince Philip wants to see me dead'"[148] – Roberto Devorik, friend and fashion designer, conversation spring 1996

---

[a] Covered in Part 5, Philip-Diana Letters section of Chapter 1C.

[b] The quotes below relate to conversations that occurred after the November 1995 *Panorama* interview.

[c] More extensive accounts of the witness evidence appear in Part 2, section on Nature of the Relationship, in the Fears and Threats chapter.

- "[Diana] pointed to the portrait of Prince Philip[a] and said 'He really hates me and would like to see me disappear'"[149] – Roberto Devorik, conversation June 1996
- "[Diana] told me that she knew Prince Philip/Prince Charles [wanted] to get rid of her"[150] – Mohamed Al Fayed, friend, conversation July 1997
- "there was ... 'a terrible anger' at the way she was being treated by ... Prince Philip.... His welcome into the Family had turned to cold hostility once the marriage had broken up"[151] (WFJ) – cameraman who recorded videos in March 1997.[b]

Brake Failure

It seems Princess Diana's fears – as expressed in the Mishcon and Burrell notes – may have been justified, because about a month later, whilst Diana was driving her Audi in London, the brakes failed.

The main account comes from Diana's friend Simone Simmons:

> **In 1995 ... [Diana] was driving unaccompanied through London in her Audi. As she approached a set of traffic lights which had just turned to red, she put her foot on the brake but nothing happened and the car kept coasting forward. When it eventually came to a halt she leapt out, abandoned [her car] where it was, and went straight back to Kensington Palace in a taxi, whose driver refused to accept his fare, and asked for her autograph instead. She rang me and said, 'Someone's tampered with my brakes'.[152] (WFJ)**

Hasnat Khan, Diana's lover, testified that around December 1995 he noticed that Diana had changed cars – from an Audi to a BMW. He told the police in 2004:

> **I asked her what had happened to the Audi as it was such a lovely car. She told me that the brakes had been tampered with so she decided to change the car.[153]**

Diana also informed her private secretary and butler.

Paul Burrell told the inquest:

> **I remember an incident with the brakes on the Princess's car. [She] felt that her brakes had been tampered with.[154]**

Patrick Jephson stated to the police:

> **During November/December 1995 the Princess of Wales stated that she thought the brakes of her Audi had been tampered with.[155]**

Simmons went on to describe Diana's reaction after the incident:

---

[a] In a London airport VIP lounge.
[b] These videos Diana recorded prior to her death are addressed later.

[Diana] wrote to her friends Lady Annabel Goldsmith, Lucia Flecha de Lima and Elsa Bowker. She also wrote to me. In the letter I received she warned, 'The brakes on my car have been tampered with. If something does happen to me it will be MI5 or MI6.'[156] (WFJ)

Elsa Bowker died in 2000 – seven years before the inquest started. But Annabel Goldsmith and Lucia Flecha de Lima were both cross-examined. They should have been asked about these letters Simmons described – but that never occurred.

The inquest heard evidence from Diana's psychic, Rita Rogers, who said in her 2007 statement: "I told Diana that somebody had tampered with the brakes on her car."[157] At the inquest Rogers said the conversation occurred "round about the time of the *Panorama* programme" – November 1995.[158]

There were efforts at the inquest to suggest Diana had made the brake tampering story up. Scott Baker introduced the topic during his Summing Up with this: "It was suggested that [Rita Rogers] was responsible for putting ideas into Diana's head..... It was she who raised the subject of Diana's brakes having been tampered with and she who was worried about the Audi." [159]

Does the concept of Princess Diana being of unsound mind fit with the evidence at the time?

On Sunday 5 November 1995 – close to the timing of this event – Diana recorded the *Panorama* interview. In the program she comes across as a person with a perfectly sound mind. If the brake tampering was a delusion, then were the four letters she sent out, the verbal notification to three other people and the change of cars also the result of a delusion?

The balance of the evidence – shown above and in Part 2[a] – indicates the brake failure incident did occur.

Palace Response

Following *Panorama* Princess Diana's public support soared to 85%.[160] (WFJ)

Within a few weeks the Queen acted.

First she punished the BBC for airing the program – she withdrew their sole broadcast rights to her annual Christmas message.[161] (WFJ)

Then, within three weeks of *Panorama* the Queen was in negotiations with prime minister, John Major, and the Archbishop of Canterbury, George Carey, trying to establish a way to enforce a Diana-Charles divorce.[162] (WFJ)

On 18 December 1995 – just under a month after Diana had gone public – she received a letter from the Queen requesting the divorce.[163] (WFJ)

---

[a] Section on Brake Tampering in the Fears and Threats chapter.

BMW Crash

Three months later, on 22 March 1996, Princess Diana was involved in a serious collision with a Fiat Uno in London.

The *Daily Mail* reported that she was "driving home alone after visiting a friend in London".

> **A Porsche 911 smashed into a parked Fiat and sent it careering into the path of [Diana's] rented BMW.... The front wing and driver's side door of Diana's car were mangled. A policeman at the scene said: 'The Fiat was propelled across the road into the path of the oncoming cars.... The BMW is too damaged to be driven away.' Diana's spokesman said: 'The Princess is shaken but she is all right.' .... A police spokesman said the owner of the Porsche had arrived at a casino in Cromwell Road and left his car with a doorman to park. 'The doorman got in and after travelling only a few yards, hit the back of the Fiat Uno'.[164] (WFJ)**

The *Mirror* also reported the crash:

> **Witnesses said Di – white-faced with shock – was lucky to escape injury as a Fiat Uno smashed into the driver's side of her car.... A passing motorist said the princess was 'extremely' lucky. The mayhem left other vehicles 'mangled' wrecks. Witness Peter Hull added: 'She looked totally dazed. Her face was shocked white.'... Passers-by said a blue Porsche pulled up behind [the Fiat Uno].... A doorman got behind the wheel but his foot slipped on the Porsche pedals, sending it flying into the Fiat which then careered across the busy two-lane road. It collided first with Di's BMW ... [which] was left with a severely damaged front wing. The driver's door was also smashed in. But Mr Hull, 25, said she climbed out unhurt. 'I saw her face as I passed a mere second after the impact,' he said. 'She looked as if she didn't know what had hit her. It was a miracle she wasn't hurt.' Another eyewitness said: 'I could not believe it when I saw all these cars in a mess. I was amazed to see Princess Diana behind the wheel. She looked really shaken up..... It was a really nasty accident – she was lucky to escape unhurt.... The accident happened the night before Diana was due to fly to the island of Barbuda on holiday with sons William and Harry.[165] (WFJ)**

Although the police investigated the crash, their report was never released. There was also no mention of this serious crash in the Paget Report or at the London inquest.

Why?

In late-October 1995 Princess Diana had alerted Victor Mishcon to a possible "accident in her car such as ... brake failure or whatever" between then and April 1996 – "efforts ... to get rid of her".

HOW THEY MURDERED PRINCESS DIANA

There may have been two attempts on Diana's life involving "her car" within the time frame she had predicted – the Audi brake failure and the BMW crash.

6 Removed From Royal Family: August 1996

Five months later – on 28 August 1996 – the Diana-Charles divorce was made final. But the Queen added extras – she stripped Diana of her HRH title and effectively removed her from the royal family.

The announcement from Buckingham Palace on the day read: "The Princess of Wales, as the mother of Prince William, will be regarded by The Queen and The Prince of Wales as being a member of the Royal Family."[166a] (WFJ)

This claim is contradicted by other evidence:

- "the Princess was no longer a member of the Royal Family after the divorce in August 1996"[167] – Miles Hunt-Davis, Philip's private secretary[b]
- "Diana, Princess of Wales … was not at the time of her death a member of the Royal Family"[168] (WFJ) – Anthony Mather, Asst Comptroller, Lord Chamberlain's Office
- Diana was "a former member of the Royal Family" at the time of her death[169] (WFJ) – Keith Moss, British Consul-General, Paris
- "the refusal [by the Queen] to lower the flags at Windsor Castle and the Tower of London [after Diana's death] was because Diana was no longer technically a member of the royal family, having been stripped of her HRH title"[170] – Tony Blair, Prime Minister

Anthony Mather, who was involved in organising Diana's post-death repatriation, told the police in 2005:

---

[a] There is no mention here of how Diana would be regarded by Philip – Diana's ex-father-in-law – or how she was to be regarded by anyone other than the Queen and Charles.

[b] As though to emphasise his point, Hunt-Davis repeated this sentiment: 13 Dec 07: 81.14: "The lady concerned ceased to be a member of the Royal Family"; 86.25: "Once the divorce had happened, what Princess Diana did was not relevant to the mainstream of the Royal Family".

There are plans in place for funerals of any member of the Royal Family.... There was never a separate plan for the funeral arrangements of Diana, Princess of Wales, as she was not at the time of her death a member of the Royal Family.[171] (WFJ)

This was supported by John Burton, royal coroner at the time. He later told Operation Paget that on the morning of the crash "I ... phoned the Buckingham Palace switchboard and spoke to a young lady who informed [me] that they were experiencing problems, as there were no contingency plans for the death of Diana Princess of Wales."[172] (WFJ)

Although the Queen's press secretary claimed the Queen still viewed Diana as a family member, other evidence reveals that she had removed the funeral plan for Diana because she was no longer a royal.

It was also the general perception that the Queen's removal of Princess Diana's HRH title effectively removed Diana from the royal family.

This perception is supported by the above independent accounts of Tony Blair, Miles Hunt-Davis, Anthony Mather, Keith Moss and John Burton.

Of these five accounts only the evidence of one – Hunt-Davis – was heard by the inquest jury.

On 28 August 1996 – just one year before Princess Diana's death – the Queen removed Diana's HRH title and expelled her from the royal family. From that point on there was no official interaction between Diana and senior members of the royal family. Meanwhile the Queen proceeded to remove Diana from the select list of people who had special royal funeral plans.[ab]

---

[a] There are other events that have occurred over the years which support the belief that the Queen no longer saw Princess Diana as a royal: According to author Christopher Andersen, Buckingham Palace staff were told after the divorce that Diana's name was "never again to be spoken in the presence of the Queen". Already in July 1996, the *London Gazette*, on the Queen's instructions, had published letters patent deleting Diana's name from prayers for the royal family in churches throughout Christendom. Earlier, in 1993, after Diana and Charles' separation and four years before Diana's death, Buckingham Palace had deleted Diana's name from the *Court Circular*, which lists official royal engagements. Following Diana's death, the Queen instructed that her name was not to be mentioned during the Sunday morning service at Crathie Kirk, near Balmoral. The Queen stated that no prayers were to be spoken in remembrance of Diana. The minister instead gave his original prepared sermon about the joys of moving house, including jokes by Billy Connolly. By 2007, 10 years after her death, Diana postcards were banned from sale at royal shops and palaces. Sources: Christopher Andersen, The Day Diana Died, 1998, p57; Anthony Holden, Charles at Fifty, 1998, pp328,352; Ken Wharfe with Robert Jobson, Diana: Closely Guarded Secret, 2002, p205; Andrew Morton, Diana: Her True Story – In Her Own Words, 1997, p276; Richard Palmer, Diana is Still Loved ... But Her Palace Postcards are Banned, Daily Express, May 8 2007.

[b] It is well known that following Princess Diana's death the Queen was reluctant to return to London from Balmoral – and didn't in fact return until the eve of the

funeral. What may be less well known is that by Thursday morning – four days after Diana's death and the day before the Queen's return to London – not one member of the royal family had signed the condolence books that members of the public had been queuing for up to eight hours to sign throughout the week. This is despite the fact that Princes Edward and Andrew were present in London and weren't at Balmoral. Palace press secretary, Dickie Arbiter, tells the story in his recent book: By Thursday morning "no-one from the Royal Family had yet gone to sign the books [and] we were skating on thin ice from a PR standpoint. I decided to take the initiative. Knowing that Prince Edward was currently staying at [Buckingham] Palace … I decided to give him an early call. [Arbiter:]'Good morning, Sir. Are you going to work today? … I suggest you stop off and look at the books of condolence in St James' Palace.' [Edward:] 'Er … I'm not sure.… I've got various things I have to do'.… [Arbiter:] 'I'm sorry, Sir, but we are getting a lot of flak from the media.… We need someone to be seen going in there.' [Edward:] 'Ah … but *will* anyone see me?'… I arranged to take him down there personally, after which time he could immediately return to work.… [Then] 20 minutes later the Prince was back on the phone. '… I'm not going down now, okay? I'm going with the Duke of York later on this afternoon instead.' …. I [next] confronted Prince Edward [in person at the palace].… I accompanied him to St James' Palace 30 minutes later.": *On Duty with the Queen*, pp187-8.

91

7 Her Year of Freedom

Prince Philip was not the only person Princess Diana feared.

In the spring of 1996 Roberto Devorik "asked her who hated her so much". Devorik later told the police Diana's answer:

> **She told me three names that she feared – Nicholas Soames, Robert Fellowes, her brother-in-law, and Prince Philip.**[173]

Nicholas Soames, a close friend of Charles who at the time was Minister for the Armed Forces, had publicly stated after *Panorama* that Diana was in "the advanced stages of paranoia".[174] There is evidence that in February 1997 he would go on to threaten Diana with an "accident".[a]

Devorik then related Diana's fear of Robert Fellowes:

> **He hates me. He will do anything to get me out of the Royals. He cost me the friendship with my sister.**[175]

Diana was referring to her sister Jane, the wife of Fellowes.

Raine Spencer, Diana's step-mother, told the inquest: "[Diana's] sister, Lady Jane Fellowes, had told her that because of her husband's position, she could not see her anymore".[176] At the time Robert Fellowes was the Queen's private secretary.

Within a few months of this conversation with Devorik the Diana-Charles divorce was finalised, the Queen withdrew Diana's HRH title and removed her from the royal family.

"I Saw Her Glowing"

Following the August 1996 divorce, witnesses describe a person who appears to have broken free – a person who has been released after years of suppression in an extremely controlled environment, the royal family.

Unfortunately only a very few family and friends were asked to comment on this.

---

[a] See later in this chapter.

Roberto Devorik, who had earlier described her fears, stated that Diana "appeared very happy in the entire year leading up to her death.... I saw her glowing".[177]

Diana's sister, Sarah, told the inquest: Diana "became much more focused.... She knew what she wanted to do. The boys were happy, sorted. It was time to go forward".[178]

Hasnat Khan, Diana's ex-lover, told the police in 2004: "In the last year of her life, Diana was just like any other normal person. The only worries she had were about her boys, as any mother would."[179]

Enter Landmines

The divorce decree nisi[a] was signed on 15 July 1996 and it was around this time that Princess Diana began to develop an interest in landmines. Diana's healer, Simone Simmons, had already travelled to war-torn Bosnia to help out her friend, Morris Power, the head of the Red Cross in Tuzla.[180] (WFJ)

On her return, Simmons told Diana what she had seen during ten days there – the carnage and suffering of the war-weary population, partly as a result of exploded and unexploded landmines.[181] (WFJ)

This started Diana – who had a natural empathy towards the suffering of others – thinking about what she could do to help. Over the following months she carried out her own research and began compiling an anti-landmine dossier.

By December 1996 Diana's research was well-advanced and Simmons received a Christmas card from Diana with the message:

The knowledge is expanding at alarming speed. Watch out world.[182]

Then on 12 January 1997 Princess Diana landed in Angola on a mission to help landmine victims and campaign for the worldwide eradication of anti-personnel landmines.

Soon after arriving Diana spoke to the assembled international media:

It is an enormous privilege for me to be invited here to Angola, in order to assist the Red Cross in its campaign to ban once and for all anti-personnel landmines. There couldn't be a more appropriate place to begin this campaign than Angola, because this nation has the highest number of amputees per population than anywhere in the world. By visiting Angola, we shall gain an understanding of the plight of the victims of landmines and how survivors are helped to recover from their injuries. We'll also be able to observe the wider implications of these devastating weapons on the life of this country as

---

[a] This is the preliminary decree. The decree absolute – the final decree – was six weeks later on August 28. See previous chapter.

a whole. It is my sincere hope that by working together in the next few days we shall focus world attention on this vital but, until now, largely neglected issue.[183] **(WFJ)**

Princess Diana stayed four days in Angola, spending time with landmine victims, visiting and walking through minefields. The trip was extensively publicised around the world, but caused a furore amongst Conservative politicians back in the United Kingdom.

Earl Howe, the Junior Defence Minister, stated publicly that Diana "is ill-advised and is not being helpful or realistic.... We do not need a loose cannon like her".[184] (WFJ)

Peter Viggers, a member of the House of Commons Defence Select Committee, declared that Diana was ill-informed and her efforts didn't "actually add much to the sum of human knowledge".[185] (WFJ)

Four days after Diana returned from Angola the royal Way Ahead Group, chaired by the Queen, convened for its twice yearly meeting.

Then during the following month the pressure against Princess Diana took a more sinister turn.

"An Accident Is Going To Happen"

In February 1997 Diana received a threatening phone call at her home in Kensington Palace. Her friend Simone Simmons was there:

I was with Diana in her sitting-room at KP when she beckoned me over and held her large old-fashioned black telephone away from her ear so that I could hear. I heard a voice telling her she should stop meddling with things she didn't understand or know anything about, and spent several minutes trying to tell her to drop her |anti-landmines| campaign. Diana didn't say much, she just listened, and I clearly heard the warning: 'You never know when an accident is going to happen.' |Diana| went very pale. The moment she put the phone down we started talking about what he had said. I tried to be reassuring which was not easy – she was clearly very worried....
When I listened into her conversation, with its apparent warning ... I was not sure |of her safety| any more. The conversation frightened Diana, and it certainly scared me.[186]

Diana told Simmons that the caller was the Minister of the Armed Forces and close long-time friend of Prince Charles, Nicholas Soames[187] – the same person who Diana had told Devorik she feared and who had accused her on national TV of being in "the advanced stages of paranoia".

Raine Spencer, Diana's step-mother, gave separate testimony that Diana "was very nervous altogether about her circumstances at that period"[188] – referring to the time around the Angola trip.

At the inquest Soames denied making this call: "it was not me who made the telephone call".[189]

But it appears significant that Soames – who was Minister of the Armed Forces at the time – failed to even recall that Diana was causing problems for the UK government on landmines: "I never thought of the Princess of Wales trespassing on any product".[190]

Soames stated that Diana's anti-landmine campaign "absolutely never came anywhere near me".[191]

Michael Mansfield, QC, asked Soames about the then Minister of Defence, Earl Howe's description of Diana as a "loose cannon". Mansfield asked: "You remember those words, don't you?" and Soames replied: "I cannot remember, no."[192]

That is a particularly significant denial because Earl Howe was a very close ministerial colleague of Soames[a] at the time, and those words – "loose cannon" – are probably the most famous descriptive words coined as a criticism of Princess Diana. Yet Soames has no recall of it: "I cannot remember, no".

Alistair Campbell[b] described the incident in his published diary entry for 15 January 1997:

> **The main story was Diana visiting Angola and doing landmines and being accused by an unnamed defence minister of being a 'loose cannon'. Everyone assumed it was Nick Soames, but it turned out to be Earl Howe.[193] (WFJ)**

Soames further denied recalling any of the public statements by the Ministry of Defence about Diana's Angola visit,[c] this despite him being a minister in that ministry.[d]

Instead Soames stated, speaking on behalf of the Ministry of Defence: "we all respected the Red Cross [anti-landmine] campaign which she was part of".[194]

This evidence runs completely contrary to the historical record as presented by the BBC which stated, during Diana's Angola trip, on 15 January 1997: "Princess Diana has angered government ministers after calling for an international ban on landmines".[195] (WFJ) This account was confirmed by journalist Richard Kay – also a friend of Diana – in an article

---

[a] Howe was Minister of Defence and Soames was Minister of Armed Forces – these are the two ministers that are responsible for the "Ministry of Defence".
[b] Labour Leader Tony Blair's Press Secretary.
[c] "I do not, no": 12 Dec 07: 75.17.
[d] It is interesting that Soames does recall Diana being angry: "I remember reading in the papers that she was angry" (12 Dec 07: 80.13). This reveals that he was reading the news and it raises the question: What does Soames think Diana was angry about?

written on the day after Diana's death, and read out at the inquest: "[Diana's] mines campaign [applying] … her simple notion of using her own fame to save lives was thrown in her face by politicians who accused her of embarrassing the Government by meddling in things she didn't fully understand".[196]

Soames' denials continued.

As Minister of Armed Forces he denied that he knew which companies in the UK manufactured landmines: "I do not know who makes landmines".[197]

He further denied any knowledge of any British support for UNITA[a]: "you are asking me about things that I knew nothing about".[198]

Soames even denied knowledge of Angola having more landmines per capita of population than anywhere else in the world: "I was not aware, no".[199]

When it came to questioning on the 1997 UK position on landmines, Soames stated: "I was not trying to argue for anything".[200] Yet at another point he said the opposite: "Our position was that we did not want to give away the use of landmines".[201b]

In summary, it is very difficult to believe that Soames has no recollection of key events that were critical to his role as Minister of Armed Forces.

Why is Soames claiming such a poor recall of anything to do with landmines?

Nicholas Soames, who is a politician, is distancing himself from an illegal phone call that it is not in his political interest to be connected to: the February 1997 call in which a threat was made to Princess Diana.

Evidence supports this: Simmons' detailed account of Diana's reaction to the call[c]; Devorik's statement that Diana feared Soames; Soames' 1995 public allegation that Diana was in "the advanced stages of paranoia"; Raine's statement that Diana was "very nervous altogether" around that particular time. Soames also agreed with Mansfield that his own voice was "quite distinctive" and therefore "difficult to confuse" with another person's.[202d]

It is evident that Soames' phone records should have been checked, but this has never occurred.

---

[a] National Union for the Total Independence of Angola.

[b] Despite Soames' major memory difficulties he managed to remember that the anti-landmine convention didn't cover "the JP22-3": 12 Dec 07: 93.25.

[c] The full evidence is in Part 2, Nicholas Soames section of the Fears and Threats chapter.

[d] Soames actually has form for making unusual phone calls to people in their homes. Alistair Campbell describes such a call in his 2007 book: Soames supported Campbell's controversial stance on the Iraq war and on Saturday 28 June 2003 phoned him at home. Campbell's son Rory answered and Soames "before realising it wasn't me went off on one – 'You sex god, you Adonis, you the greatest of all great men' before Rory said 'I'm his son'": The Blair Years, p711.

The balance of the evidence indicates that Nicholas Soames did make this phone call threatening Princess Diana with an accident.[a]

Diana was not deterred by the call and later said to Simmons:

> **It doesn't matter what happens to me. We must do something. We cannot allow this slaughter to continue.[203] (WFJ)**

Final Videos

On 7 March 1997, following the threatening phone call from Nicholas Soames, Princess Diana secretly recorded the first of 7 videos – a total of 12 hours of footage – with a former BBC cameraman who wishes to remain anonymous.

Investigative writer Gordon Thomas revealed the cameraman's account of what occurred in a 2006 article published in *Canada Free Press*.

The cameraman, who left the UK to live in the US soon after Diana's death, has gone out of his way to maintain his anonymity – he spoke to Thomas through a third party intermediary.

Thomas wrote:

> **In January 1997, Diana asked [Prince] Edward[b] if he knew of a good TV cameraman.... At the time Edward was associated with BBC broadcaster, Desmond Wilcox[c].... Wilcox was running a documentary company, Man Alive Productions in Hammersmith, London....**
>
> **Edward consulted Desmond for a suitable cameraman.... The cameraman Wilcox had suggested was described to Edward as 'old BBC. A veteran of many documentaries, the man had left the BBC to set up on his own'....**
>
> **At their first meeting, Diana close-questioned the cameraman. At this stage, she did not tell him what she planned.... Finally, in early March 1997, Diana told the cameraman what she wanted. She wanted him to film a set of videos in which she would speak directly to the camera.... She did not know, then, how many videos she would make. But after each one was completed it would be handed to her. There would be no other copy made. The schedule for filming would depend on her other engagements.**
>
> **A fee of £5,000 was accepted for the assignment. It would be paid in cash....**

---

[a] More detailed evidence and transcripts appear in Part 2, Nicholas Soames section of the Fears and Threats chapter.

[b] The article states that at the time Edward "was developing his own film company, planning to make documentaries about the Royal Family".

[c] Wilcox died in September 2000. He was co-producer of Prince Edward's 1996 documentary entitled "Edward on Edward" about the life of King Edward VIII also known as the Duke of Windsor: www.hollywod.com

The first video filming took place in early March, in the late evening. All subsequent six sessions followed the same pattern.

As instructed by Diana, the cameraman arrived by taxi at Kensington Palace. He was shown up into the drawing room where their previous discussions had taken place....

Paid in full, the cameraman never saw Diana again. But it was only after her death in Paris ... that the cameraman spoke to one person about his ultra-secret assignment -- and the momentous revelations on the tapes.

That person was Desmond Wilcox. He was sworn to tell no one – an undertaking Wilcox kept even from his own wife....

Before he died, Wilcox did tell one other person about what the cameraman had revealed. That person is still alive.... Both Wilcox and the cameraman had been questioned in the aftermath of Diana's death by MI5 security officers about the existence of the tapes. Neither had been able to throw any light as to their whereabouts....

Shortly after [Diana's] death, the cameraman who had filmed the seven videos left Britain. He first went to New York. Then to Vancouver. Today he lives on the West Coast of America.

Last week, under a guarantee of confidentiality, the cameraman's one remaining link with Britain spoke about the contents of the videos.

'They are Diana's video diaries of her marriage. In a sense they are an oral history of the Royal Family. She deals with each member in detail', he said.... He explained that the cameraman had told him last week that his abiding memory from the videos was of a very determined princess, that nothing would stand in her way.[204] **(WFJ)**

Gordon Thomas' article included detailed recollections of the contents of the 7 videos, recorded in notes taken by the cameraman at the time.

Revelations included:

- what the alleged victim of the rape by a fellow royal footman told her about the incident

- her "growing concern" about Prince Charles' relationship with Michael Fawcett[a], and how she believed it contributed to the end of her marriage

- the role Camilla Parker-Bowles played in the break-down of her marriage

- "she knew on her honeymoon that she was the odd one out in a triangle -- Charles, Camilla and Fawcett. He called Charles every day on [the] honeymoon. Charles took the calls in a separate room. When Diana asked, she was told it was all to do with work"

- "she soon became aware that in [Charles'] personal feelings towards her, there was no real husbandly emotions"

---

[a] Charles' closest aide.

- Fawcett acted as a go-between for Charles to keep secret assignations with Camilla
- "she described how she came to listen to [Charles and Camilla's] phone calls. In one, Charles was sitting on the toilet seat when she caught him"
- "she says that Camilla was the raunchier of the two. She gives examples"
- "she caught Charles and Camilla *de flagrante*" [a]
- "Diana paints a portrait of how she pleaded with [Charles] for the sake of the children to give up Camilla. She says that she turned to Anne and Andrew for help. Both, she says, refused to lift a finger"
- Diana was "highly upset" about Charles' relationship with Fawcett. "She has described how she came across them whispering to each other in the Palace corridors. She said there was something of the night about Fawcett. Diana reveals on one tape that she didn't like the way he seemed to dominate Charles, not just in a physical way, but mentally also"
- her shock at discovering the extent of Charles' dependence on Fawcett and others she did not approve of around him. "There is a group of powerful gays around Charles who have huge influence. Some are in the Queen Mother's office. Others are over at BP[b]"
- a vivid account of the group "flouncing and tip-toeing" around Charles and how he "enjoys their open adulation"
- a member of Charles' staff told her about sexual misconduct within the Royal Household staff -- and that Charles "tolerated it"
- a Royal staff party that was like "something out of Caligula"
- Charles and other members of the Royal Family -- the Queen excepted -- used to store expensive gifts in bin-liners. There was a panic when a member of the Saudi Royal Family came visiting and his wedding gift had been binned. Staff spent hours going through the bags looking for a set of gold goblets
- "I entered into a relationship with James (Hewitt). Charles knew about it and didn't care. He said it gave him the freedom to run his own life"
- Diana's deep sense of betrayal over Hewitt's subsequent behaviour. She speaks of "will I ever be lucky in love?"
- what Charles told her about Philip's relationship with the actress Pat Kirkwood

---

[a] Caught in the act.
[b] Buckingham Palace.

- relationships other members of the Royal Family have had outside marriage – accusing them of "calling the pot black when they have plenty in their kettle to answer for"
- "a terrible anger" at the way she was being treated by the Royal Family, especially Prince Philip. "She talks about how his welcome into the Family had turned to cold hostility once the marriage had broken up. On one video she quotes from letters he had sent her"
- "she attacks her brother [Charles] for refusing to give her a home on his estate"
- "she makes it clear that she would do everything possible to make sure Charles never became King. She wanted William to succeed to the Throne when the Queen died. Diana clearly saw her role as the power behind William. She had this somewhat romantic idea of being a king-maker – the mother behind the monarch".[205] (WFJ)

There is no question that the royal family would have performed miracles to ensure that these videotapes never saw the public light of day.

Profiting Out Of Misery

Meanwhile Diana continued to amass information for her anti-landmine dossier.

Paul Burrell testified:

> I knew that the Princess did compile a dossier on every fact of the landmine mission. She took it very seriously.... She learned all her facts and figures.[206]

Simmons wrote in her 2005 book:

> [Diana] did a lot of research on landmines asking questions of people on the ground, checking with those in authority whom she had met as the Princess of Wales, cross-examining anyone she met who knew something about the subject.... She compiled a dossier which she claimed would prove that the British Government and many high-ranking public figures were profiting from their proliferation in countries like Angola and Bosnia. The names and companies were well known – it was explosive and top of her list of culprits behind this squalid trade was the Secret Intelligence Service, the SIS.... 'I'm going to go public with this and name names', she declared. She intended to call her report 'Profiting Out Of Misery'.[207]

At the inquest Simmons stated that the dossier was about "4 to 6 inches" thick.[208] She said that "most of it was information that [Diana] had got from other sources [and there] were her notes as well ... on the top".[209]

In June 1997, just three months after recording the secret videos, Diana gave a copy of this dossier to Simmons, for safe-keeping.[210] Simmons believed that the original could have been kept by Diana in her elderly friend, Elsa Bowker's, safe.[211]

Simmons said she kept her dossier copy "underneath the mattress" on her bed.[212]

Immediately following Diana's death, just two to three months after Simmons was given the copy, she set fire to it.[213]

Elsa Bowker died in 2000. There was no effort by the authorities to establish what happened to the original dossier. Bowker's relatives should have been interviewed, but that never occurred.

Words of a Humanitarian

Diana delivered a landmark anti-landmine speech at the Royal Geographic Society in London on 12 June 1997. It was entitled: "Responding to Landmines: A Modern Tragedy and Its Consequences". This was to be Diana's final major address against the proliferation of landmines.

She said:

> **The world is too little aware of the waste of life, limb and land which anti-personnel landmines are causing among some of the poorest people on earth....**
>
> **For the mine is a stealthy killer. Long after conflict is ended, its innocent victims die or are wounded singly, in countries of which we hear little. Their lonely fate is never reported. The world, with its many other preoccupations, remains largely unmoved by a death roll of something like 800 people every month – many of them women and children. Those who are not killed outright – and they number another 1,200 a month – suffer terrible injuries and are handicapped for life.**
>
> **I was in Angola in January with the British Red Cross.... Some people chose to interpret my visit as a political statement. But it was not. I am not a political figure. As I said at the time, and I'd like to reiterate now, my interests are humanitarian. That is why I felt drawn to this human tragedy. This is why I wanted to play down my part in working towards a world-wide ban on these weapons....**
>
> **The human pain that has to be borne is often beyond imagining.... That is something to which the world should urgently turn its conscience.**
>
> **In Angola, one in every 334 members of the population is an amputee. Angola has the highest rate of amputees in the world. How can countries which manufacture and trade in these weapons square their conscience with such human devastation?...**
>
> **Much ingenuity has gone into making some of these mines. Many are designed to trap an unwary de-miner.... I reflected, after my visit to Angola, if some of the technical skills used in making mines had been applied to better methods of removing them....**

These mines inflict most of their casualties on people who are trying to meet the elementary needs of life. They strike the wife, or the grandmother, gathering firewood for cooking. They ambush the child sent to collect water for the family....

One of the main conclusions I reached after this experience: Even if the world decided tomorrow to ban these weapons, this terrible legacy of mines already in the earth would continue to plague the poor nations of the globe. 'The evil that men do, lives after them.'

And so, it seems to me, there rests a certain obligation upon the rest of us.

One of my objectives in visiting Angola was to forward the cause of those, like the Red Cross, striving in the name of humanity to secure an international ban on these weapons. Since then, we are glad to see, some real progress has been made. There are signs of a change of heart – at least in some parts of the world. For that we should be cautiously grateful. If an international ban on mines can be secured it means, looking far ahead, that the world may be a safer place for this generation's grandchildren.

But for this generation in much of the developing world, there will be no relief, no relaxation. The toll of deaths and injuries caused by mines already there, will continue....

I would like to see more done for those living in this 'no man's land', which lies between the wrongs of yesterday and the urgent needs of today.

I think we owe it. I also think it would be of benefit to us, as well as to them. The more expeditiously we can end this plague on Earth caused by the landmine, the more readily can we set about the constructive tasks to which so many give their hand in the cause of humanity.[214] (WFJ)

Her Year of Freedom

After Princess Diana was freed from the "royal prison" she had lived in for 16 years, she emerged a more confident person. In the words of her sister, Sarah: "She knew what she wanted to do.... It was time to go forward".

She forcefully pursued the eradication of all anti-personnel landmines.

About twelve months after embarking on this mission Diana lay dead in a Paris hospital.

This story will reveal that Princess Diana's humanitarian activities were a factor in her premature demise.

8   Crossing the Line

St Tropez Invitation

On Tuesday 3 June 1997, just nine days before Princess Diana delivered the landmark anti-landmine speech, she attended a production at the Royal Albert Hall. It was to be her final visit there and the English National Ballet (ENB) performed *Swan Lake*. Diana was present in her role as ENB patron.

At the gala dinner held in the Churchill Hotel following the ballet, Diana was seated next to long-time family friend, Mohamed Al Fayed and his wife, Heini.

Michael Cole, Harrods Director of Public Affairs, related to the British police what happened next:

> **The Princess told Mr. Al Fayed that she was concerned because she did not know where she could take her sons during their summer holidays. She said that she had asked her brother if they could use a house on the estate at Althorp.... Her brother had at first agreed but then rescinded the invitation because he considered her presence would attract the sort of media attention that would spoil the holidays for his own children.[a]... Mr. Al Fayed said that she and the Princes William and Harry were most welcome to join his family in St. Tropez.[215] (WFJ)**

Diana's friend, Rosa Monckton, told the inquest under oath:

> **[Diana] came round to our house in London on 1st June for my daughter and her god-daughter's second birthday party.[b] At the end of the birthday party she said to me, 'Can I stay because I want to**

---

[a] According to Paul Burrell – *A Royal Duty*, pp182-3 – this event between Diana and her brother occurred in June 1993. Both accounts could be true. It may have occurred in 1993 but it may still have been having an impact on how Diana spent her holidays with the boys as late as 1997. Althorp was family property – so when Diana was prevented by her brother from holidaying there that could have been a major, lasting blow to Diana. It is notable that Diana readdressed this issue in the videos she recorded in March 1997, just three months before Mohamed's invitation to holiday in St Tropez.

[b] Domenica Lawson, who has Down's Syndrome, was born on 1 June 1995. This was confirmed in a *Daily Mail* interview with Rosa Monckton in 2007: Helen Weathers, My Down's Daughter Changed My Life, *Daily Mail*, 14 November 2007.

discuss something with you?' She then said that she had been offered this invitation to go on holiday with the Al Fayeds to the South of France and she was considering accepting it because it would be fun for the boys and she would not have any worries about security. What did I think? I said that she should not even consider going on holiday with Mr Al Fayed, that it was an inappropriate thing for her to do, and at about that time, my husband came home from work and he sat down and told her the same thing.[216]

There is a serious evidence conflict between Rosa Monckton and Michael Cole.

Both witnesses have tied Diana's Mohamed holiday offer to an event – Monckton to her daughter's 2nd birthday on June 1 and Cole to the special Swan Lake production on June 3.

Both cannot be true. It is not possible that Rosa Monckton could have heard about Mohamed's offer on June 1, if the offer was not proffered until June 3.[a]

Monckton's husband, Dominic Lawson, wrote about this incident in a 2006 article in the *Mail*:

On June 1, 1997, Diana, Princess of Wales, was taking part in the second birthday celebrations of our daughter Domenica.... After the other guests had left and we were sitting down together, she told us that she'd had an invitation from Mohamed Al Fayed to spend a few days in the South of France on his newly acquired yacht, the Jonikal. She was very tempted and wanted to know whether we thought it was a good idea. My wife Rosa asked her why she was keen on taking up the invitation from the deeply controversial owner of Harrods. Diana replied that she wanted to take 'the boys' and that she knew that Fayed had a very big security operation, which would remove one of her biggest headaches - how to keep her sons protected from the Press and other intruders. I acknowledged that, but strongly urged her not to accept.... I added: 'The man is nothing but trouble.' Diana looked steadily at us with those big doe eyes, and then said: 'Thank you so much, I'm very glad I asked you.' [217] (WFJ)

Lawson supports his wife's testimony that on June 1 Diana asked whether to join Mohamed on the holiday.

However, there is also a major conflict between the Monckton and Lawson accounts.

Monckton describes an initial conversation between just her and Diana – "she said to me, 'Can I stay...'. She then said that she had been offered this invitation". Monckton said she listened and then gave her advice: "it was an

---

[a] The Royal Albert Hall website states: "On 3 June 1997 the Princess of Wales paid her last visit to the [Royal Albert] Hall, as patron of English National Ballet, to see Swan Lake." Source: Royal Albert Hall website: www.royalalberthall.com/about/history-and-archives Click on "Timeline".

inappropriate thing for her to do". It was only then that "my husband came home from work … and told her the same thing".

Lawson describes a completely different scenario. He is there before the guests left – "after the other guests had left and we were sitting down together" – and he fully describes the initial question from Diana and then a return question from Rosa. He then says it is him who proffers the advice. There is no mention of him working that day.[a]

There are major differences – despite them being husband and wife:

a)   Monckton – Lawson didn't attend the party because he was at work; Lawson – he was there before the guests left and makes no mention of working

b)   Monckton – the initial conversation is just her and Diana; Lawson – the initial conversation is the three of them: Diana, Monckton and Lawson

c)   Monckton – the initial advice comes from Monckton and is later repeated by Lawson; Lawson – the advice comes from Lawson and there is no mention of Monckton giving any advice.

Which account is true – Monckton or Lawson? Or are they both false?

Both differ from Michael Cole's account – Monckton and Lawson claim that Diana told them on June 1 about an invitation that she apparently didn't receive until two days later, on the 3rd.

It has been shown that Dominic Lawson was an MI6 agent and this book will reveal that Rosa Monckton also acted on behalf of MI6 in her dealings with Princess Diana.

It will also be shown that people who work for MI6 lie on a regular basis, particularly if they perceive it is in the national interest to do so.

Since 1997 Monckton has elevated herself – with the help of a willing media – to "best friend of Diana" status.[b] Monckton – with Lawson's assistance – could have fabricated this account of advising Diana regarding the St Tropez holiday, to exaggerate her influence. It is an example of Diana seeking out Monckton's advice on an issue of significance.

It will be shown that Rosa Monckton has lied about other aspects of her dealings and relationship with Princess Diana.[c]

---

[a] One could argue that Lawson's account is more logical – he was editor of the *Sunday Telegraph*. 1 June 1997 was a Sunday. If a Sunday paper editor had his daughter's second birthday to attend on a Sunday, one would think work commitments would not prevent that as by Sunday morning that week's paper has already been published.

[b] See later chapter: Diana's "Best Friend".

[c] Later in this book – in the Diana's "Best Friend" chapter – it will be revealed that Monckton usurped the role of Lucia Flecha de Lima in relation to the letters from Philip. In connection with the St Tropez holiday, Lucia testified to the police that she

Crossing The Line

Six days after the Mohamed invite, on Monday the 9th of June, Diana phoned Michael Cole to find out more detail about the St Tropez facilities.[218] On Wednesday the 11th she penned a letter to Mohamed:

> **Dear Mohamed, A very special thank you indeed for inviting the boys and I to stay in France next month. Needless to say we are greatly looking forward to it all and we are so grateful to you for giving us this opportunity.... I know we will speak soon, but until then, my love to you all, Diana.[219]**

Then on the next day, June 12, Diana delivered the significant anti-landmine speech in London – "how can countries which manufacture and trade in these weapons square their conscience"; "the evil that men do"; "this plague on earth caused by the landmine".

In two short days Princess Diana – who was under the constant surveillance of the British security services – had delivered two powerful messages.

First: to the British Establishment, including the royal family. Second: to the leading arms dealing nations of the western world – the US, UK and France.

On Thursday 12 June 1997 Princess Diana effectively declared war on the armaments industries of the US, UK and France – for even though Britain and France were to sign the Ottawa treaty to ban landmines, it was apparent that Diana would not have stopped at landmines: "my interests are humanitarian – that is why I felt drawn to this human tragedy". As a humanitarian, Diana – after succeeding against landmines – would have sought an end to cluster bombs and other evil – "the evil that men do" – weapons.

On Wednesday 11 June 1997 – after Princess Diana accepted the invitation to take William and Harry to Mohamed's villa – Diana, whether intentionally or not, had made a decision that sent shockwaves into the inner sanctum of the senior royals and the British Establishment.

As far as they were concerned Mohamed Al Fayed was a person of ill repute. They had repeatedly refused British citizenship, despite him having four British children. Mohamed had recently contributed to the downfall of the Tory government with his involvement in the "cash for questions" scandal. And to top it all off, Mohamed was at that time under police investigation over an alleged theft – later proven to be false – from a Harrods safety deposit box.

"told [Diana] I was not happy" about her going. There is a possibility that Monckton has again usurped Lucia's role here. Source: Lucia Flecha de Lima, Witness Statement, 1 September 2004, reproduced in Diana Inquest: The Documents the Jury Never Saw, 2010, p29 (UK Edition)

This is without adding underlying factors such as Prince Philip's racist attitude – "I can never tell the difference between you chaps".[220] (WFJ)

An Egyptian had bought the Harrods store, one of London's jewels. Philip later described Mohamed's son, Dodi, as an "oily bed-hopper".[221]

For Diana to take the future king – William – on a 10-day holiday with Mohamed Al Fayed was considered a major issue to the Queen. She had the power to veto the trip – the Queen could have prevented her grandsons from travelling to France.

It may be particularly significant that she – wearied now from over five years of trouble from Diana – did not intervene this time.

9 Rosa Monckton: Friend or Foe?[a]

Three witnesses spoke about the nature of Diana's relationship with Rosa – Rosa Monckton herself, Lucia Flecha de Lima and Simone Simmons.

Rosa-Diana Relationship

- Rosa: "we did ... become regular friends and [met] regularly"[222]
- Rosa: "you click, you become friends very quickly"[223]
- Rosa: "[Diana] did not" know that she had [MI6] connections[224]
- Rosa: "she did not know of my [MI6] connection"[225]
- Rosa: "she told me what she chose to tell me"[226]
- Lucia: "I do not think ... Diana trusted [Rosa] as much as she trusted me"[227]
- Lucia: "Diana thought maybe Rosa did have a hidden agenda as any friend of hers would have a special position"[228]
- Simmons: Diana was "aware that Rosa ... had a connection with ... MI6"[229]
- Simmons: "No, not 100%" – reply to "Did [Diana] trust Rosa Monckton?"[230]
- Simmons: "Rosa didn't have time for Diana and Diana made time for Rosa"[231]
- Simmons: "Diana was the strong one and Rosa found it very easy to off-load"[232]
- Simmons: "[Diana] would speak to Rosa about children and family things, but when it came to major issues, no"[233]
- Simmons: "[Diana] once wrongly suspected [Rosa] of spying on her"[234] (WFJ)
- Simmons: "[Diana] was understandably wary of Rosa at times"[235] (WFJ).

Three different witnesses, with three different accounts.

---

[a] See also later chapter: Diana's "Best Friend".

There are two issues – first, the overall nature of the friendship, and second and more important, whether Rosa's MI6 connections[a] influenced the friendship. This is where the key evidence conflicts occur.

Simmons confirmed that Diana was "aware that Rosa ... had a connection with ... MI6" and also has stated: "Due to Diana's concern about the ... Intelligence Services, she was understandably wary of Rosa at times."[236] (WFJ)

Lucia said: "Princess Diana thought maybe Rosa did have a hidden agenda as any friend of [Diana's] would have a special position".

Rosa stated that Diana did not know that she had MI6 connections.

The statements of Simmons and Rosa are directly opposite – Simmons says Diana was aware of an MI6 connection and Rosa says Diana wasn't aware.

If Diana wasn't aware of Rosa's MI6 connection, then clearly it couldn't influence the relationship.

But was Diana aware?

Lucia says Diana had a problem with trusting Rosa, but it was nothing to do with an MI6 connection – instead it was "a hidden agenda as any friend of [Diana's] would have a special position". In other words, any friend – including Rosa – couldn't be trusted because they could manipulate the relationship to their own ends. That is, except Lucia: "I had no hidden agenda, I was foreign and would move on."[237]

According to Lucia, Diana could trust no friends unless they were foreigners or had connections to foreign diplomats and therefore would be leaving the country. Because Rosa did not fall into that category, "Diana thought maybe Rosa did have a hidden agenda".

But Princess Diana had several British-based friends who she shared trusting relationships with over long periods of time – Carolyn Bartholomew, Annabel Goldsmith, Elsa Bowker and Elton John are a few examples.

Lucia has, however, raised the issue of Rosa's "hidden agenda" in her police statement – this does reveal that at some stage Diana voiced concerns about Rosa to Lucia.

The evidence indicates that Lucia correctly detected that "Diana thought maybe Rosa did have a hidden agenda", but deduced incorrectly the reason – that it was because Rosa "would have a special position".

When Lucia was first asked by Michael Mansfield about this[b], she refused to answer: "Nothing to do with the case".[238] Then when Mansfield said he

---

[a] It is not in dispute that Rosa has connections to MI6 and she admits that herself – see earlier in Chapter 1.

[b] The question was: "Is it right from what Diana told you that she had reservations about trusting Rosa Monckton?": 18 Dec 07: 130.19.

wanted "to read to you what you have put in your statement", Lucia interrupted: "I will not comment about a friend whose daughter is my god-daughter".[239]

If this was just about "a hidden agenda <u>as any friend of [Diana's]</u> would have a special position", Lucia may not have been so resistant under oath.[a]

Was the "hidden agenda" Lucia spoke of instead because of Rosa's MI6 connection?

Lucia should have been asked about this at the inquest – but she wasn't.

Mansfield did ask Lucia: "Did you know ... whether Rosa Monckton ... had connections with the security services, a relative?" Lucia replied: "Rosa Monckton had connections with Secret Service? I do not believe so."[240]

Mansfield's question was in connection with the "security services" – that is a general term, which covers British Intelligence, including both MI5 (Security Service[b]) and MI6 (Secret Intelligence Service). Lucia has restated Mansfield's question, before she answers – but she has changed "security services" to "Secret Service", which appears to be short for "Secret Intelligence Service", SIS or MI6.

Lucia has changed Mansfield's general "security services" to the more specific "Secret Service".[c]

It is no coincidence that it was the Secret Intelligence Service that the "relative" – Anthony Monckton – worked for. This is an indication that Lucia was aware of Anthony's employment in MI6, and therefore she was aware – contrary to what she has stated – that "Rosa Monckton had connections with [the] Secret [Intelligence] Service".

Lucia may have lied on this issue to support Rosa's assertion that Diana wasn't aware of her MI6 connection.[d]

Rosa was asked: "Diana ... knew that you had that connection, did she not?" She categorically replied: "No, she did not."[241]

Rosa's answer is completely bereft of logic.

Rosa says Diana didn't know that she had a connection with MI6. The point here is that if Diana had known, she would not necessarily tell Rosa.

So how then is it possible for Rosa to insist, "No, she did not" know.

Obviously it's not possible[ea] – yet that is what Rosa asserted under oath at Diana's inquest.

---

[a] Why was Lucia attempting to suppress evidence? Was it just that the evidence was unpalatable, or had she been told not to talk about this subject at the inquest?

[b] Singular with first letter capitals.

[c] The inquest transcriber correctly picked up that "Secret Service" had first letter capitals, whereas "security services" did not.

[d] Lucia was cross-examined on 18 December 2007 – five days after Rosa on December 13.

[e] The normal way for someone to find out would be to ask the person if they knew or not – but if Rosa had done that, then Diana would have then known.

In contrast, Simmons said that Diana was "aware that Rosa ... had a connection with ... MI6". That was supported by what Simmons wrote in her earlier book: "Due to Diana's concern about the ... intelligence services, she was understandably wary of Rosa at times".

As much as it is <u>illogical</u> for Rosa to insist that Diana didn't know about her MI6 connection, it is <u>logical</u> that if Diana did have intelligence concerns about Rosa, she could have shared that with one or two close friends.

Simone Simmons recounts a conversation about the subject – "I said, 'Are you sure about all of this?' and [Diana] said 'Yes'."[242]

As Princess of Wales, Diana had connections in high places. All it would take is for one friend – or even acquaintance – who was aware of both Rosa's friendship with Diana and her MI6 connection, to warn Diana.[b] It is not a big stretch to suggest that Diana may have been warned.

In summary, Rosa's insistence that Diana didn't know seems illogical; Lucia's evidence that Rosa's hidden agenda was having "a special position" appears flawed; Simmons' account that Diana knew about Rosa's MI6 connection seems credible and is supported by common sense.

Other evidence will later show that the Diana-Rosa relationship was not as close as it has been made out to be.

Radio Silence

Rosa Monckton stated that whenever she gave Diana advice she wasn't happy with "I would not hear from her for some time, until she had worked through it". Monckton called these periods "radio silence".[243]

Monckton went on to say that "there was definitely radio silence" after the holiday advice she and her husband gave Diana on 1 June 1997.[244]

In the context of that radio silence, Monckton was asked at the inquest: "In what circumstances did you learn that the Princess had indeed accepted the invitation from Mr Al Fayed?" She replied: "My husband ... rang me on a Saturday evening to say that there were pictures ... of Diana on Mr Al Fayed's yacht. So I said to him, 'Well that explains why I haven't heard from her because she has gone on holiday'." Inquest lawyer Ian Burnett then asked for confirmation:

> **For the whole of June and the first ten days[c] of July at least, you did not hear from the Princess?**

Monckton confirmed: "That is correct.[245]

---

[a] Rosa could have said, "I think she did not know", but Rosa's answer was categoric.
[b] This is over a period of 5½ years – Rosa first met Diana in February 1992.
[c] It is actually 12 days – the St Tropez holiday started on Friday July 11 and Monckton says she found out about it "on a Saturday evening": 13 Dec 07: 133.12

Monckton has just confirmed that she had no contact at all – radio silence – with Diana from the evening of June 1 until sometime after 12 July 1997 – a period of at least 42 days.[a] This was stated under oath at the inquest.

Yet just 10 minutes later, still talking under oath to the same lawyer, but about a different topic – the August Greek Islands holiday[b] – Monckton contradicts this account.

Burnett asks her: "The holiday to Greece ... was it organised in the period after [Diana] came back from St Tropez or was it organised long before?"[246]

This question is based on Monckton's earlier radio silence evidence – if there was a radio silence that lasted from June 1 until the St Tropez holiday[c], then it is logical that the Rosa-Diana Greek holiday would have to have been organised before the radio silence ("long before") or "after [Diana] came back from St Tropez".

Monckton replies:

I was in Hong Kong for [the handover], and we organised it on the telephone then.... I cannot remember what month that was of 1997.[247]

Monckton may have been hoping no one would check it out, but Burnett said, "That is something we can easily find out".[248] He later came back: "The handover was on 30th June 1997".[249] Burnett then asked Monckton to reconfirm her assertion: "so it is about that time that you had a telephone conversation with [Diana] to arrange the holiday". Monckton confirms.[250]

Monckton has now confirmed: a) "For the whole of June and the first ten days of July at least, you did not hear from [Diana]", and b) "so it is about [June 30] that you had a telephone conversation with [Diana] to arrange the [Greek] holiday".

One of these assertions made under oath – or both – has to be false.

There can't have been both a Monckton-Diana radio silence that lasted from June 1 to after July 10 and a phone call between Monckton and Diana on or about 30 June 1997.

What does Burnett do with this?

He tries to ease the minds of jury members, who may have been starting to doubt Monckton's evidence, while at the same time fails to challenge Monckton on an obvious conflict.

Burnett deftly ignores Monckton's confirmation of: "For the whole of June and the first ten days of July at least, [I] did not hear from [Diana]". He instead reverts back to: "In that [June 30] conversation [Diana] did not tell you that she was in fact going to St Tropez in the interval?" Monckton confirms: "No, she did not."[251] Burnett then reinforces this, probably for the

---

[a] Monckton has never actually made a clear statement about when and how this period of silence ended.
[b] This topic is addressed later.
[c] That holiday started on July 11 and finished on July 20.

"benefit" of the jury:[a] "Because you have told us that you were alerted [about the St Tropez holiday] when you became aware of press coverage a little bit later." And he quickly moves onto a new subject.[252]

Burnett moved the focus away from Monckton's categorical but conflicting evidence of a radio silence lasting well into July, instead directing focus to whether Diana had told Monckton that she was going on the St Tropez holiday.

In doing this the inquest lawyer, Ian Burnett QC, has corruptly protected a false witness, Rosa Monckton.

Why has Monckton provided such conflicting evidence on her communications with Diana?

Rosa Monckton said that after her husband alerted her to the fact Diana was in St Tropez with Mohamed, she told him: "Well that explains why I haven't heard from her because she has gone on holiday." [b]

There is overwhelming evidence in Part 2 that phone conversations between Diana and her friends didn't stop when she was on holiday.[c]

Lucia said in her statement: "The last fax [Diana] sent me was giving me the telephone number of the house in the South of France[d].... I remember that she left in July 1997. We talked on the phone but less than normal as she was in the South of France, I was in Brazil and sometimes the reception did not work. We used the house phones rather than the mobile." [253] (WFJ)

Lucia is referring to the same July 1997 St Tropez holiday that Rosa spoke of, but their evidence is completely different:

- Rosa: "I haven't heard from her because she has gone on holiday"
- Lucia: "we talked on the phone but less than normal".[efg]

---

[a] I am suggesting that Burnett is actually intending to deceive the jury and protect Rosa Monckton – see below.

[b] Supported by Lawson who describes his wife saying: "Well, that explains why I haven't heard a peep from Diana recently": Dominic Lawson, A Crucial Personal Detail ... and the Truth About Diana's Death, Daily Mail, 4 June 2006

[c] This is also addressed in the later discussion of Monckton's final phone call to Diana in the Diana's "Best Friend" chapter.

[d] Confirmed at the inquest: "Princess Diana sent me a fax giving ... her phone numbers in St Tropez.": 18 Dec 07: 99.1.

[e] The reason they talked "less than normal" was nothing to do with Lucia's criticism of Diana going – it was because "[Diana] was in the South of France, I was in Brazil and sometimes the reception did not work".

[f] Also confirmed at inquest: Burnett: "Did you and she speak while she was in St Tropez?" Lucia: "Yes, we did, but obviously not on a daily basis.": 18 Dec 07: 99.10.

[g] Lucia was in Brazil, which made communication more difficult, but presumably Rosa was in the UK – so communication for her should have been simpler.

This is despite the fact that Lucia had also conveyed her disapproval of the holiday – "neither Rosa, Richard Kay[a] nor I were very happy about it knowing of Mr Al Fayed's bad reputation.... I told [Diana] I was not happy".[254] (WFJ)

So Rosa and Lucia both expressed their disapproval of Diana joining Mohamed on holiday, but according to their evidence, Diana's reaction to each is quite different.

Diana keeps up contact with Lucia but shuts off communication with Rosa – she enters a period of radio silence. There is no mention by Lucia of any radio silence or similar.

Is this plausible?

There is no evidence from any of Diana's friends to support Rosa's testimony that there would be a falling out – "radio silence" – if they gave advice she didn't want to hear.

This includes Annabel Goldsmith, Lucia Flecha de Lima, Simone Simmons[b], Richard Kay, Susan Kassem, Roberto Devorik[c], Rita Rogers, Elsa Bowker, the Palumbos.[d] The closest we come to it is an incident with Richard Kay recounted in Simmons' book – see footnote.[e]

The general evidence[f] points to Diana's relationship with Rosa being less trusting[g] – and therefore less close and forgiving – than she had with her other known friends.

The evidence indicates:

- Monckton's timing of the Diana conversation about the Mohamed holiday offer is June 1 (her daughter's birthday), two days before the offer was proffered, according to Cole

---

[a] This cannot be checked – Kay was not asked about this at the inquest and his statement was not shown to the jury and has never been made available.

[b] There were periods of fallings out between Diana and Simmons, but not over advice dispensed. This is addressed in Part 5, section on the Greek Islands Holiday in the Monckton chapter.

[c] Devorik, whose relationship with Diana commenced in 1981, had a falling out with her in 1996, but the evidence indicates that Devorik was upset with something Diana did – it was not cutting off contact over views, as described by Rosa Monckton. See Part 5, footnote in the section on the Greek Islands Holiday in the Monckton chapter.

[d] Elsa Bowker and the Palumbos have only spoken on documentaries – there is no official police or inquest evidence. Bowker died in 2000.

[e] Simmons writes: "On one occasion the opening paragraph of a story [Kay] had written didn't meet with [Diana's] approval, she stopped speaking to him and slammed the phone down when he called.... After leaving him to stew for a couple of days [she] called him as if nothing had happened.": *Diana: The Last Word*, p199.

[f] Particularly Lucia – see earlier – but also apparently other close friends could say to Diana things she didn't want to hear without it leading to radio silence.

[g] Lucia stated: "I do not think Princess Diana trusted [Rosa] as much as she trusted me" – see earlier.

- Monckton has two conflicting accounts about when the radio silence could have ended – June 30 with the Greek holiday organisation, or sometime after July 12
- Monckton has never directly explained how the radio silence ended – just how it started
- Burnett protected Monckton at the inquest, even though it was clear she had unreconciled conflicts in her evidence
- Diana appears to have had less trust of Monckton than other friends
- Monckton stated: "I haven't heard from [Diana] because she has gone on holiday", when there is overwhelming evidence that Diana still communicated with her friends whilst on holiday[a]
- Diana kept up contact with Lucia even though she had criticised Diana for going on holiday with Mohamed
- although falling out was an issue for Diana's staff, and there are instances of it occurring at times with some friends, there is no support for Monckton's inquest account that "typically there would be radio silence" when she "gave advice or expressed views ... with which [Diana] was not very happy".

Two factors stand out:

1) that the relationship between Diana and Monckton was not particularly close or trusting

2) that there are substantial areas of conflict in Monckton's evidence – both with comparison to other people's and also within her own accounts.[b]

These factors are linked to the reality that Monckton had MI6 connections, and appears to have been working as an MI6 agent herself – see later in the book.

As part of the police investigations Rosa Monckton's phone records and bank accounts should have been checked.

This never occurred.

Why?

---

[a] See the first few chapters of Part 2 and the later discussion in this book of Monckton's final phone call to Diana in the "Best Friend" chapter.

[b] There were also conflicts in Monckton's evidence on how and when she met Diana. See Part 5, section on Meeting Diana in the Monckton chapter.

10   Pressure Builds

A fortnight after Princess Diana's landmark final anti-landmine speech, she was prevented from attending a meeting of parliament's Landmine Eradication Group. On 25 June 1997 Diana was forced to withdraw because of criticism from Conservative MPs, who stated publicly that she was "entering the political process".[255] (WFJ)

Organising A Cruise

Five days after that Tory rejection, Rosa Monckton arranged an August holiday with Diana. Monckton told the inquest: "I was in Hong Kong for [the handover] and we organised it on the telephone".[256] The handover of Hong Kong to the Chinese took place on Monday, 30 June 1997.

Monckton arranged a Greek island cruise set for the middle of August. It will be shown later that this was to be no ordinary cruise. Princess Diana returned home on August 20 – and just 11 days later she would lie dead in a Paris hospital.

Why was this holiday organised? And why did Diana agree to go on it?

Circumstantial evidence – shown later[a] – will indicate that Monckton organised this holiday on behalf of MI6, probably as an information-gathering venture – acquiring intelligence on Diana's plans and intentions. It is no coincidence that: a) the trip was arranged within two to three weeks of Diana's landmark anti-landmine speech and her decision to holiday with Mohamed Al Fayed[b]; and b) that Sherard Cowper-Coles – who it will be shown headed the Paris operation to assassinate Diana – was also present in Hong Kong for the handover.[c]

The anti-landmine speech and the St Tropez holiday decision could have triggered a mild panic in some echelons of the British Establishment.

I suggest this would have led to some high-level discussions and finally triggered an order to British intelligence – from someone in the Establishment

---

[a] See "A Greek Odyssey" chapter.
[b] Diana made inquiries about the St Tropez setup on June 9 and confirmed her decision in a letter on the 11th – see earlier Crossing The Line chapter.
[c] Cowper-Coles was Head of the Hong Kong Department in the FCO for the three years preceding the handover to China on 30 June 1997. He describes his FCO role in the handover in his 2012 book, *Ever The Diplomat*, pp145-179.

– to find out more about what Diana had in mind and possibly asking the question: Where is all this heading?

It was natural for Rosa Monckton to be used because she had connections with MI6 and also had a relationship with Diana.

Even though the Diana-Monckton relationship had run for over five years, they had never holidayed alone.

Somehow Monckton was able to convince the princess that she needed to go on a secluded holiday with her – "just the two of us", she told the inquest.[257] On the available evidence, it is impossible to know how Monckton achieved this. At face value, it certainly appears odd that Diana would allow a one-on-one holiday with a person she: a) had trust issues with – Lucia; b) thought had "a hidden agenda" – Lucia; and c) knew had MI6 connections – Simmons.

It may be that Monckton applied some sort of emotional pressure to lure Diana into agreeing to this holiday.[a]

Blair's Lies

A week after agreeing to the Monckton boat cruise, Princess Diana met with the British Prime Minister, Tony Blair, at Chequers.

Blair describes the discussions in his 2010 book:

> **I just broached the subject of her and Dodi straight out. [Diana] didn't like it and I could feel the wilful side of her bridling. However she didn't refuse to talk about it, so we did, and also what she might do. Although the conversation had been uncomfortable at points, by the end it was warm and friendly. I tried my hardest to show that I would be a true friend to her, and she would treat the frankness in that spirit.... It was the last time I saw her.[258]**

Blair fails to disclose the timing of this meeting. Nevertheless his press secretary, Alistair Campbell, revealed that it was Sunday, 6 July 1997. [259]

This poses a problem for Blair, which he has never explained.

July 6 was over a week before the Diana-Dodi relationship started (see later)[b] and over a month before it became public knowledge.[c]

So it is clearly not possible for a conversation along the lines of Blair's description to have occurred. There was no, "I just broached the subject of

---

[a] It will be shown later that the Rosa-Diana relationship was not particularly close.
[b] July 6 was eight days before the initial meeting between Diana and Dodi at the St Tropez holiday on July 14.
[c] The *Daily Mirror* broke the story of the relationship on Thursday, August 7 and the *Sunday Mirror* published "the Kiss" photo on August 10.

her and Dodi straight out" and no, "she didn't refuse to talk about it, so we did, and also what she might do".

In other words, Blair has publicly lied about the content of his Chequers communication with Princess Diana.

Why?

Blair says more:

> **I felt ... that Dodi Fayed was a problem. This was not for the obvious reasons, which would have made some frown on him; his nationality, religion or background didn't matter a hoot to me. I had never met him, so at one level it was unfair to feel nervous about him, and for all I know he was a good son and a nice guy; so if you ask me, well, spit it out, what was wrong, I couldn't frankly say, but I felt uneasy and I knew some of her close friends – people who really loved her – felt the same way....[260]**

In relation to Dodi, Blair uses words such as "problem", "frown", "nervous" and "uneasy". And the context in his memoir in which he says this is around the Paris crash.

There could be an implication to the reader that the reason Diana is dead is Dodi Fayed. And not only that, but "I warned her off him" and "if only she had taken my advice, Diana would be alive today".[a]

The evidence around the case[b] indicates that Blair did have a role in Diana's death. This falsified section of Blair's book appears to be an attempt to distance himself from involvement, in the eyes of the public.

But this argument is based on lies.

Blair says he warned Diana about Dodi at their final meeting. But the meeting took place eight days before Diana had even met Dodi.[c]

Preparatory WAG Meeting

At some point in late June or early July a decision was made to hold a special meeting of the royal Way Ahead Group (WAG) set for later in July.

In this context, a special WAG preparatory meeting was held in London on July 8,[261] just two days after Diana's final meeting with Tony Blair.

Robert Fellowes, the Queen's private secretary, told the inquest that the July 8 meeting "would have been chaired by the Lord Chamberlain, Lord Airlie, and it would have composed the Private Secretaries concerned and the Keeper of the Privy Purse".[262]

---

[a] There is a possibility – given the Chequers meeting was five days before the St Tropez holiday – that Blair may have warned Diana against taking William and Harry to Mohamed's villa. But Blair has never suggested that.

[b] See Part 5, section on Role of Tony Blair in Chapter 4. See also Early Notifications chapter in this book.

[c] Diana met Dodi on July 14 – see later.

At this meeting the groundwork was laid – by the royal household – for the later full WAG meeting involving senior royals.

The significance of the July 1997 WAG meetings is addressed later.

MPS Warning

One or two days after the preparatory WAG meeting, Robert Fellowes received a significant call from Scotland Yard.

David Davies, head of MPS Royalty Protection, informed Fellowes by telephone of police concerns regarding the imminent St Tropez holiday.[a]

Later Davies testified:

> **I told [Fellowes] that the Commissioner[b] had directed me to inform him that Her Royal Highness or Princess [Diana] was going on holiday with the two Princes, and that, in our conclusion, the matter gave us cause for concern.[263]**

Davies stated: "I was concerned as to the consequence ... for ... the reputation of the Royal Family.... The future King of England and his brother and the mother were going on holiday with a gentleman[c] who ... I had some concerns about".[264]

Davies described what occurred during the call:

> **There was a silence as I recall ... and I was not sure whether [Fellowes] had heard me ... so I repeated it."**

It was then that Fellowes replied: "Her Majesty is aware".[265]

Robert Fellowes denied under oath any recall of this phone call ever taking place: "I do not remember it".[266]

MPS commissioner, Paul Condon, was asked by Michael Mansfield if he remembered the events described by Davies. He replied: "Not in the way that that is described. I don't remember having conversations with David Davies in the way that he describes."[267]

That is an unconvincing response, so Mansfield pushed him and Condon then said: "I honestly believe I did not" participate in what Davies described.[268]

---

[a] Davies was not sure of exactly which day this phone call occurred, but it was prior to the St Tropez holiday that started on 11 July 1997. Evidence from Davies and Robert Fellowes – who denies the call took place – and Fellowes' diary, indicated that it would have been on July 9 or 10, when the Queen was at Holyrood Palace in Edinburgh. See 12 Feb 08: 41.16 to 42.19.

[b] Paul Condon.

[c] Mohamed Al Fayed.

Davies also said he informed Deputy Assistant Commissioner, Alan Fry.[269] There is no evidence Fry was ever asked about this.[a]

Davies' wife, Della, testified:

> **In early July 1997 my husband ... informed me that he was extremely worried about an issue surrounding Diana, Princess of Wales.... He said that Diana apparently was intending to go on holiday with the Fayed family to France, taking her two boys with her.... David told me that the Commissioner had asked him to phone the Royals to inform him of their joint concern.... [Later] he told me he had spoken to Sir Robert Fellowes, the Queen's private secretary, who had been very curt and arrogant.... Sir Robert Fellowes had replied 'Her Majesty is aware' and said it twice.[270]**

There are seriously conflicting accounts.

On the one hand David Davies – supported by his wife, Della – is saying that Commissioner Condon asked him to inform Fellowes about the MPS concern over the Diana-Mohamed holiday. Davies subsequently called Fellowes who curtly advised him the Queen was aware.

On the other hand Condon has denied involvement and Fellowes has denied receiving Davies' call.

At least one person is lying.

There is no evidence of any reason Davies and his wife would have to make this story up.

There is however a possibility that the Establishment would try to undermine or deny evidence indicating there were high-level concerns about this Diana-Mohamed holiday. It may not be in their interests to admit there were concerns – particularly if the planning for this holiday became a trigger for the decision to assassinate Diana.

It was also not in the Establishment's interests to be seen to be criticising Mohamed Al Fayed.

Both of these factors – the Establishment's attitude against Mohamed and disapproval of the holiday – reflect negatively in the context of the later assassination of Princess Diana.

At the inquest there were only two royal household figures[b] cross-examined – Robert Fellowes and Miles Hunt-Davis, private secretaries for the Queen and Philip, respectively. Whenever the subject of the St Tropez holiday came up it is notable that there was an air of denial or discomfort.

---

[a] Alan Fry left the MPS in 2002 and moved to Australia in 2007, the year the inquest commenced: Queensland Health: http://www.health.qld.gov.au/services/westmoreton/board/alan-fry.asp

[b] Persons who were in the royal household at the time of the crash. Paul Burrell was also cross-examined, but was not a member of the royal household at the time of the deaths.

Fellowes was initially asked by Burnett: "Presumably, you and Her Majesty, other members of the Royal Family, your family, knew well that the boys were going on holiday. Would that be right?"[271]

That should have brought about a straightforward, "Yes". But it doesn't.

Instead, Robert Fellowes – who was the Queen's private secretary and Diana's brother-in-law – tries to distance himself. He starts off: "It is hard to remember", then appears to realise what he is saying, and continues: "I am sure I was aware, but I cannot remember when I was made aware".[272]

The question wasn't about "<u>when</u> I was made aware" – Fellowes appears to have come up with that in an attempt to rescue himself from his initial, "It is hard to remember".

The question was about <u>whether</u> they "knew ... that the boys were going on holiday". The answer was, "I am sure I was aware"[a], but that's not Fellowes' initial response – "It is hard to remember".

Then later Fellowes is asked a similar question, but more directly and by Michael Mansfield this time: "You were aware of the holiday?" [b]

Again a simple "Yes" should have been forthcoming.

But no, Fellowes stalls again: "I cannot say now", then again appears to change his answer mid-sentence: "but I suppose I was, yes. I would think very likely I was".[273]

Other responses regarding the St Tropez holiday from Fellowes and Hunt-Davis were:
-     Fellowes: "I do not remember any discussion of it"[274]
-     Hunt-Davis: "I do not recollect anything about it"[275]
-     Hunt-Davis: "I cannot recollect anything specifically, but I imagine you may be right"[276] – regarding "hostile publicity about Diana and the Al Fayeds"
-     Fellowes: "no.... no.... no"[c] – regarding issues relating to Mohamed Al Fayed.

---

[a] Even the "I am sure <u>I was aware</u>" doesn't fully answer the question because Burnett was asking about the prior knowledge of "Her Majesty, other members of the Royal Family, your family".

[b] More directly because this time Fellowes is asked specifically about his own knowledge, whereas previously Burnett had asked about his recollection of the knowledge of "Her Majesty, other members of the Royal Family, your family". So this is a simpler question for Fellowes to answer.

[c] Mansfield: "Were you aware that Mr Al Fayed was under investigation?" (This other investigation is addressed later). Fellowes: "No." Mansfield: "Not at all, nothing?" Fellowes: "No." Mansfield: "No view about Mohamed Al Fayed at all?" Fellowes: "No." Source: 12 Feb 08: 98.21.

These royal denials of knowledge or discussion of the St Tropez holiday also don't fit with common sense.

William and Harry's presence at Balmoral – where the Queen was – was interrupted for ten days by the St Tropez holiday. Also, the Queen was required to authorise any overseas trips made by royals – so her approval was necessary for William and Harry to travel to France.

The denials by Fellowes and Hunt-Davis are reminiscent of the blanket denials by MI6 and embassy staff in Paris, who unanimously denied having contemporary knowledge of Diana even visiting Paris on the weekend of the crash – see Part 5[a] – and a similar blanket denial by French authorities – see Part 3[b].

If the royals were not even aware that a holiday was taking place, how could they be discussing it? And how could it have been an issue of concern? And how could it possibly have formed part of the pretext for the assassination?

The Davies' evidence then should be viewed in the light of several other factors:.

- the organisation of the Monckton-Diana boat cruise

- WAG meetings on either side of the Mohamed-Diana holiday – the preparatory meeting before and the full meeting after (see later)

- public criticism of the Mohamed-Diana holiday by other Establishment figures – see next chapter

- denials and obfuscation by the only royal household figures cross-examined at the inquest.[c]

In the light of these other events and evidence, the story put by David and Della Davies gains credence.[d]

In other words, there is credible evidence that Scotland Yard was concerned about the St Tropez holiday and sought to advise senior royals of that. But when the police called they received the cold shoulder.

And there has since been an attempt to cover up the existence of the police concern and the royal response.

Why?

---

[a] Section on Knowledge of Diana's Presence in the British Embassy chapter.

[b] Chapter on Pre-Crash Actions of French Authorities.

[c] The royal denials fit with Rosa Monckton's claims that she wasn't aware that Diana went on the holiday until the news photos came through – see earlier.

[d] The Davies-Fellowes call and surrounding evidence will be addressed in more detail in Part 7.

11 "The Best Holiday Imaginable"

Three days after the preparatory WAG meeting Diana, William and Harry travelled with Mohamed and his family to the St Tropez villa.

It was the 11th of July 1997 and the beginning of a ten day holiday.

Controversy erupted.

Harold Brookes-Baker – editor of *Burke's Peerage* – among others, spoke out:

> **This is totally irresponsible of the Princess – particularly considering the problems people have faced with the Al Fayed connection. These problems are likely to go on for a lot longer – and so it is important that she and the family she married into should be completely removed from controversy. The controversy this is creating is unnecessary for a family that has already been through so much.[277] (WFJ)**

Three days into the holiday the party was joined by Mohamed's son, Dodi. Diana and Dodi first met[a] that afternoon (July 14) on Mohamed's yacht, the *Jonikal*.

Debbie Gribble, the chief stewardess on the boat, later described the scene around that evening's dinner:

> **"They got on well enough, but I didn't think anything of it." Then a full-scale fun food fight developed at the table. "They were chasing each other and laughing and giggling like a couple of kids. Then they wrestled a bit and stopped, just staring at each other.... From that moment on something changed in the way they treated each other.... Something had passed between them – suddenly they seemed to fit as a couple."[278] (WFJ)**

The following day, Tuesday July 15: "Everyone else had gone their own way. Diana and Dodi were still deep in conversation. She was talking about her work and travels in India and Africa, and he was enthralled."[279] (WFJ)

---

[a] This was their initial meeting that led to the relationship. Over the years the two had crossed paths at official functions.

"Big Surprise"

Lee Sansum, an Al Fayed bodyguard, told the inquest what happened later that day. He was conversing with Diana on the beach: "She was talking about moving to America".[280a] Sansum then described what Diana told him after this, just before she got into a boat to meet the press out in the bay:

> **[She said] something like 'I'm going to shock them ... I'm telling them I'm going to America'.[281]**

Once out on the water, Diana never actually said this to the waiting media.

Sansum continued: "When she came back ... I remember the Royal Protection officer ... getting off the boat and saying, 'she didn't do it' and we were like 'Phew'".[282]

Diana instead had told the reporters:

> **You are going to get a big surprise with the next thing I do.[283]**

This was widely reported around the world at the time but what Diana meant remains a mystery to many to this day. Sansum's evidence – which the police could easily have at least tried to confirm with the royalty bodyguards present[b] – indicates that Diana was referring to her intention to move to the US.[c]

There is a possibility that her early rapport with Dodi – as described by Gribble – could have helped Diana realise that a trans-Atlantic move was increasingly a practical option.[d]

Diana-Mohamed: Joint Ventures

Diana was also formulating or discussing other plans during this St Tropez holiday.

Richard Kay told the inquest:

> **She told me that she had been discussing with Mr Al Fayed Senior the possibility of setting up some form of worldwide hospice network which he, she indicated, was prepared to financially underwrite.**

It was to be called "Diana Hospices".[284]

Rita Rogers, Diana's psychic, described a phone call that took place the following month:

---

[a] Sansum said that two royalty protection officers, Chris Phelan and Peter Edwards were also there: 9 Jan 08: 131.14. They have never been asked about this conversation.

[b] They were there because of the presence of the princes, William and Harry.

[c] Sansum's account fits with other evidence of Diana's intentions – see later.

[d] At that time Dodi was in the process of shifting back to the US where he had earlier lived – see later.

> When [Diana] was on the boat ... with Dodi, she rang to ask me what I thought about her and Dodi opening hospices up all around the world, and I said I thought it was a brilliant idea.[285]

Mohamed Al Fayed had a track record of sponsoring hospices – he testified that he had financed 20 in the UK over a period of 25 years.[286]

Kay also wrote in an article on the day following Diana's death:

> Mohamed Al Fayed, had agreed to finance a charity for the victims of [land]mines....

This was confirmed by Kay at the inquest.[287]

These Diana-Mohamed joint activities could have been viewed by the Establishment as an escalation in a relationship that was already causing them major concerns.

"The Best Holiday Imaginable"

The St Tropez holiday concluded on Sunday July 20. Diana, William and Harry returned to the UK – Diana to her home and the boys headed back to Balmoral.

The day after arriving back at Kensington Palace, Diana wrote to Mohamed and Heini:

> Dearest Mohamed.... Thank you both so much for an enjoyable week in France. I cannot tell you how much I loved it, waking up every morning and seeing the sun shining. The jetskis rolling was just wonderful. I really had a lot of fun with everything and everyone out there. The *Jonikal* was an amazing piece of kit. I loved sailing on it. Everyone on board was so helpful and kind and I was looked after so well. Superb holiday.... I miss you all enormously. It was with great sadness that the boys and I waved you off at Stansted last night. We were given a <u>wonderful</u>[a] and magical week and adored every minute of our stay. Thank you for your kindness, generosity and patience, particularly in the light of the behaviour of the British media. William and Harry and I had the best holiday imaginable and your family made us so welcome. Needless to say, I think your entire flock is hugely special. Mohamed, we will never be able to thank you enough for everything. You gave the three of us a great deal of happiness and a holiday to remember. Lots of love from Diana.[288]

Diana's step-mother, Raine Spencer, testified that "she had a fantastic time. She really enjoyed it."[289] Diana told Michael Cole that it had been the best family holiday of her life.[290]

But there was more.

---

[a] Underlined by Diana.

This "best holiday imaginable" was also the catalyst for the Diana-Dodi relationship.

Paul Burrell told the inquest that Diana and Dodi met "frequently" in London between July 20 and 26.[291] This was corroborated by Cole:

> **During the intervening ... week [before July 28], Dodi and Diana ... had been seeing each other. They had been meeting at his apartment; they had been to see a film in a private cinema in Soho....[292]**

But dark clouds were quickly gathering.

Greeting Princess Diana on the day she returned to London was a chilling article in the *Sunday Mirror*. It stated:

> **Speculation about Diana's future, which is as strong at Buckingham Palace as it is in the Princess's camp, comes as plans are made for the next meeting of the Way Ahead Group. The Queen, Prince Philip, their four children and senior courtiers meet twice a year to discuss new challenges facing the monarchy. <u>Top of the agenda at the forthcoming meeting is Diana</u>.[293]**

That Way Ahead Group meeting would take place three days later.

12 Special WAG Meeting

The Way Ahead Group – co-chaired by the Queen and attended by senior royals and their high-level servants[294] – only convenes twice a year. Robert Fellowes told the inquest that the WAG "met twice a year, usually in the first two months, and then in the late summer".[295]

WAG meetings were scheduled or took place on 16 September 1996[a], 20 January 1997[296], early September 1997[b] and 19 January 1998[297].

This fits with Fellowes' account – January is "in the first two months" and September is "late summer".

There were two WAG meetings scheduled for 1997 – January 20 and early September.

However the *Sunday Mirror* on 20 July 1997 revealed – based on a leak from the royal household – that there was a "forthcoming meeting" at which Diana would be "top of the agenda".[298]

At the inquest it was revealed that this special meeting took place on 23 July 1997.

In 1997 there were unusually three WAG meetings – the scheduled ones in January and September, with an extra, special meeting in July.

Royal Lies

A special meeting of the Way Ahead Group was called for Wednesday 23 July 1997. This was three days after the return of Diana, William and Harry from the "best holiday imaginable" in St Tropez with Mohamed Al Fayed and family.

Joint ventures were discussed and also a potential relationship between Princess Diana and Mohamed's son, Dodi, emerged from the holiday.

---

[a] *The Spectator* Toronto on 17 September 1996: "The Queen and her children met in council yesterday", referring to a WAG meeting: Royal Family Gathers to Chart Its Future: Way Ahead Group Talks About Church Links, Rules for Succession, *The Spectator* (Toronto), 17 September 1996.
[b] *Sunday Mirror* on 31 August 1997 – see later.

The *Mirror* printed that Diana would be "top of the agenda" at the WAG meeting.

Is it true that Diana could have been discussed at the meeting? And is there any possible link that could be drawn between the July 23 WAG meeting and Diana's premature death on August 31, just 39 days later?

What did the senior royals normally discuss at their twice-yearly WAG meetings?

Only two royal household employees – and absolutely no royal family members – were heard at the inquest: Robert Fellowes (Queen's private secretary) and Miles Hunt-Davis (Philip's private secretary).

These two men – both of whom attended the WAG meetings – outlined the WAG's purpose and the type of topics that would be up for discussion:

-       "to discuss literally the way forward, to produce a degree of coordination between their programmes"[299] – Hunt-Davis
-       "to make sure that ... the central core of what the Royal Family was doing was properly coordinated"[300] – Hunt-Davis
-       "it was really just to coordinate their programmes"[301] – Hunt-Davis
-       "the Way Ahead Group was to do with coordination.... The central theme was coordinating their public life"[302] – Hunt-Davis
-       "it was brought together as a coordinating group so that the activities, public activities, of the core members of the Royal Family ... were as purposeful and effective as possible"[303] – Fellowes
-       "it was an attempt to render more pointful ... the public appearances of the Royal Family"[304] – Fellowes.

Hunt-Davis said that the WAG was set up "really just to coordinate [the senior royals'] programmes".[305] Fellowes was more wordy: The WAG "was brought together as a coordinating group so that the ... public activities of the core members of the Royal Family ... were as purposeful and effective as possible".

Both men are singing from the same song sheet: The WAG was about coordination of the senior royals' activities and schedules.

During the preparation for the inquest the coroner, Scott Baker, had written to the royal household asking what the Way Ahead Group did. The written response – confirmed at the inquest by Hunt-Davis – was:

> **Typical topics considered [by the WAG] included the coordination of Royal diaries; priorities for forthcoming Royal visits; work with the charitable section; and the creation of a Royal website.[306]**

Between 1996 and 2011 – a period of 15 years – there was a considerable amount of media interest in the Way Ahead Group. The following is a sampling of press articles – based on leaks from within the royal household – outlining the purposes of the WAG and topics discussed:[a]

- "[the WAG] has been discussing issues such as the succession and royal marriages to Catholics"[307] (WFJ) – Washington Times, 1 September 1996

- "the Queen and her children met in [a WAG] council ... in an effort to chart the future of the Royal Family"[308] (WFJ) – The Spectator[b], 17 September 1996

- "the Way Ahead Group summit ... [meets] to consider long-term issues"[309] (WFJ) – The Independent, 23 February 1998

- "the Way Ahead group ... [is running a campaign] intended to modernise the monarchy"[310] (WFJ) – The Economist, 12 March 1998

- "one of the first [WAG] decisions was that the Queen should pay tax"[311] (WFJ) – BBC, 31 August 1998

- "the efforts of Buckingham Palace's 'way ahead group' to try to reinvent and modernise the monarchy for the 21st century"[312] (WFJ) – The Guardian, 12 June 2000

- "that [public opinion] poll was commissioned by the Way Ahead Group"[313] (WFJ) – The Mirror, 11 April 2001

- "the [WAG] makes the decisions which have shaped the Royal Family for the past decade or so"[314] (WFJ) – Daily Mail, 19 August 2006

- "the Way Ahead Group ... deals only with such paramount issues as primogeniture, the feudal rule by which the Crown passes to the eldest male heir"[315] (WFJ) – Vanity Fair, August 2011.

There is a huge conflict between Fellowes or Hunt-Davis' sworn testimony and the information that has been provided or leaked to the media repeatedly over a period of 15 years.[c]

Is the Fellowes and Hunt-Davis account true? Did the WAG focus on administrative issues or major problems that the royal family faced?

The media has consistently indicated that the WAG focus is not about coordination of schedules and activities – as stated by the private secretaries – but instead is:

- "discussing issues such as the succession and royal marriages to Catholics" – 1996
- "an effort to chart the future of the Royal Family" – 1996
- "to consider long-term issues" – 1998
- "intended to modernise the monarchy" – 1998

---

[a] More extensive excerpts from these news outlets can be viewed in Part 5, section on the Way Ahead Group, in The Royals chapter.

[b] Toronto, Canada.

[c] 1996 to 2011.

-    "to try to reinvent and modernise the monarchy for the 21st century"
– 2000
-    "makes the decisions which have shaped the Royal Family" – 2006
-    "'palace policy' and how they were going to defend themselves"[316a]
(WFJ) – 2011
-    "paramount issues [such] as primogeniture" – 2011.

This gets right to the very heart of why the WAG was set up. Was it just a group of royals discussing mundane administrative matters such as lining up schedules, or was it a top-level group that dealt with major issues facing the royal family?

If it was the latter then Miles Hunt-Davis and Robert Fellowes misled the inquest into the deaths of Princess Diana and Dodi Fayed.

Inquest lawyer Ian Burnett asked Hunt-Davis: "Was 'Diana' discussed at all at the [23 July 1997] meeting as an agenda item?"

Hunt-Davis replied: "I cannot remember. I think it would have been difficult to have done so with the senior officials there, if it was indeed a family discussion, but to be honest, I do not recall the details." [317]

Burnett then asked: "Was the Way Ahead Group considering ... an issue arising from the divorce of" Charles and Diana?

Hunt-Davis replies:

It is quite possible that it might have been. In terms of status, I would have thought that would probably be the meat of it, but I do not recall it at all.

He then confirms he is talking about Diana's "Her Royal Highness" title.[318b]

Miles Hunt-Davis knows that Diana's HRH title had been removed at the time of the divorce and her exile from the royal family in August 1996 – and there has never been any suggestion of that decision being reviewed.[c] That was around 11 months before this *Sunday Mirror* article and WAG meeting.

Therefore, if Diana was an agenda item in a July 1997 WAG meeting, it could not have been about her HRH title. Hunt-Davis has lied under oath when he indicated that was "quite possible".

---

[a] This article also does mention: "many topics were mundane, like the coordination of schedules". Given that it appeared after the inquest, it may be that Frank Prochashka, who said this, was influenced by the inquest testimony from Miles Hunt-Davis and Robert Fellowes.

[b] The fact that Hunt-Davis is accepting that this discussion "quite possibly" occurred conflicts with his general evidence that the WAG meetings dealt with administrative issues.

[c] That is, while Diana was alive. She was reinstated as a member of the royal family immediately after her death – see later and Part 4, Post-Death Status Change section of Chapter 3.

Later it was put to him that the "Royal Household"[a] had told the coroner in writing: "There is no truth in the *Sunday Mirror's* report of 20th July 1997 that 'top of the agenda for the next meeting is Diana'".

Hunt-Davis confirmed that, and also the household statement: "There were no discussions in relation to Princess Diana at these [1997 WAG] meetings."[319]

These confirmations by Hunt-Davis are in conflict with his earlier claim that a discussion re the HRH title was "quite possible".

The WAG kept their agenda documents.[b] So when Hunt-Davis was asked at the inquest about the July 1997 agenda, it seems strange that he replied, "I cannot remember" – because the household[c] had recently received a list of questions from Baker, which included that issue in it.[320]

Hunt-Davis was evasive when the specific topic of a possible 1996 WAG discussion of Diana's removal from the royal family came up.

Michael Mansfield asked: "It was discussed at the Way Ahead Group, was it not, in 1996?" Hunt-Davis: "I do not think it was discussed in that detail, no." Mansfield again: "In some little detail then?"

Hunt-Davis: "I doubt it was even in that detail, a little detail. The Way Ahead Group was to do with coordination. It was not to do with personal affairs of members of the Royal Family." He went on to say:

"I have no idea" who took "the decision to divest [Diana] of membership of the Royal Family".[321]

On the one hand, we have Hunt-Davis suggesting to Burnett that it was "quite possible" that the WAG would have discussed Diana's HRH title in July 1997, 11 months after it was removed. Yet on the other hand, Hunt-Davis indicates to Mansfield that in 1996 – when these events did happen – he doubts Diana's removal from the royal family would have been discussed "even in that detail, a little detail". And he backs this up by saying: "[The WAG] was not to do with personal affairs of members of the Royal Family.... It was not an inner sanctum where the lives and behaviour of members of the Royal Family was discussed."[322]

Then distancing himself and the WAG even further from the subject of Diana's removal, Hunt-Davis says:

---

[a] Which includes Hunt-Davis. He was still in the job at the time of the inquest – he retired in 2010.

[b] An example is 12 Feb 08: 113.20, where Baker says: "I have the minutes and agenda here" for the 23 July 1997 WAG meeting.

[c] At the time of the inquest Hunt-Davis was still in the royal household and when one considers that he had been a prominent household attendee at WAG meetings for many years, it seems likely that he would have had input into the written household responses to the coroner's questions.

I imagine Her Majesty the Queen took the decision, having taken advice, I presume. I have no idea.[323]

It is not credible that Miles Hunt-Davis – who at the time of this testimony had served 14 years as private secretary to the Queen's husband – would have "no idea" who would make "the decision to divest [Diana] of membership of the Royal Family".

There are three points here:

a)   Hunt-Davis appears to have lied when he suggests to Burnett that the WAG could have been discussing Diana's HRH title in July 1997

b)   the suggestion of discussing Diana's HRH title is a major conflict with the Hunt-Davis, Fellowes and written household evidence that Diana was not a subject of discussion in 1997 – "there were no discussions in relation to Princess Diana at these [1997 WAG] meetings"

c)   Hunt-Davis appears to have lied again when he said, "I have no idea" who would make "the decision to divest [Diana] of membership of the Royal Family".

The group is called the Way Ahead Group. This, in itself, indicates it is designed to discuss the "way ahead" for the royal family – i.e. discussing major issues of direction and facing up to challenges along that way.

The WAG meetings started in November 1992.

It is no coincidence that 1992 marked a major turning point in the relationship between Diana and the other senior members of the royal family – the Queen, Philip and Charles.[a]

The Andrew Morton book – with which Diana collaborated – was published in June 1992 and Squidgygate was published in August. On December 9 – the month following the first WAG meeting – the apparent royal family response to the Morton book was handed out: the announcement of the official separation of Diana and Charles.[b]

Following the publication of the Morton book it is possible that the Queen and Philip may have started considering Diana to be a major threat to the stability of the royal family.

Did the Queen set up the WAG so that major issues – initially, how to deal with Princess Diana – could be discussed in a group setting?

If the WAG meetings were just dealing with administrative issues, then they wouldn't necessarily have required the presence of senior royals, with the Queen in the chair. One would think that administrative issues could be dealt with in meetings between the private secretaries, who would separately consult their respective royal family bosses.

---

[a] See earlier The Watershed chapter.

[b] The full analysis of the sequence, nature and significance of these events has been covered in Part 2 – the section on Diana and the Royal Family in Chapter 6.

Hunt-Davis was asked a simple question: "Do you remember who actually attended [the WAG meetings]?" He replied: "the Queen and Prince Philip, the Prince of Wales, the Duke of York, the Princess Royal and Prince Edward". When Mansfield pushed for more, he conceded: "the Queen's private secretary, myself and possibly the Prince of Wales' private secretary".[324]

Mansfield then asked more about this – "Were there any outside advisers present?"; "Was there somebody who liaised with outside advice?"

Mansfield was obviously seeking a full answer, but Hunt-Davis instead repeated his mantra: "I mean [the WAG] was really just to coordinate their programmes".[325]

Two months later Burnett asked Fellowes the same simple question: "Who attended the Way Ahead Group meetings?"

Fellowes replied:

The Queen, the Duke of Edinburgh, their children, the Private Secretaries to the members of the Royal Family concerned, the Lord Chamberlain, who chaired it with the Queen, and the financial department, represented by the Keeper of the Privy Purse.[326a]

Given that Hunt-Davis was still working as Philip's private secretary at the time of the inquest – and Fellowes had left nine years earlier[b] – it is surprising that it is Hunt-Davis who gave the most incomplete response.

Why did he miss out the Lord Chamberlain – the co-chairperson – the Keeper of the Privy Purse[c] and the private secretaries of Anne, Andrew and Edward? [d]

Maybe he was told to.

The fewer people that are present, the more it supports the false account that this was "really just to coordinate their programmes". The presence of the Lord Chamberlain, as co-chair, and the Keeper of the Privy Purse indicate a level of formality and significance that it appears Hunt-Davis was not willing to concede.[e] In this light, it is important that Hunt-Davis fails to divulge that anyone chaired these WAG meetings.

---

[a] It is also possible that the Queen Mother attended these WAG meetings in 1997.
[b] In 1999.
[c] The Keeper of the Privy Purse meets with the Queen once a week according to Wikipedia.
[d] Anne's private secretaries in 1997 were Peter Gibbs and Rupert McGuigan (there was a changeover during that year); Andrew's was Neil Blair and Edward's was Sean O'Dwyer. Source: Wikipedia, under Royal Households of the United Kingdom.
[e] In simple terms, knowing who attended these meetings helps one understand their nature and what issues might be discussed. For Hunt-Davis to not fully answer the question indicates he is deliberately withholding information.

It may have been considered by the Queen[ab] that Fellowes – who was cross-examined two months after Hunt-Davis – should admit to a truer make-up of the WAG meetings.

Another important factor omitted by Hunt-Davis was the existence of preparatory WAG meetings. Under questioning Fellowes said the July 1997 preparatory meeting was "chaired by the Lord Chamberlain, Lord Airlie[c], and it would have composed the Private Secretaries concerned and the Keeper of the Privy Purse".[327]

Fellowes downplayed the significance of the preparatory meeting – "It was an agenda meeting really. No more than that."[328]

But the point here is that the fact a preparatory meeting took place increases the significance of the WAG meeting that it is preparing for. In other words, if a meeting requires a "preparatory meeting" before it occurs, that indicates that the meeting itself is likely to be addressing very significant issues – not "it was really just to coordinate their programmes".

Why did Fellowes and Hunt-Davis lie about the nature of discussion topics at the WAG meetings?

This is a case of excessive distancing: If the WAG only discussed administrative issues then it is clearly not possible that an assassination of Diana could be on the agenda.

But, why the excessive distancing?

Coroner's Lies

Inquest coroner, Lord Justice Scott Baker, referred to the July WAG meeting in his Summing Up.

He told his jury:

> **You will remember that some time was spent in evidence with both Hunt-Davis and Lord Fellowes on something called the "Way Ahead Group" and especially its meeting on 20th July 1997.[d] A newspaper report had suggested that Diana was top of the agenda and that a file on the Al Fayeds was produced by the security services. It is true that Hunt-Davis thought it quite likely that there was some discussion at the meeting of the perceived damage to the Royal Family. I have seen both the agenda for that meeting and the minutes. They were produced through Fellowes. I have decided not to disclose their contents because they were irrelevant; that is to say they provided no**

---

[a] Fellowes' direct boss.

[b] Bearing in mind what was already in the public domain by the time of the inquest. In 1998 the BBC had stated that "the Queen herself [was] in the chair": Paul Reynolds, Royal Family's Changing Guard, BBC News, 31 August 1998.

[c] David Ogilvy. He played a significant role in post-crash events – see later and Part 4, David Ogilvy section of Chapter 3.

[d] This date is wrong – the meeting was on 23 July 1997. See 18 Mar 08: 152.9.

support for the allegations contained in the newspaper report. Diana was not on the agenda, neither were the Al Fayeds.[329]

The above paragraph was the coroner's sole mention of the WAG in his 2½ days of Summing Up.

Baker fails to point out that the fact the *Mirror* was able to report on an upcoming WAG meeting, indicates they were receiving information from a valid and knowledgeable source – as Mansfield suggested to Hunt-Davis:

The newspaper had particularly accurate information, at least about the existence of the group and the date that it was meeting.[330a]

What Scott Baker said raises several other serious concerns:

1)   Baker stated: "A newspaper report had suggested that Diana was top of the agenda [for the July meeting] and that a file on the Al Fayeds was produced by the security services."

Whilst it is true that the paper suggested "Diana was top of the agenda", Baker has lied when he indicates the same newspaper report said "a file on the Al Fayeds was produced by the security services".

There was a later article on 31 August 1997 – the day of the deaths[b] – where the *Mirror* claimed: "MI6 has prepared a special report on the Egyptian-born Fayeds, which will be presented to the meeting."[331] This refers to a WAG meeting planned for the first week in September 1997.

Baker has stated this as though the paper was claiming the event had occurred – "a file on the Al Fayeds <u>was produced</u>", past tense. In fact the article was referring to an event in the future – "a special report on the Egyptian-born Fayeds, which <u>will be presented</u>".[c]

The articles – which both refer to the contents of future WAG meetings – are quite different from each other:

-      the 20 July 1997 *Mirror* article claims: "Top of the agenda at the forthcoming meeting is Diana". This relates to a meeting that took place three days after the article, on 23 July 1997. There is no mention of the Al Fayeds.[d]

-      the 31 August 1997 article, also in the *Mirror*, makes claims about an expected WAG meeting "next week": "MI6 has prepared a special report on the Egyptian-born Fayeds, which will be presented to the meeting. The delicate subject of Harrods and its Royal warrants is also expected to be

---

[a] Hunt-Davis failed to acknowledge this: "As I have not seen the article or don't remember seeing the article, I have no way of commenting": 13 Dec 07: 69.17.

[b] It was published in the early edition then withdrawn from distribution following knowledge of the crash.

[c] The 31 August 1997 article is reproduced below.

[d] The St Tropez family holiday concluded the same day the article was published. The Diana-Dodi relationship didn't develop until straight after that holiday – see Part 2, Chapter 1.

discussed".[332] Regarding this meeting – which was scheduled to take place after the crash – there is no mention of Diana being on the agenda, only the "Fayeds" and the Harrods royal warrants. The article – which is reproduced below – makes references to Diana, but not in connection with the WAG meeting.

So we have a late July meeting where it is suggested Diana will be top of the agenda and we have an early September meeting where Diana is no longer mentioned – instead the subject is now the Fayeds and Harrods.

The key point here is that between the two WAG meetings Diana was killed.

Therefore it is significant that the August 31 article[a] makes no mention of Diana being on the agenda – it indicates that the source where Andrew Golden from the *Mirror* was getting his information was already aware that Diana may no longer be around for the next WAG meeting in September.

There is a possibility that the Queen underestimated the depth of feeling for Diana and the effect that her death would have on the British nation.[b] It may well be that the Al Fayed-Harrods agenda for the September meeting was shelved – in fact the WAG meeting may have been shelved altogether, or instead changed to discuss the aftermath of the deaths of Diana and Dodi.

The issue here is that Scott Baker appears to be aware of the significance of the two different articles – July 20 and August 31 – and has deliberately clouded it for the jury by merging them together in his Summing Up.

> Following Page: Article that appeared in the early edition of the *Sunday Mirror* on 31 August 1997 – the morning of the crash. It revealed that at the WAG meeting at Balmoral "next week" an MI6 report on the Fayeds would be tabled and Harrods royal warrants would be discussed. There was no mention of Diana being on the agenda. In his Summing Up, Scott Baker merged the information from this article into an earlier 20 July 1997 article that said Diana would be top of the July WAG meeting's agenda.

---

[a] Although written before the crash.
[b] This is addressed in Part 4, Chapter 3.

QUEEN 'TO STRIP HARRODS OF ITS ROYAL CREST'

By Andrew Golden

THE Royal Family may withdraw their seal of approval from Harrods as a result of Diana's affair with owner's son Dodi Fayed.

The top people's store with its long and proud tradition of royal patronage may be about to lose the Prince of Wales royal crest.

Senior Palace courtiers are ready to advise the Queen that she should refuse to renew the prestigious royal warrants for the Knightsbridge store when they come up for review in February.

It would be a huge blow to the ego of store owner Mohamed Al Fayed — and would infuriate Diana, who was yesterday understood to be still with Dodi aboard his yacht, near the Italian island of Sardinia. But the Royal Family are furious about the

antics of Di, 36, and Dodi, 41, which they believe have further undermined the monarchy.

Prince Philip, in particular, has made no secret as to how he feels about his daughter-in-law's latest man, referring to Dodi as an 'oily bed-hopper'.

At Balmoral next week, the Queen will preside over a meeting of The Way Ahead Group where the Windsors sit down with their senior advisers to discuss policy matters.

MI6 has prepared a special report on the Egyptian-born Fayeds which will be presented to the meeting.

The delicate subject of Harrods and its royal warrants is also expected to

be discussed. And the Fayeds can expect little sympathy from Philip

A friend of the Royals said yesterday: "Prince Philip has let rip several times recently about the Fayeds — at a dinner party, during a country shoot and while on a visit to close friends in Germany.

"He is been banging on about his contempt for Dodi and how he is undesirable as a future stepfather to William and Harry.

"Diana has been told in no uncertain terms about the consequences should she continue the relationship with the Fayed boy.

"Options must include possible exile, although that would be very difficult an when all is said and done, she is the mother of the future King of England.

"She has also been warned to

about social ostracism. But Diana's attitude is if that means not having to deal with the royals and their kind, then she would be delighted."

There are some who believe Diana may be past caring and has decided to look towards those who can afford to keep her in the lifestyle to which she became accustomed.

The Fayed family have all the trappings of vast wealth... wherever it originated from

And Dodi has told Diana what he has told many of his other beautiful girlfriends in the past. "It's my father's store and you can have what you want. Charge it to my account and I'll just sign the bill."

But now the Royal Family may decide it is time to settle up.

Sunday Mirror, 31 August 1997

Figure 4

137

2)   Baker stated: "<u>It is true</u> that Hunt-Davis thought it quite likely that there was some discussion at the [23 July 1997 WAG] meeting of the perceived damage to the Royal Family."

This is false.

Hunt-Davis made no mention of "discussion at the [July 23] meeting of the perceived damage to the Royal Family".

Instead, as discussed earlier, Hunt-Davis said it was "quite possible that [the WAG] might have been [discussing the divorce] in terms of [Diana's HRH] status".[a]

Baker has either made this up, or plucked it out of someone else's evidence – not Hunt-Davis': see footnote.[bc]

3)   Baker says: "You will remember that some time was spent in evidence ... [regarding the WAG] meeting on 20th July 1997.... I have seen both the agenda for that meeting and the minutes. They were produced through Fellowes. I have decided not to disclose their contents...."

Earlier in the hearings, inquest QC Ian Burnett had wrongly indicated the meeting took place on 20 July 1997 – he asked Hunt-Davis: "Are you able to confirm that, in 1997, [the WAG] met on ... 20th July?"[333d] Burnett then went on to refer to the meeting as occurring on July 20.

Then later Mansfield mentioned the 20 July 1997 newspaper report, and continues: "<u>Assuming</u> that [July 20] was the [meeting] date...."[334] – so that indicates there was an awareness amongst the lawyers that the 20 July 1997 date for the meeting could have been incorrect.

Then two months later, when Fellowes is on the stand, he says: "We met in late July [1997]".[335] And Burnett then refers to "a letter that was written by the Treasury Solicitor when inquiries were made of the Palace". He indicates that the letter "suggested that the [WAG] met ... on a date which was clarified to be 23rd July." Fellowes confirmed that.[336]

Next Burnett said to Fellowes: "Indeed, the Coroner received the agenda and minutes for the meeting on 23rd July and considered them."[337]

From that point on, Burnett and Mansfield both correctly refer to the meeting as occurring on 23 July 1997.

---

[a] It has been shown earlier that Hunt-Davis appears to have lied when he said this.

[b] In a strange twist, it is possible Baker plucked this out of Sarah, Duchess of York's statement. Sarah was the next witness heard after Hunt-Davis vacated the stand, on 13 December 2007 – there was a lunch break in between. Sarah quoted from Michael Cole's statement, which read: "Diana and Sarah spoke about their fears of them both being killed because <u>of the perceived damage that they had caused to the institution of royalty</u> and to the House of Windsor in particular." 13 Dec 07: 105.13. Scott Baker said: "It is true that Hunt-Davis thought it quite likely that there was some discussion at the meeting <u>of the perceived damage to the Royal Family.</u>"

[c] Baker makes no comment on what would have caused "the perceived damage".

[d] Hunt-Davis replied: "I cannot recall the dates specifically".

Then on the last day of inquest evidence – 18 March 2008 – the Treasury Solicitor letter was read out:

> **During a search made for documents ... a memorandum dated 18th July 1997, and relating to the Way Ahead Group meeting on 23rd July 1997, was located. I attach a copy.**[338a]

That confirmed to anyone at the inquest that there was no longer any question over the date – it was definitely 23 July 1997. The coroner, Scott Baker, apparently had even more proof of that, because since before 12 February 2008[b] he had been given a copy of "both the agenda ... and the minutes".

Yet in his Summing Up Baker wrongly quoted the date of the WAG meeting as "20th July 1997", instead of 23 July 1997.

Baker had a copy of "both the agenda ... and the minutes" well before he prepared his Summing Up[c], so why does he get the date wrong? [d]

Why is the date Baker gave identical to the erroneous date put forward by Burnett earlier in the inquest – 20 July 1997?

The point is that one would presume Baker compiled his Summing Up with care.[ef] We could have expected him to check the minutes of the meeting,

---

[a] It could be significant that this document is used to confirm the meeting date, rather than the meeting's minutes or agenda documents. This could be evidence that the content of the minutes and agenda documents contained information Baker did not want the jury to see or hear.

[b] The day that Burnett stated to Fellowes: "Indeed, the Coroner received the agenda and minutes for the meeting on 23rd July and considered them." Also Burnett, Baker and Fellowes appear to be looking at copies of the minutes during Fellowes' cross-examination – this is addressed below.

[c] It is my understanding that the inquest coroner is expected to prepare thoroughly for the Summing Up. The last day of evidence was Tuesday 18 March 2008 and there was a day with the lawyers on the 20th. Easter weekend then followed. The jury didn't reappear to hear the Summing Up until Monday 1st April. So Baker had somewhere between 8 and 13 days to put together the Summing Up.

[d] Burnett had a copy of the minutes in front of him when he referred to "the minutes of 23rd July".

[e] Given that the jury are expected to rely on its accuracy to help them arrive at a verdict.

[f] In a surprising and troubling twist, Baker repeated this same mistake – dating the meeting July 20 – in his "Reasons" for not calling for evidence from Philip or the Queen. This raises serious concerns on just how deeply Baker carried out his research before drawing significant conclusions. Source: Coroner's Inquests Into The Deaths Of Diana, Princess of Wales and Mr Dodi Al Fayed, Reasons, 12 March 2008.

before writing the date into his very short section[a] of the Summing Up that relates to the WAG.

Instead Baker appears to have got the meeting date from the early transcripts involving Hunt-Davis – it is evident that Baker did not get this date from either the Treasury Solicitor's letter or the meeting's minutes.

This raises a couple of questions:

a)   When Baker put together the WAG section of the Summing Up, did he even look at the transcript of Fellowes' evidence on the subject?

Only two witnesses gave evidence on this – Hunt-Davis and Fellowes. Baker only makes reference to what Hunt-Davis said[b] and makes no mention of Fellowes' evidence.

It appears Baker did not look at Fellowes' testimony – if he had, he should have come up with the correct date (see above).

b)   When Baker put together the WAG section of the Summing Up, did he even look at the minutes of the 23 July 1997 meeting?

In it he says the agenda and minutes "were produced through Fellowes".

During the 12 February 2008 Fellowes cross-examination, Baker said: "I was not provided with page 5 [of the WAG meeting minutes] in the accompanying letter from the Treasury Solicitor".[339]

That is a conflict.

On February 12 the minutes came from the Treasury Solicitor, but a month later Baker says they "were produced through Fellowes".

The first we hear about Baker having these documents is from the inquest lawyer, Ian Burnett – "Indeed, the Coroner received the agenda and minutes for the meeting on 23rd July and considered them."[340] Burnett is talking to Fellowes, but makes no acknowledgement that he played a role in the process.

In 2008 Robert Fellowes is not the first person one would go to for a copy of the agenda and minutes of a 1997 royal meeting, because by that time he had left the Palace employ nine years earlier.[c]

The logical place to arrange to get these documents would be Buckingham Palace.

And that may be what happened and it could be that Baker was directed to the Treasury Solicitor.

The involvement of the Treasury Solicitor's Department – "the legal advisors to the Crown and the State"[341] – in WAG documentation, indicates that these meetings were about more than coordinating the royal schedules.

---

[a] 151 words out of over 80,000 in the Summing Up. By Baker's own admission in the Summing Up, during the inquest "some time was spent in evidence" on the WAG.

[b] As it turns out Baker lied about what Hunt-Davis said – see earlier.

[c] Fellowes was the Queen's private secretary from 1990 to 1999. After leaving the Palace in 1999, Fellowes became Vice-Chairman of Barclay's Private Banking.: Wikipedia, Robert Fellowes.

Are copies of the WAG documentation not kept at Buckingham Palace or in the royal archives?

Why didn't Baker simply ask Hunt-Davis – who was still working at the Palace until 2010 – for a copy of the agenda and minutes? [a]

4)   Baker said: "I have seen both the agenda for that meeting and the minutes.... I have decided not to disclose their contents because they were irrelevant; that is to say they provided no support for the allegations contained in the newspaper report. Diana was not on the agenda, neither were the Al Fayeds." [b]

Baker's basis for not passing on the agenda and minutes to the jury is "because they were irrelevant".[c] Why? Because "Diana was not on the agenda".

The point here is that a specific allegation had been made in an article published three days before the WAG meeting: "Top of the agenda ... is Diana."

That is what makes the agenda and minutes of that WAG meeting relevant – whether or not Diana is on the agenda. In other words, Baker's perception that "Diana was not on the agenda" does not make the agenda and minutes documents irrelevant.[d]

The moment the *Sunday Mirror* made the allegation on 20 July 1997, the agenda and minutes of that July 23 meeting became very relevant in the event of Diana's suspicious death.

The jury were expected to deliberate on the cause of the deaths of Diana and Dodi, yet withheld from them were the minutes and agenda of a meeting:

-       that took place just six weeks before the deaths
-       that was attended by several named suspects – the Queen (who was chairman), Philip, Charles and Fellowes
-       before which it had been publicly alleged that one of the victims was to be "top of the agenda".

---

[a] Why didn't Hunt-Davis offer to supply the inquest with a copy of the agenda or minutes after he was asked: "Was 'Diana' discussed at all at the [July] meeting as an agenda item?" and he replied: "I cannot remember."? 13 Dec 07: 60.12.

[b] It has been shown that the Al Fayeds were not mentioned in the July 20 article – they were the subject of a later article on August 31.

[c] One could argue that a more logical reason could have been for Baker to claim they were confidential, but that may have given rise to the suggestion that the information was more than about coordinating schedules.

[d] This is similar to a hypothetical situation where a witness may say they did not see an event. The fact they say they did not see the event does not make their evidence irrelevant. There may be a significant reason why the witness is saying they didn't see it.

In light of the Fellowes and Hunt-Davis evidence, the general nature of topics discussed at the WAG meeting was relevant to the jury. A question that the July 23 minutes may have answered would be: Was the meeting about coordinating royal schedules, or was there discussion of more serious challenges facing the royal family?

During the Mansfield cross-examination of Fellowes about the 23 July 1997 WAG meeting, Baker stated: "I was [possibly] not provided with page 5 [of the minutes] in the accompanying letter from the Treasury Solicitor".[342]

Burnett then says to Baker: "given that I have [a copy of the minutes] with page 5, it must have arrived with page 5 but perhaps it has not been copied onto [your copy]".[343]

And Baker told Mansfield: "I am sorry, Mr Mansfield, I gave you misleading information" about the minutes.[344]

Taken together this evidence indicates that the minutes arrived by letter from the Treasury Solicitor and upon arrival at least one copy was taken. It is possible Burnett received the original and a copy was made for Baker – but whatever happened, it is clear that Mansfield was not provided with a copy, even though he was asking witnesses questions that related to the content of the minutes.

Earlier Burnett had given the impression that only the coroner had the minutes – "Indeed, the Coroner received the agenda and minutes for the meeting on 23rd July and considered them." [345]

It is only because of the issue regarding the missing page 5 in Baker's copy that Burnett is forced into admitting he has a copy – even the original.[a]

There was a lack of openness regarding documentation. Both Burnett and Mansfield questioned this witness – Robert Fellowes – about the 23 July 1997 WAG meeting, but only Burnett was provided with the minutes from the meeting.[b]

The jury were shown absolutely no WAG documentation – nothing at all, and neither was Michael Mansfield. At one point, during Hunt-Davis' cross-examination, Mansfield said: "I do not have, as you don't appear to have either, access to any of the documentation relating to this group".[346]

---

[a] The evidence highlights the fact that Burnett received either the original or the main copy. Baker may have been embarrassed when this came to light and it is possible that led him to suggest something that is completely illogical: "I was not provided with page 5 [of the minutes] in the accompanying letter from the Treasury Solicitor or it may be that this is an error in copying at our end." Baker's first option for not having page 5 is illogical because Burnett has just shown him page 5, which Burnett could only have obtained when it came with the Treasury Solicitor's letter. Burnett points out straight after this that it is a problem in the copying. 12 Feb 08: 114.25.
[b] It is possible that the contents of the minutes were suppressed because they would have revealed that the topics discussed at WAG meetings were more than dealing with the coordination of royal schedules.

Why?

In summary, there are major problems in Baker's descriptions of the 23 July 1997 WAG meeting: he has the wrong date in his Summing Up; he says the minutes came through Fellowes even though Fellowes hadn't worked at the Palace for nine years; Baker's "irrelevant" comment lacks substance.

The key concern is that Lord Justice Scott Baker has used his claimed knowledge of the contents of the agenda and minutes of the July WAG meeting – "Diana was not on the agenda" – to neutralise the effect of the *Mirror* article – "Top of the agenda ... is Diana". But in doing this he has not allowed the Al Fayed lawyer, Michael Mansfield, or even more importantly, his own inquest jury, to view the minutes of the meeting.

This failure to show the minutes leads to the inescapable possibility that there could be truth in the article's account.

There are several ways this could happen: a) the WAG minutes could have been doctored before they are sent to the inquest;[a] b) Diana was included in the minutes and Baker has lied; c) Diana was included in the meeting's oral discussions but was deliberately omitted from the original agenda and minutes at the time they were written up.

If the contemplation of Diana's assassination was discussed at the July WAG meeting, then there is a realistic possibility that a decision would be made to omit that subject from the record – given that assassination is illegal.

Special WAG Meeting

At the inquest Robert Fellowes said that the WAG "met twice a year, usually in the first two months, and then in the late summer".[347]

Burnett stated that the Treasury Solicitor wrote to the inquest saying: "the [WAG] met twice in 1997, once on 20th January and then, again, on ... 23rd July".

Now July 23 is not "late summer" – it is mid-summer.

Fellowes' account is supported by *The Spectator* article published on 17 September 1996[b]: "The Queen and her children met in council yesterday", referring to a WAG meeting.

The 1997 timing then does not fit. If it is usual practice for the second meeting to be "in the late summer", why was the second 1997 meeting on July 23?

This evidence raises the possibility that the WAG's second 1997 meeting was brought forward. In other words, it may have been originally scheduled

---

[a] We are not told if the original minutes are loose-leaf – if they were, then they would probably be easier to doctor.
[b] The year preceding the crash.

for September 1997, but for some reason a decision was made to hold it two months early – in July.[ab]

What would trigger a decision of this nature – changing the scheduling of a WAG meeting?

The balance of the evidence has already indicated that the main purpose of the WAG was to discuss issues of importance facing the royal family.

Was there then an issue that had arisen at this time that was of urgent significance to the royal family?

Robert Fellowes gave testimony about a preparatory meeting that was held on 8 July 1997 "it was an agenda meeting really – no more than that"[348] and was "chaired by the Lord Chamberlain, Lord Airlie ... [with] the Private Secretaries concerned and the Keeper of the Privy Purse".[349c]

The earlier Timeline of Events reveals that significant events – from a royal family perspective – were happening around this time.

On 11 June 1997[d] Princess Diana wrote a letter to Mohamed Al Fayed confirming that she was intending to join – accompanied by the Queen's grandsons, Princes William and Harry – Mohamed in St Tropez in mid-July.

The preparatory meeting on July 8 was held just three days before Diana and the boys arrived in St Tropez on the holiday – and the day before the head of royalty protection, David Davies, apparently called Fellowes warning him of police concerns regarding the St Tropez holiday.[e]

The full WAG meeting was held on July 23, precisely three days after Diana and the boys returned from the St Tropez holiday, on July 20.

July 8 is the preparatory meeting; July 11, Diana, William and Harry join Mohamed in St Tropez; July 20, Diana, William and Harry return to the UK; July 23, the special WAG meeting is held.

The preparatory meeting is three days before the holiday starts and the full WAG meeting is three days after the holiday concludes.

I suggest that this is not a coincidence.

---

[a] In light of Fellowes' "late summer" comment, Baker should have sought the minutes from the 20 January 1997 meeting – they could have shown the expected date for the next meeting. I suggest that it would have been in September.

[b] Another factor that may point to this being an extraordinary meeting is that it was held on a Wednesday (23 July 1997). The only other known WAG meeting dates were both on Mondays – 16 September 1996 and 20 January 1997.

[c] Fellowes confirmed that there could be "a record of that particular agenda meeting" and Mansfield consequently requested Baker "if we might be provided" with that record. There is no evidence of Baker seeking the record of the 8 July 1997 meeting. 12 Feb 08: 99.18.

[d] Less than a month before the July 8 WAG preparatory meeting.

[e] Davies described Fellowes' initial response, after he told him about the police concerns: "there was a silence as I recall". See earlier Pressure Builds chapter.

From the Queen's viewpoint, taking Prince William and Prince Harry on a 10 day holiday with Mohamed Al Fayed was a major event.

This is supported by the reactions of other people to the news of this holiday:

- David Davies, representing the police view: "the matter gave us cause for concern"[350]
- Davies: "the holiday shouldn't go ahead"[351]
- Davies: "I was concerned as to the consequence ... for ... the reputation of the Royal Family"[352]
- Davies: "the future King of England and his brother and the mother were going on holiday with a gentleman who ... I had some concerns about"[353a]
- Lucia Flecha de Lima: "Mr Al Fayed's bad reputation as a business man and the problem over his passport being refused"[354] (WFJ)
- Lucia: "I did not think it was a proper thing to do.... [Mohamed] is a bit of a controversial person"[355]
- Rosa Monckton: "going on holiday with Mr Al Fayed ... was an inappropriate thing for [Diana] to do"[356]
- Hasnat Khan: "[Diana's] reputation was dead. I said this because I was sure that it was someone from Mohamed Al Fayed's group and that was how I felt about anyone involved with him"[357]
- Harold Brookes-Baker:[b] "this is totally irresponsible of the Princess – particularly considering the problems people have faced with the Al Fayed connection"[358] (WFJ).

WAG Cover-Up

Why is there a cover-up about the WAG discussion topics if there is nothing to cover up?

If the WAG meetings were only discussing major issues facing the royal family – even including the major challenge created by Diana's activities – there would not necessarily be a need for such information to be covered up.[c] The discussions only need to be covered up when they involve the contemplation of possible illegal activity.

---

[a] Davies' concerns were qualified. He says: "I had some concerns ... because of [an] allegation" against Mohamed Al Fayed, who was the subject of a police investigation. Davies continued: "I don't think [the allegation] has been substantiated in any way.": 31 Jan 08: 115.18.
[b] Editor of *Burke's Peerage.*
[c] There is a big difference between a discussion regarding Diana and a discussion regarding the elimination of Diana. The evidence from the Palace is that there was no WAG discussion of Diana in 1997.

So if there had been a WAG discussion – however brief – on 23 July 1997 regarding eliminating Princess Diana, then we could expect to see a cover-up of that.

There has been a cover-up regarding the WAG discussion topics.

There has to be a reason for that.

Seen in the light of the other evidence in this book, this could indicate that the assassination of Diana was contemplated at the 23 July 1997 WAG meeting.[ab]

---

[a] If MI6 were present at this meeting – and the 31 August 1997 *Mirror* article (shown earlier, Figure 4, and later in Time to Settle Up chapter) indicates that is a possibility – an order to carry out an assassination need not necessarily be overt. In fact it is likely not to be overt as there would then be no specific trail of evidence.

[b] The general evidence – particularly from the media articles – is that the WAG discussed major issues facing the royal family. It is common sense that Diana was a major issue facing the royal family – right from 1992 onwards – and therefore it is logical that she would have been a topic of WAG discussion. The fact that the Palace – through Hunt-Davis and Fellowes – has distanced itself from this, indicates there has been a cover-up regarding WAG discussion topics.

13   Exit Hasnat Khan

Meanwhile the Diana-Dodi relationship continued to develop and on July 26 the couple secretly left London for a weekend in Paris.

On her return Diana penned this letter to Dodi:

> **Dearest Dodi,**
>
> **Seldom has this particular lady ever been lost for words, but the events of the last twenty-four hours has left her speechless!**
>
> **Your organisation and sense of detail is enormously impressive & I thought I was the one with vision!!**
>
> **I am absolutely thrilled with this beautiful new addition upon my wrist & I spend many a moment just staring down on my watch in awe & am <u>so</u>[a] touched to have been thought of.**
>
> **I have always longed to stay at the Ritz, since my father loved the hotel and now, of course, I see exactly why & what with a wonderful dinner too.**
>
> **What can a girl say?!! Except perhaps to borrow a quote that was issued at 3.00 a.m. on Sunday morning, 'I love hanging out with you too: ...**
>
> **Lots of love, Dodi, & a million heartfelt thanks for all your kindness and generosity, from Diana. X** [359]

The next day Diana organised a meeting with her boyfriend, Hasnat Khan. They met twice in two days – first at Battersea Park and then the next day Hasnat visited Kensington Palace.

By the conclusion of the palace meeting Diana and Hasnat had broken up and were no longer a couple.

Why did they break up? Who initiated it? And precisely when was it?

At the inquest there was a major effort to time the Diana-Hasnat break-up to before Diana and Dodi first met. If it could be shown the break-up occurred first, then the reason for it could not have been the Diana-Dodi relationship.

---

[a] Underlining by Diana.

Hasnat's Account

The three most important issues – who initiated it? when? and why? – can all be deduced from the testimony of the only living eye-witness, Hasnat Khan.

Hasnat told the police in 2004:

> **When Diana went to St Tropez with Mr Al Fayed [July 11], everything was fine between us. I said goodbye to her the day she went, as I had stayed with her the previous night at Kensington Palace....**
>
> **After a few days, I felt something was wrong. Her mobile kept going on to answerphone. When I did eventually speak to her, unbeknown to me, she had returned from her holiday with Mohamed Al Fayed, had been at home for either one or two nights and had then gone off to Paris. When you know someone very well, you know when something is not right and that is how I felt when I spoke to her. I told her I thought something was wrong because of the way she had been acting, but she just said that because of the geography of where she was, she was having problems getting a reception on her phone. I said we would talk when she got home.**
>
> **I next spoke to Diana when she had got back from her [Paris] trip, but she was on her way with her boys to see her sister, Jane.[a] We arranged to meet up in Battersea Park when she got home again. When we did meet up in Battersea Park, she was not her normal self and she kept looking at her mobile phone. I told her that I thought she had met somebody else and it must be someone from Mohamed Al Fayed's contingent.... I was surprised when she denied to me that there was anyone else. At the end of our meeting in Battersea Park we arranged to see each other again, the following day, at Kensington Palace.**
>
> **I can't remember the exact date, but <u>we met in Battersea Park within a couple of days of her returning from Paris</u>. It was at this second meeting [at KP] that <u>Diana told me that it was all over between us</u>. She denied there was anyone else involved. I told her that <u>I strongly suspected there was someone else</u> and I remember saying to her at the time 'You are dead', meaning her reputation was dead. I said this because I was sure that it was someone from Mohamed Al Fayed's group and that was how I felt about anyone involved with him....**
>
> **It was only when I heard the news on the radio that I learned about Dodi. I think she wanted to be with someone who was happy to be seen with her in public and she could do that with Dodi....**
>
> **It is impossible to tell whether we would have got together again, but depending on what would have happened between her and Dodi, it could have been a possibility in the long run.[360]**

---

[a] There was no visit with Jane – Diana and Jane were estranged at the time. See earlier, Her Year of Freedom chapter. It is likely that Diana was instead covering for time spent with Dodi.

Diana finished the relationship around 30 July 1997,[a] because she was seeing someone else – Dodi Fayed. Diana did not tell Hasnat that she was seeing someone else, but that is something that Hasnat clearly was able to deduce because he knew her well. Later he found out it was Dodi.

The facts of the break-up are clear and simple, but that is not how the witnesses presented it at the inquest.

Lies and Misinformation

The most important issue is the immediate cause for the break-up.

The timing is closely connected to the cause: If the timing could be placed at pre-14 July 1997 then the possibility of the break-up being caused by the relationship with Dodi would be completely removed.

Outside of Hasnat, there were just three witnesses at the inquest who claimed under oath that they knew the timing of the break-up. These three people all made the identical "mistake" of placing the break-up prior to Diana's first meeting with Dodi on July 14. They either lied or provided false information.

The three witnesses are Paul Burrell, Susan Kassem – a friend of Diana – and Sarah McCorquodale – her sister.

They said:

- Burrell: "it was definitely before she went to St Tropez" (July 11)[361]
- Kassem: "it was a couple of weeks after [the Diana-Hasnat] relationship finished that she met Dodi"[362]
- McCorquodale: "it was June or July"[363].

I suggest that this misinformation is not a coincidence.

There are three possible explanations that could apply to each witness:

1) Diana misled them
2) they lied to the inquest
3) they drew their own conclusions about the timing, then claimed that they had knowledge to the inquest.

It would have been very difficult for Diana to have completely hidden the timing of the break-up from her butler, Paul Burrell. It is significant that Burrell comes across very definite that the break-up occurred before any

---

[a] Based on Hasnat's evidence that the Battersea Park meeting took place "within a couple of days of her returning from Paris" and the Kensington Palace meeting was arranged for "the following day". Diana returned from Paris on the 27th, the Battersea meeting was probably on the 29th and the KP meeting would then have been on the 30th. This timing would fit with Diana and Dodi's departure for their first cruise on the 31st. When Diana talked to her friend Annabel Goldsmith "at the end of July" the break-up had already occurred – "she told me on that last visit, end of July, that it had finished with Hasnat Khan": 17 Dec 07: 15.13.

contact with Dodi. A closer look reveals that of the three critical questions[a], Burrell gave false evidence on all three. He stated that Hasnat "didn't want to become [publicly] known, and they had reached a stalemate situation",[364] and this was "definitely before she went to St Tropez".

Burrell claimed that the break-up occurred at the Battersea Park meeting, whereas Hasnat stated that it occurred in Diana's home. It would have been common sense for this to have taken place at Kensington Palace: Diana would not have wanted a confrontation in a public park. Diana may well have sent Burrell home before Hasnat arrived at Kensington Palace on that final occasion.[b]

Why did Burrell lie about this subject?

He makes a concerted effort in his inquest evidence to undermine any importance that could be placed on the Diana-Dodi relationship.[c] It is impossible to know exactly what Burrell's motivation is, but there could be a link to a current or future benefit to himself. Evidence of Burrell admitting he lied to the inquest surfaced on 18 February 2008 – in the form of a video, after he had safely returned to the USA.[365d]

Burrell's evidence at the inquest differed significantly from the earlier account of the break-up in his 2006 book, *The Way We Were*:

1) In his book he stated that it occurred at Vauxhall Gardens,[366e] (WFJ) whereas at the inquest this had changed to Battersea Park.[367] These are two completely different locations.

2) In the book he describes hearing about it "the following morning over breakfast".[368] (WFJ) At the inquest he said "the Princess came home that night very distressed and said that she had had it" and so on.[369]

3) His timing in the book is "the first week of July"[370] (WFJ) whereas at the inquest he initially said "in the middle of July".[371f]

Burrell states in his book that Diana filled him in on the details of the break-up – "she explained what had happened, what she had said and how

---

[a] Who, when and why: see above.

[b] There is evidence that Diana did this on another occasion – when the *Panorama* interview was recorded at Kensington Palace in 1995, she made sure that she was the only one at home when the TV crew arrived.

[c] In Burrell's 2006 book *The Way We Were* he devotes a large section to "disprove" what he calls "the Dodi myth" – the belief that the Diana-Dodi relationship was developing, not concluding.

[d] A transcript of the video was read to the Court: 6 March 08: from 4.19.

[e] Vauxhall Gardens is a London park that closed in 1859. Today the Spring Gardens exist on a small part of that original site, not far from Trafalgar Square.

[f] He stated that twice to Burnett, but when Mansfield asked him he said "it was definitely before she went to St Tropez". That means before July 11, which then becomes a further conflict of evidence because before July 11 is not the middle of July.

[Hasnat] had reacted".[372] (WFJ) But it is notable that Burrell fails to support these claims by describing any of the details of what Diana actually told him.

The main problem is that Hasnat's account is that the break-up didn't occur at that public park meeting, but at KP the next day – and obviously at a time when Burrell was not present.

The inference from this evidence is that Burrell's first-hand knowledge of the break-up is either non-existent or very minimal. It could be that Diana not only didn't fill him in on the details, but she may not have, at the time, informed him that it had occurred.

Rosa Monckton never claimed precise knowledge of when the break-up occurred: "I think – I think – I think – and I am only – you know, what I can recollect is"[373] – but she still reached the same conclusion as Burrell: the cause had nothing to do with Dodi and everything to do with Hasnat – "[Hasnat] absolutely could not cope with a life in the limelight and so he ended the relationship".[374]

Monckton volunteered the information that "he ended the relationship" – all she had been asked by Burnett was an initial question relating to the timing.[a] This is significant, because there is a direct connection between timing and cause – see above – and this could indicate that Monckton was very aware of that connection.

During his Summing Up to the jury, coroner Scott Baker said: "Burrell corroborates Hasnat Khan's account that the relationship with him was broken off in Battersea Park one night in July."[375]

This is a false statement.

Hasnat stated: "It was at this second meeting that Diana told me that it was all over between us" – that occurred at Kensington Palace on "the following day" after the first meeting at Battersea Park. Hasnat clearly described two separate meetings on consecutive days. Burrell does not "corroborate" that at all.

Baker gives the timing as "one night in July" – this is technically correct, but considering the importance of the precise timing, very misleading. Burrell said the break-up occurred before July 11 and Hasnat said at the end of July.

In between times, Diana had met Dodi.

In short, Baker states to the jury that Burrell "corroborates Hasnat Khan's account" – nothing could actually be further from the truth. Burrell's account disagrees with Hasnat's on all three critical points: who, when and why.

Baker has again lied to his own jury.

---

[a] "Had her relationship with Hasnat Khan come to a definite end by the summer of 1997, as far as you were aware?": 13 Dec 07: 136.20.

Exit Hasnat Khan

In summary, it was Princess Diana who initiated the break-up with Hasnat Khan. It was because of her new relationship with Dodi Fayed and it occurred at Kensington Palace on 30 July 1997 – after Diana and Dodi had spent a weekend in Paris and before their first cruise together.

14 Romance and Landmines

The day following the Hasnat break-up Diana and Dodi travelled to the south of France where they boarded the *Jonikal* and embarked on a seven day Mediterranean cruise.

It was Thursday 31 July 1997.

Five days into this cruise Mario Brenner took the famous "the kiss" photo of the couple.

Monte Carlo Excursion

On Tuesday August 5 Diana and Dodi went ashore at Monte Carlo accompanied by their Al Fayed bodyguard John Johnson and Dodi's butler, Rene Delorm.

Delorm told the inquest: "They went [into a] jewellery store. The security guard and myself were waiting outside and they came back after 20 minutes."[376]

Johnson was asked: "Did they go into a jeweller's store while they were there?" He replied: "Not that I can remember."[377] He also had said in his statement: "If they had stopped outside a jeweller's shop, it would only have been for a few seconds".[378]

Delorm recalls a visit to a jeweller's whereas Johnson does not recall it.

The significance of visiting a jewellery store revolves around the possible viewing of engagement rings.

If a visit to a jeweller's did occur on August 5 the general evidence would suggest it was simply too early in the relationship for it to have any connection to a potential engagement.

There is no evidence that engagement rings were viewed in Monte Carlo on August 5.

That same day Diana wrote a letter addressed to "Darling Dodi":

Darling Dodi,
You spread so much happiness with your thoughtfulness – what a gift you have....
I can only imagine the look of utter joy on William & Harry's faces when they see what's arrived today.☺

As for their mother, she just beams inside & out & is deeply touched by what comes from your huge heart which holds no bounds...
Thank you, thank you, fondest luv from x Diana. X [379]

"Darling Dodi"

Diana and Dodi returned to London August 6 and Diana penned the following letter:

Darling Dodi,
Heaven knows where on earth I begin to thank you for <u>the</u> most magical six days on the ocean waves! – It is a bit of 'oh my God' situation!!
I adored it all & every possible minute was full of laughter & happiness, & that combination is a serious treat!
However, I shall always remember, in particular, the consequences of your conversation with Rita – I have never seen or felt such a huge burden being removed as what happened to you – Long long overdue, & now you are able to benefit from peace of mind in a very personal way.
This comes with all the love in the world & as always a <u>million</u> heartfelt thanks for bringing such joy into this particular chick's life,
From x Diana. x [380]

The next day – August 7 – the *Daily Mirror* broke the story of the Diana-Dodi relationship.

Bosnia

Diana arrived home from Dodi's Park Lane apartment after 1 a.m. that night and then travelled to Bosnia in the morning. This was the beginning of a three day visit to the minefields and civilian victims of landmines.

This was also confirmation to those watching that Diana was determined to disregard the threats to her life and pursue the anti-landmine campaign.

She was accompanied by 40 journalists and cameramen, Lord Deedes and her butler, Paul Burrell.[381] (WFJ) Burrell noted that while in Bosnia Diana kept in touch with Dodi using a satellite phone.[382] (WFJ)

Diana returned to London on the 10th to find "the kiss" photo published in that morning's *Sunday Mirror.*

The next day Diana penned a letter to Dilys Cheetham, a landmine campaigner working in Bosnia. She wrote that she had been "deeply moved" by her visit and it had hardened her resolve over the campaign.[383]

"Head Over Heels"

Once back from Bosnia, Diana quickly met up again with Dodi. Rene Delorm, Dodi's butler, was transferred over from Paris. He tells the story:

The Princess would be returning to London from Bosnia that day [10 August 1997], and Dodi wanted to take her immediately to his father's estate in Oxted.... On our first night [in Oxted] I set a beautiful table at the edge of the garden.... As I served the meal and later took away the plates, Dodi and the Princess continued talking non-stop. And long after ... they remained deeply engrossed in their conversation.... Finally at midnight ... they picked up their drinks and walked arm in arm into the house....

We stayed at Oxted only that one night, then returned to London. But a couple of days later [August 12], we repeated the trip. Obviously, it was a great deal easier for Dodi and the Princess to enjoy their privacy at the countryside mansion than in London, where the paparazzi had staked out their homes....

The following day [August 13][a] the two of them took the helicopter and went off on some sort of adventure... Later I found out that Diana wanted Dodi to meet her adviser, Rita Rogers, in Derbyshire....[384b] (WFJ)

Rita Rogers told the inquest: "I have never seen anyone ... look at each other like Diana and Dodi did".[385] She said Diana "loved Dodi very much. She told me that. They were her exact words."[386] Rogers also confirmed that Dodi had told her that he was "totally in love with Diana" and was "head over heels".[387]

After returning to Oxted, that same day Diana did something remarkable. As a sign of her love she gave Dodi a very special set of her father's cufflinks. With them was a loving letter:

Darling Dodi,
These cufflinks were the very last gift that I received from the man I loved most in the world – my father –
They are given to you as I know how much joy it would give him to know they were in such safe and special hands....
Fondest love, from Diana. x [388]

---

[a] Rita Rogers stated that this occurred on August 12: 17 Jan 08: 228.17.
[b] The facts described by Delorm match a similar account in Trevor Rees-Jones' book: Trevor Rees-Jones & Moira Johnston, The Bodyguard's Story: Diana, The Crash and the Sole Survivor, 2000, pages 47-54.

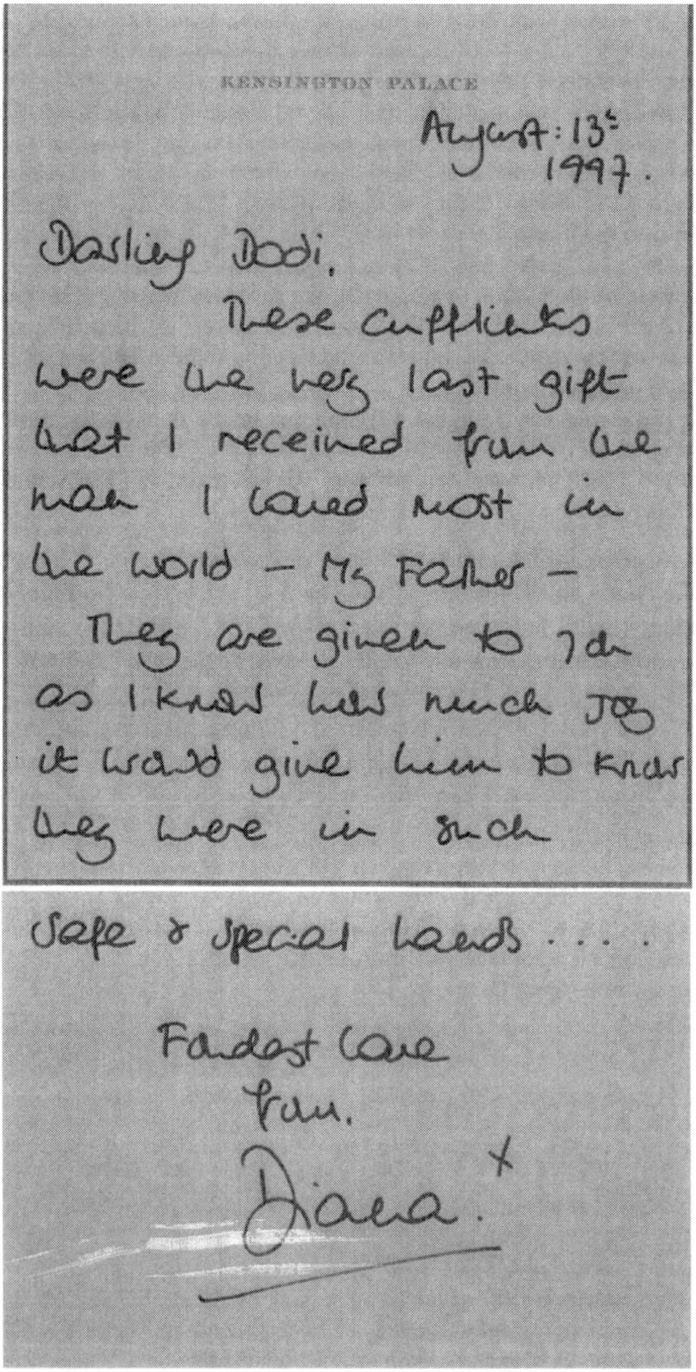

KENSINGTON PALACE

August: 13th
1997.

Darling Dodi,
        These cufflinks
were the very last gift
that I received from the
man I loved most in
the world — My Father —
        They are given to you
as I know how much joy
it would give him to know
they were in such

safe & special hands . . . .

            Fondest Love
            From.
            Diana. x

Figure 5

The next day (August 14) they returned to London.
Delorm wrote:

When we got back to Park Lane, Dodi informed me that the Princess would be joining him for dinner that night.... He was [then] planning on taking the Princess to a private screening of *Air Force One*.... The Princess in particular really loved it.[389a] (WFJ)

---

[a] The facts described by Delorm match a similar account in Trevor Rees-Jones' book: Trevor Rees-Jones & Moira Johnston, The Bodyguard's Story: Diana, The Crash and the Sole Survivor, 2000, pages 47-54.

15   Moving to Malibu

In the spring[a] of 1997 Mohamed Al Fayed purchased the Malibu property that had formerly belonged to the actress Julie Andrews.[390b] He later stated that he "bought the house, for Dodi to carry on his film-making".[391]

Quite apart from Dodi, Diana had also expressed to several people an interest in moving to the US:

- "her dream was to go to live in America"[392] – Roberto Devorik, friend
- "she talked about [moving to] ... America"[393] – Sarah McCorquodale
- "she was talking about moving to America"[394] – Lee Sansum, bodyguard
- "in America [Diana] thought she would be able to settle down"[395] – Simone Simmons, friend
- "the Princess ... very much wanted to have some kind of accommodation in America"[396] – Paul Burrell, butler
- "there was a time when she thought it would be interesting to go and live in America"[397] – Rosa Monckton, friend

Although Princess Diana did consider moving to other parts of the world, her primary focus – according to the witnesses – was on the US.

Following finalisation of the purchase of the Andrews property in June 1997, Mohamed's executive housekeeper, Dorothy Umphofr, travelled to Malibu. She was asked to "check the inventory on acquisition, the condition of the property and to start to establish what furnishing was required" for Dodi to move in.[398]

Then on August 6 Umphofr made a second visit to Malibu, this time accompanied by an Al Fayed bodyguard, Steven Griffiths. He told the inquest that he had agreed to be "based at Dodi Al Fayed's property in Malibu".[399] Umphofr said that she was responsible for supervising "the removal ... and ... unpacking of all of Dodi's possessions and to organise it as a home for Dodi".[400]

Dodi Fayed travelled from London to Malibu on August 15.

---

[a] Around April. The purchase was finalised in June.
[b] By coincidence, this was a property that Diana had contemplated purchasing in late 1995 – Simone Simmons: 10 Jan 08: 68.25.

Griffiths stated: "By the time Dodi arrived ... we had already unpacked ... most of his possessions that had been sent out from Europe".[401]

Melissa Henning, Dodi's assistant, talked at length to Dodi during his visit. She testified that Diana would also be living at the Malibu house:

> **We discussed several things that would have to be changed at the house. One was upgrading the security, of course, and perhaps building a security outpost in anticipation of [Diana's] arrival, as well as upgrading electronics. She was expected to come out mid to late September with Dodi, and at that time we were going to make further changes or whatever needed to be done, whatever she would like done to the house to make it more comfortable....[402]**
>
> **I understood that she and he would be in a continuing relationship. [Dodi] was planning to spend much more time in Malibu and he was expecting [Diana] to spend much more time in Malibu as well.[403]**

This was supported by Umphofr and Griffiths who both spoke with Dodi during that mid-August visit.

Griffiths said:

> **[Dodi] said to me, 'The next time you see me, next month', meaning September 'I will be with my special friend'... My impression from what he said was that Malibu was certainly to be his main home ... and the way he said it was that Princess Diana was not coming out in September merely for a holiday.[404]**

Umphofr stated: "Dodi certainly said that the next time he was going back to Malibu it would be with his special friend, Princess Diana."[405]

By August 15 Princess Diana and Dodi Fayed had already made the decision to live together and set up the Malibu mansion as their primary accommodation.

Just over a week later Melissa Henning spoke with Dodi during the couple's final cruise on the *Jonikal*. Dodi put Diana on the line. Henning said:

> **I believed, after speaking to [Diana], that she was going to spend a considerable amount of time in California. She was looking forward to seeing the house and ... making adjustments, [making] sure that the house was ready to receive her. And she also mentioned bringing her sons out when they were on a break from their studies.[406]**

Other witnesses also testified about this:

    - Michael Cole:[a] "[Dodi] said that he and the Princess would make the [Malibu] house their home and live in California...."[407]

    - John Johnson:[a] "[Dodi] said that 'we' would be going over to Malibu, and I took it that he meant himself and the Princess of Wales."[408]

---

[a] Harrods Director of Public Affairs.

- Mohamed Al Fayed: "I said, 'I bought the [Malibu] house, for Dodi to carry on his film-making.' And [Diana] said, 'I am not going to leave him, I am going to go with him'."[409]

- Paul Burrell: He heard Diana say in August 1997 regarding the Malibu property: "this is it, this is our dream, this is what's happening and this is where we are going to live".[410] Burrell said: "it was a given ... it was already in the pipeline".[411]

Coroner's Misrepresentations

In his Summing Up, coroner Scott Baker managed to completely leave out all the evidence from Dorothy Umphofr, Stephen Griffiths and Lee Sansum. Baker did briefly mention Melissa Henning's account on Malibu:

> **Dodi mentioned [to Henning] the <u>possibility</u> of Diana staying in Malibu in September. On one occasion, when he telephoned from the *Jonikal*, he told Miss Henning that ... he and Diana <u>might be spending some time together in the future</u>.[412]**

Baker has, at best, misrepresented Melissa Henning's evidence to the jury. Henning stated:

- "[Diana] was expected to come out mid to late September with Dodi, and at that time we were going to make further changes ... whatever she would like done to the house to make it more comfortable...."[413]

- "I understood that <u>she and he would be in a continuing relationship</u>. He was planning to spend much more time in Malibu and he was expecting her to spend much more time in Malibu as well."[414]

- "Their visit was to be mid to late September, and to me it sounded like that was <u>a firm commitment</u> by her at that point, to come out then."[415]

- "I believed, <u>after speaking to her</u>, that <u>she was going to spend</u> a considerable amount of time in California. She was looking forward to seeing the house and looking forward to ... making adjustments, make sure that the house was ready to receive her, and she also mentioned bringing her sons out when they were on a break from their studies."[416]

These are clear descriptions of conversations held between Henning and Dodi and also between Henning and Diana.

Baker has chosen to ignore the fact that Henning spoke with Diana and has clearly watered down the statements Henning made at the inquest.

In summary, Baker has misrepresented to the jury the general evidence on Malibu – he has omitted altogether the testimony of Dorothy Umphofr, Stephen Griffiths and Lee Sansum. He also misrepresented Melissa Henning's thorough account of conversations she had with Dodi and Diana.

---

[a] Al Fayed bodyguard.

16 A Greek Odyssey ... Courtesy MI6

On August 15, while Dodi was winging his way to California, Diana was getting ready to leave on the pre-planned Greek cruise with Rosa Monckton.

Diana and Monckton flew from London to Athens on an Al Fayed jet. Monckton was confronted at the inquest over whether she was comfortable with accepting Mohamed's largesse. She replied: "It did [trouble me] and I discussed it with my husband.[a] .... You can say to your friends what you believe ... but there comes a point when, if they don't accept it, you don't want to put your friendship on the line."[417]

Monckton provided the inquest with some details about the holiday:

- "we organised it on the telephone" around 30 June 1997 [418b]
- it was a "sailing holiday"[419]
- the "boat ... had been lent to [Monckton] by friends"[420]
- they were in "a very small 20-metre motorboat"[421]
- there were "three crew"[422]
- "it was just the two of us"[423].[c]

Monckton confirmed to Ian Burnett – who was basing questions on Monckton's police statement[d] – that the "boat that had been lent to her by friends".

No one asked who the "friends" were. It is interesting that the term "The Friends" is used to mean MI6, in certain circles.[a]

---

[a] Dominic Lawson, an MI6 agent – see Chapter 1.
[b] Monckton confirmed to Burnett that she "had a telephone conversation with [Diana] to arrange the holiday": 13 Dec 07: 144.7
[c] Monckton failed to provide a name for this boat – normally when people holiday on a boat, they identify it by its name. Later evidence will reveal it was named *Della Grazia*.
[d] A document we – and the jury – have never had access to.

Paul Burrell states in his book that the vessel was "hired".[424b] (WFJ) This could fit with the boat being supplied by MI6.[c] If Monckton had told Diana that it came from "friends", she may have been expected to identify them. So it is logical that she could have told Diana the boat was hired – that would not be so likely to attract questions.[d]

That then is a conflict of evidence: Monckton confirmed at the inquest – the "boat that had been lent to [her] by friends"; Burrell, whose information probably came from Monckton via Diana – "[Diana's] friend Rosa Monckton had hired a yacht with a crew of four".[425] (WFJ)

If someone wanted complete surveillance and monitoring of an entire holiday, there is actually no better way to do it than confine that holiday to a limited space – a 20 metre boat is ideal.

Where a holiday is say at a resort, only part of the time is in the room. But on a small boat, possibly the entire holiday is confined to the space of the boat. This allows bugs to be planted[e] all over the vessel[f] and it also enables MI6 to possibly plant their own agents on board – the three crew members.

---

[a] Intelligence historian, Nigel West, wrote in his 1990 book *The Friends*: "In more recent years initiated outsiders, mostly Foreign Office regulars and business contacts, have referred to the [MI6] organisation simply as 'the Friends'." *The Friends*, p1.

[b] Dominic Lawson wrote in a 2006 article: "the boat Rosa had chosen was tiny". That indicates that there was more than one boat to choose from. It raises the question: If Rosa was lent the boat "by friends" then why would she choose a "tiny" boat if a larger one was being offered? There is no suggestion in Rosa's evidence of a choice of boat being on offer. Source: Dominic Lawson, A Crucial Personal Detail ... and the Truth About Diana's Death, Daily Mail, 4 June 2006

[c] This point needs to be viewed in the context of other evidence covered in this chapter.

[d] Later evidence will indicate that the boat was chartered.

[e] Timothy Maier has written that "intelligence sources" say the 1993 APEC (Asia-Pacific Economic Cooperation) meeting in Seattle was extensively bugged by the US. "The operation was huge – more than 300 locations were bugged, including a chartered boat [Bill] Clinton and other national leaders used to visit Blake Island....": Timothy Maier, The Bugging of the APEC in Seattle, *Insight Magazine*, 29 September 1997.

[f] Mansfield asked a question about conversations Monckton may have had with Diana during the holiday regarding landmines: "So even when she does talk to you about that sort of thing [landmines], she certainly does not go into that kind of detail, does she?" Monckton replied: "It would depend upon the subject, it would depend on what else we were doing, it would depend where we were on the boat. You know, we were on holiday.": 13 Dec 07: 181.1. Monckton connects conversations on landmines to "where we were on the boat".

Media Conflict

A study of the contemporaneous media accounts of this holiday raises some serious issues.

There is a considerable amount of conflict in the reporting of what occurred on this Greek cruise:[a]

-   Rosa Monckton, at the inquest:

it was a "sailing holiday" for "just the two of us" on a "a very small 20-metre motorboat" with "three crew" – the "boat … had been lent to [Monckton] by friends"

-   Nick Buckley, Mail on Sunday:

a trip hosted by the Lemos family[b] on a Lemos yacht – the *Sunrise* – including a journey to Inousses[c], where they "were staying on the remote island" [426] (WFJ)

-   Lawrence Van Gelder, The New York Times:

a sailing trip visiting islands in the Aegean – but not including Inousses[d427] (WFJ)

-   Richard Kay and Ian Cobain, Daily Mail:

"four days" where they "drifted unseen around the Greek islands" with an "armada" of boats – "the *Della Grazia*, the *Sea Sedan* … and the *Malrala*" [428] (WFJ)

-   The News Letter:

"a quiet cruise around islands near Athens" on "the charter yacht *Della Grazia*"[429] (WFJ)

-   Stephen White, The Mirror:

"the two women boarded a motor-cruiser, the *Della Grazzia* … [and Diana] relaxed for five days" [430] (WFJ)

-   Daily Record:

they "drifted round the Greek islands … using yachts lent by friends" – "a yacht called *Sunrise*, the ocean-going cruiser *Sea Sedan* and a smaller boat, the *Malrala* … [and] the *Della Grazie*"[431].(WFJ)

The *Della Grazia* is a boat listed as available for charter on several websites – it was built in 1987, is 22 metres and comes with three crew.[432] (WFJ)

---

[a] A fuller record of the content of the articles referred to appears in Part 5, Greek Island Holiday section of the Rosa Monckton chapter.
[b] A family of Greek shipping magnates.
[c] Island which is home to the Lemos family.
[d] Inousses is across the other side of the Aegean from Athens, where Diana and Rosa apparently landed.

The other named boats are all described in promotional material as super-yachts and the three vessels are[a], or have been, available for charter.

The *Malrala* appears to be the *Marala* – it was originally launched in 1931 and is 59 metres with 18 crew. The *Sunrise* was launched in 1991 and is 90 metres with 70 crew, and the *Sea Sedan,* which was built in 1997, is 55 metres with 14 crew.[433] (WFJ)

The *Della Grazia* is the only named boat that comes close to matching the description put forward by Rosa Monckton at the inquest – 20 metres with three crew.

In summary, there are three conflicting accounts:

1)   a single small boat in which Monckton and Diana cruise for the five days – Monckton, White, *The News Letter* [b]

2)   a five day cruise involving several boats – one is small, but the others are super-yachts – Kay and Cobain, *Daily Record*

3)   a lengthy boat journey[c] to a fixed island locale where Diana and Monckton stay – Buckley.

There are three other points to consider:

-    Buckley's account was published on 17 August 1997, the third day of the holiday, and van Gelder's is on the day before it finished – the other accounts were written around the conclusion of the cruise, except for the *Daily Record*, which was published the following year

-    Van Gelder's account conflicts directly with Buckley's – Buckley states they went straight to Inousses, whereas van Gelder says that they hadn't been there by the 19th and instead lists other locations visited[d]

-    Richard Kay was a personal friend of Diana's and may have been provided personal knowledge of the holiday from her.

Bearing in mind that Rosa Monckton, the only living direct witness[e], has lied in other evidence and there is also a considerable amount of conflict in the various media accounts, it is really very difficult to determine precisely what occurred on this Greek holiday.

---

[a] In 2012.

[b] Van Gelder's account could also be included in this, but he does not have a name or size for the yacht.

[c] Buckley said the journey was from near Athens to Inousses – this is around 330 km.

[d] Van Gelder wrote: They "sailed along the eastern coast of the Peloponnesus, calling at the islands of Spetsai and Kythera. Athens newspapers featured eyewitness reports that placed her on the islands of Mykonos and Andros.": Lawrence Van Gelder, Chronicle, The New York Times, 19 August 1997.

[e] The only witness heard at the inquest – there were other witnesses, such as the *Della Grazia* crew.

MI6 could have been involved in organising this trip and possible misinformation to the media could be an indication of that.[a] What is certain is that there is a considerable amount of conflict in the available accounts.

If MI6 were involved, it is unlikely they would have wanted accurate media involvement. In that regard, only one photo of the entire trip has ever surfaced – reproduced in Part 5[b] – and some sections of the media admitted at the time that they couldn't locate Diana:
- "dozens of reporters have been sweeping the Aegean Sea since Friday, trying to find the princess, who jetted to Greece for a cruise"[434] (WFJ) – Daily Gazette
- "the Princess of Wales eluded dozens of paparazzi for a third day Monday as they scoured the Greek islands for the world's most photographed woman, believed to be vacationing incognito in the Aegean"[435] (WFJ) – The Record
- "the hunt for Diana is on" under the headline: "The Media Swarm Greek Isles, In Search Of Diana"[436] (WFJ) – Philadelphia Inquirer.

So we have: a) sections of the media who had no information and were therefore unable to describe the trip or locate Diana; and b) major conflicts between those media reports that do claim to either describe the trip or locate Diana.

Why is this?

After the Buckley article – which stated Diana was on Inousses as guest of the Lemos family – was published on 17 August 1997, media converged on that remote island which lies over 300 km east of Athens. But they found no sign of Diana and also no sign that she had been there.[cd]

The general evidence – Monckton, White, *The News Letter*, van Gelder, Kay and Cobain, *Daily Record* – is that Diana and Monckton cruised for the

---

[a] Misinformation fits with the MI6 culture – see Chapter 1A in Part 5.

[b] Greek Islands Holiday section of Rosa Monckton chapter.

[c] Van Gelder reported on August 19: "Reporters flocked to the little island of Oinousa, off Chios, in the belief that she might visit her friends in the London family of the shipowner Panayotis Lemos. 'We don't know where Princess Diana is,' Mr. Lemos told Greek television. 'We don't know whether she will come here.'": Lawrence Van Gelder, Chronicle, The New York Times, 19 August 1997

[d] Buckley stated: "Locals on Inousses ... were delighted at their surprise visitor". He continued: "Taxi driver Vassily Chryssopaido said: 'Diana is someone we would not expect to see here normally so it is a real pleasure for us.'" This would then indicate that locals were not trying to hide the presence of Diana, which makes it increasingly strange that other media – including Greek journalists – were apparently not able to confirm that Diana was there, or had been there. Source: Nick Buckley, Diana and, in the Aegean, Diana is Cruising Again, *Mail on Sunday*, 17 August 1997.

full five days, dropping ashore at various islands, but not staying at any particular location as anyone's guest.

The evidence also indicates that the two women were cruising in the small yacht[a] – even the articles (other than Buckley) that mention the presence of super-yachts[b] only claim sightings of Diana on the smaller *Della Grazia*.

The evidence raises questions about the veracity of the Buckley account:

-     no other media – including Greek media – was able to confirm that Diana was at or had visited Inousses

-     Buckley claimed to be on the island[c] at the same time as Diana, yet he does not have any supporting photos – the only published photo from the entire trip was taken on Hydra[d]

-     the Buckley account places Diana about 330 km from Athens, whereas the general evidence from the time indicates this was a relaxing cruise spent around islands closer to the Greek mainland – van Gelder: Spetsai, Kythera, Mykonos, Andros; Kay-Cobain: Hydra; White: Mikynos, Naxos, Hydra; *The News Letter*: "islands near Athens", Saronic Gulf[e]

Richard Kay, who writes for the *Daily Mail* – a paper connected to the *Mail on Sunday* that Buckley wrote for – completely ignores the information in the Buckley article, even though it was written just three days earlier.[f]

The following includes some speculation, but is based on the limited available evidence.

Although Buckley states he was on Inousses, his account does not appear to reflect that. There is a possibility that MI6 may have supplied Buckley with false information.

The effect of the Buckley article is that it removes the possibility of MI6 involvement in the Greek island cruise. In fact the trip is no longer a cruise on a small boat – it is a 330 km trip on a super-yacht to a remote island where

---

[a] Not a super-yacht.

[b] Kay and Cobain, *Daily Record*.

[c] He signed off: "From Nick Buckley on Inousses".: Nick Buckley, Diana and, in the Aegean, Diana is Cruising Again, *Mail on Sunday*, 17 August 1997.

[d] It is referred to in the Kay-Cobain article and is reproduced in Part 5, Figure 6.

[e] *The Daily Record* – the account written the following year – is the only report outside of Buckley's that mentions Inousses: "The two women made a trip from Inousses to Spetses ... and on to Hydra". Looking at this on the map, the "trip from Inousses to Spetses" is about 370 km. The article makes no mention of how they got to Inousses, which is about 330 km from Athens. There is a possibility that the reference to Inousses in this 1998 article is based on the Buckley account. Source: Diana: The Last Days; Part 8: Princess In Disguise, Daily Record, 24 August 1998.

[f] Kay also doesn't mention the *Sunrise*, which is the only vessel referred to in the Buckley article. The only other report that includes the *Sunrise* is the 1998 *Daily Record* account, which appears to have based some information on the Buckley article – see above.

Diana and Monckton stay with friends. The event is organised and financed by Greek participants – the Lemos family and the Onassis Foundation[a].

This changes the whole nature of the holiday and removes the possibility of MI6 control – a small boat bugged to record conversations throughout the five days of the cruise.[b]

Richard Kay and the *Daily Record* reported that the *Della Grazia* was accompanied by super-yachts. MI6 could have chartered these boats as security or decoys to mislead the media. The newspaper reports indicate journalists were searching the Aegean and it is likely they were looking for a super-yacht. The presence of three super-yachts in the area could certainly have distracted the media from checking out the much smaller *Della Grazia*.

Buckley's account is the only one from the time that suggests a boat provided by friends[c] – the Lemos family – but it is not primarily for a cruise, instead a journey across the Aegean to Inousses.

The *News Letter* – who apparently interviewed the crew – described the *Della Grazia* as a "charter yacht".[437] (WFJ)

The other 1997 articles give no indication of any involvement from friends.

In summary, the evidence points to a five day relaxing cruise, with stop-offs at various islands, using the chartered boat, *Della Grazia*, but with three super-yachts – acting as decoy vessels – in the vicinity.

This gave Monckton five days of peace and quiet alone with the princess – time for Diana to relax, unwind and confide plans and intentions; time for Monckton to acquire intelligence that was relevant to the spy-masters.

Rosa Monckton's inquest evidence comes across as deliberately non-specific – no mention of the name of the boat and no mention of the names of the friends she borrowed the boat from.

---

[a] The Onassis Foundation was set up in 1975 following the death of its founder Aristotle Onassis. According to its website, "culture, education, the environment, health, and social solidarity come first on [its] agenda". It states: "All projects ... relate to Greece or Greek culture and civilisation.... According to both the Foundation's regulations and the wishes of Aristotle Onassis, individual charity is not allowed.": Onassis Foundation website – www.onassis.gr/en/ It is debatable whether organising "a convoy of limousines ... [to deliver] Diana to a waiting Lemos family yacht" – as described by Buckley – would be an activity entered into by the Onassis Foundation. Article source: Nick Buckley, Diana and, in the Aegean, Diana is Cruising Again, Mail on Sunday, 17 August 1997.

[b] See earlier.

[c] The *Daily Record* account – published In 1998 – says "using yachts lent by friends" – but as indicated in an earlier footnote, that article appears to have been influenced by Buckley's.

Rosa Monckton's Role

There is a major conflict in Monckton's evidence – she claimed that there was radio silence and there had been no contact between her and Diana from June 1 to at least July 12, 1997. Yet ten minutes later Monckton says she organised the Greek Island holiday by phone with Diana around June 30.

Monckton may have fabricated the radio silence evidence to protect her role as an MI6 agent.[a]

Monckton was asked by Burnett: "In that [June 30] conversation [Diana] did not tell you that she was in fact going to St Tropez in the interval?[b]" Monckton replied: "No, she did not."

This is likely to be true – why would Diana tell Monckton about the Mohamed holiday if she knew she would not approve?

But I suggest that by June 30 Monckton already knew about the St Tropez holiday – not from Diana, but from British intelligence[c] who had asked her to organise the boat holiday.

The key effect of the radio silence account is that it distances Monckton from prior knowledge that the St Tropez holiday was going ahead – if she wasn't communicating with Diana, how could she know about it? – and therefore also distances her from having an ulterior motive in organising the Greek Island holiday.

If Monckton didn't know Diana was going on the Mohamed holiday, then how could she be accused of organising the boat holiday to try and learn more about or counter Diana's involvement with the Al Fayeds?

In turn, the radio silence protects Monckton's role in working for MI6 in her dealings with Diana – yet the evidence indicates that Monckton did perform such a role.

Rosa Monckton was faced with a quandary when she came to give her Paget and inquest evidence:

-       Monckton needed to be shown to have organised the Greek Island holiday prior to her knowledge of Diana going on the Mohamed holiday – otherwise her organising of the holiday could be seen as trying to counter the Al Fayed relationship with Diana

-       Monckton had to position herself as a close friend of Diana right up to the crash, yet come up with a reason why she was unaware that Diana had decided to go on holiday with Mohamed.

I suggest that this is the reason Monckton has fabricated both the June 1 approach by Diana asking for advice on the St Tropez holiday and the ensuing radio silence.[a]

---

[a] Lawson provided support for it, but he also is an MI6 agent – see earlier Watershed chapter.

[b] The interval between June 30 and the August 15 boat holiday.

[c] Or someone else in the Establishment.

This also explains why Monckton came up with the major conflict of evidence about her June-July contact with Diana within 10 minutes at the inquest – one minute she hasn't spoken with Diana between June 1 and at least July 12, 10 minutes later she is organising a boat trip with Diana on June 30.

In doing this Monckton avoided providing evidence on precisely how the radio silence finished. She did though support her 1997 radio silence allegation with a detailed account of an earlier instance at the time of Charles and Diana's 1992 trip to Korea. Monckton provided information about how it started – "I said, 'You have just got to pull yourself together and get on with it'"[438] – and finished – "[Diana] would pick up the telephone and say 'Come and have lunch' and off we went again".[439]

The question is: Why does Monckton provide clear evidence of how the Korea radio silence finished – when that has nothing to do with the case – and is unable to do so for the 1997 instance, which is relevant to the case?

Monckton brings up the Korea incident as support for her radio silence evidence, yet is not able to provide proper unconflicting evidence on the detail of the radio silence that she claims occurred in the months leading up to the crash.

---

[a] As noted earlier, there was no evidence of a radio silence from Lucia, who was consulted by Diana regarding the St Tropez holiday.

17   MI6 Takes Charge

On the fourth day of the Diana-Monckton cruise, Paris Ritz Hotel president, Frank Klein, received a critical phone call from Dodi Fayed.

It was 18th August 1997 – just 13 days before Diana and Dodi died.

Prior Knowledge

Klein later told the police:

> **I was on holiday in Antibes when on 18 August 1997 I received a telephone call from Dodi Al Fayed telling me that he intended to come to Paris at the end of the month.... I knew he was with the Princess, although he didn't mention her by name for security reasons.** [440] **(WFJ)**

He added: "I telephoned [Claude] Roulet and told him of my conversation with Dodi.... Mohamed Al Fayed ... called me to confirm the visit, around 18th or 19th August 1997...." [441] (WFJ)

Later evidence will reveal that Claude Roulet – who was Klein's deputy – had contacts with intelligence agencies and was working for them on the weekend of the crash.

Earlier it was shown that Princess Diana's phone calls were being monitored. It is logical to expect that once Dodi Fayed became her boyfriend, his calls would be subject to surveillance.

Claude Roulet also would have been passing on information to his intelligence handler.

So whichever way – whether by surveillance or through Roulet – the intelligence agencies[a] became aware around August 18 that Princess Diana would be travelling to Paris at the end of August.

---

[a] It will be shown later that MI6 was working together with French agencies on this case.

Method Employed

Earlier evidence indicated that MI6 could have received an order to eliminate Diana around the time of the special Way Ahead Group meeting on 23 July 1997.

The choice of the method to carry out this assassination would have been one of the earliest decisions made.

Former MI6 officer, Richard Tomlinson, told the inquest:

> **Making an operation deniable was always a consideration so that, if things went wrong, you could plausibly demonstrate that the British Government had nothing to do with it.[442]**

This certainly was relevant to this case. The assassination of Princess Diana had to be extremely deniable – it was not acceptable to kill Diana and have it credibly linked to British intelligence. It had to be made to look like an accident.

The most deniable form of death is by car accident. Every day about 3,300 people die in road traffic accidents worldwide. If Diana could be seen by the world to die in a car accident then that was the most deniable procedure that MI6 could achieve.

It is no coincidence that the method chosen was the same as Diana had been told by a source or sources, when she penned her note and spoke to her lawyer just under two years earlier. It is possible a decision about how Diana would die had been made back then, but what wasn't known was when and where – that would be determined by events.

Operational Planning

The August 18 Dodi-Klein phone call opened up the opportunity for MI6.

There were key factors that came together and made the operation to assassinate Diana achievable.

First, Frank Klein was on holiday in Antibes and would not be returning until the following month.[a] This meant that Claude Roulet – who was an intelligence agent[b] – would be running the Ritz Hotel over the critical operation period, from August 18 until the end of the month.

Second, MI6 already had experience of Diana and Dodi in Paris as they had been there for a weekend during July 26 to 27. So they had a fair idea what to expect.

---

[a] Klein was still in Antibes at the time of the crash and returned to Paris that day: 29 Nov 07: 59.23.

[b] This is shown later.

On that July visit, which was very early in the relationship, Diana had visited Dodi's apartment but stayed at the Ritz – while Dodi, according to his butler Rene Delorm, had slept at his apartment.[443] (WFJ)

It was reasonable to predict there would be trips between the Ritz Hotel, an Al Fayed asset, and Dodi's apartment – just as there had been in July.

It was logical – if a car crash was to be orchestrated – that it would take place somewhere along, or close to, that route.

Details of the actual operation that was formulated will become clearer as this story unfolds.

Sherard Cowper-Coles

Key to the operation was the choice of who would run events on the ground in Paris.

MI6 officers in each country are generally based at the embassy – and it was confirmed by the British ambassador to France, Michael Jay, that that was the case in Paris in 1997.[444a]

Each year the FCO publishes a Diplomatic List that provides information about British personnel serving in the embassies worldwide – included is a list of employees within each embassy.[b] Jay also confirmed that the MI6 personnel are included in the official Paris embassy list for 1997.[445c]

The general evidence indicates that MI6 officers in embassies worldwide are listed in two main departments, Political and Economic.[da]

---

[a] Also confirmed by MI6 Director of Operations, Richard Dearlove – 20 Feb 08: 35.20.

[b] The National Archives states: "The Diplomatic Service List published annually since 1852, ceased publication in 2006.": http://yourarchives.nationalarchives.gov.uk Search: "Diplomatic Service List".

[c] Diplomatic lists are published in January but are "based on information available in [the previous] September ... but [include] details of some later changes". For example, the 1997 List was published in January 1997, but was primarily based on information from September 1996. Source: 1997 Diplomatic Service List, Preface. This leads to confusion. To avoid this confusion, from this point on, in the text and the related footnotes the diplomatic lists are referred to by the year in which their information relates (unless otherwise specified) – so the 1998 List (FCO title) is referred to as the 1997 List in the text because the information in it is as at September 1997. In the Bibliography and footnote and endnote sources provided (and also in the inquest transcripts), the List will be described based on the FCO title. So in the note sources and transcripts, the List that is referred to in the text as 1997 is shown as 1998.

[d] Part 5 analyses the MI6 Paris personnel and their departments more thoroughly than can be covered in this book: see the Movements of MI6 Officers section in the MI6 in Paris chapter.

Referring to events at the embassy in the 24 hours following the crash (August 31), Michael Jay told the British police:

> At about 0900 [9 a.m.] in the morning of 31/08/1997, [I held] a meeting with the people available at the Embassy in order to allocate responsibilities.... The meeting was ... joined by Mr Sherard Cowper-Coles, Political Counsellor at the Embassy.... Mr Cowper-Coles had arrived at about noon on 31/08/1997, to take up his new appointment as Political Counsellor.[446] (WFJ)

Is this true – that Cowper-Coles arrived to take up his new post less than 12 hours after the crash? [b]

Sherard Cowper-Coles was the most senior infusion into the political and economic departments of the Paris embassy in 1997. He came in as the political counsellor, which means that he immediately became the head of that department.

On the surface, he did not directly appear to replace anyone – the official September 1996 list shows no person as the political counsellor.[447] (WFJ)

There is however evidence indicating Eugene Curley – First Secretary Political in September 1996[448] (WFJ) – became political counsellor at some point between January and 31 August 1997.

The Mystery of Eugene Curley

Curley's biography in the September 1996 List reads: "First Secretary Paris since March 1993".[449] (WFJ) In the following year, 1997, he has been removed from the official embassy list and his biography has been changed to "First Secretary later Counsellor Paris since March 1993".[450] (WFJ)

There are two aspects missing in the biography entries: a) there is no department shown[c] in either 1996 or 1997; and, b) the 1997 entry gives no month or year for the promotion from first secretary to counsellor.

Given that Curley appears as "First Secretary Political" in the 1996 embassy list, it is logical that his promotion to counsellor would have been in the same department and indeed it is the political department where the counsellor vacancy exists on the 1996 List.

---

[a] The Paris embassy details in the Diplomatic Lists show different fax numbers for each department, but the political and economic departments are reached on the same fax number: 44513485.

[b] The only evidence at the inquest regarding this came from Jay, as no one else present in that meeting – including Cowper-Coles himself – has ever been asked about this by any of the investigations.

[c] Departments are normally shown in the List biography entries.

If Curley was promoted to political counsellor – the head of department – sometime between January and August 1997, then, based on other evidence[a], that could have made Curley the head of MI6 France.

At the inquest, Mr 4[b] claimed that he was head of MI6 in France at the time of the crash – Burnett asked: "Were you in charge of any and all SIS staff in Paris [in August 1997]?" 4 replied: "Yes, and indeed in France."[451]

Mr 4 also described himself as "a member of the senior staff in the Embassy".[452]

During his description of the circumstances in which he learned about the crash, he mentions in passing that he was "in bed with our baby daughter".[453]

There are three key facts known about Mr 4 in August 1997: a) he was head of "all SIS staff in Paris" and France; b) he was a senior Paris embassy staff member; and, c) he and his wife had a "baby daughter".

The general evidence indicates that the head of MI6 in France would also be the head of the political department.[c]

Eugene Curley was promoted at some point in 1997 to become the head of the political department. The biography sections of both the 1996 and 1997 Lists reveal that Curley also was father to a daughter born in 1996.[454d] (WFJ) She appears to be the "baby daughter" described by Mr 4.

The inquest's Mr 4 is Eugene Curley.

By September 1997 Cowper-Coles is showing in the official Diplomatic List as the political counsellor of the British Embassy in Paris and Curley no longer appears at all on the Paris list.[455] (WFJ)

Sherard Cowper-Coles also appears on the MI6 list posted on the internet.[ef]

---

[a] Covered in Part 5 – see the section on Richard Spearman and Nicholas Langman in the MI6 in Paris chapter, particularly relating to Richard Tomlinson's evidence.
[b] Most of the MI6 officers were anonymous – they were designated numbers or letters. Numbers were used for Paris-based officers and letters for all the others.
[c] Covered in Part 5 – see the section on Richard Spearman and Nicholas Langman in the MI6 in Paris chapter, particularly relating to Richard Tomlinson's evidence.
[d] Later evidence will show that Cowper-Coles may have actually been the head of MI6 in Paris at the time of the crash – contradicting the evidence of Mr 4. The List biography reveals that in 1997 Cowper-Coles did have a daughter, but she was born in 1986 and would have been 10 or 11 at the time of the crash – i.e. not a baby. This rules Cowper-Coles out from being Mr 4.
[e] The internet list – which appeared in 1999 – is fully addressed in Part 5, section on MI6 Internet List in the MI6 in Paris chapter.
[f] UK journalist, Robert Fisk, wrote in *The Independent* in 2007: "I remember way back in the late 1970s – when I was Middle East correspondent for *The Times* – how a British diplomat in Cairo tried to persuade me to fire my local 'stringer', an Egyptian Coptic woman who also worked as a correspondent for the Associated Press and who provided a competent coverage of the country when I was in Beirut. 'She isn't much good,' he said, and suggested I hire a young Englishwoman whom he

In summary, the points that reveal Mr 4 is Eugene Curley are:
-       other evidence covered in Part 5[a] indicates that the political counsellor in the Paris embassy would also be the head of MI6 in France
-       only Curley and Cowper-Coles were political counsellors – at different times[b] – throughout 1997
-       Curley had a daughter born in 1996 – she would have been the "baby daughter" described by Mr 4. Cowper-Coles had an 11 year old daughter
-       the inquest evidence, and therefore the official MI6 account, is that Mr 4 was the head of MI6 France at the time of the crash and that Cowper-Coles didn't take up duties as political counsellor until lunchtime on 31 August 1997, after the crash. The 1997 Diplomatic List reveals that Curley was promoted to counsellor – which must have been political – prior to September 1997
-       Mr 4 stated that he left the Paris embassy in early 1998.[c] Curley appears to have left sometime before September 1997 as he is not in the September 1997 List. Cowper-Coles stayed in Paris until 1999. Mr 4 appears to have lied about the timing of his departure from Paris – this issue is addressed below.

At some point in 1997 Sherard Cowper-Coles replaced Eugene Curley as the head of the political department and head of MI6 in France.

The question is: When did this occur? Was it before or after the Paris crash?

Mr 4 – Eugene Curley – gave sworn evidence at the inquest that he was still in Paris in early 1998[d], but that does not appear to be true as he was removed from the official Paris diplomatic list published in January 1998, based on information from September 1997.

---

knew and who – so I later heard – had close contacts in the Foreign Office. I refused this spooky proposal. Indeed, I told *The Times* that I thought it was outrageous that a British diplomat should have tried to engineer the sacking of our part-timer in Cairo. *The Times's* foreign editor agreed. But it just shows what diplomats can get up to. And the name of that young British diplomat in Cairo back in the late 1970s? Why, Sherard Cowper-Coles, of course." Robert Fisk, 'Abu Henry' and the Mysterious Silence, *The Independent*, 30 June 2007.

[a] Section on Richard Spearman and Nicholas Langman in the MI6 in Paris chapter, particularly relating to Richard Tomlinson's evidence.
[b] Given that the counsellor is the head of the department, it is logical that there would be only one counsellor in a department at any one time. The official diplomatic lists support this – there is only one counsellor listed for each department in the embassy.
[c] This will be shown to be false.
[d] Mansfield asked: "Between September 1997 and possibly early 1998, were you still there?" Apparently without hesitation Curley replied, "I was": 29 Feb 08: 50.8. Curley did confirm that he had left Paris by December 1998: 29 Feb 08: 45.3.

The List published in January 1998 states in its Preface: "The List ... is based on information available in September 1997 but includes details of some later changes." [456] (WFJ)

This then indicates that Eugene Curley may have been gone from Paris by September 1997 – not during 1998 as he stated at the inquest.[a]

This is supported by Michael Jay's account that Cowper-Coles started in Paris on 31 August 1997 – it is unlikely that two political counsellors would be working at the embassy at the same time, certainly not for any lengthy period.

Why would Curley lie at the inquest about the timing of his departure?

It is not in MI6's interests to be seen bringing in a more senior section head – Sherard Cowper-Coles – just ahead of the assassination of Princess Diana.

It is a much cleaner look to have the person who has been in Paris since 1993[b] – Eugene Curley – still there at the time of the crash and then replaced by Cowper-Coles at some point after the crash.

People could start asking questions if they learned that the head of MI6 in France had changed just before the tragic crash, particularly when it is already known – see later – that Richard Spearman[c] had also arrived only five days ahead of the deaths.

Ambassador Michael Jay stated that the transition to Cowper-Coles occurred about 12 hours after the crash, on 31 August 1997, when he rushed to Paris.[d]

But is that actually how it occurred? This requires investigation.

Conflicts and Questions

Cowper-Coles was not heard from at the inquest – he was not cross-examined and there was no statement read out. This is incredible when one considers the admitted importance of Cowper-Coles' position – "head of the political section at the Embassy"[e] – and the claimed timing of his arrival – "lunchtime on 31st August" 1997.[f]

The fact that the 1997 Diplomatic List is based primarily on information from September 1997 indicates not only that Curley was gone by September,

---

[a] See above and previous footnote.

[b] The biography section of the List states that Curley had been in Paris since March 1993: Diplomatic List 1998, p167.

[c] A senior MI6 officer.

[d] Jay: "[Cowper-Coles] was in language training, I think, in the South of France, and when he heard the news, he got into his car and drove straight up.": 11 Feb 08: 93.11.

[e] Confirmed by Jay to Burnett: 11 Feb 08: 93.4.

[f] Confirmed by Jay to Burnett: 11 Feb 08: 93.8.

but also that Cowper-Coles was installed as political counsellor by September 1997.

This is logical – why would they need two heads of that MI6 section operating from inside the same embassy?

Did the transition from Curley to Cowper-Coles take place before September 1997 – i.e. before the 31 August 1997 crash?

There is no evidence from Cowper-Coles, but Curley was cross-examined, under the name Mr 4.

Curley's evidence raises several points to note:[a]

-    Curley falsely confirmed to Mansfield that he was working in the Paris embassy "between September 1997 and possibly early 1998"

-    Curley was asked: "What did you do immediately" after hearing "the news that Diana had died". Instead of directly answering, Curley replies: "Well, I suppose, like everybody else, switched on the television".[457]

-    Curley then says he called the embassy: "I cannot remember who specifically I rang up"[458]

-    Curley was speaking so softly that there were concerns his evidence couldn't be properly heard – the Coroner told him: "I think that you are dropping your voice".[459]

-    Curley appears to be uncomfortable – he doesn't apologise for speaking too softly and in fact makes no comment on it at all.

Michael Jay said in his Paget statement:

> **At about 0900 in the morning of 31/08/1997 ... [I called] a meeting with the people available at the Embassy in order to allocate responsibilities.... The meeting was ... joined by Mr Sherard Cowper-Coles, Political Counsellor at the Embassy, and I tasked him with acting as my assistant in dealing with French officials and also with those in the UK. Mr Cowper-Coles had arrived at about noon on 31/08/1997, to take up his new appointment as Political Counsellor.[460] (WFJ)**

Then at the inquest Jay elaborated on this: "[Cowper-Coles] was in language training, I think, in the South of France[b], and when he heard the news, he got into his car and drove straight up."[461]

So according to Jay, Cowper-Coles is in the South of France – that is about 700 km[c] from Paris. He hears the news of the crash, jumps in his car

---

[a] These points relate directly to his inquest evidence – they need to be seen in the light of the general context of this discussion. The picture of what has occurred will become clearer as this book develops.

[b] In a 2011 interview Cowper-Coles said he did his language training in Lille – this is addressed later in this section.

[c] This is addressed in detail below.

and heads for Paris, arriving at the embassy "at about noon" – in time to join a meeting Jay had commenced at about 9 a.m.

Eugene Curley's reaction to the news was completely different.

Curley says:

> **I was still in bed ... and I remember my wife ... telling me that it was on the news that Diana had died ... [at] about 9 o'clock.... I ... switched on the television and watched that as the events unfolded and then I rang up the Embassy. I cannot remember who specifically I rang up ... to see if I was required back, as a member of the senior staff.... I was told that there was no need for me to rush back, obviously it had nothing to do with SIS, but that the Ambassador would be holding a meeting of senior staff the following day.... There was a series of meetings [on 1 September 1997] and I went to at least one of them ... as a member of the senior management team in the Embassy.[462]**

If both Curley and Jay are telling the truth, then on 31 August 1997 the British Embassy in Paris had two heads of the political department – Eugene Curley and Sherard Cowper-Coles.

The first, Eugene Curley, had been working in the political department of the Paris embassy for 4½ years, since March 1993, part of the time as counsellor[463] (WFJ) – so he presumably would have had extensive recent experience in dealing with French authorities. With that background it would also be logical to presume that Curley spoke fluent French.

The second, Sherard Cowper-Coles, had no experience at all of working or living in Paris[a] and according to Jay appears to have cut short his French language training to rush up to Paris – "he was in language training ... he got into his car and drove straight up". Then when he arrives Jay "tasked him with acting as my assistant in dealing with French officials".

Why would Jay task a person – Cowper-Coles – who had no Paris experience with "dealing with French officials", when he had a person in the same role[b] – Curley – who was closer to Paris[c] and had 4½ years' experience working in Paris?

Bearing in mind that we are looking at the handling of possibly the most significant event in Jay's five year[d] tenure as British ambassador to France.

---

[a] Cowper-Coles' 1997 Diplomatic List biography reads: "Counsellor FCO [London] since May 1993; born 8.1.55; [started] FCO 1977; Language student MECAS [Middle-East Centre for Arab Studies] 1978; Third later Second Secretary Cairo 1980; First Secretary FCO [London] 1983; Private Secretary to the Permanent Under-Secretary 1985; First Secretary (Chancery) Washington 1987; First Secretary FCO [London] 1991; on secondment to the International Institute of Strategic Studies 1993.": Diplomatic Service List 1998, p164.

[b] Head of the political department.

[c] See below.

[d] 1996 to 2001.

Is Jay lying? Is Curley lying? Or are they both lying?

Jay said that Cowper-Coles was "in language training, I think, in the South of France". The South of France is a fairly large area – it covers four administrative regions.[a] According to LanguageCourse.net, in the south of France there is a French language school in Bordeaux, another in Toulouse, one also in Marseille, and three each in Montpellier and Nice. These schools were all operating in 1997.

All of these cities are at least 6½ hours by car from Paris – Bordeaux is approximately 6½ hours, Toulouse around 7½ hours, Marseille and Montpellier are both about 8¼ hours and Nice is close to 10 hours.[bc]

We are told by Jay that Cowper-Coles "heard the news ... got into his car and drove straight up" and he "arrived at about noon on 31/08/1997".

Princess Diana officially died at close to 4 a.m.

Given that six out of the eight language schools are in Marseille, Nice or Montpellier it seems likely that when Cowper-Coles left he was embarking on a driving journey of at least eight hours. According to his List biography, in 1997 Cowper-Coles had five children[d], the eldest was 15 and the youngest just 7 years old. I suggest this would make it unlikely for Cowper-Coles to have been accompanied by his wife. This, travelling solo, suggests that Cowper-Coles could have needed to have breaks on a long drive of this nature.

Even if Cowper-Coles had been notified of Diana's death soon after 4 a.m. one would have to add around 1½ hours for trip preparation and breaks. Added to the 8 hours, that makes at least 9½ hours for the trip. This means that the earliest Cowper-Coles could have arrived would have been 1.30 p.m. with limited sleep the previous night. Jay indicates that on arrival Cowper-Coles joined the meeting. This would have been at least 4½ hours after the meeting began at 9 a.m. – see earlier.

This evidence indicates that it would only have been possible for Cowper-Coles to have arrived in Paris by noon if he was learning French at the school in Bordeaux. But to do that, Cowper-Coles, who presumably was asleep,

---

[a] Running west to east: Aquitaine, Midi-Pyrenees, Languedoc-Roussillon and Provence-Alpes-Cote d'Azur.: www.south-of-france.com

[b] The distances by road are: Bordeaux – 583km; Toulouse – 678km; Marseille – 776km; Montpellier – 762km; Nice – 932km.

[c] Distances and times are from Himmera.com Map Distances: http://distancecalculator.himmera.com

[d] Four sons and one daughter.

would have needed to have been notified very soon after Diana's 4 a.m. death – within 30 minutes of the announcement.[a]

Meanwhile according to Eugene Curley, he was "in a hotel ... near La Rochelle". He never received any notification of Diana's death, instead learning about it from his wife at about 9 a.m.[b]

The opposite reaction compared to Cowper-Coles. Curley was in no rush – and was not put into a rush by Jay. Curley says that: a) he "switched on the television and watched that as the events unfolded"; b) "then I rang up the Embassy ... to see if I was required back"; c) "I was told that there was no need for me to rush back, obviously it had nothing to do with SIS"; d) he was told "that the Ambassador would be holding a meeting of senior staff the following day"; e) On 1 September 1997 "I went to at least one of [the meetings] ... not so much SIS as me as head of station [but] as a member of the senior management team in the Embassy".[464ca]

---

[a] If Cowper-Coles had been in Bordeaux and had left at 5 a.m. he could have had a half hour break during the 6½ hour drive and arrived in Paris at around 12 noon, as stated by Jay.

[b] I suggest that the head of MI6 in France would be contactable at all times.

[c] This conflicts with the gist of Jay's evidence that MI6 was effectively run as a separate department within the embassy. Jay said this: "Members of the SIS stationed abroad with the post receive their instructions from SIS headquarters in London" (statement reproduced in The Documents book, p636). A fuller account of Jay's statement is also near the start of the "Movements of MI6 Officers" section in Part 5. Curley has painted a picture of a dual role – head of MI6 in France and a member of senior management at the embassy. Jay's evidence indicates that as far as he was concerned those roles were one and the same – Jay just looked on MI6 as a section of the embassy. At the inquest he said: "The [reporting] relationship [of MI6] is exactly the same as with other sections of the Embassy": 11 Feb 08: 133.3; "I had overall responsibility for the conduct of the Embassy as a whole, all the different sections in it, including the MI6 station": 11 Feb 08: 133.13; "That is true for the head of that [MI6] section as for other sections of the Embassy" ; 11 Feb 08: 134.9. Jay's account is common sense – in other words, MI6 officers working inside the embassy had one job – working for MI6 – and even though their official title might be "Counsellor Political", there was no dual role. As Mansfield suggested, "it is built on authorised deceit" (11 Feb 08: 129.13) – the title "political" is a name, but the person's sole job was to work as an MI6 officer. Peter Heap, who retired in 1995 after a long career in the British diplomatic service, including a stint as ambassador to Brazil, spoke out in 2003 about the MI6 role in embassies. Heap stated: "As a diplomat who worked in nine overseas posts over 36 years, I saw quite a lot of MI6 at work. They were represented in almost all of those diplomatic missions. They presented themselves as normal career diplomats, but often, indeed usually, they were a breed apart. And it normally only took the local British community a few weeks to spot them.... In one capital, the MI6 officers rarely wore suits to the office while the rest of us did..... The MI6 station within an embassy operates on a budget that is quite separate from and kept secret from the rest of the diplomatic staff, including the ambassador....

There is a huge difference between the situation and accounts of Cowper-Coles compared to Curley:

- Curley has 4½ years' experience in Paris – Cowper-Coles had none
- Curley would have been a fluent French speaker – Cowper-Coles had just cut short his French language course
- Curley was in La Rochelle, about 5½ hours from Paris[b] – Cowper-Coles was probably at least 8¼ hours[c] away and at closest 6½ hours[d] from Paris
- Curley was already due to return to Paris on the Monday[e] – Cowper-Coles was apparently undergoing French language training; Jay doesn't say when Cowper-Coles was expected to transfer to Paris
- Curley does not receive any notification from the embassy: his first knowledge of Diana's death is from his wife[f] – Cowper-Coles has somehow learned about the death in the middle of the night.[g] It would be most unlikely that Cowper-Coles would drive "straight up" without first having communication with the embassy. It is implied that Cowper-Coles was notified very early by the embassy about the death of Diana
- Curley is told by the embassy after 9 a.m. "that there was no need ... to rush back" – Cowper-Coles appears to have been told close to 4 a.m. that he was needed urgently
- Curley attends an embassy meeting on Monday 1 September 1997 – Cowper-Coles attends a meeting at about noon on Sunday 31 August 1997.

Ambassadors and diplomatic staff saw and commented on their intelligence reports that went to their HQ in London, but could not alter nor stop them, nor know the identity of the sources." Heap's comments indicate that other people in the embassy – not just the ambassador – would know who was in the MI6 section; there was a separate budget for the MI6 section and also reports by MI6 staffers that could not be altered or stopped. Source: Peter Heap, The Truth Behind the MI6 Facade, *The Guardian*, 2 October 2003.

[a] Ms 1 describes attending a meeting on September 1 (29 Feb 08: 38.15)– she was an MI6 member, but not a "Head of Station" – see later. Ambassador Michael Jay made no mention of any meetings on 1 September 1997.

[b] Distance 470km.

[c] Marseille, Montpellier, Nice.

[d] Bordeaux.

[e] Curley said: "I was intending to go back to work some time the following Monday in any case." 29 Feb 08: 43.42.

[f] Curley: "I remember my wife ... telling me that it was on the news that Diana had died": 29 Feb 08: 42.3.

[g] Jay says, "he heard the news", but to make it to the embassy by noon, Cowper-Coles would have had to have been in Bordeaux and heard about the death very soon after it occurred – see above.

At the meeting Cowper-Coles attended, Jay entrusts him "with acting as my assistant in dealing with French officials".

This is despite Curley being an officer who had over four years' experience in dealing with French officials and also was located closer to Paris at the time of Diana's death.

Jay makes no mention of Curley in any of his evidence[a], but does refer to Cowper-Coles several times:

-   his attendance at the August 31 meeting
-   memo from Paul Johnston "dated 12/09/1997 to Mr Cowper-Coles (Head of Political Section at the Embassy)"[465] (WFJ)
-   "Mr Cowper-Coles also asked the Embassy's Drug Liaison Officer, Chief Inspector Nick Gargan to make enquiries of the French Police"[466] (WFJ)
-   "I refer to Chief Inspector Gargan's minute to Mr Cowper-Coles of 15/09/1997"[467]. (WFJ)

Michael Jay, who had access to reports drawn up at the time of the events[468] (WFJ), did state this: "One official who was not at the [31 August 1997] meeting[b] was the Second Secretary (Political), Mr Paul Johnston, who was not in Paris that weekend. On Monday 01/09/1997 I asked him to act as the point of contact with the judicial side of the French inquiry...."[469] (WFJ)

So Jay specifically mentions the absence of Paul Johnston on 31 August 1997 and then his subsequent presence on the following day, when he assigned Johnston with a responsibility.

The question is: Why would Jay mention Johnston but not Curley, when Johnston ranked far lower in the embassy than Curley[c] – and Curley was a head of department?

Johnston and Curley both missed the August 31 meeting, but both turned up on September 1. Curley is the head of the department, Johnston is a second secretary. Johnston is mentioned by Jay, but Curley is ignored.

Why?

Official Lies

There are now several points that indicate Eugene Curley was no longer employed at the Paris embassy at the time of the crash:

-   Curley does not appear on the official list of staff members drawn up from September 1997 information[470] (WFJ)
-   Jay makes no mention of Curley in any of his evidence, but he does mention, a) Cowper-Coles, the officer who replaced Curley, and b) Johnston

---

[a] His diary written at the time, his Paget statement and inquest cross-examination.
[b] Attended by Cowper-Coles.
[c] In the 1996 List Curley was ranked 16 while Johnston was 38: The Diplomatic Service List 1997, p32.

who was much more junior to Curley, but according to Jay, worked in the same political department

-     Curley's evidence regarding his movements around the time of the crash came across as diffident, at best

-     Cowper-Coles shows in the 1997 List as the political counsellor – it is unlikely that there would be two political counsellors at the same time

-     at the time of the crash Curley would have had 4½ years of experience in speaking French and dealing with the French, yet Jay said he asked the inexperienced[a] Cowper-Coles to act "as my assistant in dealing with French officials"

-     both Curley and Cowper-Coles[b] were heads of the political department yet they present opposite responses to the death of Diana

-     Curley describes a meeting on 1 September 1997 that is not mentioned in any non-MI6 evidence, particularly Jay, who provided an in depth account of the events based on written reports made at the time.[c]

Curley has fabricated an account that he was returning from holiday and was at La Rochelle on 31 August 1997 and returned to work at the embassy the following day.

Why would Eugene Curley lie about this?

Michael Jay has stated that Sherard Cowper-Coles arrived at the Paris embassy around noon on 31 August 1997. It is significant that Cowper-Coles himself has never been interviewed and was not heard at the inquest.

There is an obvious link between Curley and Cowper-Coles – Curley was made the political counsellor at some point between September 1996 and August 1997, and Cowper-Coles succeeded Curley in that role.

Curley vacated the Paris embassy at some point before the crash and it is logical that his successor, Cowper-Coles, would have taken up his new posting around the same time.

There are reasons to believe that Michael Jay has lied in his evidence regarding the circumstances of Sherard Cowper-Coles' arrival at the Paris embassy:

1)   The timing of Cowper-Coles' arrival, as stated by Jay, is in itself extremely coincidental at best.

---

[a] In speaking to and dealing with the French.

[b] If both Jay and Curley were speaking the truth – it will be shown later that neither were.

[c] Ms 1 refers to a meeting she attended on September 1 – see later. That meeting is not the "meeting of senior staff" described by Curley, but a staff meeting chaired by Jay to deal with specific details: 29 Feb 08: 38.15.

HOW THEY MURDERED PRINCESS DIANA

The suggestion by Jay is that the embassy's incoming political counsellor – the head of that department and also effectively the head of MI6 in France – took up his duties just 12 hours after the crash.

This account should be viewed in the light of other factors:

a)   that Jay indicated Cowper-Coles "was in language training" – this infers that he cut that training short to rush up to Paris. If it were true, this would mean that Cowper-Coles' appointment was made well before the crash

b)   that Richard Spearman, an MI6 officer who was also a senior employee in the political department[a], arrived in Paris on 26 August 1997, just 5 days before the crash

c)   the significance of the crash – it will be shown to be the orchestrated assassination of Princess Diana and Dodi Fayed[b]

d)   that MI6 are prime suspects for involvement in that assassination.

2)   Jay suggests that Cowper-Coles – a father to five children at the time – made an instant decision to make the approximately 700km trip: "when he heard the news, he got into his car and drove straight up".

a)   Based on the earlier calculations there is a logistical issue. Evidence has shown that distances from Paris to French language schools in the South of France range from 583km to 932km, with the majority being over 750km away.

There was not enough time[c] for Cowper-Coles to have made the trip if he had been located in the places where most of the schools are – Marseille, Montpellier or Nice.

Even if he had been in Bordeaux, where the closest school is, there are certain factors – not indicated by the evidence – that would have had to fall into place:[d]

-    Cowper-Coles would have had to be called in the middle of the night (after 4 a.m.) or otherwise – if he is a light sleeper – have woken up and switched on the news

-    Cowper-Coles would have needed to communicate with the embassy before leaving. It is very unlikely that he would have embarked on such a long drive around 5 a.m. in a foreign country without consulting the destination embassy first.[e]

---

[a] Ranked second in the political department in 1997 – see Table 2 in Embassy Tables section of Part 5.

[b] See also Parts 1 to 6.

[c] Between the death of Diana at 4 a.m. and his alleged arrival at noon.

[d] There are only 8 hours between 4 a.m. and noon and the driving time from Bordeaux to Paris is 6½ hours – see earlier.

[e] There also is a possible argument that the job Jay claims to have given Cowper-Coles after he arrived – "dealing with French officials and also with those in the UK" – doesn't logically justify the "hell for leather" rush trip that Cowper-Coles

3)   Jay's original statement account makes no comment on the circumstances of Cowper-Coles' embassy arrival – "Cowper-Coles had arrived at about noon on 31/08/1997".

I suggest that when it was determined that Jay would be subjected to inquest cross-examination, a decision was made – because of the obvious problem with the timing[a] – that his evidence would have to be fleshed out.

Jay was asked by Burnett: "Am I right in thinking that Mr Cowper-Coles arrived to take up his posting in Paris only at lunchtime on 31st August?" This is such an unusual piece of evidence that it had to be explained. This is when Jay replied with: "Yes. He was in language training, I think, in the South of France, and when he heard the news, he got into his car and drove straight up."[471]

There was no challenge to this and no further questions were asked by any of the lawyers present.

Did Sherard Cowper-Coles arrive before the crash – in a similar way to Richard Spearman – and Jay has come up with, or been told to come up with, evidence indicating he arrived after the crash?

It is logical that Cowper-Coles would have arrived at a time close to the departure of Curley, his predecessor.[b]

At the inquest Michael Jay said: "I would know the senior members of the SIS station".[472] Sherard Cowper-Coles would have been the most senior amongst the MI6 staff at the time of the crash.

In his 2005 statement Jay said: "I am not aware that any ... MI6 officers ... had been deployed in Paris during the weekend of 30/31st August 1997."[473] (WFJ) Later in the same statement Jay says: "At about 0900 in the morning of 31/08/1997 ... [I called] a meeting.... The meeting was ... joined by Mr Sherard Cowper-Coles, Political Counsellor at the Embassy, and I tasked him with acting as my assistant in dealing with French officials and also with those in the UK."

Jay has said "I would know the senior [MI6] members"[c] and he says that he wasn't aware of any MI6 working that weekend, yet he admits meeting with Cowper-Coles on the Sunday and issuing instructions.

---

undertook to get to the embassy. What difference would it have made if Cowper-Coles had not arrived at work until the following day?

[a] That the head of the political department would commence his new position about 12 hours after the crash.

[b] It could be significant that in this evidence alleging Cowper-Coles took over on the day of the crash – 31 August 1997 – there is no mention of any contact between Cowper-Coles and the person he is taking over from, Eugene Curley.

[c] I suggest that is common sense, that the person in charge of the embassy would know who the senior MI6 personnel were.

At some point in this Jay has lied.

There are different possibilities:[a]

a)   Jay doesn't know who the senior MI6 staff are – in this case, the head of MI6 France[b]

b)   Jay is aware that MI6 staff were working that weekend

c)   Jay didn't meet with Cowper-Coles and didn't issue instructions.

Jay specifically stated: "I tasked [Cowper-Coles] with acting as my assistant in dealing with French officials and also with those in the UK".

Yet earlier in the statement he had said: "It was not my role to give the SIS officers stationed at the British Embassy in Paris specific instructions. These instructions they would receive from SIS headquarters in London."[474] (WFJ)

There is no evidence linking Jay to MI6 and it is therefore illogical that he would be giving instructions to an MI6 officer – Cowper-Coles was the head of the political department and also appears on the MI6 internet list.

There is also no evidence of these "instructions" from Jay to Cowper-Coles being carried out.

The documents referred to by Jay in his statement were not reports from Cowper-Coles to Jay, but instead were minutes addressed to Cowper-Coles:

-    "I refer to [Johnston's] minute dated 12/09/1997 to Mr Cowper-Coles"

-    "I refer to Chief Inspector Gargan's minute to Mr Cowper-Coles of 15/09/1997".

Michael Jay made a very specific and thorough declaration:

I am not aware that any MI5 or MI6 officers, in which description I would include both SIS officers and any persons working with them or on their behalf, had been deployed in Paris during the weekend of 30/31st August 1997.[475] (WFJ)

---

[a] The three listed here are not mutually exclusive – more than one could be true.

[b] Richard Tomlinson wrote in his 2001 book: "Andrew Markham ... was selected for the 'Orcada' slot in Bonn. This was a deep-cover job, running MI6's most important agent in Germany, a high-ranking official in the Ministry of Finance. In return for a substantial salary, Orcada provided five-star CX on the German economy and interest rate movements.... The Orcada posting was so sensitive that only the ambassador in Bonn and H/BON were briefed and no one else in the embassy was even aware that Markham was from the 'friends' (FCO-speak for MI6). Markham thus had to learn to become a thoroughly convincing diplomat to fool his FCO colleagues, so he attended the FCO pre-posting training courses in addition to all his MI6 courses.": *The Big Breach*, pp158-9. Markham was given an unusually sensitive posting – "only the ambassador in Bonn and H/BON were briefed". This indicates that most of the time the general embassy staff were aware of who among them was MI6 – except when it was very sensitive – and the ambassador and the local head of MI6 (in this instance, H/BON) would always be made aware.

Mr 4 – Eugene Curley – stated at the inquest: "I am clear that we would have made arrangements for duty personnel, a duty officer and duty support staff" over the weekend.[476a]

Mr 4 indicates here that there would always be MI6 staff on duty, even over a weekend – and that is common sense.

It appears that Jay has again lied – it is not credible that, as ambassador, Jay would have been unaware that there were MI6 staff members on duty on weekends.

The evidence points to both Eugene Curley and Michael Jay lying in their evidence – Curley lied by stating he was still head of MI6 in France at the time of the crash and was still there in early 1998; Jay lied when he stated that Cowper-Coles had arrived in Paris at noon on 31 August 1997, just 12 hours after the crash.

Why did they do this?

What follows includes some speculation based on the known evidence.

There is a possibility that some of the senior MI6 officers in Paris, after they learned that they were needed to play a role in the assassination of Princess Diana, refused to participate.

This could account for late changes of staff in senior positions in the days or weeks leading up to 31 August 1997. It is possible that junior officers – even if they did play a role – may not have fully understood what they were involved in, because MI6 only provide information on a "need to know" basis.[b]

Eugene Curley, who was head of MI6 France, may have refused to be involved in the assassination of the princess.[c]

This could have led to a decision to transfer Sherard Cowper-Coles from London to Paris. According to Cowper-Coles' List biography he had been "Counsellor FCO since May 1993"[477] (WFJ) and the 1996 List reveals that he was the head of the Hong Kong Department in September 1996.[478d] (WFJ)

---

[a] In reply to the question: "Are you able to tell the jury whether there were any other SIS staff in Paris that weekend?"

[b] This is covered in Part 5, MI6 Culture section of Chapter 1A.

[c] The 1999 List biography for Curley indicates that he took up a post in London in February 1998 – it reads: "Counsellor FCO since February 1998". It is not known what Curley did between the time he left Paris and took up the London post – he may have been on leave. The 1997 List – published in January 1998 – reveals that whatever Curley was doing, he was not in Paris, because he is not listed in the Paris embassy staff list for September 1997. Source: Diplomatic Service List 1999, p167. (WFJ)

[d] Cowper-Coles' biography in the List reveals that he had spent a substantial part of his MI6 career in London – from 1977, 1 year; from 1983 to 1987, 4 years; from

There is a difference between prior involvement in the crash and later involvement in the cover-up. It is possible that an MI6 officer could refuse to participate in the orchestration of the crash, but agree to play a part in the subsequent cover-up,[a] as part of an agreement to stay employed in the intelligence agency.

The evidence indicates that Eugene Curley has left Paris ahead of the crash, but has agreed to testify and provide false evidence at the ensuing inquest into the deaths.

The effect of Curley's evidence has been to protect Cowper-Coles:
-    Curley helps distance Cowper-Coles from involvement in the crash.

Curley falsely states that he was head of MI6 France and was in charge – even though he was at La Rochelle – at the time of the crash. There could not be two heads of MI6 France at the same time.
-    Curley helps distance Cowper-Coles from being an MI6 officer.

Curley indicates that he was still in France into early 1998. The inquest also heard that Cowper-Coles arrived by lunchtime on 31 August 1997.[b]

If Curley was head of MI6 France at the time of the crash and into 1998, then Cowper-Coles couldn't have been, even though he was head of the political section. This helps to create a false impression that there may not even be a link between MI6 membership and the embassy's political section. In so doing – and seen in the context of Cowper-Coles being openly named at the inquest (see below) – it also could lead the jury to believe that Cowper-Coles had no association with MI6.

Scott Baker went to great lengths to ensure the names of MI6 officers were not used throughout the inquest proceedings. This would have created a perception amongst the jury members that if a name was used then that person could not have been a member of MI6.[c]

Sherard Cowper-Coles was openly named during Michael Jay's cross-examination. This could have led the jury to falsely conclude that Cowper-Coles was not an MI6 officer. Other evidence – see earlier – shows that he was.

Cowper-Coles was never himself cross-examined and has never been interviewed by any of the police investigations. Had he been cross-examined

---

1991 to 1997, 6 years. Altogether, 11 out of 20 years in London.: Diplomatic Service List 1998, p164.
[a] "It's in the national interest."
[b] If the jury had had any idea that Cowper-Coles was an MI6 officer then this could have raised questions for them – the arrival 12 hours after the crash would have appeared more suspicious. Instead the jury were led away from drawing any links between Cowper-Coles and MI6 – see below.
[c] The names of Richard Spearman and Nicholas Langman were both used, and there was never any official admission at the inquest that they were a part of MI6.

it would have been under one of the MI6 codenames, but none of those people fit with what is known about Cowper-Coles.

In summary, what occurred at the inquest was:

-    Curley[a] gave a false account that he was head of MI6 France until early 1998, when the truth is he left his Paris post prior to the crash

-    Jay gave a false account of Cowper-Coles arriving at the Paris embassy just 12 hours after the crash

-    this false evidence from Curley and Jay protected Cowper-Coles, who took Curley's place as head of MI6 France prior to the crash, and would have been in charge of the Paris MI6 staff orchestrating the crash.

Curley's false account that he was head of MI6 France and was on holiday in La Rochelle at the time of the crash had the effect of completely distancing MI6 from orchestrating the crash.

How could MI6 have been involved if their head in France wasn't anywhere near Paris at the critical time of the crash?

This strategy fits with the general cover-up that has occurred – how could the French have been involved if no authorities there even knew that Diana was in France until after the crash? How could anyone in the British embassy Paris be involved if they too had no awareness that Diana was in France?[b]

How could MI6 have been involved if their head in France was 470km from the Alma Tunnel at 12.23 a.m. on 31 August 1997?

How could Cowper-Coles have been orchestrating a crash in Paris if he didn't even arrive in Paris until 12 hours after that crash had occurred?

Some might say – "the perfect alibi".

But these are all falsehoods.

Curley wasn't the head of MI6 France at the time of the crash. Curley was no longer employed in Paris[c] – Cowper-Coles had taken Curley's place.

Cowper-Coles arrived in Paris well ahead of the crash – not 12 hours after it, as falsely stated by Jay at the inquest.

It was Cowper-Coles who organised the Paris end of the crash orchestration.[d]

---

[a] Under the codename Mr 4.

[b] These French and British claims of ignorance are covered later.

[c] It could be significant that even though Curley is completely missing from the official 1997 Paris list (he has been replaced by Cowper-Coles) – based on September 1997 – his 1997 List biography still reads: "First Secretary later Counsellor Paris since March 1993".

[d] The 1997 List biography reveals that Sherard Cowper-Coles was awarded a CMG – Commander, Order of St Michael and St George – in 1997. It is not known how or exactly when this occurred because Cowper-Coles does not appear on the official

And in a damning indictment on Lord Justice Scott Baker, it was Eugene Curley who was heard, whereas Cowper-Coles escaped cross-examination and the jury heard no evidence at all from him.[ab]

Bio Interview

Sherard Cowper-Coles was interviewed at his London workplace – at BAE systems – in March 2011.

This is what he said about his posting in Paris:

> **My reward for Hong Kong[c] was to be sent to Paris to be Political Counsellor there from 1997. I did some language training in Lille and I had a very happy just under two years there as head of the Political Section. I lived in the Gate House of the Embassy in Paris, working for Michael Jay who was the nicest of Ambassadors. We did the St Malo Agreement on Franco-British co-operation in defence but it wasn't, frankly, a terribly heavily loaded job.**
>
> **At Christmas 1998/Spring 1999 I discovered that Robin Cook was asking about me.... He decided to appoint me as his Principal Private Secretary and I went back to London in April 1999.[479]**

There are several points:

1)   The interviewer, Malcolm McBain, starts off: "We are here to talk about your Diplomatic Service career." [d]

The shortest topic in the entire interview is Cowper-Coles' 20 months as Head of the Paris Embassy Political department – all-up the interview is over 4,000 words with just 83 spent describing his time in Paris.

2)   The elephant in the room is Princess Diana.

According to Michael Jay, Cowper-Coles arrived on the day of Diana's death, 31 August 1997. Jay told the British police: "The death of the Princess

---

Queen's Birthday or New Year's honours lists for that year.: 1998 Diplomatic List, p164.

[a] Cowper Coles' biography states: "Language Student MECAS 1978" for two years. MECAS was the Middle East Centre for Arabic Studies based in Shemlan, Lebanon. It is possible that Cowper-Coles learned the French language during his college education (Hertford College Oxford). There is a further possibility that he acquired practical experience with French during his time in Lebanon where French is the second language.: 1998 Diplomatic List, p164.

[b] Cowper-Coles received no mention in the Paget Report even though the Michael Jay statement – quoted earlier – was taken by Paget officers during their investigation.

[c] Cowper-Coles was Head of the Hong Kong Department in the FCO for the three years preceding the handover to China on 30 June 1997.

[d] This interview was part of the British Diplomatic Oral History Program (BDOHP). The full interview can be viewed at: www.chu.cam.ac.uk/archives

of Wales was an event of immense importance ... momentous and unprecedented in my experience".[480] (WFJ)

Why is it that Cowper-Coles does not mention Diana's death in this lengthy interview?

Instead he suggests the whole job was low-key: "it wasn't, frankly, a terribly heavily loaded job".

Why? [a]

Cowper-Coles makes no such suggestion regarding any other diplomatic job he had – instead providing considerable detail about his various roles, but not on Paris.

In his book, written in 2012,[b] Cowper-Coles wrote that the death of Princess Diana would "dominate much of the Embassy's work for years to come".[481]

That I suggest is common sense – it was a momentous event.

So why then did he avoid Diana's death in this bio interview?

3)   Despite Cowper-Coles providing very little information on his role in France, he manages to mention: "I did some language training in Lille".

If this statement was true, then it strengthens the case that Cowper-Coles was not rushed into Paris ahead of Diana's assassination.[c] In other words, the transfer to Paris was planned and language training took place ahead of Cowper-Coles taking up the post.

Although this concurs with Jay's inquest account – "he was in language training" – there is a significant conflict on where Cowper-Coles' training took place: Cowper-Coles says Lille, but Jay stated under oath at the inquest, "I think ... South of France".

LanguageCourse.net[d] doesn't list any French language schools in Lille, but a general search on the internet reveals there would have been at least one school in Lille in 1997.[e] This account from Cowper-Coles needs to be viewed in the context of the other points mentioned here and bearing in mind that it is odd that he mentions his language training location, but fails to spend much time explaining his actual role in the Paris embassy.

---

[a] Cowper-Coles fails to explain this comment. It appears to be an explanation for why he has provided such little detail on his role in France. I suggest that this lacks common sense, as France is a key state to the UK – it is the next-door neighbour, it is an important nation in the EU.

[b] The year following the interview. His book was published seven months after the initial book that had alleged Cowper-Coles' involvement in the crash – see below.

[c] Lille is much closer to Paris than the South of France – see below and later footnote.

[d] The same site used earlier to analyse the locations of the South of France language schools.

[e] There is the French language centre in the Lille Catholic University – ICL-Clarife.

Cowper-Coles could have learned French at college and then later during his two years as a language student at MECAS (1978-80), which was in Lebanon, where French was the second language.[a]

4)   Cowper-Coles describes the posting to Paris as "my reward for Hong Kong" – he was Head of the FCO department that organised the transfer to China in 1997.

He fails to explain what he means by this – is he suggesting that Paris was a "plum job"?

Again, this would undermine the suggestion that Cowper-Coles could have been rushed to Paris to organise the assassination.

But, is it true?

I suggest that the key points are 1 and 2 – that Cowper-Coles has only spent 83 words out of over 4,000 on his role in Paris; that he has failed to mention his role in the aftermath of the Paris crash, despite it being one of the most significant events of the 20th century.

"Death on the Seine"

The first book to ever allege Sherard Cowper-Coles was heavily involved in the assassination was *Diana Inquest: Who Killed Princess Diana?*,[b] published in March 2012. Later that year[c] Cowper-Coles published his memoirs, *Ever The Diplomat*, in which he made his first public comment on his role regarding Princess Diana's death.

Cowper-Coles called the chapter *Death on the Seine*, which was clearly a take on the Agatha Christie murder mystery, *Death on the Nile*.[d]

He writes: "After packing up the Hong Kong Department three months earlier [than Diana's death[e]], I had gone straight to Lille for immersion training in French".[482]

There is a problem with the timing here.

Cowper-Coles describes being present at the Hong Kong handover ceremony – which finished in the evening of July 1 – and then says: "We … returned to London…. I cleared my desk in the Hong Kong Department…. [Then] I had gone straight to Lille".

---

[a] I suggest that it is likely Cowper-Coles would have read the Jay inquest evidence relating to him. In this interview – which was taken in 2011 – Cowper-Coles may have introduced Lille because of its proximity to Paris (about 226 km and 2½ hours travel): it makes a lunchtime arrival at the embassy more plausible.

[b] Part 5 of the *Diana Inquest* series.

[c] Late-October.

[d] An earlier chapter in the book had been called *Death on the Nile* – referring to the assassination of Egypt's President Anwar Sadat.

[e] Cowper-Coles specifically refers to the official Paris memorial service that took place ten days after the crash, on September 10.

If you allowed a week for the transition, this would place Cowper-Coles in Lille by say, July 8.

That is less than two months before Diana's death and approximately two months prior to the official Paris Diana memorial service he describes in his book.

So where Cowper-Coles indicates there was three months of language training before starting in Paris, the timing of his finishing up with Hong Kong reveals there could only have been two months, at the most.

Michael Jay creates a perception that Cowper-Coles broke off his language training to deal with the Diana death – "[Cowper-Coles] was in language training … and when he heard the news, he got into his car and drove straight up."

In his book Cowper-Coles presents it differently:

> **It had been agreed that my first day at work at the Embassy in Paris would be Monday 1 September 1997. On the morning of Sunday 31 August, I was on my way back with my children from a holiday near Perpignan, staying in a Formule 1 motel near Clermont-Ferrand. Half asleep, I flicked the television bolted to the wall over from cartoons to the news, with the sound down. Suddenly I noticed the images of a wrecked car in a tunnel and the headline "Mort de Diana". At first I thought I was watching the preview of a French television drama in poor taste. But, as I dialled the volume up, the literally unbelievable horror of what had happened started to dawn on me. I immediately phoned my wife, who had gone on ahead to Paris with one of our sons. Bridget was already installed in the Gatehouse of the Embassy … which was to be our home. She had not heard the news, but said she had heard the great gates of the Residence being opened and closed all night and had seen the Ambassador's Jaguar coming and going, and had wondered what was happening. She now knew. I rushed back to Paris and reported for duty.[483] (WFJ)**

According to Cowper-Coles the language training was over and he was on holiday and was due to start work anyway on the Monday morning, the day after the crash. He was already heading to Paris – he just sped the journey up.

According to Michael Jay, Cowper-Coles cut short the language training and rushed to Paris.

Cowper-Coles says: "I was on my way back … from a holiday" and this: "I rushed back to Paris".

But his account is that he had not yet been to Paris – so how could he rush back to Paris – a place he hadn't yet been to?

Cowper-Coles says his wife "had heard the great gates of the Residence being opened and closed all night and had seen the Ambassador's Jaguar coming and going".

Security officer, George Younes, who was on duty at the Embassy that night, revealed that "The Residence" is where the ambassador lived.[484]

The ambassador, Michael Jay, testified: "I was woken at my residence ... at about 1.45 a.m."[485] (WFJ) He then says that he and his wife were "driven ... by Tim Livesey" and "arrived at the Hospital at about 2.20 a.m." and "we were driven home ... sometime between 0700 [7.00 a.m.] and 0800".[486] (WFJ)

Keith Moss, the consul general, also was woken by the phone and attended the hospital – but he didn't live at the Embassy: "I lived in Rue Saint Jacques".[487] (WFJ)

The only disclosed movements in and out of the Residence gates would have been Livesey arriving around 2 a.m. and the Jays leaving with him before 2.20 a.m.

So what is "the great gates of the Residence being opened and closed all night" as claimed by Cowper-Coles' wife?[a]

Or is this account from Cowper-Coles a fabrication?[b]

The reality is Cowper-Coles' 2012 account does nothing to resolve the earlier issues – his failure to mention Princess Diana's death at all in his 2011 FCO bio interview; ostensibly the existence of two heads of MI6 France during the period of the assassination;[c] the lies told by both Eugene Curley and Michael Jay in their evidence and the failure of any investigation to interview Sherard Cowper-Coles.

There is no official explanation for any of this.

Why?

---

[a] Sunrise was at 7.06 a.m.: Sunrise and Sunset for France – Paris – August 1997, www.timeanddate.com

[b] Cowper-Coles' claim of being at Clermont-Ferrand places him 425 km from Paris – 4 hours driving time. (Himmera.com Map Distances: http://distancecalculator.himmera.com) He said his children were travelling with him – one was with his wife, so the remaining four were with him. To fit with Jay's claim of Cowper-Coles arriving at lunchtime, allowing for breakfast, trip preparation and getting the kids organised, it would seem the phone call to his wife would have occurred sometime prior to 7 a.m. This would place it before Jay returned from the hospital – "between 0700 [7.00 a.m.] and 0800" – and before Paul Burrell's arrival at the Residence, which was well after 7.30 a.m. See Part 4: Choice of Hospital Room section of French Embalming chapter.

[c] It's interesting that it's the account of both of the MI6 France heads – Curley and Cowper-Coles – that they were lying in motel beds hundreds of kilometres away from the Alma Tunnel at the time of the crash. And also both were scheduled to begin work after holidaying on 1 September 1997, the day following the crash.

18   Contemplating A Wedding

On the same day Dodi Fayed told Frank Klein they would be visiting Paris, US president, Bill Clinton, made a significant announcement. Clinton told the world that he would support an international ban on landmines by the end of the year.[a] Jerry White, co-founder of Landmine Survivors Network, said: "Princess Di can be very proud. She was central to pushing Clinton off the fence." [488] (WFJ)

It was Monday 18 August 1997 – 13 days before the crash.

While observers assimilated the significance of the Clinton promise, MI6 was turning its focus to the operational planning in Paris and Princess Diana and Rosa Monckton were concluding their Greek cruise.

The pair returned to London on August 20.

The following day Princess Diana paid a special visit to her local Anglican priest, Father Frank Gelli.

Consulting With Ministers

Gelli later described the August 21 meeting with the princess:

> **She stopped by my house on the way to the gym. She wanted to know if it was possible for two people of different religions to marry. I told her it was. As we spoke, [her] telephone rang. It was obviously Dodi. Her eyes lit up. As she was leaving she asked me if I would be able to perform the service when she got married. Her love was obvious. Whenever she mentioned Dodi's name her face lit up. I have only seen that look on the faces of people who are deeply in love.[489] (WFJ)**

It was around this time that Diana asked her Catholic butler, Paul Burrell, to find out what his church's position was on inter-faith marriage.

Burrell's priest, Anthony Parsons, gave this account to the British police in 2004:

---

[a] Following the death of Diana, Clinton rescinded this. He said: "There is a line I simply cannot cross": Worldwide Ban on Landmines Approved, Without US, CNN, September 17, 1997 (WFJ).

> **It was one evening in 1997 that I was ... invited round to |the Burrell's| home. This was nothing out of the ordinary....**
>
> **At some point during the course of the evening, Paul Burrell asked me, "Is it possible for a Muslim to marry a non-Catholic in a Catholic Church?"... I answered that I was "not sure, I would find out from the powers that be if you want me to". Paul Burrell said "Yes".... He said something along the lines of "Obviously I would appreciate your discretion" and the sentiment I understood was that this was connected in some way to the Princess of Wales....**
>
> **I am not sure exactly when Paul Burrell asked me this question, but I never followed through with it because it was around the time of the Princess of Wales's death....**
>
> **I remember I mentioned the theory in passing with my Carmelite Brothers, but I certainly did not mention the provenance of the question posed. The question was passed over and simply laughed off. If I had wanted to find out whether marriage under these circumstances was a possibility, I would have needed to approach the Bishop or members of his Marriage Tribunal at the Diocese of Westminster.**[490]

Parsons was asked by Burrell to find out whether a Muslim – Dodi – could marry a non-Catholic – Diana – in a Catholic church. Parsons couldn't answer but told Burrell he would find out.

Before Parsons did this, Princess Diana was dead.

These accounts from both Anglican and Catholic priests are evidence that by August 21 Diana was not just in a serious relationship with Dodi, but marriage between the two was being contemplated.

Frank Gelli has never been interviewed by the police and his evidence was not heard at the inquest.

Dr Lily

Later that day Diana visited her Chinese doctor, Lily Hua Yu.

Dr Lily told the police in 2005:

> **Diana was very happy the last time I saw her |August 21| and was in a very positive mood.... She mentioned Dodi. He appeared at the right time.... She said she felt very good.**[491]

The next day Diana and Dodi slipped away together via Stansted airport – they were headed for the South of France.

The two lovers would never see England again.

19   Final Holiday

On Friday August 22, Diana and Dodi embarked at St Laurent-du-Var starting their final cruise together – again on the *Jonikal*, and again in the sparkling summer waters of the Mediterranean.

The next day the *Jonikal* moored off Monte Carlo.

Monte Carlo Excursion

On Saturday Diana and Dodi headed for the shore. Myriah Daniels, the couple's on-board holistic healer, described what happened:

> [Diana and Dodi] took off without the bodyguards and the bodyguards were somewhere else in the boat. By the time they said 'Gee, we are going', the guys did not have enough time to get from one end of the boat to the tender to go with them. The bodyguards were livid.[492]

Trixi Chall, a former journalist with the German *Bild* living in Monaco, saw Diana and Dodi come ashore:

> I was surprised to see Diana the Princess of Wales hand in hand with a man I had never seen before. It was amazing because there were no bodyguards.... They looked like a very normal young couple in love.... I just remained on the other side of the road and they walked on a bit ahead of me on the other side of the road. They were going in the same direction as I was.... She was so beautiful and so happy and at one point he put his arm around her shoulder.... They were dressed very casually.... I felt that Love was in the air.... I followed Diana and this handsome man as I was fascinated and nobody was aware of them and they were aware of nobody, as if they were the only ones in the world!... They were not in any hurry, were chatting happily and they were strolling casually which is probably why no one noticed them.... They walked towards the Hermitage, which is where I thought they were going. They went to the shop situated on the left of the Hermitage hotel which is Repossi the Jeweller. They looked in the window and Diana was pointing with her finger at something. As they had stopped, I felt I should continue on my way, but as I turned round to glance once more at them, I saw them entering the shop.[493]

In 2005 Claude Roulet told police that he received a call at the Ritz: "Dodi told me that he had been for a stroll with [Diana] in Monte Carlo and that the Princess liked a ring that she had seen in the window of the jewellers,

Repossi. He asked me to ensure that this ring be available for them in Paris."[494]

Identification Panic

At some point the specific description of the ring seen by Diana and Dodi became confused. This led to a series of moves – on the same day (August 23) – to try and precisely identify it.

The detailed evidence of this is in Part 2[a] – below is a summary of what occurred.

Dodi called Frank Klein in Antibes stating that Diana had seen a "simple ring in gold[b] ... close to a platinum watch",[495] "to the rear at the right" in the window[496] of Repossi's in Monte Carlo. Dodi requested that this ring be available for Diana and him to view when they came to Paris at the end of the month.[497]

Klein called Claude Roulet passing on the information from Dodi.[498]

Roulet then requested Ritz Operations Manager, Franco Mora, to call Repossi's in Monte Carlo and ask them to have the ring put aside.[499]

Mora phones Repossi's in Monte Carlo and speaks to an unidentified female salesperson, who is unable to identify the ring. She provides Mora with details of the jewellery in the right rear area of the window. Mora writes down this information.[500]

Mora shows the list of the Repossi window jewellery to Roulet, who adds in writing that the listed jewellery is near a platinum watch. He then asks Mora to fax the list to Klein. Mora does this and dates the fax, 23 August 1997.[501c]

Roulet then phones Dodi to try to establish a more specific description of the ring, but does not appear to learn any more detail than what he already knows.[502]

Repossi is asked to open the Paris store for Diana and Dodi's visit at the end of the month.[503]

In summary, the evidence shows that Diana and Dodi saw a ring in the Repossi window, which later, based on a vague description from Dodi, was not able to be identified.[d] The "solution" was for Alberto Repossi to be available in Paris, with jewellery from Monte Carlo, for the visit of Diana and Dodi at the end of the month.

---

[a] Section on 23 August 1997, in the Engagement chapter.

[b] This description is from Claude Roulet and is discussed later.

[c] The fax from Mora to Klein is INQ0005932 on the website. It is also reproduced in Part 2, section on Mora Fax to Klein, in Engagement chapter.

[d] Roulet described it as a "plain gold ring" – this evidence is discussed later.

Planning An Engagement

Later in the day (August 23) Diana phoned her Anglican priest, Frank Gelli. He recalled their conversation:

> **She said she had some very good news and seemed very excited. She invited me to go to Kensington Palace on her return.... After all the things that she had previously told me about their relationship, I could only imagine that she was about to announce her engagement to Dodi.** [504] **(WFJ)**

Gelli was not alone in his perception a Diana-Dodi engagement would be announced.

Raine Spencer, Diana's step-mother, testified that she spoke with Diana on August 15 – eight days before the Monte Carlo excursion:

> **[Diana] was very effusive, very excited about [Dodi] ... incredibly happy. And she said really she had never been so happy for years. She was really blissful. That was the moment when I really felt that it was highly likely that she and Dodi would get engaged and then married.** [505]

Early in this final cruise Dodi's assistant, Melissa Henning, was told by Dodi "quite specifically that he was definitely going to ask the Princess to marry him". [506] She testified that he said "he was going to 'ask the question'". [507]

Then later in the cruise – on August 29 – Dodi phoned his close friend Barbara Broccoli. She was producing the James Bond movie *Tomorrow Never Dies* being shot at Frogmore, outside London.

Broccoli told the inquest:

> **Dodi said ... "I have never been so happy in my life. We are flying to Paris tomorrow and coming back Sunday evening. I have something very important to tell you, but I can't tell you over the phone". Dodi also said that we, which I understood to mean Diana, Princess of Wales and him, would like to see me on Monday, 1st September 1997. I told him that we were filming at Pinewood Studios the following Monday and we agreed that they were going to come to see me there.... My impression at the time was that the very important news which Dodi wanted to tell me related to his personal life and his relationship with Princess Diana and not to any other matter such as a business matter. That was my impression at the time and remains my impression now.** [508]

On the same day Dodi phoned Stuart Benson, who was the Al Fayed General Legal Counsel.

Benson later recalled:

> **[Dodi said]: "Can't really talk over the telephone, but my friend and I have very exciting news. Are you around on Monday [September 1] to**

have lunch as it will mean lots of issues to talk about, to discuss?" ... I was absolutely in no doubt – went home that evening, and said, "I have had this call from Dodi and I am pretty sure he is getting engaged".[509]

Then as the cruise finished the next morning – Saturday August 30 – Sardinian taxi driver, Tomas Muzzu, transported Diana and Dodi from the yacht to the Olbia airport. He described a loving couple planning a future together: "They spoke in English, very loving words.... My impression was of a couple very much in love and making plans for their future." [510] (WFJ)

The couple would fly by private jet to Le Bourget in Paris.

But within 18 hours both their lives would be snuffed out – preventing any of these plans from coming to fruition.

20 Final Controversy

Three days before the final cruise finished *Le Monde* in Paris published a bombshell interview with Diana, Princess of Wales.

It was Wednesday 27 August 1997.

This was Princess Diana's final interview.

Journalist Annick Cojean quoted Diana:

- regarding the royal family: "from the first day I joined that family, nothing could be done naturally anymore"

- on upsetting the Establishment: "it's because I'm much closer to the people at the bottom than the people at the top, and the latter won't forgive me for it"

- on her role: "if I must define my role, I'd rather use the word 'messenger'"

- on her independence: "Nobody can dictate my conduct. I work on instinct. It's my best adviser."

- on leaving England: "I think that in my place, any sane person would have left long ago. But I can't. I have my sons to think about." [a]

- on handling criticism: "Over the years, I had to learn to ignore criticism. But the irony is that it gave me strength that I was far from thinking I had. That doesn't mean it didn't hurt me. To the contrary. But that gave me the strength I needed to continue along the path I had chosen."

- on her love towards others: "Nothing gives me greater happiness than trying to help the weakest in this society. It's a goal and, from now on, an essential part of my life. It's a sort of destiny. I will run to anyone who calls to me in distress, wherever it is,"[511] (WFJ)

---

[a] This interview was recorded on 13 June 1997 – see below. The general evidence indicates that Diana became more willing to leave the UK throughout July and August, as she underwent increasingly severe criticism over her activities. There is evidence of Diana and Dodi – besides moving to Malibu – seeking out part-time accommodation in Paris, which would have been much closer to her sons. See Part 2, Future Location and Living section of Future Plans chapter.

But what caused great controversy was Cojean's quote of a political comment regarding landmines: The new Labour government's "position on the subject was always clear. It's going to do tremendous work. Its predecessor was so hopeless."[512] (WFJ)

Tories were quick to respond.

Sir James Hill, a one-time chairman of the Conservative backbench committee on constitutional affairs, said Diana must keep out of politics – and that if she would not, she should be "disciplined" by the Royal household.[513] (WFJ)

Tory MP Sir Patrick Cormack said the Princess was "an inexperienced young woman" making "partisan, political" comments.[514] (WFJ)

Backbencher David Wilshire was quoted in *The Mirror*: "It's seriously dangerous to drag the Royal Family into party politics. I don't think we ought to allow one young to coming up to middle-aged woman to alter the British constitution."[515] (WFJ)

Diana denied saying that the Tories were hopeless on landmines. She released a strong defence to *Daily Mail* journalist Richard Kay. Diana's private secretary Michael Gibbins had been present during the interview at Kensington Palace on June 13. On August 15 the draft article by Cojean had been faxed to him for vetting.[516] (WFJ)

Kay wrote:

> **Mr Gibbins, a fluent French speaker, read it all closely. His task was to ensure that the written answers[a] were reported faithfully and that other quotations accurately reflected the conversation he had observed. They did. Most important of all, the article did not include those five words attacking the Tories. They were not there because, said Kensington Palace, the Princess did not utter them.[517] (WFJ)**

Gibbins had retained the draft article.[518] (WFJ)

Whilst the debate over Princess Diana's alleged words raged, the planning for her assassination in Paris continued unabated.

---

[a] Diana had separately provided written answers on July 4 to some follow-up questions from Cojean.

21   An Assassin Prepares

The day before the controversial *Le Monde* article, MI6 chief David Spedding transferred his personal secretary – a senior officer – to Paris.[519]

His name was Richard Spearman and the date was Tuesday 26 August 1997 – just five days ahead of the crash.[520]

Then the next day – August 27 – a strange, seemingly unrelated event occurred in the South of France.

Enter James Andanson

Throughout the final Mediterranean cruise Diana and Dodi were pursued by a flock of paparazzi.

Amongst them was the notorious French photographer, James Andanson.

It will be shown later that this man was the driver of a white Fiat Uno that was involved in the August 31 crash that killed Diana and Dodi.

Andanson had various characteristics that helped him stand out from the normal throng of snappers.

Born "Jean-Paul" Andanson, he changed his name to James as an adult.[521] This action reflected his love of things British[a] and by 1997 Andanson had actually placed a Union Jack on his central France property.[522]

Françoise Dard, who knew James Andanson over a period of 30 years, testified that he had told her he was Irish – even though he was French. She only discovered this lie well after he died.[523]

Hubert Henrotte, the head of Andanson's photo agency, told the inquest that "he was feared, in fact; he was feared" by the other paparazzi, because he was extremely competitive.[524]

Andanson was not popular amongst those who crossed paths with him. He died prematurely in 2000.[b] People often talk well of the dead, but in Andanson's case the adjectives used by witnesses at the inquest were:

  - "not a very likeable man" – Pierre Suu, fellow photographer[525]

---

[a] His wife Elisabeth was quoted in 2000 saying James had a "great affection for Britain": 11 Feb 08: 156.4.

[b] See later.

- "highly competitive" – Henrotte[526]
- "feared" – Henrotte[527]
- "not the kind of person to go unnoticed" – Suu[528]
- "a loner" – Christophe Lafaille, journalist and friend[529]
- "he made jealousies" – Lafaille[530]
- "did not have a good reputation ... with colleagues" – Jean-Claude Mulès, French investigating officer[531]
- "he was always saying ... that he was very clever" – Françoise Dard[532]

Andanson mixed in high circles and had been linked to the premature 1993 death of former French Prime Minister Pierre Bérégovoy. [533] (WFJ)

"Dropped the Couple"

James Andanson had also taken an interest in Princess Diana and part of that involved chartering boats to pursue her and Dodi during their final holiday.[534] An excerpt from a letter Andanson sent his agency boss reveals just how important the Diana-Dodi story was to him – he wrote: "The reporting of Lady Di ... in my eyes is the greatest news story of the last 50 years...."[535a]

Those words were typed by Andanson on Saturday, 30 August 1997 – less than 24 hours before the death of Princess Diana.

Yet three days before this letter, Andanson had prematurely terminated his Mediterranean pursuit of Diana and returned home – three days before the cruise finished on August 30.

Andanson's diary for Wednesday 27 August 1997 reads, at 8 p.m. "Dinner Manoir"[b].[536]

Why did he leave early?

Andanson's son, James Jnr, was working with his father throughout the Diana pursuit that summer. He told the French police in February 1998:

We followed the Princess's boat until 25.08.97.... Two days later we returned to Lignières[c], my father and I. That must have been on 27-28 August 1997. From that day on, my father dropped the couple. He did not know exactly where they were in Paris, but he knew that his colleagues were covering their movements."[537] (WFJ)

So we learn that not only did James Andanson leave early but he "dropped the couple" – Diana and Dodi: he did not follow the rest of the cruise and he didn't follow Diana to Paris.

---

[a] It is notable that the inquest jury were not shown the English translation of this letter – see later.

[b] Le Manoir was the name of Andanson's home property.

[c] The location of their family home.

All this, despite his belief that Diana and Dodi was "the greatest news story of the last 50 years".

Witnesses have proffered reasons for Andanson dropping the Diana-Dodi story.

Hubert Henrotte, his boss, stated that Andanson was no longer interested in following Diana because "the kiss" photo had been published – "it was not anymore of such an interest because this coup had been done, it was over".[538]

Henrotte also said that Andanson had his mind set on doing his next job – a shoot of Gilbert Bécaud[a] – and that "there was no way that we could talk him out of doing it".[539]

There are problems with Henrotte's account.

In Andanson's own words the Diana-Dodi relationship was the "greatest news story of the last 50 years" and he stated that in an August 30 letter to Henrotte. It is difficult to imagine how the Bécaud assignment[b] – the photos of which apparently were never published[c] – could have superseded the Princess Diana story.

Further to this, "The Kiss" photo was first published in London's *Sunday Mirror* on 10 August 1997. This was 13 days <u>before</u> Andanson and other paparazzi started on their Mediterranean pursuit of Diana, on the 23rd of August. Henrotte is suggesting that Andanson gave up following Diana because of the kiss photo, yet it was published much earlier – before Andanson started following her.

Andanson's wife, Elisabeth, says that she agrees with Henrotte about her husband focusing on the Bécaud assignment. But then she added that as soon as they knew Diana would be flying out "what they knew was that for them it was over".[540]

This occurred "in Portofino".[541]

According to James Andanson's diary, he was in Portofino on the 25th and 26th of August.[542] This was still four days before Diana and Dodi left the Mediterranean area. It was inevitable that the Diana-Dodi cruise was going to come to an end at some stage. Particularly considering Andanson's competitive personality (see earlier) it is not logical that he would simply close up shop, just because he hears that Diana is going to be flying out in a few days.

Elisabeth says that "another team of photographers ... was going to take care of it",[543] but it is clear from Henrotte's evidence that fellow paparazzo

---

[a] Gilbert Bécaud was a French singer/song-writer who was aged 70 and lived in Corsica in 1997. He died in 2001.

[b] This assignment was carried out by Andanson on August 31 – it is addressed later.

[c] See Part 1, Bécaud Assignment section of Chapter 5C.

Stéphane Cardinale was present in both the South of France and Paris.[544] Why wouldn't Andanson have done the same?

Andanson was not averse to driving long distances overnight to get a job done.[a] He had just made the trip home from St Tropez, a distance of over 400 km, so one could imagine he would not have considered the approximately 280 km trip to Paris, to follow Diana, too difficult.

There is another conflict in Henrotte's evidence. He states that Andanson following Diana to Paris was "not at all something that we discussed".[545] Yet Henrotte said that "there was no way that we could talk him out of doing" the Bécaud shoot.[546] The implication from the latter statement is that Sygma[b] did try to talk Andanson out of doing the Bécaud job, presumably because Henrotte would have wanted him in Paris to follow Diana and Dodi.

James Andanson Jnr, who worked with his father that summer, stated that from 25 August 1997 "my father dropped the couple". What did he mean by that? Why did his father drop Diana and Dodi?

These questions were not asked of Andanson's son at the inquest.

In summary, between Elisabeth and Henrotte there were three reasons proffered for Andanson returning early and not going on to Paris: "the kiss' photo had stolen his thunder; he was focused on the Bécaud shoot[c]; he gave up once he knew Diana was going to fly out.

The reality is that none of these reasons stack up – none of them reveal why Andanson went home on Wednesday August 27.

Then the person who is most likely to know the answer – James Jnr, who was with his father during that period – has never been asked about why he departed early.

Why?

Mystery Trip

James Andanson's diary reveals that he had lunches and dinners at home – Le Manoir – on Thursday and Friday, August 28 and 29.[547]

Hubert Henrotte told the inquest that Andanson informed him on the Friday evening or Saturday that Diana would be flying into Paris.[548]

Then on the Saturday – August 30, the final day of Diana and Dodi's lives – Andanson rose very early. Departing from home well before 5 a.m. James Andanson made an unexplained 126 km return car trip to the Vierzon East motorway interchange.

The purpose of this trip is apparently a complete mystery.

---

[a] See Part 1, The Logistics section of Chapter 5C.
[b] Henrotte's agency that Andanson worked for.
[c] The timing will later reveal that Andanson could have done both – Diana in Paris and Bécaud in Corsica.

Andanson left home sometime before 4.30 a.m., drove over 25 minutes and was recorded exiting the toll road at Vierzon East at 4.55 a.m.[549] This is a very early start, with the suggestion, from an exit toll receipt at Bourges[a] at 5.08 a.m.,[550] that Andanson also made a fairly quick return home. The distance from Vierzon East to Bourges is about 24 km, so he covered that distance, including carrying out whatever he needed to do in Vierzon, in 13 minutes. There would not be much traffic at that time on a Saturday morning.

Andanson booked this trip to the Bécaud photo assignment job,[551] but in responding to this, Elisabeth Andanson testified that her husband would book up his own "private journeys or even journeys that [she] made".[552] This indicates that she is aware that the journey would have had nothing to do with the Bécaud job. Yet under later questioning Elisabeth stated: "I have no idea about that trip".[553]

If Elisabeth has no idea about the trip then why does she indicate it was not to do with the Bécaud assignment – the job Andanson booked it to? [b]

Is Elisabeth Andanson withholding information from the court?

If James Andanson's Uno was the car that was in the Alma Tunnel at 12.23 a.m. on August 31[c], then it would have had to get there somehow, without drawing undue attention. Could Andanson's early morning trip on August 30 have been connected to this?

Ian Croxford's questioning of Elisabeth brought out the fact that there was a train line that ran to Paris through Vierzon.[554] He also established that Andanson was no stranger to the French train or road transport system – he used it for moving his motorbike around the country.[555d]

The toll receipts only register when the vehicle exits from the tollway. Therefore it is unknown whether the trip to Vierzon took longer than the return trip. We also are not able to tell if there were two vehicles – the second one paid by a different credit card – on the initial trip. It is clear that if Andanson was involved in the Paris crash, he would have been operating as part of a much larger organised operation. It will be shown that the resources of MI6, DGSE or DST or all three were behind this.

---

[a] Andanson's home tollway exit.

[b] It makes sense that it would not be connected to the Bécaud job, which was a normal photo shoot. The question though is: What was this mystery trip connected with?

[c] The time of the crash.

[d] There is a conflict in Elisabeth Andanson's evidence regarding the mode of transportation of the motorbike. Earlier in Croxford's cross-examination, she confirmed that the motorbike would be collected from the train: 21 Feb 08: 72.10. Later she states that "it was not by railway, it was by road": 21 Feb 08: 82.12.

The Uno could have been transferred to Vierzon at that early hour on August 30 and loaded onto a train or covered truck bound for Paris.

The above is of course speculation, and there are other possible explanations for this trip. Andanson may have arranged to meet someone near the Vierzon East interchange. He may have been collecting a cash payment for his role, similar to what Henri Paul received in the hours before the crash.[a]

Andanson included in his diary details of trips he made, even to the specifics of where he ate lunch and dinner each day, and also some phone calls – this early morning August 30 trip does not, however, receive a diary entry.

The factors that draw attention to this outing are the timing – 4.30 a.m. on a Saturday morning; the distance – a 126 km return trip; the short duration at the destination; and the lack of desire by the French investigation to find out the purpose of the trip.

Jean-Claude Mulès shied away from any responsibility to know about this mystery trip, despite the fact that he was the commander on the case. When asked if he was aware of it, Mulès responded: "I would like to recall you what was my role.... There were more than 2,994 pages of statements in this investigation. I could not see everything."[556]

It is clear from Elisabeth's questioning that in 1998 the French were provided these receipts from the toll company.[557]

Yet, despite having this documentary evidence, the French investigation failed to ask James Andanson about the purpose of the trip.

Why?

Mystery Letter

After returning home from this mystery trip, James Andanson wrote a lengthy letter to his boss, Hubert Henrotte, regarding Princess Diana.

Given that this letter was addressed to Henrotte, it is unbelievable that he was not asked anything about it during the inquest.

The inquest is about the death of Diana, and this letter was:
- about Diana
- written under 24 hours before Diana's death
- authored by a person who is suspected to have been involved in the circumstances of Diana's death.

Yet the London jury were never provided with the English translation of the letter,[b] and only the first page (in French) of what was a five or six page letter has ever been posted to the inquest website.[c]

---

[a] See later.

[b] The jury were told by the coroner that "it may not be necessary to go into the detail": 21 Feb 08: 60.11.

[c] The evidence reference is INQ0009206.

The few people heard who have read this letter were in conflict over its content.

Andanson's diary describes it as: "The Letter: Report on Lady Di's voyage".[558] Inquest lawyer, Jonathon Hough said it "focuses upon Lady Di, as the diary suggested it did".[559] Elisabeth Andanson says that the letter is about James' feelings regarding "his relationship with the Sygma agency".[560] Inquest lawyer, Nicholas Hilliard, says that it is a criticism of how Sygma handled the Diana pictures from the cruise.[561] Jean-Claude Mulès, the French case commander, talks as though he has never seen the letter in his life.[562]

Scott Baker suggested that the jury may not need to see the letter, as it "simply bears out what the witness [Elisabeth] has been saying".[563]

I have had the first page of this letter[a] translated into English. The letter starts out: "My dear H, After a little peace and quiet I'm writing you this long letter my dear H, whom I consider a friend. I only have a few friends in my life, but you are one of them." It goes on to describe the Diana-Dodi events as "the greatest news story of the last 50 years". Andanson states that he felt there had been a bad failure in "the reporting of Lady Di", and he wanted to inform Henrotte on how things occurred as he experienced them "on the ground". He then starts getting more specific about the issues regarding the Diana reportage.

The tone of the letter appears to be very friendly and it does not seem to be a letter written with his resignation from Sygma in mind.[b] Of course, it is impossible to know for sure, without seeing the entire letter.

Why weren't the contents of this letter revealed to the jury, so that they could make their own decision on its level of relevance?

And why wasn't Hubert Henrotte – the person who received the letter – asked about its contents?

---

[a] That is all that is publicly available.

[b] After 24 years' service, Andanson resigned from Sygma on September 5 – just five days after the crash. It is both Henrotte and Elisabeth's contention that James knew he would resign ahead of the crash and that the timing is simply a coincidence. Elisabeth told the court: "I want to specify that my husband did not decide to leave the Sygma agency because of the Lady Di work. There had been a conflict going on for some time between my husband and Mr Henrotte.": 21 Feb 08: 59.18.

22   Agents at the Ritz

In 1997 there were two full-time Ritz Hotel employees working on behalf of intelligence agencies.

They were the Ritz Vice-President, Claude Roulet and the Acting Head of Security, Henri Paul.

Both of these men were used by MI6 to help bring about the assassination of Princess Diana and Dodi Fayed. They played key roles in the events, yet neither would have been aware that they were involved in such a sinister and heinous operation. This is because of the intelligence principle called "need to know". Basically the left hand has no idea what the right hand is doing.[a]

Claude Roulet's specific role will emerge as this story progresses.

Secretive and Discreet

Ritz colleagues[b], close friends and acquaintances viewed Henri Paul as discreet or secretive, or both:
-       Henri was "discreet and not the type to confide"[564] – Frank Klein
-       "he was quite secret and he did not speak too much about his private life"[565] – Claude Roulet
-       "Henri Paul was very discreet and … [I] knew nothing about his private life"[566] – François Tendil, Ritz Night Security Manager
-       "[Henri] was fairly secretive and did not recount his weekends"[567] (WFJ) – Catherine Esperandieu, Ritz Head of Human Resources
-       "he never spoke about his private life. He kept a lot of things to himself and did not talk about himself much"[568] (WFJ)[a] – Jean Henri Hocquet, Ritz Former Head of Security

---

[a] Former MI6 Chief, Richard Dearlove, testified that "the principle of 'need to know' is applied throughout the organisation. Therefore your knowledge is compartmentalised in terms of the activity for which you are responsible, but of course the further up the service you go, the more you need to know what everyone else is doing.": 20 Feb 08: 27.1. Bearing in mind that agents like Henri and Roulet were at the bottom of the organisation.
[b] Henri Paul had worked at the Ritz since 1986 – 11 years.

- "Henri Paul was confidential about his work and didn't mention any names"[569] (WFJ) – Claude Garrec, Henri's closest friend[b]
- "he had some secrets and that's normal. I could see some things, but he didn't tell everything"[570] – Claude Garrec
- "to sum up Henri's personality for you, he was a secretive man.... He did not talk about his professional or his private life"[571] – Dr Dominique Mélo, Henri's female doctor and friend
- "Henri was very discreet about his private life.... Henri was very discreet professionally. He didn't talk about his work"[572] – Jean-Claude Morere, friend of Henri
- "M Paul was very discreet as far as his work was concerned"[573] – Myriam Lemaire, Manager of Le Bourgogne[c]
- Question: "Did [Henri] ever speak to you about the work he did?" Answer: "No, as a matter of fact, never.... He was discreet...."[574] – Josiane Le Tellier, Owner of Le Champmeslé Lesbian Bar

Being secretive and discreet does not make a person an intelligence agent. However all intelligence work involves secrecy and discretion. MI6 Chief John Sawers said publicly in 2010: "Secrecy is not a dirty word.... Secrecy plays a crucial part in keeping Britain safe and secure."[575] (WFJ)

Secrecy is a vital characteristic of employees working for intelligence.

But there is much more to this than Henri Paul's secrecy and discretion.

Henri's Finances

Following Henri Paul's death the following was established:
- Henri's Ritz income was 17,000FF[d] per month[576]
- he was separately banking on average an additional 38,867FF per month[577e] – so his total monthly income was 55,867FF – in 1997 this equated to approximately £5,587
- he was operating 17 separate bank accounts, spread between three banks
- his combined bank balances totalled in excess of 1,252,771FF or about £125,277[578f]
- he owned a Barclay's share portfolio valued at 431,485FF[579] (WFJ)

---

[a] Evidence followed by (WFJ) means that it was withheld from the jury at the inquest.
[b] They were friends since their teenage years in the early 1970s.
[c] A bar frequented by Henri.
[d] French Francs.
[e] A full table revealing Henri's banking history from December 1996 until his death is in Part 1, section on Finances in the Henri Paul chapter.
[f] A full breakdown of Henri's bank accounts and balances at the time of his death is in Part 1, section on Finances in the Henri Paul chapter.

- he operated five credit cards[580]
- he owned a flat in Paris that he rented out[581]
- he had a safety deposit box with 30,000FF in it[582]
- he had clocked up 605 hours of flying time at an average cost of 3,000FF per hour[583] (WFJ) – a total cost of 1,815,000FF or about £181,500
- he was carrying 12,565FF on his person at the time he died[584].

Where did all this money and assets come from? How did Henri finance this lifestyle?

Certainly not from 17,000FF per month at the Ritz. Henri would have had to work for nearly nine years just to pay for his flying time – with no money allocated to food, rent, clothing, car expenses, etc.

Investigative Failure

The most striking factor regarding the official investigation into Henri Paul's financial dealings is the lack of actual investigation.

The following points are worth noting:

1) The records don't go back before late 1996. This is less than a year before the crash. If the police had really wanted to establish a pattern – and after seeing the figures above they should have been – they would have gone back at least two or three years.

2) Paul Laffan, the MPS financial investigator, saw a signature on a 49,900FF deposit into one of Henri's accounts and stated: "I have no way of knowing that that is [Henri's] signature".[585] This has to be one of the most ridiculous statements of the entire inquest, and yet it went unchallenged. How hard would it have been for Laffan to find a document with Henri Paul's signature on? He had at least four places he could have gone to: the French investigation; the bank; the Ritz Hotel or Henri Paul's parents. Then Laffan could have compared the signature to establish whether it was Henri's. It is unbelievable that Laffan has carried out a full investigation of Henri Paul's financial records and yet is unable to establish the look of Henri Paul's signature.

3) It is very basic bank and police work to establish the source of funds[a] – particularly where a cheque has been banked – yet in the case of Henri Paul, neither the French nor British investigation were able to establish the source of any of the funds Henri deposited. There is no reason at all why a 30,000FF cheque deposited on 26 March 1997[586] was not traced – that is, unless the police just didn't want to find out.

4) It would have been a simple matter for the French police to have established who the 80,000FF cheque drawn on Henri Paul's account on 21 May 1997[587] was payable to – yet this was never established.

---

[a] I have 25 years of experience as an accountant.

5)   On reviewing Michael Mansfield's cross-examination of Laffan, it becomes apparent that Laffan has not bothered to inquire of the French banks regarding their individual policies on checking deposits. The two cash deposits of 49,900FF made in 1996 on December 18 and 19,[588] certainly indicate that there could be an effort by the depositor not to bank over 50,000FF on the one day.

Laffan made statements like "we never had that information",[589] but very little attempt appears to have been made to secure any information beyond what he was originally given.

The best slant on this financial "investigation" by Paul Laffan is to say that this was very lazy police work, but when one considers that this is part of the investigation into the death of the mother of the future King of England, it becomes unbelievable. It seems very much like this police work was conducted by people who did not want to – or had been told not to – find out the answers to the relevant questions.

In the final analysis, one point is very clear: Whoever was paying Henri Paul these large sums of money – and stopped paying them after he died – has not come forward to explain the mystery. Why not? Their failure to do so indicates that they would have a reason not to reveal themselves.

When this is considered in conjunction with other evidence regarding Henri Paul's activities – see later – it would appear there could be a connection between Henri's unexplained income and the Alma crash.

Tips

It has been suggested that the unexplained funds comprised of Ritz tips.

According to Operation Paget, Henri Paul's mother, Gisèle, told John Stevens in a meeting that "on one occasion [Henri] … [was] given a FF 5,000 tip".[590] (WFJ)

Inquest lawyer, Jonathon Hough, appeared to deliberately misquote Gisèle during his cross-examination of Claude Garrec.

Hough said that Gisèle told the police that "Henri Paul was <u>often</u> given tips as large as 5,000 francs". What the jury didn't hear was that Gisèle actually told the police that she knew of "<u>one occasion</u>" when this had occurred. There is a huge difference. The indication could be that Henri recounted to her something that was unusual, and not at all a regular occurrence. At the inquest, when the Pauls were asked how often Henri received these very large tips, they replied "We don't know at all. We don't know".[591]

When the Pauls were reminded by Ian Burnett of the example of the FF 5,000 tip, they stated that Henri used that money to purchase a camera.[592] So clearly, that tip did not get banked or form part of the large account balances that Henri Paul had at the time of his death.

Frank Klein testified that "maybe once or twice" Henri could have received tips, but not large amounts.[593] His mother Gisèle said that "clients left tips for him in envelopes with the hotel reception or the concierge".[594] Other Ritz staff – like the concierge and reception – could and should have been interviewed on this subject. This has never happened.

The questions about tips should have been asked of the Ritz Head of Security or other staff in the security department. This was not done – by the French or British police, or the inquest.

Garrec stated to the British police that Henri invested the tips into the share market.[595] (WFJ) If that were the case, then this would have been additional money, in excess of the large amounts that were going into Henri's bank accounts.

When Michael Mansfield questioned Garrec on how sure he is about the tips being banked, he stated: "It's the explanation I feel is sound because I do not have any other explanation".[596] After ten years, this is hardly a convincing reason to believe that Henri's large cash inflows were coming from tips.

Common sense – based on the size, timing and method of the deposits[a] – suggests that the money was not from tips. The cash deposits were almost exclusively FF500 notes[b] – if these amounts had been from tips then the denomination notes banked would have been more diverse.

From 29 May to 5 August 1997 Henri deposited seven separate amounts of exactly FF 40,000 – FF 280,000 in total.[c] Mansfield put it succinctly: "Very clearly … these are sums far in excess of an accumulation of a myriad of tips which come to an exact figure of 40,000 each time".[597]

Credit Cards

The Paget Report made one comment about Henri Paul's credit cards: "Transactions on these cards were not provided in the French dossier."[598] (WFJ)

A key element of the investigation of Henri Paul's activities would have to be an analysis of the five credit cards he was running at the time of his death – yet the French police did not provide the transaction list on any of those cards to the British.

---

[a] Full details of the deposits are in Part 1, Finances section of the Henri Paul chapter.
[b] Where the denomination breakdown is known, the cash deposits were all in FF500 notes e.g. the first deposit of FF 49,900 on 18 December 1996 was paid in with 99 FF500 notes and 2 FF200 notes – 5 Feb 08: 82.8 (the inquest was told 2 FF400 notes, but that must be a mistake as it doesn't add up correctly). FF500 was the largest note denomination in circulation. Refer Laffan: 5 Feb 08: 97.15.
[c] At least five of these deposits were in cash. Full details of the deposits are in Part 1, Finances section of the Henri Paul chapter.

Paul Laffan apparently asked for the details, but when asked if he knew about the status of those inquiries, he replied "I do not, no".[599]

The question is: Why are Henri Paul's credit card transactions not known? If the French police really wanted to know what he was up to, it would have been a simple process for them to get the transaction details on each card. So why didn't they?

The next question is: Why does Laffan not follow up on any of his queries? When Hilliard asked about balances, Laffan says it was his "first piece of work, I requested that they find that information".[600] So, when he doesn't get a response from the French police, why doesn't Laffan go back to them and ask what is happening?

If someone in the UK police had sat down and asked: "What is the minimum activity we can do and still look as though we are doing something?" then what Laffan has done would be it. Laffan is then able to stand up in front of the jury and say "Well, I asked the questions".

Then the final question in this series is: Why doesn't the Coroner then ask Laffan to follow up on it? Why didn't Baker say: "Look, we've got six weeks still to go in this inquest: Could you please go back to the French and get these transaction details? Even if we have to go to Henri's parents or the card companies ourselves, let's get to the bottom of this."

Why didn't Baker do that?

Safety Deposit Box

Paul Laffan said he asked the French about Henri's safety deposit box – and admitted that he received no answer.[601] Once again the question is: Why did Laffan not follow up on this?

The Paget Report reads: "Henri Paul's parents stated that there was some cash inside [the safety deposit box] – around FF 30,000 – and a few letters and papers, given to ... Claude Garrec, for safekeeping."[602] (WFJ)

Garrec told the police: "When [the deposit box] was cleared after his death, there was an amount of cash, not a fortune, but it is for Henri Paul's parents to tell you what the sum was. Otherwise, there was nothing else."[603] (WFJ)

Henri's parents stated that there were "letters and papers". Garrec appears to go out of his way to say that there was only cash in the safety deposit box.

There is a conflict of evidence here that has never been addressed – not by the French, the British or the inquest. It is common sense that if "letters and papers" are kept in a safety deposit box, then they must be of some importance. Why did Garrec say "there was nothing else" besides the cash?

Is there a reason why Garrec – and possibly Henri's parents – did not want the police to see the content of the safety deposit box?

Why didn't the French or British police ask to see these documents? Why did Laffan not follow up?

Tax Returns

Under cross-examination Claude Garrec confirmed that he had seen Henri's tax returns after he died – and that the unexplained income was "of course" not declared.[604]

In contrast, in the last piece of evidence heard by the inquest, it was stated that the Pauls' French lawyers "had not as yet been able to trace any former tax returns" for Henri Paul.[605]

Analysis of tax returns is a critical part of piecing together a dead person's financial situation.

The fact is that Henri Paul's tax returns exist, or did exist, and Claude Garrec states that he has seen them. So, why has it been so hard for the French or British police to find them? If they couldn't see the copy Garrec had, why didn't they enquire of the French taxation authorities?

Why is the most basic police work so impossible to accomplish when it comes to investigating the death of this much-loved humanitarian Princess?

Coroner's Deception

Coroner Scott Baker told his jury during his Summing Up:

> **At the start [of the inquest][a], I told you it was not necessary to solve every sub-plot in the story and unravel every thread. You may think that there are certain matters relating to Henri Paul that simply cannot be resolved with any clarity…. Where the money in his possession when he died had come from; and … where all the money had been coming from that had been going in fairly regularly to his bank account. You may have speculative ideas, but these are, I suggest, quite simply mysteries that cannot be solved on the evidence. In any event, are they mysteries that are relevant to any verdict?[606]**

In tying the "mysteries" surrounding Henri Paul to his early suggestion that the jury don't put the effort into trying to resolve every issue, Baker has effectively put Henri Paul's finances into the "too hard" basket. He then suggests that this subject may not be relevant to the verdict anyway.

The question that was crying out to be asked was: Why is the issue of Henri Paul's large cash inflows still unresolved ten years – and two full investigations by the elite police forces of two modern nations – after the crash?

The answer to this starts to become clearer when one studies the evidence of Paul Laffan and the early approach taken by the French police. The failure by the French to ask the right questions of Henri Paul's banks indicates that

---

[a] Coroner's Opening Remarks: 2 Oct 07: 27.15: "You do not have to unravel every issue that emerges in the evidence to solve every sub-plot."

they had very little interest in determining where the unexplained money was coming from.

Laffan was a financial investigator for Scotland Yard. His failure to basically carry out even the slightest level of investigation into these matters indicates that he is either lazy, completely incompetent or part of a huge cover-up that is determined the source of Henri Paul's funds will not be uncovered.

Scott Baker tends to confirm the latter possibility, when in his Summing Up he steers the jury away from any attempt to study these issues, suggesting that they may not be relevant to the verdict anyway.

If there was a connection between the large money inflows to Henri Paul's bank accounts and his possible links to British and French intelligence agencies – when taken in conjunction with other evidence in this book – then that information could be <u>very "relevant</u> to any verdict".

Henri Paul and MI6

At the inquest MI6 became very sensitive around its connections with the Ritz Hotel.

Eugene Curley insisted that MI6 had no "interest in the movements and meetings of people at the Ritz".[607]

If that was true then any questions regarding Ritz guests or staff should not have been a problem for MI6.

Yet when Michael Mansfield started asking more specific questions – "members of the Middle Eastern community … who might be staying there"[608] – Robin Tam, the MI6 lawyer, intervened before the question was complete.

Even on a basic question of common sense – whether the security department would provide information about who was in hotels – Mr 4 refused to answer.[a]

Richard Spearman[b] stated that he "never visited the [Ritz] Hotel during my four years in Paris",[609] whereas his claimed boss[c] said "I used and other colleagues used the Ritz Hotel as clients and customers. It was a very

---

[a] Mr 4: "We did not have time to go round hotels and look at who was staying there and see who was of interest."
Mansfield: "No therefore the obvious way into some of these key places [hotels] would be, do you agree, this much, through the acting head of security for information?"
Mr 4: "I think that might lead me into an area where I would find it difficult to answer.": 29 Feb 08: 49.24.
[b] Mr 6 at the inquest – see later.
[c] Mr 4. Spearman's actual boss was Cowper-Coles – see earlier.

agreeable meeting place".[610] Spearman was posted to the Paris embassy on 26 August 1997[611], only 5 days before the crash. This indicates that MI6 avoided the Ritz Hotel for at least the four years after the crash. One could ask: Why would this be?

Spearman tied himself in knots over MI6 links with the Ritz Hotel. He confirmed that it is his understanding that "at no stage, in all the time that Henri Paul was at the Ritz, did the British security services contact him at all – [there was] no record of anything".[612]

When Spearman is then told that is incredible, he indicates the reason for this is "because we would be working with our French colleagues jointly".[613] Then when Mansfield wants clarification of that, Spearman says that "the details of that joint working would be properly recorded".[614]

On the one hand, Spearman is saying that the reason there was no contact with Henri Paul was because they would use their French colleagues to liaise for them – he says: "I am aware of other examples" of this sort of thing.[615] On the other hand, Spearman is saying that the British would have records of these joint liaisons, and there are no records of any contacts regarding Henri Paul.

On 29 November 2007 Ritz Hotel president, Frank Klein, told the inquest: "It does not surprise me at all … that [Henri] would have links with foreign security services."[616]

Two months later inquest lawyer, Jonathon Hough, referred to this. When cross-examining Claude Garrec on January 31, Hough altered Klein's "foreign security services" to: "French security services and with the embassies of other countries".[617]

Then the following week, on February 4, Hough went a step further, eliminating any foreign aspect, changing Klein's testimony to "the police and the security services of France".[618]

This is a critical distinction. MI6, the British security intelligence service, have outrightly denied any links with Henri Paul.[a] Klein's evidence points to the possibility of a connection between Henri Paul and MI6: Klein says "foreign security services" and given that Britain is a next door neighbour and closely connected to France, it is logical that MI6 could have been one of the security services included in Klein's statement.

Hough's misquoting of Klein limits Henri's intelligence involvement to French agencies, and thus excludes MI6 as a possibility.

There is a huge conflict of evidence between MI6 employees, on the one hand, and most other witnesses – Frank Klein, Claude Garrec, Claude Roulet and Richard Tomlinson – on the other.

---

[a] See below.

MI6 is either denying outright any relationship with the Ritz Hotel at all – Richard Dearlove, Mr 4 – or refusing to comment – Miss X.[a][b]

Klein, Roulet and Garrec all say that they expected a relationship between Henri Paul, on behalf of the Ritz, and MI6, would have been normal.[c] Tomlinson says that he recalls seeing a specific MI6 file on someone who worked at the Ritz Hotel in the early 1990s, and had a very similar profile to Henri Paul.[619]

The Pauls stated that it was "totally wrong" that their son worked for British intelligence.[620]

It appears though that if Henri had a relationship with MI6, his parents would not have known about it. They have said that "he never spoke to us about" his links with French intelligence,[621] yet Henri had DST contact numbers in his phone list.[622] The parents were also asked the question in a very confronting manner – "your son worked for the British Security Services".[623] It would be only natural for them to defend their son against allegations.

Evidence from intelligence agencies always has to be read in the context that what they say depends on whether it could adversely affect the national (UK) interest. If it could, then the truth won't be forthcoming.[d]

It is common sense that MI6 would have an interest in some of the people who stay at the Paris Ritz. Whenever the cross-examinations headed in this direction, the MI6 witness would either completely deny any interest or in

---

[a] Dearlove stated that "there would have to be a record [of MI6 using Ritz security] and I have told you in the case of the Ritz there was no record": 20 Feb 08: 138.21. Eugene Curley (Mr 4) insisted that MI6 had no "interest in the movements and meetings of people at the Ritz".: 29 Feb 08: 47.10.

Miss X was asked by Mansfield: "Mr Tomlinson ... would have been surprised if the Secret Intelligence Service did not have an interest in the Ritz, considering who stayed there from time to time. Can you help?" X replied: "I cannot on that matter, I am afraid.": 26 Feb 08: 133.12.

[b] It is difficult to work out exactly what Spearman is saying, but he appears to be indicating that there was no relationship – see above.

[c] Klein: "It does not surprise me at all ... that [Henri] would have links with foreign security services.": 29 Nov 07: 105.7.

Garrec confirmed that Henri Paul "would have contact with ... security services relating to other countries whose dignitaries, diplomats or whatever were coming to France": 31 Jan 08: 148.20.

Roulet confirmed: "If it is [a hotel guest] from abroad bringing [their own] security, then if it is a British person, British security services might need to contact Henri Paul": 5 Dec 07: 132.1.

[d] This is an issue that is addressed in Part 5 – it is shown that MI6 officers lied repeatedly under oath, in the "national interest".

some way would avoid answering the question.[a] The only MI6 witness who strayed from that line was Spearman, and he tied himself up in knots – see earlier.

If one presumed that MI6 would have an interest in the Ritz, the evidence indicates that the security department is the natural link. The accounts of Klein, Roulet, Garrec and Tomlinson point to Henri Paul being the primary contact for MI6 at the Ritz. Roulet said that relations with intelligence agencies were normally with the head of security but as deputy[b] "Henri Paul had very good contacts with the French police", and he was therefore the main contact.[624c]

Coroner's Misrepresentation

During his Summing Up for the jury Scott Baker said:

> **There is no evidence from any of the SIS witnesses that Henri Paul was ever of any interest to them. It may, of course, be a different matter with regard to the French security services, but we have not been able to explore that in evidence with the French and, <u>in any event, so what</u>?**[625]

Baker distances Henri Paul from any relationship with French or British security services. This is not a true reflection of the evidence.

Baker makes no mention of the clear evidence that: a) Henri had links to the DST in his phone list[626] and b) the DST had stated in a letter to the British investigation that "Henri Paul has been in touch with members of the DST".[627] According to the evidence, it is these dealings that would be expected as part of Henri's role at the Ritz. Nevertheless, it is relevant that Henri had links to the DST, proven from both sides.

The alleged relationship between Henri Paul and DGSE or MI6 has the most relevance to the crash. In his Summing Up, Baker does mention the Gerald Posner testimony of Henri's alleged pre-crash meeting with DGSE.[628d] The Coroner also includes Tomlinson's recollections of the MI6 file he saw.[629] However he omits the clear evidence – Klein, Roulet and Garrec – that supports Tomlinson's account. He instead puts to the jury Tomlinson's evidence standing alone against the avalanche of MI6 department evidence denying any relationship.

To top his arguments off, Baker, referring to the lack of courtroom evidence from the DST and DGSE, says "in any event, so what?" What is he

---

[a] The MI6 testimony on this is shown in more detail in Part 1, section on Links to Intelligence Agencies in the Henri Paul chapter.

[b] He had been acting head of security only since the end of June 1997.

[c] Prior to his employment Henri Paul had been recommended to the Ritz Hotel by a member of the French police: 29 Nov 07: 118.16.

[d] Gerald Posner is a US journalist – his evidence is addressed in Part 1, section on DGSE Meeting in the Henri Paul's Movements chapter.

suggesting here? Is Baker inferring that whether Henri Paul had connections with intelligence agencies is really completely irrelevant?

The whole concept of a staged crash relies on it being orchestrated by an organisation with resources. The crash – as this book will show – was too complex to have been carried out by any one individual.

Whether Henri Paul had connections to intelligence agencies gets to the very heart of the case Scott Baker was meant to be helping solve.

On balance, the evidence points to a direct connection between Henri Paul and DST, DGSE and MI6.

Were those connections beyond what would have been normal contact between a leading hotel's security department and an intelligence agency?

If the answer to that question is "yes" then one would expect Henri to have been paid well for his services.[a]

Henri's State of Mind

At the end of July 1997, Henri Paul joined some of his closest friends for a few days holiday at Cadaques in Spain.

Claude Garrec testified that during the break Henri was "tense" and was "on the phone to work … a lot".[630]

Henri's friend Dr Dominique Mélo was also there and spoke to the police in September 1997:

> **I found him tired and tense. In the course of our conversations, I learned that this was due to the great pressure he was under in his job at the Ritz, as he was having to manage the security single-handedly.**[631]

Mélo then added that she called Henri around the middle of August 1997: "He told me that he had a lot of work on, and that he could not get any weekends off."[632]

Both Garrec and Mélo directly connected Henri's increased stress level to his Ritz work. Henri had however worked in security with the Ritz for 11 years, so one would expect he would have been familiar with the ropes.

Henri's Ritz colleagues should have been asked about this. Were there a lot of phone calls to or from Henri during this end of July break? Did he seem stressed about his responsibility as acting head of security for the Ritz?

They were not asked. Why?

During this summer period, June to August, Henri received FF 240,000 – FF 80,000 per month – in extra unexplained and undeclared income. This represented a large acceleration in the rate of payments to Henri: in the

---

[a] See earlier section on Henri's Finances.

previous <u>six</u> months – December to May – he had banked net unexplained income of only FF 110,000.[a]

It is most unlikely that Henri was receiving this extra income for doing nothing. It is also evident that he was not sharing with his best friends the knowledge of whatever it was that he was doing to earn this money.

There is a possibility that Henri's increased stress at this time was connected to the large amounts of unexplained income he was receiving.

Medical Examination

On Thursday 28 August 1997 – three days before the crash – Henri underwent a medical examination for the continuation of his pilot's licence.

It was carried out by Dr Diane d'Ivernois who certified that "M Henri Paul ... fulfils the conditions of physical and mental fitness required of non-professional pilots.... Glasses must be worn for distance work."[633]

Two weeks after the crash Henri's personal doctor, Dominique Mélo, told the French police:

> I can tell you that as a health professional, I know that the medicals for pilots are very thorough and detailed – testing for signs of exogenisation, palpitation of the liver, a thorough neurological examination – and consequently a doctor authorised to perform such an examination could not overlook symptoms of alcoholic impregnation.[634]

Dr D'Ivernois has never been interviewed by the French or British police and was not heard from at the inquest.

Agents At The Ritz

Later evidence will reveal that during the weekend of 30-31 August 1997 both Henri Paul and Claude Roulet were working for a second employer – someone in addition to the Ritz Hotel.

Other evidence will indicate this mystery employer was an intelligence agency – British or French intelligence, or both.

---

[a] This figure is after deducting an unexplained cheque withdrawal of FF 80,000 on May 21. Without that, the figure would be FF 190,000 over the six months or nearly FF 32,000 per month. This is still under half the rate of income Henri received in the final summer period.

Timeline of Events: 30 August 1997 to 10.06 p.m.[a]

August 30
a.m.

4.25   James Andanson leaves home and drives to Vierzon then back home

p.m.

12.30   Claude Garrec drops Henri home after tennis and a drink at Café Pelican
        Henri tells Garrec he will be working and can't make it to dinner that evening

12.45   Badia Mouhib calls Henri – he says he won't be able to see her till after 3 p.m. Sunday

3.20   Diana and Dodi land at Le Bourget airport – travelling in the Harrods Gulfstream jet

4.35   Diana and Dodi arrive at Ritz Hotel after visiting Villa Windsor

5.30   Diana calls Rita Rogers and tells her they will be dining at the Ritz

5.32   Claude Roulet arrives at Repossi's jeweller in Place Vendôme – he waits for Dodi

5.44   Dodi arrives at Repossi's

5.50   Dodi leaves Repossi's

6.45   Roulet delivers Tell Me Yes engagement ring to Dodi

6.57   Diana and Dodi leave the Ritz heading for Dodi's apartment

7.01   Henri leaves Ritz Hotel

7.15   Diana and Dodi arrive at the apartment

7.30   Henri calls Didier Gamblin – he lets him know the couple will be leaving the apartment around 9 p.m.

8.15   Olivier Lafaye parks the Mercedes S280 in the Vendôme car park

8.20   Roulet leaves Ritz Hotel

8.33   Roulet phones Henri's home number

8.35   Roulet tries Henri's home number again

---

[a] Some timings are approximate – based on the available evidence.

HOW THEY MURDERED PRINCESS DIANA

8.45	Dodi calls his uncle and invites him to join them for after-dinner coffee at the Ritz
9.30	Diana and Dodi leave Dodi's apartment
9.45	Phone call to Roulet from the Mercedes 600
	Roulet calls the Ritz
	Henri visits Le Champmeslé Lesbian Bar
9.50	Diana and Dodi arrive at Ritz Hotel
9.57	Roulet tries to call Henri's mobile
9.58	Roulet tries to call Henri at home
9.59	François Tendil calls Henri
10.06[a]	Henri returns to Ritz Hotel

---

[a] A detailed Timeline of Events for the Ritz Hotel between 10.06 p.m. and 12.24 a.m. appears later in the book.

23   Driving Mission

Henri Paul enjoyed a relaxing summer's Saturday morning – a game of tennis with his best friend, Claude Garrec, followed by a drink at the Café Pelican. Garrec later told the police that "Henri drank a Coca-Cola".[635]

Henri regularly went to the Garrec's house for Saturday night dinner – but not this week. Garrec recounted that Henri told him: "This evening I'll surely be getting off work late."[636]

After leaving the café Garrec dropped Henri off outside his apartment, at 12.30 p.m.[637]

Soon after that – before 1 p.m. – Henri's new female friend, Badia Mouhib, phoned him. She later related that he could not see her until after Sunday at 3 p.m.[638] That was just after the time that Diana and Dodi were expected to leave Paris for London.

Unprecedented Behaviour

After lunch, Henri went into work and met with Philippe Dourneau and they headed out to Le Bourget airport to meet the arriving VIPs – Dourneau chauffeuring in the premier vehicle, the Mercedes 600, and Henri driving the back-up Range Rover.

In doing this though, Henri's behaviour was most unusual – even unprecedented.

Ritz president, Frank Klein, later said that Henri was not even meant to be at work that weekend – "no, he was not on duty".[639] Yet his close friend, Dr Dominique Mélo, said: "As soon as Henri learned Dodi and Diana were coming to Paris, he cancelled a short break that he had fixed in Lorient to see his parents."[640]

Witnesses also stated that in Henri's 11 years working for the Ritz, he had never before driven guests on behalf of the hotel. This was to be the first time.

Jean Hocquet, Henri's direct boss up to June 1997, stated that "it was not at all part of M. Paul's duties to drive cars, or to chauffeur people".[641] Frank Klein confirmed that "Mr Paul had never driven a guest at the Ritz before". He added: "It was not part of his job and he knew that full well".[642]

Rene Delorm had lived with and worked for Dodi in Paris for three years – since June 1994 – yet never even knew who Henri Paul was before 30

August 1997.[643] Not only did Henri Paul not drive guests, but he also did not drive for Dodi. Instead Philippe Dourneau was Dodi's regular driver in Paris.

Claude Garrec told the British police:

> [Henri] didn't particularly like driving cars.... If he could avoid driving he would.... Henri Paul only drove me on rare occasions....[644]

So Henri was not meant to be working, never drove Ritz vehicles, and avoided driving.

Yet on Saturday August 30 it was Henri Paul who drove the back-up car to the airport to meet Diana and Dodi.

Planning For Saturday

Henri Paul paved the way for this on the Friday.

Philippe Dourneau, Dodi's regular Paris driver, told the French police in 1998 that on the Friday Henri had asked him to have a Mercedes ready in order to collect Diana and Dodi and Henri himself would be driving the Range Rover back-up.[645] (WFJ)

And also on the same day – Friday, August 29 – Henri informed Jean-François Musa, the normal back-up driver, about the arrangements. Musa told the French police on September 1, the day after the crash, that Henri had asked him to "make himself available for chauffeur duties outside the Ritz Hotel at about 5 p.m. the next day."[646] (WFJ)

This timing left Henri the opening to be the back-up driver for the 3 p.m. arrival of the VIPs from Sardinia.

Airport Meeting

Why did Henri Paul – who wasn't meant to be working, never drove Ritz vehicles, and disliked driving – drive the back-up vehicle to the airport?

It will be shown later that during the journey into Paris with the couple the back-up car – driven by Henri – stopped following the Mercedes 600 and instead headed for a different location.

If Henri was involved in ensuring the safe transportation of Diana and Dodi from the airport, he would have arranged for a back-up car with Jean-François Musa at the wheel. This would have been a proper back-up car – one that stayed behind the Mercedes for the duration of the journey.

Henri had to have an important reason not to ask Musa, who was available, to carry out this task.

At the airport there is witness and photographic evidence of a close, intense discussion between Dodi Fayed and Henri Paul – this is despite the fact Dodi was travelling in the Mercedes, not the car Henri was driving.

Rene Delorm, Dodi's butler, who arrived with the couple, stated: "My boss stopped to talk to a heavy-set balding man in a grey suit and dark glasses. It was Henri Paul."[647] (WFJ) Bodyguard Trevor Rees-Jones also described it in his book: "Dodi walked directly up to [Henri Paul], shook hands and chatted."[648] (WFJ) And it was noted by a waiting paparazzo, Fabrice Chassery: "I even saw Mr Paul, who was talking to Dodi Al Fayed. The celebrities remained in the vehicle for a while – still on the tarmac – before departing."[649]

It is impossible to know exactly what was said as both witnesses – Henri and Dodi – died later that night. But it is clear that it was not in the Ritz's interests for Henri to be driving the back-up car – he was not a chauffeur. It is then common sense that Henri was doing this on behalf of his other employer, MI6. This would have been a meeting that was essential for Henri to have, if the plans for the rest of the Paris visit were to go smoothly. I suggest that Henri would have been told what to say by his intelligence handlers. It could have been along the lines of: "We're expecting a lot of pressure from the paparazzi on the ground and we have the security in hand. Please just trust us if we have to make recommendations on actions to take during your stay here to ensure the complete safety of you and the princess."

It will be shown that it was critical to the MI6 plan that Dodi would make decisions based on information from their agents, Claude Roulet and Henri Paul. Later that day, Henri and Roulet provided advice to Dodi – which he did follow – and it led directly to the deaths of Diana, Dodi and Henri.

Figure 6

Dodi Fayed listening intently to what Henri Paul has to say immediately after Diana and Dodi's arrival at Le Bourget airport on 30 August 1997.

Coroner's Misstatements

Lord Justice Scott Baker told the jury in his Summing Up:

[Henri Paul] seems to have been one of, if not the, central figure in coordinating arrangements and he went to Le Bourget to meet them. That was hardly surprising because he was acting head of security at the Ritz, but he was also close to Dodi and trusted by him.[650]

Baker said to the jury that it was "hardly surprising" that Henri Paul went to the airport. At best, this is very misleading and flies in the face of the evidence. It is true that Dodi and Henri had a very good relationship[a] but Delorm, who had three years of living and working with Dodi in Paris, never knew who Henri Paul was.

The evidence speaks for itself: Henri Paul was not allowed to drive for the Ritz and never did. Therefore it was a most unusual event for Henri – who didn't like driving – to turn up at the airport driving the back-up car. What is even more unusual is that this act was clearly premeditated by at least a day or two.[b]

Baker attempts to suggest that Henri's appearance at the airport was normal. The reality is that there was nothing normal about it at all.

---

[a] Several witnesses supported this. Jean Hocquet, Ritz Head of Security to June 1997, said: "Although Mr Dodi Al Fayed did not shake hands with virtually anyone, he did do so with M. Paul. They got on well fairly quickly, each of them clearly knowing where they stood.": Paget Report, p164. Other witness evidence is in Part 1, Employment section of Henri Paul chapter.

[b] There is separate evidence of Claude Roulet organising Henri Paul as back-up driver to the airport by the Thursday, August 28. This is included in Part 1, the Driving section of chapter 2C.

24 "We Didn't Know She Was Here"

Princess Diana and Dodi Fayed concluded their final cruise on Saturday morning, 30 August 1997.

Their Harrods Gulfstream jet departed from Olbia, Sardinia in the afternoon headed for Paris. The couple landed at Le Bourget airport at 3.20 p.m.

Apart from Philippe Dourneau and Henri Paul, a few uninvited personnel awaited the couple's arrival – a clutch of paparazzi, a police car and several police motorbikes.

Trevor Rees-Jones revealed in his 2000 book:

> **The airport had not received a sigma signal, which alerts that it is a state or VIP flight – no special instructions of any kind had been given. The Princess had not advised the British Embassy of her presence in France and had not requested any particular protection from the French authorities.... Trevor led his charges down the [aeroplane] stairs.... He could see several gendarmes and motorcycle police standing by....[651] (WFJ)**

Police Escort

The French police received prior warning that Princess Diana was coming.

A police officer in Le Bourget immigration control, Pascal Winieski, testified in 1997: "A few minutes before the aircraft touched down, a gendarme informed him that the Princess of Wales was due to arrive at Le Bourget airport that day".[652] (WFJ)

Operation Paget also described the 1997 statement of Chef Delebecque, Maréchal de Logis at Airport Gendarmerie, Le Bourget: "Delebecque stated that the flight was unannounced. The status of occupants was given to the Gendarmerie only five minutes before the Gulfstream aircraft landed. He did not state where that information came from." [653] (WFJ)

Rees-Jones told the inquest that they received a police escort that "peeled off at the edge of the airport grounds".[654]

The paparazzi also described the police presence. David Odekerken told the police five days later: "The people who met [the plane] ... [included] uniformed police officers, two motorcyclists. A marked police car was also present...."[655]

Rene Delorm, who travelled in the back-up car, stated: "We had a police escort until we hit the A1 autoroute, but no farther." [656] (WFJ)

An Ambassador's Investigations

Despite this clear evidence of French police knowledge of Princess Diana's presence, there has been a concerted effort to claim that French authorities had no idea the princess was in Paris.

Philippe Massoni, the Paris Prefect of Police, told Paget: "I did not know prior to the accident that the Princess of Wales was in France".[657]

British ambassador, Michael Jay, stated that following the crash one of his earliest moves was to investigate the level of French knowledge of Diana's presence in France. On the day of the crash he wrote in his diary: "None of us here knew the Princess was in Paris and nor did the French authorities."[658]

At the inquest Jay confirmed this under oath: "I certainly remember, by the end of that [first] day, as I said in the diary entry ... I was aware that the French were not aware of the visit...."[659] He said this was based on what he "had been told by the French authorities".[660]

Then on September 11 *Le Monde* published an article which threw doubt on the French position.

Jay immediately asked his private secretary, Paul Johnston, to investigate. Johnston wrote up an internal embassy memo the following day:

> **Sir M. Jay asked me to check with the [French] Interior Ministry whether the suggestion in *Le Monde* of 11 September that the Ministry had been warned of the Princess's visit to Paris on 30 August was true. I spoke to Gouyette (Diplomatic Adviser) who rang back today having checked with the relevant departments to confirm that neither the Ministry nor the Préfecture de Police had been aware of the Princess's visit. The first they had known was when the accident was reported around 00.30 [12.30 a.m.] the following morning.[661] (WFJ)**

Michael Jay confirmed at the inquest that "the French authorities did not know [about Diana's presence] and that followed the investigations made by ... Mr Cowper-Coles".[662] .

In his police statement Jay said: "Mr Cowper-Coles also asked the Embassy's Drug Liaison Officer, Chief Inspector Nick Gargan to make enquiries of the French Police as to whether protection had been requested for the Princess of Wales".[663] (WFJ)

Gargan wrote a minute to Cowper-Coles on September 15:

> **I spoke to Vianney Dyevres of the Brigade Criminelle this afternoon. He has spoken to the Chef d'Etat Major of the French Police VIP Protection Unit. They have assured him that the first they heard of the**

Princess of Wales' visit was when they learned of the accident at the Pont d'Alma.[664] (WFJ)

By 15 September 1997 – 15 days after the crash – four investigations into the level of French knowledge of the visit had been carried out by the British Embassy. There was Jay's initial investigation on the day of the crash, Paul Johnston's investigation on September 11-12, Cowper-Coles' investigation and Nicholas Gargan's investigation that was completed on September 15.[a]

MI6 Non-Intelligence

The French were not alone in this claimed state of ignorance.

Ambassador Jay had also written in his diary on August 31: "None of us here knew the Princess was in Paris"[665] – "us" being the British Embassy staff.

This indicates that Jay ensured that all the Paris embassy staff were interviewed or asked about this on the day of the crash. Outside of this diary entry there is actually no evidence of that occurring.

Operation Paget stated:

> **Neither the FCO in London, nor the British Embassy or Consulate in Paris, with the exception of Brigadier Charles Ritchie,[b] were aware of the presence of the Princess of Wales and Dodi Al Fayed in Paris [until] ... around 12.50 a.m. and 1.10 a.m. on Sunday.[666c]**

There are about 40 diplomatic staff in the British embassy[d], not including security and other service staff.

How many of these staff did the police interview?

Paget states: "Operation Paget has interviewed staff at the British Embassy who had a role in the events after the crash." [667e] (WFJ)

---

[a] Some may argue that Cowper-Coles' and Gargan's investigation were one and the same, but they were addressed separately at the inquest during Jay's cross-examination – see 11 Feb 08: 93.2 and 93.18. The lawyer also uses the term "all of those inquiries" to describe these multiple investigations: 11 Feb 08: 93.22.
[b] Ritchie stated that he became aware of Diana and Dodi's presence in Paris at "almost exactly five [minutes] to midnight" on 30 August 1997. That is about 30 minutes before the crash. Ritchie told the inquest that he and his wife were walking near the Ritz Hotel and his wife "went up to one of the paparazzi ... and asked who it was who was in the hotel and she was informed, 'It is your Lady Di and Mr Fayed'." 12 Feb 08: 142.10.
[c] This is around half an hour after the crash.
[d] See Diplomatic Service lists shown in Part 5, Movements of MI6 Officers section of MI6 in Paris chapter.
[e] The police indicate that they have been thorough in doing this – in the case of Steven Gunner, Paget says: "Wing Commander Gunner is posted abroad. Operation

This strategy is fundamentally flawed ... or very lazy investigation.

There is no connection between pre-crash knowledge of Diana's presence in Paris and an employee having "a role in the events after the crash".

We effectively have a situation where Paget has – by its own admission – not interviewed all embassy employees who could have known Diana was in Paris on 30 August 1997.

The Paget Report includes the statement accounts of nine embassy staff – Michael Jay, Keith Moss, Charles Ritchie, Keith Shannon, Stephen Donnelly, Timothy Livesey, Steven Gunner, Paul Johnston and George Younes.[668] (WFJ)

Of those nine, Paget only provides the first person evidence of one – Steven Gunner. The other accounts are all Paget descriptions of excerpts of their statements with Scotland Yard.

Gunner told Paget: "The first I heard of the <u>death of Princess Diana</u> was ... early on Sunday morning."[669] (WFJ) That is not saying that he was unaware of the <u>presence of Diana</u> in Paris – it is confirmation of when he found out about <u>Diana's death</u>.

The only embassy employee witness whose original words Paget published[a] is Steven Gunner. But Gunner has not said what Paget has claimed he said.

Gunner said he first heard of Diana's death on Sunday morning – not her presence in Paris. This then leaves open the possibility that Gunner could have been aware of Diana's presence in Paris at some point prior to the crash.

Although Paget did not provide the original words of any other witness statements, some of those have since been published, either through the inquest or *The Documents* book: Michael Jay, Keith Moss, Stephen Donnelly and George Younes.[b]

Those four people have all stated that the first they heard of Diana's presence in Paris was when they found out about the Alma Tunnel crash.[c]

The statements of Ritchie, Shannon, Livesey and Johnston have never been published – and of those, only Ritchie was cross-examined at the inquest. Ritchie admitted that he became aware of Diana's presence in Paris about half an hour before the crash.[d]

Paget officers have spoken to him, and [have received] correspondence".: Paget Report, p611.

[a] Rather than a Paget description of their evidence.

[b] Jay and Moss' statements were published in *The Documents* book; Donnelly and Younes' statements were heard at the inquest.

[c] These accounts are all shown in Part 5, the Knowledge of Diana's Presence section of the British Embassy chapter.

[d] See earlier footnote.

Paget expects the public to rely on them providing a truthful description of evidence for the accounts of Keith Shannon, Tim Livesey and Paul Johnston – all suggesting they were unaware of Diana's presence before the crash.[a]

Nicholas Gargan was also cross-examined at the inquest and he said the same.[b]

Paget says that "all SIS staff in post in Paris in August 1997, including those who have subsequently retired ... have provided signed statements".[670] (WFJ) The statements of Ms 1 and Mr 5 were read out at the inquest and Mr 6 and Mr 4 were both cross-examined.

Those four MI6 employees claim that pre-crash they were also unaware of Diana's presence in Paris.[c]

Out of the approximately 40 diplomatic staff in the embassy at the time of the crash, Paget has obtained and allowed to be declared evidence on this issue from just 12 – Jay, Moss, Ritchie, Shannon, Donnelly, Livesey, Gunner, Johnston, Spearman, Ms 1, Mr 5 and Mr 4.

There are up to 28 embassy diplomatic staff that Paget apparently never interviewed or took statements from.[d]

In turn, this leads to the inescapable conclusion that Paget has dishonestly claimed:

-        "staff at the British Embassy ... all stated that they personally had no prior knowledge of the Princess of Wales' visit"[671] (WFJ)

-        "neither the ... British Embassy or Consulate in Paris, with the exception of ... Ritchie, were aware of the presence of [Diana and Dodi] in Paris until ... somewhere between around 12.50 a.m. and 1.10 a.m. on Sunday 31 August 1997".[672] (WFJ)

The reality is that Paget cannot honestly make these claims because:

-        Scotland Yard interviewed well under a third of the embassy staff

-        at least one of the employees interviewed by the police – Steven Gunner – did not say they were unaware pre-crash of Diana's presence in Paris, as claimed by Paget.

---

[a] These accounts are all shown in Part 5, the Knowledge of Diana's Presence section of the British Embassy chapter.

[b] Gargan's account is shown in Part 5, the Knowledge of Diana's Presence section of the British Embassy chapter.

[c] There were more than four MI6 employees in the embassy that weekend, but the exact number is not known – see Part 5, MI6 in Paris chapter.

[d] It is difficult to be precise about the degree of Paget's failure to interview staff because a) Paget said it had taken statements from all MI6 staff but failed to declare the number; and b) we are not privy to the numbers of non-diplomatic staff at the embassy. Examples of non-diplomatic staff are George Younes and Nicholas Gargan. Younes was interviewed by Paget, but Gargan was not.

Why This Claimed Ignorance?

The general thrust of this evidence appears to be an attempt to distance the British embassy staff from involvement in the orchestration of the Alma crash. If the Paris embassy staff had no awareness that Diana and Dodi were even in France, then how could they possibly have been involved in an assassination plot to remove them in a Paris car crash?

The evidence from embassy employees is very similar to that claimed by the French authorities – they had no knowledge that Princess Diana was in France.

Is this possible?

When Princess Diana's plane touched down in Paris at 3.20 p.m. on Saturday afternoon, was there suddenly a media blackout?

We know the paparazzi were present and there is famous video footage of that arrival.

Are we seriously expected to believe that the video footage and paparazzi photos of Diana and Dodi arriving in Paris didn't make the television evening news on 30 August 1997?

The French media carried daily reports of Diana's movements, but as soon as she arrived in their capital, did they suddenly stop reporting it?

Was the "sea of people"[673a] (WFJ) present outside the Ritz Hotel at 10 p.m. – see later – aware that Diana was in town, but none of the 40 plus British embassy employees were? [b]

The general British embassy employee evidence that was taken – and the Paget claims[c] – don't really add up.

On Sunday 31 August 1997 Michael Jay wrote in his diary: "None of us here knew the Princess was in Paris and nor did the French authorities." [d]

---

[a] Philippe Dourneau, 3 September 1997 statement.

[b] The Roulet and Klein testimony doesn't make specific reference to Diana's presence in Paris, but they do recall the atmosphere of the time. Klein confirmed to Mansfield: "there would not have been anybody in France, unless they had their eyes shut, that would not have known that [Dodi] was there [on the *Jonikal* in the south of France] with Princess Diana": 29 Nov 07: 100.5. Roulet confirmed to Mansfield: "all the newspapers spoke about it ... virtually every day": 5 Dec 07: 111.2.

[c] Bearing in mind that Paget failed to interview most of the embassy staff – see above.

[d] When Jay did his Paget statement he addressed the issue of embassy knowledge of Diana's presence, yet he made no mention of this diary entry. Jay actually said nothing at all in his statement about his diary, but he did list embassy reports and other evidence. There is a possibility that Jay's 31 August 1997 diary could have been altered or updated well after the event. The evidence has been addressed in this section based on the presumption that has not occurred – in other words, it has been presumed that the diary entry Jay read out at the inquest was how it was written up on 31 August 1997. When Jay was asked by Burnett: "Do you keep a personal diary?"

Why did Michael Jay write this?

Is there a connection between knowledge within the British embassy of Diana's Paris visit and the ensuing crash?

There are two major reasons why this information could have – at that time – seemed important enough to record:

1)   Security concerns.

One could argue that Jay put this in because there may have been an expectation for the British or French to provide security for Princess Diana after her arrival in Paris. The claim that no one knew Diana was there would then release the authorities from any security responsibility.

Paul Johnston wrote to Judge Stéphan[a] in January 1999: "Following her divorce[b], the Princess had not wanted to have protection except for high profile public engagements. On this occasion, a private visit, she did not ask for protection."[674] (WFJ)

There was then an awareness in the embassy that Diana "had not wanted to have protection" – at least not provided by the UK authorities.

Even if Diana had sought official UK security protection for this trip to France, it wouldn't have been provided by the embassy, but by the UK police, possibly the Royalty Protection division.[cd]

There does not appear to be any logical basis for Michael Jay, or his Paris embassy staff, to have had concerns about providing security protection for Princess Diana in France.

2)   Knowledge of an orchestrated crash or assassination.

If Michael Jay knew that Diana and Dodi had been deliberately eliminated, then that could have led him to leave documentary evidence that the embassy was not involved.

A diary entry along the lines of: "None of us here knew the Princess was in Paris", could suffice.[e]

---

he answered: "I did when I was in Paris." 11 Feb 08: 102.6. The implication then is that Jay didn't necessarily keep a diary at other times. Why did Jay keep a personal diary in Paris, but not at other times in his life?

[a] Head of the French judicial investigation.

[b] In late-August 1996. Diana requested reduced protection in 1994 – see earlier.

[c] Diana's security protection issues are covered in the Surveillance chapter of Part 2.

[d] Ritchie detailed the extent of the embassy's role whenever an official visit – which this was not – took place: "We would not be informed of an unofficial visit; official visits, yes, because we often had to look after the Royal Air Force flight coming in, look after the crew and the bill would come to the defence section.": 12 Feb 08: 143.14.

[e] The full quote – shown earlier – includes a reference to the French: "None of us here knew the Princess was in Paris and nor did the French authorities." This book

HOW THEY MURDERED PRINCESS DIANA

This is a case of what I call "excessive distancing". It should have been enough for the British embassy not to have received any notification of the visit.[a] But Jay – and subsequently other embassy officials – took it an incredible step further, by claiming no knowledge of Diana's presence, even though she had been in Paris for around nine hours by midnight on 30 August 1997.

If the deaths of Diana and Dodi had been accidental then it would not have mattered whether the embassy staff knew Diana was present in Paris pre-crash. This issue of awareness of her presence only becomes significant if there is already evidence the crash was orchestrated. It has the effect of distancing anyone who was ignorant pre-crash of Diana's presence, of involvement in the assassination.

Michael Jay has indicated that he spent time and embassy resources on the first day trying to establish people's – both British and French – pre-crash levels of awareness of Diana's presence. According to his evidence, Jay appears to have done this, while neglecting to spend time ensuring the protection of Princess Diana from an invasive French embalming (see later) while she lay lifeless in the Paris hospital.

This indicates that Jay was more interested in distancing himself, the embassy and the French authorities from involvement in the crash, than in protecting the body of the dead princess.[b]

---

reveals that there had to be a close coordination between the British and the French, to both, succeed with the assassinations, and then also the huge cover-up. Jay's diary comment that the French didn't know about Diana's presence in their capital – and his continued enquiries in the following days to that effect, described in his statement (see earlier) – appear to be a part of the post-crash cover-up. Jay has effectively, in just a few words in his diary, provided a same day alibi for all French authorities – if they had no idea that Diana was in Paris, then they too could have had no part in orchestrating the crash. At the inquest Jay stated: "I received assurances from [my staff] that nobody among the French authorities was aware of her presence".11 Feb 08: 91.21. An "assurance" is "a statement ... intended to give someone confidence" (Oxford). The question is: Why did Jay need confidence that the French weren't aware of Diana's presence in Paris? If the Alma crash was just an accident then it would not have mattered whether the French knew Diana was there, or didn't know. This issue of knowledge only becomes significant if there is already evidence the crash was orchestrated.

[a] I am not suggesting that the embassy didn't know in advance – the evidence shows they would have – but "no notification" would be more believable than claiming no knowledge of Diana's presence until after the crash had occurred.

[b] In his 2012 book Cowper-Coles states: "The first question was why we had not known that the Princess was in Paris". Despite raising this issue, Cowper-Coles then proceeds to effectively ignore it – only mentioning Ritchie's account of finding out just before midnight (shown earlier). *Ever The Diplomat*, p182.

French Knowledge

The evidence from individual police officers is that they were aware of Diana and Dodi's visit even before the plane landed – Winieski, Delebecque.

This is confirmed by substantial eye-witness evidence from people who were present at the airport arrival – Delorm, Rees-Jones, Dourneau, Odekerken, Chassery.[a]

Trevor Rees-Jones says that the police were waiting for the plane even though there had been no communication that could have alerted French authorities that it was "a state or VIP flight". [675] (WFJ) This shows that the police had been tipped off about the arrival of Diana and Dodi from another source – Delebecque "did not state where that information came from". [676] (WFJ)

Why didn't Paget ask him?

The point is that both Delebecque and Winieski obviously should have been subjected to cross-examination at the inquest. Not only did that not happen, but the jury didn't even get to hear their statement evidence.

Why?

At the very least five police knew of Princess Diana's arrival in advance: the three drivers of the police car and two motorbikes, Winieski, Delebecque and probably their source for the information.

Are we then expected to believe that over the following nine hours these five or six police kept the information that Diana, Princess of Wales was in the city to themselves?

The conspiracy theory is that from 3.20 p.m. on Saturday through to 12.23 a.m. on Sunday – the time of the crash – both the media and the police present at the airport suppressed the knowledge that Princess Diana had arrived in Paris.

The media suppressed it from the general population and the police suppressed it from their bosses.

Yet the media's job is to disseminate information to the masses and a critical part of a policeman's job is to inform his or her bosses of vital security information of this nature.

"We Didn't Know She Was Here"

The suggestion that Massoni, Jay and Johnston have put forward is that there was a major suppression of information regarding Princess Diana's visit to Paris that day.

Such a notion is so ridiculous it is laughable – if it wasn't so serious.

---

[a] The full evidence from these people is in Part 3, Pre-Crash Actions chapter.

HOW THEY MURDERED PRINCESS DIANA

Why have the British and French taken this line of deception?

Because it simplifies the conspiracy denial: if the authorities could be shown to have no knowledge of even Diana's presence in Paris, then it turns any suggestion of their complicity in the crash into a fanciful theory.

The problem though is that it has never been proven that they had no knowledge and in fact the evidence shows that such a denial is a lie:

-       it's common sense that Diana and Dodi's presence in the French capital was a major news item for people in Paris, and this was supported by the media presence at the airport[a]

-       the couple were greeted by a "sea of people" when they arrived at the Ritz Hotel at 10 p.m., 2½ hours before the crash – see later

-       the police were already waiting at the airport for the plane as it landed.

The evidence then is not just that the police were aware of Diana's presence in Paris ahead of the crash – which they have consistently denied – but that they were aware that she was on her way even before the plane landed at 3.20 p.m.[b]

The jury never got to hear any of this key evidence – the "sea of people" comment and the police accounts of prior knowledge.

Why have the authorities lied about this?

To cover-up the truth: the neck-deep involvement of both French and British authorities in the crash, evidenced most graphically by their massive jointly-orchestrated cover-up.

This will become clearer as the story develops.

---

[a] When writing to his boss, James Andanson described the Diana-Dodi story as "the greatest news story of the last 50 years" – see earlier.

[b] Alain Guizard, a Paris photographic agent, received a couple of hours' notice of the impending arrival of Diana and Dodi's plane. He testified: "At around 12.30 or 1300 hours, I received a telephone call from Max Colin, a photographer in Corsica who told me that he had received information from the Olbia control tower in Sardinia that Princess Diana's aeroplane would be landing at Le Bourget in 40 minutes' time." 3 Sep 97 Statement read out 10 Mar 08: 142.6.

25   Airport to Paris

After landing at Le Bourget airport, Diana, Dodi and Trevor Rees-Jones set out for the Villa Windsor in the Mercedes 600 driven by Dodi's regular chauffeur, Philippe Dourneau. They were followed by Henri Paul driving the back-up Range Rover heading to Dodi's apartment – it also carried the luggage, Kez Wingfield, Rene Delorm, Debbie Gribble and Myriah Daniels.

Joining the procession were the police escorts and several paparazzi vehicles that had been waiting at the airport.

Witnesses saw black motorbikes, a black Peugeot 205 and photos being taken.[a]

"Dangerous Manoeuvres"

There were two identified paparazzi motorbikes: Stéphane Darmon and Romuald Rat (pillion) were on a blue Honda 650 and there was a white bike from the Angeli agency.

But witnesses clearly described more than two motorbikes.

Trevor Rees-Jones – the bodyguard in the Mercedes – gave a graphical account in his 2000 book:

> **They were surrounded by screaming motorcycles darting around the target vehicles, sometimes two to a bike so that the photographer could wield his camera and focus the powerful zoom lens.[677] (WFJ)**

Kez Wingfield, the other bodyguard, was in the front passenger seat of the back-up Range Rover. Three days later he told the police there were "numerous motorcycles"[678] and said:

> **The paparazzi's vehicles embarked on a series of dangerous manoeuvres in order to get photos. Indeed [a black Peugeot] 205 … overtook us very quickly on the right and then very suddenly cut in, in front of the Mercedes in which Mr Dodi and the Princess were travelling, braking very hard as it did so. This manoeuvre enabled the motorcycles following us to get very close to the Mercedes on both sides and to get some pictures. Meanwhile [the motorcycles] were constantly trying to squeeze between the Mercedes and the Range Rover.[679]**

---

[a] Full witness accounts are in Part 1, section on Journey from Le Bourget in Chapter 2A.

> **The black 205 ... made us brake very sharply, so much so that I was propelled forward and felt the pressure from the seat-belt on my chest. This was the first time in my experience that I had seen the paparazzi behaving so dangerously.**[680]

Rene Delorm saw the same black car:

> **A black car sped ahead of us and ducked in front of the Mercedes, braking and making us slow down so that the paparazzi on motorcycles could get more pictures. It was really frightening to see how aggressively these people could behave – all in the name of getting what would probably be a pretty lousy picture. They were risking their lives and ours just to get a shot of Dodi and Diana riding in a car. Unbelievable.**[681]

Debbie Gribble was sitting near Delorm and saw the motorbikes:

> **There were two or three motorcycles whizzing in and out between us[a] in a sort of S-shaped manoeuvre. I definitely thought that one of them was going to get knocked off. It was like a chase.... These motorbikes ... were black.**[682]

Darmon's bike was dark blue and the Angeli motorbike was white.

The witness evidence indicates strongly that there were several black motorbikes present – other than the two paparazzi bikes.

The driver of the black Peugeot 205 that cut off the Mercedes has never been identified.

Philippe Dourneau, the chauffeur in the Mercedes, told the inquest: "I remember the flashes of the cameras on motorbikes".[683] Other witnesses – Rees-Jones, Wingfield, Delorm – described photos being taken by pillions on the motorbikes.

Where are the Photos?

It is clear that photos were taken on this trip from Le Bourget, and it is also clear that if they were published they would be worth a great deal of money. If these photos had been taken by the paparazzi[b], then in some way, somehow, they would have found their way into the public domain. An example of this is the photos taken of an injured Diana in the crashed car – they eventually were published (see later). So why is it that the photos taken on the airport trip – that have no direct connection to the crash – have never been published?

This fact, when considered with the other clear evidence that there were non-paparazzi motorbikes present, indicates that the photos were taken by these other motorbikes. These motorbike riders were behaving worse than normal paparazzi: Kez Wingfield said: "This was the first time in my

---

[a] "Us" being the Mercedes in front and the Range Rover Gribble was in.
[b] The paparazzi have denied that any photos were taken.

experience that I had seen the paparazzi behaving so dangerously". He also said that even the paparazzi-hardened Diana[a] "was concerned that one of the chaps on the motorbikes was going to fall under one of our vehicles".[684]

As this story of August 30 unfolds it will become clear that aggressive behaviour by pursuing large black motorbikes becomes a theme of that day in Paris.

It is true that the paparazzi followed Diana and Dodi during the afternoon and evening of August 30 – but there is also repeated evidence of these big dark motorbikes. It will become clearer that they were not paparazzi, but were extremely aggressive and were flashing photos right up to those taken just before the entrance to the Alma Tunnel.[b]

Where are the photos?

Were these big bikes ridden by people who were pretending to be invasive paparazzi trying to build pressure on the visiting group – pressure that later in the evening would escalate to a crescendo that eventually led to unusual decisions being made, and which in turn culminated in the tragic crash?

The truth of what occurred will emerge as this book progresses.

The Non-Back-Up Car

Range Rover passengers and the following paparazzi revealed that at one point along the freeway Henri Paul made a rapid exit and stopped following the Mercedes 600.

Myriah Daniels said Henri "cut across all lanes of traffic and … barely made it [to] the off-ramp".[685] This was supported by Debbie Gribble who confirmed that "there was one manoeuvre when the driver drove across a number of lanes quite suddenly".[686]

Fabrice Chassery viewed this as part of the following paparazzi. He told the police on September 4: "Suddenly the Range Rover, which was 200 metres in front, effected a sudden, even dangerous manoeuvre, going from the extreme left-hand lane to leave directly towards Neuilly".[687]

After shaking off the pursuing vehicles, the Mercedes 600 carrying Diana and Dodi proceeded to the Villa Windsor, where the couple spent approximately half an hour being shown around.[c]

---

[a] She had 17 years' experience of being pursued by the paparazzi.

[b] See later.

[c] There has been some debate about whether Diana and Dodi visited the Villa Windsor with a view to living there. The general evidence – see Part 2, section on Future Location and Living Arrangements – indicates that by August 30 Diana and Dodi had already ruled out Villa Windsor as a potential home. Frank Klein stated: "The Villa Windsor at the end of August and September/October 1997 was still under

Meanwhile Henri Paul drove the staff and luggage to Dodi's apartment. After offloading, he and Kez Wingfield continued on in order to catch up with the group at the Villa Windsor.

---

renovation/restoration". 29 Nov 07: 67.21. Diana and Dodi may have visited Villa Windsor on August 30 to check out the possible acquisition of antique furniture.

26   Preparing the Decoys

After leaving Villa Windsor, the Mercedes 600 headed for the Ritz Hotel and CCTV footage shows the couple entering the rear of that building at 4.35 p.m.

Some of the paparazzi, who had followed the Range Rover from the airport, were already at the Ritz. Other paparazzi had started assembling out the front from about 4 p.m.

Once at the Ritz, Princess Diana had her hair done and made at least two phone calls – one to her journalist-friend Richard Kay and another to Rita Rogers.

Dinner Arrangements

Rogers told the inquest that Diana called around 5.30 p.m.[a688] and said: "I am having dinner at the Ritz".[689] This was supported by Dodi's uncle, Hasseen Yassin, who received a call from Dodi at about 8.45 p.m. He said Dodi invited Yassin "to join him and Diana at the [Ritz] restaurant for coffee after their dinner". [690] (WFJ) Mohamed Al Fayed also testified that it was his belief that "they were going back to the Ritz" for dinner.[691]

Claude Roulet stated under oath:

> **Dodi asked me to find some interesting restaurant. I proposed him a choice of restaurants. Among them was not Benoît.... But Dodi told me that he made another choice, he would like to go to Benoît,[b] and he asked me to reserve there for them.... I booked under my name to be sure that no one knows who was coming.[692]**

Why is there a conflict here?

---

[a] Paris time.
[b] A local restaurant, called Chez Benoît.

HOW THEY MURDERED PRINCESS DIANA

Why do people close to Diana and Dodi – Rita Rogers, Mohamed, Dodi's uncle – say the dinner was to be at the Ritz, when Roulet says Dodi asked him to book Chez Benoît? [a]

Why has no investigation ever interviewed any staff from Chez Benoît?

Preparing the Decoys

There is a period of nearly an hour – between around 4.40 and 5.30 p.m. – when Claude Roulet, Henri Paul and Dodi Fayed were all in the hotel and appear to have discussed arrangements for that evening.

Later evidence will indicate that there would have been a discussion about paparazzi pressure. It was shown earlier that there was a key meeting between Henri and Dodi at the airport – but since then there had been the horrific ride from the airport, where fake paparazzi had been acting dangerously and aggressively around the Mercedes. [b]

The evidence will also show that two other issues must have been discussed at this point – first, letting Dodi know about a decoy restaurant plan to let people know the couple would be dining at Chez Benoît, when they actually were planning dinner at the Ritz Hotel.

The second discussion point was around their plans for the after-dinner journey back to Dodi's apartment near the Arc de Triomphe. Henri or Roulet would have told Dodi that if necessary they could use a decoy plan for that trip – leaving the main Mercedes out the front and departing in a different car out the back of the hotel. Later evidence indicates that Dodi was told to let Henri know if he felt pressured by the paparazzi and wanted to employ this decoy plan.

The restaurant decoy plan would have been to let Dodi know the paparazzi and staff would be informed of the false dinner destination – Chez Benoît. Ostensibly the purpose would have been to help relieve the paparazzi pressure on Diana and Dodi.

What actually occurred is the staff were told Chez Benoît (see later) but the paparazzi weren't. Instead there is evidence – shown later – that the paparazzi were aware dinner would be at the Ritz.

The real purpose of this plan appears to have been to help set up the eventual cover-up. If it could be shown the couple were intending to dine at Chez Benoît, then it helps remove the possibility for assassination.

Effectively Henri Paul could not be the driver[c] – he was at the Ritz. Also there would be no opportunity to switch to the second Mercedes – as occurred

---

[a] It will be shown later that there was an expectation amongst some of the Ritz staff that Diana and Dodi were going to Chez Benoît for dinner – this is something they were told by Henri Paul and Claude Roulet.

[b] See previous chapter.

[c] The importance of Henri Paul as driver will become clearer later.

at the Ritz. That was an essential part of the assassination because it enabled the seat belts to be tampered with and also ensured there was no back-up car.

The plan was to pin critical decisions on Dodi, who would be dead – Chez Benoît was chosen by him (Roulet) and he decided on the Mercedes decoy plan that led directly to the deaths – see later.

The methods used by MI6 to set up and bring about both these decoy plans – apparently communicated to Dodi between 4.40 and 5.30 p.m.[a] – will become clearer as the evidence revealed in this book develops.

---

[a] Although there is no direct evidence of Dodi being informed of these plans at the Ritz, there is substantial later evidence that indicates this is what must have occurred. The reason for the lack of evidence is that there were only three witnesses – Dodi, Henri and Roulet: two of them are dead and the third, Roulet, was an MI6 agent.

27   "Tell Me Yes"

During the late afternoon of Saturday August 30, Dodi Fayed's primary concern appears to have been the purchase of the Repossi engagement ring, "Tell Me Yes" – the one Diana had seen a week earlier in the Monte Carlo window.

To that end, Dodi had told Roulet "to ensure that [the] ring be available for them in Paris."[693]

The Repossi Paris store was actually closed for the holidays.[694] Alberto Repossi, the owner, testified: "I went with my wife and my brother-in-law from Monaco to Paris and I called the [Paris] staff to have everything to be prepared" for Dodi's visit.[695]

CCTV footage from the store reveals that Dodi arrives at 5.44 p.m. and joins Roulet, who had been waiting there for him since 5.32.[696]

Determining exactly what occurred in the Paris Repossi store on 30 August 1997 is very difficult, primarily because the two main living witnesses – Claude Roulet and Alberto Repossi – are proven liars.[abc]

Repossi's Lies

Alberto Repossi's account has always been – since his first interview in 2005 – that Diana and Dodi selected the "Tell Me Yes" ring in early August, but it needed to be resized in Italy, and Dodi collected it from the Paris store on August 30.[697]

If this account was true, then it would have been unlikely that Dodi needed to visit the Repossi store on August 30 – the ring could have been simply delivered to the Ritz, or Roulet could have just picked it up. In other words, if August 30 was just a straightforward "ring pick-up" then it would not have required the Repossis to:[d]

---

[a] Re Repossi, see Part 2, Engagement chapter; re Roulet, see later in this book.
[b] Alberto's wife Angela Repossi's evidence was not heard at the inquest but a third person account of her 20 April 2006 statement can be read in the Paget Report pp73-75. Her evidence basically corroborates her husband's accounts and is contradicted by the CCTV footage and other evidence.
[c] Repossi's inquest testimony is at 10 Dec 07: from 1.22. Operation Paget included his statement evidence in the Paget Report pp65-71.
[d] At the inquest Repossi suggested that Diana had requested him to restyle some of her own jewellery and that was why they were to meet on August 30: 10 Dec 07:

1) specially open up their Paris store, which was closed for the holidays
2) interrupt their holidays to travel to Paris to be present in the store[698]
3) organise the extra staff required to serve Dodi and Roulet.[699]

In his 2005 statement Repossi paints a picture of Dodi collecting the "Tell Me Yes" ring on August 30: "I showed him the ring which he had chosen. We laughed about the name of the ring, 'Say Yes'.... He thanked me for opening the shop for him. He told me that he liked the ring very much and that it was 'to announce the engagement with Princess Diana'." [700] (WFJ)

The CCTV footage[a] reveals an entirely different picture of the visit: Dodi arrives and Alberto, Angela and two staff are milling around showing Dodi various items – the CCTV images are not clear enough to tell what these items are. There is a lot of walking back and forth and viewing in a short period of a few minutes.

Repossi said that Dodi put the "Tell Me Yes" ring "in his pocket"[701] (WFJ) but the CCTV shows that never occurred – Dodi left the store without any merchandise.

Repossi then said that he "accompanied him to the door" as he left[702] (WFJ) – the CCTV reveals that Dodi shook hands with Repossi at the viewing table and went upstairs unaccompanied and left the store.

Repossi's accounts are littered with inaccuracies similar to the above.

The question becomes: Why has Alberto Repossi lied from his earliest police statements, right through to the inquest?

The answer will emerge as we progress.

Roulet's Lies

In Claude Roulet's earliest 1998 statement[b] he described this first Repossi visit[c] and said that Dodi "chose four or five rings ... and I myself took the rings to the hotel".[703] (WFJ)

This evidence is significant for two reasons:
1) Roulet only mentions rings – he makes no suggestion of Dodi looking for other jewellery
2) Roulet said he took the rings back to the Ritz – but the CCTV reveals that all he carried away from that first visit was a piece of paper.

22.16. The fact that Diana had not met earlier with Repossi, and did not meet with him on the 30th, indicates that this could not be correct.

[a] The CCTV footage is viewable on the inquest website – see Evidence for 5 Dec 07: Repossi visits - CCTV camera footage.

[b] Roulet had made other earlier statements but this was the only occasion on which the French investigation asked him about the engagement.

[c] Roulet made two visits to Repossi's on August 30 – see below.

Roulet's various accounts for the reason Dodi visited the store on August 30 have been:

Aug 1998: French statement – "he chose four or five rings"[704] (WFJ)

Mar 2005: British statement – "he made a choice of four to six rings"[705]

Oct 2005: British statement –   "Dodi tried to describe to us what the ring was like. They got lots of rings out, but they did not look like the one that Dodi wanted.... Dodi ... chose four or five"[706] (WFJ)

Jan 2006: British statement –   "Dodi ... was looking for the ring that he had seen with Diana, Princess of Wales, in Monte Carlo.... Dodi ... chose a few pieces that he took with him"[707] (WFJ)

Jul 2006: British statement –   "he is looking for the ring which he saw in the window of the Repossi boutique in Monte Carlo"[708] (WFJ)

Dec 2007: Inquest – "Dodi explained what ring they saw in Monte Carlo"[709] and "he started to ask for bracelets, when [Repossi] did not find a ring suitable for him"[710]

In Roulet's two earliest statements he makes no mention of Dodi visiting Repossi's on August 30 to collect a ring that Diana and him had seen in Monte Carlo, yet in his four other accounts he does. It is difficult to know why this would be, except that the French (in 1998) did not ask much about this issue and the Paget March 2005 statement comes across as an overview.[a] Having said that, this is a fairly major fact Roulet has left out.

   Other evidence[b] – a fax from Mora; phone calls between Klein, Roulet, Repossi Monte Carlo and Dodi – strongly indicates that this was the case: that Dodi visited the Repossi Paris store on August 30 to identify and collect the ring the couple had already seen.

   The question then becomes: Was this an engagement ring that Diana and Dodi had seen and that Dodi was on August 30 trying to track down?

   In March 2005, when Roulet was asked: "Did the purchase of that ring suggest to you a planned engagement?" he answered: "Yes, although officially nothing had been settled as far as I know."[711]

   On other occasions Roulet said:

Oct 2005 British statement – "this ring was more in keeping with what Dodi was looking for in giving this present"[712] (WFJ)

Jul 2006 British statement – "Dodi ... wanted a gift for the Princess of Wales"[713] (WFJ)

Dec 2007 Inquest – "it was nothing special, very definite"[714]

   Shop assistant Emanuelle Gobbo, who was present on both the Paris store visits on August 30, gave very clear evidence at the inquest: "we presented various diamond rings, because we realised that it was for an engagement ring".[715]

---

[a] See Paget Report p59.

[b] See earlier, section on Identification Panic in the Final Holiday chapter.

Seen in the light of Frank Gelli's account of Diana's August 23 phone call[a] and other earlier evidence, it becomes clear that Dodi was not just seeking a gift, but an engagement ring.

Roulet's evidence in 4 of his 5 statements prior to the inquest was that Dodi was specifically looking at rings. His evidence on this differed for the first time in January 2006 when he said that "all the items that had been originally selected" were written "on the back of Mr Mora's fax".[716b] (WFJ) Then at the inquest he said for the first time: "[Dodi] started to ask for bracelets, when he did not find a ring suitable for him".[717] This directly conflicts with his four earlier accounts – which the jury didn't hear – and also Gobbo's account: "it was for sure, yes, understood that he was looking for a ring".[718]

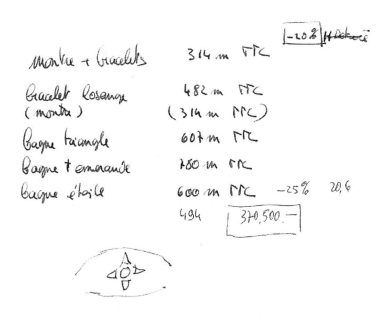

Figure 7	Priced jewellery list, on the reverse side of the Mora fax, compiled by Claude Roulet while at Repossi's on 30 August 1997. At the foot of the list is a drawing which appears to be Roulet's representation of the "Tell Me Yes" ring.	

[a] See earlier Final Holiday chapter.

[b] This list on the back of the fax is reproduced below. Roulet said it was written whilst in the Repossi store – see later.

It is clear that the priced list Roulet said was written by him on the back of the fax during the initial store visit[719] (reproduced above) included two items (out of five) that weren't rings – two watch bracelets.[720] This documentary evidence runs against the four Roulet statements, Repossi and Gobbo's evidence, and also a "ring sign" that Roulet made to Repossi at 6.36 p.m. during the second visit.[721a] It may simply be that Dodi was seeking the ring they had seen in Monte Carlo, but may have seen the watch bracelets in passing. It is obvious, in the final outcome, that they were not purchased. On balance, the general evidence is clear that Dodi was seeking a particular ring and was looking at rings.

In various statements Roulet has provided differing accounts of what occurred after Dodi chose the rings:

Aug 1998: French statement – "I myself took the rings to the hotel. At Dodi's request I returned to the jeweller's to negotiate a discount"[722] (WFJ)

Mar 2005: British statement – "he asked me to go back [to the store] and negotiate a reduction"[723]

Oct 2005: British statement – "I returned to the hotel with the rings.... I brought them to Dodi ... [who] asked me if I had negotiated a price on the rings"[724] (WFJ)

Jan 2006: British statement – "Dodi Al Fayed chose a few pieces that he took with him and I stayed behind"[725] (WFJ)

Jul 2006: British statement – After shown the CCTV footage: "[I returned] to negotiate a price for Dodi Al Fayed, on the items of jewellery he had chosen during his first visit. I also had to know if Dodi Al Fayed could pay for these with an American or British credit card.... From memory, I had to collect these items of jewellery."[726] (WFJ)

Dec 2007: Inquest – Before the CCTV footage is shown: "I did take the jewels" on the first visit.[727]

After the CCTV footage is shown: "I gave [Dodi] the prices. He asked me, 'What are these prices in dollar and in UK pounds?' and then he told me, 'Can you get a discount more?' So that is why I returned to Repossi – to ask, what was an additional discount they could give on these items?"[728]

In all of Roulet's accounts prior to being shown the CCTV footage in July 2006, he had claimed that the rings were taken back to the Ritz at the conclusion of the first visit – in 1998 and 2005 he says he took them back himself and in January 2006 he says Dodi took them back. In July 2006 Roulet is forced to admit that the rings were taken later, but again at the inquest he reverts to his earlier mantra that "I did take the jewels" on the first visit – until the footage again proves otherwise.[b]

---

[a] Roulet returned to the store without Dodi on the second visit – see later.

[b] Later in this book a parallel will emerge with the way in which Roulet provided his evidence regarding the time he left the hotel on the Saturday night – again proven

This evidence is significant, because had Roulet been correct in saying that Dodi or Roulet took the rings back after the first visit, this would have been proof that Dodi was seriously looking at purchasing a ring other than the "Tell Me Yes" ring. The importance of this distinction should become clearer later.

Roulet has given accounts of Dodi requesting a price reduction via Roulet after the first visit – Roulet often gave this as the sole reason for the second visit. In his evidence Roulet has stated that this was "on the items of jewellery he had chosen during his first visit"[729] (July 2006) (WFJ) and "on these items"[730] (inquest).

It is significant that there is only one item on the Roulet list with discount calculations right next to it, and that is the Étoile ring. A close look at these calculations is very revealing – this is addressed below. This assessment of Roulet's calculations proves that, contrary to his evidence, he was working only on the Étoile ring.

This evidence becomes significant when it is seen in the light of Gobbo's testimony regarding the Étoile ring, which the jury didn't hear: "He ... explained that in his view 'Étoile' and 'Tell Me Yes' are the same range of rings."[731a] (WFJ)

In other words, the sole ring Dodi requested Roulet to seek a discount on was a ring from the same range as the "Tell Me Yes".

This is even more significant when we establish which rings Claude Roulet actually took to Dodi after his second store visit.

Roulet's account has consistently been that several items were taken back to the hotel: at the inquest he said: "Maybe four or five".[732] He also said, referring to the Repossi receipt for the two rings signed by Roulet (see below): "I am persuaded that there is another sheet which reported the other item I took".[733]

Repossi: "Mr Roulet never went out, except with two rings".[734]

Gobbo: "the only pieces he took away were the two rings".[735]

The only documentary evidence is the Repossi receipt, signed by Roulet, which reveals that two rings were taken by Roulet – the Étoile and the "engagement" ring, which was the "Tell Me Yes" ring that Dodi bought.[b]

---

wrong by the CCTV shown to him by the police, and again reverting to his previous mantra at the inquest, until proven wrong for a second time by the footage.
[a] Gobbo's evidence was presented in the Paget Report in the third person.
[b] Repossi was asked by the inquest to procure the receipts on either side of this receipt – 10 Dec 07: 92.6. This evidence was never produced, but that is not evidence of additional rings being taken. Repossi was treated rather shabbily by the inquest and it may be that he decided not to cooperate any further.

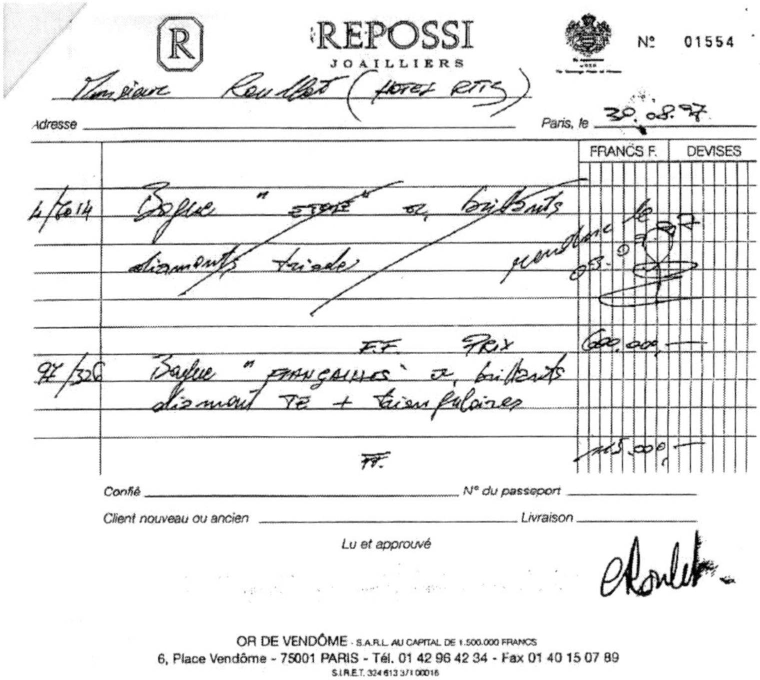

REPOSSI
JOAILLIERS
N° 01554

Adresse

Paris, le 30.08.97

	FRANCS F.	DEVISES

Confié ________ N° du passeport ________

Client nouveau ou ancien ________ Livraison ________

Lu et approuvé

OR DE VENDÔME - S.A.R.L. AU CAPITAL DE 1.500.000 FRANCS
6, Place Vendôme - 75001 PARIS - Tél. 01 42 96 42 34 - Fax 01 40 15 07 89
S.I.R.E.T. 324 613 371 00016

Figure 8

Repossi receipt for two rings signed by and given to Claude Roulet on 30 August 1997. The ring purchased by Dodi Fayed was the second one listed. “Bague fiancailles” means “engagement ring”.

At the inquest Roulet appeared to diverge from his insistence that there were several items taken back to the Ritz, when he quoted Dodi: “He said, ‘I take this one, put <u>the other one</u> in the safe and give them back to Repossi’.”[736]

It is fair to conclude that only two rings were taken by Roulet to Dodi after the second visit:

1) The Étoile ring – a ring from the same range as “Tell Me Yes”
2) The “Tell Me Yes” engagement ring which Dodi purchased.

The evidence is that Dodi went to the Repossi store on August 30 seeking a specific ring that had been seen and liked by Diana in Monaco on August 23. The evidence from Roulet in July 2006 – not heard by the jury – is that “he does not find it and he is very disappointed”.[737] (WFJ)

This makes sense: Dodi has sought out a ring he knows Diana likes – firstly, by telephone from the boat immediately after the Monte Carlo store visit on August 23, and now secondly, in person, and he is frustrated because

Repossi's are unable to produce the ring that both Diana and he had already seen. "Very disappointed" may even be an understatement.

Why is it that Dodi picks out the Étoile ring from the other rings he is shown, when he is not able to locate the original ring he saw?

The link is given in Gobbo's police statement: "'Étoile' and 'Tell me Yes' are the same range of rings". [738a] (WFJ)

In other words, there is an indication here that Dodi had already seen the "Tell Me Yes" ring on August 23, couldn't now locate it, so had shown an interest in the nearest looking ring: the Étoile ring.

This is supported by Dodi's reaction when Roulet finally produced the correct ring: "I showed [it] to Dodi, telling him that it was called 'Tell Me Yes'. Dodi immediately said, 'that's the one I have chosen'." [739] Roulet said that Dodi took that ring "without seeing it". [740b]

Why would Dodi react like that? The only reason he didn't look at it would be if he already had seen it before – he recognised that name and had already seen that ring a week earlier, and knew it was the one that Diana liked.

At the inquest the insinuation was made by Richard Horwell[c] and Claude Roulet that Dodi immediately chose the "Tell Me Yes" ring because it was cheap – Roulet said: "I remember that I mentioned that it is less expensive than the other items". [741] In all his previous statements Roulet had never suggested this.

It does not make much sense that Dodi, who was a wealthy man, would skimp on the purchase of a ring for Diana. There is however a possibility that Diana, who was very aware of her public image and was not comfortable with ostentatious displays of wealth, may have deliberately shown an interest in a less expensive engagement ring – it may have been a romantic choice for her.

There are a number of unusual coincidences:

1)   Diana and Dodi see a ring in Repossi's Monte Carlo store, yet no one is able to locate it even though Dodi arranges for the store to be rung later that same day

2)   Repossi's still can't locate the ring in Paris, even though Dodi is there in person to describe it

3)   Suddenly the Repossis produce a ring that Dodi – when told the name of it – is instantly happy with and chooses.

---

[a] This is confirmed on the Repossi September 3 invoice for the "Tell Me Yes" ring – shown below – which is described as "Étoile".

[b] Roulet is possibly lying about Dodi's reaction – Roulet didn't mention this until his third statement in October 2005, but his earlier accounts were not as detailed.

[c] MPS QC.

"It Was Not So Significant"

Why is it that Repossi's were unable to identify a ring in their window even though they were rung about it on the same day?

Roulet's evidence of how Dodi described the ring on August 23 was: "Very vaguely. He said it is a simple ring in gold".[742] We only have Roulet's account on this: why wasn't Klein – who received the original call from Dodi – and Mora – who described the ring to Repossi's – asked specifically about this?

In this context, it is significant that when Roulet was first shown the "Tell Me Yes" ring on Angela Repossi's finger, the CCTV shows he immediately started to draw it – no doubt to show Dodi the drawing.[743abc] This is an indication that he recognised the design as being similar to what Dodi had earlier described to him. This suggests that Dodi had not described a "simple ring in gold" – see the photo of the "Tell Me Yes" ring.[d]

Alberto Repossi stated in his evidence:

1)   "I also suggested to [Dodi] and showed him the same ring but one larger and more impressive [Étoile], saying to him that it was a better proportion for Princess Diana."[744] (WFJ)

2)   "I thought that for a lady like the Princess of Wales, we could have given a ring which was the same size but more significant."[745]

3)   "the ['Tell Me Yes'] ring was not so significant"[746]

4)   "I had two other clients, some significant clients, two Royal Families to take care about at that very moment, and these sales were much more significant than this one"[747]

Repossi has made it very clear, several times, that in his opinion Diana was suited to a more expensive and significant ring than the "Tell Me Yes".

---

[a] Roulet's drawing was made at the foot of the list he wrote on the reverse of Mora's fax – reproduced earlier.

[b] This is confirmed from the Paget Report, where it describes Repossi's reactions to watching that section of the CCTV footage: "As he watched the footage Alberto Repossi stated, '[Roulet]'s in the process of taking it…. He's taken it. He puts it to one side and then he starts writing. Or perhaps he did that diagram there, that drawing.' It was confirmed to Alberto Repossi that Claude Roulet agreed that he was making the diagram. (Paget Note: The diagram is that of an oblong shape with a triangle on each side – representative of the shape of the 'Tell me Yes' ring.)": Paget Report, p68 (WFJ).

[c] At the inquest Roulet claimed that the drawing was of "the last item" on his priced list (5 Dec 07: 71.8) even though he had earlier admitted to Paget that it was the "Tell Me Yes" ring – see previous note. It was only when he was confronted with that reality by Mansfield that he backed away from that claim, and admitted that it was a "very close" representation of the "Tell Me Yes" design: 5 Dec 07: 118.15.

[d] Reproduced in Part 2, Figure 6.

Scenario

Something similar to the following scenario may have occurred:

When Repossi's Jewellers Monte Carlo received a call from the Ritz Hotel relating to a ring that Diana, Princess of Wales was interested in, I believe that Alberto Repossi would have been made aware of that call, before a response was made to the Ritz Hotel.

There is a possible explanation for why Repossi's couldn't locate the ring Diana and Dodi saw: It appears that the "Tell Me Yes" ring was described[a], but Repossi believed that Diana should have been getting a more expensive ring.

Repossi then agrees to open the Paris store in the hope of selling a "more significant" ring. Instead, when Dodi finally arrives at the store his mind is set on the "Tell Me Yes" ring and he is "very disappointed" when he doesn't see it. Six minutes later Dodi walks out of the store and returns to the Ritz with no rings.

Later, when Roulet returns to the hotel with his priced list, Dodi expresses an interest in only one ring – the Étoile[b] – but by no means says that he will purchase it. Dodi asks Roulet to see what discount he can get on it. Dodi sends him back with an instruction to still seek out the original ring he and Diana had seen in Monte Carlo.

When Roulet arrives at the store on the second visit the CCTV reveals that he is still looking at merchandise. I suggest that it is only when Repossi realises that he may not be making any sale at all, that the "Tell Me Yes" ring finally emerges.

Immediately Roulet sees it on Angela Repossi's hand he starts drawing it onto his piece of paper – see earlier. This is because Roulet has now finally been shown a ring that meets the description that Dodi has been telling him about from August 23.

Roulet then takes both the rings[c] back to the hotel "on approval" and Dodi immediately recognises the "Tell Me Yes" ring when Roulet mentions the name.

Why has Repossi lied so extensively in his evidence?

Repossi is clearly not a party to the conspiracy or cover-up of the events – if anything his lies could be used by people wishing to prove that engagement

---

[a] I am not suggesting Dodi would have necessarily remembered the name at that stage, but he may have described the ring. I believe that when Roulet eventually told him the name at the Ritz on August 30, then that may have triggered a memory of it.

[b] This needs to be viewed in the light of the analysis of Roulet's calculations on the back of the fax – see below.

[c] The Étoile and the Tell Me Yes.

could be a motive for murder. Unfortunately his lies and fabrications have led to most of his evidence lacking credibility. In saying this, I don't discount the fact that Repossi's evidence may have served to further confuse the inquest jury. In the final analysis, it may even have had the effect of undermining the evidence relating to an engagement.

Such a scenario (as related above) could have created a situation where Repossi felt he needed to fabricate a different story, in order to protect his reputation.

It is significant that the Repossis' niece, Alice, who was present during the Paris store visits on August 30, serving both Dodi and Roulet, has never been interviewed by French or British police and was not heard from at the inquest.

Roulet's Calculations

The following relates directly to Roulet's written workings on the reverse side of Mora's fax – reproduced earlier.

There is a direct connection between the figures close to the Étoile ring – "bague étoile" – and the conversion calculations further down the page: FF494,000 with a 25% discount equals FF370,500.

Taken at an exchange rate of FF6 to the $, this equals $61,750.

At FF9.8 to the £, this equals £37,806, which Roulet appears to have rounded down to £37,800.[a]

The "20.6" on the right hand side is the French VAT rate of 20.6% – this is calculated on the price before tax (as revealed in the final Repossi invoice for the "Tell Me Yes" ring (below). It is a difficult calculation for the average person to work back from the price after adding the tax – in this case on the Étoile ring, FF600,000 – in order to establish what the price before tax would be. Roulet appears to have used a crude method to calculate this 20.6% tax figure:

He seems to have taken the 20% first – 20% of FF500,000 would have given him FF100,000.

Next, he appears to have tried to calculate the 0.6%, but very crudely – he apparently has quickly calculated this basing it on the FF100,000, and arrived at an additional FF6,000.

He has added the 6,000 and the 100,000 together, making FF106,000.

Roulet has then deducted the 106,000 from the FF600,000 to arrive at FF494,000[b], which is the figure he has used to calculate the discount – see above.

---

[a] Roulet of course is using French figuring, which is why his "7" sometimes looks like a "2".

[b] The correct and exact figure before tax is actually FF497,512 – 20.6% of 497,512 equals FF102,487. FF497,512 + FF102,487 = FF600,000. The calculations are rounded to the nearest FF.

"Tell Me Yes"

Alberto Repossi travelled to Paris, from Monaco, to open their Place Vendôme store especially for Dodi. Dodi visited the shop at 5.45 p.m., but Repossi, who had also employed extra staff for the viewing, was in no mood to allow Dodi to purchase what he saw as a cheap ring, FF115,000 (£12,000). Repossi later said: "I thought that for a lady like the Princess of Wales, we could have given a ring which was the same size but more significant". So six minutes later, after only being shown other more expensive rings, Dodi left the store empty-handed.

It took another hour of Claude Roulet toing and froing between the Ritz and Repossi's before Repossi relented and handed over the ring Dodi had requested. Roulet finally delivered the Tell Me Yes engagement ring to Dodi in the Imperial Suite at 6.45 p.m.

Twelve minutes later, at precisely 6.57 p.m., Diana and Dodi left the hotel heading for Dodi's apartment.

REPOSSI
JOAILLIERS
MONTE-CARLO

COURRIER REÇU LE
25. SEP. 1997
HOTEL RITZ PARIS
DIRECTION

Paris le 03 Septembre 1997

Monsieur Frank J. KLEIN
THE HOTEL RITZ LIMITED
15, place Vendôme
75001
PARIS

FACTURE

Une bague en or et diamants model " ETOILE ".

Or 18 KT	grs.	7,60
Brillants	cts.	1,56
1 diamant TE	cts.	1,46

PRIX H.T. .... 95 357 F.F.
T.V.A. 20,6 % .... 19 643 F.F.
PRIX T.T.C. .... 115 000 F.F.

(Cent quinze mille francs)

ref. 97/326
Signé REPOSSI
Poinçon d' Etat
Poinçon d' atelier REPOSSI

REPOSSI
6. PLACE VENDOME
75001 PARIS

PARIS
6, PLACE VENDÔME, PARIS Iᵉʳ - TÉL. 01 42 96 42 34

Copy of exhibit CR/4

Figure 9

Repossi invoice raised on 3 September 1997 for the "Tell Me Yes" ring. Its description confirms that it was from the "Étoile" range.

28   MI6 Non-Intelligence

MI6 officers in Paris stated that no one was on duty on the weekend Princess Diana died.

Identifying MI6 Officers

At the inquest the Paris-based MI6 officers who gave evidence were provided with code numbers to protect their identities – Ms 1, Mr 4, Mr 5 and Mr 6.

Several factors indicate Richard Spearman and Mr 6 are one and the same person:

1)   Both men have said they went out to dinner with their wives.

Mr 6 confirmed at the inquest: "My wife and I were out at dinner ... on the evening of 31st August".[748ab]

---

[a] Mr 6 confirmed the date of the dinner as "the evening of 31st August" – this is not the critical evening. The crash occurred at 12.23 a.m. on 31 August 1997, therefore the critical evening – just prior to the crash – is Saturday, 30 August 1997. Paget does not specify the exact date of the dinner – it reads "that evening". The Paget Report states on p767: "Richard Spearman was in Paris on the weekend of 30/31 August 1997. That date coincidentally was his birthday (as confirmed in the British Diplomatic Service List) and he was out that evening for a meal with his wife at a named restaurant." Paget says: "That date coincidentally was his birthday" – but "that date" was "30/31 August 1997". People are born on a specific day – either 30 or 31 August, but not both. Although the 1998 Service List (p294) does state that Spearman's birthday is August 30, the other evidence indicates he may have gone to the restaurant with his wife, but not on the critical evening before the crash (August 30), and instead on the evening following the crash, Sunday, 31 August 1997.
[b] Mr 5 also had dinner at a restaurant with his wife, but they took their child with them (see point 2 below re babysitter): "During the evening I had a meal with my wife and child at the Thoumieux Restaurant in Rue St Dominique.": 29 Feb 08: 37.18. The only other MI6 witness who has admitted to being in Paris was Ms 1. She said in her statement: "the [30 August 1997] Saturday evening [diary] entry is blank, which indicates to me that I was at home with my husband": 29 Feb 08: 36.5. Being female, Ms 1 couldn't be Spearman anyway.

The Paget Report – not available to the jury – stated: "Richard Spearman ... was out that evening for a meal with his wife at a named restaurant".[749] (WFJ)

2) Both men employed a babysitter.

Mr 6 confirmed to Burnett: "I had indeed ... left [our] children at home with a babysitter".[750]

The Paget Report stated: "[The Spearman's] children were left at home with a babysitter".[751] (WFJ)

3) Both men were in Paris for four years.

Mr 6 said: "I never visited the hotel during my four years in Paris".[752]

The Paget Report stated: "Richard Spearman ... moved to Paris on Tuesday 26 August 1997 to begin a four-year posting...."[753]

4) Both men had a pre-Paris job at the centre of MI6.

Mr 6 confirmed at the inquest: "Prior to ... going to Paris ... I occupied a central position, a position of trust, at the centre of the [MI6] organisation."[754]

Richard Tomlinson stated in his 1999 affidavit: "Mr Spearman ... had been, prior to his appointment in Paris, the personal secretary to the Chief of MI6 Mr David Spedding."[755]

Mr 6's pre-Paris role was addressed again during Mansfield's cross-examination. Mansfield said he had a question "I am asking you because of your seniority at the time".[a] Spearman replied: "It is less seniority than a position with a wide-ranging vision of what is going on".[756]

That again fits with Spearman's role of "personal secretary to the Chief of MI6" – that's a position that is not necessarily very senior, but enables a wide vision of activities within MI6.[b]

5) By the time of the inquest, both men had served up to 20 years in MI6.

Mr 6 said to Mansfield: "I have been in the [MI6] organisation nigh on two decades".[757]

The MI6 officer list that was anonymously posted onto the internet includes a reference to Spearman: "Richard David Spearman: 92 Istanbul, 97 Paris; dob[c] 1960." [d]

This entry indicates that Spearman was born in 1960, so at the time of the 2008 inquest would have been age 48. It also reveals that Spearman's initial

---

[a] Referring to 6's position prior to his transfer to Paris.

[b] Spearman also transferred to Paris just a few days before the crash – see later. At one stage during Mansfield's cross-examination Mr 6 said: "... the proposition that we were involved in [the crash is] preposterous. I am talking now from my own perspective. So there is the business of timing of folks' arrivals within Paris....": 29 Feb 08: 74.5.

[c] Date of birth.

[d] The MI6 officer list can be viewed at: http://cryptome.org/mi6-list-276.htm

international MI6 posting was to Istanbul in 1992 – 16 years before the inquest.

This then fits with Mr 6's passing reference at the inquest to his time in MI6: "nigh on two decades".

Mr 6 was none other than Richard Spearman, one of the two[a] prime named MI6 suspects for involvement in the orchestration of the Princess Diana assassination.

It is more difficult to identify Ms 1 and Mr 5, than Mr 4 (Eugene Curley)[b] and Mr 6 (Richard Spearman)[c] – 1 and 5 were never cross-examined[d], and there is less known information about the other people who were in the political and economic departments at the time of the crash: Sherard Cowper-Coles, Valerie Caton, Colin Roberts, Caroline Copley, G.J. Hendry, Robert Fitchett, Andrew Wightman, P.J.E. Raynes, Nicholas Langman and Hugh Powell.[e]

In the above list, there are two females – Valerie Caton and Caroline Copley.

Ms 1 states: "the Saturday evening [diary] entry is blank, which indicates to me that I was at home with my husband".[758] There is no mention of any children.

The 1997 List reveals that Caton had a son born in 1994[759], and a British government press release at the time of her 2006 appointment as ambassador to Finland states: "Children: One daughter (1992) & one son (1994)".[760f]

Caroline Copley's 1997 List biography reveals that she was married in 1996 and has no children listed.[761]

Ms 1 is very likely to be Caroline Copley.

We are then left with the remaining eight males – Cowper-Coles, Roberts, Hendry, Fitchett, Wightman, Raynes, Langman, Powell – one of which should be Mr 5.

Mr 5 said in his statement: "During the day I may have gone shopping with <u>my wife and child</u>.... During the evening I had a meal with <u>my wife and child</u> at the Thoumieux Restaurant".[762]

---

[a] The other is Nicholas Langman.

[b] See earlier MI6 Takes Charge chapter.

[c] See above.

[d] They provided written statements that were read out.

[e] Other personnel have been left off this list because their 1997 biography states they left Paris before the crash: Peter Ricketts – April 1997; Anna and Matthew Kirk – March and April 1997; Julia Nolan – June 1997; Simon Fraser – March 1997. The Diplomatic Service List 1998, pp190, 228, 261, 278.

[f] It is not known why there is a conflict between the List and the press release.

Of the eight men listed above, there are two who are not included in the List biography section, even though they are on the official 1997 embassy list[a] – they are first secretaries G.J. Hendry (political) and P.J.E. Raynes (economic).[b]

Of the remaining six men, only one is described in the 1997 List biography section as married with one child[c] – he is Hugh Powell, who had been second secretary political at the Paris embassy since April 1993. Powell's biography reveals that he was married in 1993 and had one son born in 1996.[763]

I suggest it is likely that Hugh Powell is Mr 5, but one can't be certain because the biographical details of Raynes and Hendry remain unknown (see above).[d]

Where Were The Spooks?

There is a significant conflict in the MI6 evidence regarding who was on the ground in Paris on the Saturday night, 30 August 1997.

Eugene Curley (Mr 4) was asked by Ian Burnett QC: "We have heard read to us the evidence of Witnesses 1 and 5 who were in Paris that weekend. We are also going to be hearing from witness 6, who was in Paris that weekend. Are you able to tell the jury whether there were any ... SIS staff [other than Ms 1, Mr 5 and Mr 6[e]] in Paris that weekend?"

Curley replied:

> **I know that – I remember well that witness 6 was in town, and I am clear that we would have made arrangements for duty personnel, a duty officer and duty support staff, but in terms of who specifically was doing what, I cannot clearly remember that.[764]**

Curley has failed to answer the question.

The question is about "whether there were any other SIS staff in Paris that weekend". Burnett has just told Curley that Ms 1, Mr 5 and Mr 6 have already said they were in Paris – but was there anyone else?

---

[a] Reproduced in Part 5, section on Movements of Officers in MI6 in Paris chapter. Also on inquest website: INQ0049222.

[b] Hendry and Raynes also don't show on the MI6 internet list.

[c] The others are: Sherard Cowper-Coles – married in 1982, 5 children, born in 1982, 1984, 1986, 1987 and 1990; Colin Roberts – single, no children; Robert Fitchett – married in 1985, 3 children, born in 1987, 1988 and 1993; Andrew Wightman – married in 1988, no children; Nicholas Langman – married 1992, 2 children, born in 1994 and 1995.: Diplomatic Service List 1998, pp164, 186, 230, 279, 316.

[d] It is not known why Raynes and Hendry do not have biographical details published. There is a possibility that they were undeclared MI6 officers, but I suggest it is unlikely that undeclared officers would appear on the official list for the Paris embassy.

[e] Richard Spearman.

Instead of answering the question, Curley: a) reiterates part of what he has already been told – "witness 6 was in town"; b) makes a general comment[a] – "we would have made arrangements for duty personnel, a duty officer and duty support staff"; c) says he doesn't remember "who specifically was doing what".

Basically Curley's answer, despite being lengthy, completely sidesteps the question.

Why?

All the information Curley has given could have been provided by a former head of MI6 France who by 30-31 August 1997 was no longer involved in what was happening with MI6 in Paris:[b]

-       Curley says: "witness 6 was in town" – Burnett has just told him that
-       Curley relates general weekend duty arrangements – that is something Curley would have known from his general past experience as political counsellor in Paris
-       Curley says he doesn't remember "who specifically was doing what" – this is completely unrelated to the question[c] and adds to the perception that Curley wasn't involved.[d]

All Burnett was trying to ask was: who amongst the MI6 staff was in Paris on the weekend of 30-31 August 1997?

Burnett, who already knows the answer[e], now comes at the same question from a different angle. He asks if Curley has "had an opportunity of reading the [Paris MI6 Paget] witness statements". Curley confirms.[765]

Then Burnett asks if "Paget took statements from all [Paris] SIS members". Again Curley confirms.[766]

Next Burnett tells Curley the answer to his original question about "whether there were any other SIS staff in Paris that weekend". Burnett states to Curley: "All the others in their statements set out where they were that weekend and none was in Paris." Burnett asks Curley to confirm that – Curley: "That is right."[767]

---

[a] It's non-specific – doesn't name anyone who could have been there, by codename or otherwise.

[b] As was Curley's situation – this has been shown earlier in the MI6 Takes Charge chapter.

[c] The question was about "whether there were any other SIS staff in Paris that weekend" – not what they were doing.

[d] Some might argue that Curley was still on holiday in La Rochelle. I suggest that even if he was in La Rochelle but was still in charge in France and wasn't aware of "who specifically was doing what" on the weekend Princess Diana was assassinated, he would have made it his job to find out after he returned to work.

[e] He gives it to Curley below.

In this period of cross-examination one simple question – were MI6 staff in Paris? – was not answered and then turned into a series of four questions. In all of this, Curley provided no information at all from the perspective of a person who was actually in charge of the personnel he was meant to be commenting on.

Instead all the information came from Burnett – "witnesses 1 and 5 ... were in Paris that weekend"; "witness 6 ... was in Paris that weekend"; "Operation Paget took statements from all [Paris] SIS members"; "all the others ... set out where they were that weekend and none was in Paris".

I suggest that when Burnett asked Curley the original question – "Are you able to tell the jury whether there were any other SIS staff in Paris that weekend?" – the true answer would have been "No".[a]

That would not have been a good look for MI6 – Mr 4 was claiming to be the head of MI6 in Paris, so why would be not be able to answer such a simple question?

This was an easy question for someone who knew the official answer[b] – "Yes" and then "There were no other SIS staff in Paris that weekend".

But Curley was not able to answer it. He didn't – and possibly never did – know the answer. The reason being that he had already left his posting in Paris at some point prior to the crash – see earlier.

Instead of answering "No" (see above), Curley had to bungle his way through territory he "should" have known but didn't.[c]

Curley starts off his answer: "I know that – I remember well that witness 6 was in town". Now Curley had just been told by Burnett that "witness 6 ... was in Paris that weekend".

Curley may have started off with "I know that" and then reminded himself that he was supposed to be portraying a person who was a witness recalling events that they were a part of. He then starts again "I remember well", but then he doesn't provide anything more than what Burnett has just told him. For example, why or how does he remember it so well? [d]

Curley can "remember well" something he has just been told by Burnett, but is unable to remember the answer to the question.

I am not suggesting that Curley – if he had been near La Rochelle – would remember from on location knowledge, because he is not claiming to have been in Paris. But the point is that if Curley was the head of MI6 Paris – as he

---

[a] "No, I am not able to tell the jury whether there were any other SIS staff in Paris that weekend."

[b] This is the official answer provided by MI6 – I suggest that the evidence indicates this is not the truth (see earlier and later).

[c] He "should" have known it if he had been in charge, but the earlier evidence indicates that he was no longer in charge – Cowper-Coles, who wasn't cross-examined, had taken over.

[d] Bearing in mind that Curley has said that he was near La Rochelle at the time.

claims – then when he arrived back at the office he would have been finding out where his staff had been over that weekend. The Diana assassination was so big, and Curley's officers have been labelled as suspects right from early on – it is clear that if MI6 were not involved from the top, then they would be finding out who was involved. They would be asking questions like: "Do we have rogue officers in Paris?" or "Where were all our officers that weekend?"

If Curley was still in charge and MI6 were not involved in orchestrating the crash, then I suggest Curley would have made it his business to find out where his officers had been that weekend.

The reality though is: a) that Curley was no longer in charge in Paris – Cowper-Coles was; and b) MI6 were involved – from the top on down.[a]

The assertion that Curley was no longer in charge is supported by his failure to provide an answer to Burnett's simple question: "Are you able to tell the jury whether there were any other SIS staff in Paris that weekend?"

Nevertheless, in his initial answer Curley did provide critical evidence regarding MI6 Paris staffing on any given weekend – "I am clear that we would have made arrangements for duty personnel, a duty officer and duty support staff".

"A duty officer and duty support staff" – that's three or more people: one duty officer and two or more duty support staff.

Mr 5 has stated: "I believe I was the duty officer on call that weekend".[768]

Ms 1 has stated: "I was in Paris ... as I was on call and had to be in the city".[769]

There is a critical difference between being on "duty" and on "call".

The Oxford Dictionary states under "on duty": "doing one's regular work" – so in the current scenario, that would mean an officer working for MI6 Paris during the weekend of 30-31 August 1997.

The definition for "on call" is: "available to provide a professional service if necessary".

Curley – who had before this been the head of MI6 France – does not say anything about staff being on call, he says: "duty personnel, a duty officer and duty support staff". He then adds: "but in terms of who specifically <u>was doing what</u>, I cannot clearly remember that".

Curley describes staff "doing" things – this would fit with the above dictionary definition for "on duty".

Mr 5 and Ms 1 describe something quite different – they portray themselves doing nothing workwise, following their normal weekend pursuits, but being "on call".

---

[a] This will become clearer as this book progresses.

My understanding of intelligence – from extensive research – is that it does not shut down come the weekend.

Even when a major event does occur right in the middle of their territory, these "on call" MI6 officers do not let it affect their weekend – Ms 1: "I was not asked to carry out any tasks in relation to the crash as it had no connection to SIS work";[770] Mr 5: "I took no action because I believed the response to the incident was not an SIS responsibility".[771]

The point here is that the primary stated function of an intelligence officer is to gather information – otherwise known as intelligence. If MI6 wasn't involved in the assassination of the British princess, then MI6 would have been making it an urgent priority to covertly find out who had eliminated their princess.

And Mr 5 and Ms 1, being on the ground "on call" in Paris, would be where MI6 would start its post-event secret gathering of intelligence regarding this unexpected disaster.

Ms 1 has stated she was "on call", but has never suggested she was on duty – she has instead provided evidence that: "I had friends staying ... who left ... on Saturday morning";[772] "on Sunday morning, one of the Embassy locally employed staff ... telephoned my home to confirm arrangements for a pre-arranged barbecue at his country home".[773]

Mr 5 has described himself as "the duty officer on call that weekend", but later goes on to say: "I had the impression that I was the only SIS member of staff around Paris that weekend, but do not know the movements or locations of any of the other staff."[774a]

Although he has used the same term – "duty officer" – as Curley, 5's evidence does not fit with Curley's. Curley does not say anything about "on call" and he also indicates there would be at least two "duty support staff" – by inference the support staff would be supporting the duty officer.

Yet, Mr 5 has claimed to be the "duty officer on call", with apparently no support staff that he knew of – "I was the only SIS member of staff around Paris" and "[I] do not know the movements or locations of any of the other staff".

Evidence has also been heard from Mr 4 and Mr 6.[b] This is a key part of an MI6 officer's evidence – if they were on duty on the weekend of the crash then that would be one of the first things they would divulge in their account.

Neither of these officers – 4 (Curley) and 6 (Spearman) – have indicated that they were on duty or on call: 4 said he was near La Rochelle; 6 arrived in

---

[a] 5 also said he went shopping and to a restaurant with his wife and child: 29 Feb 08: 37.16.

[b] There were other MI6 officers who were heard, but they were not part of the Paris MI6 station – they gave evidence in connection with a plot to kill Serbian leader, Slobodan Milosevic.

Paris just five days before the crash and was at a restaurant birthday celebration with his wife.

I suggest it is unlikely that Mr 6 would have been on duty or on call, if he was out on a birthday celebration with his wife, and he has never said that he was on duty.[775] (WFJ)

Eugene Curley confirmed – see above – that "all the others[a] ... set out where they were that weekend and none was in Paris".

This evidence – from the MI6 officer accounts – indicates that <u>no one was on duty</u> and Mr 5 and Ms 1 are the only personnel who were on call in Paris on the weekend of 30-31 August 1997.

This is a major conflict with Curley's evidence – "I am clear that we would have made arrangements for duty personnel, a duty officer and duty support staff".

Curley's account is common sense – it is ridiculous to suggest that a key organisation like MI6 would have no staff members on duty in a city the size of Paris on a normal weekend.

Curley has at least three people on duty, whereas the evidence supplied by the MI6 officers in Paris shows no one on duty and just two people on call – Mr 5 and Ms 1.

There are two possibilities:

1)   Curley is wrong and the other MI6 officer statements are all true – this would mean that there were no MI6 officers on duty[b] on the weekend of 30-31 August 1997

2)   Curley is right – there are three or more duty staff on a normal weekend.

It would be ridiculous to conclude that there would be no MI6 officers in Paris on duty in a normal weekend – Curley is correct, which also is common sense.

This then leads to one of two inescapable possibilities:

1)   that MI6 officers have lied in their accounts – not just one, but three or more have stated that they were out of Paris or not working, when in fact they were on duty in Paris. This is not to say they were involved in orchestrating the crash, but that the officers have lied in their evidence

2)   that MI6 was involved in the orchestrated assassinations of Princess Diana and Dodi Fayed and there has been a major cover-up in the statements and inquest evidence of Paris-based MI6 officers.

---

[a] Other than Ms 1, Mr 4, Mr 5 and Mr 6.

[b] And only two on call – Ms 1 and Mr 5.

If point 1 was true, it would mean that these three or more officers have lied in unison for no apparent reason, because they have nothing to cover-up – they were not involved in the assassinations.

That is very unlikely – why would three or more MI6 officers lie for no reason?

The evidence points to number 2 above and the question is: Why is there a cover-up if there is nothing to cover up?

This adds to a building dossier that will lead to the conclusion that MI6 were not innocent bystanders, but instead had been involved in previous assassination plots,[a] made sure that the right people were stationed in the Paris embassy before the weekend of the crash, were involved in the orchestration of the assassinations of Princess Diana and Dodi Fayed and have been a major party to the ensuing massive cover-up.

In summary, there are two main issues that indicate the MI6 evidence is not credible:

1)   Taken together, all the MI6 witnesses are saying that no one was on duty in the MI6 Paris station on the weekend of 30-31 August 1997 – this is simply not believable[bc]

2)   Even if one does choose to believe the MI6 accounts that no one was on duty, then if MI6 were not involved in the orchestration of the crash, there would have been personnel on duty following the crash.[d]

---

[a] A list of MI6's historical involvement in assassination plots is included in Part 5, section on Does MI6 Murder People? in the MI6 Culture, Methods and Secret Operations chapter.

[b] This type of evidence fits with the thematic way the general cover-up has been conducted. The French unanimously said they never knew Diana was in France – see earlier; the British Embassy staff unanimously said they never knew Diana was in France – see earlier; and here, MI6 staff are unanimously saying they were not working that weekend – most even were out of Paris. How could they possibly have been involved if no one was aware or on duty? In this way, the authorities in both France and the UK have attempted to distance themselves from involvement in the crash.

[c] The British Embassy staff interviewed – which included all the MI6 staff – all (except Ritchie and Gunner – see earlier) said they weren't aware Diana was in France until after the crash had occurred. The reality is that Diana and Dodi arrived in Paris at 3.20 p.m., with paparazzi and police at the airport to welcome them. This means that we have people like Mr 5 – who said "I am a light sleeper.... On that night I recall listening to BBC5 Live and at about 2 or 3 am I first heard reports of the crash" (29 Feb 08: 37.25) – listening to the news in the early hours, but not during the afternoon or evening, when Diana's arrival would have been reported.

[d] The MI6 evidence – Curley and Ms 1 – indicated that meetings involving MI6 officers didn't take place until Monday, 1 September 1997, the day following the crash. (29 Feb 08: 38.15 and 43.8) This tends to also have the effect of undermining

In other words, MI6 was either involved in the crash, or would have taken a very keen interest following the crash – to establish through intelligence whether it was an accident, or who actually was responsible.

MI6 witnesses in Paris have said that they were not involved in the crash and also took no specific interest following the crash[ab] – this also is not credible.

We have a situation where there were 11 political and economic department staff[c] working in the British Paris embassy around the time of the crash. Other evidence indicates that these staff are the people that made up the MI6 Paris station.

Of those 11 – Cowper-Coles, Caton, Spearman, Roberts, Copley, Hendry, Fitchett, Wightman, Raynes, Langman, Powell – only one (Spearman, Mr 6) was cross-examined at the "thorough" inquest held by Scott Baker.[def]

Not one of these 11 people – who are alleged suspects involved in the assassinations – have ever had their alibis for the night of 30-31 August 1997 properly checked.

For example, Spearman says he produced his credit card statement – "when I was asked for it, I was able to produce it"[776] – substantiating he was

---

the significance of the crash regarding MI6 and reinforces their mantra: "We had nothing to do with it".

[a] In addition to the reactions of Ms 1 and Mr 5 shown above, Mr 6 (Richard Spearman) has also admitted to being in Paris at the time of the crash. When he was asked at the inquest: "On that Sunday, so that is Sunday 31st August 1997, did you make any contact with the British Embassy?" He replied: "I did not, no." 29 Feb 08: 55.8.

[b] One could argue that Sherard Cowper-Coles is the exception – he rushed up to Paris from the South of France (see earlier). Cowper-Coles though has never been interviewed by any of the investigations – that evidence came from Michael Jay who has been shown at times to have lied under oath. At the inquest it was also never admitted that Cowper-Coles was in MI6. Other evidence indicates that he was, and that he was already in Paris at the time of the crash – see earlier.

[c] Excluding Curley, who has been shown to have left ahead of the crash and is not in the official 1997 List.

[d] Others, Ms 1 and Mr 5, had statements read out, but were not subjected to cross-examination.

[e] Eugene Curley, Mr 4, was cross-examined, but he was not part of the Paris embassy staff at the time of the crash – see earlier.

[f] It is significant that while only one Paris-based MI6 officer – Spearman (Mr 6) – was cross-examined, three MI6 officers who were part of the Balkans team – Mr A, Mr E and Mr H – were cross-examined in connection with a 1992 piece of paper (which has since been destroyed) outlining the Milosevic plot. This is despite the fact that Diana was assassinated in Paris and not in the Balkans.

269

at a restaurant, the Bistro d'a Côte. It is shown in Part 5[a] that this may have been for a dinner on the night following the crash, not before it.

Why was this credit card statement – which is crucial to Spearman's alibi – not shown to the inquest jury who were investigating the deaths?

Spearman does not tell us <u>who</u> "asked for it". Paget makes no comment about Spearman providing a credit card statement or any corroborating documentary evidence[b], even though they normally were very keen to state they had supporting evidence where they could.[c]

Ms 1's alibi is: "The Saturday evening[d] [diary] entry is blank, which indicates to me that I was at home with my husband".[777] This is not a particularly convincing alibi – there is no evidence of Ms 1's husband being questioned on this.

Mr 5 said: "During the evening [of 30 August 1997] I had a meal with my wife and child at the Thoumieux Restaurant in Rue St Dominique".[778] Again, there is no evidence this has ever been checked out with: a) the restaurant; and, b) 5's wife. There was no documentary evidence proffered.

Sherard Cowper-Coles – who it has been shown was the head of MI6 France at the time of the crash – has never been asked for an alibi. Michael Jay has said that Cowper-Coles was "in the South of France" and "arrived [in Paris] at about noon on 31/08/1997" – 11½ hours after the crash.[e]

Why has Cowper-Coles never been interviewed by any police and was not heard from at the inquest?

The jury was told by inquest lawyer, Ian Burnett:[f] "All the others[g] in their statements set out where they were that weekend and none was in Paris".[779]

Why were the jury not shown these statements from "all the others"?

Not only have the alibis from these people not been properly checked, but the jury have not even been told what their specific alibis are.[h]

---

[a] In the Richard Spearman and Nicholas Langman section of the MI6 In Paris chapter.
[b] Paget only state that the restaurant was named, without supplying the name. See next footnote.
[c] Paget's account of this is on page 767 of the Paget Report: "Richard Spearman was in Paris on the weekend of 30/31 August 1997. That date coincidentally was his birthday (as confirmed in the British Diplomatic Service List) and he was out that evening for a meal with his wife at a named restaurant. Their children were left at home with a babysitter (named)." (WFJ)
[d] 30 August 1997.
[e] Earlier evidence in this volume has raised issues regarding the timing of Cowper-Coles' trip.
[f] Confirmed by Curley, who wasn't in Paris – see earlier.
[g] Paris MI6 employees.
[h] Paget gave an alibi for Nicholas Langman – not heard by the jury: "Nicholas Langman was on leave on the weekend of 30/31 August 1997, staying with relatives in England. Statements corroborating his account have been obtained." (Paget Report, p767) (WFJ). Who actually gets to see these corroborating statements Paget talks

Why is this?

Why this casual disregard of key evidence from suspects for the assassinations of Princess Diana and Dodi Fayed?

---

about? They are not shown in the Paget Report, they have never been made public and the jury were never even told that Langman said he wasn't there, let alone hearing corroborating statements.

29   Dodi's Apartment: 7.00 to 9.30 p.m.

At 6.57 p.m. Diana and Dodi left from the rear of the Ritz Hotel in the Mercedes 600, chauffeured by Philippe Dourneau – they were headed for Dodi's apartment on the Rue Arsène Houssaye. Immediately behind was the Range Rover driven by Jean-François Musa and several paparazzi vehicles.

Some of the witnesses say this trip went smoothly. However paparazzo Fabrice Chassery makes an interesting comment. Four days later he told the police: "All the professionals [paparazzi] … were there, plus the fans who were behaving like madmen".[780]

Chassery knows who the fellow paparazzi are, and views any other vehicles present as "fans". They may have been unidentified people masquerading as paparazzi and continuing to build pressure on the occupants of the Mercedes. Chassery was not cross-examined during the inquest.

Rees-Jones recalled the paparazzi "became more intrusive on that journey to Dodi's Apartment".[781] He said:

> **One of the motorcycles had actually come alongside the principals' vehicle and [after arriving] … we spoke to the press and asked them to lay off during the journey and take the photographs when we got to the location.[782]**

Rees-Jones should have been afforded the opportunity to identify the motorbike or the rider(s) that drew alongside – that didn't happen.

There was a continuing problem with photos being taken in transit: initially on the Le Bourget to Paris trip and then also on this 7 p.m. trip to the apartment.

As with the earlier journey there have never been any photos published. If the photos had been taken by paparazzi there was no reason for them not to have been published.

Where are these photos?

"Have Some Champagne Ready"

The convoy arrived at the apartment at around 7.15 p.m.

Whilst there Diana and Dodi relaxed.

Dodi's butler Rene Delorm described under oath an incident that occurred:

[Dodi] came to the kitchen…. He took a look at the other side of the apartment to make sure that the Princess was not close by and he said, 'Rene, have some champagne ready because when we come back, I am going to propose to the Princess'. The next thing he did, he reached in his pocket, he opened a box and I saw the ring.[783]

This indicates Dodi was intending to formally propose to Princess Diana after they returned from the Ritz Hotel that night. The crash occurred on that return trip back from the hotel and the ring was found in the apartment by Delorm on the following day.[784]

30   Dinner Decoy: Chez Benoît

Claude Roulet and Henri Paul had set up – with Dodi's acquiescence – a decoy plan involving the couple's anticipated location for dinner that night. Some Ritz staff were told that they would be dining at Chez Benoît, when their actual intended location was the Ritz Hotel restaurant.

Dodi would have been led to believe the paparazzi would be told Chez Benoît – but the evidence indicates they were not.

There is no evidence at all of paparazzi waiting at or travelling to Chez Benoît – instead they were either waiting at the Ritz or outside Dodi's apartment.

Paparazzo Thierry Orban told the French investigation in September 1997:

> **On the evening of Saturday 30th August 1997, I was at home having dinner with friends.... At about 9 or 9.30 [p.m.], I had a phone call from my duty chief editor, Guillaume Vallabregue. He told me that there was a rumour of an announcement that Lady Diana was getting married or having a baby and <u>asked me to go to the Ritz</u> to take a few photos of Diana with Dodi Al Fayed. I refused because I wasn't on duty and I had people to dinner at my place.[785]**

The media somehow knew that Diana and Dodi would be returning to the Ritz. Thierry Orban's name was never mentioned in the Paget Report and this statement was not included.

Investigators should have interviewed Orban's boss, Guillaume Vallabregue, to establish how he knew that photos of Diana and Dodi would be obtainable at the Ritz.

That never occurred.

Confusion Over Destination

Meanwhile, there was confusion over the dinner destination amongst the staff present at the apartment or on the subsequent journey.

Of those asked, Philippe Dourneau, the driver of the Mercedes 600, is the only one who was consistently clear that the destination was Chez Benoît. He told the police three days later: "François [Musa] and I waited in the cars for instructions to go to Chez Benoît".[786] Then he confirmed at the inquest that "during the journey ... Dodi decided to go to the Ritz rather than to Chez Benoît ... because of the activities of the paparazzi".[787a]

Jean-François Musa, the driver of the Range Rover, in his 1998 statement indicates he knew about "a restaurant",[788] (WFJ) but at the inquest he said, "what I understood was that we were going back to the hotel".[789]

Earlier at the Villa Windsor Diana had told Rees-Jones that they would be "going out to a restaurant"[790] (WFJ) – that could mean one of two possibilities: Diana didn't know the venue yet or Diana did know, but wasn't in a position to say. "A restaurant" could mean a restaurant at the Ritz or a restaurant elsewhere. He said: "Zero information was coming from Dodi".[791] (WFJ) Despite repeated efforts to find out the destination, Rees-Jones said that he only learned "as we were travelling en route" that they were heading for the Ritz.[792] (WFJ)

Kez Wingfield's evidence has similarities to Rees-Jones' except that in Wingfield's 2005 statement he recalled that Dodi withheld the destination information until immediately before they left, when he recollects "Dodi said that we were going to the Ritz". He added: "I was never told about any other intended restaurant or destination."[793] (WFJ)

Wingfield's evidence at the inquest also conflicted with Dourneau and Musa's: He said the drivers told the bodyguards before the departure: "We believe it's the Ritz".[794]

It is unfortunate that only a short and confusing excerpt of Wingfield's earliest 2 September 1997 statement has been made public. He states that he informed his "superiors[b] of our itinerary" but says that Dodi never told him what the itinerary was.[795] (WFJ) Wingfield was not asked about this at the inquest.

What is clear from Wingfield's Paget statement and inquest testimony is that he believes he knew the destination to be the Ritz before the vehicles left the apartment. It should though be noted that that is contrary to what it says in Rees-Jones' 2000 book: "As the two vehicles drove off, Kez called London on the car phone: 'We're on the move'. 'Where?' 'We have no idea!'"[796] (WFJ)

Dodi's butler, Rene Delorm, was also not aware of the destination. He told the police: "I knew that they were going for dinner but I didn't know where".[797] (WFJ) This fits with Rees-Jones' account – he said: "Through Rene Delorm we were trying to get the name of [the restaurant] [but] we never managed to get the information."[798] (WFJ)

---

[a] The fake paparazzi were again active on this trip – see later.
[b] Superiors in London.

Didier Gamblin, a Ritz fire safety officer assigned to the apartment, indicated that he was told about the Benoît destination by Henri Paul. Whilst describing a call from Henri at 7.30 p.m. Gamblin stated: "[Henri] also said that my job would be finished when the couple left the flat to go to a Paris restaurant, le Benoît."[799]

Ritz night security manager, François Tendil, testified that Diana and Dodi "had to go to the restaurant, Chez Benoît".[800] He said: "Nobody [at the Ritz] thought that they would come back. I asked [Henri] ten times the question and, according to him, it was impossible that they would be back."[801]

Ritz night manager, Thierry Rocher, said that he knew nothing about Chez Benoît but was also not expecting the couple to dine at the hotel.[802]

One aspect is clear from all of this evidence: there was a significant amount of secrecy and confusion regarding the destination for the couple's dinner, even amongst the people in the vehicles heading to that destination.

Mercedes 600 driver, Philippe Dourneau, stated three days later: "Once we got to the hotel, there was a sea of people."[803] (WFJ) This indicates that somehow word had got out ahead of time that the couple were expected to return to the Ritz that evening.

Importance of Decoy

Dodi may have been told – by Roulet, Henri or both – that using Benoît as a decoy would be a good tactic to deal with the paparazzi, but the real motive for such a plan may have been quite different.

The importance of Chez Benoît is that if it was the intended destination then it effectively counters the conspiracy. This is because the conspiracy relies on prior knowledge by intelligence that the couple intended to visit the Ritz before returning to Dodi's apartment.

If the staged crash was organised by an intelligence agency, they would have been thinking ahead to methods of deniability, disinformation and cover-up, before the plan was actually implemented. An ideal part of a premeditated cover-up would be to establish an intended destination, like Benoît, which would have made the key ingredients of the assassination plan – switching of the Mercedes and driver, elimination of the back-up car – impossible to carry out.

What also would have made Benoît ideal is that from Dodi's apartment the initial route heads towards the Ritz, so the convoy could have looked as though it was heading for Benoît, even though it was actually going to the hotel.

The final coup is that people like John Stevens and Scott Baker would be able to conclude: "They were heading for Chez Benoît, not the Ritz Hotel, so how could the perpetrators have known in advance that they would travel from the Ritz to the apartment?"

Roulet's Role

Claude Roulet stated that he was outside Chez Benoît for "at least an hour" waiting for the couple to arrive.[804]

Dourneau told the inquest that he knew about Chez Benoît "because the booking had been made".[805] He also confirmed that he remembered "that M Roulet was to wait at the restaurant".[806]

Roulet stated he received a call "from Dodi, saying that they were surrounded by too many paparazzi and that they prefer to go in the Ritz".[807a]

Dourneau told the French investigation on September 3 that "during the journey, Mr Dodi asked me to inform Mr Roulet, who was at the restaurant, that he would rather dine at the Ritz given the pressure from the paparazzi who were following us".[808] (WFJ)

Roulet says the call was made by Dodi, whereas Dourneau says he was asked by Dodi to make it.[b]

Dourneau told Paget in 2005: "I do not remember who notified [Roulet]". He was then asked if he remembered any phone calls made by Dodi during the journey. His answer: "No, not at all."[809] (WFJ)

Rees-Jones was in the car and should have been asked about this. He wasn't.

It is possible that Dourneau's earliest account – three days after the crash – is correct: that Dodi requested him to call Roulet. Dodi was definitely "in on" the Benoît decoy plan and he would not have wanted Dourneau to know that he had been involved in deceiving him regarding the dinner location.

Why weren't details of the phone records of Dourneau, Dodi and Roulet provided to the jury?

Was Roulet ever actually waiting outside Chez Benoît?

The entire Chez Benoît scenario hangs on the evidence of Claude Roulet. It is Roulet's evidence that he booked Benoît – there are no other living witnesses to this action.[c] There has never been any support for this from the restaurant and no Benoît staff member has ever been interviewed by the French or British police.

---

[a] Roulet said just before this that he had received an earlier call "by Philippe, the driver of Dodi" informing him they were leaving for Chez Benoît: 5 Dec 07: 94.7.

[b] Dourneau has never stated that he actually made the call – just that he was asked to make it. He was not asked about this at the inquest.

[c] In his March 2005 statement to Paget, Roulet said: "It was I who made the reservation in my name, on 30 August in the morning I think, and I kept Mr Mohamed Al Fayed informed from the Ritz Hotel." Paget Report, p209 (WFJ) At the inquest Mohamed maintained that he was told the couple were having dinner at the Ritz. Since the conclusion of the inquest, it has been confirmed to me that the first Mohamed heard of Chez Benoît was after the crash had occurred.

Why weren't these people interviewed?

It is Roulet's evidence that he waited outside the restaurant for over an hour – once again there is no support for this from the restaurant and there are no other witnesses.

Roulet said at the inquest that, while waiting, he rang the staff at Dodi's apartment "many times, many times".[810] There should be phone records to back that statement, but that aspect was not looked at during the inquest.

Roulet said that Delorm was his contact there.[811] Delorm has never made any mention of any of these phone calls – in his book, statement or cross-examination – but he did say to the British police that he had no knowledge of the specific destination.[812] (WFJ) It becomes clear that Delorm had no idea where Roulet was, or why he would have been making these "many" calls – if Roulet did in fact make them.

Even if Roulet did make these calls – and there is no evidence he did – that would not necessarily mean they were made from outside Benoît. If Roulet was working for an intelligence agency, he could just as easily have been meeting with a minder, monitoring what was happening.

It is clear that Roulet's "at least an hour" wait evidence contributes to the widespread acceptance that Benoît must have been the real destination. It will be shown below that the timing does not actually allow Roulet to have waited for that length of time before Benoît was cancelled.

Roulet's Timing Problems

Over the years Claude Roulet has maintained repeatedly that he left the Ritz Hotel before 7.30 p.m.

At the inquest he swore on oath that "it must [have been] around 7[pm] or something like this".[813] In 2005 he told the British police:

I finished work and left the Ritz at around 19.00 [7 p.m.] or 19.15 [7.15 p.m.], having asked Dodi if there were any further instructions. Dodi and the Princess left ... before I left.[814]

In saying this, Roulet linked his Ritz exit to Diana and Dodi's 6.57 p.m. departure.

In December 2006 the Paget Report stated (in brackets):

According to the CCTV footage, Claude Roulet left the hotel at about 8.20 p.m., a fact he acknowledged in a later statement.[815] (WFJ)

Operation Paget had received an acknowledgement from Roulet that he didn't leave the hotel until 8.20 p.m. So why then did Roulet again start his testimony to the inquest saying that he left the Ritz around 7 p.m.?

Richard Keen QC arranged for the CCTV footage to be shown to Roulet. He then was forced to publicly confirm that he "left the Ritz not at 7 o'clock or 7.15, but at about 8.20 pm".[816]

But the inquest was never told that Roulet had already been shown this 8.20 p.m. footage by Paget around two years earlier.

Instead Roulet was allowed to falsely reinforce the perception that he had never been previously told about the 8.20 departure:

Mr Keen, during ten years, no one knew that I left the hotel at 20 past 8. You bring this to me ten years later.[817]

Why has Claude Roulet attempted to stick to the 7.15 p.m. Ritz departure, rather than the 8.20 p.m. shown on the CCTV?

Roulet has maintained that after leaving the Ritz he saw Henri Paul in a bar at around 7.30 p.m.[a] When pressed on timings he said that it would have taken about seven minutes to walk from the Ritz to the Bar de Bourgogne where he met with Henri.[818] Then before going to Chez Benoît, he walked home – about 20 minutes from the Ritz when you include his brief time spent with Henri Paul.[819b]

Roulet said he told Henri: "I wanted first to pass at home to have a bite because I am sure I will not eat tonight."[820]

Separately Roulet had said that if he walked direct from the Ritz to Benoît it would take around 25 minutes.[821]

There is no suggestion that Roulet was in a rush – he had made the booking for 9.30 p.m., he stopped by his house to eat and he walked the whole way. The very minimum one could estimate for his home visit would be 15 minutes, but it is likely it would be longer than that.

Roulet stated: "Philippe Dourneau ... called me ... ten minutes [after leaving] to ask me to cancel Benoît's".[822] This would time that call at about 9.40 p.m.

The table below reveals that Roulet could only have been waiting for 45 minutes, at the most, if he left the Ritz at 8.20 p.m. – which we know he did.

It becomes obvious that the long wait outside the restaurant is much easier to substantiate with a 7.15 departure than with the actual 8.20 departure.

---

[a] This is addressed later.

[b] The detail of this Roulet-Henri meeting is addressed in the later Missing Hours chapter.

279

HOW THEY MURDERED PRINCESS DIANA

Event	Timing: Roulet	Timing: CCTV
Ritz Departure	7.15	8.20
Henri Meeting	7.22 to 7.24	8.27 to 8.29
Arrival Home	7.35	8.40
Eats Meal etc	50 minutes	15 minutes
Leaves Home	8.25	8.55
Arrives Benoît	8.32	9.02

This table shows that Roulet's true departure time from the Ritz of 8.20 p.m. did not allow him enough time to have waited for "at least an hour" outside Benoît before the restaurant visit was cancelled at 9.45 p.m.

There is another significant factor that could have caused Roulet to lie about the timing of his departure from the Ritz. It is addressed in the next chapter.

Dinner Decoy

Scott Baker's Summing Up does not include any reference to Roulet's evidence of booking Chez Benoît and his long wait outside the venue.

Using Benoît as a decoy would have required the compliance of Dodi, just as the final decoy plan employed after midnight needed his approval.[a] The pressure from the paparazzi – both real and fake – was clearly providing an atmosphere where Dodi was open to novel ideas on how to deal with it. It is very possible that suggestions of this nature were coming from both Henri Paul and Claude Roulet – starting right at Le Bourget airport where Dodi is shown in a photo intently listening to what Henri Paul (who wasn't meant to be there)[b] has to say.[c]

Claude Roulet was available to advise or assist Dodi after the couple's arrival at the Ritz around 4.35 p.m. It is during this time that Dodi could have agreed to using Benoît as a decoy restaurant.

At the inquest Tendil said he asked Henri ten times whether Diana and Dodi would be coming back to the hotel. Was Tendil suspicious that he wasn't getting straight answers from Henri? Why did he feel that he needed to repeatedly ask the same question?

Tendil said that Henri was saying "it was impossible that they would be back". How could Henri be so sure that Diana and Dodi wouldn't be returning to the Ritz? Was he providing Tendil with incorrect information? It will be shown later that Henri went missing for three hours. Henri's

---

[a] See later.
[b] See earlier Driving Mission chapter.
[c] Photo reproduced earlier in Driving Mission chapter.

movements towards the end of that disappearance are relevant to the couple's return.[a]

Dodi withheld the destination information from both bodyguards – the couple's immediate protection – until possibly just before they got into the cars (Wingfield[b]). If Dodi had told them Benoît, with the knowledge that wasn't true, he may have risked getting himself into trouble for deliberately misinforming the couple's key protectors. Instead he left them uninformed.

The people who were told early that the destination was the Ritz[c] – Mohamed, Rogers, Yassin – were all safe with the knowledge. None of them – from Diana and Dodi's viewpoint – were at risk of being hassled by the media or others for the information.

What is clear and is an underlying theme of this case: the phone calls were being listened to. Diana's call to Rogers, Dodi's calls to his father and Yassin would all have been monitored. There would have been an early understanding amongst the assassins that the dinner arrangement was for the Ritz Hotel, not Chez Benoît. This knowledge could have led to the situation that Dourneau described as a "sea of people" outside the hotel when they arrived. The pressure on the group increased as the evening progressed.

In outlining this scenario, I am not suggesting that either Henri Paul or Claude Roulet were directly culpable for the crash – they were both used as pawns and neither would have had any concept of what the consequences of their actions would be. It may well be that they were following intelligence agency directions in the belief that their actions were improving the security of Diana and Dodi, not stripping that security away.

---

[a] See Henri's Missing Hours chapter.
[b] Wingfield recalled: "Dodi said that we were going to the Ritz": Paget Report, p213 (WFJ).
[c] See earlier Preparing the Decoys chapter.

31   Choosing the Car

The Mercedes 600 and Range Rover were used as decoys for the final journey from the hotel – Diana and Dodi were driven in a third car. This will be addressed later.[a]

The regular driver of that third car – the Mercedes S280 – was a chauffeur called Olivier Lafaye.

It was this car – Lafaye's Mercedes S280 – that was involved in the crash later that night.

But why? Why was this particular Mercedes chosen?

Lafaye's Evidence

Olivier Lafaye's evidence was never heard at the inquest. In September 1997 he told the French investigation:

> **At exactly 6 p.m. I did the last job of the day, a trip to Roissy II for my client Mrs Mataga, who was leaving for Tokyo. I left the airport again at about 7.40 to take the car back to the Ritz. When I got to the hotel I asked my colleague Gérard Pratt if I was supposed to do the usual standby duty, which is always from 7 to 9.**
>
> **Since obviously it was about 8.15 when I got back to the Ritz, Gérard was doing the standby duty. Anyhow I asked the car valet if I was still needed that day. It was a goodwill gesture on my part because any job that's needed after 7 in the evening is done by the person on standby, who in this case was Gérard.**
>
> **The valet, who that evening was a man called Jacques, told me there were no more jobs, so I decided to park the Mercedes on the 3rd level of the Vendôme underground car park as I did every evening.**
>
> **After that I returned the car keys to the valet in a sealed envelope. I had written "688*" on the envelope. Those were the first three figures of the number plate and the star stood for Étoile Limousine. I left the Ritz and walked home. I should say that the Étoile Limousine chauffeurs normally take the luxury cars home with them if they have**

---

[a] See Decoy Mercedes chapter.

a garage. Since I don't have one I always park the car in the Vendôme car park.

In theory the Mercedes 280 S was not due to go out again on the evening of 30 August 1997, unless anything unexpected came up. That's why I always leave the keys with the doorman.[823] **(WFJ)**

This vital testimony – withheld from the jury – reveals that certain factors were known in advance.

First, it was known that Lafaye's would be the only Ritz vehicle available – the other chauffeurs "normally take the luxury cars home with them". Second, it was known that Lafaye normally would be finished by 9 p.m. – "any job that's needed after 7 in the evening is done by the person on standby". Even the standby operation "is always from 7 to 9 [p.m.]". Third, it was known that the car was always parked in the same place – Lafaye parked his Mercedes "on the 3rd level of the Vendôme underground car park as I did every evening". Fourth, it was known that the keys for the Mercedes would be readily available – "I always leave the keys with the doorman".

It was also known that this Mercedes S280 had untinted windows, something that later would assist with the operation – it enabled the pursuing motorbikes to be more intimidating and take invasive photos of Diana and Dodi through the clear glass.[a]

These factors – that Lafaye's vehicle would definitely be available, that it would be in a predetermined location, that the keys would be easily accessible – all enabled a premeditated operation to occur.

All these factors were known or obtainable by inside agents, Henri Paul or Claude Roulet.

And all these factors were withheld from the jury.[b]

---

[a] See later.

[b] On 20 April 1997 this Mercedes was stolen from outside a Paris restaurant. It was recovered on May 6 and some significant parts had been stripped: the power steering and the antilock braking system, the linings and inner workings of the doors, the wheels and tyres. The car was repaired and passed an MoT test on July 7. Lafaye has been reported saying there were still problems with the car: "You had to know it to drive it safely and Henri Paul had never driven it." (WFJ) The timing of the theft – over four months before the crash – would appear to preclude any direct link to the deaths: it occurred three months before the Diana-Dodi relationship commenced. It could therefore not have been known that Princess Diana would be visiting the Paris Ritz and potentially travelling in this Mercedes S280. Both Musa and Lafaye have commented on the theft: Musa – 4 Dec 07: from 65.2; Thomas Sancton and Scott MacLeod, Death of a Princess: An Investigation, 1998, page 194; Lesley Hussell, Diana 1961-1997: Mirror Investigates: The Fiction and the Facts, The Mirror, 11 September 1997; Lafaye – David Montgomery, Chauffeur Tells of Faults with Diana

Roulet's Timing

Claude Roulet left the Ritz that night at 8.20 p.m. – contrary to Roulet's repeated accounts that he had left by 7.15 p.m.[a]

Lafaye states that "it was about 8.15 [p.m.] when I got back to the Ritz" in the Mercedes S280. He added that he parked it in the regular spot and left "the keys with the doorman". (WFJ)

This was just five minutes before Roulet left the Ritz Hotel. It is possible that he may have waited for Lafaye's arrival and then assisted agents in identifying the vehicle. Roulet may have even been told that tracking equipment was being fitted to assist with protection from a security threat. Later evidence will show that it is likely the seat belts – particularly Diana's – were tampered with.

Roulet's lying insistence on a 7.15 p.m. Ritz departure time, along with a 7.30 meeting with Henri[b], would distance Roulet away from anything to do with the Mercedes. This may have been an attempt to cover up his possible role – probably unwitting – in assisting with tampering of the Mercedes.

If the French had conducted a serious investigation they would have seized the CCTV footage from the Vendôme car park for the four hour period that the car was sitting there, from 8.15 p.m. to 12.15 a.m.[c]

It will become clear as this story progresses that the presence of this Mercedes S280 was an integral part of the plan for a staged crash.

The CCTV footage of Roulet leaving the hotel at 8.20 p.m. is not showing on the inquest website.[d] This makes it impossible to know if he accessed the car key cabinet before leaving the hotel. Even if Roulet didn't get the keys for the Mercedes S280, it is possible that part of his "job" on that night may have been to stay at the hotel until he was able to confirm that the third car – the Mercedes S280 – had arrived.

Death Car, The Scotsman, 28 July 1998. This theft is also briefly mentioned in the Paget Report, p424.

[a] See previous chapter.

[b] Which also will be shown to be false – see later.

[c] The approximate time the Mercedes was moved to the rear of the Ritz ahead of the final journey – see later.

[d] Why is this?

32 Apartment to Hotel: 9.30 p.m.

At around 9.30 p.m. Diana and Dodi left the apartment in the Mercedes 600 and returned to the Ritz Hotel. Philippe Dourneau was at the wheel and they were followed by Musa, Rees-Jones and Wingfield in the Range Rover, with a contingent of paparazzi vehicles.

"Coming From All Angles"

Dourneau was the only person travelling in the Mercedes with Diana and Dodi. His account is very clear – the paparazzi were a major disruption on this trip. Three days later he told the French investigation:

> **There were lots of paparazzi. They were coming from all angles, from front and behind. They were all over the place – some of them were recceing, travelling in front of our vehicle to see where we were going.**[824]

At the inquest Dourneau elaborated: "There were motorbikes everywhere. I remember that; on the pavement, on the roads, everywhere."[825]

Didier Gamblin was on duty at the apartment. He described what he saw as the Mercedes 600 left:

> **They went completely crazy. They called their motorbikes and set off like lunatics to follow the car. They could have knocked pedestrians over on the pavement. People had to press themselves against the wall to let the paparazzi's motorbikes past. They were driving on the pavement.**[826]

Changing Their Evidence

On 1 September 1997 Jean-François Musa, the driver of the Range Rover, told the police that the paparazzi were "a little more aggressive".[827]

But by the time of the inquest his evidence had changed. Musa now said there were "very few" paparazzi and "there was no aggressivity issues – it was a rather quiet journey".[828]

Then when reminded of his description of aggressive behaviour made the day following the crash, Musa replied: "It is a little bit old, I do not really remember."[829]

Under pressure Musa did admit that "there were paparazzi taking photographs".[830]

Kez Wingfield, who was in the Range Rover with Musa, has also inexplicably changed his evidence.

Two days after the crash Wingfield told police: "On the way we were followed constantly by 15 or so paparazzi."[831] But by the time of the inquest he changed this to "possibly one or two" and "there were certainly no problems during that trip".[832]

Wingfield was confronted at the inquest with his "15 or so" statement account. He then confirmed it – contradicting his "one or two" evidence – then added: "it's nowhere near as many as there were there in the afternoon and … it was nowhere near as intrusive".[833]

Wingfield doesn't explain what he means by the "afternoon" move and it is surprising that no one asks him. Their only earlier trips where they were dealing with paparazzi were the initial Le Bourget to Paris trip and the 7 p.m. Ritz to the apartment journey. There were clearly not more than 15 on the airport trip, and Wingfield had described the 7 p.m. move as "no problem".[834] Wingfield should have been pressed on what he meant by his "nowhere near as many as … the afternoon" statement.

Wingfield's assessment of the presence of 15 paparazzi is corroborated by Pierre Suu – "there [were] … about 15 journalists"[835] – who along with all the other paparazzi, said that the trip took place at a normal pace and with no press intrusion.

Breaking the Rules

Rees-Jones has never been asked for his recollections regarding the paparazzi on this trip from the apartment to the Ritz. In his statement to Operation Paget, taken on 21 December 2004, he said this:

> **On that last trip from the apartment to the Ritz I decided with Kez to travel in the backup vehicle with him.... This was because Dodi and the Princess were getting stressed by the whole press business and I decided to let them have more space. We were right behind so there was no compromise in their security.[836] (WFJ)**

Why is Philippe Dourneau's assessment so different to that of all of the other witnesses?

It is possible that the situation on this trip for the Mercedes 600 was quite different to what was encountered by the Range Rover.

Did the Range Rover fall behind in the traffic, leaving the Mercedes to be isolated and harassed by fake "paparazzi" – similar to those that had troubled the convoy on the earlier trip from Le Bourget?

If something like that happened, it is likely that Musa, Wingfield and Rees-Jones would not be prepared to admit to it, as it could reflect badly on all three of them: Musa, because as he said, it was his job to "drive very closely behind, to make sure that no one can get in between";[837] Wingfield and Rees-Jones, because they know full well that one of the bodyguards should have been in the Mercedes with the principals, and that was not the case on this particular trip.

If this is a case of Rees-Jones and Wingfield covering for themselves for a misjudgement, it will not be the only occasion, because there is clear evidence that they did something similar much later in the evening at the Ritz.[a]

The fact that both Musa and Wingfield changed their evidence indicates they are not comfortable around this subject.

The statements taken from the paparazzi were made under pressure – they were under arrest, or in some cases they were about to be arrested.[b] As with the Le Bourget to Paris trip, none of the paparazzi describe anything untoward happening on this apartment to Ritz trip. From the witness evidence of the earlier Le Bourget trip, it was clear that there were non-paparazzi motorbikes present, and this trip may have been similar. Suu describes "three motorbikes [and] two scooters" amongst the paparazzi,[838] whereas Dourneau said there were "many motorbikes".[839]

Apartment To Hotel

Of the non-paparazzi testimony, Dourneau's has been the most consistent right from the day after the crash through to the inquest ten years later. It is common sense that if his account is true, then it is so graphic that it is the sort of picture that would leave a strong imprint on a person's mind: paparazzi "coming from all angles". Also, Dourneau does not appear to have any particular reason to lie about this evidence.

Dourneau was not asked by the French police to describe these motorbikes, and there is no apparent attempt to secure any identification of the participants from him.

The full transcript of Gamblin's statement reveals that a month after the crash, he was able to identify quite a few of the paparazzi who were present outside the apartment. Gamblin was shown 34 photos, but was not asked how many there were that he couldn't identify.[c]

---

[a] See later.
[b] Darmon was the only paparazzo who was subjected to inquest cross-examination – and he was a driver, not a photographer.
[c] See Inquest Transcripts: 7 Mar 08: From 104.17

Musa stated that "there were paparazzi taking photographs" during the trip.[840] If this is true, and the photos were taken by the paparazzi, why have they never been published?

Dourneau's evidence is supported by François Tendil, who was at the hotel when the convoy arrived. He testified: "It was just crazy…. When they came back in the hotel, there were more than 100 paparazzi behind them".[841]

Dourneau's account fits with the pressure and tension that was mounting throughout the afternoon and into the evening – pressure that is seen as coming from the paparazzi, but in reality may have been coming from people who were pretending to be paparazzi.

This manufactured environment could have been the catalyst for decisions made later in the evening that eventually led to the crash.

33　Henri's Missing Hours

Ritz CCTV footage shows Henri Paul walking out of the hotel via the front entrance at 7.01 p.m., four minutes after Diana and Dodi had left for the apartment from the rear exit, at 6.57 p.m.

Then three hours later – at 10.07 p.m. – the same CCTV camera records Henri reentering the hotel.

One of the most important mysteries around this entire case is: What did Henri Paul do during those three hours, from 7 to 10 p.m. on 30 August 1997?

Prior Knowledge

On September 1 Jean-François Musa told the French police that on Friday August 29 Henri had asked him to "make himself available for chauffeur duties outside the Ritz Hotel at about 5 p.m. the next day."[842] (WFJ) And in 2006 he told Paget: "I got to the Ritz late in the [Saturday] afternoon. I was with the Range Rover by about 17.00 hrs [5 p.m.] or 18.00 hrs [6 p.m.]."[843] (WFJ)

By August 29 Henri knew that he would be driving the back-up car to the airport,[a] but he had no intention of driving after 5 p.m.[b]

Henri would be free for other activities. Musa would be doing any further back-up car driving required.

The jury heard neither Musa's September 1 nor his Paget account – and these were also withheld from Musa himself at the inquest.

Instead what happened is the jury were provided with a confusing conflict, as Musa tried to recall events from ten years ago.

They first heard Musa say: "I had to be available probably on the Saturday, at noon, in front of the hotel"[844] and "I think … I was there around lunchtime".[845]

---

[a] See earlier Driving Mission chapter.
[b] Earlier evidence showed that Henri Paul arrived at the Ritz driving the back-up vehicle at around 4.30 p.m.

Then under later questioning with a different lawyer, they heard Musa confirm that Henri had asked him "to make yourself available … at the Ritz between 3 and 6 in the afternoon".[846]

So the jury heard noon, then the conflicting 3 to 6 p.m. – the closest to the truth would have been the early account of 5 p.m., not heard.

Henri drove the Range Rover from the airport to the apartment, then to Villa Windsor and on to the Ritz, but then did not want to continue driving it. In 2006 Musa indicated to the police that he was mystified by Henri Paul's actions: "As far as I know there was no reason why Mr Paul couldn't have driven later that day if required, but I didn't ask why he couldn't have driven that evening, as I felt it was an honour for me." [847] (WFJ)

Jumping ahead for a moment, it is clear that Henri was once again available for driving duties after he arrived back at the hotel at 10 p.m., because it was he who took the wheel of the Mercedes at 12.18 a.m. – even though Musa and Dourneau were still clearly available to drive.

How did Henri know on the Friday that he wouldn't be intending to drive from around 5 p.m. on the Saturday?

Common sense suggests that he knew there was something else he had to do, or somewhere else he had to be, for a period on the Saturday evening.

Is there a connection between Henri's request for Musa to be available from 5 p.m., and Henri's disappearance between 7 and 10 p.m.?

This is not a question the jury would have asked themselves, because they were never given the evidence that Musa was requested to arrive around 5 p.m.

Needless to say, this issue is omitted from Baker's 80,000 words of Summing Up.

Was He Still Working?

Henri's boss, Claude Roulet, told Paget in 2005: "[Henri] finished work at around 1900 hours [7 p.m.], and he was not due back in until Monday, 1 September 1997."[848] (WFJ) This was confirmed by Frank Klein who told the inquest: "[Henri] left the job at 7 o'clock [Saturday] and his work was finished".[849]

Had Henri really stopped working at 7 p.m. on Saturday?

Didier Gamblin was on security duty at Dodi's apartment – he described three work-related phone calls involving Henri that took place between 7 and 7.30 p.m.

First, Gamblin said: "My colleague and I had been told by M Paul that the car was leaving the Ritz to go to the flat" – this was at around 7 p.m.[850]

Next, he phoned Henri after the couple arrived at 7.15 p.m.: "I [asked him] … if we should … stop the photographers taking any pictures".[851]

Then finally Henri called him "at around 7.30". Henri told Gamblin that "the couple were due to come out at 9.00 p.m.… Mr Paul had come to the end of his day and he was going home … [and] my job would be finished when the couple left the flat to go to a Paris restaurant, le Benoît."[852]

Gamblin's evidence is clear and there is an unmistakable time sequence to these phone calls – they tie in to the arrival of Diana and Dodi, which we know was around 7.15, after leaving the hotel at 6.57 p.m.

Henri was still in work mode around 7.30 p.m., and was very much aware of what was happening with Diana and Dodi.

Henri indicated to Gamblin that he was still at the Ritz and was heading home. The CCTV shows that he had already left the Ritz half an hour earlier, and other evidence indicates he never went home – see later.

It is incredible that Didier Gamblin was never interviewed by the British police and was not called for cross-examination at the inquest.

Working Sunday

In October 1997 Gamblin stated:

Mr Paul would definitely have come and joined me in Rue Arsène Houssaye at about 8 o'clock [Sunday morning], as he had told me. We were going to look after the couple in the daytime on Sunday and when they left the flat.[853]

Henri Paul had made a definite arrangement to work with Gamblin from around 8 a.m. on the Sunday.

Jean-François Musa told the French investigation in 1998:

When we parted company [Henri] had said to me 'Call me when you get finished this evening so that I can make arrangements for tomorrow [Sunday]'.[854] **(WFJ)**

At that stage – just before 7 p.m. on Saturday – Henri was unaware whether he or Musa would be driving the back-up car the next day.

According to the limited amount of what has been shown of Musa's 10 police statements[855] in the Paget Report, there is no reference to Henri confirming the Sunday arrangements with Musa, when he saw him much later on the Saturday evening (see later). Does that indicate that he was expecting to be driving again himself the next day?

No one at the inquest or in any of the police investigations has asked Philippe Dourneau the obvious question: What were the arrangements for the Sunday?

Henri indicated to his friend Badia Mouhib that "he could not see her that [Saturday] evening, but says that she should ring him Sunday at 3 p.m." [856] (WFJ)

This ties in directly with Diana and Dodi's intended arrival time in the UK[a], revealed in the cross-examination of Colin Tebbutt, Diana's driver. On Saturday he received a "message from [the] Princess of Wales' [office] to meet her at Stansted airport with BMW ... the next day [at] 2 o'clock".[857]

This suggests that Henri expected to be involved with the couple's visit right up until the time they left.

This is directly contrary to the evidence of Roulet and Klein, who said that Henri's work for the weekend was finished at 7 p.m. on Saturday. Klein was on holiday in Antibes, and he may have relied on retrospective communications from Roulet on this subject.

Someone Is Lying

It is clear from Gamblin and Musa that Henri Paul was not being secretive about the fact he was expecting to continue working on the Diana and Dodi visit. Yet Roulet's evidence was not "I don't remember": it was very definite that "he was not due back in until Monday".[858] (WFJ)

There are three possibilities:
  a) Roulet presumed Henri was finished for the weekend, but wasn't actually told this
  b) Henri misled Roulet by telling him he was finished, but in fact Henri knew that he wasn't finished
  c) Roulet has said that Henri was finished, but knew that it wasn't true.

If Roulet had only made a presumption it would seem unlikely that he would make such a definite statement on oath.

If possibility "a" is taken out, the other two possibilities indicate a sinister action.

If Henri lied to Roulet about this, he may have had a reason to want to keep working without Roulet being aware that he was doing so. One would still have to ask: Why would Henri tell Gamblin and Musa if he was trying to hide the information from Roulet?

If Roulet lied on oath about this, he may have had a reason to distance himself from any knowledge that Henri Paul was actually still working after he left the hotel at 7 p.m.

As the story progresses other evidence will come to light that indicates "c" is the most likely scenario.

Roulet's Meeting

Claude Roulet stated that he met Henri Paul by accident during the period between 7 and 10 p.m.

---

[a] France is one hour ahead: 2 p.m. in London is 3 p.m. in Paris.

On Monday 1 September 1997 – the day after the crash – Roulet told the French police: "I myself saw [Henri] at about 19.30 hours [7.30 p.m.] in a cafe called 'Le Bar de Bourgogne' in the Rue des Petits Champs."[859]

The following day – September 2 – in a separate police statement, he said this: "I do not know where Mr Paul was between the end of his shift and his return to the hotel."[860]

One of these is a lie – both cannot be true.

At the inquest Roulet was confronted with this clear conflict – all he said was: "Yes".[861]

Then on September 8 Roulet said: "I remember that Henry was at the [Bourgogne] bar, I called him and he came out and chatted with me for a few moments."[862]

In 2005 – eight years later – he had a more detailed recollection for Paget:

> **I saw Henri Paul in the Bar de Bourgogne…. He was on his own in the bar by the glass door which was open. He was drinking something, but I cannot say what it was. We very briefly exchanged a few words. I told him that I was in a hurry because I wanted to grab a bite to eat before going to wait for the couple outside Chez Benoît.[863]**

He confirmed this fuller account at the inquest.[864]

Roulet's problem is that the Bourgogne staff were interviewed by police on the 4th and 5th of September 1997, and their evidence is very clear – Henri Paul was not at their establishment at all on 30 August 1997. Head waiter, Bernard Lefort – who described Bourgogne as a "small" bar – said: "I did not see M Paul on Saturday 30th August throughout the entire day".[865] The manager, Myriam Lemaire, testified: "I worked from 11 am to 1 a.m. I did not see M Paul".[866]

There is no apparent reason why Lefort or Lemaire would lie, and given that Roulet's evidence has lacked credibility in other areas of this case, it is reasonable to conclude that Henri was not there.

At the inquest Frank Klein was asked whether he made enquiries about Henri's missing hours. He mentioned that "Claude Roulet has made some enquiries" but no information had come back.[867]

Yet Roulet was telling the police that he had seen Henri at the Bourgogne at 7.30 p.m.

Was Claude Roulet giving the police a different story to what he was telling his boss, Frank Klein?

The question is no longer whether Claude Roulet is lying, but rather: Why is Claude Roulet lying?

From 1 September 1997 onwards Roulet stated a definite recollection that he saw Henri at around 7.30 p.m., when years later the CCTV footage revealed that Roulet was at the Ritz until 8.20 p.m.[a]

Roulet's mobile records indicate that he was trying to phone Henri at home at a time very close to when he was supposed to have met him – see later.

Roulet may have been told by his intelligence handlers to fabricate false evidence of seeing Henri Paul in a bar. It will be shown later that Henri was framed for causing the crash with false evidence of him being a drunk driver.

Bribing a Witness

Bourgogne's Lemaire gave her statement on 4 September 1997 and Lefort was interviewed the following day, September 5.

Lefort told the police about an incident the previous evening:

> **At around 8.00 pm, two journalists who [Lefort] believed by their accent to be English, came into the bar.... They submitted me ... press cards.... One of them then said ... "Tell me that [Henri Paul] drank two whiskies and I will give you whatever you want." ... I ... called the police at the time to tell the police officer about it.[868]**

This incident occurred on September 4 at 8 p.m. This is the evening after Lemaire has given her evidence that Henri wasn't there, but before Lefort testified on September 5.

This approach to Lefort appears to have been made by people who had inside knowledge of what was happening in the French investigation. They seem to know to make the offer to Lefort, who hadn't yet given evidence, rather than Lemaire, who had. The two men also know the significance of the Bourgogne bar – Henri Paul frequented several bars and restaurants in the general area, but there is no record of any similar bribery occurring at any of those. The Bourgogne only gained importance to the investigation after the evidence of Roulet was taken on September 1, and this was not public knowledge on September 4.

Lefort was concerned enough about the approach that he called the police and also included the incident in his statement the next day. Lefort was not asked at the inquest what the response of the police was to his phone call.

It appears that the two "journalists" were desperate to prove that Henri was drinking during the hours of his disappearance. If they had been able to elicit a statement from Lefort that Henri had been drinking, Lefort would have been under pressure to make the same statement official to the police the next day. This then would have corroborated Roulet's evidence and provided "proof" – when combined with the autopsy results (see later) – that when Henri arrived at the Ritz later that night he had already "had a few" drinks.

---

[a] See earlier Dinner Decoy chapter.

On 5 September 1997 Lefort made a very serious allegation that he, an important witness, had been the subject of attempted bribery.

Why didn't the French police follow up on this?

Why did the 832 page official British police Paget Report leave out any mention of this attempted bribery that occurred four days after the crash?

Coroner Baker failed in his Summing Up to mention the attempted bribery on September 4. Baker also omits any mention of Lemaire's evidence that Henri wasn't there, thus pitting only Lefort's evidence against Roulet's conflicting account.[869]

This is misleading – the truth is that out of the three witnesses, there are two that say Henri was not there.

Phone Records

Roulet's phone records indicate that it was unlikely that he met Henri around 8.30 p.m.

An analysis of his mobile calls reveals that he phoned "the landline for Henri Paul at home" twice within a few minutes of the alleged meeting – at 8.33 and 8.35 p.m.[870]

Nevertheless Roulet stood by his evidence that he saw Henri at Bourgogne – right to the end.

Roulet said that "it maybe means that he told me he was going home",[871] but other evidence – see later – indicates that Henri never actually went home at all.

If the earlier scenario of Roulet leaving the hotel at 8.20 p.m., immediately after the Mercedes S280 arrives back, is correct, then there is a possibility that Roulet's attempts to contact Henri may have been to confirm the availability of the third car.[a] It is clear – see later – that the decoy plan could not have taken place without this car.

Baker intervened to shut down the Pauls' QC Richard Keen's cross-examination of Roulet at a critical moment. Keen says: "There is also the confusion about <u>why</u> you were phoning [Henri] at home" when Baker breaks in to say: "Can we move on, please".[872]

Roulet's evidence was that at 7 p.m. Henri had already finished work for the weekend.

The issue of why Roulet would be trying to phone Henri 1½ hours later has never been addressed.

Operation Paget wrote in 2006:

---

[a] The third car was the Mercedes S280. The first two cars were the Mercedes 600 and the Range Rover.

> **Claude Roulet made <u>two attempts that evening</u> to speak with Henri Paul on the telephone.... [He] rang Henri Paul's mobile telephone number at 9.57 p.m. and immediately after, at 9.58 p.m., [a] his home telephone.[873] (WFJ)**

Paget misses out the two phone call attempts to contact Henri just after 8.30 p.m.[b]

Mark Stokes, the mobile phone expert employed by Paget, was asked about "telephone data for Claude Roulet". He replied: "I do not even know who the name is".[874] He was not challenged on this despite the Paget Report saying: "These calls[c] were confirmed by telephone data from Claude Roulet's telephone."[875]

There appears to be a concerted effort by Scotland Yard to conceal the evidence of those two Roulet phone calls at 8.33 and 8.35.

Why?

The existence of those phone calls helps dislodge Roulet's chance meeting evidence – the <u>main evidence that places Henri Paul drinking in a bar between 7 and 10 p.m.</u> This – along with other evidence still to be looked at – undermines the very heart of the Paget police finding that the crash was caused by a driver influenced by drink, Henri Paul.

Paget's statement that Roulet made only two calls to Henri – 9.57 and 9.58 – also misses out a later call he made to Henri at the hotel at 11.30 p.m. This is dealt with later in this book.[d]

Coroner's Deception

Scott Baker stated in his Summing Up:

> **[Roulet's phone records] showed that he had phoned Henri Paul's flat at 8.33 p.m. and 8.35 p.m., and the point was made that he would hardly have been doing so if he had seen Henri Paul in the Bar de Bourgogne around 8.20 to 8.25.[876]**

---

[a] These two later calls are addressed later.

[b] The Paget Report also stated on page 205: "Myriam Lemaire and Bernard Lefort, two of the staff at 'Bar de Bourgogne', interviewed on 4 and 5 September 1997, stated that Henri Paul <u>was in their bar</u> on Saturday 30 August 1997." (WFJ) This was at best an inadvertent mistake, but when looked at in the context of the MPS treatment of the phone call evidence, it seems more likely to be a deliberate lie.

[c] At 9.57 and 9.58 p.m.

[d] Mansfield noted that on Claude Roulet's phone account "there are other initials of HP [Henri Paul]. I do not know who wrote them on, but they are not all Henri Paul's numbers." 17 Mar 08: 15.14. This indicates that there were other phone calls on the account for August 30 where someone – possibly even Roulet himself – had noted "HP" alongside. They may have been numbers called by Roulet during his efforts to locate or contact Henri Paul.

If the jury were confused over this issue of the Roulet meeting with Henri, Baker added to it by getting the timing wrong.

The CCTV shows Roulet leaving the Ritz at 8.20 p.m. Roulet's own evidence is that the walk from the hotel to Bourgogne would take "approximately 7 minutes but it could have been 8 or 9 minutes this evening".[877] Taking the shortest option, 7 minutes, that places the meeting between 8.27 and 8.29.

By falsely stating "8.20 to 8.25" Baker has effectively distanced the phone calls from the meeting, enabling the meeting to look more plausible, as it comes up to 15 minutes before the calls (8.33 and 8.35).

The reality is that the calls would have been placed just a few minutes after the meeting – that is, the meeting that never actually took place.

Changing His Story

Claude Roulet's 2 September 1997 statement – made two days after the crash – is the only time that he didn't describe the 7.30 meeting with Henri. In that statement he appears to come up with an entirely different scenario regarding Henri's three hour disappearance: "I have just heard that he might have been with friends."[878ab] In his statement the day before this, he had said: "I myself saw him ... in a cafe called 'Le Bar de Bourgogne'...."[879] On September 8 Roulet said: "I remember that Henry was at the bar".[880]

Both of these scenarios – with friends or in a bar – have a common factor: The likelihood that Henri Paul was drinking alcohol between 7 and 10 p.m.

Claude Garrec stated that often on a Saturday night Henri would socialise at Garrec's house, but on this particular Saturday Henri had said that he would be working late, so couldn't make it.[881] (WFJ) As Henri's parents said: "If he was having a drink with a friend, it was with Claude Garrec, and Claude Garrec was not with him during this period of time.".[882]

Why has Roulet consistently tried to connect Henri's three hour absence with being in a place or situation where he could have had alcohol? [c]

---

[a] Roulet should have been asked about this claim at the inquest, but wasn't. Roulet never said where he heard this from. There has never been any other evidence to suggest this was ever a possibility.

[b] "The Friends" is an in-house term for MI6: Nigel West, *The Friends*, p1.

[c] In the last couple of days of inquest hearings Roulet came up with completely new but fabricated "evidence" that Henri was drunk when he took the wheel. This is addressed in Part 1, the Dourneau and Musa section of Chapter 3B.

Visit to Le Champmeslé

Josiane Le Tellier owns the Le Champmeslé Lesbian Bar, a short distance from Henri's apartment. She gave evidence that he visited the bar late on 30 August 1997.

Three weeks after the crash Josiane stated that she saw Henri at 9.45 p.m.[883] (WFJ) She told the British police in 2004: "He made an appointment to meet up with friends from the Bar de Bourgogne later that evening at around midnight."[884a] (WFJ)

He Didn't Go Home

Claude Garrec confirmed he listened to Henri's landline answering machine messages – he said there were "three to four"[885] and they were "just phone calls from friends".[886b]

Henri's friend, Jean-Claude Morere, told the French police on 17 September 1997:

> **I did phone [Henri] at home on Saturday 30th August to ask him to come to dinner with me and a friend that evening. I left a message on his answering machine asking him to call me back. When I had not heard from him before dinner time, I rang him at home again at about 8 in the evening. There was no answer.... I must say I was surprised that Henri didn't ring me back after I left the message on his answering machine – that makes me think he didn't go home again, because he would have been bound to call me on my mobile when he got my message.[887]**

Henri didn't reply to Morere's early message. It seems that Morere would have expected a courtesy response – even if Henri had still been in work mode – if he had heard the message.

Corroborating this was the MPS evidence that "telephone records ... of Henri Paul's home telephone reveal no [outgoing] calls being made between 7 and 10 [p.m.]".[888]

Morere also stated: "When we went out, [Henri] usually changed whenever he could get home before meeting us". He added that he would "put on casual clothes, jeans and a bomber jacket – it was quite different from the suit that he normally wore".[889]

The CCTV footage viewed at the inquest revealed that when Henri re-entered the Ritz at 10.07 p.m. "he [was] wearing exactly the same clothes that he was wearing when he went off duty [at 7.01 p.m.] ... suit, blue shirt and [the same] tie".[890]

---

[a] This evidence indicates that Henri expected he would be at work for a couple of hours.

[b] The French carried out a pathetic "investigation" into Henri's answering machine messages – see Part 1, section on Phones in the Henri Paul chapter.

This affirms that a) he didn't go home and b) he still considered that he was in work mode.[ab]

The only possible evidence pointing to Henri going home is in Josiane Le Tellier's earliest statement where she says that at around 9.45 p.m. "he arrived from the direction of his home, and he was holding a small white bag".[891] (WFJ) Given that Henri lived very close to Josiane's bar, the implication is that Henri was walking, but at the inquest Josiane said that "he parked his car right in front of my bar, and just came in".[892]

Josiane should have been asked about this possible conflict, but never was. It is also neglectful questioning that Josiane was never asked about the white bag at the inquest.

In the final analysis Josiane did not know whether Henri had been home or not. There is the possibility that Henri had quickly slipped in and out of his flat without checking the answering machine.

Whatever the case, the balance of evidence indicates that Henri was certainly not at home for any prolonged period.

The Missing Hours

The reality is that there is some knowledge about Henri's movements during the mysterious three hour period.

We know that Henri:
- had told Claude Garrec that he would be working late that night
- phoned Didier Gamblin about work at around 7.30 p.m.
- didn't spend the time at home
- didn't spend the time with friends or family
- entered Josiane Le Tellier's bar for a short time at around 9.45 p.m.
- drove off in his car from Josiane's just after 9.45 p.m.[c]

There is something else that we know that is very significant: We know that Henri either spent the disappearance time on his own or with a person or persons.

Whoever Henri did spend the time with, does not want us to know who they are and what Henri was doing – otherwise they would have come forward. So he, she or they have something to hide.

---

[a] Earlier evidence also indicated Henri was still working after 7 p.m.
[b] This also fits with evidence from Francois Tendil that Henri told him "Just call me on my <u>mobile</u> phone" if Diana and Dodi returned to the hotel. 3 Dec 07: 52.11. This indicates that around 7 p.m. Henri already knew he may not be going home.
[c] Josiane: "He waved and drove off very calmly.": 5 Sep 97 statement read out 13 Mar 08: 93.18.

If Henri spent the time on his own somewhere, then why hasn't someone from the Paris public come forward with a sighting?

If he had been at a loose end he would have gone to Garrec's place, where he regularly went on Saturday nights.

Henri considered himself to be working, in one form or another: he phoned Gamblin at 7.30; he didn't change his clothes; he told Josiane that he was "on call"[a] and he didn't spend any time with friends.

---

[a] Josiane: "He said that he was on call and that he would be back around midnight" 13 Mar 08: 91.3.

34   Henri's Mysterious Ritz Return

Diana and Dodi arrived back at the Ritz Hotel at 9.50 p.m. and Henri Paul parked his Mini outside the front and walked back in at 10.07 – 17 minutes later.

Josiane Le Tellier gave evidence that at around 9.45 Henri paid a short visit to her lesbian bar, before driving off in his car.[a] This was approximately 15 minutes before Ritz Night Security Manager, François Tendil, phoned Henri on his mobile to inform him that Diana and Dodi had arrived back at the hotel – Tendil's 1½ minute phone call finished at exactly 10.00 p.m.[b] Henri parked his Mini outside the front of the hotel at 10.06 – precisely six minutes after the completion of Tendil's call.

The Ritz CCTV evidence is clear: Tendil's call was completed at 10.00 and Henri arrived at 10.06.[893]

On 2 September 1997 Claude Roulet told the French police that "it took [Henri] 15 minutes by car to arrive from the time of the [Tendil] telephone call."[894] (WFJ)

Just two days after the crash, and Roulet has converted 6 minutes into 15 minutes. Roulet appears to be attempting to distance Henri Paul from prior knowledge of a return by the couple to the Ritz.

Josiane Le Tellier, Owner of Le Champmeslé Lesbian Bar, saw Henri Paul around 15 minutes before Tendil's phone call.

Josiane's evidence indicates that as early as 9.45 p.m. Henri Paul was preparing to go back to work, for about two hours – "he said that he was on call and that he would be back around midnight".[895]

---

[a] See previous chapter.
[b] CCTV footage showed Tendil on the phone from 9.58.28 to 9.59.57: Inquest Timeline Summary of Key Events. According to the Paget Report (p214) this call was registered on Henri's mobile at 10 p.m. (WFJ)

Could it be that Henri was expecting a call from François Tendil – a call that would be triggered by the 9.50 return of Diana and Dodi to the hotel?

Roulet's Calls

After being told by Dourneau and Dodi that the Mercedes is now heading for the Ritz, Claude Roulet describes making three phone calls. First, a call to the Ritz Hotel, and then two attempted phone calls to Henri Paul.

There are inconsistencies in his accounts of what occurred.

Roulet's earliest September 1 statement is the most straightforward. He calls the hotel after 9.45 p.m. – "I then called the hotel to cancel the booking at Benoît's, to let the Ritz restaurant know, and to inform Security that they would be coming." He adds: "[The couple] had just arrived when I got through to Security".[896] (WFJ)

He gives three reasons for the call to the Ritz: 1) to get the hotel (concierge) to cancel the booking at Benoît's; 2) to let the Ritz restaurant know to set up for Diana and Dodi; 3) to notify security of the impending arrival. By the time he got through to the third location – security – it must have been after 9.50 p.m., because the couple had already arrived. There is no mention of any delay in getting through to security.[a]

In this first statement Roulet leaves out the two calls to Henri. We know these calls occurred because they are on Roulet's phone records.

It is on September 10, in Roulet's fourth statement[b], that he introduces the Henri Paul phone calls into his evidence – "I ... tried to contact Mr Paul without success on his mobile at 9.57 in the evening and at home (landline) at 9.58".[897] (WFJ)

It is not until Roulet's seventh statement, almost a year later to the French magistrate, that he first draws a direct connection between his phone call to the hotel and the Henri calls. Roulet suggests that he felt it of immediate importance to "tell him that it was not good enough that it took so long to get through to the security officer in the lobby".[898c] (WFJ)

In support of this new evidence, Roulet changed the timing of the Dourneau-Dodi phone call from 9.45 to 9.40 p.m.[899] (WFJ) – thus allowing for an extra five minutes of delay in him getting through to security.

From Roulet's first statement it appears that he received the Mercedes phone call at 9.45 p.m. He would have rung the Ritz, asked for and spoken to the concierge, asked for and spoken to the restaurant, and then asked for

---

[a] He introduces this delay later – see below.

[b] Roulet gave six statements to the French police in the first few weeks after the crash.

[c] In his statement on September 10, Roulet said he was calling "to inform him of a problem with a temp", but he does not connect it to the earlier Ritz call, and does not flesh out any detail: Paget Report, p216 (WFJ).

security. It is logical that by the time he was put through to security it could already have been 9.50 p.m., and the actual arrival of Diana and Dodi may well have contributed to any delay he had in being answered.[a]

Roulet doesn't mention any specific problem with a particular staff member in his 1998 statement – just that he rang Henri to complain that it "took so long to get through".

In his 2005 Paget statement he reverts back to omitting the Henri calls – he states: "On my mobile I then immediately phoned the Ritz.... After that I went directly home."[900] (WFJ)

In the course of 11 statements[b] plus the inquest, the name of this employee and the exact mechanics of what he or she did wrong have never been explained. Despite that, Roulet has insisted on that mystery employee's negligence being the reason for the two late-night attempts to reach Henri Paul.[c]

It is amazing and significant that at the inquest Roulet was never actually asked about the purpose of those Henri Paul phone calls, and he never volunteered the information for the jury.

Roulet's 9.57 p.m. call to Henri's mobile takes on more significance in the light of François Tendil's call to Henri just after this – Tendil dials Henri at 9.58.28.[d] Tendil's call is answered, but Roulet's is not, even though it was at least a minute earlier.

When tied in with Josiane's evidence and the speed with which Henri returned to the hotel, there is an indication that Henri may have been sitting in his car near the hotel, waiting for Tendil's phone call.[e] This would be an explanation for why Roulet's call went unanswered – Henri not wanting to have a busy line when the anticipated call from Tendil came through. Tendil stated that he "did not hear any background noise",[901] and this could have been the case if Henri had been waiting in his car with the windows up.

Why would Roulet have wanted to call Henri?

If there was a prearranged plan for Henri to return to the hotel after Diana and Dodi, Roulet may have been intending to inform Henri that it was now definite that the couple had already returned. In Roulet's 1998 statement he felt he needed to add: "I had no intention whatsoever of asking him to come back to the Ritz."[902] (WFJ)

---

[a] The length and precise timing of the phone call would have appeared in Roulet's mobile phone records, but that information has never been divulged.

[b] 7 French and 4 British.

[c] A similar reason was also given by Roulet to explain an 11.30 p.m. call to Henri – see later.

[d] Ritz CCTV footage in Key Events Timeline.

[e] This possibility is discussed below.

Why Did He Return?

Tendil's call to Henri was terminated at precisely 10.00 p.m. Henri arrived by car outside the front of the Ritz at 10.06 – six minutes later.

The evidence – Josiane, speed of arrival, Roulet's unanswered call – indicates that Henri was expecting Tendil's call.

The question is: Why?

He had told Tendil that "it was impossible that they would be back" at the Ritz,[903] yet the most likely reason for a call from Tendil would be the couple's return. After all, Henri had also told Tendil: "Call me on my mobile phone" if they return.[904]

If a plan had been formulated, as the evidence indicates, then Henri would have had prior knowledge of the return to the Ritz – and indeed may have known from earlier in the afternoon, that would be occurring. If the plan dictated that Henri was required to be at the Ritz, then all Henri needed was the phone call from Tendil, and in the meantime he would be on standby ready for a quick return – which occurred.

If Henri returned on Tendil's phone call then, probably unbeknown to Henri, that would assist in the ease of a later cover-up. John Stevens and Scott Baker would be free to say: "The first Henri Paul knew that Diana and Dodi were back at the Ritz was when he received a call from François Tendil."

One could argue that the only reason Henri acquiesced to getting Tendil to call him on their return, was because Tendil hassled Henri. The answer to this conundrum appears in the evidence of a person who was never heard from at the inquest, David Bevierre.

Much has been said – at the inquest and in the Paget Report – to distance Henri Paul from the possibility that he could have expected Tendil's phone call.

David Bevierre – a security officer at the Ritz – told the French investigation just ten days after the crash: "In cases like this, we always notify the Head of Security or his deputy."[905] (WFJ)

This reveals that it would have been normal procedure to contact Henri in such an event as the couple's return. If Henri had prior knowledge of Diana and Dodi's destination being the Ritz, he already would have known that a call to notify him would be forthcoming.

It is incredible that David Bevierre was not called at the inquest, and even more so, that his statement was not even read out.

In August 1998 Claude Roulet told the investigation:

> **Henri Paul decided to return to the hotel off his own bat, and without being asked by Mr Tendil or myself, <u>that anyway is what he said to me himself</u> over the phone.**[906a] (WFJ)

---

[a] Roulet spoke to Henri on the phone at 11.30 p.m. – see later.

Yet at the inquest Richard Keen QC put this to Roulet: "It would appear from what we have heard ... [that Henri] simply volunteered to go back into the Ritz that evening and did so." And Roulet replied: "That is what was said. He did not say this to me."[907]

There is a clear conflict in Roulet's evidence. In 1998 Henri told him that he returned "off his own bat". At the inquest Roulet is saying the opposite: Henri did not tell him that.

Both can't be true.

Missing Hours and Rapid Return

Scott Baker summed up to his jury: "The evidence is that [Henri] was not expecting to return to work that night"[908] and this: "Henri Paul went off duty at 7 p.m. and ... he thought he had finished for the day."[909]

The implication of this for the jury is clear: when Henri Paul left the Ritz Hotel at 7 p.m. he had no idea that Diana and Dodi would be returning. As a result, if he was working with plotters, Henri would have been unable to help them because he had no relevant information to impart.

An analysis of the events and evidence, as we have done, reveals that Baker's simplistic approach – which may be appealing to some – lacks substance.

There is substantial evidence that by 7 p.m. Henri was planning to continue working that weekend – Garrec, Badia, Musa, Gamblin, Morere and Josiane. Musa's evidence also shows that on the Friday Henri organised him to come in to drive from 5 p.m., covering the period when Henri disappeared for three hours.

Possibly the most important aspect in this area is the significant amount of evidence showing Roulet's testimony falling down on several key points:
- his departure time from the hotel (CCTV footage)
- the accidental meeting with Henri Paul (Lefort. Lemaire, phone evidence)
- his four attempts to contact Henri Paul – 7.33, 7.35, 9.57 and 9.58 p.m.
- the timing of the wait outside Chez Benoît.

The unreliable nature of Claude Roulet's evidence effectively removes him from any lists of credible witnesses.

But it does more than that: it raises the issue of what his reason for lying would be, and when studied along with other evidence, Roulet becomes implicated as an accessory to an assassination, albeit probably unwilling and unknowing.

There has been an orchestrated attempt to suggest that Henri was probably drinking during his period of disappearance. Roulet is involved in this – his evidence of Henri being with friends (2 Sep 97) and also bumping into Henri in the bar environment of Bourgogne. Both of these accounts are fictitious.

The attempt to bribe the Bourgogne barman on 4 September 1997 is along the same theme, as is the evidence of Posner that Henri drank alcohol with a DGSE agent.[a]

Operation Paget concluded in its report:

No matter which scenario one takes to account for Henri Paul's whereabouts in the three hours from 7 p.m. to 10 p.m.: at home alone or with a companion; in a restaurant or other establishment; or even in the company of some form of security service officers, he would have had no reason not to drink alcohol. He did not expect to return to work that evening. In all of these scenarios, there was no reason to believe that anyone at the Ritz Hotel would have known that Henri Paul had a level of alcohol in his body when he returned to the Ritz Hotel just after 10 p.m.[910] (WFJ)

The Coroner reinforces this pattern in his Summing Up: "[Henri] certainly had the opportunity to drink and the evidence is that he was not expecting to return to work that night."[911]

The reality is that there is no credible evidence that suggests Henri was drinking during this period, and any suggestion that he was appears to be based on smoke and mirrors.

On the other hand, on a comparison of Josiane's various statements, it becomes apparent that at around 9.45 p.m. Henri was preparing to return to work for about two hours. Josiane saw Henri drive off in his car at that time. Henri's extremely quick response to Tendil's phone call – six minutes in Saturday night traffic – indicates that he was already in his car and close to the hotel, when he received the call.

When Claude Roulet's evidence becomes shaky, and he himself becomes implicated, the Chez Benoît destination scenario no longer looks convincing. The possible use of Chez Benoît as a decoy plan would tend to fit with the evidence of another decoy plan later that night – see later.

There is evidence from those who weren't at the scene – Mohamed, Rogers, Yassin – that the real predetermined destination was the Ritz. The evidence that there was a huge crowd build-up outside the Ritz before their arrival supports this – it also indicates that inside information was being picked up in some way. Earlier evidence showed that the phone calls were being monitored, allowing this destination information to be readily available to intelligence agencies.

One of the most telling facts surrounding Henri Paul's disappearance is that a substantial part of the evidence relating to it was never heard by the jury. If you look back through these last two chapters you will notice that a lot of the most shocking evidence that has been discussed has "WFJ"[b] next to

---

[a] Gerald Posner is a US journalist – his evidence is addressed in Part 1, section on DGSE Meeting in the Henri Paul's Movements chapter.

[b] Withheld From Jury.

it. Although the evidence was given by the witness, this was not at the inquest, and the jury neither heard nor had access to the witnesses' statements.

The jury were expected to draw conclusions regarding Henri's missing three hours without even being able to hear some of the most significant evidence.

Timeline of Events: Ritz CCTV: 10.06 p.m. to 12.24 a.m.

Time	Event
10.06	Henri parks his Mini out the front of the Ritz
10.07	Henri enters Ritz
10.08	Henri enters Bar Vendôme
10.10	Rees-Jones exits Bar Vendôme and Ritz and makes a mobile phone call
10.19	Dodi exits Imperial Suite and meets Rocher Dodi & Rocher talk for 1½ minutes
10.21	Dodi enters Imperial Suite Rees-Jones concludes his phone call and re-enters Ritz and Bar Vendôme
10.25	Henri exits Bar Vendôme
10.30	Henri talks with Rocher for about a minute
10.34	Henri exits Ritz
10.36	Henri walks into Place Vendôme and out of CCTV range
10.43	Henri comes back into range, and enters Ritz
10.45	Henri enters Bar Vendôme
11.09	Rees-Jones, Wingfield & Henri exit Bar Vendôme Rees-Jones & Wingfield head upstairs to the Imperial Suite foyer area
11.10	Henri exits Ritz and talks to paparazzi
11.13	Henri enters Ritz
11.14	Henri talks to Rees-Jones & Wingfield for several minutes outside the Imperial Suite
11.18	Rocher arrives upstairs and talks to Dodi at Imperial Suite door for 30 seconds, then leaves
11.20	Henri heads downstairs
11.21	Wingfield throws out his arms, clasps his hands together and slumps forward Henri exits Ritz and talks to paparazzi Rees-Jones & Wingfield talk continuously for six minutes

11.26	Henri enters Ritz
11.27	Henri rejoins Rees-Jones outside Imperial Suite
	Wingfield goes downstairs and looks outside
11.29	Wingfield returns upstairs and talks to Henri & Rees-Jones
11.30	Rocher comes upstairs to get Henri for a phone call
	Henri heads downstairs and takes phone from Tendil
	Henri goes out of CCTV range with the phone
11.34	Henri finishes phone call
11.36	Henri goes back upstairs
11.37	Henri talks to Rees-Jones & Wingfield
11.38	Rees-Jones makes a phone call with Henri standing next to him for 2 minutes
11.41	Rees-Jones finishes the call and talks to Henri
11.42	Rees-Jones & Wingfield head downstairs
	Henri paces around outside the Imperial Suite for 3 minutes
11.43	Rees-Jones & Wingfield exit Ritz with Tendil & Rocher and stand outside
11.44	Rees-Jones, Wingfield, Tendil & Rocher enter Ritz
11.45	Henri heads downstairs
	Rees-Jones, Wingfield & Rocher walk upstairs and then to the rear of the Ritz
11.46	Henri exits Ritz
	Rees-Jones, Wingfield & Rocher exit Ritz at rear and walk down Rue Cambon to Salon de Nuit exit and back
11.47	Rees-Jones, Wingfield & Rocher enter Ritz at rear
	Henri stands in front of the paparazzi
11.48	Rees-Jones, Wingfield & Rocher walk (inside) to Salon de Nuit exit and back
	Dourneau & Musa start dummy run circuit of Place Vendôme
11.49	Rees-Jones, Wingfield & Rocher return to the front of the hotel
	Dummy run ends
11.50	Henri enters Ritz
	Rees-Jones, Wingfield & Henri head upstairs
11.51	Rees-Jones, Wingfield & Henri talk outside the Imperial Suite
	Henri paces back and forth between standing and talking for 9 minutes
12.00[a]	Henri returns downstairs

---

[a] A more detailed Timeline of Events from 12.00 to 12.12 a.m. appears later in this book.

	Imperial Suite door opens and Dodi talks to Rees-Jones & Wingfield for 28 seconds
12.01	Henri goes to the restroom
	Rees-Jones & Wingfield go to the top of the stairs
12.02	Rees-Jones beckons Tendil & Rocher who meet him half way up the stairs
	Rocher & Tendil descend the stairs and exit Ritz
12.03	Henri meets with Rocher, Tendil, Dourneau & Musa for 20 seconds as they enter Ritz
	Henri exits Ritz
12.04	Henri talks to the paparazzi
	Dourneau & Musa ascend the stairs and talk to Rees-Jones & Wingfield at the top
12.05	Dourneau & Musa return downstairs
	Rees-Jones & Wingfield walk towards the rear of the hotel then return
12.06	Dodi & Diana exit Imperial Suite and are met by Wingfield
	Henri enters Ritz
	Rees-Jones descends the stairs and beckons Henri
	Rees-Jones & Henri head upstairs
	Dodi, Diana & Wingfield head towards the rear of the hotel
12.07	Henri & Rees-Jones meet Dodi, Diana & Wingfield
	Henri, Dodi, Diana & Rees-Jones head to the rear
	Wingfield descends downstairs and meets Tendil & Rocher
12.08	Wingfield & Rocher exit Ritz
	Wingfield & Rocher meet with Dourneau & Musa outside[a]
12.09	Henri, Dodi, Diana & Rees-Jones arrive in the service area at the rear
	Wingfield & Rocher enter Ritz and meet Tendil
	Henri exits Ritz at rear and then re-enters
12.10	Dourneau, Musa & Cavalera enter the hotel and go to the key cabinet
	Henri exits Ritz at rear and then re-enters
12.11	Cavalera exits Ritz
	Dourneau & Musa join Wingfield, Rocher & Tendil
	Wingfield phones Rees-Jones and talks for over a minute
	Henri exits Ritz at rear and then re-enters
12.12	Dourneau & Musa exit Ritz
	Henri exits Ritz at rear and then re-enters
12.13	Wingfield to Rees-Jones phone call finishes

---

[a] This meeting does not show on the CCTV footage on the inquest website. This is discussed later in the Decoy Drivers chapter.

	Henri exits Ritz at rear, waves to the paparazzi, puts his fingers to his mouth and then re-enters Ritz
12.14	Henri exits Ritz at rear and then re-enters
12.15	Henri talks to Dodi and Diana
	Diana salutes Henri
	Wingfield receives a call on a Ritz phone
12.16	Henri exits Ritz at rear and then re-enters
	Wingfield finishes phone call
	Wingfield exits Ritz
12.17	Henri exits Ritz at rear and looks back
	Diana, Rees-Jones & Dodi exit Ritz at rear
	Henri, Diana, Rees-Jones & Dodi walk along Rue Cambon[a] and get in the Mercedes S280
	Wingfield talks to Musa then to Dourneau, who are both in their decoy cars
12.18	Mercedes S280 departs with Henri driving
	Wingfield gets into Mercedes 600
12.19	Both decoy vehicles – Mercedes 600 & Range Rover – leave from the front of the Ritz
12.22	Mercedes 600 & Range Rover pull up at rear of Ritz
12.24	Mercedes 600 & Range Rover leave from rear of Ritz

---

[a] This walk was necessary because of road works which were being carried out at the rear of the Ritz.

35   Pressure Takes Its Toll

On the day of the crash – August 31 – paparazzo Nikola Arsov told French police he had "found a crowd of people" outside the Ritz at around 8 p.m.[912]

When Diana and Dodi arrived, nearly two hours later – at 9.50 p.m. – chauffeur Philippe Dourneau described a "sea of people" outside.

There had been a build-up of "paparazzi" pressure – right from the airport – "it was really frightening to see how aggressively these people could behave"[a] – to the later drives to and from the apartment – "they went completely crazy"[b]. Then as they returned to the Ritz, François Tendil reported that "there were more than 100 paparazzi behind them".[913]

The evidence indicates this pressure was having an effect on Diana and Dodi.

Ritz CCTV shows the couple entering the downstairs restaurant at 9.51 p.m., but just ten minutes later – at 10.01 – they leave it and head for the privacy of their Imperial Suite. Kez Wingfield noted that "the princess was crying" as they left the restaurant.[914]

Ritz night manager, Thierry Rocher, stated in 1997 that Dodi remarked that "he was finding it increasingly difficult to cope with the pressure of the paparazzi".[915] He elaborated at the inquest: "[Dodi] was very irritated and he seemed to be tired, to be nervous".[916]

It will be shown that the decoy Mercedes plan[c] required Dodi's approval. The fact that the plan was implemented reflects the effect of the pressure that had built up throughout that afternoon and evening.

Knowledge of a Return Trip

Rene Delorm told Paget: "I knew [Diana and Dodi] were going to return around midnight...."[917] (WFJ)

It was evident to anyone closely following events that the couple's luggage had been delivered from the airport to the apartment. It is common

---

[a] Rene Delorm.
[b] Didier Gamblin.
[c] See next chapter.

sense that was where they intended to sleep that night. Therefore it was inevitable that after the Mercedes 600 left Dodi's apartment at 9.30 p.m., at some stage Diana and Dodi would be returning.

Prior knowledge of a final journey was also confirmed by several members of the paparazzi. Nikola Arsov stated: "The English bodyguards ... said the couple were having dinner and would be coming out again later".[918]

36   Decoy Mercedes[a]

An unusual plan for the implementation of Diana and Dodi's return from the Ritz to the apartment, surfaced during the final hours at the hotel.

Essentially the arrangement was for the couple to leave the Ritz from the rear exit in a third car driven by Henri Paul, with one bodyguard – there was to be no back-up car. Simultaneously, the two cars and drivers that had been used throughout the day would remain out the front of the Ritz, acting as decoys to deceive the paparazzi.

At the inquest there was a great deal of conflicting evidence regarding how this strange plan came about.

Dodi-Rocher Meeting: 10.20 p.m.

Exactly half an hour after Diana and Dodi's arrival at the hotel, Dodi met with night manager Thierry Rocher outside the Imperial Suite.

Ten days later Rocher told the French investigation:

> **[Dodi] asked me to let Mr Paul know that a third car would be ready in rue Cambon and that they would leave via that [rear] exit.**[919] **(WFJ)**

Then in 2005 he elaborated:

> **[Dodi] did not ask me to organise that third car – he simply told me that it would be there and that only Mr Paul was to be informed about it.**[920] **(WFJ)**

At 10.20 p.m. on 30 August 1997 Dodi stated to Rocher:
1) There would be a third car
2) It would leave from the Ritz rear
3) Diana and Dodi would be in it

Rocher was to tell this to Henri Paul only.

Rocher-Henri Meeting: 10.30 p.m.

Nine minutes later Rocher passed this information on to Henri Paul.

Henri's reaction to this is noteworthy. Rocher told Paget: "He asked no questions whatsoever and seemed to simply accept the instruction."[921] (WFJ)

Henri didn't react to Rocher.

---

[a] A key aspect of the decoy plan was the availability of the third car. This has been covered in the earlier chapter on Choosing the Car.

He doesn't ask for clarification from Rocher – he asks no questions about it.

The extensive Ritz CCTV footage reveals that Henri also didn't get clarification from Dodi – neither by phone nor in person. Henri's first contact with Dodi after this conversation didn't occur until 12.07 a.m., when they were already walking towards the rear of the hotel, preparing for departure.

The fact that Henri Paul didn't seek clarification indicates that he didn't need clarification. This means that there was enough information in what Rocher had said for Henri to know how to carry out what was needed, without asking any further questions of Rocher or Dodi.

The information given from Dodi to Rocher is significant for what it did say and also for what it didn't say. Dodi said "that a third car would be ready in Rue Cambon". Rocher clarified this in his 2005 statement: Dodi "did not ask me to organise that third car – he simply told me that it would be there".

The critical information that is excluded from Dodi's instructions to Rocher:
- Who will drive the third car?
- Will there be any back-up car?
- Will there be one, two or no bodyguards in the car?

How was Henri able to proceed with organising what Dodi had suggested without seeking answers to the above three questions?

There is only one logical explanation for this: There had to already be some understanding between Dodi and Henri prior to the conversation between Dodi and Rocher at 10.20 p.m. Henri already knew the answers to the above three questions – or was able to find out the answers without consulting Dodi.

It is clear from Rocher's evidence that Dodi wasn't asking if a third car could be made available – Dodi said "a third car would be ready in rue Cambon". Dodi was stating a fact: a third car would be there.

It was not Dodi's job to organise cars. The only way that Dodi could confidently state that the car would be there, was if someone had already told him that was what would or could happen. The strong inference from the evidence is that that "someone" was Henri Paul.[a]

If Henri Paul had already told Dodi that the third car had been or could be arranged, then Dodi's instructions to Rocher were an indication that he was confirming acceptance of that alternative plan.[b] Since the plan was being

---

[a] Claude Roulet could have been involved in this as well, but at this point he was no longer in the hotel – see earlier.
[b] On the subject of interaction between Henri and Dodi, the earlier evidence surrounding Henri Paul driving to meet with Dodi at the airport in the afternoon

organised by Henri, it was not necessary for Dodi to provide the answers to the above questions, as they would be dealt with by Henri.

In other words, the fact that Dodi never passed on, and was never asked for, the structure of the decoy plan is evidence that the plan was not actually his – it came from Henri Paul.[a] This fact will become increasingly evident as this story progresses.

Henri thanked Rocher for passing on the information and then said "I am going to finish my Ricard with the Englishmen".[922][b] The CCTV footage actually reveals that this did not happen straightaway: it is 11 minutes before Henri gets back to finish his first drink. The Rocher-Henri conversation was interrupted when Rocher received a phone call, then Henri and Rocher were joined briefly by Tendil. At 10.34 Henri exited the hotel and is seen smoking out the front, near his parked Mini. At 10.36 Henri disappears for seven minutes[c] and doesn't rejoin "the Englishmen" until 10.45 p.m.[923]

Henri's comment to Rocher that he was going to finish the Ricard indicates that he had left the drink part way through.

Why had he left that first drink unfinished?

The CCTV footage shows Henri exiting the Bar Vendôme 18 minutes after he entered it, at 10.25 p.m. – precisely four minutes after Dodi had finished giving the instructions to Rocher. After exiting the bar area, Henri heads straight for Rocher, who is in conversation with Tendil.

While Henri was in the bar area with the bodyguards, he appears to have one eye on what was going on in the main hall and stairs area.

Coroner's Manipulations

Scott Baker told his jury in the Summing Up that the 10.20 p.m. Dodi-Rocher conversation was "clear evidence … that the initiative to depart from the normal practice of having a car and back-up vehicle leaving from the front came from Dodi."[924]

When Dodi's conversation with Rocher is closely analysed and taken in context with the other evidence – as shown above – it becomes clear that the plan may not have come from Dodi, but instead from Henri Paul.

Baker pins the arrangement for no back-up car on Dodi, but it is clear that Dodi's instruction to Rocher made no mention of a back-up car – either way.

---

should be considered. Henri Paul and Claude Roulet were also both present in the hotel after the couple's arrival at 4.35 p.m.

[a] It is clear from witness evidence shown in Part 1 – Musa, Roulet, Hocquet – that Dodi and Henri had a close relationship, and Dodi would not appear to have had any reason not to trust Henri. See Part 1, section on Work Relationships in the Henri Paul chapter.

[b] Henri was having a Ricard at the bodyguards' table in the Bar Vendôme – see later.

[c] See below.

Then addressing the subsequent Rocher-Henri conversation, Baker stated: "Rocher said he told Henri Paul what Dodi had said."[925]

In saying this, Baker managed to completely leave out Rocher's critical evidence regarding Henri's reaction to the instruction received through Rocher.

The coroner also told his jury: "There is no basis for saying that [Henri] had any idea of the third car plan until he was told by M Thierry Rocher at about half past 10."[926]

When the evidence is looked at in balance, it can be seen this is a presumption that Baker was not justified in making. It is clear that Rocher only told Henri that there would be a third car leaving from the rear.

Where did the rest of the decoy plan come from, if not Henri Paul?

Henri's 7 Minute Disappearance: 10.36 p.m.

At 10.36 p.m. Henri Paul is seen striding purposefully across the Place Vendôme when he disappears out of the Ritz CCTV range. He reappears 7 minutes later, again walking with purpose, returning from a similar direction.[a] During the inquest this period of disappearance was generally described as being for eight minutes. The true length of time Henri Paul was missing from the CCTV was actually between 6½ and 7 minutes.

The timing of this disappearance is significant: it is within minutes of Henri hearing Dodi's confirmation of the decoy plan from Rocher.

It is clear from the CCTV that when Henri sets out on this walk and returns, he is moving fairly quickly.

It is possible that Henri left the scene to meet an intelligence officer in a predetermined location, within reasonably close walking distance of the hotel. He may have needed to clarify something based on what Rocher had told him, or he could have been secretly notifying his intelligence handlers that the decoy plan had been confirmed by Dodi and all systems were go.

I am not suggesting that Henri would have had any idea what he was getting himself and others into – he was getting paid very well not to ask too many questions. He may also have been led to believe that the decoy plan would have strengthened security for the Princess, because it had the intelligence agency's backing.

Henri's short disappearance started precisely half an hour after his arrival at the Ritz. He can be seen looking closely at his watch on the CCTV at 10.34 p.m. just before leaving the hotel. Did he have a prior arrangement to meet with his handlers after being back for 30 minutes?

---

[a] This footage can be viewed on the inquest website as part of the "Movements of Henri Paul" video.

Coroner's Deceptions

Scott Baker made several mentions of this unexplained Henri disappearance in his Summing Up[927] – maybe it was an issue that he thought might cause some concern for the jury.

Baker told the jury that "it is pure speculation that during the eight ... minutes ... [Henri] had slipped off to make contact with someone intent on staging a crash".[928]

I suggest that it is also speculation, when one looks at his purposeful stride on the CCTV, to assume that he was hanging around somewhere in the Place Vendôme, out of camera range.

Throughout Scott Baker's Summing Up there is a theme of isolating each event rather than looking for connections between events. If each event is taken by itself it may prove nothing, but when the event is looked at in the context of the surrounding events, a completely different picture emerges.

The Coroner dismissed any relevance that the disappearance could have had, and it is evident that when taken in isolation it proves nothing. The disappearance has to be looked at in the context of the events that occurred before and after it. Possibly the most relevant circumstantial evidence to the disappearance is the timing – within minutes of the news being relayed to Henri that Dodi has confirmed acceptance of the decoy plan.

As this story develops it will become even clearer that the actions of Henri Paul consistently confirm that on that night he was working on behalf of someone outside of the hotel, and not on behalf of Diana and Dodi or the Ritz.

Telling the Bodyguards: 10.45 p.m. Onwards

There are significant areas of conflict in the various accounts that Trevor Rees-Jones and Kez Wingfield have put forward – their explanations of how they became aware of the decoy plan.

There are two major issues:
1)   Who came up with the decoy plan?
2)   Is the evidence of the bodyguards credible?

Kez Wingfield

The Ritz CCTV footage[a] reveals that the bodyguards were made aware of the decoy plan by Henri Paul. At 11.45 p.m. the bodyguards are shown carrying out a recce of the walk to the rear of the hotel. It is evident, and admitted by the bodyguards, that the only reason for doing this was because of their knowledge of the decoy plan.[929] The footage reveals there was no contact between the bodyguards and Dodi before 12 midnight, but Henri is

---

[a] Viewable on the inquest website as part of the "Key Events" video.

shown talking to the bodyguards on at least two occasions before the recce – their knowledge of the decoy plan must therefore have come from Henri.

Two days after the crash Kez Wingfield gave a sworn statement to the French police. The Ritz CCTV footage has since revealed that earliest statement contains serious errors.

At the inquest Wingfield repeatedly claimed "lapses of memory" as being the reason for conflicts in his statements[a] – this would suggest that his earliest 2 September 1997 statement should be the most accurate one.

That statement is proven wrong by the CCTV in the following areas. Wingfield said:

- "at around 23.15 [11.15 p.m.] ... Dodi opened the door of his suite to ask me how many paparazzi were there"[930]
- "I told him, after checking, that there were at least 30 or so of them opposite and roughly 100 passers-by and onlookers"[931]
- that the Princess was present when Dodi told him about the decoy plan.[b]

The CCTV reveals that the Imperial Suite door was only opened three times in the period after the bodyguards went upstairs following their dinner:[c]

1) At 11.18 p.m. when food was delivered and Rocher briefly talked with Dodi – Wingfield was not talked to during this; 2) At midnight when Dodi talked to the bodyguards for 28 seconds; and 3) At 12.06 a.m. when the couple exited.

Two days after the crash Wingfield has fabricated this evidence about Dodi requesting paparazzi numbers.

Why would Wingfield do that?

It appears that at a very early stage – before 2 September 1997 – Wingfield made a decision that if he was able to pin the decoy plan on to Dodi, then he and Rees-Jones – who was still unconscious – could not be blamed for letting Henri Paul take over the arrangements on the night. The evidence points to the decoy plan having been put together by Henri, under the direction of people outside the Ritz.[d] The CCTV evidence clearly shows that the plan must have been passed on to the bodyguards from Henri.

Wingfield's fictional account of Dodi requesting paparazzi numbers appears to be an attempt to show that Dodi was personally working out strategies on how to cope with the paparazzi pressure for the return trip to the apartment. If it had been true, this would have been supporting evidence for

---

[a] Wingfield used this excuse six times – 29 Jan 08: 110.16, 114.6, 121.11, 160.4, 161.14, 207.1.
[b] He said: "When [Dodi] told me of his plan to leave the hotel via the rear, he was happy, as was the Princess." 2 Sep 97 Statement read out 29 Jan 08: 59.12.
[c] They went upstairs at 11.09 p.m.
[d] See earlier.

the decoy plan having been decided by Dodi. In that first Wingfield statement, Henri was attributed no input at all into the formulation of the plan – he states: "Dodi explained <u>his plan</u> to me".[932]

At the inquest, when Wingfield was confronted with other errors in his September 2nd statement, he responded: "I think the only possible explanation is that ... because this statement was so close to the accident, I had just lumped all the information together and I have put it all together".[933]

By 1998, in front of the French judge, Wingfield's evidence had completely changed on this: there is no longer any mention of Dodi requesting paparazzi numbers and Henri Paul has now been given a role as messenger – "M Paul went off upstairs to the suite where Dodi and the Princess were, and a few minutes later he returned and told us that there had been a change of plan. He told us what the new arrangements were".[934] Wingfield also introduces the new scenario of the plan having Mohamed's approval: "Henri Paul told us that ... Mohamed Al Fayed had given the plan his blessing" – this absolved the bodyguards of any responsibility to have notified London about a severely flawed plan.[935]

The CCTV footage shows that the trip by Henri from the Bar Vendôme to Dodi's suite, as described in the 1998 statement, is fictitious. Nevertheless, by introducing Henri into this account, Wingfield had arrived at something a little closer to the truth, but still insisted that the plan originally came from Dodi.

Wingfield's 1998 account was also the first time any of the bodyguards had suggested that the original decoy plan called for no bodyguards.[a] This concept made the bodyguards look better, because it showed that at least they had argued the point and negotiated a compromise – "Dodi then agreed that one of the bodyguards could go in the car".[936] (WFJ) In other words, they hadn't taken such a flawed plan lying down.

If the original plan was no bodyguards, then why didn't Wingfield say so in the September 2 statement? This would have been a key omission – not just that the plan called for no bodyguards, but he also forgot to mention that the bodyguards had talked Dodi into providing a bodyguard.

Why did Rees-Jones also leave out this point in all three statements he gave to the French in 1997 – see below – only switching over to agree with Wingfield's 1998 account in his Paget evidence?

By the time Rees-Jones' book was published in 2000, Henri is now telling the plan to the bodyguards outside the Imperial Suite,[937] a little closer again to the truth.

---

[a] Wingfield stated that they later confronted Dodi on the plan: "We dug our heels in ... telling [Dodi] that it was impossible for him to go off in a vehicle without a bodyguard". Paget Report, p233 (WFJ).

Wingfield's later account in 2005 defies the imagination. It is as if he really has forgotten what he had said in earlier statements, and in fact, at the inquest he said that when he made that 2005 statement "I deliberately didn't go through any of my previous statements because I wanted to give the memory as I had it in 2005".[938]

In that statement Wingfield strongly pins the plan on Dodi with no involvement at all from Henri Paul: "I would emphasise that it was Dodi's plan",[939] and this: "I don't remember [Henri] having any input into the arrangements".[940] In this account Wingfield came up with a brand new concept: "Trevor knocked at the door" – not on the CCTV – to remonstrate with Dodi over the plan.[941] He also removes Henri Paul from any involvement saying he came upstairs "just before we left".[942]

During his inquest cross-examination Wingfield was forced to concede that the decoy plan must have been given to the bodyguards by Henri Paul, but he clung to his evidence that it originated from Dodi Fayed.

Wingfield said: "In any statement I have ever given, the key points always remain the same".[943] The reality is that when his first two statements on this subject – 1997 and 1998 – are compared (see table below), there is conflict on all the key points of evidence.

The truth is that over the years Wingfield has given five accounts, and no two have been exactly the same on the key points.

Kez Wingfield's Decoy Plan Evidence					
Evidence Date	2 Sep 97	3 Jul 98	2000 Book[a]	15 Feb 05	29 Jan 08[b]
Who from?[c]	Dodi	Henri	Henri	Dodi	Henri
Henri-Dodi Contact	No	Yes	Yes	No	No
Location	Outside Suite[d]	Bar Vendôme	Outside Suite	Outside Suite	Outside Suite
Time	After 11.15 p.m.	Before 11.08 p.m.	11.40 p.m.	12.03 a.m.	11.14 or 11.37 p.m.
Bodyguards[e]	One	None	None	None	None
Authorised by MAF[f]?	No	Yes	Yes	Yes	Yes
Did Jury Hear?	Yes	Part Only	Yes	Yes	Yes

The above table summarises the key areas of Wingfield's evidence on the communication of the decoy plan to the bodyguards.

Trevor Rees-Jones

Trevor Rees-Jones ended up in a coma as a result of the crash and only regained a limited ability to communicate verbally over two weeks later, on the 15th of September 1997. Two days earlier, on the 13th, Wingfield had flown into Paris and was put on standby to visit Rees-Jones in hospital at the first available opportunity. Wingfield got to spend time with Rees-Jones by the 16th, three days <u>before</u> the first official French police interview was conducted with Rees-Jones, on 19 September 1997.[944]

This visit by Wingfield prior to Rees-Jones' initial interview gave him an opportunity to tell Rees-Jones what he had already said to the police.

One of the main points that Rees-Jones emphasised in this short hospital interview was that the decoy plan was Dodi's: "Dodi changed the plan".[945] In

---

[a] The book quotes from Wingfield, but the author was Rees-Jones: Trevor Rees-Jones & Moira Johnston, *The Bodyguard's Story: Diana, The Crash and the Sole Survivor*, 2000.
[b] At the inquest after viewing the CCTV footage.
[c] Who told him about the plan?
[d] Imperial Suite.
[e] The number of bodyguards initially included with the third car.
[f] Mohamed Al Fayed.

fact, the key points in this first Rees-Jones interview align <u>completely</u> with Wingfield's initial September 2 account:
- it was Dodi's plan
- no Henri-Dodi contact
- one bodyguard in the initial plan
- no mention of Mohamed authorising it.[a]

The French judge asked Rees-Jones a logical question, based on his evidence that Henri did not have a part in the decoy plan: How was Henri summoned to drive, and by whom? His answer was a fabrication: "Dodi called [Henri] so that he could drive us from the back of the hotel".[946] The CCTV shown at the inquest revealed that it was actually Rees-Jones that descended the stairs to summon Henri at 12.06 a.m.

Rees-Jones appears to have suggested Dodi had summoned Henri to strengthen his evidence that it was Dodi's decoy plan.

In his two remaining 1997 statements Rees-Jones managed to maintain some consistency on the key points, sticking very much to his account that Henri Paul had nothing to do with the decoy plan. In both his October and December 1997 accounts he places Henri with the bodyguards outside the Imperial Suite as they hear the plan from Dodi.[947b] The CCTV clearly reveals this as another lie: Henri left that area to go downstairs just before the only occasion when Dodi opened the door, at midnight, to communicate with the bodyguards.

Why did Rees-Jones place Henri Paul in the foyer with the bodyguards when they heard the plan? By putting all three there together, the implication is that prior to this there was no knowledge of the plan outside of Dodi – i.e. this was the first that anybody else got to hear of the plan. This concept helps solidify the bodyguards' evidence that the plan originated from Dodi.

Rees-Jones may also have been trying to align the story to his early account of Dodi summoning Henri. Or, possibly he was suggesting that Dodi chose Henri as the driver because he was right there.

When Rees-Jones provided his evidence to the British police in 2004, his account regarding Henri Paul's role changed dramatically. He said: "Henri Paul had been into the suite to see Dodi on a number of occasions".[948] The

---

[a] The transcript of the released section of this statement appears in Part 1, section on Telling The Bodyguards in the Decoy Plan chapter. It is also in the inquest transcripts: 24 Jan 08: from 33.10.

[b] The October statement was read out – see endnote – but the December one was withheld. On 19 December 1997 Rees-Jones stated: "While all three of us [Rees-Jones, Wingfield, Henri] were outside the suite, Dodi opened the door and said that we would be leaving in a third car and that the Mercedes and the Range Rover should remain outside the Ritz." Paget Report, p231 (WFJ).

CCTV evidence reveals that this statement is completely fictional. There was actually no contact between Dodi and Henri during the period Rees-Jones was talking about.

In this Paget account Rees-Jones tries to cover all the bases when he says: "I don't know if Henri Paul took any part in deciding how the couple were going to leave the hotel".[949] Even though he gives more prominence to Henri Paul at that time, he still maintains that the plan was Dodi's and the communication of it to the bodyguards was from Dodi[a] – this was later proven to be false by the CCTV.

Rees-Jones then introduced a brand new concept to his testimony: Dodi's "original idea was just him, the Princess and the driver in one vehicle"[950] – i.e. no bodyguards. This was an idea that Wingfield had come up with in 1998 and had stuck with it since, but Rees-Jones had previously never said that. In October 1997 Rees-Jones had actually said the exact opposite: "I was not happy as Dodi was separating the two security officers"[951] – referring to himself and Wingfield.

Rees-Jones even elaborated on this by recalling Dodi's precise words: "You and Kez stay at the front to [make it] appear that we are leaving from there".[952]

The idea of putting this into the story must have appealed to Rees-Jones because it strengthened the position of the bodyguards – they won a hard-fought concession and without their intervention the bad scheme would have been even worse. In a dramatic account he states that if Dodi had had his way there definitely would have been no security at all. Rees-Jones basically attempts to paint a picture of himself rescuing the reckless Dodi from his own stupidity: "I had to decide on the best compromise that I could reach with [Dodi] without throwing him into making another rash decision to go alone."[953]

Wingfield's fabrication of the "Mohamed approval" idea has never been claimed by Rees-Jones. This means that if Wingfield was somehow correct in this assertion, Rees-Jones has forgotten that the bodyguards threatened to phone London and that Mohamed's authority had been invoked by – according to Wingfield at the inquest – both Henri and Dodi at separate times.[b]

Even though Rees-Jones had viewed the CCTV the evening before he testified at the inquest, he started off saying: "Either Dodi told me directly or

---

[a] Rees-Jones stated: "The verbal command came from Dodi": 21 Dec 04 Statement read out 23 Jan 08: 123.4.
[b] Wingfield: "Dodi said to us, 'It's been okayed by MF, it's been okayed by my father', those were his exact words": 15 Feb 05 Statement read out 29 Jan 08: 113.1. "We decided to call our boss in London.... However, Henri Paul told us that it was not worth contacting [London] as Mohamed Al Fayed had given the plan his blessing": 3 Jul 98 Statement read out: 29 Jan 08: 206.15.

Henri Paul would have told me" about the decoy plan.[954] Later he was forced to retract his ten year Dodi mantra, finally admitting: "I accept that it was communicated via Mr Paul".[955]

Trevor Rees-Jones' Decoy Plan Evidence						
Evidence Date	19 Sep 97[a]	2 Oct 97	19 Dec 97	2000 Book[b]	21 Dec 04	23 Jan 08[c]
Who from?[d]	Dodi	Dodi	Dodi	Henri	Dodi	Henri
Henri-Dodi Contact	No	No	No	Yes	Yes	No
Location	NA	Outside Suite[e]	Outside Suite	Outside Suite	Outside Suite	Outside Suite
Time	NA	11.45 p.m.	NA	11.40 p.m.	Before leaving	11.40 p.m.
Bodyguards[f]	One	One	One or Two	None	None	None
Authorised by MAF[g]?	No	No	No	Yes	No	No
Did Jury Hear?	Yes	Most Of	No	Yes	Yes	Yes

The above table summarises the key areas of Rees-Jones' evidence on the communication of the decoy plan to the bodyguards.

Dodi's 28 Second Conversation: 12.00 a.m.

At precisely 12 midnight the door to the Imperial Suite opened and Dodi talked with the bodyguards for 28 seconds.

The problem for the bodyguards is simple: 28 seconds is not long enough for their description of what was said.

The discussion, as Rees-Jones described it, would have taken a minimum of 90 seconds to occur.[a] Likewise Wingfield's September 2 account of the

---

[a] This was Trevor Rees Jones' first interview and was conducted in hospital. The full transcript has never been made available to the jury or the public.
[b] The book quotes from Wingfield, but the author was Rees-Jones.
[c] At the inquest after viewing the CCTV footage.
[d] Who told him about the plan?
[e] Imperial Suite.
[f] The number of bodyguards initially included with the third car.
[g] Mohamed Al Fayed.

same conversation could not have occurred in 28 seconds – it times out to a minimum of 75 seconds.[b]

Under cross-examination in front of the jury Rees-Jones said: "I have been quite consistent all along that I insisted that I would go with the couple from the rear of the hotel. I believe that's a consistent memory I have."[956] The truth is that Rees-Jones has been anything but consistent on this point: in three interviews in 1997 he never made the claim that the original decoy plan called for no bodyguards, and therefore there was no insisting that he should go. The first time that this appeared in his official evidence was in 2004, seven years after the crash.

Kez Wingfield suggested under oath that he "fleshed out" the "bare bones" and "made a couple of assumptions" in his story for the French two days after the crash.[957] This indicates that Wingfield is aware that his early 2 September 1997 statement is not a true account of the facts.

In the end Wingfield explains why he made errors in that first account: "Because this statement was so close to the accident, I had just lumped all the information together".[958]

If Kez Wingfield was not able to tell the truth two days after the crash, why should any credence be given to any of his other accounts, including his evidence at the inquest?

Telling the Bodyguards

The irrefutable CCTV evidence has revealed flaws in several of the statements made over the years by Rees-Jones and Wingfield, regarding the actions of Henri and Dodi on the night. This realisation naturally raises doubts over the other evidence that they have given, which is unable to be verified or discounted by the CCTV footage.

Their evidence at the inquest appeared to reveal a desire to place their knowledge of the plan as close to the departure as possible. Are we able to determine precisely when the bodyguards were told of the decoy plan?

Henri Paul was the person who told them of the plan. He would have realised that the two bodyguards, who travelled everywhere with their principals, were on a very short "need to know" list.

The CCTV reveals a discussion that took place outside the Imperial Suite at 11.14 p.m. Henri is shown standing and talking to the two seated bodyguards for several minutes. A minute after Henri leaves the area, Wingfield is shown throwing out his arms, clasping his hands together and slumping forward. He and Rees-Jones are seen talking continuously for six

---

[a] Rees-Jones' description is in his 2004 Paget statement, read out 23 Jan 08: from 122.18.

[b] Wingfield's account of this conversation was read out 29 Jan 08: from 58.4.

minutes. This could be the sort of reaction that one may expect from bodyguards who have been presented with the decoy plan.

Both bodyguards insisted that this evidence did not fit with their recollection of when they heard the plan. But then, they would say that, wouldn't they? It is obvious that the later Rees-Jones and Wingfield heard about it, the better they look – they would have had less time to protest the dangers of it.

You may ask: Why did the bodyguards accept the plan without putting up too much of a fight?

Any suspicions regarding Henri Paul would have soon been dispelled at midnight, when it became apparent to them that Dodi had already agreed to his plan.

There had also already been laxness in the way security had been conducted earlier in the day:
- no back-up car for part of the trip from Le Bourget to Villa Windsor
- both bodyguards in the back-up car on the 9.30 p.m. trip from the apartment to the Ritz
- no security presence outside the Imperial Suite while the bodyguards had dinner.

So Rees-Jones and Wingfield may not have actually looked on the decoy plan as being that particularly flawed.

Another issue is: What were Dodi's expectations regarding security for that final journey?

Rocher said: Dodi "asked me to let Mr Paul know that a third car would be ready in Rue Cambon and that they would leave via that exit". There was no mention there of who would be driving that car and whether there would be a back-up car.

It is quite possible that Henri or Roulet had earlier told Dodi something like: "Don't worry if the paparazzi get too difficult. We can organise a third car to leave from the rear – we'll leave the other cars and drivers out the front and no one will know any different".

If this was the case, by the time Dodi got inside the Ritz just before 10 p.m., such a plan could have looked reasonably attractive. He realises Henri is now back in the hotel, and he instructs Rocher to confidentially tell Henri that is the plan he will go with.

Dodi may never have realised at that stage that Henri Paul was going to drive and that there was no back-up car.

Consideration on the detail of exactly how Dodi was getting from A to B in Paris was not really Dodi's concern. Other people were paid to take care of those things. It became a concern for him when the paparazzi pressure built up, but even then he may well not have been fully aware of the decoy plan detail until much later in the piece. When and if he did find out there was no back-up car, he may not have felt particularly threatened – he would have believed that Henri had gone to the trouble of organising the third car to avoid the paparazzi. Dodi would probably not have been envisioning other worst case scenario threats, like what eventually occurred. There is no evidence of him – or anyone else – kicking up a fuss when Henri stopped following Dourneau on the route from the airport earlier in the day.

Common sense would suggest that if Dodi felt there was a problem with the paparazzi, getting rid of security – no back-up car or bodyguards, as outlined by Rees-Jones and Wingfield – would not be a logical solution. This alone would indicate that the plan wouldn't have been Dodi's idea. It is clear that the person or people who came up with this flawed plan were interested in removing the security of a back-up car from Princess Diana and Dodi.

The issues surrounding the bodyguards' evidence hit right at the very heart of the investigation of the crash. The bodyguards have consistently lied on a central pillar of evidence: From whom did the decoy plan originate?

The decoy plan, which included having no back-up car, effectively stripped away critical protection for the couple. This was central to the assassination plot – with a back-up car the motorbikes would not have been able to so easily intimidate the Mercedes S280.[a]

If the decoy plan had originated from Dodi, then obviously there could not have been a murder plot – no one could possibly suggest that Dodi would have helped orchestrate the crash.

If Henri Paul was the originator of the flawed decoy plan, then it was the bodyguards' clear responsibility to ensure the plan couldn't be put into effect.

If the plan originated from Dodi, the bodyguards still had a responsibility to notify London.[b] However, since Dodi was their boss, it would be understandable that in the pressure of the circumstances on the night, they allowed the plan to go ahead.

Thus, it was in the bodyguards' interests that the plan came from Dodi – it goes directly to their level of culpability for the crash.

The evidence above shows that Rees-Jones and Wingfield's accounts are riddled with lies and conflicting testimony. They have lied on this very central issue – the originator of the plan – in order to protect themselves. In doing this, the bodyguards have directly contributed to the cover-up of one of the most extraordinary assassinations of the 20th century.

Wingfield must have assessed his situation in the period between the crash and September 2, when he gave his first evidence. There were only six

---

[a] See later.
[b] John Macnamara, Al Fayed's Director of Security, gave evidence that this should have been the bodyguards' course of action: 14 Feb 08: 107.21. Rees-Jones also concurred with this in his book *The Bodyguard's Story*, p19.

witnesses to the way in which the decoy plan came to be: Wingfield, Rees-Jones, Henri, Dodi, Diana and Rocher. Of these, three – Henri, Diana and Dodi – were dead. Wingfield would probably have been unaware of Rocher's limited involvement, and may have believed that with Rees-Jones in a coma in hospital, he was the only conscious witness of the plan. I suggest that these circumstances made it tempting for Wingfield to construct his own version of events, and that is precisely what happened.

When Rees-Jones emerged from his coma in the middle of September it became imperative for Wingfield that he got to his colleague before the French police took their first statement. During Wingfield's hospital visit, about three days ahead of the statement, he would have told Rees-Jones the main points of what he had already told the police. The most important of these points was that the plan came from Dodi, and that was emphasised in Rees-Jones' account given on September 19.[a]

No Back-up Car

The Al Fayed policy was that when Princess Diana was travelling with Dodi there was to be a back-up car.

John Macnamara, Al Fayed's Director of Security, testified that the policy "was absolutely laid down. You could not or should not ever have the principal's car travelling without the back-up car."[959]

This was confirmed by Trevor Rees-Jones.[960]

Despite a clear policy on this, the bodyguards have never explained why there was no back-up car for a significant part of the trip from Le Bourget airport to Villa Windsor.

This rule was flouted for a second time when Henri Paul drove the Mercedes S280 from the rear of the Ritz later that night, with no back-up car.

The Driver: Henri Paul[b]

Should Henri Paul have been behind the wheel of the Mercedes S280 when it left the rear of the Ritz at 12.18 a.m. on 31 August 1997?

Witnesses stated that in Henri's 11 years working for the Ritz, he had never before driven guests on behalf of the hotel.

Jean Hocquet, Henri's direct boss up to June 1997, stated that "it was not at all part of M. Paul's duties to drive cars, or to chauffeur people".[961] Frank Klein confirmed that "Mr Paul had never driven a guest at the Ritz before". He stated: "It was not part of his job and he knew that full well".[962]

---

[a] There was also a change made to Rees-Jones' perception of whether Henri Paul had been drinking in the Bar Vendôme – see later.

[b] This subject has already been touched on in the earlier Driving Mission chapter.

Others confirmed that it was not part of Henri's duty to chauffeur guests:

- Claude Roulet: "M Paul was not authorised to drive for the Ritz in these circumstances"[963]
- Philippe Dourneau: "it was the first time since [I] had been employed driving Dodi ... that someone else had driven him" in Paris[964]
- Jean-François Musa[a]: "it was something which was totally unusual, to have a car of the [Étoile] company being driven by an external person"[965]
- François Tendil: "[I told Henri] that it was not for him to drive the car"[966]

The witness evidence is overwhelming that Henri Paul had no right to be behind the wheel of the Mercedes S280 on the final journey.

Étoile Limousine, run by Jean-François Musa, supplied the cars and drivers that the hotel required.

Henri Paul's late night drive was:
- the first time in 11 years that he had ever driven a Ritz customer
- the only time ever that an Étoile car had been supplied without their own driver[967]
- the only time ever that an Étoile car has been driven by a driver without a Grande Remise licence – see below
- the first time ever that Dodi had been driven in Paris by someone other than Dourneau.

When this evidence is looked at, one begins to realise just how unusual it was that Henri Paul was the driver of Diana and Dodi that night.

This is why, when Tendil challenged Henri just before he left, Henri "just looked at [him] and said nothing".[968]

Grande Remise Licence

Henri Paul did not possess a Grande Remise Licence, which chauffeurs in France require to be able to drive limousines.

Musa told Paget:

> **This was the <u>only time</u> that one of the Étoile Limousine cars was ever driven by a driver without a 'Grande Remise' licence.[969] (WFJ)**

He told the French police three days after the crash:

> **I was reluctant to hand over the keys [to Henri Paul] but I realised that I did not have much of a choice as ... I could not really see myself saying 'no' to my employer.[970]**

Musa's evidence reveals an insight into some of the pressure of the moment. It may well be that Dodi himself did not know that Henri was to be the driver, yet the players were manipulated or pressured into allowing the situation to occur.

---

[a] Owner of Étoile Limousines, the company that leased the Mercedes to the Ritz.

By the time Musa was confronted with having to hand over the keys, events were already set in motion and it would have been very difficult for him to refuse.[a]

Coroner's Deceptions

Scott Baker told his jury:

> **The plan that Henri Paul should drive may have come from Dodi through Rocher, although this is not Rocher's recollection, or it may have been a decision made by Henri Paul himself on the assumption that that was what Dodi wanted.[971]**

Baker only provides the jury with two possible options: 1) Dodi requested Henri, or 2) Henri assumed that Dodi wanted him to drive.

Both of these suggest that the decision was based on Dodi's wish that he wanted Henri Paul to drive. The question that isn't answered is: Why would Dodi have a particular wish to have Henri drive, above anyone else, including qualified drivers?

Lord Justice Baker doesn't allow for any other possibilities, like whether Henri was working for someone else – even though Baker is well aware that Henri was receiving large amounts of money from an unknown source.[b]

Baker also fails to address the volumes of evidence that Henri was not a practical or logical choice as the driver. He ignores the fact that Henri driving that car went against the policies of both Étoile and the Ritz Hotel.

Rocher was very definite that Dodi did not request anyone to be the driver of the third car, but Baker suggests that his recollection ten days after the crash could have been faulty. Rocher does not appear to have any particular motive to distort the record of these events.

Baker also told the jury:

> **You may think that [Henri Paul driving] is not something that can be resolved with any clarity. It is not relevant, from the viewpoint of gross negligence on the part of Henri Paul ... how he came to be in the driving seat. He was a free agent. It can only have been of relevance if you think ... Henri Paul [was] driving for the purpose of creating a staged accident in the tunnel.[972]**

There may have been a relevance regarding gross negligence on the part of Henri Paul, relating to his lack of a Grande Remise licence. Baker ignores the evidence regarding this licence in his 80,000-word Summing Up.

Baker suggests here that Henri driving is relevant if it was a murder, yet in a cruel irony he had already taken away that option from the jury.[a]

---

[a] There is more on this later.
[b] See earlier Agents at the Ritz chapter.

Henri As Driver

Claude Roulet testified that if he had been there, he would not have allowed Henri to drive.[973] That is precisely the reason why Vice-President Roulet was not there at the Ritz, because questions would have later been asked as to why he didn't veto the decoy plan.

There are a number of reasons why Henri Paul shouldn't have been driving the Mercedes S280 that night:

-    it was against Ritz policy for Henri to drive clients
-    it was against Étoile policy to supply cars without their own driver
-    Henri didn't possess the necessary Grande Remise licence
-    there were other qualified drivers present who could have driven the couple.

Add to this evidence the fact that Henri Paul didn't even like driving, and one begins to realise that there must have been an overriding and compelling reason why Henri decided to drive the Mercedes.

This is more evidence that points to the fact that Henri Paul was neither working for the Ritz nor Dodi on the night of 30 August 1997. Henri was being paid very well to ensure that he was the person driving the Mercedes as it pulled away from the rear of the hotel.

There were forces at work that were much greater than Henri Paul, and he would have had no idea that his determination to drive the couple on that journey was essential to setting in motion the build-up to one of the most shocking crimes of our time.

---

[a] It will be shown later that Baker removed murder as a possible verdict for the jury.

37   The Ricards

On entering the Ritz Hotel at 10.07 p.m. Henri immediately located the two English bodyguards in the Bar Vendôme, and joined them at their table.

Then he ordered a Ricard. Later in the evening he ordered a second Ricard.

There was some debate at the inquest about whether the Ricards were measured as 4cl[a] or 5cl.[b] Calculations in this work are based on the larger measure: 5cl – the balance of the evidence indicates that this is the most likely measurement. Ricard has an alcohol content of 45% and is normally diluted with water before drinking.

Barman, Philippe Doucin, described the first Ricard as "nearly empty" when he cleared the table.[974] (WFJ) There is a possibility that the second glass may not have been fully drunk. At the inquest the bodyguards and the waiter who finally cleared the table after 11.08 p.m. were not asked about how much was left in the second glass. This is an incredible oversight, and it raises the possibility that Henri may not have completely drunk two Ricards.

Pathology and toxicology experts working on the case stated in 2006:

> **A calculation based on [consumption of two Ricards of 5cl (50ml)] would give a blood ethanol concentration [in Henri Paul] of 0.64g/L. By midnight[c], metabolism would have reduced this level to approximately 0.34 g/L, which ... is below the legal limit in France and is considerably below that of the blood alcohol tests allegedly carried out on [Henri's] body samples.[975d] (WFJ)**

If Henri Paul had not had any previous alcohol that evening, but completely consumed both Ricards at the Ritz, by midnight[e] he would have had a blood alcohol reading of about 0.34 – significantly below the French legal limit, and less than half the UK limit of 0.80.

---

[a] Centilitres
[b] Klein 29 Nov 07 from 56.12; Trote 11 Dec 07 from 49.4; Doucin 11 Dec 07 from 101.6; Willaumez 20 Dec 07 from 76.16.
[c] Just before the Mercedes left on the final journey.
[d] The results from Henri's body samples are addressed later.
[e] Just before the departure on the final journey.

38   Was Henri Drunk?

The French and British police investigations both concluded that Henri Paul was under the influence of alcohol when he took the wheel of the Mercedes S280 at 12.18 a.m.

There is a great deal of evidence regarding his condition that night.

"He Wasn't Drunk"

Josiane Le Tellier saw Henri at about 9.45 p.m. She stated: "I've been tending bar for 25 [years] and I can tell when somebody's drunk. He wasn't."[976] (WFJ)

François Tendil, who had known Henri for ten years, conversed with him during the final two hours at the Ritz. He spoke ten days after the crash: "At no time did Henri Paul appear to me to be under the influence of alcohol".[977]

Thierry Rocher also had conversations with Henri throughout that period. He confirmed he couldn't "smell the Ricard that he had … been drinking".[978]

Sébastien Trote and Philippe Doucin both served Henri in the Bar Vendôme. Trote confirmed that Henri didn't appear "to have had too much to drink".[979] Doucin testified that "he did not seem to be drunk".[980]

These five witnesses all had interaction with Henri Paul in the last two to three hours of his life – and all stated that he was not drunk.

The Bodyguards

The witnesses who had the closest and longest interaction with Henri Paul after 10 p.m. were the two bodyguards, Trevor Rees-Jones and Kez Wingfield.

There are two separate issues when reviewing their evidence: a) Was Henri drunk? and b) Was Henri drinking alcohol at all?

It was part of Rees-Jones and Wingfield's job to ensure that their principals were not chauffeured by a person who had drunk <u>any</u> alcohol.

If it became known that they were aware that Henri had two Ricards, given the tragedy that later occurred, the question would inevitably be asked: "Why did you let him drive?" From the bodyguards' professional perspective, this could be an issue, even though the drinks that Henri had at the hotel left him well below the legal driving limit.[a]

Both bodyguards have stated that they didn't know that Henri Paul was drinking alcohol – even though he had two serves of Ricard, and they were sitting at the same table. Wingfield even claimed that he went so far as to ask Henri "what he was drinking".[981b] Rees-Jones stated: "I did not take any interest in what Henri Paul was drinking. I have absolutely no idea what drink it was."[982]

Is it true that they didn't know Henri was drinking alcohol?

There are several factors that raise doubts over the veracity of the bodyguards' evidence on this:

1)   Ricard is served with a large glass that includes only the 5cl of Ricard – this is a small amount in the bottom of the glass – accompanied by a carafe or jug of water. The customer pours the water in to fill the glass. The evidence of Trote, Doucin and Wingfield confirms that is precisely the manner in which these drinks were served to Henri. Wingfield told Paget: "The barman brought it with a carafe of water and Henri Paul poured water into it."[983] (WFJ) Wingfield also said that Henri told him that he was drinking "'ananas', which is French for 'pineapple'".[984] Ricard is quite unique in that the substance itself is orange in colour and undergoes a substantial colour change when the water is added.[c] It is only then that the drink could have taken on a look resembling pineapple cordial.[d] Bodyguards are trained to be observant. It is a stretch of the imagination to accept that both Rees-Jones and Wingfield missed the manner in which Henri's drinks were served, twice. It may be that Henri did say it was "pineapple", but one would tend to see that as a joke. Rocher's evidence reveals that Henri was not hiding the fact that he was drinking – he told Rocher he was going to "finish my Ricard with the Englishmen".[985]

2)   In Trevor Rees-Jones' 2000 book *The Bodyguard's Story* some of his initial reactions[e], after he regained consciousness in mid-September, are described:

> **Jill and Ernie [Trevor's parents] told [Trevor] what the papers were saying about Henri Paul being drunk. 'He only had two drinks' Trevor wrote, sending fear into his parents' hearts.... Later, Kez**

---

[a] See previous chapter.

[b] Henri's alleged reply appears below.

[c] This can be observed at the Ricard website: www.ricardpastis.com/saveur/index_rituel.html

[d] Wingfield told Paget: "I thought it was pineapple cordial": Paget Report, p220 (WFJ).

[e] These were written down by him, as he was still unable to speak at this early stage.

calmed their fears[a], explaining that both of them had thought the drinks were just pineapple juice.[986]

There are three points that this excerpt raises:

a)   Rees-Jones' initial reaction "He only had two drinks" appears to be an inadvertent acknowledgement from him that he knew it was alcohol that Henri was drinking.

b)   Wingfield asserts that both he and Rees-Jones believed the drinks were pineapple juice. This has never been mentioned in any of Rees-Jones' statements.

c)   The substance that Wingfield describes has evolved. In the book he has described the drinks as "juice", whereas in his 2005 police statement he said it was "cordial".

3)   Wingfield said that his attention wasn't on Henri – "the focus of attention was to get a sandwich down my neck as quickly as I could, and then get back on the job".[987] The CCTV evidence reveals that Wingfield and Rees-Jones entered the bar area at 9.58 p.m.[b] They leave the area at 11.08 p.m., so approximately one hour and ten minutes from when they entered. If there really was a rush to get back on the job, why didn't they get the food and drinks delivered to the foyer outside the Imperial Suite, where their principals were? The reality is that the table receipt shows that on top of the "sandwich" they had four "Schweppes Tonics" between them, two "Patisseries of the Day" and two coffees.[988] The situation is more relaxed than Wingfield's description. In his 2nd October 1997 statement Rees-Jones had said: "Dodi told us to go back to the bar for dinner...."[989] The fact is that Dodi had given the bodyguards some time out while he and Diana ordered their own dinner in the Imperial Suite. Wingfield said to the inquest: "Henri Paul was sat here, to my left, but I was facing to my right, looking for an indication from the Paris Ritz security staff, that there was maybe a change and the couple were moving".[990] The couple were not moving – they were having a relaxed dinner in their suite.

If Wingfield's focus was not on Henri Paul, why did he ask him what he was drinking?

4)   The Coroner asked Wingfield a pretty simple question: "So if you had realised that Henri Paul was drinking Ricards, how would that have affected the way you would have acted later in the evening?"[991] If you check the inquest transcript, you will notice that it takes another four questions

---

[a] This occurred on the 14th of September, 2 days before Kez's first visit to the hospital, and 5 days before the first police interview of Trevor Rees-Jones, on the 19th.

[b] There is a two minute period between 10.02 and 10.04 p.m. when both bodyguards leave to escort Diana and Dodi from the restaurant to their hotel suite.

before Wingfield properly answers the question. He appears to be attempting to evade the issue, not really in a rush to answer such a direct question.

5) At 10.10 p.m. – just two minutes after Henri had joined the bodyguards – the CCTV shows that Rees-Jones exited the Bar Vendôme to make a phone call outside the hotel. He was on the phone for about ten minutes.

This call was to Ben Murrell, the security officer at Villa Windsor. Murrell described it to Operation Paget officers in 2006:

> **The next call I got from Trevor was from the Ritz, when they were having a meal in the small restaurant.... Trevor had observed [Henri Paul] taking a drink and offered drinks to Trevor and Kez, which they thought was highly unprofessional. Trevor did not specify that it was an alcoholic drink, but the fact that this was mentioned led me to believe that it was an alcoholic drink.[992]**

Rees-Jones was questioned about this and accepted that the call could have been to Murrell.[993] He should have been asked what the ten minute conversation was about, but that didn't happen.

Murrell's account fits with the CCTV evidence:
- a phone call on a serious subject like this could take ten minutes
- the footage shows Rees-Jones walking away out of camera range for five minutes while talking. If he was discussing such a sensitive topic, he would not want the conversation overheard
- the precise timing shows Henri entering the Bar Vendôme 1 minute and 36 seconds before Rees-Jones exits it. That is long enough for Henri to have at least ordered the Ricard and offered drinks to the bodyguards.

This phone call was never mentioned in any of the bodyguard statements and it only appeared in Murrell's 2006 account[a]. It is also omitted from Rees-Jones' 2000 book.

Whilst the evidence of Rees-Jones and Wingfield that Henri was not drunk is clearly backed up by other witnesses, their testimony that they were unaware that he was drinking alcohol does not appear to be a true account. It is obvious that it is in the bodyguards' interests for them not to have been aware of Henri consuming any alcohol: by allowing him to drive, they could be made to look careless or negligent in the conduct of their duties, ahead of a tragedy. It may be that they have portrayed this picture to protect their own interests.

This is not the only instance of the bodyguards misrepresenting the evidence – see the earlier Decoy Mercedes chapter.

_____

[a] Murrell's only statement was in 2006 – he was never interviewed by the French police.

CCTV Footage

The CCTV footage of Henri at the hotel from 10.06 p.m. was viewed in detail at the inquest. He was shown carrying out activities in a normal fashion.

Expert forensic toxicologist, Professor John Oliver, was asked for his opinion of what the video revealed:

> **When [Henri] parked his vehicle, it was with elan ... [or] competently.... The behaviour I saw of Henri Paul when he descended the staircase in the Ritz Hotel was not of a man struggling to control his actions. He came down there steadily, with a steady gait, with no obvious attempt, it would seem, to ensure that he was actually placing his foot in front of the other..... There was no hesitancy. That was not, in my view, an intoxicated individual that came down that staircase. I then saw Henri Paul down tying his shoelace, where he is taking down a very narrow base on his feet and then tying his shoelace and then moving, tying the other shoelace, a narrow base. Again this could be akin to the field impairment test of a one-leg stand.... I find that test very difficult myself, and Henri Paul, there was no sign whatsoever of any movement within that.[994]**

The Ritz CCTV footage indicates that Henri Paul was not drunk throughout the two hour period before leaving on the final journey.

Gait[a] Analysis

Haydn Kelly[b], a forensic gait analysis expert, completed a detailed assessment, based on the CCTV footage, of Henri Paul's movements during the final hours at the hotel. He wrote:

> **Mr Henri Paul's gait, body movements and functions do not appear to be impaired and are wholly consistent with those of a man who at all times appears well coordinated and fully in control of his actions. The footage of Mr Henri Paul ... shows him performing a number of different movements and functions which include standing, walking, walking down stairs and upstairs at different speeds, walking up steps, bending to tie his shoelace, parking a motor car and exiting and entering a car. Some activities are performed in combination; for example, walking down a curved staircase unaided whilst removing notes from his jacket pocket. Such activities as these combinations ... require an increased level of motor co-ordination due to the number of**

---

[a] Walking pattern.

[b] Haydn Kelly is based in London and has been performing clinical, biomechanical gait analysis for over twenty years. He is the Lead Assessor for Forensic Podiatry at The Council for the Registration of Forensic Practitioners and an Examiner in Forensic Human Identification at The Society of Apothecaries, London. Kelly also lectures internationally on Forensic Gait Analysis.

tasks being performed simultaneously. If a person was under the influence of alcohol, drugs or both, one would expect to see at least some indications of this in their movements. At no time, even when performing these combinations of activities, did Mr Henri Paul show signs of any impairment or loss of coordination to his gait or body movements and in particular no characteristics are seen which one would associate with a person who has consumed excess alcohol, taken drugs, or both.[995] (WFJ)

This report was passed onto me by someone close to the inquest who prefers to remain anonymous. The analysis carried out by Haydn Kelly was submitted to Scott Baker who rejected it as superfluous to the requirements of the inquest.

Considering that the autopsies on Henri Paul found that he was driving just minutes later with an alcohol reading three times the legal limit[a], this approach by Baker appears rather strange.

Was Henri Drunk?

There is substantial evidence regarding Henri Paul's condition as he went about his business in the Ritz Hotel during the two hours before the crash.

What is known for sure is that Henri was served two Ricards. From the evidence available, it is not known whether he finished the second one. Whether he did or not, it is clear that if those were the only alcoholic drinks he had that night, then he would have been well under the legal driving limit.

The bodyguards were the closest to and spent the most time with Henri Paul in the hours leading up to the crash. Yet their evidence regarding his condition is virtually worthless, because if they had said he was drunk then they would be placing themselves in the frame for helping enable the crash to occur. The bodyguards even have clear and understandable difficulties with admitting that they were aware Henri was drinking alcohol at all. In this aspect the evidence of Rees-Jones and Wingfield has been shown to not be credible. This fits with their evidence regarding the formulation of the decoy plan – see earlier: that evidence also fails the credibility test.

The accounts from the witnesses who don't appear to have any axe to grind – Josiane, Tendil, Rocher, Trote, Doucin – was that Henri appeared to be sober.

When the evidence is taken on balance – witness, CCTV, gait analysis – it would be very difficult to conclude that Henri was inebriated when he took the wheel at 12.17 a.m. This becomes significant in the light of the post-crash autopsies conducted on Henri Paul's body which found that he was three

---

[a] This is addressed later.

times over the legal blood alcohol limit for driving. This huge conflict is dealt with later in this book.

One could ask: If Henri knew that he was going to be driving Diana and Dodi – evidence will suggest that he did know – then why did he drink any alcohol at all?

It would appear that Henri did not consider himself to be "on duty" for the Ritz when he returned at around 10 p.m. It was a Saturday night and Henri had just received a considerable sum of cash – the equivalent of around £1,200 – and maybe a promise of a lot more, for effectively what was a weekend's work. It is clear from other evidence that Henri was definitely not a teetotaller, but he was also not an alcoholic.[a]

The impending reality of driving the Princess of Wales may have been daunting for anyone who is not a professional chauffeur, and yet that was the job he had been given. Making this job even more difficult was the fact Henri didn't particularly like driving.[b] He also would have been very aware that it was not logical that he should be the driver, particularly when he didn't have the required chauffeur's licence. Frédéric Lucard, the car jockey who delivered the Mercedes S280 from the Vendôme car park to the rear exit,[c] may have been a much more appropriate choice. Henri simply could have felt he needed a drink or two to relax and to be able to deal with the situation.

It would be ridiculous to suggest that because Henri had two alcoholic drinks over a period of two hours, that he was putting at risk the lives of the people he was transporting. There are other factors, yet to be dealt with, that did jeopardise their lives, but the two drinks is not one of them. The expert evidence indicates that based on those drinks Henri was well under the limit, and the limits – which are strict in France – are in place to determine what is safe and what is unsafe driving.[de]

---

[a] See Chapter 5 of Part 3.

[b] See earlier Driving Mission chapter.

[c] See later.

[d] More detailed evidence on Henri's condition is in Part 1, section on Was Henri Drunk? in the Henri Paul Movements chapter. Aspects such as paparazzi evidence and post-crash conversations amongst Ritz employees are covered there.

[e] Autopsy evidence was later used by the French and British investigations to indicate Henri Paul was drunk on the night. The autopsies and the treatment of the evidence is addressed later in this book.

39   Henri and the Paparazzi

The paparazzi were mainly set up out the front of the hotel, with only a few at the rear. Ritz outdoor CCTV footage reveals that between 11.10 p.m. and 12.06 a.m.[a] – a period of 56 minutes – Henri made four separate visits to the paparazzi out the front of the hotel.

Why?

Visiting the Enemy

Most witnesses who were asked said that Henri's behaviour was unusual.

Ritz president, Frank Klein, stated that it was Henri's job to keep the paparazzi away.[996] Jean-François Musa put the unusual behaviour down to the special occasion.[997]

Christophe Lafaille, a French journalist who had heard from paparazzi there, said "normally [Henri] would not do that".[998]

The paparazzi present have unanimously stated that this behaviour had never occurred before:

- Pierre Suu: "it did not seem right to me.... I felt it was strange"[999]
- Fabrice Chassery: "[Henri] never spoke to the photographers, he was not really friendly. That evening he wasn't like that at all"[1000]
- Romuald Rat: "[it] shocked me … that [Henri] should come and talk to us. At the Ritz, the drivers and doormen must not speak to us and I think that is normal. His attitude was completely the opposite"[1001]
- Serge Arnal: "this was not the way [Henri] normally behaved from what I knew of him previously"[1002]
- Serge Benhamou: "[Henri] is generally someone who never speaks to us, he … does not talk"[1003]

It may also be telling that most of the paparazzi said they did not know who Henri Paul was before that night.[b]

---

[a] At 12.06 a.m. Henri re-entered the hotel and immediately was summoned to walk to the rear of the Ritz with Diana and Dodi, ahead of the final drive.

[b] The full transcripts on the inquest website reveal this.

The Ritz CCTV reveals that these four paparazzi visits were definitely made. The paparazzi told the police what Henri told them during these encounters:

- David Odekerken: "he informed us of the countdown regarding the couple's exit.... He said 'ten minutes' and then the following time, 'five minutes' and then 'two minutes'"[1004]

- Pierre Suu: "Paul was providing snippets of information about the couple's movements, saying that they would be out in five or ten minutes"[1005]

- Fabrice Chassery: "Mr Paul kept us informed of the imminence of the departure in an ironic manner"[1006] "Mr Paul ...started coming out two, three times, each time repeating the same thing, namely 'they are coming out in 10 minutes, they are coming out in 5 minutes'"[1007]

- Stéphane Darmon: "he was saying that Lady Di would be arriving in a quarter of an hour, then ten minutes – he was trying to create ... an atmosphere of anticipation.... Then he said that the couple was going to be there in five minutes"[1008]

- Romuald Rat: "he came out two or three times in front of the photographers who were lined up and signalled to us 'in five minutes' or in ten minutes"[1009]

- Stéphane Cardinale: "he went in and out of the hotel several times, indicating an imminent departure for our benefit, which he reckoned would be a matter of minutes".[1010]

This consistent paparazzi evidence – that Henri was providing them with a countdown to the departure – is backed up by Thierry Rocher who said that Henri told the group[a] that he would warn the paparazzi that "they would leave within ten minutes".[1011]

The main questions are: Why did Henri provide regular updates for the paparazzi after 11 p.m.? Klein said Henri's job was to try and get rid of the paparazzi, so why was he so friendly towards them on this particular night?

Common sense would suggest that it is not the job of a high class hotel's security manager to rev up the paparazzi ahead of an impending movement by a couple of their high profile guests.

If Henri had been working for the Ritz that night he would have been discouraging the presence of the paparazzi, not encouraging them. Why wouldn't he have said, as it got later: "Sorry, it looks like the couple have decided to stay the night here – see you tomorrow"?

It was not in the interests of Diana and Dodi to have the paparazzi milling around ahead of their departure: they had already had a hell of a day with the build-up of paparazzi pressure – real and fake. Little did they know that while

---

[a] Tendil, Dourneau and Musa were also present during this conversation at 12.03 a.m. – see earlier timeline.

they relaxed over dinner, their soon-to-be driver was assisting to stir up the paparazzi pressure, as the final journey of the night drew nearer.

If you look at the CCTV footage[a] of Princess Diana as she left from the rear of the hotel after midnight, you can see that as she heads towards the Mercedes she has her left arm raised, shielding herself from the cameras.[b] Diana didn't want the paparazzi there – yet only a matter of minutes before, Henri had been cheerfully waving to the same cameras.[1012] Why?

As one becomes more familiar with the circumstances of the build-up to the crash, there is an aspect that stands out – the mounting pressure of the paparazzi. As this story progresses, it will become increasingly apparent that the paparazzi pressure was a key background element to this staged crash. Without the paparazzi presence on the night, the post-crash cover-up would not have been able to be so successfully carried out. To this day many people still believe that the paparazzi were responsible for the crash – the later eye-witness evidence will show that this could not have been the case.

The presence of the paparazzi was critical to the plot. They were required to not just be present on the night, but to actually be right there at the start of the final pursuit. For that to occur, the paparazzi had to be kept waiting outside the Ritz Hotel – it would have been a disaster for the conduct of the assassination plot if the paparazzi had called it a night and gone home. If the paparazzi were not present in the pursuit, it would have been impossible for them to have been blamed and held accountable for the crash – shifting the focus from the real unidentified assassins.

It appears that Henri was given the role of ensuring the paparazzi stayed. He kept up their interest by making regular trips out to them as the night wore on: 11.10; 11.21; 11.46; 12.03 – each visit apparently providing the paparazzi with a new prediction for the departure. He made sure that the paparazzi realised that Diana and Dodi were going to be leaving – just in case they got tired of waiting and thought the couple might have decided to stay the night after all.

Henri was with the paparazzi right up until the minute before Diana and Dodi left the Imperial Suite area, headed for the rear of the Ritz. Henri joined them and then in fact led the way during the walk to the rear. The group arrived into the rear service area at 12.09 a.m.

---

[a] Viewable on the inquest website.

[b] This also is viewable in the two photos of Diana leaving included in Part 1, section on Paparazzi in the Henri Paul Movements chapter.

Waving to the Enemy

The first move Henri then makes is to exit at the rear, look up the road towards the paparazzi and then re-enter. During the eight minutes that the couple are waiting at the rear, Henri exits and re-enters a total of seven times – at 12.09; 12.10; 12.11; 12.12; 12.13; 12.14 and 12.16.

At 12.12 the CCTV shows Henri waving to paparazzi across the street.[1013]

The concept behind the decoy plan – see earlier – was to divert the paparazzi to the front of the hotel, while Diana and Dodi exited out the back. Why then was Henri so keen to make his presence known to the paparazzi waiting at the rear of the hotel? It would have been no secret that the paparazzi all had mobile phones and they were communicating with each other, between the front and the rear of the Ritz.

Why were the couple made to wait for eight minutes before the Mercedes S280 arrived? After all, they were not catching public transport. Why is it that Diana and Dodi left the suite at 12.06, but it was not until 12.10 that the hotel's key cabinet is accessed? That is a minute after the couple had already arrived at the rear.

It is difficult to know whether this delay was due to incompetence on the part of the staff at the front, or whether Henri had planned this delay and the staff were following instructions. It is notable that Henri doesn't appear to phone the front to ask why there is a delay after the couple arrived at the rear.

The evidence – Henri's paparazzi interaction, his seven rear exits, the delay – taken together, indicates that the plan of the plotters may have been to get as many paparazzi as possible to the rear of the hotel, before the eventual departure.

It's significant, because this is the exact opposite of the claimed goal of the decoy plan.

Some paparazzi moved from the front to the rear of the hotel, as a result of the actions of Henri Paul. Some of those that didn't move were alerted to the departure and caught up at the Place de la Concorde as a result.

The following excerpts reveal some of the paparazzi responses to what was happening before their eyes:

- Christian Martinez: "Guizard telephoned me to tell me that they would be leaving via the rear." [1014]
- Jacques Langevin: "I noticed the hotel's head of security standing at the hotel exit in the Rue Cambon so I thought they were coming out that way." [1015]
- David Odekerken: "Fabrice [Chassery] called me on the telephone. He was talking in a low voice and was telling me, 'They are both outside, standing and waiting without a bodyguard'.... Fabrice then asked me to come round, which I did. So I took my vehicle and rejoined him in Rue Cambon."[1016]

- Romuald Rat: "I called [Odekerken] on my mobile. He must have told me that they had come out by the back...." [1017]

In a way, given the signals that were provided to the paparazzi, it is rather surprising that there were still quite a few out the front of the Ritz at the time of the rear departure.

Henri's actions regarding the paparazzi were not in the interests of the Ritz or the couple. This is further evidence that Henri was working that night for other people – people who paid him very well and wanted to use the paparazzi as a cover for causing what was a planned crash.

Framing and blaming the paparazzi has been a critical cornerstone of the cover-up, but the paparazzi were not there when the Mercedes S280 entered the tunnel, and the eye witness evidence will prove that point.

40   Roulet Phones Henri: 11.30 p.m.

At 11.30 p.m. Claude Roulet made a phone call to the Ritz Hotel. He spoke with Henri Paul for four minutes.

There are two important issues:

1) Who was the call initially made to?
2) What was the purpose of the call?

More Roulet Lies

In his first statement on September 1, Roulet said "I called Monsieur Paul ... to find out how things were going".[1018] (WFJ)

By September 10, Roulet's story had completely changed. Now he said: "I rang ... to speak to Mr Tendil and I actually got Mr Paul".[1019] He gave no reason for why he wanted to speak to Tendil.

Then at the inquest Roulet's story changed again. This time the call was intended to tell Henri about the behaviour of a new security department employee: "I wanted to tell ... Henri Paul that this behaviour was not a correct one and that people should know who is who".[1020a]

Only three known accounts exist, and they all give a different story.

It doesn't particularly ring true that Roulet would have gone home after Benoît, waited for 1½ hours and then decided to ring Henri again about the employee problem. Not only that, but he rings him at the Ritz. Roulet later told Richard Keen[b]: "I did not know that Henri Paul was back at the hotel" when he made that 11.30 phone call.[1021]

There is some logic to the argument that Roulet may have been ringing Tendil to find out how things were going with the couple – this is possible to put together from his September 10 evidence.

---

[a] Evidence from Roulet claimed that two attempted phone calls to Henri just before 10 p.m. were also about the behaviour of the new employee – see earlier Henri's Mysterious Ritz Return chapter. This difficult employee has remained anonymous and has never been interviewed. He or she also has never been mentioned in any other person's evidence.

[b] QC for the Pauls.

The problem is that his very earliest – September 1 – account does not concur with that.

The September 1 account – calling Henri to check how it was going (not heard by the jury) – is probably the closest to the truth, but it has two major problems with it:

1)   How did Roulet know Henri Paul was at the hotel? Since Henri had returned at 10.06 p.m., Roulet had had no contact with the hotel or with Henri

2)   Roulet's explanation of the content of the phone call – he "told me that he was in perfect control of the situation" and "he did not say anything to me about the couple's intentions for the rest of the evening" – does not come anywhere near describing a conversation that according to the CCTV lasted for four minutes.[1022] (WFJ)

The strong inference is that: 1) Roulet was already aware that Henri was at the hotel, possibly through his intelligence connections, and 2) Roulet had something important to discuss with Henri, possibly connected with Roulet's role in the decoy plan.[a]

---

[a] See later evidence in the Decoy Drivers chapter.

Timeline of Events: 12.00 to 12.12 a.m.

Time	Event
12.00	Henri leaves Imperial Suite foyer to go downstairs Dodi opens the door to tell Rees-Jones & Wingfield they will be leaving shortly
12.01	Henri goes to the restroom Rees-Jones & Wingfield go to the top of the stairs looking for Henri
12.02	Rees-Jones beckons Tendil & Rocher and meets them halfway down the stairs. He asks them where "the driver" is. Rocher & Tendil exit Ritz seeking Musa & Dourneau, thinking they are the drivers Rees-Jones is referring to
12.03	Rocher & Tendil re-enter Ritz with Dourneau and Musa and meet Henri at the entrance Henri exits Ritz
12.04	Henri talks to the paparazzi Dourneau & Musa ascend the stairs and talk to Rees-Jones & Wingfield, who tell them they are seeking the "third chauffeur – the one with the grey hair"
12.05	Dourneau & Musa return downstairs Rees-Jones & Wingfield walk towards the rear of the hotel seeking Henri, then return
12.06	Dodi & Diana exit Imperial Suite and are met by Wingfield Dourneau & Musa exit Ritz Henri enters Ritz Rees-Jones descends the stairs, finally sees Henri and beckons him Rees-Jones & Henri head upstairs Dodi, Diana & Wingfield head towards the rear of the hotel
12.07	Henri & Rees-Jones meet Dodi, Diana & Wingfield Henri, Dodi, Diana & Rees-Jones head to the rear Wingfield descends the stairs and meets Tendil & Rocher
12.08	Wingfield & Rocher exit Ritz

	Wingfield & Rocher meet with Dourneau & Musa outside Ritz <u>or</u> Musa meets with Roulet[a]
12.09	Wingfield & Rocher enter Ritz and meet Tendil
12.10	Dourneau, Musa & Cavalera[b] enter Ritz and go to the key cabinet
12.11	Cavalera exits Ritz with the Mercedes S280 keys
	Dourneau & Musa join Wingfield, Rocher & Tendil – Wingfield tells them about the decoy plan, and instructs the drivers about their role
	Wingfield phones Rees-Jones and talks for over a minute
12.12	Dourneau & Musa exit Ritz

---

[a] See evidence in later Decoy Drivers chapter.
[b] Sébastien Cavalera, Ritz doorman.

41   Decoy Drivers

The evidence of what occurred at the front of the Ritz Hotel after midnight is very surprising.

By midnight events were moving rather quickly and witness recall at the inquest was somewhat limited and confused – some witnesses were not even cross-examined on this vital area.

The clearest accounts of what happened were given in the earliest statements of the central players.[a]

Henri Goes Missing: 12.01 to 12.06 a.m.

At 12.00 a.m. Dodi opened the Imperial Suite door. This took place 17 seconds after Henri had left the area, heading downstairs to the toilet. Dodi told Rees-Jones and Wingfield that they would be "leaving the hotel in the next few minutes"[1023]. At the conclusion of that 28 second conversation, the bodyguards had to set about finding the couple's driver – Henri Paul. The CCTV shows them both walking to the top of the stairs. Rees-Jones catches the eye of Tendil or Rocher and beckons them both – he meets them halfway down the stairs. He conveys the message that they are seeking the driver, presuming they know who he is referring to.

Tendil and Rocher know very little – nothing in the case of Tendil – about the decoy plan, and they think Rees-Jones is referring to Dourneau and Musa, the normal drivers. They immediately set about locating the drivers, who are outside of the hotel. They find Dourneau and Musa and head back into the hotel with them. As they enter they meet Henri, who is on his way out to visit the paparazzi – Henri cannot be seen by Rees-Jones and Wingfield who are at the top of the stairs. Dourneau and Musa ascend the stairs, but find out from the bodyguards that it's not them they are after – Dourneau said: "They asked us where the third chauffeur was, the one with the grey hair".[1024] (WFJ) Initially the drivers don't know who they are talking about. Musa told the police: "I did not understand the question for there was no question of any other driver." He then added: "Trevor [Rees-Jones] told me that they were

---

[a] Not all of these statements have been made available. Where the subject has not been covered in the excerpts of the early statements shown in the Paget Report, I have had to show the record from later statements.

speaking about the driver [from] Le Bourget and I understood that they were speaking about [Henri] Paul."[1025]

Rees-Jones and Wingfield next head down the corridor looking for Henri, then probably decided they should be back at the Imperial Suite. Wingfield is back in time to meet the couple as they exit the suite, while Rees-Jones heads downstairs to continue the search for Henri. He finally spots him as he re-enters the hotel after visiting the paparazzi.

Rees-Jones beckons Henri Paul and they both ascend the stairs and join up with Diana and Dodi for the walk to the rear of the hotel.

It is amazing that neither of the bodyguards were cross-examined about the search for Henri at the inquest, and neither have they ever been asked about it in any police interview. The evidence is obviously significant – from the bodyguards' viewpoint, the driver (Henri) went missing for five long minutes just as Diana and Dodi are preparing to leave.

The interaction between the bodyguards and the drivers (Dourneau and Musa) was clearly visually recorded on the CCTV.

Dourneau and Musa's evidence reveals two important facts:
1) At 12.04 a.m. – just 13 minutes before departure – both decoy drivers are still unaware that there is a decoy plan[a]
2) The bodyguards appear to be unaware that the drivers are unaware – they may have presumed that Henri had told them.

The bodyguards were asking for the "third chauffeur", but that wouldn't have indicated to Dourneau and Musa that Henri would be driving the couple.

Why did Henri withhold the decoy plan information from the decoy drivers?

The success of the murder plan relied on Henri driving the Mercedes S280 – Henri was being paid well to ensure that he was behind the wheel of that vehicle when it left. Musa, as Étoile owner, owned the S280, and his approval was required for Henri to drive the car. Musa's evidence shows that after he did eventually find out, he was uncomfortable with the proposition: "I was worried about Henri Paul driving – I knew he didn't have a 'Grande Remise' licence".[1026] Henri would have been aware in advance of Musa's likely reticence, so rather than risk giving him the opportunity to come up with a more appropriate or qualified driver, he (or his handlers) decided to not let Musa know of the plan until it was too late for him to do anything about it.

It will be shown that Musa was told about the requirement for the third car by Roulet, who as Vice-President carried more weight than Henri. This occurred at a time that was so late that Musa had no option but to acquiesce.

---

[a] They weren't told about it till after 12.06 a.m. – see below.

It is also of interest that neither of the bodyguards knew Henri Paul's name – "the one with the grey hair" – even though they had spent a considerable amount of time with him during that day and evening.[a]

Telling the Decoy Drivers: 12.06 to 12.12 a.m.

Who told the decoy drivers about the decoy plan?

Not Henri Paul.

There was no contact between the drivers and Henri after the 12.04 a.m. conversation with the bodyguards described above. At 12.06 the drivers went outside the hotel and Henri came in from talking to the paparazzi, but was immediately summoned upstairs to meet up with Diana and Dodi, and walk towards the rear departure point.

Philippe Dourneau told Paget:

> **I only learned a few minutes before [Diana and Dodi's] departure through Trevor Rees Jones or Kez Wingfield that I was to remain in front of the hotel at the wheel of the Mercedes, with François Musa at the wheel of the Range Rover, and that during that time the couple would leave by the rue Cambon in another Mercedes belonging to Étoile Limousine.[1027] (WFJ)**

Dourneau's police statements – which the Coroner and inquest ignored – reveal that he was told by one of the bodyguards "a few minutes before" the departure.

In Jean-François Musa's account to the police a day after the crash, he said this:

> **At around a quarter past midnight, Mr Roulet, the Director of the Ritz, came and asked me if I had a vehicle ... available. I then went and looked at the board ... and I saw the keys to the petrol-engined Mercedes S280. I took them and gave them to a car jockey.... I returned to the front of the hotel, where an English bodyguard, the one out of the two who did not get in with Diana and Dodi [Wingfield], came and explained to me how things were scheduled for the end of the evening. It had been arranged ... that Philippe Dournon (sic) and I should create a diversion by making out that we were preparing to leave from the front of the hotel in the Mercedes and the Range Rover, whilst Dodi and Diana left via the Rue Cambon in the S280 Mercedes driven by Henri Paul, with Trevor, the other bodyguard, alongside him.[1028] (WFJ)**

In this early police statement – again ignored at the inquest – Musa reveals a clear picture of what happened. When this account is put together with Dourneau's evidence, the truth of how and when information was conveyed to the drivers becomes apparent.

---

[a] Trevor Rees-Jones has also said that he "had met [Henri] before": *The Bodyguard's Story*, p90.

Three days after the crash, Dourneau said the bodyguard told them about the plan <u>after</u> the key had been passed to the doorman.[a] On 1 September 1997 Musa had said that Roulet asked him for the car, he dispensed the key and then Wingfield described the decoy plan and the drivers' role in it.

At the inquest Rocher described his ten-years-on impression of the conversation that took place after the key had been passed on to Sébastien Cavalera[b]:

> **Mr Wingfield asked Mr Dourneau and Mr Musa if everything was ready for the third car.... Mr Dourneau and Mr Musa looked very amazed and they asked Mr Wingfield what is it about exactly. Mr Wingfield then explained them that a third car would leave from Rue Cambon so that the paparazzi think that there are two cars leaving from Place Vendôme.[1029]**

The accumulated evidence – Musa, Dourneau, the CCTV – shows that the order of events was: 1) Request to Musa for the key; 2) Dispensing of the key to Cavalera; 3) Wingfield tells Musa and Dourneau about the decoy plan and their role.

Why did the jury not hear or have access to Musa and Dourneau's earliest statements on how they heard about the decoy plan?

Roulet Reappears: 12.08 a.m.

Jean-François Musa's evidence has consistently been that he met and talked with Claude Roulet outside the hotel, before entering and dispensing the key to Cavalera.

The CCTV does not reveal any movement towards accessing the key cabinet until 12.10 a.m. – 4 minutes after Diana and Dodi have already left the Imperial Suite.

What is it that precipitates the action to go to the key cabinet?

Whatever it was has not been described in the inquest timelines and does not appear on the CCTV footage shown on the inquest website.

Musa's account is that he was approached by Roulet outside of the Ritz Hotel and it was Roulet who officially requested the use of the third car. On September 1 Musa stated:

---

[a] Dourneau on September 3 to French police: "François [Musa] discreetly gave the key to the Mercedes 280 to the doorman. Then, a bodyguard came to see each of us in order to get us to put on an act and make out we were leaving: we were to put the headlights on and switch on the engine attracting the paparazzi's attention, while the couple left via the rear." Paget Report, p247.
[b] The doorman.

At around a quarter past midnight, Mr Roulet, the Director of the Ritz, came and asked me if I had a vehicle, specifically a Mercedes 300, available.[1030] (WFJ)

Musa gave this account the day after the crash and has stuck religiously to it up to the present day.[a] He would have been familiar with Roulet's appearance, as he had worked with the hotel for around eight years.[1031]

Musa describes the meeting with Roulet occurring outside the hotel.[b] It is significant that the inquest website does not provide CCTV footage of the critical time period outside the hotel prior to 12.10 a.m. Even if the footage was available, it is very difficult to establish identities on the Ritz outside-CCTV because it is long view footage.[c]

The inquest was provided with CCTV footage of what is titled "The Meetings to Arrange the Third Vehicle".[d] It is important to note that the footage shown omits the movements of Musa and Dourneau for a very critical time period: 12.06 to 12.09 a.m. The footage shows Musa and Dourneau just before 12.06 exiting the Ritz after talking with the bodyguards, who were looking for the missing Henri. The next footage of the drivers is near 12.10 a.m. when they enter the hotel walking towards the key cabinet. This omission is significant because it is the period when the actual request for the key must have taken place.

In a separate CCTV-based timeline titled "The Movements of the Bodyguards" – describing footage which is not available on the website – there is a very interesting entry: 12.07.38 to 12.09.09: "Place Vendôme: <u>Long View</u> Camera: Wingfield and Rocher meet with Dourneau and Musa outside the hotel".

This meeting has never been mentioned in any witness evidence from the alleged participants – Wingfield, Rocher, Dourneau and Musa. The timing clashes with the approximate time that Musa describes himself meeting with Roulet – just prior to entering the hotel to access the key cabinet at 12.10 a.m. It is obvious that if this CCTV timeline is correct, then it would cast serious doubt on Musa's adamant testimony that he met Roulet outside the hotel.

The Bodyguard Movements video has not been posted onto the website[e], and therefore is not open to scrutiny. There are other examples on the website of film from the same Place Vendôme long view camera – when looking at

---

[a] Musa's detailed evidence on this is in Part 1, section on Request for the Key in the Decoy Plan chapter.

[b] In 1998 Musa to the French investigation: "I then went out of the hotel. A few moments later, Mr Roulet came….": Paget Report, p249 (WFJ).

[c] See below.

[d] This is included as part of the Key Events video on the website.

[e] This is despite a specific emailed request to Andrew Tuff, Web Manager, Judicial Communications Office, on 18 March 2008.

the footage, it is impossible to identify particular individuals as the images are too small and indistinct.

The Paget Report stated that Musa had mistaken Rocher for Roulet:

> **The actions [Musa] referred to related to Thierry Rocher but Jean-François Musa is convinced it was Claude Roulet.**[1032] **(WFJ)**

Rocher has never claimed to have been involved in requesting the S280. Rocher's inquest evidence reveals that up until 12.11 a.m., the only knowledge he had of the decoy plan was what Dodi had told him at 10.20 p.m. The Paget claim is completely fictional.

Musa told Paget in 2006:

> **It was definitely Claude Roulet who I spoke to. It was definitely not Thierry Rocher. I've known Claude Roulet well for a long time and I am not mistaken; he was wearing a suit and tie.**[1033]

No other players – Wingfield, Tendil – have claimed that they asked for the third car.

Is Musa's consistent account that Roulet requested the third car true or false?

The third car with Henri driving was critical to the murder plan and the plotters would not have been able to risk the possibility of Musa refusing to provide it, or providing his own driver. Musa's evidence reveals that he was not keen to release the Mercedes' keys but felt pressured and compelled to do so. As Ritz Vice-President, it is Roulet who could have provided the authority that made it very difficult for Musa to say "No". When this is combined with the late notification – Diana and Dodi were already arriving or waiting at the rear – Musa would have been left with very little option but to acquiesce.

A day after the crash Musa stated that Roulet asked "specifically [for] a Mercedes 300".[1034] (WFJ) Why would Roulet say that? If Roulet had been aware that the S280 was sitting in the car park and he had been instructed that was the car, Roulet may have stipulated a 300 to ensure there could be no mix up – even though the S280 was the only car there, Roulet may not have been aware of that.

There is also no apparent motive that Musa would have to lie about this meeting – he really has nothing to gain or lose regarding who requested the third car. What is clear is that <u>someone requested it</u>, yet there is no witness who has put their hand up for that.[a] This indicates that someone is lying, and Roulet certainly has every reason to be that person. If it is shown that Roulet knew about the flawed decoy plan and failed to pull the plug on it – or even

---

[a] At the inquest Roulet claimed that Musa "is wrong" about him being there: 5 Dec 07: 96.12.

failed to attempt to do so – then he would be placed in a situation of indirect culpability for the crash.

Cavalera was never cross-examined at the inquest, and neither was his statement heard. It should have been obvious that because he was right there and received the key from Musa, his account is extremely important. He may have been able to verify whether he saw Roulet or not.

During his Summing Up Scott Baker told his jury:

> **[Musa] said Roulet asked him for the key for the third vehicle face to face, but he must be wrong about that because Roulet was <u>not in the hotel</u> at the time.**[1035]

What the coroner didn't say was that Musa never stated that he saw Roulet "in the hotel" – the meeting took place outside the hotel.

The balance of the evidence indicates that Roulet did meet with Musa at around 12.08 a.m. He told him that they needed a third car, which "Henri Paul would be driving".[1036] (WFJ) Musa objected saying that he could drive it, but Roulet told him he "should remain at the wheel of the Range Rover in order to keep the paparazzi occupied in the Place Vendôme".[1037] (WFJ) At 12.10 a.m. Musa went to the key cabinet, got the keys for the S280 and passed them to Cavalera, who took them out of the hotel and gave them to the car jockey, Frédéric Lucard.[1038] As Lucard was proceeding to the car park to collect the S280, Musa and Dourneau were meeting with Wingfield, learning about the detail of the decoy plan and their role in it.

The presence of Claude Roulet out the front of the Ritz before the couple left is additional evidence that Roulet's activities on the night were quite different to the story he has told the authorities. His account was that he returned home after waiting outside Chez Benoît, phoned the hotel at 11.30 p.m. and after 1 a.m. received a phone call advising him of the crash.[1039]

42   The Decoy Plan

The decoy plan appears to have been instigated by people outside of the hotel – an intelligence agency – who employed Claude Roulet and Henri Paul to implement it.

Henri Paul was instructed to:
- make sure that the paparazzi didn't go home
- make sure that he drove the Mercedes S280
- make sure that there was no back-up car
- take the normal chauffeur's route to Dodi's apartment.[a]

The bodyguards have been far from truthful in their accounts of what took place in the hotel. The lies of Rees-Jones and Wingfield have been orchestrated to protect their own interests and have included:
- stating that the decoy plan was Dodi's idea and was conveyed to them from Dodi
- stating that the original decoy plan was to include no bodyguards
- suggesting that both Dodi and Henri claimed the decoy plan had been approved by Mohamed Al Fayed
- claiming that they had no idea that Henri Paul was drinking alcohol at the Ritz.[b]

Following the crash there was a presumption that the evidence of the bodyguards – particularly Wingfield who had no crash-induced memory difficulties – was reliable. At the inquest the evidence of both Rees-Jones and Wingfield has proven that this trust was misplaced.

Because they were the key witnesses, their claim – now shown to be false – that Dodi was the originator and conveyor of the decoy plan has provided fuel to those who claim that the crash was an accident. This is because the allegation of murder and the decoy plan are inextricably linked. Without the decoy plan, there would have been a back-up car, and a lethal crash brought on by the pursuing motorbikes[c] would have been much harder to pull off.

If the decoy plan is proven to have come from Dodi, then that precludes premeditation of the plan. The truth is that the bodyguards knew that the plan

---

[a] See later.
[b] More complete coverage of the bodyguards' evidence is in Part 1, The Decoy Plan chapter.
[c] See later.

came from Henri Paul, but they have denied this to protect their own interests – to remove themselves completely from any culpability for the crash and instead put the blame on the dead Dodi Fayed.

The role of Claude Roulet in the later events – his phone call to Henri at 11.30 p.m. and his instructions to Musa at 12.08 a.m. – show that he was intimately aware of the decoy plan despite his denials.[a] When these events are combined with the earlier evidence – Roulet's 8.20 p.m. departure from the Ritz, his phone calls at 8.30 and 10.00 p.m., his fictional meeting with Henri Paul, his claimed long wait outside Chez Benoît – it becomes clear that Henri Paul was not the only one working for an outside employer. Roulet's financial records should have been checked as part of the investigations into the crash.[b]

Although the decoy plan came from Henri, he would have only been carrying out instructions from his intelligence employers. Henri would have had no idea that his actions were going to lead to tragedy and contribute to his own death. He may have been working for an intelligence agency that had promised him that he was playing a part in increasing the safety of Princess Diana and Dodi Fayed – not diminishing it. Henri may have been told that the security would be provided by the intelligence agency, when actually their real objective was to bring about the murder of the occupants of the Mercedes S280.

---

[a] More complete coverage of Roulet's evidence is in Part 1, The Decoy Plan chapter.
[b] Claude Roulet gave evidence to Paget that he had passed on information to RG (police intelligence): "When Claude Roulet passed on information to the RG, he would leave an envelope addressed with a false name with the hotel concierge. This was the normal routine." Paget Report, p190 (WFJ). This evidence was not heard by the jury.

43   Final Journey

The Mercedes S280, driven by Henri Paul and carrying Princess Diana, Dodi Fayed and Trevor Rees-Jones, departed from the rear entrance of the Paris Ritz Hotel headed for Dodi's apartment.

The time was 12.18 a.m., 31 August 1997.

Within minutes of Diana's Mercedes departing, Philippe Dourneau and Jean-François Musa left in the two decoy vehicles, also heading to Dodi's apartment.

Dourneau and Musa followed the same route as the Mercedes S280 – the normal chauffeur's route, along the embankment. Musa told the inquest: "It was the usual journey taken by the drivers to go to the apartment, Rue Arsène Houssaye."[1040] Geographically it would have been more direct to turn right onto the Champs Élysées from the Place de la Concorde. Dourneau stated: "It was a Saturday night and there is always a lot of traffic on the Champs-Élysées on a Saturday night, so [the embankment] was a quieter road."[1041]

The route of the Mercedes S280 along the riverside expressway was not unexpected, and would already have been known ahead of time.

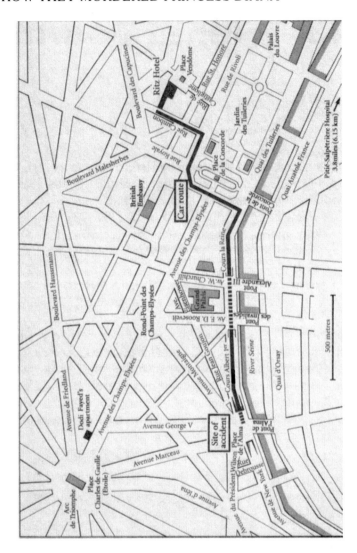

Figure 10

Map of Central Paris showing the route of the final journey of the Mercedes S280 carrying Diana, Princess of Wales, Dodi Fayed, Trevor Rees-Jones and Henri Paul. Original map reproduced from *Death of a Princess: An Investigation.*

Prior Knowledge of the Route

Even equipped with prior knowledge of the Paris visit, how likely would it be that assassins could predict in advance that Diana and Dodi would travel down the riverside expressway?

Trevor Rees-Jones stated: "I assumed [in advance] that they would go to the Ritz [and] I assumed they would be staying at Dodi's apartment".[1042]

To Rees-Jones the movements of Diana and Dodi in Paris were reasonably predictable.

It is not possible to calculate the exact odds, but one could assume that if the arrangement was to stay at Dodi's flat – which it was, from as early as the 18th [a] – then the chance of the occurrence of a late night trip from the Ritz (owned by Mohamed) to the flat had to be high.

Musa's earlier evidence was that on the 29th of August Henri Paul was in a position to predict that he would be required for "chauffeur duties [from] outside the Ritz". [1043] (WFJ) Other evidence showed that Dodi would be visiting Repossi's (near the Ritz) to pick up or look at a ring.

The preferred chauffeur's route from the Ritz Hotel to Dodi's flat was the riverside expressway. If the plotters were able to predict a late night trip between the hotel and the flat, then they would have had to arrange a blocking of the exit before the Alma Tunnel, to ensure that the couple travelled through the tunnel.

Later evidence in this book will show that this is precisely what happened.

---

[a] Dodi was told on the 18th that the Ritz was booked out: 29 Nov 07: 60.17.

44 Ritz to Place de la Concorde

Hotel employee, Frédéric Lucard, was given the responsibility of moving the Mercedes S280 from the Vendôme car park to the rear of the Ritz – where Henri Paul took over.

"You Won't Catch Us"

Lucard reported to the French investigation:

> **Henri "said to [the paparazzi] something like, 'Don't try to follow us; in any case you won't catch us'".** [1044]

He told the inquest that this took place while Henri was "standing next to … the driver's door" of the Mercedes. [1045]

Lucard is the only person to report this widely publicised last minute challenge to the paparazzi. He states that it was directed to "two or three photographers on motorbikes or scooters". [1046]

The paparazzi in the Rue Cambon[a] at the time of the departure were Serge Benhamou, Alain Guizard, Jacques Langevin and David Odekerken. Of these, only Benhamou was on a scooter – the rest were in cars. The motorbikes Lucard saw were evidently ridden by unidentified people.

In their statements, none of the paparazzi acknowledged hearing Henri Paul's challenge. Benhamou specifically mentioned it:

> **I have heard it said in the press that [Paul] apparently said to some journalists that he was going to lose us. I did not witness any of that and I do not know if it was true.** [1047]

At the time their statements were taken, the paparazzi were either under arrest or, in the case of some, about to be arrested. Regarding other issues, their statements show a uniform interest in trying to distance themselves from blame for the crash – often by deflecting culpability towards Henri Paul. It would have been in paparazzi interests to pin a statement like this on Henri, as it would imply he had an intention to speed – and this could be seen as a

---

[a] At the rear of the Ritz Hotel.

contributing cause of the crash. They did not do this, which indicates strongly that they didn't hear the statement.

Was the statement made?

Paget Officer Paul Carpenter pointed out that the CCTV footage indicates that Henri Paul did not speak to the paparazzi during the short period Lucard alleges the statement was made.[1048]

The slow speed of the initial section of the journey[a] indicates that Henri Paul did not initially have the intention to speed.

The jury never got to hear Lucard's original French statement, which was taken eight months after the crash. This was his first mention of this quote of Henri Paul, and in it he comes across more tentative on the detail of the statement – "I could not be absolutely precise as to his words"[1049] (WFJ) – than when he gave his inquest account ten years later.

Lucard really was a key witness to the events and he should have been interviewed by French police within days of the crash. This never happened.[b]

Speed

The CCTV footage of the Mercedes leaving the Ritz Hotel along the Rue Cambon can be viewed on the inquest website.[c] The video shows the vehicle departing with normal acceleration.

This was supported by the paparazzi.

Alain Guizard stated: "We drove at a very moderate speed as far as the Crillon Hotel" – the Place de la Concorde.[1050] Serge Benhamou said: "I followed on my scooter. We were not going very fast."[1051]

Unidentified Motorbikes

The first unidentified motorbikes were seen following the Mercedes right from when it left the rear of the Ritz Hotel.

Frédéric Lucard testified that when he arrived at the rear of the Ritz with the Mercedes S280 "there were three motorcycles or scooters with their riders waiting there".[1052] He added that as the Mercedes carrying Diana and Dodi moved off "they left at once to follow the car".[1053]

Serge Benhamou was the only paparazzo at the rear on a motorbike or scooter. Lucard identified him to the French police, but the remaining two riders were unidentified.[1054]

---

[a] See below.
[b] Lucard's first statement was taken in April 1998. By that time, it had been widely publicised that the French police believed Henri Paul was drunk at the wheel.
[c] In the evidence for 4 October 2007. Click on "Part of TJS/36": Footage of two views of the Mercedes' departure is towards the end of that video.

Paget officer, Paul Carpenter, supported Lucard during his description of the CCTV footage of the Ritz rear departure – he confirmed there were "several other vehicles" following the Mercedes. Carpenter added: "We have not been able to identify [any] of those."[1055]

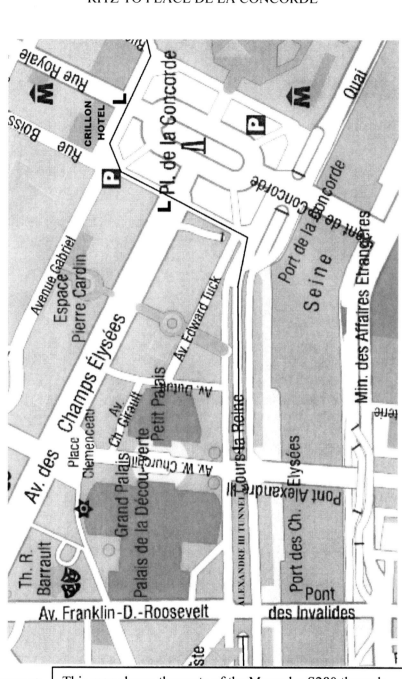

100m

Figure 11

This map shows the route of the Mercedes S280 through the Place de la Concorde, onto the riverside expressway and through the Alexandre III Tunnel. The two sets of traffic lights where the Mercedes stopped are denoted with "L". Original map from Hot Maps: www.hot-maps.de

45   Crillon Hotel Lights

The Mercedes stopped at two sets of traffic lights in the Place de la Concorde – first at the lights near the Hotel Crillon and the Naval Museum and a second set at the corner of the Champs Élysées.

There were unidentified motorbikes near the Mercedes at the Hotel Crillon lights.

Unidentified Motorbikes

Photo agent[a] Alain Guizard stopped behind the Mercedes. Three days after the crash he stated that "there were three or four [riders] on two bikes".[1056]

Guizard described the scene after the lights changed:

> **Two motorcycles thus chased after the Mercedes. Behind them were Martinez and Arnal and some other photographers' cars but I could not say how many. I remember seeing Benhamou on a scooter at the Place de la Concorde – he must have [been] following the convoy.[1057]**

Guizard couldn't identify the riders on the pursuing motorbikes: "I am unable to say who they were".[1058]

Later at the inquest Paul Carpenter[b] and Tom de la Mare[c] pointed out to the jury that one of those motorbikes was Romuald Rat (and Stéphane Darmon, his driver).[1059] However, this could not be correct as Rat and Darmon left from the front of the Ritz and did not arrive at the Place de la Concorde until the Mercedes was already waiting at the Champs Élysées lights.[d] Guizard confirms this when he points out that after the convoy had already left the Hotel Crillon lights, "I then saw some photographers who had been waiting in front of the Ritz arrive".[1060]

---

[a] Technically Guizard was not a paparazzo – he didn't have a camera with him. He was a photo agent and his main interest was in helping his photographer Christian Martinez to get into a good position, to be able to follow behind the Mercedes. 3 Sep 97 Statement read out 10 Mar 08: 145.16.

[b] Paget officer.

[c] Lawyer for the Ritz Hotel.

[d] See next chapter.

De La Mare points out that the French police interviewing of Guizard is severely deficient:

He is not pressed ... to try to identify the motorbikes in terms of ... their cc, shape, colour ... [and there is no] attempt to describe their clothing.[1061]

Just three days after the crash, the French completely failed to ask the questions that could have helped lead to any possible identification of the unidentified motorbikes.

Camera Flashes and Speed

The first unidentified camera flashes near the Mercedes were seen at the Crillon traffic lights.

Alain Guizard stated: "There were some flashes ... in the direction of the Mercedes". He said that he could not see "where they were coming from".[1062]

Guizard is the only person who gives clear evidence of camera flashes at the Crillon traffic lights. The paparazzi who had been at the front of the Ritz hadn't caught up yet. Martinez was the first of them to arrive – he had early phone warning from Guizard, who had been around the back.[1063]

The camera flashes that Guizard saw are the first evidence that the occupants of the Mercedes S280 (which had untinted windows) were being put under pressure. It is also during the departure from these lights that the first evidence emerges of the Mercedes being in a hurry. Prior to this, the pace had been normal. It is probable that the Mercedes left the Crillon lights quickly as a direct result of the camera flashes.

Guizard said that the Mercedes "drove off very quickly" from the lights.[1064] This was confirmed by Martinez, who said: "The Mercedes sped off".[1065]

46 Champs Élysées Lights

After making the rapid take-off at the Crillon lights the Mercedes S280 was again impeded by a red light at the Champs Élysées intersection.

This was to be the last stop before the fatal crash in the Alma Tunnel.

Unidentified Motorbikes

Mohammed Rabouille, a waiting taxi driver in the Place de la Concorde, stated in an interview published in *USA Today* on September 5:

> **There was a limousine, a Mercedes, with several motorcycles behind and near it. I thought it was an escort, but there were too many [motorcycles] for one car.** [1066] **(WFJ)**

The paparazzi were primarily in cars, but Serge Benhamou was on a scooter and Romuald Rat (driven by Darmon) was on a motorbike. Benhamou, who was at the intersection, mentioned the presence of "Rat and Darmon's motorbike" and "a second [unidentified] motorbike … [with] two people on".[1067]

Rat also saw a scooter[1068] – possibly Benhamou's – and another motorbike. He told the police on September 1: "Darmon and I were not the only ones on a motorbike at the lights".[1069]

Camera Flashes

Jean-Louis Bonin was stopped at the lights right next to the Mercedes S280. The next day he wrote a letter to the French police:

> **Having stopped at the traffic lights … a large black Mercedes stopped on my right. A scooter with two persons on it quickly came between our two cars. The passenger on the back of the scooter started photographing the occupants of the Mercedes. Intrigued by this behaviour … I looked in the back of the Mercedes. I immediately recognised Princess Diana and, on her left, Dodi Al Fayed.**[1070]

After posting that letter Bonin travelled abroad for three weeks – he gave a more detailed statement after his return to France:

My attention was drawn by ... a black scooter registered in [department] 75 ridden by two persons with dark helmets.... The passenger on the scooter ... was taking one photograph after another with his flash in the direction of [the left rear] window. It was not tinted.[1071]

In a later interview Bonin confirmed it was a scooter he saw: "I saw only one scooter. I did not see any motorbikes."[1072]

Bonin witnessed a pillion on a black scooter registered in department 75, taking repeated photos of Diana and Dodi through the untinted windows of the Mercedes.

The only identified scooter present was Benhamou's, and it was registered department 75. But Benhamou was travelling solo on a dark green scooter[1073] – Bonin saw a black one with two riders: so it was clearly not Benhamou's.

Bonin was shown photos of the paparazzi on 24 September 1997, and was unable to identify the riders on the scooter.[1074]

The scooter and its riders were unidentified, yet the passenger was "taking one photograph after another" of the couple.

Bonin stated that the Mercedes was on his right and the scooter was in between the two cars.[1075] Rees-Jones recalled "a motorcycle [that] arrived on the right-hand side of the [Mercedes] and ... stopped".[1076a]

Clearly Bonin and Rees-Jones saw different vehicles. Rees-Jones also described "lots of flashes", but doesn't say where they were coming from.[1077]

Despite Bonin seeing a photographer "taking one photograph after another" – supported by Rees-Jones – no photos from the final journey have ever been published.

Why?

Blocking Car

Bonin testified that a dark car in front of the Mercedes deliberately blocked it from progressing.

Three weeks after the crash Bonin told the police:

The Mercedes was behind a dark car and there was no one in front of me.... Then the lights changed to green and I started off normally, thinking that the car stationary in front of the Mercedes was not moving forward as if blocking it. Then, in my interior mirror, I saw the Mercedes which was pulling out and I heard its engine roar loudly and its tyres spin.[1078]

---

[a] Rat stated that he and Darmon "drew level with" the Mercedes at the lights: 1 Sep 97 Statement read out 11 Mar 08: 20.6. There is a possibility that the motorbike Rees-Jones saw was Darmon's.

Then in 1998 Bonin was asked: "Did you get the impression that this [dark] car was obstructing the Mercedes deliberately?" He answered:

Definitely. When you are a driver and you see someone behind you who is obviously in a hurry, the reaction is to give them room, but this car really was not doing that.[1079]

Darmon supported Bonin on the position of the Mercedes: "in the second position in their line".[1080]

Darmon also confirms that there was a delay in the departure of the Mercedes after the lights changed: "they waited to have some space".[1081]

Cross-examination of Jean-Louis Bonin would have been useful at the inquest – unfortunately he died before it took place.[1082]

Speed

The Mercedes was not speeding prior to reaching the Place de la Concorde. At the Hotel Crillon traffic lights the camera flashes started and when the lights turned green the Mercedes left quickly. It was then held up for a second time at the Champs Élysées lights.

At that point, the pressure on the occupants of the Mercedes escalated in several ways:

      1)   intensified photo taking using a camera flash through the untinted windows

      2)   a car deliberately blocking the Mercedes' progress at the lights change

      3)   if Rabouille is correct – he was never interviewed by the French, British or the inquest – the Mercedes around this time had "several motorcycles behind and near it".[a]

Bonin was able to view what was happening inside the Mercedes: He stated:

Dodi Al Fayed ... had his ... right hand shielding his face.... Princess Diana ... was sitting back into her seat to conceal herself.... The bodyguard ... seemed very annoyed, turning his head a lot, and I guess he wanted the car to move off.[1083]

Diana and Dodi were exposed to the camera flashes because of the untinted windows. Rees-Jones appeared frustrated and anxious to get away from the intersection. The blocking car would have exacerbated the situation.

With this combination of factors, the occupants of the Mercedes may have already felt threatened in the Place de la Concorde.

These circumstances would have contributed to Henri Paul's very rapid departure from the Champs Élysées traffic lights, as described by the witnesses:

---

[a] Rabouille said he was in the Place de la Concorde when he saw the Mercedes. The Champs traffic lights was the Mercedes' last stop in the Concorde area.

- Bonin: "I had [driven] about 10 metres [from the intersection] when Diana's Mercedes overtook me at very high speed"[1084]

- Lopes-Borges[a]: "when the lights changed ... the [Mercedes] went very fast"[1085]

- Darmon: "the Mercedes accelerated radically. It took off just like a plane"[1086]

- Rat: "it took off again like a shot".[1087]

---

[a] Antonio Lopes-Borges – he was in a car well-back from the Champs-Élysées intersection, but with a view of the Mercedes.

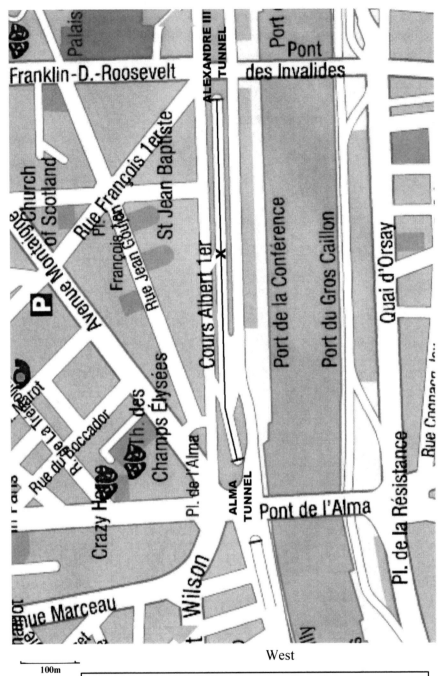

Figure 12   Map showing the route taken by the Mercedes S280 along the riverside expressway, after leaving the Alexandre III Tunnel. The intended exit is marked with an "X". Original map from Hot Maps: www.hot-maps.de

47 Expressway to the Intended Exit

Leaving the Place de la Concorde the Mercedes turned right onto the westbound riverside expressway. It then proceeded to enter the Alexandre III tunnel.[a]

Unidentified Motorbikes

Thierry Hackett was driving in the Alexandre III tunnel when he was overtaken by the speeding Mercedes and motorbikes.

Later on the same day Hackett told the French police:

> **[The Mercedes] was clearly being chased by several, I would say between four and six, motorcycles. There were two riders on some of the bikes. These motorcycles were sitting on the vehicle's tail and were trying to get alongside it.**[1088] **(WFJ)**

At the inquest Hackett testified that he was scared because of the proximity of the motorbikes to the Mercedes. He said: "I would say very close, very close. I was a bit scared. They were really close. I would say between 10 to 15 feet."[1089]

In his August 31 statement, Hackett said: "They were motorbikes, not scooters".[1090] (WFJ) The jury never heard that, but this becomes relevant in the later discussion as to whether these motorbikes could have been paparazzi.

---

[a] The expressway tunnel that precedes the Alma, where the crash occurred.

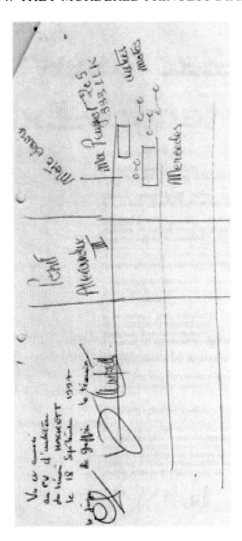

Figure 13

Drawing made by Thierry Hackett on 18 September 1997.
It shows the Mercedes in the Alexandre III tunnel pursued
by 4 motorbikes as it overtook his Peugeot. One of the
motorbikes was alongside the Mercedes as it passed him.

Blocking The Exit

The inquest cross-examination of Thierry Hackett failed to bring out the context of the chase along the expressway: the Mercedes was heading for Dodi's apartment, and to reach it they had to leave the expressway at a particular exit to the right – this exit is about 300 metres past the end of the Alexandre III tunnel.

Hackett was in the right lane. In his September 1997 statement, he clearly states that the first motorbike "was in between me and the Mercedes at the time of the overtaking manoeuvre".[1091] (WFJ)

He goes on to say that "after having passed the Alexandre III tunnel" the Mercedes "was still in the left hand lane. I could still see the light coloured [first] motorcycle at the same level as the Mercedes on the right".[1092] (WFJ)

The Alexandre III underpass is 330 metres long. In his statements to the French, Hackett said "I must have been travelling at around 80 kph"[1093] and he estimated the Mercedes' speed at "around 120 or 130 kph".[1094] Based on these estimates Hackett would have been past the Alexandre III tunnel at around the same time as the Mercedes and the motorbikes were passing the exit that would have taken Diana and Dodi to Dodi's apartment.

At this point, Hackett describes the Mercedes in the left lane and the first motorcycle on its right, with "the others following".[1095]

Hackett also testified on the day of the crash:

> **I noticed that the [Mercedes], which continued travelling in the left hand lane, was veering from side to side and having trouble keeping its line. Clearly, the driver of the vehicle was being hindered by the motorbikes.[1096]**

Hackett's testimony – the motorbikes were hindering the Mercedes; the first bike was "at the same level as the Mercedes on the right" – points to the motorbikes (particularly the first one) preventing the Mercedes from taking the exit that it needed to, in order to reach Dodi's apartment.

This action would have forced the Mercedes to change its intended route – not taking the exit, but instead heading directly towards the Alma Tunnel.

In his August 31 statement Hackett was unequivocal: "Clearly, the driver of the [Mercedes] was being hindered by the motorbikes." By September 18, this has changed to: "I think, but this is only an interpretation, that he could have been hindered by the motorcycles that were surrounding him...."[1097] This change may have been a result of pressure from the French investigators.

Hackett's description of the Mercedes "veering from side to side and having trouble keeping its line" was supported by Christophe Lascaux, who saw the Mercedes whilst travelling in the opposite direction, towards the Alexandre III tunnel.

Lascaux told the police on the day of the crash that the "large black Mercedes ... was "swerving or, to be more precise, it was doing a wide zigzag".[1098a]

Hackett's testimony of a motorbike on the right hand side of the Mercedes is also supported by the driver of a vehicle that entered the expressway just before the Alma Tunnel, François Levistre.

Levistre's statement was taken the day following the crash. He stated: "I saw in my mirror, but from a distance, a car that was escorted on each side by motorcycles".[1099]

Trevor Rees-Jones, who had access to the French investigation file, stated: "One of [the French investigation's] conclusions [was] that Henri Paul may have been forced into the Alma Tunnel because motorcycles blocked the exit he intended to take."[1100] (WFJ)

Ritz president, Frank Klein, told the inquest he had been travelling that route for 20 years: "After a long tunnel [Alexandre III], there is an exit.... Every person would exit there to go to the Champs Élysées[b]. There [are] no other solutions."[1101]

Failure to take the exit off the expressway, and instead driving through the Alma Tunnel, put Henri Paul on a course where he would have to drive twice as far to reach Dodi's apartment.

Something prevented the Mercedes from taking that exit. The evidence indicates that it was the "hindering" motorbikes seen by Hackett, which he fully explained in his earliest statements.

The jury did not get to hear most of this evidence.

---

[a] Lascaux should have been cross-examined at the inquest, but that never occurred.
[b] The location of Dodi's apartment.

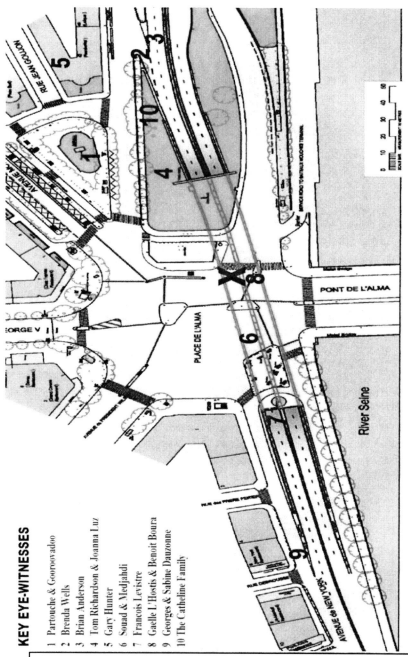

KEY EYE-WITNESSES

1 Partouche & Gooroovadoo
2 Brenda Wells
3 Brian Anderson
4 Tom Richardson & Joanna Luz
5 Gary Hunter
6 Souad & Medjahdi
7 Francois Levistre
8 Gaelle L'Hostis & Benoit Boura
9 Georges & Sabine Dauzonne
10 The Catheline Family

Figure 14 · Map of crash scene showing the positions of the key witnesses at the time of the crash (except the Dauzonnes' position reflects when they witnessed the Fiat Uno post-crash). The crash impact point at the 13th pillar of the Alma Tunnel is denoted with an "X". Original map produced by the inquest Property Services Dept.

48 Intended Exit to the Alma Tunnel

After failing to use the exit that would have taken them towards Dodi's apartment, the Mercedes S280 continued heading west on the expressway, towards the Alma Tunnel.

Unidentified Motorbikes

François Levistre was travelling along the service road parallel to the expressway just before joining the expressway ahead of the Alma Tunnel.

In his statement taken the day after the crash Levistre said:

> **I could see in the distance in my rear view mirror a vehicle surrounded on either side by motorbikes.... I joined the embankment[a] via a slip-road and the convoy drew closer.... I realised that the motorbikes were not police motorbikes, as there were no flashing lights. There were more than two motorbikes, travelling in tandem on each side of the car.**[1102b]

Off-duty chauffeur, Olivier Partouche, was standing in the Place de la Reine Astrid, near the Alma Tunnel, when he saw a Mercedes accompanied by motorbikes. He described seeing "a group, a compact group, with a car and motorcycles just behind". He elaborated:

> **In front of the group [was] the car, and the motorcycles [were] just behind, [all travelling] at the same speed.**[1103]

---

[a] The expressway.

[b] Levistre gave a completely different account ten years later at the inquest, aged 63. It is fair to say that his evidence taken a day after the crash would be the most accurate. It is important to note that Levistre's early statements, that there were several motorbikes, are supported by the accounts of other witnesses – Rabouille, Hackett, Anderson and Partouche (see earlier and later). The jury should have been given access to Levistre's earliest statement, but this never happened. The key conflicts in Levistre's testimony are addressed in Part 1, Intended Exit to Alma Tunnel section of Chapter 4A.

US businessman, Brian Anderson, was a passenger in a westbound taxi just before the Alma Tunnel, when he was overtaken by the Mercedes and three motorbikes.

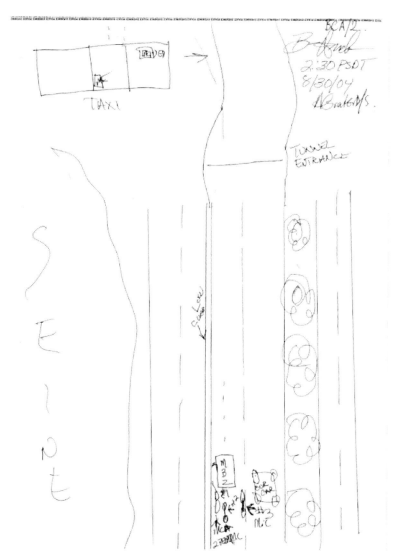

Figure 15

> Drawing made by Brian Anderson
> for British Police on 30 August 2004.

Figure 16

> Close up of Anderson's drawing showing the 3 motorbikes close
> behind the Mercedes (MBZ) as it overtook his taxi. The diagram
> shows MC (Motorcycle) 1 on the left starting to overtake, MC2
> in the centre and MC3 on the right rear of the Mercedes.

Brian Anderson saw three motorbikes "in a cluster, like a swarm around
the Mercedes".[1104] Referring to the Mercedes and the three bikes, he told the
inquest:

> **There were four moving objects in close proximity and somewhat in
> concert in their movement forward.**[1105]

He added: "One motorbike had two people and two ... just had single
passengers".[1106]

Thierry Hackett, François Levistre, Olivier Partouche and Brian Anderson
all provided a graphic and consistent account of several motorbikes
surrounding or closely pursuing the Mercedes S280 as it headed down the
expressway towards the Alma Tunnel. These witnesses described "a cluster",
"a swarm", "a compact group", "the convoy", "motorbikes travelling in
tandem on each side of the car", "motorcycles sitting on the vehicle's tail".

Camera Flashes

In Partouche's statement taken two hours after the crash he says that he clearly saw a dark car in front "trying to make the Mercedes slow down".[a] He further states that "the object of this manoeuvre was to make it possible for the paparazzi to take photographs"[1107]. He said:

> **I saw flashes before the vehicles disappeared into the [Alma] underpass.[1108]**

By the time Partouche's third statement was taken at 9.05 a.m., he is qualifying his account: "I thought that there were flashes coming from the motorbike.... However, I cannot be certain, given that the ... expressway is very well lit.".[1109]

Inquest lawyer, Jonathon Hough, next states that Partouche said in his first statement that he "saw the reflections of flashes from a camera as you were looking towards the group of vehicles".[1110] This is not a true account of what Partouche said – it is a blending of two completely unrelated recollections.

In his earliest statement Partouche said:

1) " I think that I saw flashes before the vehicles disappeared into the underpass"[1111]

2) "The motorcyclist that I saw pursuing the Mercedes was taking photos of it in the tunnel: I could see the reflections of flashes from a camera."[1112] (WFJ)

The first quote is relating something he saw before the crash, while the second one is describing what he saw after the crash.

In blending these two statements together, Hough has effectively watered down the meaning of what Partouche was saying in his 2.25 a.m. statement.

The phrase "reflections of flashes" makes sense in the context in which Partouche was using it: after the crash he was outside the tunnel and would not have been able to see the flashes themselves – it was the reflections that told him that photos were being taken inside the Alma Tunnel.

Prior to the crash, when Partouche saw the photos being taken before the Mercedes reached the tunnel, he would have directly seen the flashes – he was not seeing reflections.

This distinction is important.

There is a big difference between Partouche's initial and categoric "I saw flashes" and his later back-down – possibly under pressure from the French police[b] – "I cannot be certain, given that the ... expressway is very well lit".

---

[a] This blocking car is covered later in the Overtaking the Mercedes chapter.
[b] There is evidence indicating Partouche and Gooroovadoo were pressured by the French police into changing their accounts. This is addressed in Part 1, Intended Exit to Alma section in Chapter 4A.

The transition in the jury's mind is easier to make when coming from "reflections of flashes" – as falsely introduced by Hough – than from seeing the flashes themselves.

Coroner's Deceptions

There are several problems with the way in which Scott Baker summed up Partouche's evidence for the jury:

1)   Baker twice related the statement about the expressway being well lit – "[Partouche] could not say [there were flashes] because the expressway was well lit";[1113] quoting Partouche: "I cannot be certain [there were flashes] given that the ... expressway is very well lit".[1114]

Conversely, Baker fails to mention that when Richard Keen[a] put to Partouche his earliest statement about the dark car "trying to make the Mercedes slow down.... for the paparazzi to take photographs", Partouche replied "I think I was accurate".[1115]

2)   Baker stated that Partouche "said he had seen reflections of flashes from a camera as he was looking towards the group of vehicles".[1116]

This is a virtual word for word repetition of Hough's false blending of the two unrelated statements by Partouche (see above) and Baker dishonestly tells the jury that this was what Partouche had said "in his very first statement, written within hours of the collision".[1117]

3)   Immediately after Baker's misrepresentation of Partouche's account[b] he then states to his jury:

> **How much all of this fits with the known involvement of the Fiat Uno in the path of Mercedes evidenced by marks on the road is something you will no doubt want to consider.[1118]**

Baker suddenly introduces the white Fiat Uno into a section of evidence that is completely unrelated to that subject.[c] This is an extremely complex case already. The evidence from Partouche is dealing with camera flashes and a blocking car[d] outside the tunnel. To introduce the Uno into the thinking of the jury in this area could presumably have the effect of confusing them –

---

[a] QC for the Pauls.

[b] In point 2 above.

[c] It will be shown later that the Mercedes collided with a white Fiat Uno just inside the Alma Tunnel. The blocking car seen by Partouche and Gooroovadoo, and overtaken by the Mercedes, was before the tunnel. Those witnesses did not have a view into the tunnel. Partouche said it was "maybe a Ford Mondeo ... [and] a dark colour". 24 Oct 07: 10.3.

[d] Partouche thought it could have been a Ford Mondeo – see previous footnote.

particularly since earlier in the day Baker had already told the jury there was "no evidence" of the Fiat Uno being a part of any deliberate collision.[ab]

Changing the Evidence

Clifford Gooroovadoo[c] told the police in his initial statement – made just two hours after the crash:

> He "saw a motorbike with two people on it and ... the pillion passenger ... taking one photo after another".[1119]

By the 12th of September he states that he is sure there was a motorbike, but then this: "I cannot say how many people were on this motorcycle".[1120]

That effectively then removes any possibility of Gooroovadoo seeing "one photo after another" being taken.

In answer to an unknown question in his 2.30 a.m. statement Gooroovadoo says "Reply to question: I would like to correct something. I do not remember if there were any flashes".[1121] In his 6 a.m. statement he reverts to having seen flashes but says this:

> On the wall that leads into the tunnel, there are neon lights and so I cannot say whether the passenger on the motorbike was taking pictures with a flash gun or whether it was a reflection of the neon lights that I could see, producing a flashing effect.[1122]

Gooroovadoo's statements appear to have been made under pressure from the French investigators. It would be particularly interesting to know what the question was at the conclusion of the first statement – it is that question that appears to have encouraged him to alter his evidence.

There were, and are, no neon lights on the wall leading into the Alma Tunnel.

Gooroovadoo was not cross-examined during the inquest, but should have been.

Other Witnesses

Brian Anderson, talking about the pillion passenger on one of the motorbikes he saw, stated: "I strongly believe that it was a photographer or someone acting in that type of role, observer".[1123]

Benoît Boura[a] was driving eastbound[b] towards the Alma Tunnel when he saw "flashes from cameras used by photographers" in the distance.[1124]

---

[a] "No one disputes that a white Fiat Uno collided with the Mercedes.... Did that [Uno driver] deliberately collide with the Mercedes? There is, I suggest, no evidence from which you could draw such an inference." 1 Apr 08: 31.2

[b] The white Fiat Uno is dealt with later.

[c] Off-duty chauffeur standing near Partouche.

In summary, several witnesses – Partouche, Gooroovadoo, Anderson, Boura – all provided evidence indicating photos were taken just before the Alma Tunnel.

Once again none of these photos have ever been published.

Why?

The following chapter will show that the motorbikes pursuing the Mercedes were not paparazzi, but instead were people acting as paparazzi.

Following the crash this deception was a critical factor in blaming the paparazzi for the crash, even though they were nowhere near the Mercedes as it entered the Alma Tunnel.

---

[a] Once in the tunnel, Boura witnessed the crash happen – see later.

[b] The opposite direction to the Mercedes.

49   Were the Motorbikes Paparazzi?

Some of the paparazzi followed the Mercedes S280 from the Ritz Hotel and others caught up at the Place de la Concorde.

The eight witnesses – Lee, Hackett, Lascaux, Levistre, Anderson, Partouche, Gooroovadoo and Wells[a] – who saw the Mercedes with following vehicles after the Place de la Concorde and before the Alma Tunnel, unanimously described those following vehicles as motorbikes.

Could those pursuing motorbikes have been paparazzi?

Coroner Baker told the jury in his Summing Up:

> **You have heard that the photographers who certainly were in a position to have been following the Mercedes closely were Rat, Benhamou, Arnal, Martinez and Odekerken. It is unclear whether Chassery and Langevin could have been.[1125]**

Paparazzi in the Place de la Concorde	
Person	**Vehicle**
Arnal	Black Fiat Uno
Benhamou	Green Honda 80 cc Scooter
Darmon	Blue Honda 650 Motorbike
Guizard	Grey/Blue Peugeot 205
Martinez	With Arnal
Odekerken	Mitsubishi Pajero
Rat	With Darmon

This table shows the paparazzi who were present with the Mercedes in the Place de la Concorde and which vehicle they were in or on.

[a] The evidence of Eric Lee, Christophe Lascaux and Brenda Wells is covered in Part 1, Chapter 4A.

Fabrice Chassery was driving alone in his dark grey Peugeot 205, but paparazzi police statements and mobile phone evidence reveal that he was not involved in this final pursuit of the Mercedes.[a]

Paparazzi statements and CCTV evidence also rule Jacques Langevin out from the pursuit of the Mercedes. Langevin was driving a grey VW Golf.[b]

The witness evidence of the pursuit of the Mercedes right up to the Alma Tunnel is clear. There were 15 witnesses who saw unidentified vehicles near the Mercedes at various points of the journey – 14 of these described the vehicles as motorbikes and one, Bonin, saw a scooter.[c]

There are two mentions of unidentified cars close to the Mercedes, and both of these were blocking vehicles – at the Place de la Concorde and immediately before the Alma Tunnel. Bonin describes the dark blocking car as following the Mercedes "at the same speed".[1126] It would appear though, that it was unable to keep up, as no witnesses describe any close pursuing car along the expressway – this includes Lee, Hackett, Lascaux, Levistre, Anderson, Partouche, Gooroovadoo and Wells.

Bonin also witnessed the scooter with two people aboard giving chase from the Place de la Concorde.[1127] The only paparazzi scooter present at the Place de la Concorde was Benhamou, who was not carrying a passenger. His scooter was an 80 cc Honda and would not have had any hope of keeping up with the Mercedes. It is clear that the scooter Bonin saw could not have been ridden by paparazzi.[d]

None of the witnesses between Concorde and the Alma Tunnel saw a scooter close to the Mercedes – the implication is that the scooter Bonin saw was also not powerful enough to keep up with the Mercedes.

As the above table shows, there was just the one paparazzi motorbike in the Place de la Concorde – the 650 Honda with Darmon and Rat aboard.

Speed Tests

The French police conducted vehicle acceleration and speed tests.

Darmon's Motorbike

Paget investigator, Anthony Read was asked to provide details of the French testing. He said this:

> **Read: They ... used a similar Mercedes. They used a Honda 650 motorcycle ... the type ... ridden by Rat and Darmon, a Yamaha 850 motorcycle, a BMW K75 motorcycle, a BMW GS100 motorcycle and ... another BMW 1100 motorcycle....**

---

[a] Refer Transcripts 13 Mar 08 36.12 to 40.18
[b] Refer Transcripts 12 Mar 08 72.18 to 73.14
[c] The full list of 15 and their evidence is in Part 1, Chapter 4A.
[d] See earlier Champs Élysées Lights chapter.

Hilliard:[a] Were you satisfied that, with one possible exception, they were all capable of maintaining contact with the Mercedes along the expressway?

Read: Yes, they were. All bar the motorcycle ridden by Darmon and Rat had comparable or better performance over that distance.[1128]

This little period of "cross-examination" between Nicholas Hilliard and Anthony Read has some similarity to the infamous story of the "Emperor With No Clothes".

Both Hilliard and Read would only be too aware that there was only the one paparazzi motorbike (Rat & Darmon's) present in the Place de la Concorde, and therefore only one paparazzi motorbike (Rat & Darmon's) could possibly have been in a position to pursue the Mercedes. Yet Hilliard and Read, like they are performing some sort of charade, keep up the pretence that somehow there was a small fleet of paparazzi motorbikes that were in a position to keep up with Diana's Mercedes.

The fact that the French tested five motorbikes, with four of them having no connection to the paparazzi present, is deceptive and misleading of itself.

The evidence from the French speed tests reveals that over the 1,400 metres from Concorde to the tunnel, at top speed, Darmon's motorbike would have been 17% slower than the Mercedes – a full 7 seconds behind over that distance.[1129bc]

This fact however did not stop the Ritz lawyer, Tom de la Mare, from describing Darmon's motorbike as "the speed machine on the block".[1130d] De la Mare also falsely declared that "the French testing of the various motorbikes established that the bike … Mr Darmon was driving would have no difficulty whatsoever in keeping up with the Mercedes".[1131]

This was then confirmed by Paul Carpenter, another Paget officer, who proceeded to blatantly lie under oath:

---

[a] Inquest lawyer Nicholas Hilliard.

[b] To make a direct comparison, the French tests should have been conducted with a pillion passenger on the motorbike. It was not revealed whether this was done.

[c] The evidence of Levistre and Anderson – see next chapter – shows that one of the motorbikes present didn't just have the power to keep up, but was able to carry out a difficult overtaking manoeuvre to get in front of the Mercedes.

[d] This was four months after the jury had been told there was a 17% difference and critically, De La Mare's comments were made during the last few days of inquest testimony.

> **[The French] established that of all the vehicles being used by the paparazzi, [Darmon's] was the slowest and he would still be able to keep up [with the Mercedes].**[1132a]

The fact that Carpenter was not made to account for that – or charged with perjury – is indicative of the corrupt nature of this inquest, a reality which will be increasingly exposed as this story continues.

Both Rat and Darmon have provided consistent evidence – right from their first interviews on the day of the crash – that they were unable to keep up with the Mercedes.[1133]

Other Motorbikes

As the paparazzi list[b] reveals, there were five two-wheeled vehicles ridden by the paparazzi who were outside the Ritz Hotel on the night. Of these, only two were present at the Place de la Concorde – Darmon's Honda 650 and Benhamou's 80 cc scooter. The two wheelers that didn't follow Diana's Mercedes were: Arsov's BMW R100 TS; Tomic's BMW K1000 and Veres' Piaggio scooter.[c]

Of the motorbikes that the French tested – claiming that they matched the paparazzi motorbikes – only the Honda 650 actually did match a paparazzi motorbike: Darmon's. There is no evidence for how or why the French actually decided to test motorbikes that had no relevance to the models of motorbikes ridden by the paparazzi.

At the inquest this deception was continued by Read, who pretended to the jury that all the motorbikes tested were the equivalent of those ridden by the paparazzi.[d]

The reality is that of the five motorbikes the French tested, only one had any connection to the paparazzi motorbikes.

French Logic

Jean-Claude Mulès, the head of the French police investigation, stated: "I assume these motorbikes [witnessed by Partouche near the tunnel] were … the paparazzi".[1134]

Michael Mansfield QC then rightly asked: "Why do you assume that?"

This was Mulès' stunning reply – stunning because this is from a person who spent two years running the investigation:

> **It seems logical. Everybody knows that the Mercedes could not manage not to have any photographer, any paparazzi, behind it, and**

---

[a] This was stated four months after the jury had heard about the French testing – it was again during the last few days of inquest testimony.

[b] Near the beginning of this book.

[c] The paparazzi vehicles were also listed at the inquest: 11 Oct 07: 56.4.

[d] See above.

> so they grouped – all the paparazzis grouped together because news in
> this profession spreads quite quickly and they were all behind the
> Mercedes.[1135]

Mansfield went on to ask Mulès: "Did you ever consider that one or more
of the motorcycles ... may not have belonged to paparazzi?"

Mulès: "No."[1136]

Why not?

The French knew that there was only the <u>one</u> paparazzi motorbike at the
Place de la Concorde. They had the clear statements of Hackett, Partouche
and Levistre stating that there were <u>several</u> motorbikes surrounding the
Mercedes. Why did they not ask: "How can this be?"

How could the surrounding group of motorbikes be paparazzi if there was
only one paparazzi motorbike in the Place de la Concorde?

Coroner's Deceptions

The final verdict available to the jury was gross negligence of the
"following vehicles".[a] In Scott Baker's Summing Up for that jury, he
conveyed that these "following vehicles" were the paparazzi.

He told them:

> There is evidence of a number of paparazzi vehicles following the
> Mercedes to the Place de la Concorde, [and] that a number [were] still
> behind it at the Alexandre III tunnel and on the approach to the Alma
> Tunnel.[1137]

Unless "behind" means a long way behind, Baker has ignored irrefutable
evidence that "a number" of paparazzi vehicles were not close to the
Mercedes on the approach to the tunnel.

And this: "It is not relevant from the viewpoint of <u>gross negligence</u> on the
part of Henri Paul or the <u>paparazzi</u>, how he came to be in the driving seat."[1138]

"[Henri Paul] was racing to get away from the paparazzi."[1139]

"There is evidence that the paparazzi continually accelerated to follow the
Mercedes."[1140]

"Did the paparazzi try to take flash photographs on the journey or <u>are
some of the eye witnesses mistaken</u>? If they did try this, did their photographs
come out? If they did, what has happened to them? This is an intriguing
subplot, but it may well take you nowhere."[1141]

The Coroner only provides the jury with two possible options here: Either
the paparazzi were taking photos or the seven independent eye-witnesses
have got it wrong – meaning that all seven never saw any camera flashes.[a]

---

[a] Murder was removed by the coroner – see later.

The third option, not considered by Baker, is that there were camera flashes, and the photos were not taken by paparazzi, but by people posing as paparazzi.

Baker concludes that the discussion "may well take you nowhere" – yet this discussion is at the very heart of what was happening in central Paris on the night of 30 August 1997.[b]

Soldier N

In late-August 2013 Scotland Yard detectives interviewed the wife of a former SAS soldier – known only as Soldier N – at an undisclosed location in the UK.[1142]

Mrs N alleged that in 2008 Prince William had visited her then husband's regiment's headquarters. Later in the day, after N had returned to their home in Hereford, during conversation N had confided to his wife that the SAS had been involved in the murder of William's mother, Princess Diana.

N told his wife that Diana was killed by an SAS hit team on motorbikes, one of whom flashed a high-powered light into the face of the Mercedes driver, Henri Paul.[1143]

Mrs N went into hiding in October 2013 after being advised by SAS officers that her life was at risk.[1144c]

MI6 and SAS

Would MI6 employ an SAS team to assist in carrying out an assassination?

There are several points:

1)   In 1956 MI6 devised a "plan to use SAS troops in the run-up to [an] invasion to kill or capture [Gamal Abdel] Nasser", the president of Egypt.[1145] (WFJ)

2)   In March 1988 MI5 employed four SAS personnel to kill three unarmed IRA terrorists in Gibraltar.[1146] (WFJ)

3)   Intelligence experts Jonathan Bloch & Patrick Fitzgerald wrote in 1983:

---

[a] The seven are Guizard, Bonin, Rees-Jones, Odekerken, Boura, Partouche and Gooroovadoo. The full evidence is in Part 1, Chapter 4A.
[b] French journalist Christophe Lafaille stated: "A professional photographer would never overtake a car to take pictures through the windows. It is not worth it, you have the glass and its reflection and they don't take risks like that." 7 Feb 08: 31.18.
[c] Scotland Yard released the results of their Soldier N investigation on 16 December 2013. The report can be viewed at:
http://princessdianadeaththeevidence.weebly.com/scotland-yard-report.html

> **Close cooperation is required between MI6 and the SAS before and during overseas campaigns and SAS squadrons receive briefings from MI6 before departure.**[1147] (WFJ)

4)   Intelligence journalist Richard Norton-Taylor stated in 1990:

> **The Special Air Service (SAS) is ... now firmly established as a highly-trained, armed unit permanently available to the security services and the prime minister. The SAS has become the armed military wing of the security and intelligence services.**[1148] (WFJ)

5)   Ex-MI6 officer, Richard Tomlinson, testified in 1999 that he saw an MI6 outline of a plan to assassinate Serbian leader Slobodan Milosevic. He said that the 1992 document was circulated to several senior officers, including "the SAS liaison officer to MI6 (designation MODA/SO)".[1149] (WFJ)

6)   Tomlinson stated in his 1999 affidavit that "a strobe flash gun [is] a device which is occasionally deployed by special forces[a]"[1150] (WFJ) At the inquest he said that "a very bright flashing light ...was used [by the SBS] ... to disorient, for example a helicopter pilot, on landing".[1151][b]

Tomlinson states in his 2001 book *The Big Breach* that a select group from the SAS and SBS called The Increment are employed by MI6. He wrote:

> **To qualify for the increment, SAS and SBS personnel must have served for at least five years and have reached the rank of sergeant. They are security vetted by MI6 and given a short induction course into the function and objectives of the service.... They learn how to use improvised explosives and sabotage techniques.**[1152] (WFJ)

Avoiding The Increment

MI6 and Scott Baker were notably nervous about any mention of the increment at the inquest.

Michael Mansfield asked Richard Dearlove – MI6 Head of Operations in 1997 – about the increment, on four occasions.

Dearlove initially reacted very strongly, on the second occasion Baker intervened, on the third Dearlove simply refused to comment and on the fourth MI6 lawyer Robin Tam intervened:

1st instance: Dearlove: "can I cut to the quick, Mr Mansfield? I am not going to speculate on SIS's various operational capabilities...."[1153]

---

[a] SAS and SBS.
[b] MI6's relationship with strobe lights is addressed in the later chapter on the Powerful Flash.

2nd instance: Baker cut Mansfield off mid-sentence and said: "I do not really see why we are spending so long on ... a matter which really must be speculation"[1154]

3rd instance: Dearlove: "I am not going to speculate or comment"[1155]

4th instance: Tam: "my learned friend [Mansfield] is getting into operational details and methods which are sensitive and should not be asked about" followed by Dearlove: "the service's capability is the service's capability".[1156]

There are several serious concerns about what occurred during this critical period of cross-examination:[a]

1)   Speculation.

Dearlove's initial reaction, when Mansfield suggested that MI6 "employ an increment" for "tasks abroad", was "I am not going to speculate on SIS's various operational capabilities".[1157]

Baker later supported that: "I do not really see why we are spending so long on this, on a matter which really must be speculation".[1158]

Just in case we didn't get it, Dearlove repeated it: "I am not going to speculate".[1159b]

Speculation[c] – the point here is that Richard Dearlove is on the stand. Dearlove: 38 years' experience in MI6, Director of Operations for 5 years and MI6 Chief for another 5 years, 11 years on the MI6 board.[d]

Dearlove is being questioned on a key aspect of MI6 operations – critical to the current case[e] – so it is ridiculous to suggest that any answer on this from him would be speculative. Yet we have both Dearlove and Baker suggesting just that – "I am not going to speculate"; "a matter which really must be speculation".

2)   MI6 capabilities.

Dearlove states that "the court does not need to know about ... [the] SIS's various operational capabilities".[1160] And later: "I am not going to confirm or

---

[a] The reader should bear in mind that this subject – the use of others, e.g. the SAS, to carry out operations for MI6 – is possibly central to the Paris crash. There is a realistic possibility that MI6 would have used other people to operate on their behalf. Other evidence has shown or will show that on the night of the crash and the following day people such as Henri Paul, Claude Roulet, Jean-Marc Martino, Dominique Lecomte, Gilbert Pépin and Jean Monceau appeared to be working on behalf of an outside organisation. Despite extensive witness evidence of riders on powerful motorbikes pursuing the Mercedes S280, none of these riders have ever been identified.

[b] On the third occasion "the increment" came up.

[c] To speculate is to "form a theory or opinion without firm evidence" – Oxford.

[d] Dearlove joined MI6 in 1966: 20 Feb 08: 4.4. Dearlove's background was covered on 20 Feb 08: 4.4 to 5.15.

[e] See earlier footnote regarding the use of others.

deny whether the [capabilities] you are mentioning are part of the service's capability".[1161]

Dearlove finished up by stating: "the service's capability is the service's capability".[1162]

The inquest jury were investigating the circumstances of the Paris crash. MI6 had been named as a prime suspect for having orchestrated it. Yet Dearlove is trying to tell the jury they are not entitled to be told about MI6's "operational capabilities".

This type of evidence tends to make a sham out of even having MI6 witnesses cross-examined at this inquest. If the jury aren't allowed to know about the capabilities of a prime suspect in the investigation, then how can they be expected to reach an informed verdict on the circumstances of the crash?[a] If there were concerns that national security was threatened by revealing this information, then why wasn't it told to the jury in a closed court?

3)   Dearlove's control.

Dearlove strongly states on three occasions that the jury needed to know that he was in control:

-    "what the court does need to know is that all of these capabilities, every single one of them, were under my personal control"[1163]

-    "anything that is referred to ... was under the control of the director of operations"[1164b]

-    "there is no part of SIS ... which is not fully under the control of the operational director".[1165c]

Dearlove is suggesting that everyone should rest easy because in 1997 – at the time of the deaths of Princess Diana and Dodi Fayed – the operational

---

[a] One of the key questions regarding the crash was: Was it possible for a crash of this complex nature to be orchestrated? In other words, was there any organisation that would actually have the capabilities to pull such an operation off? In that light, it was important that the jury got to hear this type of critical information. Linked to this was the knowledge – indicated by the accumulated facts of the case – that various operatives appeared to be working for an outside organisation.

[b] Dearlove was MI6 Director of Operations at the time of the Paris crash.

[c] Dearlove used various phrases to emphasise this point: "every single one" (20 Feb 08: 116.20); "whether you have heard of it before or whether you have not heard of it before, whether it has a strange name or whether it has not got a strange name" (117.1); "let's be absolutely crystal clear" (117.5); "it is important that the jury understands that" (117.6); "I am going to repeat this" (125.21); "whether it is deniable or not" (125.24); "I do not know how many times I am going to have to emphasise this" (126.7); "I have said it four or five times already" (126.8); "it is unproductive to go on banging on about this" (126.10).

capabilities of MI6, whatever they may be, were under Dearlove's personal control.

What Dearlove, or anyone else, fails to tell the jury is that in the previous year, 1996, under Dearlove's watch as Director of Operations, MI6 had been deeply involved in two high-level assassination plots – Muammar Gaddafi and Saddam Hussein.[a] (WFJ)

What this means is that the knowledge that Dearlove was in control at the time of the Paris crash is not a cause for comfort, but instead a cause for concern.[b]

It raises the inevitable question: If Dearlove – and Chief Spedding[c] – presided over the assassination plots of Muammar Gaddafi and Saddam Hussein, did these same men also preside over the assassination of Princess Diana?

4)   Subject change.

On the second occasion that Mansfield mentioned the increment, Baker interrupted him midstream, pointing out that even if the increment was used an operation would still be "under the approval of SIS" and then continued: "the whole point is that this [Milosevic] plan is not one officer on a frolic of his own going to carry it out on his own. It has been put up through the system for approval."[1166]

If we go back to Mansfield's question, we can see that it has nothing to do with what Baker is suggesting: "What I wanted to put to you is deniability means this, doesn't it: it means there will be a secret operation abroad, carried out by an increment, not SIS officers but SAS officers or SBS officers – "[d], at which point Mansfield was cut off by Baker.[1167]

Mansfield's question focuses on the issue of deniability and he mentions just before this – see previous footnote – "I am asking ... whether in 1993 there were discussions which involved the concept of deniability". He then

---

[a] The evidence regarding MI6 involvement in these plots is covered in Part 5, section on Does MI6 Murder People? in Chapter 1A.
[b] The jury would not have realised this because they were prevented from hearing about the Gaddafi and Saddam plots.
[c] David Spedding was MI6 Chief for the same period as Richard Dearlove was Director of Operations – 1994 to 1999. Spedding was never interviewed in any police investigation. He died in 2001.
[d] The full question started at 120.10: "But now you see why I am asking the questions about what discussions even take place at an official level. That is all I am asking, whether in fact – before we even get to unofficial levels, whether in 1993 there were discussions which involved the concept of deniability. What I wanted to put to you is deniability...." For the full context, refer to the inquest website. The fuller context does include discussion regarding MI6 officers conducting independent operations, but by the time Mansfield asked this question he was focusing on the issue of deniability "at an official level" – see discussion below.

puts it to Dearlove that deniability "means there will be a secret operation abroad, carried out by ... SAS officers or SBS officers".

This is where Baker cuts Mansfield off and changes the subject to the issue of: "one officer on a frolic of his own".

Mansfield was not suggesting anything like that – he was describing a "secret operation abroad, carried out by an increment" on behalf of MI6, which could later though, if necessary, be denied by MI6: the issue of deniability.

Mansfield was effectively describing a possible scenario for the way the Paris crash could have been organised, had MI6 done it – a deniable operation.

Yet we next find Baker saying: "I think we need to focus on what happened in the tunnel, not on other ephemeral matters." [a]

In doing this, Baker was able to deftly – but dishonestly – shut down Mansfield's line of questioning and he was forced to move on to the next subject.[b]

Later, when Mansfield brings up the increment for the fourth time, Dearlove then emphasises his argument by appearing to copy a similar line from Baker: "There is not a bit of SIS that acts independently or goes off and does its own thing. This does not exist...."[1168]

The point is that no one has ever suggested that the increment – the use of the SAS or SBS to conduct operations for MI6 – was ever acting independently. In all the mentions of this in the literature, including Tomlinson, the actions of the SAS and SBS – when operating on behalf of MI6 – are under the control of MI6.

If the SAS conducts an operation for MI6, then the fact that MI6 is not directly carrying it out makes it easier for them to deny involvement. That does not however mean that MI6 is not in control of the conduct of that operation.

5)   Relevance.

Both Baker and Dearlove suggested that the issue of the increment had nothing to do with the current case – the deaths of Princess Diana and Dodi Fayed:

-        Baker: "I think we need to focus on what happened in the tunnel, not on other ephemeral[a] matters"[1169]

---

[a] This is from the person who spent around three days of the inquest focusing on the Milosevic plot, where the only documentary evidence was apparently destroyed by MI6.

[b] And Dearlove was saved from having to address the increment ... until Mansfield's next attempt.

- Dearlove: "I do not think [MI6's capabilities] has anything to do with this inquest into the death of Princess Diana". [1170]

MI6 was alleged to be one of the prime suspects for the orchestration and conduct of the Paris crash. Therefore, if the jury were to be allowed to do a proper job of determining the cause of the deaths of Diana and Dodi, it would be imperative for them to understand the capabilities – including use of the increment – of MI6.[b]

Baker, who was in control of the inquest, appeared very determined – with the help of Tam and Dearlove – to ensure that his own jury were not privy to such information.

Why is this?

Despite the refusal by Baker, Dearlove and Tam to divulge this to the jury, other evidence, mostly not heard at the inquest – Tomlinson, Dorril, Bloch and Fitzgerald, Norton-Taylor – reveals that the SAS and SBS are used to conduct operations on behalf of MI6.

The evidence of Mrs N indicates that the increment may have been deployed to assist with the assassination of Princess Diana.

---

[a] Ephemeral was a favoured word by both MI6 and Baker – it means: "lasting or living for a very short time": Oxford.
[b] Even if this meant that such evidence should be heard in closed court, to protect national security.

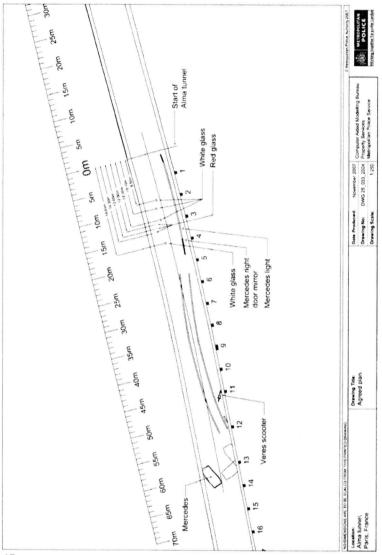

Figure 17

MPS forensic map of the Alma Tunnel crash scene, used at the inquest – it shows the skid marks, debris spread and movements of the Mercedes. Although this is a very useful diagram, the inclusion of "Veres scooter" close to the impact point is a complete mystery – this was never explained to the jury and there has never been a mention of Veres' scooter in connection with the crash. The Ritz CCTV shows that Veres actually didn't leave the Place Vendôme until 12.25 a.m. – 2 minutes after the crash had already occurred. Refer transcripts: 11 Mar 08: 183.9.

50   Overtaking the Mercedes

Witnesses saw a blocking car sitting in the right-hand lane – possibly a dark-coloured Ford Mondeo – which forced the Mercedes S280 to switch into the left lane.

Blocking Car

In his earliest statements made on the day of the crash Olivier Partouche said:

> **In front of the Mercedes was a car.... It was dark in colour and clearly this car was trying to make the Mercedes slow down.[1171]**
> **The first vehicle was visibly travelling in such a manner as to slow down the Mercedes that was following it.[1172]**
> **I could quite clearly see a dark coloured car travelling in front of a Mercedes limousine brake in order to enable a motorbike to draw level with the VIP vehicle [the Mercedes].[1173] (WFJ)**

Clifford Gooroovadoo was standing near Partouche and saw the same blocking car: He told the police on the day of the crash:

> **In front of [the Mercedes] there was a car ... travelling at a considerably slower speed.... I did see the Mercedes pull out, whilst accelerating even harder to overtake on the left.[1174]**

Baker told the jury in his Summing Up: "A blocking vehicle could have been involved. However ... there is no forensic scientific evidence to support such a possibility."[1175]

Baker correctly states there is no forensic evidence, but he ignores the fact that there is clear early witness evidence of a blocking vehicle – Partouche and Gooroovadoo.

Overtaking On the Left

After seeing the blocking car brake, Partouche stated that action enabled "a motorbike to draw level with the VIP vehicle" – the Mercedes.

Partouche was viewing this from a nearby park and was unable to see what happened next, as the Mercedes entered the Alma Tunnel.

But other witnesses did.

Brian Anderson

Brian Anderson was a passenger in a taxi which was now behind the Mercedes.

Anderson has provided a very clear and graphic account of the events he witnessed – firstly, two weeks after the crash to the ABC, then later to Operation Paget in 2004 and finally to the inquest. He also outlined that he was interviewed several times by the French police in the first days after the crash – the French have categorically denied that these interviews took place.[a]

During Anderson's inquest testimony, an unusual line of questioning by Ian Burnett, the inquest QC, emerged. Burnett asked Anderson about what motorbikes he saw, but it was only in relation to the motorbike on the right rear side that Burnett asked "What was it trying to do?" Anderson answered this question by saying "I do not know". He then proceeded, presumably in an effort to be helpful, to start speculating that this right rear motorbike could have been trying to overtake the Mercedes.[1176]

Burnett did not ask this question ("What was it trying to do?") regarding the other two motorbikes he saw.[b] By omitting to ask, Burnett did not give Anderson, who was remembering events from ten years previous, the opportunity to describe fully what he saw, to the jury. The jury were left with a confusing picture, because they later heard Anderson's evidence given to the ABC two weeks after the crash. In that interview Anderson outlined:

> **One [motorbike] proceeded with two people to make a move quickly to the left side of the [Mercedes] and get in front of the automobile.**[1177]

The jury were shown a drawing Anderson had made, but not the enlarged version of the vehicles themselves in the second image (see drawings shown earlier). And they also did not hear Anderson's critical statement to the British police, where he provided more detail:

> **[There] was a bike which had a passenger.... I noticed this bike was accelerating on and off the throttle and was to the rear left hand side of the Mercedes as it travelled forward. It appeared that it was trying to get in between the Mercedes and the low kerb in the centre of the road, which separated our two lanes from traffic flow in the opposite direction. I remember at this point saying to the taxi driver 'The guy's fucking crazy'. I was referring to the driver of motorcycle number**

---

[a] Refer to Part 1, the chapter on "Undermining of Key Witnesses" for the detail of statements on this from Anderson and the French police.

[b] Anderson saw three bikes altogether – see earlier Intended Exit to the Alma Tunnel chapter.

> 1[a].... **The left of the Mercedes was only about a foot and a half from the central low kerb I have described and there was no way in my opinion that the driver of ... bike [number 1] was going to be able to pass the Mercedes in between it and the low kerb.**[1178] **(WFJ)**

Then in Scott Baker's Summing Up of Anderson's account, he told his jury:

> **There was a ... motorbike to the <u>rear right</u> of the Mercedes. It appeared to be trying to overtake the Mercedes.**[1179]

Baker dishonestly failed to mention anything about the actions of the motorbike that Anderson saw overtake on the left. This serious omission was despite Baker being aware of both the content of Anderson's Paget statement and his earlier ABC interview.

By the time the jury retired it is very likely that they would have been left with the false view that Anderson had seen only the motorbike on the right attempt to overtake the Mercedes.

This is significant because the fact that Anderson saw the motorbike with two riders overtake on the left hand side corroborates the evidence of François Levistre from inside the Alma Tunnel.

François Levistre

François Levistre also described a motorbike overtake the Mercedes on the left:

> **I saw a motorbike accelerating. It was to the left of a large car that was behind me. The motorcycle, it was large and the two riders had full-face helmets on, cut up the large car in order to get in front of it.**[1180] **(WFJ)** [b]

---

[a] Motorcycle 1, as depicted in Anderson's drawing shown earlier.

[b] At the inquest the jury did hear Levistre say the motorbike overtook the Mercedes (15 Oct 07: from 91.3) but his clearest account was to the French investigation in 1998, which was withheld.

51   Fiat Uno Collision

Witness and forensic evidence indicates the motorbike was overtaking the Mercedes S280 just as Henri Paul was about to enter the Alma Tunnel and see a white Fiat Uno straddling the lanes in front of him.

Henri was confronted with a stark, but split-second, choice – either risk hitting the motorbike on his left or the Fiat Uno ahead on his right. Before he could take any action the powerful motorbike was in front of him and the Mercedes side-swiped the Fiat Uno.

The evidence of the Uno collision is incontrovertible – Uno debris in the tunnel, Uno paint on the Mercedes.[a]

Was the Fiat Uno's presence in the tunnel orchestrated or coincidental?

Waiting for the Mercedes

David Laurent was approaching the Alma Tunnel in his Volkswagen Polo about ten seconds[b] before the Mercedes S280 arrived. In October 1997 he described what confronted him:

> **At the entrance to the tunnel, I suddenly came upon a car that was driving slowly in the right-hand lane. I was taken by surprise, but even so, I had time to pull the steering wheel to the left to avoid it.... It was a small light-coloured hatchback car.... I think it was an old model.... I was doing 70 to 80 kilometres per hour and I think that car was doing 30 to 40 [kph]. I do not know why it was going so slowly. It did not seem to be broken down or damaged.**[1181]

Laurent's girlfriend, Nathalie Blanchard, was also in the Polo and told police the "small car [that was] driving slowly ... was light-coloured, beige, grey or white ... [and] was something like an Austin Mini or a Fiat Uno".[1182]

---

[a] See later.

[b] This timing is based on Laurent's approximate speed – 70 to 80 kph – and the time at which Laurent heard the noise of the crash – "when I came out of the tunnel". 14 Oct 97 Statement read out 11 Oct 07: 23.24 & 24.18. The tunnel length is about 130 metres – at 75 kph Laurent would have been emerging from the Alma Tunnel about 10 seconds after entering it.

Is there a reason this car was moving so slowly? Was it waiting for the Mercedes S280?

Getting Into Position

Seconds later Souad Moufakkir – passenger in her boyfriend's grey Citroen BX – entered the tunnel just ahead of the Mercedes S280. She also witnessed the Fiat Uno acting strangely:

> **I saw through the back window a Fiat Uno driving very fast up to us, in the outside [left] lane – but rather than hurtle past, it slowed down so we were side by side. It was very strange behaviour, and I got frightened. The white car was only centimetres from ours.... [The driver] had a very strange expression, like his mind was thinking about something else. His whole manner was odd. It troubled me.... I became very scared. I thought he was a madman, and I told Mohammed[a] to speed away. We did that and a moment later we heard the screech of tyres. [1183] (WFJ)**

If the driver of this white Fiat Uno was not anticipating the arrival of the Mercedes, then why was he acting so strangely? And why has he never come forward?

The Collision

Just moments after Souad's boyfriend accelerated away the Mercedes S280 sideswiped the Fiat Uno, immediately after entering the Alma Tunnel.

There is substantial forensic evidence of this collision – debris from the Fiat Uno,[b] white Uno paint on the Mercedes[c] – but only one person saw the moment of impact: Benoît Boura.[d]

Boura was travelling eastbound through the tunnel[e] and looked across when he heard the screech of tyres. He told the police on the day of the crash:

---

[a] Souad's boyfriend, Mohammed Medjahdi.

[b] Forensic discussions regarding the debris found can be viewed on the inquest website for the 7th, 8th and 12th of November 2007. There were three investigators cross-examined: Anthony Read, MPS; Peter Jennings, TRL (Transport Research Laboratory); John Searle, independent.

[c] The paint was analysed by both the French and British police. There is an analysis of their conclusions in Part 1, Police Analysis section in Chapter 5B. This is also mentioned later when establishing who owned this white Fiat Uno.

[d] Other people heard the small impact of the two vehicles colliding. For example, David Le Ny was walking near the tunnel entrance and recalled hearing "braking [then] a shock which was not so significant". 15 Oct 07: 10.6. Jean-Claude Catheline was walking near Le Ny – he stated that he heard a "first noise ... as if the [Mercedes] was bumping into something, but something light". 15 Oct 07: 47.19.

[e] Opposite direction to the Mercedes.

> **I heard the noise of the tyres, and then a little impact. At that moment, I saw in the opposite [westbound] lane, two vehicles.... I think that the Mercedes, which was driving very fast, struck the saloon.**[1184] **(WFJ)**

At the inquest Boura was specifically asked: "What did you see in the opposite lane?" He answered:

> **A car that bumped into another and then bumped into a pillar in the tunnel.**[1185]

David Laurent had to swerve to avoid a slow-moving white Fiat Uno in the right lane. Then a few seconds later Souad witnesses a white Fiat Uno in the left lane come "very fast up to us" before "it slowed down" to be alongside her. Souad's car sped up then "a moment later [she] heard the screech of tyres". Boura, travelling on the other side, heard the same "noise of the tyres" and then saw the Mercedes-Uno collision.

Were the actions of the Uno driver premeditated? Or was this all a coincidence?

There is other evidence to assess.

52   Powerful Flash

The motorbike with two riders on board overtook the Mercedes on the left, pushing Henri Paul to the right. Once inside the tunnel Henri was confronted with the slow-moving white Fiat Uno, straddling the two lanes.[a] The motorbike got in front of the Mercedes which sideswiped the Uno. Three independent witnesses saw a powerful flash. The Mercedes S280 then went out of control.

The Witnesses

Just three witnesses saw the powerful flash – they were in the cars travelling in a line with the Mercedes S280, two ahead and one behind.

On the day following the crash François Levistre – who was ahead of the Mercedes – told the police:

> **I could distinctly see one motorbike cut across the front of the [Mercedes]. There was a large white flash.**[1186] **(WFJ)**

Brian Anderson – who was behind the Mercedes in a taxi – told the Paget inquiry:

> **I saw a flash coming from … in front of us…. It was an intense flash … so bright like magnesium igniting.**[1187] **(WFJ)**

At the inquest Souad Moufakkir – who was in front of the Mercedes – testified that she saw a flash "during the collision, when the car was hurtling".[1188]

Identifying the Flash

In 1998 a Fulcrum documentary on Britain's ITV tried out two different flashes for François Levistre to assess. When they tested the second one, Levistre confirmed it was the type of flash he saw in the Alma Tunnel.

The documentary then stated:

> **The first flash was from a paparazzi camera. But Monsieur Levistre identified the much bigger flash, the second one and that came from …**

---

[a] The location of the Mercedes-Uno collision was a point of debate at the inquest – see Part 1, section on Point of Uno Impact in Chapter 4C. Witness and forensic evidence reveals that it occurred inside the Alma Tunnel.

an anti-personnel device.... It sets off one enormously powerful flash of light. Shine this in somebody's eyes and they are stunned, blinded, disabled for several minutes. If you're driving a car when it happens, you'll almost certainly crash.... It's used by army special forces – including the British – around the world.[1189]

If the police – French or British – had been serious about establishing the cause of the crash, they would have conducted their own flash testing with the three witnesses and compared the results.

That never occurred.

Why?

MI6 and Powerful Flashes

Does MI6 use portable equipment that could have been deployed in the Alma Tunnel on 31 August 1997 to produce the significant, bright flash that was described by witnesses?

As with everything to do with MI6, the evidence is conflicting:

- Tomlinson: "I remember [during training at an SBS briefing] ... a piece of equipment that could give a very bright flashing light ... that ... was used ,,, to disorient"[1190]

- Dearlove: "no there were not" to Mansfield's: "was there training which involved them seeing and watching the use of strobe lights?"[1191]

- Miss X: "no, they were not" to Burnett's: "were any strobe lights used or shown to you?"[1192]

- Mr A: "I had never heard of blinding strobe lights until ... this year"[1193] – in an undated document written sometime after the Paris crash

- Mr A: "absolutely not" to Burnett's: "you were not trained in the use of strobe lights or blinding lights?"[1194]

There are several points to note from Dearlove's cross-examination:

1) Mansfield's initial question on what occurred in MI6 training was: "Was there training which involved [trainees] seeing and watching the use of strobe lights for disorientating –".[1195a] Dearlove interrupts, not letting Mansfield finish. Mansfield's last word is "disorientating", but Dearlove doesn't give him a chance to say or ask who might be disorientated or the potential uses of the strobe lights.

2) Dearlove appears to be in two minds about the integrity of his evidence around strobe lights – "I can say, I think with confidence";[1196] "under oath, I think I am very confident";[1197] "I am judging from my knowledge";[1198] "I think ... in my view".[1199]

---

[a] There is a dash at the end of the question which indicates the witness interrupted before Mansfield had finished talking.

3)   When Mansfield asks if "any inquiries [have] been made in relation to" Tomlinson's recollection, Dearlove appears dismissive – "it was believed in the services that it is not part of SIS's training".[1200] In other words, the account was dismissed by Dearlove, or MI6, as "a Tomlinson construction"[1201] and apparently not investigated.

4)   Just as Mansfield starts his next question about that, he gets one word out – "believed", before Dearlove interrupts again, this time with an attack against Tomlinson – "Tomlinson made many, many allegations"; "a very clear intention, of causing mischief for the service" then, "the strobe light allegation is, in my view, spurious[a]".[1202b]

X was evasive at times.

Burnett asked X: "Had you undergone similar training [to Tomlinson] or been involved in training at about that time [of Tomlinson] or just before?" X didn't answer this – she said: "I have been involved in training,[c] yes." Burnett: "When were you involved in training?" X is again evasive: "Sort of intermittently over the years."[1203]

X states she was "involved" – see previous footnote – with "that initial training course".[d] Without finding out what "involved" means, Burnett then asks X: "In that capacity, did you attend the SBS briefing?"[1204]

What "capacity"?

The jury is hearing X's answers without being privy to what her role was at the SBS briefings.[e] For example, X may have had a role that wouldn't have brought her in contact with a strobe light, whether such lights were there or not.

So when Burnett finally asks: "Were any strobe lights used or shown to you?" X is not evasive: "No, they were not."[1205]

---

[a] Oxford lists two meanings for "spurious": 1. "not being what it seems to be; false"; 2. "(of reasoning) apparently but not actually correct".

[b] Mansfield then moved on to the next subject.

[c] When X says she was "involved in training" she appears to mean in a role other than as a trainee. For example, she could have been a helper in some way. When Burnett asked: "Did you work on that initial training course?" X replied: "I was involved with that, yes." 26 Feb 08: 71.4. X fails to explain what she means by "involved" and Burnett fails to ask her.

[d] There is also no explanation from Burnett or X as to what is meant by "that initial training course".

[e] When finally Burnett establishes X attended the SBS briefing at around the same time as Tomlinson, there appears to be a conflict on how often – at the inquest: "probably about three or four times" 26 Feb 08: 71.8; in her statement – (not shown to the jury and not seen by the author): "two occasions in the late 1980s" 26 Feb 08: 71.12.

What was X's role at the SBS briefings? Why did Burnett not even try to find out what her role was? Would X's role have brought her in contact with strobe lights had any been there?

Mr A stated[a]: "I had never heard of blinding strobe lights until ... this year[b,1206] – this is an interesting statement from an experienced MI6 officer, who was Head of the MI6 Balkan Target Team during the Yugoslav war.[1207] A gave the strongest denial[c] evidence from any of the MI6 witnesses – he is not just saying that blinding strobe lights weren't shown or heard about during training, but he is denying that he had ever heard of them in his life up to when he "saw some conspiracy theory television programme after the crash in Paris".[1208]

Tomlinson stated in his affidavit: "Dr Fishwick[d] suggested that one way to cause the crash might be to disorientate the chauffeur using a strobe flash gun...."[1209] (WFJ)

It may not be a coincidence that the MI6 officer who provides the strongest denial – complete ignorance of the existence of strobe lights – is the very one who is alleged to have put forward the proposal to use a strobe light in an assassination plot.

Tomlinson has never suggested that MI6 keeps stocks of strobe lights. His evidence is that SBS uses them, or something similar, in their work and he saw one during his training at an SBS display in Poole. By inference, the lights could be used on behalf of MI6 – see earlier evidence of MI6 using SBS and SAS to conduct field operations.[e]

The official SAS website includes a "Strobe Light Pouch MkIII[f]" in its list of equipment products.[1210ghi] This is independent supporting evidence for

---

[a] In a statement not seen by the jury or the author.
[b] Sometime after 1997.
[c] A emphasises this by using the term: "for the record".
[d] Mr A is named as Dr Simon Fishwick – the person who showed the Milosevic plot document to Tomlinson: see Tomlinson's affidavit in Part 5, Chapter 1A.
[e] This would fit with Tomlinson's 1999 affidavit: "a strobe flash gun ... is occasionally deployed by special forces". Special forces being SAS and SBS. Richard Tomlinson, 12 May 99 Affidavit to the French Investigation.
[f] "MkIII" could indicate there were earlier versions of this product – MkI and MkII.
[g] The SAS Equipment website was present on the internet during the research for Part 5 in 2012. Since the publication of Part 5 the website had been removed from the internet by May 2014.
[h] Product Code P19.
[i] There is also another listed product called "AW Modular Minimi Pouch" (Product No. 9000502) which includes "2 molle strips on top of pouch to attach smaller pouches such as micro accessory, strobe or multi tool".

Tomlinson's sworn affidavit account – see earlier – that "a strobe flash gun [is] a device which is occasionally deployed by special forces[a]".[b]

Tomlinson has provided a logical reason why the SBS had the "piece of equipment that could give a very bright flashing light" – it was: "this was used ... to disorient ... a helicopter pilot, on landing for example".

One could argue that since strobe lights exist, and apparently they have since 1931[1211], why wouldn't they be used by special forces and be known to intelligence agencies?

If the SAS and SBS do not use strobe lights in their line of work, then one could ask, why? Why wouldn't SAS and SBS include strobe lights as part of their useful equipment?

The attempts by MI6 to distance themselves from knowledge of or use of strobe lights would tend to arouse suspicion, rather than be seen as credible evidence.

Coroner's Deception

Scott Baker stated in his March 2008 "Ruling On Verdicts" document:

While various witnesses recall 'bright lights', the evidence is simply not sufficient for a jury to conclude that a light was flashed deliberately to disorientate Henri Paul.[1212] [c] (WFJ)

"Bright lights" or "bright light" have never been terms used by any witness in describing the powerful flash seen after the Mercedes entered the Alma Tunnel. Changing it into the plural "bright lights" is completely foreign to what has been described by the witnesses: a single powerful flash. This could cause confusion.

"Bright light(s)" is a term used by Scott Baker six times in his Summing Up to the jury[1213] – each time regarding evidence relating to the powerful flash.

The above conclusion is part of Baker's reasoning to eliminate murder as an available verdict. Exactly how much evidence of a flash would Baker require? Would he need an independent photo taken of the flash being flashed?

There are three independent witnesses who testified that they saw a flash. Two of these – Anderson and Levistre – provided enough detail to show that the flash they saw occurred at a time when a motorbike, with two riders on,

---

[a] SAS and SBS.

[b] If SAS and SBS have strobe lights in their equipment – and this evidence indicates they have – it is not logical to suggest they wouldn't be used on missions carried out on behalf of MI6.

[c] Baker used this document to remove murder as a possible verdict for the jury. This is addressed later in the book.

had cleared the front of the Mercedes.[a] When taken in conjunction with other witness evidence[b] this would have also been very close to the point where the Mercedes started to lose control.

Souad should have been asked further questions regarding the flash, but wasn't.

The circumstantial and witness evidence indicates that a deliberate flash was at the very least a possibility. Events happened extremely quickly in the tunnel – there are some witnesses who didn't see the flash, but there are also some witnesses who didn't see the Fiat Uno, but we know the Uno was there, from the forensic evidence.

It is common sense that the jury should have been allowed to decide whether the flash was deliberate or not. Yet this is not what happened – Scott Baker withdrew from the jury the ability to decide on this.

Powerful Flash

The evidence from Mrs N was that one of the SAS hit team flashed a high-powered light into the face of the Mercedes driver, Henri Paul.[1214]

Other evidence indicates that the SAS sometimes use strobe lights during operations.

Mrs N's account is also supported by the crash eye-witness accounts of François Levistre, Brian Anderson and Souad Moufakkir – all of whom were in a direct line with the Mercedes S280 at the time they saw the flash.

---

[a] The full witness evidence is in Part 1, chapter on Events in the Alma Tunnel.
[b] See next chapter.

53 Loss of Control

Three witnesses described the point where the Mercedes lost control – Benoît Boura, Gaëlle L'Hostis and François Levistre. All were inside the tunnel.

Brian Anderson commented that he believed the motorbikes "contributed to something happening that caused the [Mercedes] to lose control"[1215] – but he does not claim to have actually witnessed the loss of control. This would make sense in that in his evidence he stated that he was "looking to the right" when he saw the flash: "I caught the flash out of the extreme corner of my left eye. It hit me on the left of my face".[1216] (WFJ)

On the day following the crash Levistre stated:

> **I could distinctly see one motorbike cut across the front of the [Mercedes]. There was a large white flash.... I saw the [Mercedes] zigzagging.[1217] (WFJ)**

Levistre effectively states that he saw the Mercedes lose control straight after the flash, which he said came from the motorbike.[a] This is supported by what Anderson said, although of course Anderson did not directly witness it.

Neither Boura nor L'Hostis saw the flash. Boura said:

> **The Mercedes, which was driving very fast, struck the saloon and lost control.[1218] (WFJ)**

He added that the saloon in front "accelerated brutally" at the same moment.[1219] (WFJ)

Boura's girlfriend, Gaëlle L'Hostis, told the police 17 days after the crash:

> **The car in front of the Mercedes was small.... She described it as accelerating as the Mercedes lost control.[1220] (WFJ)**

What these three witnesses saw occurred within the tunnel. The angle of vision of Boura and L'Hostis – they were on the opposite carriageway – along with the positioning and size of the centre strip pillars, meant that anything they witnessed occurred inside the tunnel.[b]

---

[a] At the inquest Levistre called the flash "this major white flash of the motorbike in front of the Mercedes" 15 Oct 07: 92.19.

[b] It was the conclusion of the Paget Report that the point of the Mercedes losing control occurred well before the entrance to the Alma Tunnel, and therefore whatever occurred within the tunnel itself – collision with Uno, flash – was irrelevant, as it would not have changed the course of events. This, and the confusing expert accounts

Levistre saw the motorbike in front and the flash, but did not see the car in front. Boura and L'Hostis saw the car in front, but did not see the motorbike in front[a] or the flash. The flash occurred at around the same time as the collision between the Uno and the Mercedes witnessed by Boura.

The loss of control of the Mercedes did not occur until both the collision with the car in front and the powerful flash had taken place.

---

heard by the jury, is addressed in Part 1, section on Point of Loss of Control in Chapter 4B.

[a] Boura and L'Hostis witnessed a different motorbike which was behind the Mercedes – see Part 1, section on Unidentified Motorbikes in Chapter 4B.

54 Smoke in the Tunnel

After losing control at around 100 kph the Mercedes S280 swung left then right and back to the left before crashing into the 13th central pillar of the Alma Tunnel. It bounced back from the pillar, swung around 180 degrees and finally came to rest near the wall and facing the tunnel entrance.

The earliest witnesses saw lots of smoke.

Grigori Rassinier, a passing photographer, was descending eastbound into the Alma Tunnel when he heard an "extremely violent crash".[1221] He told the French investigation:

> **I saw grey smoke that was coming from the [Mercedes] and which fairly rapidly engulfed this part of the tunnel.[1222]**

Joanna Luz was one of the first two pedestrians to enter the tunnel after the crash:

> **Directly following the accident, as we entered the tunnel, we saw lots of smoke.[1223]**

Jean-Louis Bonin was heading westbound and said:

> **There was a lot of smoke and you could not see very much.[1224]**

There was enough smoke in the confined area of the Alma Tunnel to have affected some witnesses' views of post-crash events.

Figure 18

This photo, taken by Serge Arnal, was stated at the inquest to be the first paparazzi photo of the crash scene. It is obvious that the smoke level in it does not match the early witness descriptions (see above). This is further proof that the paparazzi were not present at the time of the crash – see earlier Were The Motorbikes Paparazzi? chapter.

55 Early Photographers

The earliest witnesses saw unidentified photographers taking pictures at the crash scene.

Noe da Silva

Noe da Silva, a trainee reporter with Radio France, entered the Alma Tunnel heading eastbound, immediately after the crash had occurred.

Da Silva was one of the most significant witnesses of post-crash events yet was not cross-examined at the inquest, was never interviewed by Operation Paget and was not mentioned at all in the Paget Report.

The French investigation recorded his graphic account on 23 September 1997. This is what he said:

> When I got to the Alma Tunnel ... I noticed before going down into the underpass that the cars in front of me were slowing down. Right from then, at the point where the road starts to slow down into the tunnel, I noticed bluish flashes which looked like sparks.... I was in the right-hand lane and there was no one in the left-hand lane. My lane slowed down. It did not stop.
>
> As I went down [into the tunnel] I could still see these blue flashes.... One of the first cars in my lane on the right, which was near the tunnel exit, started to reverse to stay in the tunnel.... Cars in the right-hand lane were stopping.... The horn of the Mercedes was stuck and it was hooting. When I drove past the crashed car, I wound down my window and immediately noticed smoke. I do not know where it was coming from.
>
> When I saw what had happened, I realised where the sparks were coming from. There were actually three or four people taking photos of the car with flashes. The photographers were in a circular arc behind the car on the right. None of the car doors was open on the side I could see. I also saw some motorbikes parked in front of and behind the crashed car... I cannot say how many there were. As well as the photographers, there was a man near one motorbike phoning on a mobile. I think this was an off-road motorbike, something like a 'Tenere'....

[A] man ... who seemed to have got out of [a] light-coloured car, parked at the tunnel exit, went up to the photographers and physically pushed them back. Then he looked towards the cars on my side and gestured to us to drive faster and get out of the tunnel. The man was fairly thick set.... He looked European, fair skinned....

I thought the accident had happened a long time before I got there because people were taking photographs of it.... I certainly did not realise what I was seeing a part of. As I drove forward to get out of the tunnel, I turned round and saw the windscreen of the Mercedes. It was only then that I saw blood, airbags and silhouettes in the car. I was very shocked because I could even see people very clearly through the windscreen. It gave me a shock. When I started to drive out of the tunnel, I saw that the driver of the car in front of me seemed to be phoning from his car. Then, further down outside, I saw people running to get into the tunnel. I was very shocked at seeing the casualties and, as I was driving along, I realised that the accident had only just happened. Then I said to myself that if people were taking photos, the injured must have been taken out and the people I saw were dead....

When I arrived outside the Louvre, I heard the France info news at 12.30. From that I assume it was about 12.20 or 12.25 when I was in the tunnel....

When I was going through the tunnel, I did not see anyone helping the people in the car at all.... I did not find out who the people in the car were until about 8.30 on the Sunday morning from my sister.... She told me that Princess Diana had been killed in a car accident that night on the Pont de l'Alma near the Eiffel Tower. I immediately realised the connection with what I had seen. The same day I wrote my statement down in order to be able to tell you what I remembered soon after the accident....

In answer to your question, I might be able to identify the man in the light-coloured car or the one who was making a phone call near a motorbike if I saw them again. I note that you are showing me a photograph album with photographs in it.[a] After looking at it, I can tell you that I recognise photographers who were speaking on the television after they had been questioned. They are numbers 21 to 22 [Romuald Rat] and 29 to 30 [Laslo Veres].... I do not recognise any of the people I described to you before.

In answer to a question:... I do not remember there being a hold-up at the tunnel exit going towards Concorde-Trocadero.[1225]

Noe Da Silva is one of the most important post-crash witnesses. He was a trainee journalist, and the next morning as soon as he realised it was Princess Diana in the crash, he wrote down his eye-witness account of what he saw.

---

[a] These are photos of the paparazzi.

Da Silva arrived very soon after the crash:

1) the eastbound traffic flow had slowed, but not yet stopped
2) the Mercedes doors were closed on the right hand side (Diana's side)
3) the horn was blowing[a]
4) there was smoke
5) Dr Mailliez had not arrived yet[b]
6) pedestrians are running to get into the tunnel
7) based on a news broadcast he timed his passage through the tunnel to 12.20 to 12.25[c]

Da Silva's statement reveals he is quite observant, so it is significant that when shown photos of the paparazzi by the French police, he did not recognise any of them as the photographers he saw in the tunnel. He states that he did recognise Rat and Veres from seeing them on TV. This is important because Rat was the first paparazzi photographer to arrive at the scene.

Da Silva saw motorbikes parked in front of and behind the Mercedes. There was only the one paparazzi motorbike that arrived early – that of Darmon and Rat. Darmon stopped to drop Rat off and then rode the bike another 10 to 15 metres past the Mercedes, before walking back.[1226] Da Silva saw "a few motorbikes which were stationary"[1227] and "three or four people taking photos ... in a circular arc".

He describes cars in his lane stopping once he was in the tunnel – he had a very slow trip through the tunnel, enabling him to observe what was happening.

It beggars belief that Da Silva was not called as a live witness for cross-examination in the inquest.

He was not able to identify any of the photographers he saw. He arrived just after the crash had occurred. He saw "some motorbikes parked in front of and behind the crashed car".

Only one of the paparazzi arrived on a motorbike – Romuald Rat driven by Stéphane Darmon.[d] Da Silva describes "some" and "a few" motorbikes – so at least three.

Who were the photographers – the "three or four people taking photos ... in a circular arc" – that he witnessed?

---

[a] Other witnesses described the horn blowing for a minute or so after the crash. It could be significant that whoever turned it off – or disconnected the battery – has never come forward.
[b] See later – Dr Mailliez was a passing emergency doctor who arrived quickly after the crash.
[c] The crash occurred at around 12.23 a.m.
[d] Benhamou was on an 80 cc scooter – see earlier Were The Motorbikes Paparazzi? chapter.

Other Witnesses

Amel Samer drove eastbound into the Alma Tunnel, after the crash. She didn't encounter traffic delays as she entered, but said once inside the traffic stopped for "less than one minute, just the time for me to give a call for the emergency services".[1228]

The Mercedes' doors are closed[1229] and no one is providing assistance to the passengers[1230] – Dr Mailliez has not yet arrived. This, along with the registering of her call to emergency services at 12.24 a.m.,[1231] places her as a very early post-crash witness. Samer stated that she didn't hear the sound of the crash, but she did have her radio on.[1232]

She said that she saw "about 11 or 12 people in the tunnel, on the other side.... Eight of them being in an arc around the car and three or four in front of it." She added that they "were taking pictures".[1233]

Samer was not able to identify any of the photographers or people she saw from the police paparazzi photo line-up, even though there is at least one that she thought she should have been able to recognise.[1234]

Samer and Da Silva were both travelling in the same direction, and it would seem at a similar time to each other. They appear to be describing the same scene – an arc of photographers around the as yet untouched Mercedes, constantly taking pictures.

Samer was never asked if she saw any motorbikes.

Benoît Boura confirmed that "before [he] got into the tunnel … [he saw] flashes up ahead".[1235]

Boura also confirmed that once in the tunnel he "covered about a third of the tunnel without seeing any other flashes and then [he] started to hear [the] sounds" that led to the crash.[1236]

He added:

> **"I got into the tunnel and saw the photographers" and only then realised the "flashes [were] from cameras used by photographers".[1237]**

This evidence infers that Boura was a witness to photographers at work after the crash.

He should have been cross-examined about the photographers he saw in the tunnel, but wasn't.

Brian Anderson stated that his taxi passed through the tunnel after the crash. He told CBS in June 1998:

> **I saw one motorcycle down on the ground and people running towards the car and flashing as we left out of the tunnel.[1238] (WFJ)**

Tom Richardson and Joanna Luz were American tourists walking near the Alma Tunnel entrance. After hearing the crash they were the first pedestrians to rush into the tunnel. Both were interviewed by CNN within hours of the events they witnessed.

Luz said:

> **There was a photographer on the scene within 5 seconds of the crash happening.... His equipment was very professional – his camera was a foot and a half tall. It definitely was not a tourist camera.** [1239] **(WFJ)**

Richardson told CNN that within seconds "the paparazzi [were] snapping off pictures." [1240] (WFJ)

Tom Richardson has never been interviewed by the French or British police, and was not called at the inquest. Joanna Luz (now Da Costa) was also never interviewed by the French police. She provided a statement to Operation Paget in August 2004,[1241] but there was no mention of her in the Paget Report. Luz also gave evidence at the inquest, but she was not asked about her comments to CNN, which were made live on the morning of the crash.

Two hours after the crash Olivier Partouche[a] told police:

> **The motorcyclist that I [had earlier seen] pursuing the Mercedes was taking photos of it in the tunnel: I could see the reflections of flashes from a camera.**[1242b] **(WFJ)**

He also said:

> **A few moments [after hearing the crash], I went down into the underpass and I saw that the ... photographers had already left.**[1243] **(WFJ)**

On hearing the crash Partouche rushed towards the tunnel – on the way he saw the reflections of camera flashes,[c] but by the time he actually got into the tunnel the flashes had stopped and the photographers had gone.

Partouche saw early post-crash camera flashes from the same photographer(s) he had seen taking photos as the Mercedes approached the Alma Tunnel.[d]

Early Photographers

The witness evidence – Da Silva, Boura, Anderson, Samer , Richardson, Luz, Partouche – indicates that there were unidentified photographers taking pictures immediately following the crash. Within a minute or so, these photographers appear to have vacated the tunnel and after that the earliest identifiable paparazzi – Rat, Darmon, Martinez and Arnal – have arrived.

---

[a] A pedestrian in the Place de la Reine Astrid, near the tunnel entrance.
[b] A few hours later Partouche clarified this: "I have seen flashes before the vehicles disappeared into the tunnel. Then, after the crash, I saw many flashes that came from it". 31 Aug 97, 6.55 a.m. Statement read out 24 Oct 07: 36.25.
[c] He said "many flashes" in his second statement – see previous footnote.
[d] See earlier Intended Exit to the Alma Tunnel chapter.

This scenario would fit in with the picture that has been pieced together of the journey from the Ritz Hotel – pursuing motorbikes that were taking photos, presumed by any witnesses to be paparazzi. We know that they weren't paparazzi because they remain unidentified, and the paparazzi only had one motorbike in pursuit – and it was not powerful enough to keep up with the Mercedes. These early motorcyclists may have stayed in the Alma Tunnel, taking photo after photo immediately after the crash – a minute (or even less) doing this would have been enough to strengthen the perception that paparazzi were responsible for the crash.

In his Summing Up to the jury, Scott Baker fails to include Partouche's references to seeing post-crash flashes coming from the tunnel. Noe Da Silva and Amel Samer did not rate any mention at all in the Summing Up. Boura was not cross-examined regarding the photographers he saw in the tunnel. The evidence of Tom Richardson was never mentioned in the inquest.

The entire subject of early post-crash camera flashes from unidentified photographers in the tunnel was left out of Baker's Summing Up.

Why?

56 Fleeing Motorbikes

Any vehicle that passed the crash scene without stopping was breaking French law and was at risk of prosecution. Eva Steiner, the inquest expert on French law testified: "This is very clear, you have to stop." She added that "under the ... Code Penal, there have [over the years] been a number of motorists who have been prosecuted because they did not stop".[1244a]

Nevertheless witnesses saw motorbikes and cars fleeing the scene immediately after the crash.

No one has ever been tracked down or prosecuted.

"It Took Off Like A Shot"

Grigori Rassinier "saw a motorbike emerge from the smoke. It swerved as if it were avoiding the crashed car.... Once it had swerved [it] continued on its way.... It did not stop and took off like a shot".[1245]

Séverine Banjout was a passenger in a westbound vehicle ahead of the Mercedes. As she was leaving the Alma Tunnel, she said she "heard the crash and almost simultaneously saw a motorcycle with one person aboard pass them at high speed." [1246] (WFJ)

Benoît Boura told the police: "I saw a motorcycle or a big Vespa ... pass the Mercedes.... The motorcycle slowed down, then accelerated and left."[1247] (WFJ)

Boura's girlfriend, Gaëlle L'Hostis, said the motorbike she saw "slowed down fast, maybe to try to see what was happening with the Mercedes, and then accelerated and left".[1248]

François Levistre stated that after he was "outside the tunnel ... [he] saw a motorbike coming out of the tunnel. It was a powerful machine, with two people on board." [1249]

The full witness descriptions of the motorbikes seen fleeing are in Part 1[b]. They reveal that witnesses were seeing different motorbikes – for example, some had just one rider while others saw a motorbike with two riders.

---

[a] Steiner was referring to instances outside of this case.
[b] Fleeing Vehicles section of Chapter 4D.

"You Have to be Careful with Witnesses"

At the inquest it was put to Paget officer Paul Carpenter that "witnesses [saw] bikes driving away immediately from the scene without stopping". Carpenter's reaction was:

You have to be a bit careful with the witnesses.[1250]

This comment is typical of the condescending attitude of Operation Paget and the inquest towards witnesses.

There were five witnesses – Rassinier, Banjout, Boura, L'Hostis and Levistre – that saw a fleeing motorbike. All of them were in the Alma Tunnel and gave their statements either on the day of the crash or the day following – yet Carpenter seeks to undermine the relevance of their evidence.

Why?

57 Fleeing Cars

Gary Hunter, a London solicitor, was positioned on the third floor of the Royal Alma Hotel at 35 Rue Jean Goujon, less than 100 yards from the Alma Tunnel. In October 1997 Hunter described to police what happened a minute or two after he heard the noise of the crash:

> I was ... alerted by ... tyres screeching at the bottom of the road from where the crash sound had originally emanated. I immediately returned to the window and looked left to see that a small dark vehicle had completed its turn into Rue Jean Goujon, immediately followed by a larger ... vehicle ... a white Mercedes. The Mercedes completed its turn immediately behind the smaller dark vehicle. The two vehicles then proceeded in tandem, along the Rue Jean Goujon, passing under my bedroom window towards the [roundabout] junction in the Rue Jean Goujon.... Both vehicles were travelling at inordinate speed. The white vehicle was almost touching the rear bumper of the smaller dark vehicle. I thought the white car was shielding the small black car from behind. At the junction with the roundabout, with wheels screeching, they turned right and out of my sight. Whilst all of this was happening, and from my position, the street lighting was good and it was a dry humid night, I noticed that the Mercedes was not manoeuvring or signalling to pass the smaller dark car. It was this that makes me believe that the Mercedes was shielding the rear of the small black car.[1251]

Following the crash Hunter tried to provide his testimony to the French police, but they refused to take it.[a]

On September 21 he told the *Sunday Times*:

> My own feeling is that these were people in a hurry not to be there. I am confident that car was getting off the scene. It was obvious that they were getting away from something and that they were in a hurry – it looked quite sinister.[1252] (WFJ)

---

[a] "Hunter did go [back to Paris] on 7 September [1997], but the French judicial authorities declined to take his deposition.... Some investigators laughingly dismissed Hunter's story by saying he couldn't even see the tunnel from his hotel window.": Thomas Sancton and Scott MacLeod, Death of a Princess: An Investigation, 1998, p227. See also Part 3, Gary Hunter section of Chapter 13.

And on NBC's *Dateline* in early October Hunter said: "My initial reaction was here are people in a hurry to get away from that particular spot.[1253] (WFJ)

Gary Hunter's statement to the police, despite his efforts, wasn't taken until nearly two months after the crash. The delays by the police were not addressed during the inquest.

The earliest accounts of Hunter's evidence are from the media statements, which reveal that his opinion was that the cars he saw were purposely fleeing the crash scene. The jury only got to hear the official police statement, which was not quite as clear on that particular aspect of his account.

Gary Hunter was not able to be cross-examined at the inquest, as he died in February 2004, aged 47. His wife, Teresa, who was interviewed by the British police in July 2004, should have been called to give evidence at the inquest. Although she slept through the events, Hunter related what he had seen to her after she woke up, on the morning of the crash.[1254] Baker went on to completely ignore Gary Hunter's evidence in his Summing Up for the jury – his name did not even rate a mention.

The dark car seen blocking the Mercedes before the tunnel entrance – Partouche, Gooroovadoo – could be the dark car that Hunter witnessed fleeing.

Souad Moufakkir confirmed that following the crash she saw "six or seven" cars that "drove around the Mercedes ... to avoid it".[1255]

The dark blocking car could have been one of those. Two of those six or seven vehicles could be the cars that Hunter saw heading up the Rue Jean Goujon.

Souad has never been asked to describe the vehicles she saw.

58   Fiat Uno Post-Crash

Souad Moufakkir stated that immediately after the crash she "looked for the Fiat [Uno] but it had disappeared".[1256]

Other witnesses testified that the Fiat Uno was never overtaken by the Mercedes S280.

Benoît Boura told the police:

> **This vehicle accelerated at the time that the Mercedes lost control. I then saw it drive off and when I arrived level with the Mercedes it was already a long way away. We did not see it again afterwards.**[1257] **(WFJ)**

Gaëlle L'Hostis said:

> **This [smaller] car, in my opinion, was never passed by the Mercedes.... I don't know what became of it.**[1258] **(WFJ)**

Souad said that she witnessed the cars that overtook the already crashed Mercedes[a] and was actually looking for the Uno[b] – it appears to have left the scene while Souad's attention was focused on what was happening to the Mercedes.

The balance of the witness evidence indicates that the Fiat Uno accelerated ahead of the Mercedes, probably passing the cars immediately in front –Souad and Levistre[c] – as the Mercedes crashed.

The next people to see the white Fiat Uno were outside the Alma Tunnel.

"It was Zigzagging and Backfiring"

Around the time of the crash Georges and Sabine Dauzonne travelled in their Rolls Royce across the Pont d'Alma[d] and through the Place de l'Alma. They turned left onto the slip-road which took them onto the expressway westbound, just after the Alma Tunnel.

---

[a] See previous chapter.
[b] She said: "I looked for the Fiat [Uno] but it had disappeared.": Alexander Hitchen, I Saw Fiat Driver Kill Di, The People, 18 January 2004.
[c] Levistre has consistently testified that he never saw a white Fiat Uno.
[d] Alma Bridge that crosses the Seine River.

Georges stated in 1998:

> My attention was caught by a vehicle travelling level with us, coming out of the tunnel, which was zigzagging and backfiring – [like] the exhaust pipe was cracked or in bad condition. The driver didn't see us at all – he was so busy watching what was going on in his inside rear-view mirror and his left hand wing mirror, especially the rear-view. He wasn't paying attention whatsoever to what was happening in front of him. The vehicle almost smashed into us as we were reaching the end of the slip road, at the exit of the tunnel.... The driver carried on zigzagging and if I hadn't braked, he'd have rammed us, because ... he was only watching what was going on behind him. I let him go ahead and then I passed him.... He'd stopped by the pavement security railings on the corner of the next street, as if, when he looked up, he hadn't known where he was and had pulled over, lost.... I'd thought that either he must be drunk – or that, from the way he was looking in his rear-view mirror, perhaps he was expecting someone to be following him. He was very jumpy.[1259] (WFJ)

Sabine told the French police in September 1997:

> My husband tried to overtake him but the man swerved to the left again, as if he was sort of trying to stop us getting past and he nearly hit us again.... The man got in the right-hand lane, as if he was going to stop. But I don't know what he actually did, because I didn't turn round.... The man ... was leaning so far to look behind him that I thought he must be waiting for someone a long way behind in the Alma Tunnel. I saw the car stop by the last restaurant there, about thirty metres from the tunnel exit.[1260] (WFJ)

During his Summing Up Scott Baker told his jury that Georges said "the Fiat driver seemed to be bothered by something in his rear-vision mirror and you may think that he was aware that he had been in a collision and was weighing up whether to stop".[1261]

Baker only gives the jury the one alternative.

The Uno driver may have been waiting for someone to come out of the tunnel – both Dauzonnes suggested that possibility.

From earlier evidence – Souad, Boura, L'Hostis – it appears that the Uno left the tunnel very quickly, but the Dauzonnes witness the Uno after it has emerged from the tunnel, and at that stage it was moving slower and zigzagging.

59   Crash Scenario

The eye-witness evidence speaks for itself.

The Evidence

Fourteen separate witnesses saw unidentified motorbikes closely pursuing or surrounding the Mercedes, along the route. Multiple witnesses saw camera flashes from photographers at the Place de la Concorde, then just prior to the Mercedes entering the Alma Tunnel and also immediately following the crash. These photographers have been proven to be unidentified and no photographs of the final journey after leaving the Ritz have ever been published.

Vehicles impeding the progress of the Mercedes were witnessed at the Place de la Concorde, at the intended exit on the expressway, just before entering the Alma Tunnel and inside the tunnel itself.

Two witnesses, one in front of and one behind the Mercedes, saw a motorbike with two people aboard overtake the Mercedes – which was in the left lane – on the left. Both saw a powerful flash after that dangerous manoeuvre. Others saw the Mercedes lose control at around that time, inside the Alma Tunnel.

The witness and forensic evidence regarding the white Fiat Uno is clear: it collided with the Mercedes after straddling the two lanes, inside the tunnel. A white Fiat Uno was also seen acting in an unusual fashion, both before and after the crash.

Possibly the most telling evidence of all is that the only identified vehicle in all these events is the crashed Mercedes S280. All other vehicles fled the scene, and in over seventeen years no driver or rider has ever come forward.

Why have the French and British police, after years of investigations, never been able to identify one motorbike or car seen by the many witnesses?

Crash Scenario

The following scenario is based on the eye witness testimony and the forensic evidence found in the tunnel and on the Mercedes:

As the Mercedes approaches the Alma Tunnel in the right hand lane, Henri Paul quickly comes up behind a dark Ford Mondeo. A large motorbike with two riders is now moving up on Henri's left side. Even though he is travelling at around 100 kph, Henri downshifts the automatic transmission in order to accelerate away from the motorbike at the same time as rapidly changing lanes to pass the Mondeo.

Henri successfully manoeuvres the Mercedes around the dark car but the motorbike simultaneously accelerates trying to overtake him on his left, even though Henri is now in the left lane. At the same time, as they enter the tunnel, Henri encounters a slow moving white Fiat Uno straddling both lanes. The motorbike on his left is pushing him towards the Fiat Uno. Henri brakes heavily but can't avoid a minor collision with the Uno. The Mercedes connects with the Uno, then scrapes along its side, while the motorbike accelerates to the front, successfully overtaking the Mercedes on the left. The motorbike cuts in front of the Mercedes, then there is a powerful single flash of white light from the rear of the motorbike, using an anti-personnel device in the dimly-lit tunnel – this is aimed at Henri Paul. The flash is something Henri has never encountered before and is completely unprepared for. Shining directly into his eyes, it stuns, completely blinds and disables him. Being totally disoriented and suddenly unable to see anything, Henri loses direction and control of the Mercedes. He attempts to maintain control but the Mercedes skids out of control, swinging left and right, then left again, crashing into the 13th pillar of the Alma Tunnel at around 100 kph.

On the huge impact the Mercedes rebounds off the pillar, spinning 180 degrees anti-clockwise, and comes to rest facing the tunnel entrance, diagonally close to the wall. The white Fiat Uno, which accelerated after the contact with the Mercedes, manages to stay ahead of it, and exits the tunnel. The motorbike keeps moving, hesitates to survey the scene as it passes and then accelerates quickly out of the tunnel. The dark Mondeo followed by a white Mercedes, which has now entered the tunnel, pass the crash scene very slowly, assessing the damage and confirming that there are no movements inside the black Mercedes. They then both exit the tunnel quickly, together turning right onto Rue Debrousse, then right onto Avenue du President Wilson, across the Place de l'Alma, then both accelerating to speeds in excess of 100 kph along the Rue Jean Goujon.

Timeline of Events: 31 August 1997[a] from 12.23 a.m.

Aug 31 – Time Since Crash
a.m.

12.23	Mercedes S280 crashes into the 13th pillar of the Alma Tunnel
12.24 – 1 min	Paparazzi start arriving
12.25 – 2 min	Passing emergency doctor arrives – Dr Mailliez
12.26 – 3 min	Dr Mailliez returns to his car
	Passing police patrol car arrives – Dorzée & Gagliardone
12.27 – 4 min	Dorzée assists Diana
12.28 – 5 min	Mailliez returns to the Mercedes to treat Diana
12.32 – 9 min	Two Fire Service ambulances arrive – Gourmelon & Boyer
	Dr Mailliez hands over to them and quickly leaves the tunnel
12.40 – 17 min	SAMU ambulance arrives – Dr Martino
	Prefect of Police, Philippe Massoni, is notified of the crash
	Police arrest 7 paparazzi in the tunnel
	1st SAMU report to base – Dr Martino
12.42 – 19 min	Dr Derossi leaves the base and heads to the crash scene
	Auxiliary wakes Dr Lejay who takes over SAMU control
12.43 – 20 min	Dr Fuilla of Fire Service arrives
	2nd SAMU report to base – Dr Martino
12.50 – 27 min	Medical dispatcher arrives – Dr Derossi
	Prefect of Police Philippe Massoni arrives at the crash scene
12.53 – 30 min	French accident investigators arrive
	Patrick Riou, Head of Judicial Police, sighted in the tunnel
	Maud Coujard, Deputy Public Prosecutor, sighted in the tunnel
12.55 – 32 min	Massoni notifies British ambassador Michael Jay about the crash
1.00 – 37 min	Diana is removed from the Mercedes
1.01 – 38 min	Diana becomes "pulseless" for a few seconds
1.02 – 39 min	Diana is anaesthetised, intubated and ventilated

---

[a] Some timings are approximate – based on the available evidence.

1.06 – 43 min   Diana is transferred into the ambulance
1.10 – 47 min   Duty officer at Elysée Palace notifies George Younes at the
                 British Embassy about the crash
                 Consul-General Keith Moss is notified about the crash
1.20 – 57 min   3rd SAMU report to base – Dr Derossi
1.25 – 1 h 2 m   SAMU base notification to the hospital
1.29 – 1 h 6 m   SAMU base call to the ambulance
1.30[a] – 1 h 7 m Prime Minister Tony Blair is notified about the crash
1.41 – 1 h 18 m Diana's SAMU ambulance leaves the Alma Tunnel
2.00 – 1 h 37 m Ambulance stops for 5 minutes near hospital
                 Photographer Lionel Cherrualt in London receives call
                 from Sipa notifying him of the crash
2.06 – 1 h 43 m Diana arrives at La Pitié Salpêtrière Hospital
2.10 – 1 h 47 m Cardio-Thoracic surgeon is telephoned at home
2.12 – 1 h 49 m Diana's heart stops beating: effective time of death
2.15 – 1 h 52 m Keith Moss arrives at La Pitié Hospital and is met by
                 Massoni and Chevènement
                 Cherrualt receives a call from Mark Saunders in Florida
                 offering him pictures of the crash
2.20 – 1 h 57 m Moss sets up a British Government incident room
2.22 – 1 h 59 m Cardio-Thoracic surgeon arrives at hospital
2.30 – 2 h 7 m   Michael and Sylvia Jay arrive at the hospital with Tim
                 Livesey
3.40 – 3 h 17 m Henri Paul's body received at the IML
4.00 – 3 h 37 m Resuscitation efforts cease: official time of Diana's death
4.10 – 3 h 47 m Death of Diana, Princess of Wales is officially announced
4.20 – 3 h 57 m Completion of death certificate for Princess Diana by
                 Bruno Riou
4.30 – 4 h 7 m   Faxing of "JM/12" death certificate from Riou to Coujard
                 Phone call from Malcolm Ross to the president of
                 Kenyons requesting French assistance with same-day
                 repatriation and ordering an embalming of Diana's body
                 by a female practitioner
4.35 – 4 h 12 m Discussion between Bestard and Coujard regarding
                 carrying out body examinations on the Mercedes'
                 passengers
4.45 – 4 h 22 m Formal request from Maud Coujard to Dominique
                 Lecomte to conduct body examinations of Princess Diana
                 and Dodi Fayed

---

[a] 12.30 a.m. in the UK.

HOW THEY MURDERED PRINCESS DIANA

4.55 – 4 h 32 m Mercedes S280 removed from the crash scene

5.00 – 4 h 37 m 1st cleaning of crash scene

President of Kenyons in London phones the PFG president, Racine, in France – passes on instructions from Ross

Conference call between Robert Fellowes, Alastair Campbell and Angus Lapsley[1262a]

5.20 – 4 h 57 m Meeting between Lecomte, Riou & Pavie at La Pitié Hospital

5.25 – 5 h 2 m Alma Tunnel reopened to traffic

5.30 – 5 h 7 m Dominique Lecomte conducts autopsy on Princess Diana's body at La Pitié Hospital

Racine phones Chapillon to pass on instructions from Kenyons

5.48 – 5 h 25 m Andanson exits the motorway at La Folie-B/Paris heading for Orly airport

5.55 – 5 h 32 m Press conference at the hospital, held by Jay, Chevènement and Riou

6.09 – 5 h 46 m Buckingham Palace announces the Queen and Charles are "deeply shocked and distressed by this terrible news"

6.20 – 5 h 57 m Diana's French autopsy concludes

6.21 – 5 h 58 m Tony Blair announcement: "I am utterly devastated. The whole of our country, all of us, will be in a state of shock and mourning"

6.23 – 6 h 0 m James Andanson purchases a plane ticket to Corsica at Orly airport

6.30 – 6 h 7 m Lecomte travels from the hospital to the IML

Chapillon of PFG phones Launay telling him to stand by

6.45 – 6 h 22 m Dominique Lecomte conducts autopsy on Dodi Fayed's body at IML

7.00 – 6 h 37 m Diana is moved to a room with no air conditioning

Chapillon phones Plumet, passing on instructions from Racine

Malcolm Ross in Scotland phones Anthony Mather advising that he needs to organise Diana to be repatriated that day

7.06 – 6 h 43 m Sunrise in Paris

7.15 – 6 h 52 m Dodi's French autopsy concludes

7.20 – 6 h 57 m Tassell of Levertons is notified by Mather of a death in Paris

---

[a] Fellowes – Queen's Private Secretary; Campbell – Tony Blair's Press Secretary; Lapsley – Private Secretary, Home Affairs in the Blair Government.

	Andanson flies out of Orly airport headed for Corsica
7.30 – 7 h 7 m	Tassell phones Keith Leverton, telling him to phone Mather at home
	Tebbutt and Burrell fly out of London heading to Paris
	Kingsmill flies out of London heading to Paris, intending to carry out advance organisation ahead of the Charles trip
	Jay leaves the hospital heading to the embassy
7.40 – 7 h 17 m	Keith Leverton phones Mather who tells him Diana has died in Paris. Mather instructs Levertons to instigate Operation Overstudy and repatriate Diana that day
7.45 – 7 h 22 m	Plumet of PFG phones Monceau of BJL – requests embalming of Diana
	Keith phones Clive Leverton to advise him of the death of Diana
7.55 – 7 h 32 m	Keith phones embalmer Green
	Clive phones embalmer Fry
8.00 – 7 h 37 m	Westbound lanes of Alma Tunnel closed for second time
	2nd cleaning of crash scene
	Pourceau arrives at Alma Tunnel to remeasure a tyre mark
8.15 – 7 h 52 m	Monceau phones Hauffman instructing her to call a female embalmer – complying with the original request from Ross
	Meeting between Bestard and Coujard
	Coujard receives Lecomte's body examination reports for Diana and Dodi
8.20 – 7 h 57 m	Moss phones Donnelly with request for ice for Diana's body
	Henri Paul autopsy commences
8.30 – 8 h 7 m	Coujard issues burial certificates for Diana and Dodi
8.45 – 8 h 22 m	Mme Chirac views Diana's body with the Jays
9.00 – 8 h 37 m	Donnelly phones Caltiau of PFG requesting ice for Diana's body
	Hauffman calls Amarger to tell her she will be needed to carry out the embalming
	Monceau leaves his house heading to the hospital
	Launay phones his assistant, Dupont
	Chapillon phones Jauze to ask him to be ready to handle Dodi's repatriation
	Royal coroner, John Burton, calls Buckingham Palace and is told that Diana is being repatriated that day via RAF

Northolt and it is likely she will be buried at Windsor Castle

9.20 – 8 h 57 m A police Commissaire phones Plumet "a number of times"

Lionel Jospin, PM, views Diana's body with Michael Jay

9.30 – 9 h 7 m   Mather arrives at Buckingham Palace

9.35 – 9 h 12 m Monceau arrives at the hospital

9.45 – 9 h 22 m Hauffman calls Amarger to give specific instructions to attend the hospital

Moss phones Plumet to officially engage PFG for the repatriation

10.00 – 9h 37m Westbound lanes of Alma Tunnel reopened for second time

Pourceau leaves tunnel area

Monceau enters Diana's room for the first time

Henri Paul autopsy concludes

10.05 – 9h42 m   Jauze arrives at work at PFG

10.15 – 9h 52m   Plumet calls Launay to confirm PFG are handling the case

10.30 – 10h 7m   Amarger leaves for the hospital

First post-death phone call between Tony Blair and the Queen

10.45 - 10h22m   Amarger arrives at the hospital

11.00 - 10h37m   Plumet calls Jauze and tells him to go to the Ritz Hotel

Clive Leverton meets with Keith and Tassell – they learn from Mather that they have to leave the UK at 2 p.m.[a]

Royal Standard from Lord Chamberlain arrives at Levertons

Levertons are told that the plane with Diana's body will arrive at RAF Northolt at 7 p.m. (8 p.m. French time)

Amarger enters Diana's room for the first time

Tony Blair's tribute to Diana – the "People's Princess"

11.15 - 10h52m   Charrier arrives at the hospital

11.30 - 11h7m   Tebbutt and Burrell arrive at the hospital

Plumet calls Launay to inform him a coffin will be arriving at Villacoublay and Charles will be coming on another plane, which will be met at Villacoublay by Jay, and they will come to the hospital

Robert Thompson arrives at Fulham Mortuary and finds "several men in dark suits" who appear to be "police officers from Royalty Protection"

11.45 - 11h22m   Launay calls Dupont to tell him to work on the Dodi body repatriation

---

[a] French time.

Tebbutt finds the room "getting hotter" and he is told
Diana is "melting"

p.m.

12.00 - 11h37m Blankets are put up in Diana's room to shut out the media
Air conditioners are put into Diana's room

12.15 - 11h52m Monceau talks with Moss

12.25 - 12h2m Charles' bodyguard, Peter Von-Heinz, and an advance
officer enter Diana's room and put black sticky tape over
the blinds

12.30 - 12h7m Commencement of Paris embalming
Royal family arrives at Crathie church for service that fails
to mention Princess Diana

1.15 - 12h52m Launay leaves his house heading to the airport

1.30 - 13h7m Conclusion of Paris embalming

1.45 - 13h22m Kingsmill arrives at the hospital

2.00 - 13h37m Launay arrives at Villacoublay Airport
Dr Bernard Kouchner[a] views Diana's body
Meeting at the hospital to organise security and media for
Charles' visit

2.05 - 13h42m Clive Leverton, David Green and Bill Fry leave from RAF
Northolt

3.15 - 14h52m Call from Jeffrey Rees in Rutland to John Burton advising
of "problems in France in releasing bodies"

3.22 - 14h59m Charles leaves Aberdeen on the royal flight

3.30 - 15h 7m Plumet and Jauze arrive at the IML
Stoneham receives a call from Rees notifying him of the
Scotland Yard pre-post-mortem meeting
Michael Burgess phone call to John Macnamara advising
of delay in repatriation of Dodi's body

3.40 - 15h17m Patrick Launay, Clive Leverton, David Green and Bill Fry
arrive at the hospital

4.00 - 15h37m Macnamara phone call to Frank Klein regarding delayed
repatriation

4.05 - 15h42m Repatriation of Dodi's body held up by Lecomte

4.15 - 15h52m Coffin porters arrive at the hospital
Macnamara phone call to Burgess advising of delay

4.29 - 16h 6m Burgess phone call to Surrey Police advising of delay

4.35 - 16h12m Dodi's body released from IML – witnessed by Jauze and
Plumet

---

[a] French Minister of Health.

HOW THEY MURDERED PRINCESS DIANA

4.40 - 16h17m Jauze and Plumet leave IML
Burgess arrives at Fulham Mortuary

4.44 - 16h21m Burgess phone call to Surrey Police advising of body release

4.50 - 16h27m Jauze and Plumet arrive at the hospital

5.00 - 16h37m Charles, Sarah and Jane's royal flight arrives at Villacoublay airport

5.15 - 16h52m Pre-post-mortem meeting held at New Scotland Yard – attended by Jeffrey Rees, Philip Stoneham, Richard Wall and Dennis Sharp

5.30 - 17h7m Keith Leverton leaves for RAF Northolt

5.40 - 17h17m Charles, Sarah and Jane arrive at the hospital
Klein & Roulet visit Patrick Riou

6.00 - 17h37m Maud Coujard oversees raid of Sygma agency – 23 crash-related photos are confiscated

6.15 - 17h52m Diana's body leaves the hospital

6.25 - 18h2m Dodi's body arrives at Fulham Mortuary

7.00 - 18h37m Diana's body arrives at Villacoublay

UK time[a]

6.00 - 18h37m Commencement of Dodi's London post-mortem

6.30 - 19h7m Remembrance service at St Paul's Cathedral

7.00 - 19h37m Diana's body arrives at RAF Northolt
Maud Coujard oversees raid of Sipa agency – 12 crash-related photos are confiscated

7.13 - 19h50m Charles reboards plane for return trip to Balmoral

7.15 - 19h52m Conclusion of Dodi's London post-mortem

7.25 - 20h2m Dodi's coffin leaves Fulham Mortuary

7.35 - 20h12m Diana's body arrives at Fulham Mortuary accompanied by Sarah and Jane

7.55 - 20h32m Chain and 4 photographs removed from Diana's body

8.05 - 20h42m Chain and 4 photographs given to Michael Walker

8.15 - 20h52m Burgess and Keith Brown leave Fulham Mortuary heading home

8.21 - 20h58m Commencement of Diana's UK post-mortem

8.30 - 21h7m Departure from Fulham Mortuary of Sarah and Jane with Paul Mellor

10.00 - 22h37m Burial of Dodi Fayed

11.20 - 23h57m Conclusion of Diana's post-mortem

11.40 - 24h17m Diana's body moved to St James' Palace

---

[a] From this point all times are UK – all previous times were Paris.

Sep 1
a.m.

12.30 - 25h7m DS Richard Wall places head hair samples from Diana and Dodi into a locked safe at New Scotland Yard

1.00 - 25h37m Thompson leaves the Fulham Mortuary

4.00 - 28h37m Conclusion of UK embalming of Diana

4.15 - 28h52m Sipa-connected royalty photographer Lionel Cherrualt's home is burgled – computer equipment containing photos is stolen

9.50 - 33h27m Wall deposits the head hair samples into a sealed bag in the OCG store at New Scotland Yard

60   Diana's Condition

As the Mercedes S280 came to rest the two occupants on the driver's side – Henri Paul and Dodi Fayed – were already deceased. The two on the passenger's side – Trevor Rees-Jones and Princess Diana – had survived.

Several witnesses described Diana's condition during the first minutes after the crash – before any ambulances arrived.

The earliest paparazzi arrived around a minute or so.

Romuald Rat said that after arriving he checked on Diana and shouted out "she's alive".[1263] Christian Martinez said: "I could see that she was alive. She was moving, her eyes".[1264] David Odekerken told the police: "I could see that Diana was only injured, because she was moving."[1265]

Police officers Lino Gagliardone and Sébastien Dorzée were in their patrol car in the area and were beckoned by passers-by to the crash scene. They arrived around 3 minutes after the crash.

Dorzée stated:

> **She moved, her eyes were open, speaking to me in a foreign language. I think that she said 'My God'.**[1266]

He also said that Diana "appeared ... to be in the best shape of all of them [in the car]".[1267]

All up there are seven witnesses[a] – outside of Dr Mailliez[b] – who have described Diana's early condition.[c]

During the first few post-crash minutes Diana was conscious, moving and talking.

None of these early witnesses to Diana's post-crash condition – Rat, Martinez, Odekerken, Redjil[d], Gooroovadoo, Gagliardone, Dorzée – were cross-examined at Baker's "thorough" inquest. Neither were any of them

---

[a] Listed below.

[b] See next chapter.

[c] Their evidence is covered more fully in Part 2, section on Diana's Condition: 12.23 to 12.32 a.m. in Chapter 9A.

[d] Abdelatif Redjil, a pedestrian in the Place de la Reine Astrid at the time of the crash.

interviewed during the earlier "extensive" British Paget investigation.[a] Gagliardone and Dorzée, the first two police officers on the scene, should have appeared at the inquest, but didn't.

Cardio-thoracic expert, Tom Treasure, explained to the inquest the nature of what may have occurred internally to Diana during the moments after crash impact. Using a diagram not available on the inquest website, he showed how after the initial trauma and injuries, the body can find a "new balance" where loss of blood is "contained".[1268]

She Was Talking

In 1998 Trevor Rees-Jones told the French judge:

I remember having heard somebody moaning and the name 'Dodi' was uttered…. I conclude that it was Princess Diana as it was a female voice.[1269]

Abdelatif Redjil and Belkacem Bouzid were both pedestrians in the Place de la Reine Astrid at the time of the crash. They attended the scene quickly. Redjil said:

She repeated words like 'My God, my God'.[1270]

Bouzid testified:

She was moaning and said a few words in English, 'my God, my God'.[1271]

Damien Dalby was a volunteer fireman travelling eastbound a few minutes after the crash.[b] He stopped the car and rushed over to provide assistance. He testified:

She was saying, 'Oh my God, oh my God'.[1272]

The police officer Sébastien Dorzée stated:

I think that she said 'My God' on seeing her boyfriend dying.[1273]

There is a consistent recollection that Diana was repeating the words "My God" during the initial minutes after the crash – she was evidently taking in the enormity of what had occurred.

---

[a] Dr Mailliez arrived within about 2 minutes – he was cross-examined and his evidence is covered in the next chapter. He also was not interviewed by Operation Paget.
[b] Dalby arrived between Dr Mailliez and the police: 25 Oct 07: 76.4 and evidence from his passenger, Sébastien Pennequin: 25 Oct 07: 62.23.

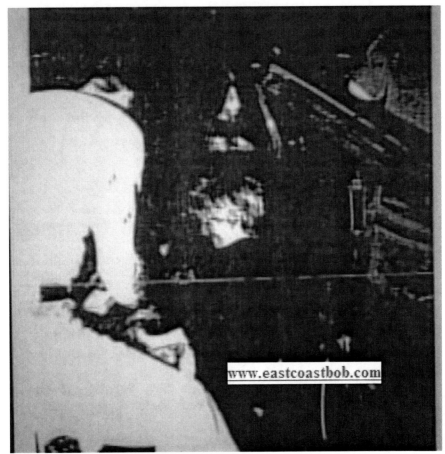

Figure 19

Photo that shows Diana conscious and grimacing in the back of the Mercedes just after the crash. Dr Mailliez is on the left.

61   The Passing Doctor

Dr Frédéric Mailliez, a passing emergency doctor travelling eastbound, arrived around two minutes after the crash had occurred. He was carrying a passenger, Mark Butt.

Butt said that after stopping the car Mailliez "told me to stay in the car, to put on the blue beacon light and to stay with the car and he was going to go see what was going on".[1274]

Changing His Evidence

Dr Frédéric Mailliez's various accounts are laced with conflicts and inconsistencies.

One Piece of Equipment

Mailliez was driving an official SOS Médécins emergency medical car, yet did not have the normal medical equipment with him.

On the day following the crash he told France 2 TV that he had "some of [his] equipment" with him[1275] (WFJ) but he testified at the inquest that a "respiratory bag ... was the only equipment I had ... that night".[1276]

In a 1998 interview Mailliez stated:

> **There is nothing worse ... it's so stupid ... to find yourself there when you know exactly what you could do further, if you had the right equipment.[1277] (WFJ)**

By the time of the inquest this had changed to:

> **I was not on duty that night and, for a question of security, I never carried – I never had this kind of [doctor's] bag because that cost a lot of money.[1278]**

So a year after the crash it is a "stupid" mistake, but at the inquest it was intentional – "a question of security".

Which is it? Or is it neither of these?

In his Summing Up coroner Baker said: "Obviously, being off-duty, [Mailliez] did not carry full equipment".[1279]

It wasn't just a question of not having the "full equipment" – the reality is that Mailliez had only one item, a respiratory bag. As he said in 1998: "I didn't even have a blood pressure cuff. No, not even my blood pressure cuff".[1280a]

Diana's Condition

When it comes to the early medical assessments of Diana's condition in the Mercedes, there are two separate issues: 1) Her visible external condition, and 2) Her actual internal condition.

It is Diana's visible condition that Mailliez primarily assessed. However he has also alluded to her internal condition. At the inquest he stated: "I was just suspecting a brain damage or ... chest damage".[1281]

Six weeks after the crash Mailliez had told *Newsweek*: "Her heart had been ripped out of its place in her chest."[1282] (WFJ)

That is a grossly false assessment.[b]

Mailliez's ability to determine Diana's internal condition must have been limited without basic equipment like a blood pressure cuff.

Regarding Diana's external condition: Dr Mailliez described her as "unconscious and weak" at the inquest[1283] and as "unconscious" in his original statement taken on the day of the crash.[1284] (WFJ) The Oxford dictionary's definition of unconscious is "not awake and [not] aware of and [not] responding to one's surroundings".

This perception conflicts with the evidence of the other witnesses who saw Diana during the same time period.[c] Police lieutenant Dorzée, who, apart from Mailliez, had the closest early contact with Diana, described a person who was awake, aware and responding to her surroundings: in other words, conscious, not unconscious.

Mailliez has painted a picture – from his earliest statement right through to the inquest – of Diana being in a worse visible external condition than she actually was.

This conflict becomes clearer with the evidence of the fire service medical witnesses that attended the crash following Mailliez.[d]

Why did Dr Mailliez paint this more negative external picture?

Her Words

Dr Mailliez has made the following comments to the media – none of these were heard by the jury.

-    To *Impact Quotidien*[a] in September 1997: When he spoke to her he "obtained no response".[1285] (WFJ)

---

[a] Also confirmed at the inquest: 13 Nov 07: 23.7.

[b] See later.

[c] See previous chapter.

[d] See next chapter.

- On *Larry King Live*, 23 September 1997: Question: "Did she say anything to you?" Mailliez: "No".[1286] (WFJ)
- To *Reuters* 12 October 1997: "When you're in that kind of pain, you don't think about giving testaments to the next generation – the only thing you think of expressing is the pain." [1287] (WFJ)
- In *Newsweek* 20 October 1997: "Mailliez would not tell *Newsweek* what Diana said: 'I must respect the privacy of the patient.'" [1288] (WFJ)
- To *The Times* 22 November 1997: "She kept saying how much she hurt as I put a resuscitation mask over her mouth" She said "I'm in such pain" and "Oh God, I can't stand this".[1289b] (WFJ)
- To CNN TV: "She was semiconscious, muttering, but never said anything precise."[1290] (WFJ)
- To an August 2006 documentary *Who Killed Diana?*:[c] "When I arrived she was not conscious.... She couldn't speak words." [1291] (WFJ)

Dr Mailliez told the inquest: "I do not remember any words."[1292]

Michael Mansfield suggested that Mailliez might have been "concentrating on [Diana's] physical condition" and missed the fact that she was communicating.[1293] This scenario is illogical for an emergency doctor, because one of the central ways they have to determine the patient's condition is by their verbal responses.[d]

There is a clear conflict between what Mailliez recollects when compared to other witnesses.

5 out of 6 witnesses from the first 7 minutes – Rees-Jones, Redjil, Bouzid, Dalby, Dorzée – recollected Diana talking.[e] The remaining witness who commented on this subject was Gooroovadoo and he stated that Diana "tried to speak" but "nothing came out".[1294]

Mailliez's evidence is that Diana did not speak a word. However in an interview to *The Times* on 22 November 1997 he contradicted this position by stating that Diana did speak – he then retracted this the following day in an interview with the *Associated Press*, alleging that he had been misquoted. Mailliez said: "I never said she was crying in pain – that she spoke to me of her pain. She was semi-conscious, muttering, but never anything precise."[1295]

---

[a] A French medical magazine.

[b] In an interview the following day Mailliez retracted this statement, saying he had been misquoted. This is discussed below.

[c] Shown on Sky One TV.

[d] The international standard Glasgow Coma scale, used by emergency teams, evaluates a patient's condition on a score of 15 points – 5 of these are an assessment of "verbal response". When the SAMU ambulance arrived at 12.40 a.m., Diana had a rating of 14 – see later.

[e] See previous chapter.

Meanwhile, *The Times* journalist, Bill Frost, stood by his original 22 November 1997 story. [1296]

Mailliez's interview published in *Newsweek* on 20 October 1997 also conflicts with his other statements. By refusing to relate what Diana said in the interest of patient privacy, he automatically indicated that Diana did actually have something to say.

Mailliez's evidence that Diana wasn't speaking at all also conflicts with the statements of later medical witnesses.

Why has Mailliez maintained the line that Diana didn't speak?

This gets right to the centre of the issues regarding Diana's condition after the crash. If she was coherently putting words together, this would show that she was conscious. Mailliez has consistently maintained that Diana was unconscious and it is obvious that his statements suggesting she wasn't speaking back up this position.

Why is it that Mailliez has insisted that Diana was unconscious when most other evidence – including photographic[a] – strongly indicates that she was conscious during the short period in which he was present at the scene?

Emergency Phone Call: 12.26 a.m.

At 12.26 a.m. Dr Mailliez returned to his car and phoned the Fire Service. That call was recorded.[b]

There was conflicting evidence over the phone number that Dr Mailliez dialled.

Under oath to the French police Mailliez said that he dialled '18'[1297] and under oath at the inquest Mailliez insisted: "I am absolutely certain that I called the direct phone number".[1298]

The Paget Report stated that Mailliez said "he had dialled the Fire Brigade control number (0147 546835)".[1299] (WFJ) It is not explained where Paget got this from, as Mailliez said in his statement that he dialled "18".[c]

The call transcript records Mailliez's instruction: "We'll need at least two ARs[d]".[1300] That also was Mailliez's recollection when he was interviewed in 1998.[1301]

Why did Mailliez consider that he, the only doctor present, needed to call the Fire Service? Why did he not ask other people present to do that, or even Butt, his passenger?

It is not as though Mailliez was providing the Fire Service with any special medical information – he said: "There are one or two who appear to be dead and two others seriously injured. I can't tell you any more than

---

[a] See earlier photo in previous chapter.
[b] A transcript appears in Part 2, section on Dr Mailliez in Chapter 9A.
[c] Operation Paget did not interview Mailliez.
[d] Ambulances.

that."[1302] That was not any more information than an ordinary person who looked inside the Mercedes could have provided.[a]

Mailliez was an experienced Parisian emergency doctor[b] so why does the call transcript[c] reveal he was unfamiliar with the location of the crash? At the inquest Butt indicates that Mailliez was familiar with the location: "I think he knew where he was".[1303]

Mailliez apparently checked the map of the area,[1304] but he still managed to give the Fire Service the incorrect location when he rang through. The operator, who had already been notified of the crash, said: "You are on the Alma Bridge, aren't you, by the Place de la Concorde?" To which Mailliez said "It's before that, before." Operator: "Before it?" Mailliez: "Oh yes, we're before it."[1305]

The Fire Service operator already had the correct location, but Mailliez was adamant that they had it wrong. This could have created confusion and delay for any attending Fire Service ambulances.

Treatment of Diana: 12.28 to 12.32 a.m.

Dr Mailliez returned to the Mercedes and set about fitting the respiratory mask onto Diana's face.

There is again conflict in his evidence regarding Diana's reaction.

At the inquest Michael Mansfield asked Mailliez: "Was Diana resisting you putting on the mask?" Mailliez replied: "No."[1306]

The Paget Report description of Mailliez's French statement, which the jury didn't get to hear, stated the exact opposite: "She would not accept it".[1307] (WFJ)

In a TV interview on the day after the crash, Mailliez said: "I ... helped her breathe with an oxygen mask." [1308] (WFJ)

Why did Mailliez tell the French police that Diana wouldn't accept the oxygen mask?

Recognising His Patient

Dr Mailliez has consistently claimed that he didn't realise at the time that he was treating Princess Diana.

An analysis of the evidence indicates his recollection has evolved.

On the day following the crash, he said: "I did not recognise her immediately."[1309] (WFJ)

---

[a] There were non-medical witnesses who quickly assessed the scene and drew the same conclusions in their early statements.
[b] Mailliez said he had worked for three years for the Fire Service (13 Nov 07: 19.15) and he also worked concurrently with SAMU: 13 Nov 07: 6.14.
[c] See below.

In 1998 Mailliez stated:

> **I was very close to [Diana] – inches from her face ... but her face was always in profile, or tilted at [an] angle away from me, so that I never looked at her square in the face. But even if I had, I'm not sure it would have dawned on me who it was. I was too busy doing my job.[1310] (WFJ)**

He added that on his way home after the crash he "still didn't know it was Princess Diana".[1311] (WFJ)

Then when he did a 2004 interview with CNN, Mailliez said this:

> **When I woke up the next morning, my friend Mark [Butt] told me – he turned on CNN and he saw the car accident and he realised that the person I've been treating last night was Princess Diana. So he told me, and it was a big shock for me to understand that.[1312] (WFJ)**

At the inquest under oath Dr Mailliez testified: "The next day I discovered that the woman I was treating was Princess Diana".[1313]

In 1997 Mailliez didn't "immediately recognise her; in 1998 he still didn't know on his way home; in 2004 he found out after waking the next morning; in 2007 it was the next day.

To CNN's Larry King, Mailliez said "I had four victims on my hands I had other things to think about than trying to recognise who were my victims".[1314] (WFJ) But there has only ever been evidence of Mailliez treating Diana – he had no contact with Rees-Jones and both Dodi and Henri had already died on impact.[a]

At the inquest, Mailliez was asked by Burnett: "Were you able immediately to see that ... the bodyguard in the front passenger seat was alive?" Mailliez replied: "Obviously he was alive because he was screaming.... He was alive but severely injured."[1315]

If Mailliez didn't recognise Diana, why didn't he, as the only doctor present, go to the assistance of the most seriously injured – Rees-Jones? Instead he went to assist Diana, a person whose "condition did not seem desperate to me".[1316][b]

The French police asked Martinez in his earliest interview if he recalled Mailliez being told that the passengers didn't speak French and that he was

---

[a] At the inquest Mailliez said "the driver and Mr Al Fayed were obviously dead": 13 Nov 07: 12.11

[b] Mailliez later said: "The bodyguard was already helped by a volunteer fireman, so the only victim I could help was the young lady":13 Oct 07: 13.10. This conflicts with the reason he gave for assisting Diana to *Impact Quotidien* in September 1997 – "I thought her life could be saved". The evidence is that the volunteer fireman, Damien Dalby, arrived at "the same time" as Mailliez – see Sébastien Pennequin 25 Oct 07: 59.13. It is common sense that the passing emergency doctor would treat the most severely injured patient – not the passing volunteer fireman.

treating Diana. No other paparazzi have ever been asked about this. Martinez's response was: "I did not hear any of that".[1317]

Mailliez's 1998 account was that the paparazzi were repeatedly telling him to speak English:

> **Speak to her in English! Speak to her in English!' they kept repeating. 'So I started speaking English to her'.[1318] (WFJ)**

So why does Martinez not recall that when specifically asked around ten hours after the crash? And why did the French police not then go on to ask the same question of the other paparazzi present?

There is no substantiation for Mailliez's claim that he was not aware that the surviving occupants of the Mercedes were English-speaking.

Pedestrian Abdelatif Redjil directly contradicts Mailliez's story. He told the French investigation:

> **I saw a kind of 'SOS Médécins' car arriving.... I went to see the driver [Mailliez] and explained to him what was going on and told him that one of the casualties was the Princess of Wales.[1319]**

Redjil also recalls Mailliez's response: "She was a casualty like any other".[1320] It is obvious that Redjil should have been cross-examined at the inquest.

He wasn't.

Under cross-examination Mailliez was asked about the presence of photographers. He replied: "They were behind me. They were close to me. They were taking a lot of pictures with a lot of flash".[1321] One could think that even if Mailliez hadn't been told, common sense would have suggested to him that there was a high profile person present in the Mercedes: Why was there such a photographic interest in a crash at 12.30 a.m. on a Sunday morning?

It is evident that Mailliez should have been confronted with Redjil's account and also the issue of whether French or English was being spoken to Diana should have been addressed. Neither of these lines of questioning occurred.

Why?

In his various accounts, Mailliez has distanced himself from knowledge of who was in the Mercedes: Firstly, by denying that he knew he was treating Diana and secondly, by suggesting that he was talking in French until being persuaded to speak English by the surrounding photographers.

Why would Mailliez do this?

His ignorance of who was in the vehicle until the following day would completely preclude him from involvement in a premeditated plot. His account that he was speaking French would back up that position.[a]

The problem for Mailliez is that his evidence is directly contradicted by Redjil, who has no apparent motive to lie about this. Mailliez's recollection that he was speaking French until repeatedly reminded by the paparazzi to speak English has never been corroborated by any of the witnesses at the scene.

Mailliez gave four statements to the French police. Not one of these has ever been made public and his evidence only rated about ten lines in the 832 page Paget Report.[1322] Yet Mailliez was the first medical person at the scene.

Why is this?

Who is Dr Mailliez?

At the inquest Dr Frédéric Mailliez provided some unusual answers to some straightforward questions.

He was asked: "We know that you are a doctor. Could you tell us your qualifications please?". He replied: "I am an emergency physician."[1323]

Mailliez went on to say that he worked "also for the SAMU".[1324] Then afterwards he is asked if he had worked a long time for the SAMU and he answered: "I did not work for the SAMU".[1325]

He was asked: "What vehicle were you driving Dr Mailliez?" His answer: "It was my own vehicle, my own car."[1326]

Then less than a minute later says the car was "belonging to the SOS Médécins corporation".[1327] .

Mailliez told the inquest that he "had to cancel a day of work" when "some media invited [him] to a restaurant".[1328]

Why was getting Mailliez's version of events out so important that he "had to cancel a day of work" to conduct an interview?

Mark Butt

Mark Butt was the sole passenger in Dr Mailliez's car. Mailliez instructed him "to stay with the car" while he attended the crash scene.[1329]

Butt's account is quite remarkable.

He admits to being a "bit nervous [and] a little bit freaked out" at the time of the crash. He also said that "a lot of stuff was going on that I did not understand and I was just dealing with it".[1330] It is amazing that at the inquest he was not asked to explain what he meant by these extraordinary comments.

If Mailliez did play a role in a premeditated plot, then Mark Butt who was in the car with him, may well have been in a situation where "a lot of stuff was going on that I did not understand and I was just dealing with it".

---

[a] This is another instance of excessive distancing.

Rapid Departure: 12.32 a.m.

Mailliez left the scene very quickly after the arrival of the fire service at 12.32 a.m.

Xavier Gourmelon from the Fire Service stated:

As soon as we arrived, [Mailliez] presented the situation quickly and then he left.[1331]

Mark Butt testified:

After the fire services arrived, we quickly left.[1332]

Mailliez made a quick departure from the crash scene, but he stated in 1998 that they "decided to take a detour on the way home and drive by the Ritz".[1333]

Why was Mailliez – the only qualified doctor present at that time – in such a hurry to leave the scene?

The Passing Doctor

There is a great deal of conflict surrounding the testimony of Dr Mailliez. The evidence raises the following issues:

-        Mailliez was driving an official SOS Médécins car without the normal medical equipment

-        Mailliez described Diana as unconscious while photo evidence and other witnesses suggest she was conscious. He paints her condition as worse than it actually was

-        Mailliez has repeatedly said that Diana never spoke a word. This directly conflicts with the other witness accounts

-        Mailliez said in an interview in November 1997 that Diana did speak, then retracted his remarks the following day

-        Mailliez has given two completely different accounts of which number he dialled when he called the fire service

-        Mailliez said he checked the map, but the call transcript shows he then directed the fire service to the incorrect location

-        Mailliez told the French police that Diana would not accept the oxygen mask, but told the media that it helped her to breathe

-        Mailliez insists that he didn't know he was treating Diana, yet Redjil said he told Mailliez that Diana was in the car as he arrived

-        Mailliez said that he worked for SAMU and later said he didn't work for SAMU

-        Mailliez cancelled a day's work to conduct a media interview

-        Butt stated that at the time of the crash "a lot of stuff was going on that I did not understand and I was just dealing with it"

- Mailliez left rapidly after the fire service arrived.[a]

Most of the above factors on their own don't suggest anything sinister, but the picture is different when they are looked at in context. There is a pattern of conflict between the evidence of Mailliez and the other witnesses, who were at the scene around the same time as him.

Mailliez stated that:

1) Diana was unconscious
2) Diana never spoke any words
3) He didn't know it was Princess Diana he was treating.

These three statements are proven by the accounts of other witnesses – who have no apparent reason to lie – to be false.

Why has Mailliez painted a false picture of the events that occurred in the Alma Tunnel?

There is a possibility that Dr Mailliez was working for an additional employer whose intention was to harm Princess Diana.[b] This does not by any means suggest that Mailliez would have been aware that Diana was going to be dead within hours of him treating her.

When studying the post-crash medical treatment of Princess Diana, there is a theme that is very apparent: time was of the essence. This will become clearer as this story progresses.

For the assassins orchestrating the events, it would have been of paramount importance that a medical person they could trust be present to control Diana's situation, during the critical minutes after the crash. It may be that Mailliez's primary role could have simply been to ensure that no one attempted to transport Diana away from the crash scene. This function would have been completed once the fire service arrived, and that is when he quickly left.

As an emergency physician – driving the official car – any decision he made would have overridden that of anyone else who happened to appear at the scene, even that of a normal doctor.

There is a possibility that Mailliez's role extended to being a critical spokesman to the media. Over the years he has conducted many interviews

---

[a] There is a further conflict in Mailliez's comments regarding the paparazzi presence. In the interview with France-2 TV on 1 September 1997 he said: "[The paparazzi] were just like the people you find milling around the site of serious accidents." The following day he was quoted in the *Seattle Times*, from wire services: "The paparazzi swarmed over the scene clicking pictures, the light bursts from their flashes ricocheting through the tunnel." At the inquest Mailliez said: "They were behind me. They were close to me. They were taking a lot of pictures with a lot of flash, but they did not hamper me doing my job. They were just behind me." 13 Nov 07: 14.6.
[b] This is a theme that runs through the evidence surrounding the Paris crash – it was shown earlier that both Henri Paul and Claude Roulet were working for an additional employer on the weekend of the crash.

for the press and at one point "had to" take a day off work for a media encounter.

Scott Baker, in his Summing Up, never mentioned any of the issues surrounding Dr Mailliez and Butt's testimony.[a] Why is this?

As Mailliez was the first medic to have contact with and treat Diana post-crash, the importance of his role and evidence cannot be overstated – yet his evidence is riddled with conflict, with other witnesses and within his own accounts. Why?

Did Mailliez receive payments from another organisation, similar to Henri Paul and possibly Claude Roulet? When Mailliez's evidence is assessed in the cold light of day, it becomes clear that his financial records should have been looked at as part of a thorough investigation. They weren't.

On 29 September 1997 Mailliez was asked by *The Scotsman* whether Diana would have survived if she had reached hospital earlier. He replied:

> **That's very controversial. It's impossible to say. I don't want to be drawn on that. I've already said too much and I don't want to say any more.**[1334b]

Why would he say that he had "said too much"?

Some of Dr Mailliez's media comments indicate that he was answerable to someone else: the switch in his evidence regarding the paparazzi between September 1 and 2 implies that he may have received overnight instructions. A similar scenario occurred in November 1997 regarding his account of Diana speaking.

---

[a] Butt does not receive any mention at all in Baker's 80,000 word address to the jury.
[b] The issue of whether Diana could have survived is dealt with later.

62 Sapeurs-Pompiers

At 12.32 a.m. two Sapeurs-Pompiers – Paris Fire Service – ambulances (Nos. 94 and 100) from the Malar Medical Emergency Centre, arrived. Neither of these ambulances had doctors on board, but each was manned with five staff.

Dr Mailliez immediately handed over responsibility for Princess Diana's medical treatment to Xavier Gourmelon, a Paris Fire Service First Aid Instructor.

The Sapeurs-Pompiers took control for eight minutes – from 12.32 to 12.40 a.m. when the first SAMU ambulance arrived.

Diana's Condition

Gourmelon stated that Diana "was conscious, she could speak to me".[1335] He also confirmed that she was "moving her limbs".[1336]

Philippe Boyer was in charge of the second Fire Service ambulance and spent more time with the princess. He testified: "She was agitated. It seemed that she had understood what had happened."[1337]

Boyer added:

> **She had trauma on the right shoulder because her arm was trapped in between the two front seats, but that was the only visible injury.**[1338]

Boyer also confirmed that Diana's pulse was "fine and quite strong" and her breathing was normal.[1339]

Diana's Words

Xavier Gourmelon recalled Diana saying, "My God, what's happened?"[1340] (WFJ)

Philippe Boyer told the inquest:

> **She said 'My God' several times, it was repeated. But the other things that she said, I could not hear or understand. I was told later on.**[1341]

No lawyer asked Boyer what these "other things" were, but two factors are evident:

1) Boyer heard Diana speak words other than "My God"
2) Boyer "was told later on" what the words were.

Boyer revealed that the reason he couldn't understand everything Diana was saying was because his "understanding of English is not very good".[1342]

Why was there no attempt at the inquest to find out what these other words were?

Treatment

There is no evidence of the Fire Service ever checking Princess Diana's blood pressure. Mailliez was obviously aware of the importance of doing so – he had said in 1998: "I didn't even have a blood pressure cuff.... If I had had it with me, I would have known already" that there was an internal injury.[1343] (WFJ)

Why did Mailliez not tell Gourmelon to take Diana's blood pressure before he left the scene?

The first evidence of this being done is just before Diana was removed from the Mercedes at around 1.00 a.m., and that reading wasn't recorded.

A simple blood pressure check – as is standard procedure on visits to the doctor in many places in the world – could have helped reveal a clearer picture of Diana's internal injuries.

Boyer stated:

> **I tried to assess her health condition. I started putting on a surgical collar.... We checked the heartbeat, the level of ventilation.... We looked for possible traumas.[1344]**

He also confirmed that the Sapeurs-Pompiers gave Diana oxygen and wrapped her in an isothermic blanket.[1345]

Sébastien Dorzée – the police officer present – testified:

> **One of the fire officers asked me to look after the Princess and to keep her awake when she fell asleep.... The other fire officers attended to the front right-hand passenger[a].[1346]**

Although ten people had arrived in the two Fire Service ambulances, Dorzée – a non-medic – still found himself to be Diana's primary carer during the critical minutes before SAMU arrived at 12.40 a.m.

By then, it was already 17 minutes since the crash.

Sapeurs-Pompiers

Scott Baker told his jury during the Summing Up that "[Mailliez] handed over to the doctor in the fire rescue vehicle that arrived at 12.32 a.m."[1347]

This is a direct lie: Baker says that Mailliez "handed over to the doctor". The truth is that there was no doctor present and that was a theme of the Fire Service evidence. Gourmelon confirmed that there was no doctor in his

---

[a] Trevor Rees-Jones.

451

vehicle[1348] and Boyer said that they were waiting "for the [SAMU] physicians".[1349]

Dr Mailliez did not hand Diana over to the care of a doctor and that is an issue of concern.[a]

There are several serious issues around the Sapeurs-Pompiers response to the crash.

The central problem is that two ambulances arrived at the scene at 12.32 a.m., 7 minutes after the crash, but neither had a doctor aboard. It's not that the Fire Service didn't have doctors – both of these ambulances actually came from a medical centre, the Malar Medical Emergency Centre.[1350]

Fire Service doctors did attend the scene, but they did not come until later – Dr Fuilla arriving at 12.43 a.m. and Dr Le Hot a minute later, at 12.44.[1351]

Gourmelon insists that "it is for certain that the seriousness of the crash had been taken into account"[1352] – this then raises the question: Why is it that the two ambulances were sent off without doctors? Dr Fuilla, the first Fire Service doctor to leave for the scene, didn't depart until 12.34 a.m.[1353] – 11 minutes after the crash.

Dr Mailliez, an experienced emergency doctor who had worked for both the Fire Service and SAMU, gave the following evidence:

> **The ambulances belonging to the SAMU and the ambulances belonging to the firemen brigade are exactly the same, with an emergency physician on board and a driver and a nurse and the same kind of equipment.[1354b]**

What Dr Mailliez is stating – that the Fire Service ambulances have a doctor on board – did not actually happen on the night. Two ambulances rolled up with no doctors aboard.

Why?

Both of the ambulances were described by Gourmelon as containing "rescue" teams – five persons in each.[1355]

The question is: Who were these ten people rescuing?

Obviously not Princess Diana.

The evidence shows that after arriving at 12.32 a.m. Gourmelon put Boyer in charge of Diana.[1356] Boyer carried out a few tests, put on a surgical collar, gave her oxygen, wrapped her in an isothermic blanket and then said "our job was done by then – we had to wait for the physicians from ... SAMU."[1357] Boyer then handed the care of Diana over to Dorzée, the policeman, instructing him "to keep her awake".[1358]

---

[a] See below.
[b] This evidence was backed up by the findings of the Paget Report: "The...Sapeurs-Pompiers have fully qualified doctors as part of their emergency response teams." – p525.

SAPEURS-POMPIERS

If the Paris Fire Service had been serious about rescuing Diana they would have moved her out of the Mercedes at the earliest opportunity. This should have been immediately after making the initial patient assessment after their arrival at 12.32. As it turned out, Diana wasn't moved out of the car for another 28 minutes – 1.00 a.m. – a full 37 minutes after the crash.[a]

Dr Mailliez phoned the Fire Service rather than SAMU, and it was the Fire Service who turned up first. Mailliez, an experienced emergency professional, must have realised that the person he was handing Princess Diana over to wasn't a doctor. Yet the evidence is – Butt, Gourmelon – that he left the scene quickly.[b]

Why is this?

One could be forgiven for wondering why a medical centre despatched two ambulances with no doctor. The problem is that practical and logical issues like that were not always raised by the lawyers at the inquest. It was basically accepted that the fire service ambulance teams sat there at the scene for eight minutes, effectively doing nothing to advance the treatment of Diana, Princess of Wales: "We had to wait for the [SAMU] physicians" is what Boyer told the courtroom.

Why did they have to wait for the SAMU doctor? Is there a rule in France that only a doctor can move a patient at a crash scene? If that is the case, then what is the point of having ambulances that don't have a doctor on board?

Why did Mailliez disappear in such a hurry, when he knew that he was the only doctor in the vicinity?

Mailliez's main defence for why he didn't do anything has always been that he had no equipment. When the equipment arrived – in the form of two ambulances – Mailliez cleared out very quickly.

Why is it that the two Fire Service doctors – who did eventually arrive at the scene, Dr Fuilla and Dr Le Hot – have never been interviewed by any police inquiry and were not heard from at the inquest?

The evidence points in one direction: The Fire Service may have been instructed not to proceed with effective treatment – i.e. the removal of Diana from the Mercedes to a waiting ambulance – until the SAMU ambulance arrived.

Why?

---

[a] See next chapter.
[b] See earlier The Passing Doctor chapter.

453

63   Diana in the Mercedes: 37 minutes

The crash occurred at 12.23 and Princess Diana – who was not trapped – was removed from the Mercedes at 1 a.m.?

Why did this operation take 37 minutes?

The Crawling Ambulance

Even though the SAMU ambulance left two minutes before the Fire Service ambulances, it arrived eight minutes after the Fire Service.

The inquest heard that the first notification calls to SAMU were at 12.23 a.m. but the "first call recorded in the [SAMU] transcript ... was at 00.26 [12.26 a.m.]".[1359]

Two minutes later, at 12.28, Paris Fire Service headquarters called Paris SAMU headquarters.

The call transcript indicates that the SAMU ambulance had already left before this phone call took place. The SAMU operator says "we're on our way" twice and also "we have sent an ambulance".[1360] Michel Massebeuf the driver confirmed this when he told the French investigation "we set off straightaway" after being informed.[1361]

The inquest was told that Dr Martino – the ambulance doctor in charge – wrote on his observation sheet that the ambulance didn't leave until 12.34 a.m.[1362] When one looks at the observation sheet – as shown to the jury in English[1363] – the "leave base" time is recorded as "00[?]4", and not 0034 as stated by Jonathon Hough, the inquest lawyer.

If one presumes that 0034, or 12.34 a.m., was the written time on the observation sheet, the question would then be: Why did the ambulance delay leaving by around 7 or 8 minutes? Lejay suggests an answer to this:

> **You need to have the time for the call, the time to perform an analysis of the call, the time to call the teams, and roughly all these steps may take up to five to seven minutes.**[1364]

This does not sound particularly convincing.

The 12.28 a.m. call suggests that all of these steps had already taken place in the period since the original accident notification call. Hough said that the earliest notification call was received at 12.23 a.m.[1365] If this was the case, then by 12.28 SAMU had already known about the crash for up to 5 minutes. This is common sense: the crash occurred just prior to 12.23 a.m. and in the era of mobile phones, why would witnesses wait 3 minutes to phone the ambulance?[a]

The SAMU ambulance came from the Necker Hospital[1366] and arrived at the crash scene at 12.40 a.m.[1367]

Based on the evidence from the call transcript and Massebeuf, the journey, which measures 2.3 kilometres, took around 12 minutes – this means that the ambulance was travelling at an average speed of only 11½ kph. Even if Martino was correct, and they did wait an additional six minutes at the Necker Hospital before departing, the average speed would still only be approximately 23 kph, or 14 mph.

This raises question marks over driver Massebeuf's testimony that the ambulance "went very quickly".[1368b]

Witnesses said that traffic at the time was fairly light,[1369] and after all, this was an ambulance rushing to a serious accident scene – so there was no requirement to stop at traffic lights or follow the normal road rules.

Compared to the expectations that the average person would have – that of an ambulance speeding to the crash scene – 11½ kph, or 7 mph, is actually a snail's pace.

The importance of this information is clear when it is coupled with the testimony from Philippe Boyer of the Fire Service[c] that they were waiting at the scene for up to 8 minutes for a doctor to arrive.

The jury were never told that the distance from Necker Hospital – the SAMU base – to the crash scene was only 2.3 km.

It is obvious that Massebeuf should have been cross-examined at the inquest, but he wasn't.

It is also a major concern that the French investigation waited until six months after the crash before interviewing Martino and Massebeuf on 12 March 1998.[1370]

---

[a] The inquest heard several early witness accounts of people either calling emergency services themselves or witnessing others doing so.
[b] The Paget Report also stated on p526: "In this instance, Dr Martino, the SAMU doctor, arrived at the scene quickly."
[c] See previous chapter.

Coroner's Intervention

Just before the cross-examination of Dr Martino – the doctor who controlled Diana's treatment between 12.40 and 2.06 a.m.[a] – Scott Baker announced to the court:

> **Mr Hough will ... spend his lunchtime shortening [the cross-examination of] Dr Martino as much as he possibly can.**[1371b]

This was an incredible statement for the judge to make prior to the cross-examination of such a vital witness, as Dr Martino was.

SAMU Treatment: 12.40 to 1.00 a.m.

After Dr Jean-Marc Martino's SAMU ambulance arrived at 12.40 a.m., Diana remained in the Mercedes S280 for a further 20 minutes.

Even though there was an abundance of medical personnel at the scene[c], no results were recorded for any tests that were administered in the car.

In 1998 Martino told French investigator Andre Lienhart that he was "doing his best to remember" what Diana's arterial pressure and heart rate were.[1372] Lienhart replied that the results were rough estimates that were "reported afterwards", but he doesn't say when, and there is no record of them in any of the inquest evidence.

We are left with inquest lawyer Nicholas Hilliard's reading of the Lienhart-Martino interview[d] – Martino was "doing his best to remember".

Dr Martino said under oath that "we didn't give [Diana] an injection" while she was in the car.[1373] This conflicts with what he told Lienhart in 1998 – he "re-injected her himself and put the drip in".[1374] This occurred after an initial drip line had been inserted in Diana's wrist by the female "student in medical studies" working with Martino – that line had been pulled out by Diana.[1375]

When Lienhart is asked if the student was qualified to insert the drip, he asserts "Yes, indeed".[1376]

This student has never been interviewed by the police, was not heard from at the inquest and was never identified to the jury.

Lienhart stated that sedating Diana enabled her removal from the car "more quickly".[1377]

The reality is that Diana was left in the car for 37 minutes after the crash.

---

[a] One hour 26 minutes.

[b] This was one of many comments made by Baker throughout the inquest aimed at rushing proceedings to meet his self-imposed deadlines. This issue is addressed in Part 7.

[c] By 12.45 a.m., there were three Fire Service ambulances as well as Dr Fuilla and the Martino ambulance – there were around 20 medical staff in the Alma Tunnel. By 12.50 a.m. an additional SAMU ambulance and two doctors had arrived.

[d] The transcript was not shown to the jury and has never been made public.

It's not as though Diana was trapped: post-crash photos of the scene reveal that the structure of the area of the Mercedes where Diana was sitting was not adversely affected by the impact of the crash.[a] When Mailliez was confronted with this issue in September 1997, he didn't say "I couldn't remove her". Instead he said: "I don't have the right to [remove Diana from the car] without first giving the patient an intravenous drip and making sure they're conscious."[1378] (WFJ) At the inquest Mailliez categorically stated: "Princess Diana was not blocked inside the wreckage".[1379]

Some of the statements made by the French participants in the medical treatment appear to emerge straight out of fantasyland.

Lienhart suggests that Diana's removal from the car had an element of quickness about it. He states that SAMU worked with Diana in the car for "several minutes"[1380] – the truth is it was 20 minutes before she was removed (from 12.40 to 1.00 a.m.). Massebeuf said that the ambulance "went very quickly" – the reality is that it was travelling at about 11½ kph.

Glasgow Coma Scale

The ambulance report reveals that at the time of SAMU's arrival Princess Diana scored a Glasgow Coma rating of 14.[1381]

Professor Tom Treasure, the inquest expert cardio-thoracic surgeon, told the courtroom:

> [Diana] was very definitely alive when first encountered and the head injury aspect, of a scale of 15, she scored 14.[b] In spite of this terrible accident, there was only one point that she dropped.... 14 out of 15 is very good. The only point she dropped, I think, is she could open her eyes, she was moving, she was responding, but the answers – she was speaking, but the answers were not coherent. That drops you a point.... It is a scale of prediction of head injury and it was very favourable.[1382]

Diana's Injuries

After arriving at the scene Dr Martino viewed the Mercedes wreckage and Diana's position[c], and was immediately aware that Diana had been involved in "a high-speed accident, the technical wherewithal capable of operating in thoracic, cardiac and abdominal regions was needed".[1383]

---

[a] See earlier Figure 18 in the Smoke in the Tunnel chapter. A better shot of this is on the inquest website: INQ-JB1-00000053c.

[b] This figure of 14 appears in the report drawn up by Dr Martino – reproduced later in the Transfer to Ambulance chapter.

[c] He would have realised Diana had not been wearing a seat belt – see next chapter.

Martino was aware of the high Glasgow coma rating, which is a simple visual and audio appraisal – he excluded severe head injury from his assessment.

From around 12.40 a.m. Dr Martino was aware that Diana could have serious internal injuries and would require an operation in the "thoracic, cardiac and abdominal regions".

This information was not conveyed to the SAMU base.

First Report: 12.40 a.m.

Dr Martino called the SAMU base at 12.40 a.m.

The inquest was told about this initial report: "There is a request for additional units, but there is no mention of the injuries".[1384]

It was also pointed out that the accident involved "VIPs, including Princess Lady Di".[1385]

After receiving this report Dr Arnaud Derossi – who had been operating the SAMU base phones – headed to the crash scene. An "auxiliary woke Dr Lejay at 00.42 [12.42 a.m.] and told him that [Derossi] had already left".[1386]

Dr Lejay took over the phones.

Dr Fuilla from the Fire service arrived at 12.43 a.m.[1387]

The actions of Drs Martino and Derossi will later reveal that they were both working on behalf of an intelligence agency on the night of the crash.

The Second Victim

After Dr Martino submitted this first report there was a further delay of three minutes before attending to Princess Diana.

In 1998 Martino stated:

> **I asked my crew to take care of the front right hand seat passenger [Rees-Jones], who seemed the more seriously injured of the two, whilst calling for back up from the Mobile Emergency Service [SAMU] in order to attend to the second victim [Diana].**[1388] **(WFJ)**

Martino says that he started his team working on Rees-Jones ahead of "the second victim". Earlier in the statement he said he had already recognised that second victim was "Lady Di". [1389] (WFJ)

As a result of this decision, there was an additional period of three minutes – from 12.40 to 12.43 a.m. – when nothing happened with Diana's treatment. At the inquest Martino confirmed that it was only after Dr Fuilla from the Fire Service arrived that Martino started treating Diana.[1390]

This evidence raises a major query over Dr Martino's early actions in the tunnel.

At 12.40 a.m. he directed his team to work on Rees-Jones, as Martino considered him the "more seriously injured of the two". This means that by

12.43, when Dr Fuilla arrived, Martino and his team had already been working on Rees-Jones for three minutes.

As he was the first doctor to arrive, Martino was evidently in charge of the scene.[a] At 12.43 Martino handed Rees-Jones over to Fuilla but fails to explain why he didn't just get Fuilla to start working with Diana, whom he considered to be the second victim – the one least in need of treatment.

Why did Martino switch his own team from Rees-Jones to Diana when Fuilla, the second doctor, arrived?

The natural progression of events would have led to Fuilla being Diana's doctor at the scene, but that is not what occurred. At 12.43 a.m. Martino interfered with this logical outcome and shifted his own team from Rees-Jones to Diana, then directed Fuilla to work with Rees-Jones.

This evidence, when seen in the light of the earlier evidence that the Fire Service did very little for Diana during the period they were in control of the scene, suggests that there was an undisclosed requirement for Martino to be the doctor who dealt with Diana.

There is a further issue surrounding Martino's early actions.

At 12.40 a.m. after Martino's initial assessment of the situation he decided to focus on Rees-Jones and called the SAMU base for a back-up ambulance "in order to attend to the second victim", Diana. Martino's evidence indicates that he was only going to start treating Diana when the back-up SAMU ambulance arrived. The records show that ambulance didn't reach the scene until 12.50 a.m.[1391]

Does this mean that at 12.40 a.m. Martino was preparing to leave Diana for a further ten minutes untreated in the back, while he dealt with the more critical Rees-Jones in the front?

The 12.43 a.m. arrival of Fuilla forced a change from that plan.

As this story develops it will become apparent that Martino's actions were not in the interests of his high profile patient, Princess Diana. The evidence will indicate that Martino may have had allegiance to another employer he was working for on the night – an employer that took priority over his work for SAMU.

Dr Fuilla has never been interviewed by either of the "thorough" police investigations and his evidence was also not heard at the inquest.

Second Report: 12.43 a.m.

Dr Martino called the SAMU base for the second time at 12.43 a.m. He reported to Dr Lejay:

---

[a] Mailliez had arrived earlier but had already vacated the scene – see earlier The Passing Doctor chapter.

Two dead and a passenger trapped, having hit the windscreen. Very severe facial injuries, requiring intubation, ventilation and at the scene. Rear passenger, would seem an arm, the right arm, completely turned backwards. We are trying to sedate and initial treatment. Over.[1392]

This call took place immediately after the arrival of Dr Fuilla, and it confirms that nothing occurred in the treatment of Diana – the "rear passenger" – between 12.40 and 12.43 a.m.

This was because Martino and his team were working on Rees-Jones, the "trapped" passenger – who was considered a priority.[a]

This initial official report of Princess Diana's condition, passed on 20 minutes after the crash, is more significant for what it doesn't say than what it does say. One could be forgiven for thinking, on reading the report, that Martino is describing a patient in the back with an injured arm.

There is a huge conflict between Martino's initial assessment and what he conveyed back to base in his report.

Martino told the French investigators that his "initial assessment" was:

[Diana] herself had a facial injury, frontal according to the journey log, and was trapped with her right arm bent to the rear, at first glance possibly with a fracture in the upper third. However, she may have had all sorts of other internal injuries, abdominal or thoracic, which might decompensate at any time.[1393]

So essentially three injuries detected:
1) "Facial injury"
2) Fractured right arm
3) Possible "internal injuries, abdominal or thoracic".

Why did Martino lie in his initial injury report to the SAMU base?

Just the fact that Martino did lie in this report is a major source of concern: the primary post-crash care doctor for Princess Diana was not providing a true report on her condition back to base. In fact, Martino's report could hardly have been more erroneous: an injured arm is mentioned, but possible life-threatening internal injuries are not.

The second SAMU ambulance didn't leave until 12.45 a.m.,[1394] two minutes after this second report. After seeing this report, there would have been no reason for that ambulance, with Dr Vivien aboard,[1395] to be in any particular hurry to reach the scene.[b]

There appears to have been a plan for Martino to have been the central person in control of Diana's care, right from early on after the crash.

This initial injury report that Martino dispatched back to base would have quelled any possible alarm by senior staff there. This would in turn have then

---

[a] See above.

[b] Dr Vivien has never been interviewed by any of the investigations.

given Martino more control at the scene – there was no need for any interference from the SAMU base as the situation was completely under control.

The main cause for concern would have been that Princess Diana was involved in the crash, but her only injury was to her right arm.[a]

---

[a] Staff at the base would have been completely unaware that Diana hadn't been wearing a seat belt. See next chapter.

64   Seat Belts

At the time of the crash, only one of the four occupants of the Mercedes S280 was wearing a seat belt – Trevor Rees-Jones.

Witness Evidence

Princess Diana always travelled with her seat belt fastened:
- she "always" wore a seat belt and "made me put on a seat belt as well"[1396] – Michael Gibbins, Diana's Private Secretary
- "[wearing] a seat belt … was a natural reaction whenever she got in the car, whether driver or passenger – it was automatic"[1397] – Ken Wharfe, Diana's bodyguard
- "she was always very particular about putting her seat-belt on"[1398] – Hasnat Khan, Diana's ex-boyfriend
- "I remembered how meticulous the Princess had always been about … belting up"[1399] – Dickie Arbiter, Diana's press secretary
- "she normally [would] wear a seat belt"[1400] – Colin Tebbutt, Diana's Driver and Security.

Witnesses also said of Dodi:
- "when I drove a few times with him … he was wearing a seat-belt"[1401] – Rene Delorm, Dodi's butler
- "the first thing he would always say when you would get into a car … it was always 'Myriah, buckle your seat-belt'. Always. He would do the same"[1402] – Myriah Daniels, Dodi's holistic healer
- "it would be automatic for him getting into the vehicle to place the seat belt on"[1403] – John Johnson, Dodi's bodyguard.[a]

Why No Belts?

The question – which wasn't asked at the inquest – is: If Diana always wore a seat belt, why wasn't she when the Mercedes S280 crashed on 31 August 1997?

Was it because she had been drinking and had reduced inhibitions? Not according to Dr Robert Chapman, the pathologist who conducted the UK

---

[a] Laurence Pujol, Henri Paul's ex-girlfriend, also testified that Henri "would always insist on my wearing" a seat-belt: 31 Jan 08: 176.23.

autopsy of Diana, who said at the inquest: "No alcohol was found in either the blood or the vitreous humour samples".[1404a]

Even if Diana and Dodi didn't have their belts on at the start of the journey, why didn't they reach for them as the pursuit – evidenced by many witnesses – hotted up?

Trevor Rees-Jones, the bodyguard in the front passenger seat, didn't usually wear a seat belt when working, because of the nature of his job – bodyguards require flexibility of movement in a vehicle.[1405]

According to the Paget Report the French investigation found that "Trevor Rees-Jones may have been in the process of putting on his seat belt at the moment of impact".[1406] (WFJ)

Without explaining how the French had discovered that, the British report stated: "From the nature of marks found on his seat belt, it is considered unlikely that he was even in the process of attempting to put it on at all at the time of the crash".[1407] (WFJ)

In saying this Paget ignored the statements of two of the earliest Sapeurs Pompiers personnel to arrive at the crash scene – Xavier Gourmelon and Philippe Boyer.[b]

Their inquest evidence shows that Rees-Jones was either wearing a seat belt, or at the very least was in the process of putting it on at the time of the crash.

Gourmelon said:

The front passenger, he had a safety belt.[1408]

Boyer testified:

I was the one who cut the safety belt of the passenger on the right-hand side of the car in the front.[1409]

So, how is it that Rees-Jones was putting his seat belt on while his principals sat in the back without seat belts?

Tampering

Were the rear seat belts on the Mercedes S280 tampered with?

The S280 was standing in the Vendôme car park from 8.15 p.m. until the party left at 12.18 a.m. This gave assassins a period of four hours in which the vehicle could have been tampered with.

---

[a] There is actually evidence of Diana drinking a moderate amount of alcohol. This discrepancy is addressed in the later Fraud at Fulham chapter and also in Part 4, Alcohol section of UK Post-Mortems chapter.

[b] They both provided statements to the French investigation that weren't heard by the jury and have never been made public.

CCTV evidence shows that Claude Roulet left the Ritz Hotel at 8.20 p.m., and it is possible that he could have assisted assassins in identifying the target car.[a] Roulet may have been under a misapprehension that a tracking device, or something similar, was being fitted by an intelligence agency to assist in security. In reality, he may have helped enable the couple's security to be compromised.

The Paget Report stated that TRL investigator David Price, who the inquest did not hear from, found that Diana's seat belt was jammed:

David Price's examination of the seat belts showed that they were in a good operational condition with the exception of the rear right seat belt, which was found to be jammed in the retracted position because part of the internal mechanism had become displaced.[1410] (WFJ)

Paget suggests that this malfunction occurred "after the collision". They invoke the evidence of French investigator Serge Moreau – also not heard from at the inquest – to support this: Moreau "found it to be in proper working order ... in October 1998".[1411][b] (WFJ)

There are several questions:

Why did the French leave it for over a year before they checked the seat belts?

What event occurred between 1998 and 2006 that caused the seat belt to malfunction?

Why did the jury not get to hear that a fault was found in Diana's seat belt?

Anyone investigating this is faced with the following factors:
- consistent evidence from all of Diana's friends or staff – that have been asked – that she always used a seat belt
- clear witness evidence that Rees-Jones was, at least, in the process of putting his belt on
- substantial evidence that along the expressway the Mercedes was under immediate threat from the pursuing motorbikes
- neither Diana nor Dodi were drunk – under autopsy, Diana had no alcohol level[c] and Dodi registered .078[a]

---

[a] See earlier Choosing the Car chapter.
[b] The book *Cover-up of a Royal Murder: Hundreds of Errors in the Paget Report* reveals (on page 287) that in September 1997 the French had reported that the right front tyre was deflated, but Moreau reported in October 1998 that it was inflated. When Price looked at it in 2006 he reported that it was deflated, and there was a cut in the side wall of the tyre. This evidence raised questions about just how thorough Moreau's examination of the Mercedes was, and indicated that Moreau stating a seat belt was working was not really a reliable indication that it actually was.
[c] There is actually evidence of Diana drinking a moderate amount of alcohol. This discrepancy is addressed in the later Fraud at Fulham chapter and also in Part 4, Alcohol section of UK Post-Mortems chapter.

- the inadequacies of the French and British police investigations into the Mercedes S280
- the failure in the inquest to advise the jury of Diana's defective seat belt
- the failure by the inquest to cross-examine David Price and Serge Moreau.

The only logical explanation is not that Diana was unwilling to wear a seat belt, but that she was unable to.

There is every indication – unless it can be proven otherwise – that the defect in the right rear seat belt, found by Price, could have been present in advance of the crash. The Paget Report failed to explain exactly why or how they believed the defect in the belt occurred after the crash.[b]

Paget Investigator Anthony Read was cross-examined on the condition of the Mercedes, but was not able to properly answer the questions because the full vehicle examination had been conducted by Price – "I would like to point out to you that most of that work was done by Mr Price"[1412].

Yet Price's evidence, in the form of cross-examination or report, was not heard at the inquest.

Why wasn't the vehicle report shown to the jury?

---

[a] 26 Nov 07: 12.4: 78 mg for 100 ml of blood – 2 mg below the British legal driving limit.
[b] Paget says: "The evidence strongly supports this displacement occurring after the collision" (Paget Report, p421) – but then fails to describe the nature of that evidence.

65   Removing the Media

At 12.40 a.m. just as the Martino ambulance was arriving, the French police rounded up the paparazzi present in the tunnel. Ten minutes later they were formally arrested.[1413]

Those arrested in the tunnel were: Romuald Rat, Stéphane Darmon, Serge Arnal, Christian Martinez, Jacques Langevin, Nikola Arsov and Laslo Veres.[1414a]

Martinez stated:

> **Then the BAC[b] (Crime Patrol Group) arrived. It was then that we were asked to remain at the scene and we were rounded up in a group on the other side of the central reservation.**[1415]

The paparazzi were removed from the scene and from that point there was no journalistic record of the treatment of Princess Diana in the Alma Tunnel.

They were released several days later.

The paparazzi were not found culpable for the crash in any of the investigations – the French, Paget and the London inquest.

The jury at the inquest found the "following vehicles"[c] were guilty of unlawful killing – they were referring to the pursuing motorbikes that chased the Mercedes S280 as it entered the Alma Tunnel.

---

[a] Other paparazzi – Serge Benhamou, Fabrice Chassery, David Odekerken – had already left the scene. They later handed themselves in and were arrested on September 5.
[b] BAC: Brigade Anti-Criminalite.
[c] These were unidentified.

66   Bees to a Honey Pot

The crash occurred in the middle of the night but senior law enforcement figures in Paris converged quickly onto the scene.

Paris Prefect of Police, Philippe Massoni, told Paget: "At 0040 hours [12.40 a.m.], the headquarters of Public Safety informed me of the accident.... I arrived [at the crash scene] at 0050 hours [12.50 a.m.]".[1416]

Massoni continued:

> **I was very quickly joined at the scene by M Patrick Riou, Director of the Judicial Police for Paris, M Berlioz, Assistant Director of Public Safety, and Mr De Keyser, the Chief of Staff of the Judicial Police [and] Madame Coujard, Deputy Public Prosecutor.**[1417]

Central Accident Bureau police officers, Thierry Brunet and Thierry Clotteaux, attended the crash at 12.53 a.m. They reported that when they arrived "the Deputy Public Prosecutor Maud Coujard, the Préfet de Police Philippe Massoni and other senior officers as well as officers from the Brigade Criminelle[a] were present."[1418] (WFJ)

There is a major contradiction in the French post-crash emergency response to this crash.

On the one hand there are the actions of the people who actually had a job to do – Mailliez, Gourmelon, Boyer, Martino, Derossi – who at best provided a very ordinary standard of at-the-scene medical treatment for Princess Diana. As he arrived Dr Mailliez told a concerned witness that the Princess of Wales "was a casualty like any other".[1419]

On the other hand, senior officials were quickly drawn to the Alma Tunnel in the dead of the night, like bees to a honey pot.

How many senior public officials does it require to handle the scene of a road crash?

The answer is: normally zero.

Inquest QC Ian Burnett stated:

---

[a] Elite section of the French police – see later Enter Brigade Criminelle chapter.

HOW THEY MURDERED PRINCESS DIANA

French Police Lieutenant Bruno Bouaziz[a] "lists quite a number of public officials who ... were present at the scene. Unless anyone would like me to read all of those out, I would not propose to do so. I doubt it will assist the jury.[1420]

Burnett said it wouldn't "assist the jury" to read the names out, so he didn't.

Some of the names can be gleaned from other witness evidence:[b]

Philippe Massoni - Paris Prefect of Police
Patrick Riou - Director of Judicial Police
M Berlioz - Assistant Director of Public Safety
Mr De Keyser - Chief of Staff of the Judicial Police
Martine Monteil - Head of Brigade Criminelle
Olivier Bonneford - Area Director of Judicial Police
Maud Coujard - Deputy Public Prosecutor
M. Guidat - Fire Service Lieutenant-Colonel
M. Courvoisier - Fire Service Lieutenant-Colonel
M. Gury - Fire Service Lieutenant-Colonel
M. Bignand - Fire Service Colonel
M. Chivot - Fire Service Battalion Commander

These 12 people all attended the crash scene, on top of the 23 medical staff[c], the lighting and relief vehicle team[d], Captain Chalifour who controlled Fire Service operations,[1421] the police crash investigation teams and the unnamed public officials in the Bouaziz list.

All up there would have been in excess of 50 official people at the crash scene, not including paparazzi, witnesses and bystanders from the public.

Massoni said he was phoned at 12.40 a.m. and he was on the scene at 12.50. This account is supported by Brunet and Clotteaux who say that Massoni was already in the tunnel when they arrived at 12.53.

Massoni arrived within 10 minutes of notification – that was substantially quicker than Diana's ambulance which was notified at 12.23 a.m., travelled 2.3 km and arrived at 12.40 a.m., 17 minutes after notification.[e]

This, despite the fact that Massoni was presumably either asleep or in a state of relaxation when notified – whereas the ambulance crew, on a Saturday night, should have been in a state of high alert.

---

[a] Not interviewed by Paget and not cross-examined at the inquest.
[b] The source details are in Part 3, Early Presence section of the Actions in the Tunnel chapter.
[c] 16 Fire Service (3 ambulances of 5 and 1 extra doctor) and 7 SAMU (2 ambulances of 3 and an extra doctor)
[d] They removed the roof of the Mercedes to free the trapped Rees-Jones.
[e] See earlier Diana in the Mercedes chapter.

Massoni wasn't the only official to arrive with great speed – Brunet and Clotteaux also state that Maud Coujard and "other senior officers as well as officers from the Brigade Criminelle[a]" were already there when they arrived at 12.53 a.m. Coujard said that Patrick Riou was already there when she arrived[1422] – this would also then place Riou at the scene before 12.53 a.m.[b]

Coujard appeared to try and distance herself from an early arrival, when she told the inquest that she was at home and wasn't notified until "about 1 o'clock in the morning"[1423] – but the police report completed soon after the crash, but not heard by the jury, places her in the tunnel before 12.53 a.m.[c]

A fuller understanding of precisely who was at the crash scene was available to the inquest in the form of Bouaziz's 31 August 1997 statement, but Burnett chose not to read it out.

---

[a] There may be significance in the early presence of Brigade Criminelle officers, because they actually weren't designated with control of the investigation at that stage – see later Enter Brigade Criminelle chapter.

[b] This is supported by Massoni who said that he was "very quickly joined at the scene by M Patrick Riou" and Coujard's Paget statement: Paget Report, p572.

[c] In Coujard's statement – not heard by the jury – she said: "I must point out that at no time did I see the Princess of Wales or Mr Trevor Rees-Jones, who had already been transferred to the hospital." (WFJ) This is clearly untrue as Coujard arrived before 12.53 a.m. at a stage when Princess Diana was still in the Mercedes. Diana's ambulance didn't leave the tunnel until 1.41 a.m. – at least 48 minutes after Coujard's arrival.: Source: Maud Coujard, Witness Statement, 15 Nov 06, reproduced in The Documents book, p48.

67 Early Notifications

At around 12.55 a.m. Philippe Massoni "notified the British Ambassador" Michael Jay "as soon as we knew that the Princess of Wales was one of the victims of the accident". He said this was "done on my behalf by Nicola Basselier, my assistant private secretary".[1424]

Michael Jay has claimed that he was not notified until 1.45 a.m. – and not by Massoni. He told the British police:

> I was woken at my residence … at about 1.45 a.m. in the morning of Sunday 31/08/1997. I received two telephone calls in quick succession. The first was from Keith Moss my Consul General and the second was from Tim Livesey the Embassy's Press Officer.[1425] (WFJ)

There is a detailed analysis of the evidence in Part 5[a] – Massoni's account is shown to be credible, whereas Jay has lied in an apparent attempt to distance himself from early knowledge of the crash.

If Jay was not notified until one hour and 22 minutes after the crash – and also was not aware that Diana was in Paris until then[b] – then how could he have had any prior knowledge or involvement in the deaths?

British Consul-General Keith Moss said: "At around 0110hrs [1.10 a.m.] I was sound asleep at my home in Paris when I received a telephone call" notifying him about the crash.[1426] (WFJ)

Moss continued:

> I immediately telephoned the Resident Clerk / Duty Officer at the FCO. I asked him to inform Buckingham Palace, number 10 Downing Street, and others, including the FCO News Department, and the Foreign Secretary who was at that time in Manila.[1427] (WFJ)

Distancing Blair

Tony Blair has claimed that he was first told about the crash at around 2 a.m. – 3 a.m. Paris time.

He wrote in his 2010 book:

---

[a] Section on Phone Calls in the British Embassy chapter.
[b] See earlier "We Didn't Know She Was Here" chapter.

At about 2 a.m. something most peculiar happened.... I woke to find a policeman standing by the bed.... As I struggled into consciousness he told me that ... Princess Diana had been seriously injured in a car crash; and that I should immediately telephone Sir Michael Jay, the British ambassador in Paris.[1428] (WFJ)

If Moss called the FCO officer at around 1.20 a.m. – 12.20 in the UK – and the officer called Buckingham Palace first and then Downing Street, we could be looking at a call to Downing Street by 12.40 at the latest.

What was the response from 10 Downing Street when the officer phoned?

The FCO officer remains anonymous, has never been interviewed by police and wasn't heard from at the inquest.

No one from Downing Street has ever been interviewed.

Other evidence (including Moss) indicates that Downing Street may have already heard about the crash before 12.40 a.m.[a] – at least one hour 20 minutes before Blair's claimed wake-up time.

Why would Blair lie about his crash notification time?

Blair's account is strikingly similar to Michael Jay's: "I was woken at my residence ... at about 1.45 a.m."

The point again being: If Blair didn't wake up until 2 a.m. then how could he possibly have been involved in the assassination crash which occurred at 11.23 p.m.[b], 2½ hours earlier?

The evidence indicates otherwise. It indicates that Blair woke up well before 2 a.m., possibly around midnight and at least before 1 a.m.

Keith Moss declared in his 2004 statement that he told the FCO duty officer "to inform Buckingham Palace, number 10 Downing Street, and others, including the FCO News Department, and the Foreign Secretary".

At the inquest Moss stated:

My first telephone call was to the ... Foreign Office ... duty officer ... to ... ask him if, through his channels, a range of contacts could be put in the picture, namely the Royal Household ... that the Foreign Secretary should be informed ... and probably a number of other contacts as well. I cannot remember the precise detail ... oh and the news department in the Foreign Office.[1429]

Missing in Moss' inquest list is any reference to Downing Street or the prime minister – even though he specifically mentions "the Foreign Secretary" and "the news department in the Foreign Office".

Moss had his statement in front of him – and was accessing it – while he gave this inquest testimony (see footnote).[a]

---

[a] The evidence is covered in detail in Part 5, section on Role of Tony Blair in the Role of British Government chapter.

[b] UK time.

Despite Moss' statement account being very precise on this[b], Moss now says at the inquest: "I cannot be precise";[1430] "I am fairly certain";[1431] "I cannot remember the precise detail".[1432]

It is no coincidence that even though Moss had four phone call destinations written down in the statement in front of him – "Buckingham Palace, number 10 Downing Street ... the FCO News Department, and the Foreign Secretary[c]" – he "recalls" three of them at the inquest and the one he misses out is "number 10 Downing Street".

This indicates that Moss has been told at the inquest not to mention that the UK prime minister was one of the first persons notified after the Paris crash.

It is further evidence of a concerted attempt to distance Tony Blair from the 31 August 1997 events in Paris.

---

[a] Moss says: "my statement says 10 past 1" – 22 Nov 07: 9.4; "I think in my statement I said that he did" – 10.7. Moss' answer about his call to the FCO duty clerk is immediately after both of these quotes, at 10.19.

[b] See Moss' full statement excerpt on this in Part 5's Embassy chapter, the Phone Calls and Missing Records section.

[c] Foreign Secretary, Robin Cook, was in the Philippines and went public with an early press statement after Princess Diana's death.

68　Enter Brigade Criminelle

While Philippe Massoni's secretary was informing Michael Jay and the French leadership[1433] about the crash, Massoni himself had another significant agenda to fulfil.

Along with Massoni, deputy public prosecutor Maud Coujard was at the crash within 30 minutes of it occurring. She was a "junior official"[1434] – a lowest level magistrate[1435] – who was entrusted with a major responsibility regarding the crash.

Coujard stated that it was her job "to choose which police force is going to be responsible for the investigations".[1436]

Choosing the Police Force

Coujard was placed under pressure by top police officers to choose the Brigade Criminelle – the elite section of the police that deals with murders, kidnappings and terrorism.

The Brigade Criminelle was appointed and carried out the investigation into Diana's death – but that was not the decision made in the tunnel following the crash.

Witnesses have said:
- "the Brigade Criminelle took the responsibility for this inquiry"[1437] – Patrick Riou
- "Coujard ... appointed the Brigade Criminelle ... to conduct the investigation"[1438] – Philippe Massoni
- "my department was considered for taking on this investigation.... This appointment was confirmed by the Paris Public Prosecutor"[1439] (WFJ) – Martine Monteil, head of Brigade Criminelle
- "the instructing magistrate asked for the Brigade Criminelle to deal with this case"[1440] – Jean-Claude Mulès, head of the crash investigation
- "the decision [was] initially to place the investigation in the hands of the Brigade Criminelle"[1441] – Nicholas Gargan, British police liaison in Paris.

Thierry Brunet, a Central Accident Bureau police officer who attended the scene, told the British inquest:

> **What you have to know is that ... I have put been put aside from this procedure and it was the Criminal Brigade which was involved.**[1442]
>
> **I was just in charge of drawing a map of the scene of the collision and everything was given and the rest was done by the Criminal Brigade.**[1443]

In a joint report not seen by the jury Thierry Brunet and Thierry Clotteaux wrote: "The BCA[a] were told that the Brigade Criminelle would be completing the full description and investigation of the scene".[1444] (WFJ)

It is clear from Brunet and Clotteaux that the BCA was initially called to the tunnel but they were fairly quickly removed from the investigation – and replaced by the Brigade Criminelle.

There is major conflict over the context and content of a key conversation at the Alma Tunnel around 1 a.m. – a conversation involving Patrick Riou, Philippe Massoni and Maud Coujard.

Coujard told the British police in 2006:

> **I immediately attended the scene where I found Mr Massoni ... and Mr Riou.... The first question I had to resolve was which investigative unit I was going to assign to conduct the investigations. At that time, I telephoned Mr Bestard the Public Prosecutor.... I indicated to him that I was considering to appoint the Brigade Criminelle to conduct the enquiries, in association with ... the [police] department [that] specialised in road traffic accidents.... The Public Prosecutor approved my choice.**[1445] **(WFJ)**

Under cross-examination at the inquest in the following year, Coujard's account changed.

She stated: "I remember that [Riou's] preference went to the criminal police[b],"[1446] – Coujard had made no mention to Paget of any input from Riou before ringing Bestard.

Coujard told the inquest: "I did not call [Bestard] to seek his approval"[1447] and "[Bestard and I] thought that the best solution would be to appoint jointly those two divisions"[1448] – the BCA and the Brigade Criminelle.

Earlier she had told Paget that Bestard "approved my choice", whereas to the inquest she didn't seek his approval and the joint investigation idea was arrived at by both her and Bestard.

Riou's account of the discussions that occurred on the night was completely different to Coujard's. He stated:

> **I was joined at the scene ... by ... Mrs Coujard. My first objective was to convince her and [Massoni] of the requirement to instruct the Brigade Criminelle to conduct the investigations.... They were both quickly convinced that this was the only sensible choice to be made. The Public Prosecutor [Bestard] personally approved this choice.**[1449]

---

[a] Central Accident Bureau.
[b] Brigade Criminelle.

There were four people involved in these negotiations – Bestard, Coujard, Riou and Massoni. Of those, only Coujard has been subjected to cross-examination, Riou and Massoni gave their only statements nine years after the crash and Bestard has never been asked to provide an account.

Even if it was true that the Public Prosecutor's department decreed that it should be a joint investigation, that is not actually what occurred – instead the investigation was very quickly completely taken over by the Brigade Criminelle.

Brunet stated that all the BCA did was draw the map then "in the afternoon Major Farcy gave it to the Criminal Brigade" and that was it.[1450]

Why the conflict between what Coujard says compared to the other witnesses?

It was Patrick Riou, Head of the Judicial Police – not Maud Coujard or Gabriel Bestard – who was calling the shots: it was Riou who ensured the investigation would be handled by the Brigade Criminelle:

-    Riou: "My first objective was to convince [Coujard], and the Prefect of Police, of the requirement to instruct the Brigade Criminelle to conduct the investigations" [a]

-    Coujard: "I remember that [Riou's] preference went to the criminal police"

-    Mulès: "the director of the judicial police [Riou] asked me and appointed me there".[1451]

Even though Martine Monteil was the Head of the Brigade Criminelle, it was Riou who enlisted Mulès, a Brigade Criminelle commander, to investigate the crash.[b]

Reading between the lines here, deputy Public Prosecutor Maud Coujard turned up to the crash scene expecting it to be a serious car accident involving the Princess of Wales. As such, the normal course would have been for the investigation to be conducted by the BCA – there is no evidence of the Brigade Criminelle ever having investigated a previous car crash.

Coujard admitted she "had no [previous] knowledge of [a car accident] being transferred to" the Brigade Criminelle.[1452]

In 23 years Mulès – the person who headed this investigation – "had never investigated a road traffic incident".[1453]

It seems that Coujard may have been taken by surprise when Riou pushed strongly for the Brigade Criminelle to conduct the investigation. She was then forced to call her boss – Gabriel Bestard, the Public Prosecutor – in the

---

[a] This evidence should be seen in the light of the earlier evidence that Brigade Criminelle officers were on the scene as early as 12.53 a.m. – Brunet and Clotteaux.
[b] This should be viewed in the light of the way Mulès was chosen to be present at the 1st Henri Paul autopsy – see Part 3, Choice of Police Officer section of Chapter 1.

middle of the night, to inform him of what was happening. It appears that Coujard and Bestard made a decision that the best procedure would be for a joint investigation between the BCA and the Brigade Criminelle.

From that point on the decision was practically taken out of Coujard's hands – the BCA who had carried out initial investigations were given the job of completing a map of the scene, but later that day that map was passed on to the Brigade Criminelle and "the rest was done by" them.[1454]

There was no joint investigation along the lines of what Coujard was telling the inquest.

Why the Brigade?

Why was the investigation handed to the Brigade Criminelle?

The two people who have claimed to be the ones who made the decision – Riou, Coujard – have provided conflicting reasons.

Riou gave two reasons – "the technical aspect of the investigation, and the significant resources that [the Brigade] has at its disposal".[1455]

When these reasons were put to Coujard she said that she couldn't "remember if we discussed the technical aspects" and ignored the mention of resources.[1456a]

Coujard claimed that the reasons were skills, "legal safety"[b][1457] and VIP involvement.[1458] She also added that the investigation would be delicate, long, particularly difficult and thorough.[1459]

Monteil indicated that the reason was the complexity of the investigation.[1460] (WFJ)

The conclusion of the French investigation was that it was a straightforward car accident caused by a speeding, drunk driver.

Why was it so important to give control of the Alma crash inquiry to an organisation with virtually no experience in the investigation of car crashes?

Riou stated that handing control to the Brigade Criminelle was a "requirement" and "the only sensible choice to be made".[1461] Yet Riou is the same person who gave "technical aspect" as his first reason to involve the Brigade Criminelle. When one considers that the Brigade Criminelle had little or no experience in dealing with the technical aspects of a car crash – Mulès had never investigated a car crash before – it becomes evident that Riou's argument holds little or no logic.

---

[a] Massoni told the inquest that "the Prefect of Police in Paris has some 33,000 men under his authority": 20 Nov 07:55.5. It is very difficult to find information on the Brigade Criminelle on the Paris police website, but according to the French Wikipedia site the Brigade Criminelle in Paris "has about 110 men": http://fr.wikipedia.org "Brigade Criminelle".

[b] Coujard never explained what she meant by "legal safety" and was not asked to.

Coujard stated that the Brigade Criminelle was "the most appropriate" organisation to lead the investigation.[1462] She also insisted that there was nothing unusual about this decision:

- "it was not unusual"[1463]
- "and it was not unusual"[1464]
- "it is not something that is unusual".[1465]

Monteil stated: "The Brigade Criminelle was the only department capable of conducting such an investigation reliably and meticulously and in a manner that would not be able to be called into question" and she "was not surprised" that it was chosen.[1466] (WFJ)

It is common sense that Paris car crashes were investigated by the BCA and indeed this is what started to happen on the night – initially with the work of Brunet and Clotteaux who arrived 30 minutes after the crash. It was only at Riou's insistence that this normal procedure got changed and the Brigade Criminelle took control of the investigation.

Coujard's initial story was that the Brigade Criminelle "had been in charge of rather few car crashes".[1467] When challenged by Mansfield on this, she admitted: "I had no knowledge of such a matter being transferred to them".[1468] Soon after that, Coujard confirmed that she already knew that Mulès "had never investigated a road traffic incident" during his 23 years in the Brigade Criminelle.[1469]

Monteil admitted that the Brigade Criminelle "usually deals with terrorism and murders".[1470]

So why did Riou and Massoni rush to the scene arriving within half an hour of the crash?

Their early presence enabled them to ensure that the Brigade Criminelle, and specifically Jean-Claude Mulès, would be leading the official French investigation into the crash. Riou and Massoni were so keen to make this happen that even when Coujard told them it was to be a joint investigation, they ignored that decision and carried out the remainder of the investigation under the control of the Brigade Criminelle.

Brunet's inquest evidence indicates that he was not comfortable with the way this was done – he said to Nicholas Hilliard: "what you have to know is that ... I have ... been put aside from this procedure".[1471]

BCA officers Brunet and Clotteaux stated that "officers from the Brigade Criminelle were present" in the tunnel when they arrived 30 minutes after the crash.[1472] (WFJ)

This indicates that a very early decision was made to have the Brigade Criminelle conduct the investigation – without consulting the Public Prosecutor's Office.

Why?

69   Transfer to Ambulance: 6 minutes

While Riou and Massoni were pursuing the agenda to have Brigade Criminelle control this investigation, Princess Diana had been left in the Mercedes for over half an hour.

After 37 minutes Diana was finally removed at around 1 a.m.[1473]

Diana was not trapped in the car[1474] and her removal was a straightforward operation.

The ambulance driver Michel Massebeuf stated: "The firemen got the Princess out of the damaged vehicle and I came up with our stretcher, onto which she was immediately placed."[1475]

Philippe Boyer from the fire service said that it was not a difficult exercise: "We are quite used to doing it…. We always do it."[1476]

"Cardiac Arrest"

A significant medical incident occurred immediately following Diana's removal from the Mercedes.

Dr Jean-Marc Martino told the French investigation that during the removal Diana "went into cardiac arrest and I had to intubate and ventilate her and massage in order to resuscitate her."[1477]

Other evidence indicates that Martino has misrepresented the situation – Diana didn't have a cardiac arrest and it wasn't necessary to intubate her.

Dr Arnaud Derossi testified that there was a "drop of pressure … she very briefly received cardiac massage, and then pressure increased again".[1478]

Inquest expert and cardio-thoracic surgeon Tom Treasure – who studied what occurred – told the inquest that it was brought on by her position in the Mercedes:

> What she had … [is called] electromechanical dissociation – [meaning] that there was so little blood in the circulation at that point that the heart could not fill. The heart was beating – electrical activity, normal

**beat, normal rhythm – but because it was completely empty, it had
nothing to push into the circulation, so she was pulseless. Having then
some time later, having got out of this difficult position in the car, laid
flat, her own reflexes come into action, some fluid given, the heart has
volume again, the pulse returns.**[1479]
**The period during which she was pulseless was very brief, and having
got her out and settled her down, the pressure came back. So at that
point the heart was maintaining a circulation adequate to deliver a
pulse at the periphery. So the brisk bleeding was controlled.**[1480]

On balance the medical evidence – Martino, Lienhart[a], Derossi, Pavie[b],
Treasure[c] – is clear that what occurred was a loss of pulse and blood pressure,
but Diana's heart was still beating. It appears that this loss of pressure
occurred because of Diana's position in the Mercedes – Pavie, Treasure –
sitting on the floor with her back against the front seat and her legs up on the
back seat.[d]

Although not addressed at the inquest, it is common sense that this
incident may have occurred because of the length of time Diana was left in
this position – 37 minutes. Had she been removed more quickly, this loss of
pressure or pulse may not have happened at all.

The evidence from witnesses is that cardiac massage was applied.
Treasure told the inquest:

**You can keep [the heart] going just by tapping it and that is just
enough to trigger the beat. That is what they mean by a tap. Massage
is sustained pressure repeatedly 80 times per minute to generate a
pulse. He[e] showed you what he was doing. He did not do massage; he
said "tap" and you saw him do it on the screen.**[1481]

The evidence indicates that Martino responded to the loss of pulse
situation with three treatments: a) manual cardiac massage – although at the
inquest it was described as "tapping",[1482] the French investigator described it
as "knocking the thorax"[1483] and the witnesses who were there said it was
"massage";[f] b) an increase in the drip serum fluid;[1484] and c) intubation and
ventilation.

---

[a] André Lienhart, French Medical Investigator.
[b] Alain Pavie, Cardiac and Thoracic Surgeon, La Pitié Hospital.
[c] More detailed evidence is in Part 2, section on Cardiac Arrest in Chapter 9C.
[d] Because Diana was not wearing a seat belt, she basically swung 180 degrees during
the crash, finally ending up in the position described.
[e] Treasure appears to be referring to the inquest testimony of French investigator
André Lienhart, who was cross-examined earlier the same day. This word was
translated as "knocking" in the transcript: 19 Nov 07: 10.15.
[f] See below.

There is an issue around the administration of manual cardiac massage on a patient who could have internal chest injuries.

Why is there a conflict between the witnesses at the scene – they described cardiac massage – and the experts employed – they described tapping (Treasure) and knocking (Lienhart).

Did Martino conduct cardiac massage to the pulseless Diana, when he should have been just tapping her thorax?

There is also conflict over how long this massage occurred for.

The eye-witness evidence is:

Martino – "a couple of minutes"[1485]

Gourmelon – "we gave her manual heart massage … [for] a very few seconds"[1486]

Boyer – "they gave her heart massage … it was just a matter of a few seconds"[1487]

Derossi – " she very briefly received cardiac massage".[1488]

Dr Martino's Lies

On balance the evidence is that the period of massage was very short.

Why did Martino say in 1998 that "she regained a satisfactory heartbeat in a couple of minutes"?[1489]

Lienhart stated, based on Martino's evidence to him, that after Diana's removal from the car "her condition was much more serious".[1490] At the inquest Martino said: "Her heart stopped beating, so we had to ... try to resuscitate her with massaging and everything".[1491] The Paget Report, based on Martino's 1998 statements said: "She then went into cardiac arrest. Following external cardiopulmonary resuscitation the Princess of Wales' heart started beating again." [1492]

Tom Treasure says that Diana's heart would never have actually stopped beating, but she was pulseless because of the blood circulation problems caused by her post-crash posture, which she had been in for 37 minutes. This opinion was supported by the evidence of Alain Pavie, also a cardio-thoracic surgeon who told the inquest:

> **When your legs are up, all the blood goes to the heart and to the brain. When you lay the legs down, part of the volume of blood is perfusing[a] the legs.... [Diana] was easily treated and she was easily stabilised.**[1493]

Dr Martino has overstated the seriousness of the situation faced after Diana's removal. This position is supported by his lie that it took a couple of minutes for Diana's heart beat to normalise – the other witnesses clearly say it was only a few seconds.

When this is viewed in the context that Martino had at this stage told the SAMU base that Diana only had an arm injury,[a] it becomes more apparent

---

[a] Spreading to.

that Martino's agenda did not include the best interests of Princess Diana or SAMU.

Martino appears to have told the base that there was only an arm injury to enable himself to maintain control of the situation, without interference from more senior officials at the base.

Conversely, later on Martino seems to have exaggerated the "removal from the car" incident in an effort to portray Diana's situation as more serious and life-threatening than it was.

This had the effect of: 1) justifying whatever drastic measures he took from that point onwards, and 2) painting a situation where Diana's eventual death is not as shocking: events beyond Martino's control were starting to take hold, after Diana's removal from the Mercedes.

Martino added to his dramatisation of the event by saying: "After she was taken out of the car ... we had to take her out of the tunnel because my ambulance was at the other end of the tunnel."[1494] This has never been corroborated by any other witness, and frankly, it defies logic. It is a little bit like taking the mountain to Mohammed.

Why wouldn't Diana's ambulance be near the Mercedes? It should have been obvious to all concerned that her ambulance was at that stage the most critical vehicle at the scene, and they had plenty of time to organise this – Diana was 20 minutes in the car after the SAMU ambulance arrived.

Martino said:

> **It's very hard to assess the time. As I have stated on many occasions in my statements, I did not have a watch on me and it is the same debate that comes back again and again.**[1495]

An emergency doctor without a watch is an interesting scenario.[b] He complains that the debate "comes back again and again" – this is because time was of the essence during the final hours of Princess Diana's life.

It is a convenient cop-out for Martino to claim he didn't have a watch. Did none of his professional team have a watch, as well?

Why didn't Martino make it his business to provide a full record of what occurred, after he found out that the most famous woman on the planet had died, after being in his care?

Intubation and Ventilation

Immediately after the "cardiac arrest" Martino took the additional measure of intubation and ventilation.

---

[a] See earlier section on the Second Report in the Diana in the Mercedes chapter.
[b] Emergency doctors are generally expected to time their reports and actions.

Intubation and ventilation – it rolls easily off the tongue, but it is quite an extreme process. This involved placing a flexible plastic tube down Princess Diana's windpipe. For this to occur, Diana had to be sedated.

There is some conflict over why Diana was intubated and ventilated:

- Martino's March 1998 statement: "I had to intubate and ventilate her … in order to resuscitate her"[1496]

- Martino at the inquest: It was done "according to the norms" to maintain her breathing[1497]

- Derossi's September 1998 statement: "there were indications to intubate her on grounds of a suspected inter-cranial haemorrhage or cerebral oedema"[1498]

- Derossi at inquest: "protecting the lungs against any regurgitation"[1499] and "it is certainly keeping the patient breathing but also improving the quantity of oxygen going to the blood"[1500]

- Massebeuf's March 1998 statement: "she was intubated in order to help her breathe"[1501]

To summarise, there have been three main reasons given for carrying out the intubation and ventilation:

1) To resuscitate Diana from the "cardiac arrest" – Martino 1998
2) To assist with breathing – Massebeuf 1998, Derossi 2007, Martino 2008
3) Suspected head injuries – Derossi 1998

When the original 1998 statements of the three key witnesses are analysed, they reveal that Martino, Derossi and Massebeuf all gave a different reason for the intubation and ventilation. Martino said it was to resuscitate her from the "cardiac arrest" – which was not a cardiac arrest;[a] Massebeuf said it was to assist breathing and Derossi said it was because of suspected head injuries.

It is significant that Derossi said head injuries because Diana's Glasgow Coma reading in the Mercedes was 14 out of 15. As the Glasgow scale is used to determine if there are possible head injuries, the indication was that this was not a consideration at the time the intubation took place.

Dr Bruno Riou, a senior French anaesthetist, confirmed that head injury could not have been a logical reason for instigating the intubation: "In general, one considers that a Glasgow of less than 8 necessitates as such the intubation and ventilation operations".[1502]

By the time of the inquest the three witnesses' accounts have become more closely aligned, with all agreeing that the intubation was carried out to assist with Diana's breathing.

That of course raises the question of whether she was actually having any problems with breathing. Treasure, who as an expert has studied the evidence

---

[a] See earlier.

closely, believes that any possible breathing problems were not enough to justify the drastic step of intubation:

> **She was after all breathing, with a Glasgow coma scale of 14 out of 15.... There is no reason why, with simple manoeuvres, oxygen to breathe and if she is holding the chin forward and encouraging her, she could not have breathed her own way to hospital.**[1503]

Treasure's assessment is based on the evidence: Boyer (Fire Service) had said that Diana was breathing "normally"[1504] and the SAMU evidence – Martino, Massebeuf, Derossi – regarding Diana's condition in the Mercedes makes no mention of any breathing difficulties. A possible breathing issue crops up when Diana was removed from the vehicle, but this was righted within a few seconds.

Sedation

There are differing reasons given for why Princess Diana was sedated:

- Martino: "to allow the Princess to be freed quickly from the car"[1505]
- Lienhart based on Martino's evidence: "we decided to inject some drugs to reduce the agitation and for her to accept the treatment"[1506]
- Lienhart again: to move her out of the car "more quickly, and without altering her brain function"[1507]
- Derossi: "some anaesthetic drugs are given, just to put the patient into what we call a therapeutic coma so that we can put a tube in the trachea through the mouth with a tool called a laryngoscope"[1508]
- Treasure: intubation "requires the use typically of two sorts of drugs. One is to sedate and calm the patient and the other is indeed to briefly paralyse them."[1509]

The reasons from the French witnesses therefore are:

1) To reduce agitation – Lienhart
2) To accept the treatment – Lienhart
3) To move her out of the car "more quickly and without altering her brain function" – Lienhart
4) To free her "quickly from the car" – Martino
5) To induce a coma to enable the intubation – Derossi

Lienhart, who is basing his testimony on what Martino told him in 1998[a], provides three reasons for administering the sedatives to Diana: one of them matches Martino's evidence but none of them relate directly to the intubation – the sole reason given by Derossi.

---

[a] It was a major oversight that Martino was not asked about the sedation at the inquest.

There is a clear conflict between the two SAMU doctors present at the scene.

Lienhart's testimony appears to reveal desperation to come up with a valid reason that justifies the extreme measure of sedation, or anaesthetising (Treasure), or putting Diana into a coma, as Derossi put it. Martino and Lienhart suggested that she was sedated so she could be removed "more quickly" from the car, when it is clear that Diana was left in the car for 37 minutes.

Treasure makes it abundantly clear that intubation of a person in Diana's condition would have been impossible without drugs to sedate and paralyse.[a] Treasure also says that in the UK the rule is that "ambulance crews are [only] able to put a tube in if the patient is actually so obtunded[b] that they can do it without giving drugs".[1510]

Clearly the rules in France are different because doctors accompany ambulances in France, but the evidence – Treasure, and the breathing accounts of Boyer, Martino, Derossi, Massebeuf – shows that to suggest Diana was in need of intubation would be profoundly wrong.

And if Diana did not need the painful intubation, then the logical implication is that she would not have needed sedation – if the purpose of that sedation was to achieve intubation.

Martino's evidence, supported by Lienhart, that Diana was sedated inside the car raises the possibility that Martino was preparing for intubation before the loss of pulse occurred when Diana was removed.[c]

The initial reaction of the SAMU base doctor Marc Lejay, who is himself a specialist in anaesthesia and intensive care[1511], is significant. At 1.20 a.m., when Lejay finally was told about the sedation[d] he responded that the "anaesthesia was rather strong for the circumstances".[1512]

Treasure also states that anaesthetising the patient makes "them much harder to analyse in terms of their brain injury and so on".[1513]

Anaesthetising or sedating should be done as a last resort, but that is clearly not what occurred in the Alma Tunnel.

Why Sedate and Intubate?

The circumstances that confronted Martino and Derossi at the time of the sedation and intubation were:

---

[a] Treasure's evidence is covered in more detail in Part 2, Intubation and Ventilation section of Chapter 9C.

[b] Incapacitated.

[c] The SAMU form completed by Martino (reproduced below) reads: "Sedation Hypnovel 20g Fentanyl 150γ – removed from vehicle". This indicates that Diana may have been sedated prior to removal from the Mercedes.

[d] See later regarding communication blackout throughout this period.

- Diana had a Glasgow rating of 14 out of 15
- Diana was breathing normally
- Diana had been left holed up on the back floor of the Mercedes for 37 minutes
- Diana encountered a "pulseless" episode that only lasted for a few seconds just after she was moved from the Mercedes. This was directly attributable to the position she had been in for so long.

The evidence strongly indicates that the anaesthetising, intubating and ventilating of Princess Diana in the tunnel was treatment that did not match the circumstances being faced by Dr Martino and Dr Derossi.

If it wasn't medically necessary, why did Martino carry out the anaesthetisation, intubation and ventilation?

The inquest heard that Martino was a specialist in anaesthesia and resuscitation[1514], so he obviously knew what he was doing.

One reason could be that these measures are an effective method to prevent a patient from talking – both the sedation and the fact there was a tube stuck down Diana's windpipe ensured this.

If Martino had a sinister agenda regarding Diana, then his job would have been made easier if Diana was sedated and not in a position to speak. Later evidence will suggest that Martino was employed by an intelligence agency or other organisation that was intent on Diana not surviving the night.

It is difficult to come up with an innocent explanation for Dr Martino's treatment of Princess Diana: firstly leaving her in the Mercedes for 20 minutes after he arrived and secondly, for his sedation and intubation of Diana immediately after her removal from the vehicle.

These events occurred during a 37 minute communication blackout between the Alma Tunnel and the SAMU base.[a]

Why did Dr Derossi, who was the only other SAMU doctor immediately involved with Diana[b], not intervene when he witnessed Martino taking extreme measures in the treatment of Princess Diana?

Later evidence regarding the role of Dr Derossi may shed some light on this issue. There is evidence to suggest that he may have played a role of complicity in the events of the night.

Dr Lejay, the dispatcher at the base, expressed some disquiet, but he was not at the scene.

---

[a] See next chapter.

[b] Dr Fuilla from the Fire service was dealing with Rees-Jones. Dr Le Hot arrived with an ambulance a minute after Fuilla, and it would be logical to presume that he assisted Fuilla. Neither of these doctors have ever been interviewed by the police and neither appeared at the inquest. It is obvious that they should have.

HOW THEY MURDERED PRINCESS DIANA

TELEPHONES

URGENT LINE: ▓▓▓▓
NON URGENT LINE: ▓▓▓▓
TELEX: ▓▓
FAX: ▓▓▓

PARIS AMBULANCE SERVICE [SAMU]
Necker U.C.H. – Sick children
149, rue de Sèvres
75743 PARIS CEDEX 15

NECKER S.M.U.R. [Mobile Emergency and Resusitation Service]

DATE | | | | | | |

ASSISTANCE RENDERED AT THE SCENE

NONE ☐ PARAMEDIC ☐
DOCTOR ☐ AMBULANCEMAN ☐
STATE REGISTERED NURSE ☐

SURNAME | L | A | D | Y | | D | I | A | N | A | | | 1ˢᵗ Name | | | | | | | Age | | Year ☐ Month ☐ Sex ⊙ M

Address   Code | | | | | Locality   Tel

Person to be informed   Mr, Mrs, Miss   Tel   S.S. No.

Doctor attending Dr   Tel   Centre n°   Adr

ORIGIN :   DESTINATION :   HOSPITAL RECEIVING:

Alma Bridge   Pitie Salpetriere   RTA

DEPARTMENT:

Public road ☐   Public place ☐   Place of work ☐   Home ☐
School ☐   Doctor's surgery/disp. ☐   Hospital ☐   Recovery

SMUR INTERVENTION

TEAM: Doctor   MARTINO   Ambulanceman   MICHEL   Assisting   KAPFER   FADI

METHOD: Ambulance | N | 02 | Light vehicle | P | | Helicopter ☐   Plane ☐

TERRESTRIAL | 0 | 0 | [?] | 4 | | 0 | 0 | 4 | 6 | | | | | | | | | | | | | | | | | | | | 0 | 4 | 1 | 1 | | 0 | 4 | 1 | 7 |

   Leave base   Arrive at scene   Report   Leave scene   Arrive hospital   Leave hospital   Return to base

TIMETABLE :
AIR | | | | | | Outward | | | | | | | | | | Return | | | | |

   Departure   Arrival   Departure   Arrival

DECISION

TRANSPORTATION WITH DOCTOR ☐   TRANSPORT NO DOCTOR ☐ Entrusted to Ambulance ☐ [VSAB] ☐ Police ☐ Other ☐
LEFT AT SCENE ☐   Comments:

Dear colleague, please find below the medical observations on the patient that we deliver to you. Please be kind enough to forward a copy of your hospital admission report to the following address

SAMU DE PARIS   Yours
149 rue de Sèvres 75730 Paris CEDEX 15   The transportation doctor, Dr.

REASON FOR IMMEDIATE DEPLOYMENT OF SMUR   [MEDICAL OBSERVATION]
Requiring urgent medical assistance ☐ / Requiring transport with doctor ☐ / Other ☐
for:
Female of ? – rear passenger not wearing a seatbelt and projected forward. Right frontal trauma. Right arm bent to the rear – alert upon our arrival,
INITIAL CAUSE   Glasgow 14
(consecutive to.....) venous access 18g left forearm [blood pump] – sedation Hypnovel 26g Fentanyl 150γ – removed from vehicle.
Findings: upper 1/3 of right humerus fractured affecting vasculo-nervous package, fracture to right wrist. Thoracic trauma with sub-cutaneous
emphysema, wound to right leg with cutaneo-muscular damage from the iliac crest to the mid 1/3 of the right leg. Right femoral route of
administration in the presence of unmeasurable pressure. Oro- tracheal intubation No 7.5 – under dopamine 7γ [?] then 16μg/kg/00. On our arrival
in the resuscitation unit given a drop in arterial pressure.
ANTECEDENTS
- pathology linked to critical state and treatment
   - pathology not linked to critical state and treatment

Figure 20

> Reproduction of the sole document presented at the inquest that relates directly
> to Diana's medical treatment. This SAMU form is incomplete and unsigned. It
> was presumably filled in by Dr Martino. The names "Kapfer" and "Fadi"
> appear next to "Assisting" – these are two female interns who assisted Martino
> on the night: neither have ever been interviewed by any investigation and were
> not heard from at the inquest. This form also states that the ambulance stayed
> at the Pitié Hospital until 4.11 a.m. A close-up of the bottom section can be
> viewed on the next page. Inquest document INQ0004774. The full four page
> report is reproduced in The Documents book pp326 to 330.

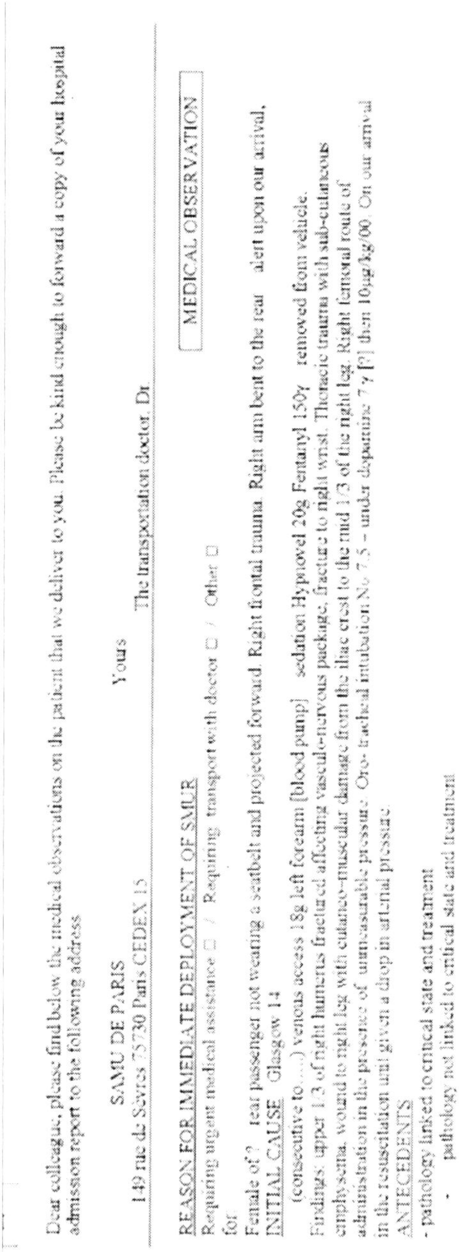

Dear colleague, please find below the medical observations on the patient that we deliver to you. Please be kind enough to forward a copy of your hospital admission report to the following address

SAMU DE PARIS
149 rue de Sèvres 75730 Paris CEDEX 15

Yours
The transportation doctor Dr

MEDICAL OBSERVATION

REASON FOR IMMEDIATE DEPLOYMENT OF SMUR
Requiring urgent medical assistance ☐ / Requiring transport with doctor ☐ / Other ☐ for
Female of ? tear passenger not wearing a seatbelt and projected forward Right frontal trauma Right arm bent to the rear alert upon our arrival,
INITIAL CAUSE Glasgow 14
(consecutive to.....) venous access 18g left forearm [blood pump] sedation Hypnovel 20g Fentanyl 150γ removed from vehicle.
Findings: upper 1/3 of right humerus fractured affecting vasculo-nervous package. fracture to right wrist. Thoracic trauma with sub-cutaneous emphysema. wound to right leg with cutaneo-muscular damage from the iliac crest to the md 1/3 of the right leg. Right femoral route of administration in the presence of unmeasurable pressure. Oro-tracheal intubation No 7.5 - under departure 7 [?] then 10µg/kg/00 On our arrival in the resuscitation unit given a drop in arterial pressure
ANTECEDENTS
- pathology linked to critical state and treatment
· pathology not linked to critical state and treatment

Figure 21

Close up of bottom section of the document on the previous page. This is the only documentary evidence shown to the jury of SAMU's 1 hour and 25 minutes spent treating Princess Diana.

HOW THEY MURDERED PRINCESS DIANA

70   Communication Blackout: 37 minutes

There is no record of any communication between Martino's team and the SAMU base for a period of 37 minutes, from 12.43 to 1.20 a.m.

The central issue is the quality of information that the SAMU base were being provided from the crash scene.

Derossi's Phantom Report

Dr Arnaud Derossi, who was a dispatcher, was at the scene primarily to dispatch.[a] This means that he was to report to SAMU base on what was happening at the scene of what SAMU must have considered – with the presence of Princess Diana – a top priority crash.

Derossi testified in 1998 that he did make a dispatch soon after he arrived at 12.50 a.m.:

> **After making these [initial] checks, I returned to the [Renault] Espace in order to make an initial telephone report to Dr Lejay, informing him essentially who and what the victims were. I do not recall if I then requested an additional intensive care team, but in any event a team arrived....[1515]**

In 1998 Dr Lienhart asked Derossi why there was no evidence of this report. Derossi answered that it could have been made on "a different radio channel".[1516] This conflicted with his initial account that it was a "telephone report".

At the inquest Derossi started off by again suggesting the radio idea: "I guess the first [report] was done over the radio".[1517] As the questions increase, he starts backing away from the story that there even was an earlier report: "Most likely, but I cannot confirm."[1518]

In 1998 Derossi introduced the possibility that he could have ordered "an additional intensive care team". There was only ever one additional SAMU team and it arrived with Dr Vivien at 12.50 a.m.,[1519] very close to the time

---

[a] Dr Derossi's role is discussed later.

Derossi himself had arrived. It is obvious that Derossi could not have been the person who ordered it.[a]

There is no documentary evidence of this early report Derossi claimed to have made and Lejay denies that it occurred:

> **I have no information on that, neither on the transcript of the tapes nor from my recollection.**[1520]

The first report from Derossi listed on Lejay's timeline was at 1.20 a.m.[1521]

This extra report did not actually occur and Derossi's 1998 account of it is fictional.

Why did Derossi make this up?

And why did Derossi, who after all was a dispatcher, not make a dispatch until he had been at the scene for 30 minutes?

Communication Blackout

The SAMU base was receiving miniscule information.

Their only injury report received before 1.20 a.m. was from Martino at 12.43 a.m., where he told them that Diana had an injured arm.

No doubt when any senior officials at the base heard that report there would have been a collective sigh of relief, as one of the most high profile patients they had ever dealt with was basically okay.

The result of the conveyance of that early information would have been to give Martino effective control of the scene, without the threat of the base breathing down his neck seeking updates or asking questions about what was happening or why it was all taking so long.

This, along with the very slow trip to the tunnel,[b] enabled Martino to leave Diana in the "medically abnormal" post-crash position[1522] for what was effectively 37 minutes since the crash – without having to answer to anyone. No doubt Martino would have known that a delayed removal of Diana from the Mercedes could have led to a loss of pulse, as happened.

It was this loss of pulse that was then used by Martino to introduce the critical anaesthetisation, intubation and ventilation of Diana. By approximately 1.06 a.m., when Diana was transferred into the ambulance, she was now unable to speak and was in a state of induced coma.

All of this was able to occur without the SAMU base knowing anything about it because of two critical factors:

1)   Martino's 12.43 a.m. call to base saying that the extent of Diana's injuries was damage to her right arm

---

[a] Earlier evidence showed that it was ordered by Dr Martino at 12.40 a.m.

[b] See earlier Diana in the Mercedes chapter.

2)   Derossi's 30 minute silence from the Alma Tunnel – not calling the SAMU base even though he was well aware that Diana's condition was quite different to what Martino had conveyed at 12.43 a.m.

Martino did not act alone in his questionable treatment of Princess Diana, but was assisted by Derossi. Derossi is recorded as leaving the base at 12.42 a.m. and it is very likely that he would have been made aware of the contents of Martino's 12.43 call during the eight minutes he was in transit.

Inquest lawyer Jonathon Hough asked Dr Derossi what his knowledge of injuries would have been after he had been in the tunnel for 5 minutes – this would have been at 12.55 a.m. Derossi replied:

> **Very limited knowledge. Only the fact that it was a very severe accident with severely injured patients, but it would have been the only information.**[1523]

This is an incredible remark.

One would expect that after Derossi's arrival he would have consulted with Martino who had by that stage been there for 10 minutes. By 12.50 a.m. Gourmelon and Boyer had already been at the scene for 18 minutes, and they also had the input from Dr Mailliez who had arrived two minutes after the crash.

Derossi is suggesting that by 12.55 a.m. – 32 minutes after the crash – the sum total of knowledge would have been "a very severe accident with severely injured patients" – in other words, no different than what a non-medical passer-by would have been able to determine immediately after the crash.

71 Five in the Ambulance

There were five people in the ambulance – not counting Princess Diana. The driver was Michel Massebeuf.

The role of the four others is not so clear.

The head of the ambulance team, Dr Jean-Marc Martino, qualified as a doctor in September 1997[1524] – after the crash which occurred on 31 August 1997.

Dr Arnaud Derossi was operating the phones at the base and transferred himself to the ambulance soon after its arrival in the Alma Tunnel. He denied being in the ambulance during the journey to the hospital – other evidence revealed later, indicates he was.

Both doctors, Martino and Derossi, have lied repeatedly about the events on the night of the death of Princess Diana.

Deceiving the Jury

On 12 May 2005 Dr Martino was interviewed in Paris by Scotland Yard. He was asked who was in his ambulance team. He replied:

The driver, Michel Massebeuf, a non-resident medical student, Barbara Kapfer [and] a young female student undergoing training, whose name I have forgotten.[1525] (WFJ)

At the inquest Martino changed this to just the one intern – "Myself and the student who was with me".[1526]

Lienhart was asked "who was the someone else", but he failed to answer that.[1527]

Page 1 of the ambulance report[a] records two names of people "assisting": "Kapfer" and "Fadi".

This supports Martino's Paget account, but also reveals that he lied under oath at the inquest.

---

[a] Reproduced earlier in Transfer to Ambulance chapter.

The inquest jury were deceived into thinking there were just three people travelling in the ambulance to the hospital – Massebeuf, Martino and an unnamed intern.

The reality is that there were not three, but five – Massebeuf, Martino, Kapfer, Fadi and also, it will be shown later, Derossi.

Kapfer and Fadi have never been interviewed by any investigation and were not heard from at the inquest.

These two interns were in the closest proximity to Diana, and yet their identities were withheld from the inquest jury.

Why?

And why was the jury deceived into thinking there were just three people, when there were actually five?

72 Ambulance in the Tunnel: 1 hour 1 minute

Dr Jean-Marc Martino's SAMU ambulance arrived at 12.40 a.m. – 17 minutes after the crash – and remained in the Alma Tunnel for 61 minutes, until 1.41. It departed from the tunnel one hour 18 minutes after the crash.

Diana was removed from the Mercedes at 1.00 a.m. and transferred into the ambulance at 1.06.

Arnaud Derossi posted his first report to the base at 1.20, after Diana had been in the ambulance for 14 minutes.

This was the third report to the SAMU base.

Third Report: 1.20 a.m.

This phoned report to Dr Lejay at the base – made 57 minutes after the crash and 40 minutes after SAMU arrived at the scene – was the first knowledge at the SAMU base that Diana had more than just an injured arm.

Derossi told Lejay that:[a][b]
-   Diana had been intubated and ventilated[1528]
-   Diana had "obvious cranial trauma"[1529]
-   Diana was "showing agitation and confusion"[1530]
-   Diana should be referred to the neuro-surgical unit at the Pitié Salpêtrière Hospital[1531]
-   Diana had been given Hypnovel and Fentanyl to anaesthetise her[1532]
-   There was "at first appearance, nothing to report for the thorax" [1533][c]
-   There were no lesions in the pelvic level[1534]
-   Diana appeared to have a broken arm[1535]
-   Diana's Glasgow coma rating was now 12[1536]

---

[a] This list is shown in the order in which the information was given.
[b] The jury were not provided with the actual transcript of this call and it also has never been made public.
[c] Derossi actually said this twice within this one conversation – see later.

- Diana was very agitated and confused[1537a]
- Diana's blood pressure was 70[1538]
- Diana's pulse rate was 100[1539]
- Diana was being reinflated using a G suit[1540]
- Diana was being given catecholamines[1541]
- They needed Lejay to find a hospital place quickly[1542]
- The ambulance would be ready to go in a few minutes.[1543]

Head Injury and Thoracic Trauma

There are two major diagnostic issues that emerge from this report, made approximately 14 minutes after Diana had been transferred into the ambulance.[b]

Firstly, there is a clear emphasis on head (cranial) trauma. During this conversation Derossi twice emphasised that Diana was agitated and confused. I am not a medical expert, but that evidence appears to conflict with the fact that Diana had by this stage been sedated with Fentanyl[c] and Hypnovel.

Derossi links the agitation and confusion to the head injury – he mentions it immediately after "obvious cranial trauma". He then uses this information to state that Diana should be sent to the "neuro-surgical unit at the Pitié Salpêtrière Hospital".[d]

At the inquest, when Derossi is confronted with this, he replies:

Actually, the recommendation was to get to La Pitié Salpêtrière as they have got a trauma centre, with all the appropriate facilities, plus the neurosurgery.[1544]

That is what he said at the inquest, but that is not what he told Lejay at the scene. The lawyer Jonathon Hough, who is getting his information directly from the transcript, says that Derossi specifically stated the "neuro-surgical unit".

Dr Martino's documented report did not include mention of head or cranial injuries.

Secondly, Derossi specifically states: "at first appearance, nothing to report for the thorax". Mansfield said that Derossi made this remark twice in the conversation.

This is a significant remark from several perspectives:

---

[a] Stated twice in the report – see above.

[b] The ambulance remained stationary throughout.

[c] Fentanyl has "a potency approximately 80 times that of morphine": Wikipedia under "Fentanyl". Lejay's immediate reaction was that the sedation was too strong – see earlier Transfer to Ambulance chapter.

[d] This critical issue of hospital choice is dealt with later.

1) One would expect the reporting doctor to be focusing on the areas that are problems, not the areas where there aren't problems.

2) Martino said in 1998 that when he first examined Diana, after undressing her in the ambulance, he saw that she had a "right-hand side thoracic trauma".[1545]

3) Martino's documented report described his "findings" after Diana was "removed from [the] vehicle": "thoracic trauma".

Dr Martino's inquest reaction, when confronted with the major conflict over the thorax evidence, is significant. He states that Derossi gave this report "whilst she was still in the car",[1546] even though he had just agreed that it was made 20 minutes after Diana's removal from the Mercedes.[1547]

When Martino is told that can't be true, then he comes up with another lie: "Dr Derossi reiterated my initial report because he didn't see what happened after she was taken out of the car and resuscitated and put in the ambulance."[1548]

There are two problems with this comment: a) Martino's "initial report" was that Diana only had an injured arm, so Derossi couldn't possibly have been reiterating that; and b) Suggesting that Derossi, who was at the scene to report back to base, "didn't see what happened after she was taken out of the car and resuscitated and put in the ambulance" is an absolutely ridiculous remark, which is obviously untrue.

If this statement by Martino were true it means that Dr Derossi would be an incompetent, lying fool – giving a detailed report to base on the condition of a patient, who happens to be a British Princess, about which he knows virtually nothing.

Inquest lawyer Jonathon Hough then moves on to the next topic and Martino is not challenged any further on this by any of the other lawyers.

This is desperation from Martino, under oath, to "prove" that Derossi's statement that there was no thorax injury was logical in the circumstances.

In other words, defending the indefensible.

Why did Derossi, at 1.20 a.m., talk up a head injury and specifically state that there was "nothing to report for the thorax"?

By this stage – around 14 minutes after Diana had been transferred to the ambulance – an examination had been carried out and Martino was aware of thoracic trauma. The evidence is clear that Derossi was reporting to base after that examination and must have had full knowledge of it.

Derossi was lying on both counts: the importance of a head injury and the non-existence of a thorax injury.

Why would Derossi lie to the base about these critical issues?

Up to this point all the knowledge the SAMU base had received, was that Diana had an injured arm. At the base, this 1.20 a.m. phone call was a sudden huge explosion of information regarding Diana's condition.

Derossi starts the conversation with three shocking bombshells of new information: Diana's been intubated and ventilated; she has <u>obvious</u> cranial trauma; she is agitated and confused.

Next Derossi ventures outside his area of responsibility and tells the base not just which hospital Diana should go to, but also which department.[a]

The situation had now drastically changed from 12.43 a.m. when Martino sent a report to base that completely understated the situation regarding Diana.

Now, when Derossi calls 37 minutes later, Diana is completely ensconced in the ambulance, and even though the ambulance is not going anywhere,[b] there is now nothing that the SAMU base would be able to do to intervene – at this stage Martino and Derossi have total control of any treatment of Diana.

Derossi feeds the base information that would have had the effect of creating a panic, even asking Lejay towards the end of the call, to find a hospital place quickly.

The information Derossi gave the base would have the following effects:

1) It would account for why Diana was in such a bad condition, in fact nearly dead, when she finally arrived at the hospital 46 minutes later.[c]

2) It would force the base to quickly choose and organise the hospital, taking Derossi's recommendation on board, because there was really no time to consider alternatives anyway.[d]

3) It would ensure that any instructions given by the base to the receiving hospital would not include having a thoracic specialist present on Diana's arrival.[e]

After 1.20 a.m., 57 minutes following the crash, the understanding at the SAMU base was false on two critical counts: a) They believed Diana had a major head injury; and b) They believed that Diana had no thorax injury.

By the time Princess Diana was in the ambulance she was under the care of people who were probably being paid by an outside employer – an intelligence agency – to ensure that she would not survive to see in the next day.

---

[a] The process of hospital choice is dealt with later.

[b] The ambulance doesn't leave the crash scene until 1.41 a.m., 21 minutes after this phone call.

[c] At 2.06 a.m.

[d] The choice of hospital and the reason why it was Derossi that chose it is discussed later.

[e] The effect of this is discussed later.

Thoracic Lies

Knowledge of the thoracic trauma was restricted to those in the ambulance.

The base doctor Marc Lejay testified that he was never told about the thoracic trauma.[1549] He was asked: "How [was it] that you were never told about one of the most important findings?" Lejay replied:

> **I have no explanation for that. The only thing I can tell you is that in the assessment I received at 1.19 [a.m.], the thorax was normal.**[1550]

When Dr Martino was presented with this deception of the base, he responded:

> **Dr Derossi had arrived at the scene and he was dealing with the communications with the hospital regulators.**[1551]

After Dr Derossi is confronted with it, he states:

> **I guess this finding by Dr Martino was done within the ambulance, whereas the first report – this report given to the medical dispatching was done maybe just before or at the moment she was taken inside the ambulance.**[1552a]

The courtroom discourse continues,[1553] and Michael Mansfield outlines the position, but Derossi completely fails to give any explanation for why he twice told the SAMU base that Diana did not have a thoracic trauma – when Martino had actually found just the opposite.

When Dr Lienhart is told about the problem, he states:

> **At that time there was no evidence of any thorax trauma, at that time, at that very time.**[1554]

If Derossi had the best interests of the Princess in his considerations, then even if he had been unaware of thoracic trauma at 1.20 a.m., when he did become aware he would have immediately notified the base. That never happened. Derossi spoke again with the base at 1.29 a.m. – see later – but failed again to mention the thoracic trauma.

To an independent observer, just the fact that Derossi specifically stated twice that Diana <u>didn't have</u> thoracic trauma, would sound suspicious.

Why would he need to mention the thorax area twice if no trauma had been detected there?

---

[a] This is a possible reason why Martino falsely stated in 1998 that Diana "was moved to the SAMU ambulance at 1.18 a.m.": Paget Report, p514 (WFJ). This would have helped preclude Derossi from having knowledge of the thoracic trauma at the time he made the 1.20 a.m. phone call. The timing of the transfer from Mercedes to ambulance is addressed in Part 2, Transfer into the Ambulance section of Chapter 9C.

Low Blood Pressure

During the 1.20 a.m. ambulance-base phone call Derossi told Lejay that Diana "has blood pressure of 70, with a pulse rate of 100". Lejay asked if the pressure was low "due to the anaesthesia" and asked what type it was. When told it was "Hypnovel and Fentanyl" Lejay then suggests that is "a bit violent". He adds that "if necessary, catecholamines would be appropriate" to increase Diana's blood pressure.[1555]

In short, Lejay, who is an anaesthesia specialist,[1556] told Derossi that the sedation they had given Diana[a] was too strong and could have caused the blood pressure drop. So he tells them to use catecholamines to increase the blood pressure, if necessary.

Lejay's advice to increase the blood pressure was predicated on the fact he had not been told about the thoracic trauma.

Dr Martino revealed in 1998 that he administered dopamine – a catecholamine – even though he was aware of the thoracic trauma and internal bleeding. Dr Lienhart, the investigator, stated:

> Martino "could see that there were signs of a thorax wound" and "measured the rate of haemoglobin[b] within the blood [which] showed that there was bleeding somewhere". He used "dopamine ... [and] her arterial pressure got back to between 8 and 11 centimetres of mercury"[c] and Martino then "allowed the transfer to the hospital".[1557]

There is no documentary or verbal evidence of what quantities of catecholamines were being administered.

Inquest expert Tom Treasure pointed out to the inquest the effect of that treatment on the patient:

> If you give a [patient] ... dopamine, it narrows the blood vessels.... You tighten up the circulation, you don't reduce bleeding, you actually tend to increase it. So pushing up the pressure would tend to push blood out of the circulation through any torn blood vessels....
> Struggling to get a perfect pulse and blood pressure may be wrong; you want one that is just good enough. A blood pressure that is high enough to sustain life, then stop the bleeding[d] and now get the pressure up makes more sense than pushing the blood pressure up when you still have a hole for the blood to come out of....
> The vasoconstrictors [catecholamines] being counterproductive, they are flogging the heart, they are tightening the circulation. But the real

---

[a] Which was administered to allow for the unnecessary intubation – see earlier.
[b] Red protein that transports oxygen in the blood.
[c] Equivalent of 80 to 110.
[d] An operation to stop the bleeding could only be carried out in a hospital.

problem is the hole in the blood vessel and, if anything, you are making other things worse.[1558]

After the transfer to the ambulance and subsequent examination there were two major issues: 1) Diana's blood pressure was low; and 2) Martino discovered a thoracic trauma.

One of these issues was passed on by Derossi to the SAMU base – the low blood pressure – but the other – the thoracic trauma – was not passed on.

Treasure's evidence reveals that in the circumstances – thoracic trauma and low blood pressure – a doctor would not aim for perfect blood pressure, but just "high enough to sustain life, then stop the bleeding". When Treasure says "stop the bleeding" he means getting to a hospital, because that was the only place where this bleeding was going to be stopped – it required an operation using the facilities that only a hospital could provide.

Treasure is saying that the low blood pressure shouldn't be raised when there was an awareness of thoracic trauma and internal bleeding (Lienhart).

Why?

Because the dopamine, which was administered by Martino, had the direct effect of constricting the blood vessels – that is how it increases the blood pressure. This constriction of the vessels, as Treasure points out, is counter-productive when there is a torn blood vessel, because it increases the pressure on the tear, and therefore more blood is lost through the tear.

Because Derossi only passed on half the story to the base, the advice that Lejay gave to increase the blood pressure was based on an incomplete picture. An analysis of what was happening, in the context of Treasure's evidence, reveals that Lejay would not have suggested that, if he had been told there was thoracic trauma.

It becomes evident that:

-      the combination of thoracic trauma and low blood pressure was an emergency that could only be dealt with at a hospital

-      the infusion of adrenalin would only be productive if Diana were rushed to hospital, otherwise it would become counter-productive.

Princess Diana was not rushed to hospital – she arrived at 2.06 a.m., exactly one hour after she had been transferred to the ambulance. Martino's administering of the dopamine would have been okay if he had left for the hospital, but he didn't leave until 35 minutes after Diana had entered the ambulance, at 1.41 a.m.

Given that they were not in a rush to get to hospital, the dopamine treatment then becomes "counter-productive" – or another word would be "life-threatening", when one considers that Martino was aware that Diana had a thoracic trauma.

Sinister Actions

Why did Derossi not tell the base about the thoracic trauma?

If one presumes that Derossi and Martino were interested in the welfare of Princess Diana then, there is no logical reason for that omission.

If one considers that Derossi and Martino had plans that were not in Diana's interests and were working for an outside employer, an intelligence agency, then yes, there are at least two valid reasons:

1)   Knowledge of a thoracic trauma would have given Lejay the opportunity to alert the hospital to have a thoracic surgeon present on Diana's arrival

2)   If the base had known there was both thoracic trauma and a loss of blood pressure and had detected that the ambulance was in no hurry to get Diana to a hospital, they may have panicked and instructed another doctor to take over, or even possibly sent out a helicopter which could have rushed Diana to the hospital.

Instead what happened was that Derossi told the SAMU base twice that there was no thoracic trauma.

This had the effect of:

1)   Diana reaching hospital with no thoracic surgeon present[a]

2)   Dr Lejay suggesting to Derossi that they use catecholamines (dopamine) to increase the blood pressure.

Lejay asked if the ambulance was "ready to roll" at 1.20 a.m.[1559] even though he had no knowledge of the thoracic trauma. Had he known of that, it is obvious – when one considers the medical evidence – that the base would have been demanding an immediate departure for hospital.

SAMU Base Call: 1.29 a.m.

Dr Lejay called the ambulance at 1.29 a.m. Although the ambulance didn't arrive at the hospital for another 37 minutes, this short call was the final communication between the ambulance and the SAMU base.

Lejay asked Derossi "whether the blood pressure had been restored". Derossi's answer was: "Oui, actuellement 70 de systolique, en cours de remplissage."[1560]

At the inquest he was asked to translate this. He said: "the blood pressure status is better and ... she is receiving fluid".[1561]

The blood pressure is the same as what it had been 9 minutes earlier – 70 – yet Derossi has lied under oath by deceiving the inquest – telling the jury the blood pressure was "better".

The true translation is: "Yes, currently the blood pressure is 70 and she is receiving fluid".

---

[a] See later Alive in the Hospital chapter.

At 1.20 a.m. Lejay had asked Derossi if the ambulance was "ready to roll". This showed that even though Lejay knew that the blood pressure was low, he was still expecting the ambulance to be leaving the scene.

At that point Derossi had replied that they would leave "in a few minutes".[1562]

Now at 1.29 a.m. Lejay asks if they are "en route yet", even before asking about Diana's condition.[1563] It is clear that Lejay was expecting the ambulance to leave without waiting for Diana to be fully stabilised.

This time Derossi replied that they would leave "in two minutes"[1564] despite his admission that the blood pressure hadn't increased.

The ambulance actually didn't leave for another 12 minutes.[a]

---

[a] During this call Lejay also "told the ambulance that the Pitié-Salpêtrière were ready to take the Princess of Wales": 11 Dec 07: 19.15.

73   Inordinate Delays

Princess Diana was transferred into the ambulance at around 1.06 a.m., but that ambulance did not leave the Alma Tunnel until 1.41 – 35 minutes later. Why the delay?

A Stable Patient

Once Diana was in the ambulance, how long did it take to stabilise her? Dr Martino argued:

> **After examining her ... giving her the right medicine, resuscitating her, it probably took up to 30 minutes.**[1565]

However, a clear difficulty emerges. When Mansfield asked what Martino's "definition of stability" was, Martino replied:

> **Blood pressure between 60 and – a minimum of 70 to 80 units of arterial blood pressure and a heartbeat between 60 and 100.**[1566]

A quick look back by the reader to Derossi's 1.20 a.m. report to the base reveals that both those criteria had already been met at that stage – Diana had blood pressure of 70 and a heartbeat of 100.[a] At 1.29 a.m. Diana's blood pressure was still reported to be 70.

So Diana was resuscitated and stabilised – using Martino's own criteria – by 1.20 a.m. at the latest. This meant that she was in a situation of being ready to leave for the hospital and that is supported by the expectation of the base when Lejay asked if they were "ready to roll" at 1.20 a.m.

Mansfield went on to quote from Martino's 1998 statement:

---

[a] A direct effect of dopamine is to increase the heart rate – that could account for Diana's rate being at the upper end of Martino's window. Increased heart rate is also an uncommon side effect of Fentanyl, one of the sedatives Diana had been given. Sources: South African Electronic Package Inserts: http://home.intekom.com re Dopamine; www.virtualmedicalcentre.com re Fentanyl.

> **I placed her in my ambulance in order to carry out a closer examination and to continue resuscitation during the journey to the designated hospital.**[1567]

In 1998 Dr Martino told Dr Lienhart that he would continue the resuscitation during the ambulance journey to the hospital. At the inquest he said that Diana had to be completely resuscitated and stabilised before departing:

> **Once all the parameters are restored and maintained for three to five minutes and everything seems to be stable, then I can give the order to move.**[1568]

When Mansfield requests an explanation of this major conflict in Martino's evidence, the witness effectively refuses to answer and he is not made to do so by the Coroner. Martino obfuscated: "I missed the gist of the question";[1569] "What I cannot understand is what am I not supposed to be doing."[1570]

At that stage Mansfield gave up on his cross-examination of Martino.[a]

The problem for Dr Jean-Marc Martino – and it is the same for Claude Roulet and others – is that when a witness is telling lies and is covering up what really happened, they can get away with it only if their various accounts are not scrutinised. The death of Princess Diana was too important an event for these actions not to eventually be subjected to close scrutiny.

This scrutiny, as conducted at the inquest and in this book, reveals that Martino has lied under oath – and in his various statements he has tied himself up in knots.

Yet it was during Martino's period of care – 12.40 to 2.06 a.m. – that Princess Diana's condition underwent an incredible deterioration: from a Glasgow rating of 14 and blood pressure of 110[1571b] to being close to death on arrival at the hospital.[c]

It becomes evident that the 35 minutes of additional delay in the tunnel – during which Diana was stable from at least 1.20 a.m.[d] – is further evidence that Martino was not operating in the best interests of his patient, Princess Diana.

---

[a] It was conducted by video-link with Martino in Germany.
[b] 11 centimetres of mercury.
[c] See later Death By Ambulance chapter.
[d] 21 minutes before the departure of the ambulance.

74 Choosing the Wrong Hospital

From very early, it was known that the surviving occupants of the Mercedes would require a hospital.

La Pitié Salpêtrière

The hospital chosen for the treatment of Diana, Princess of Wales was La Pitié Salpêtrière, 5.7 km from the crash scene.

During the process of choosing that hospital there were three significant deviations from the norm:

1)   In response to Mansfield's questioning, Dr Derossi stated: "What we usually do in such a situation is to prepare a destination [hospital]. Even so, we know it cannot be confirmed before we get a full assessment."[1572]

Derossi is saying that an initial preparatory call is made in a very serious crash like this, and when the injured are fully assessed inside the ambulance, then the hospital destination is confirmed.

In this case, that initial preparatory call never occurred.

2)   It is common sense that the decision regarding hospital choice would be made by the dispatcher at the base, Dr Lejay.

What happened in this case was that Derossi, who was at the scene, decided not only that Diana should be sent to La Pitié, but he also told Lejay which department to send her to – the "neuro-surgical unit".[1573]

Lejay suggests that it wasn't all Derossi's idea: "I had already made my opinion at that time [12.43 a.m.]"[1574] and "I had already planned to send her there".[1575] He even states that Derossi did "not directly" ask him to send her to La Pitié.[1576]

The fact is that the phone transcript is hard evidence showing that the idea of sending Diana to La Pitié did come from Derossi.[a]

3)   When Dr Derossi finally gave his full assessment at 1.20 a.m., he lied about Diana's injuries: He stated that Diana had "obvious cranial trauma" and that there was "nothing to report for the thorax".

---

[a] See earlier Ambulance in the Tunnel chapter.

HOW THEY MURDERED PRINCESS DIANA

Derossi himself stated: The hospital is given the injury assessment from the scene to "make sure that all the [necessary] surgical teams are available and ready to receive the patient".[1577] If the hospital is told "cranial and not thoracic", then they won't be going out of their way to ensure there is a thoracic surgeon on hand at the time of arrival.[a]

Why was La Pitié Salpêtrière the hospital chosen on the night?

Various reasons were put forward at the inquest:

- "we have all the specialties within the hospital"[1578] – Derossi
- "the quality of this hospital in terms of welcoming injured people"[1579] – Lejay
- it "is validated by the US Presidency"[1580] – Lejay
- it "is able to take in care the various traumas, skull traumas, from the Paris citizens"[1581] – Lejay
- "on duty was the neurosurgical department"[1582] – Lejay
- "on duty that night was one of my masters, Professor Riou"[1583] – Lejay
- Riou is "one of the best intensive care specialists"[1584] – Lejay
- "it was the nearest hospital which was adapted for these multiple traumas"[1585] – Lienhart
- it is "the most important hospital in the Paris area for people suffering from multiple traumas"[1586] – Riou
- "if a foreign head of state has a problem in Paris, that is where he is sent"[1587] – Riou

The main reason given was that La Pitié dealt with multiple trauma victims.

Yet on the night, when Diana was finally delivered to the hospital at 2.06 a.m. – 1 hour and 43 minutes after the crash – the thoracic trauma surgeon that she needed to see was not present.[b]

Dr Lejay stated that La Pitié "is validated by the US Presidency" – God only knows what he meant by that, and he was never asked to explain it. There is no mention of the US President on the La Pitié website and there is no mention of La Pitié on the White House website.

Lienhart said that "it was the nearest hospital which was adapted for these multiple traumas" – this statement is not true, as the Val de Grâce was closer (see below).

Riou suggested: "If a foreign head of state has a problem in Paris, that is where he is sent – he is sent to the Pitié Salpêtrière."

That is a bald-faced lie. When I wrote the book *Cover-up of a Royal Murder* in 2007, I extensively researched news stories back to the early 1980s

---

[a] Even if Lejay had not passed on the "not thoracic" information – the full call transcript has never been revealed – he clearly told the hospital that they were increasing Diana's blood pressure: 29 Nov 07: 20.23. This would have possibly indicated to the hospital that there was no thoracic problem.

[b] See later Alive in the Hospital chapter.

and found that there were no cases of a foreign head of state being sent to La Pitié – in all cases they are delivered to the Val de Grâce.[ab]

Val de Grâce

The Val de Grâce Hospital was put forward as an alternative destination at the inquest. It is situated 4.6 km from the crash scene.

Only two witnesses – Dr Lejay and Dr Riou[c] – were asked about the Val de Grâce. Dr Derossi, in particular, should have been – since he was the one who made the La Pitié decision – but he wasn't.

Between them, Lejay and Riou came up with several reasons why the Val de Grâce would have been a bad choice for Princess Diana:
- "it does not take care of as many people suffering from multiple traumas"[1588] – Riou
- "the likelihood of someone suffering from multiple traumas surviving is higher if he is sent to the Pitié Salpêtrière"[1589] – Riou
- "it is a hospital that you need to warn before" going there[1590] – Lejay
- "it is quicker for somebody from the public to reach La Pitié Salpêtrière"[1591] – Lejay
- it "is a military hospital" – Lejay[1592] and Riou[1593]

There are two difficulties with Lejay's statement that "it is quicker for somebody from the public to reach La Pitié Salpêtrière at night than reaching Val de Grâce":[1594] 1) Diana wasn't "somebody from the public" – she was a British Princess; and 2) the Val de Grâce was closer to the crash scene by about 1.1 km.

Lejay said the Val de Grâce "is not equipped to take patients with multiple injuries" in his Paget statement,[1595] (WFJ) but failed to mention that in his reasons at the inquest.

Riou states that a person with multiple traumas has less chance of surviving if sent to Val de Grâce, yet he admits that Val de Grâce "is the hospital that takes care of the President ... or the Prime Minister".[1596]

Does this mean that if the French President was involved in a crash and ended up with multiple injuries, that he (or she) would have less chance of surviving than an ordinary member of the public in a similar situation?

---

[a] See below.

[b] There has only ever been one documented case of a French leader being treated at La Pitié: in April 2008 (five months after Riou testified at the inquest) ex-President Jacques Chirac was admitted for the installation of a pacemaker. The French leadership are generally sent to Val De Grâce, where Chirac has received medical treatment on four occasions – see table below.

[c] The receiving doctor at La Pitié.

HOW THEY MURDERED PRINCESS DIANA

If a military hospital is particularly set up to handle VIPs – which the Val de Grâce is (see below) – then it would need to be ready 24/7 for any range of possible emergencies, including multiple trauma.

In May 1993, when ex-French Prime Minister Bérégovoy was shot in the head in Nevers, he was rushed by air to the Val de Grâce Hospital, even though it was a journey of around 200 km. When Paris was struck by five terrorist bombs in September 1986, the victims were rushed to the Val de Grâce. When an envoy was shot at the German embassy in Paris in January 1988, he was rushed to the Val de Grâce.

A study of the records relating to VIP visits to Paris hospitals reveals that there is one main hospital in Paris that caters for VIPs – and it is the Val de Grâce.

VIP Visits to the Val de Grâce Hospital		
Date	**Country**	**Position or Person**
Jan 1984	Vietnam	Ex-Prime Minister Tran Van Huu
May 1993	France	Ex-Prime Minister Bérégovoy
Nov 1995	France	Ex-President Mitterrand
Jul 1997	Vietnam	Ex-Emperor Bao Dai
Dec 1997	France	Justice Minister
Sep 1998	France	Interior Minister Chevènement
June 1999	Guinea Bissau	President Vieira
Nov 1999	Egypt	President Mubarak
Feb 2001	Egypt	President Mubarak
Oct 2003	Mauritania	Ex- President Daddah
Oct 2004	Palestine	Leader Yasser Arafat
Apr 2005	France	President Jacques Chirac
May 2005	France	Prime Minister Raffarin
Sep 2005	France	President Jacques Chirac
Nov 2005	Algeria	President Bouteflika
Apr 2006	Algeria	President Bouteflika
May 2006	France	President Jacques Chirac
Feb 2007	Chad	Prime Minister Pascal Yoadimnudji
Apr 2007	France	Ex-Prime Minister Raymond Barre
Aug 2007	France	Ex-Prime Minister Pierre Messmer
Oct 2007	France	President Nicolas Sarkozy
Jun 2008	Zambia	President Levy Mwanawasa
Dec 2008	France	Ex-President Jacques Chirac

The Val de Grâce did not rate a mention in the Coroner's 2½ days of Summing Up.

If Baker was serious about establishing which was the most suitable hospital to send Diana to, why didn't he arrange for a statement to be taken from a doctor at the Val de Grâce?

Hospital Comparison		
Item	La Pitié Salpêtrière	Val de Grâce
Distance from Scene	5.7 km	4.6 km
Treats VIPs	Not normally[a]	Yes
Multiple Trauma	Yes	Yes

Making the Choice

Why did Arnaud Derossi choose to send Princess Diana to La Pitié Salpêtrière?

The decision was left until quite late, 1.20 a.m. By that time Martino had established precisely what Diana's injuries were, and particularly that she had a thoracic trauma with low blood pressure – a life-threatening condition unless operated on quickly.

Drs Derossi and Martino may have had, or been provided with, information about which hospitals had specialists on duty that night.

La Pitié did not have a thoracic specialist on duty that night.

Derossi and Martino – working on behalf of an intelligence agency, and aware of Diana's condition and injuries – may have chosen La Pitié precisely because they knew there was no thoracic surgeon on duty at the time.

Derossi twice told Lejay at 1.20 a.m. that there was no thoracic trauma. That would have ensured that la Pitié would not have taken steps to organise a thoracic specialist to be there for Diana's arrival. If Diana had been sent to a hospital with a thoracic specialist on duty, then that would not have been an issue.

The suggestion by *The People* early on 31 August 1997 that Diana was "believed to be in the French VIP Val de Grâce hospital in central Paris"[1597] (WFJ) indicates that: 1) the Val de Grâce is the "French VIP" hospital, and 2) *The People* presumed – or had been told – that the Val de Grâce was the logical choice of hospital for Diana.[b]

---

[a] The only documented instance of La Pitié providing medical treatment to any Head of State was to Ex-President Jacques Chirac in April 2008 – see earlier note.
[b] It is possible that *The People* had an early editorial deadline and because the ambulance took so long to leave the tunnel, they may have been "forced" into guessing the destination hospital.

75   Dr Arnaud Derossi: In the Shadows

Dr Derossi, who was working as a base dispatcher on the night, left for the crash scene, arriving at 12.50 a.m.

There was a common theme in the inquest evidence: a bold attempt to understate Arnaud Derossi's role in relation to Princess Diana.

Derossi asserted that he was at the scene to deal with both Diana and Rees-Jones:

> I [was] actually some time with the medical team in charge of the Princess and some time with the fire brigade medical team – working, caring for the other patient in the car.[1598]
> I was monitoring what was done for the two patients.[1599]

The phone calls made – Derossi to the base at 1.20 a.m.; Lejay to La Pitié at 1.25; Lejay to Derossi at 1.29 – reveal that SAMU, and particularly Derossi, had nothing more to do with Rees-Jones after Dr Fuilla from the Fire Service arrived at 12.43 a.m.[a] At that point Rees-Jones became the Fire Service patient, and Princess Diana became the SAMU patient.[b]

Dr Lienhart makes a concerted effort to downplay the role of Dr Derossi at the scene.

Lienhart, who carried out a full investigation (with Professor Lecomte) of the medical treatment of Diana in 1998, said: "Dr Derossi does not perform any medical report. It was not his function to do so."[1600] And: "The one who made a report was Dr Martino".[1601] At one stage Lienhart said: "We felt it was significant for us to interview [Derossi] because he was an additional witness at the scene."[1602]

---

[a] Derossi didn't arrive until seven minutes after Fuilla – at 12.50 a.m.
[b] If the Fire Service doctors had appeared at the inquest they could have been asked about this. The Fire Service employees who were at the scene and also appeared at the inquest – Boyer and Gourmelon – were not asked about this.

In saying this, Lienhart effectively relegated Derossi's significance to being merely that of a witness of the events, but not actually someone with any significant role.

When Mansfield points out that Lienhart's evidence is conflicting with his 1998 report – which said that Derossi "served as an interface between the teams treating the casualties and [SAMU] control in order to find suitable trauma centres for the casualties to be taken to" – Lienhart suggested that was a "general description of his role" but not an accurate one.[1603]

Both Lienhart and Derossi lied under oath at the inquest about the nature of Derossi's role.

Why?

Some background information: In February 1998 French Judge Stéphan assigned Professor Lienhart to "review and report on all medical aspects of the treatment provided to the Princess of Wales" – but this was not a sole responsibility, it was assigned jointly to Lienhart and Professor Dominique Lecomte[a].[1604]

By that time Lecomte's role in the post-crash events was becoming legendary, particularly in that she personally carried out the first autopsy on Henri Paul's body – an autopsy which included 58 basic errors.[b] Her autopsy was so poorly conducted that Stéphan ordered a second autopsy on Henri Paul 4 days later.[c] It will be revealed that Lecomte played a critical role in the French post-crash cover-up.

Lecomte was not heard from at the inquest.

When this evidence is seen in the light of Lienhart's obvious lies at the inquest, it raises the question of whether Lienhart himself was providing evidence based on instructions from an outside employer.

The reason Derossi and Lienhart have underplayed Derossi's role could be an attempt to divert attention away from what his actual role on the night was.

It was Derossi, at 1.20 a.m., who conveyed the hospital destination to Lejay. When that is looked at in the light of early British Embassy phone calls,[d] it becomes clear that Derossi must have had some communication with a person outside of the tunnel regarding the destination (see last footnote).

---

[a] Head of the Paris IML – Institute of Forensic Medicine.
[b] Listed in the book *Cover-up of a Royal Murder: Hundreds of Errors in the Paget Report*.
[c] This is dealt with later.
[d] There were three phone calls: Elysée Palace to the embassy's George Younes – 1.10 a.m.; Younes to Shannon – after 1.15 a.m.; Shannon to Moss – around 1.20 to 1.25 a.m. This is addressed in Part 2, Prior Knowledge section of Chapter 9D. In essence they show that at 1.10 a.m. the British Embassy already knew that Diana was going to La Pitié – 10 minutes before Lejay was told.

Derossi's role also involved feeding incorrect medical injury information regarding Diana – obvious head injury, no thoracic trauma – to Lejay at 1.20 a.m. There is also evidence that indicates Derossi stayed in the ambulance on the trip to the hospital and played a role in events that transpired on that journey.

Derossi actually played a major medical role in the treatment of Diana, but on the surface he appeared to just have a background role. The perpetrators of her death – MI6 in association with other intelligence agencies – would not have wanted Derossi's role made public at the inquest.

Lienhart has made a particularly bungled attempt to cover up Derossi's role – even to the point of outrightly denying that Derossi even made the report to Lejay at 1.20 a.m.: "Dr Derossi does not perform any medical report".

When people tell lies, their evidence tends to come unstuck at some point along the way – if it is scrutinised.

76 2nd Communication Blackout: 37 minutes

Diana's ambulance left the Alma Tunnel at 1.41 a.m. – this was 1 hour and 18 minutes after the crash. Dr Martino's SAMU ambulance had been stationary in the tunnel for 1 hour and 1 minute.

There was no communication between the ambulance and the SAMU base after 1.29 a.m.[a], including the entire period of the journey to the hospital. This shutdown lasted for 37 minutes.

If Dr Martino was working on behalf of an intelligence agency that was intent on assassinating Diana, then the shutdown of communication with the base would be a logical course of action.

Michel Massebeuf, the ambulance driver, stated that once en route "in order to ensure as much privacy as possible, we no longer transmitted any information by radio."[1605]

Dr Marc Lejay told the inquest:

> **At 1.29 a.m. we got this information, but then afterwards they were told not to give any information any longer by radio.**[1606]

He said the shutdown was "for privacy and confidentiality reasons".[1607] And later he said: "I do not have the exact [departure] time because the times were no longer communicated for reasons of discretion."[1608]

Dr Martino has denied knowledge of such a shutdown. When asked at the inquest he said: "If such a decision was taken, it was taken independently of me".[1609]

Dr Derossi wasn't asked about it because he wasn't in the ambulance during the journey ... or was he? Although Martino denies knowing about any shutdown, he does go on to say that Derossi was responsible for any blackout on transmissions during that period – "afterwards it was Dr Derossi that was dealing with ... any transmission".[1610]

---

[a] This was the time when Lejay confirmed the hospital acceptance to Derossi.

That evidence indicates that Martino was aware that Derossi was present in the ambulance during the journey.

77 A Trundling Ambulance

The ambulance driver, Michel Massebeuf, was instructed to go slow. He stated: "The doctor instructed me to drive slowly because of the condition of the Princess."[1611]

How fast should an ambulance carrying seriously injured patients travel to a hospital?

The inquest heard from several French medical witnesses who said that it should be a slow ride.

The jury never got to hear the other side of the argument, as outlined by US cardio-vascular surgeon Dr John Ochsner:

> **Shocks and bumps? You know, if you're trying to save a life, you have to get them to the operating room quickly.**[1612] **(WFJ)**

How slow is "slow"?

The journey from the crash scene to the La Pitié Hospital is 5.7 kilometres. The ambulance left the Alma Tunnel at 1.41 a.m. and arrived at the hospital at 2.06. If one allows for a 5 minute stop during the journey (see next chapter), this would make actual driving time about 20 minutes. A simple calculation reveals that the average speed of Diana's escorted ambulance was 17 kph – this is less than half the speed Massebeuf told the police he was driving at: "40 or 50 kilometres per hour".[1613a]

Journalist Pierre Suu, who followed the ambulance, stated that it "was being driven at walking pace".[1614]

As the driver, Massebeuf must have been aware that he was driving significantly slower than the speed he declared under oath to the French police.

Why did Massebeuf lie?

Massebeuf was never cross-examined at the inquest.

---

[a] Massebeuf also testified that the earlier ambulance journey to the crash scene was "very quick" (14 Nov 07: 21.14) even though evidence shows the ambulance was travelling at around 11½ kph – see earlier Diana in the Mercedes chapter.

78 Stopping the Ambulance

The ambulance stopped for five minutes, less than 500 metres before the hospital entrance.

Dr Martino told Paget:

> **I took that decision [to stop the ambulance] because the arterial pressure was dropping.**[1615] **(WFJ)**

Lienhart told the inquest that after Martino stopped the ambulance he "increased the quantity of the drip volume ... and he also increased the dopamine".[1616]

Is this true?

Did what was happening in the ambulance justify stopping for five minutes close to the hospital gates?

Tom Treasure made it clear that he had his doubts:

> **Whether within a minute of the hospital you would put your foot on the accelerator or you would put your foot on the brake is open to some debate.**[1617]

What was it that actually triggered Martino to stop the ambulance?

The various witness accounts are:

- Massebeuf: "to provide treatment that required a complete absence of movement"[1618]
- Martino: "to find out why there was such a drop in the blood pressure"[1619]
- Martino: "we were afraid that [the blood pressure drop would] ... lead to a cardiac arrest, a heart arrest, and it is very hard to resuscitate a patient in these conditions whilst the ambulance is moving"[1620]
- Martino (with MacLeod's[a] help): Diana "needed to be stabilised before the ambulance moved"[1621]
- Martino: "to re-examine the Princess [because] there was something abnormal going on" [1622] (WFJ)

---

[a] Police lawyer Duncan MacLeod.

- Lienhart & Lecomte: to adjust the dopamine drip after a drop in blood pressure.[1623] (WFJ)

At the inquest some alarming adjectives were used for the blood pressure drop. These did not come from witnesses, but instead were fabricated by the coroner Scott Baker and Duncan MacLeod, the police lawyer.

MacLeod referred to "a <u>catastrophic or near catastrophic</u> fall in arterial blood pressure"[1624]

Baker claimed in his Summing Up: "During the journey, there was another <u>near-catastrophic</u> fall in blood pressure." [1625]

MacLeod: "The patient's arterial blood pressure fell to <u>dangerous</u> levels"[1626] and "the <u>critically low</u> blood pressure".[1627]

In his police statement, Martino, who was the only eye-witness to give evidence,[a] said that "the arterial pressure was dropping" [1628] (WFJ) The jury never got to hear that.

If the investigation carried out by Lienhart and Lecomte (which also the jury never heard) was correct – that the only action taken was to increase the dopamine – then that would strongly indicate that Martino needn't have stopped the ambulance. Martino could have easily increased the dopamine in a slow-moving ambulance – and if he did require a stationary ambulance, why did he take 5 minutes?

In 2004 Martino stated:

> **I had the vehicle stopped in order to re-examine the Princess. There was something abnormal going on, and the vehicle had to be stopped, so that I could understand that abnormality.[1629] (WFJ)**

The jury never heard this account and Martino was not asked at the inquest to explain this mysterious "abnormality" comment. He clearly should have been.

This stoppage was far from "normal", and Martino's "abnormal" remark confirms that.

The Ambulance Was Followed

The most shocking evidence came from the two witnesses who were watching from outside of the ambulance – Pierre Suu and Thierry Orban. Neither of these journalists were cross-examined at the inquest, but it is obvious that they should have been.

Suu and Orban describe actions occurring which are quite different to the accounts provided by the French medical witnesses. They said:

---

[a] There were other eye-witnesses – the two female interns, Barbara Kapfer and "Fadi" who were in the back of the ambulance with Martino. Neither of them have ever been officially interviewed.

- the ambulance "was rocking, as if they were doing a cardiac massage"[1630] – Orban
- "the driver got out hurriedly and got into the back"[1631] – Orban
- "a doctor jumped out of the passenger side of the vehicle and rushed round the back of the ambulance and got inside. He was wearing a white doctor's jacket."[1632] – Suu

The evidence indicates that Suu and Orban were reasonably close to each other – "Orban and I looked at one another"[1633] – so they probably viewed the ambulance from a similar angle.

The Second Doctor

Orban describes the driver getting out and going to the back and Suu says it was a doctor.[a] Although he is giving this evidence in 2006[b], it is Suu who appears to have the more specific recollection. He states: a) that he got "out of the passenger side"; and b) that "he was wearing a white doctor's jacket."

In support of Suu's account, Massebeuf never stated that he was asked to assist in the treatment, and common sense would suggest that – if there was any urgency to get Diana to hospital, which I admit is in serious doubt – the driver would be left in the driver's seat, ready for action.

Presuming that it was Suu's account that is correct[c] there would be three possible scenarios:

1) Dr Martino was sitting in the front of the ambulance, leaving Diana in the care of the student interns, Barbara Kapfer and Fadi
2) An unknown and anonymous doctor sat in the front of Diana's ambulance
3) Dr Derossi didn't remain at the crash scene (as he said, see below) but instead stayed with the ambulance after it departed from the Alma Tunnel.

At the inquest Martino was asked by Hough: "I think for all that time that the ambulance was on the road, you were in the back and busy with your patient?" His reply was a simple "Yes".[1634] Unless Martino was lying about this, his evidence would preclude the first option above. It is common sense that Martino would have remained in the back of the ambulance, regardless of whether his intentions towards Diana were positive or sinister.

Regarding the second option, there was one other SAMU doctor who arrived at the scene with an ambulance at 12.50 a.m.: Dr Vivien. He had been

---

[a] Bearing in mind that Martino already had two assistants with him in the back of the ambulance, it should be considered that none of the actions during this stoppage, as described by the French medical witnesses – primarily Martino – comprised of anything that required a fourth person, be it a doctor or a driver.

[b] Orban's account is from 23 September 1997.

[c] It is obvious that both witnesses should have been cross-examined, but neither were.

originally summoned after Martino first arrived at the scene. There is no evidence of Vivien carrying out any function regarding the crash, and it is possible that when he found the Fire Service dealing with Rees-Jones, he may have left the scene before 1.41 a.m.[ab] There is another possibility that his ambulance may have been used to transport the two deceased, Henri Paul and Dodi Fayed. There is no evidence to suggest any motive he may have had for switching himself into Martino's ambulance.

Derossi told the police that after Diana's ambulance left "I myself remained at the scene in order to supervise the operations to assist the front seat passenger", Trevor Rees-Jones.[1635] (WFJ) At the inquest he said that the first he heard about the stoppage of Diana's ambulance was when he "got back to the medical dispatch of the SAMU" – the base.[1636]

There are however several points that bring Derossi's account, which the jury never heard, into question:

1)   Martino's evidence was that Derossi was responsible for any communication blackout for the period from 1.29 a.m. onwards: "afterwards it was Dr Derossi that was dealing with ... any transmission".[1637]

2)   Derossi's official role – despite Lienhart's denials[c] – was to report back to the base. It is common sense that he would have stayed with the ambulance to conduct communications if required.

3)   Derossi's account that he stayed at the scene has never been corroborated by any other eye-witness. Fire Service witnesses – Gourmelon, Boyer – should have been asked at the inquest about this.

4)   Derossi's description of what happened with Rees-Jones – viewable in his 1998 French statement[1638] (WFJ) – is very generalised and contains no information that he couldn't have learned through media reports of the events.

5)   Derossi states: "I myself remained at the scene [after Diana's ambulance left] in order to supervise the operations to assist" Rees-Jones.[1639] (WFJ)

There is a major problem with this claim: Dr Fuilla – who arrived at 12.43 a.m. and immediately took over the treatment of Rees-Jones – was described by Gourmelon as the DSM, or "Director of Medical Rescue Services" and the "officer in overall charge at the scene".[1640] Dr Le Hot had also arrived with his Fire Service resuscitation ambulance at 12.44 a.m., a minute after Fuilla.[1641]

---

[a] The time of the departure of Diana's ambulance.
[b] Lejay's "Deployment Report" makes no mention of the role played by Vivien's ambulance. The Deployment Report is reproduced in Part 2, Figure 14. It is also on the website: INQ0053176.
[c] See earlier Dr Arnaud Derossi chapter.

At the inquest, Dr Derossi described himself as "a part-time doctor" working for SAMU as a dispatcher.[1642]

Would Dr Fuilla, who was evidently a senior doctor and had been working with his team on Rees-Jones for 58 minutes[a] at the time Diana's ambulance left, hand supervision responsibilities over to Dr Derossi, as soon as he became available?

It is common sense that from 12.43 a.m., when Martino transferred his team to dealing with Diana after the arrival of Dr Fuilla, Rees-Jones then became the patient of the Fire Service.

This is an issue that should have been addressed at the inquest, but wasn't.

The evidence from Suu is clear that he saw an extra doctor at the scene.

If that person wasn't Dr Derossi, then who was it?

In considering Derossi's account, the significance of the failure to interview both Dr Fuilla and Dr Le Hot, by the French and British police and the inquest, becomes increasingly clear.

Massebeuf, Orban and Suu were not cross-examined at the inquest. Additionally important is the fact that the Paget Report missed out all of Suu's evidence on the ambulance trip, completely omitted Massebeuf's statement altogether and never included any evidence of Orban, failing to even mention that he existed.

Added to this is the failure to officially identify the two female student interns present in the ambulance.

Why has there been such a cover-up of the critical evidence around this very strange stoppage within sight of the destination hospital?

What Were They Doing?

Orban witnessed a "rocking" ambulance during the stoppage.

Massebeuf stated that the ambulance "stopped for about five minutes, in order for [Martino] to be able to provide treatment that required a complete absence of movement".[1643] Massebeuf does not describe what that treatment was and it may be that he didn't know – he may have stayed in the driver's seat and was not necessarily a witness to what occurred in the main ambulance compartment.

Orban described an ambulance that "was rocking, as if they were doing a cardiac massage".[1644]

Martino testified in his Paget statement – not heard by the jury – "I did not do any cardiac massage at that moment".[1645] (WFJ)

What did the people in the ambulance do that:
1) required four people, including two doctors
2) took five minutes
3) led to Orban seeing an ambulance that "was rocking"?

---

[a] From 12.43 to 1.41 a.m.

None of these three factors fit with the conclusion drawn by the French medical investigators, Lienhart and Lecomte: the only action that took place was an adjustment of the dopamine drip. [1646] (WFJ) That could have been carried out by one doctor acting alone, would have taken less than a minute and wouldn't have resulted in a rocking ambulance.

If Dr Martino and Dr Derossi had been given the job of ensuring that Princess Diana didn't make it through that night – and there is a significant amount of evidence[a] that indicates that was the case – then this point, less than 500 metres from where they had to hand over responsibility to the hospital, was a very critical juncture.

This may have been the moment when Martino and Derossi realised that if they handed Diana straight over to the hospital, there was still a chance that she could have been revived.

As will be seen later, Diana was in such bad shape when she finally arrived at the hospital – following the five minute stoppage – that she was already close to death.

---

[a] There is additional evidence in Part 2, Section 3 on Medical Treatment.

79 Alive in the Hospital: 6 minutes

Princess Diana arrived at La Pitié Salpêtrière Hospital unconscious – it was 1 hour and 43 minutes after the crash.

Professor Bruno Riou, the receiving doctor, told the French investigation:

The Princess was alive, unconscious, and receiving mechanical ventilation. She was in a state of traumatic shock.[1647] **(WFJ)**

Daniel Eyraud, an intensive care doctor who assisted, said that "her blood pressure was very low, but ... her heart was still beating."[1648]

Riou told the inquest that Diana's condition on arrival was "very bad because a filling operation had been done – catecholamines had been administered and despite that, her blood pressure was extremely low".[1649]

This corroborates with the assessment by inquest expert Tom Treasure that the object should have been to get Diana to a hospital quickly, even though her blood pressure was low, and not administer catecholamines, which would have the effect of increasing the pressure on any source of internal bleeding.

Before Princess Diana's arrival a medical team was drawn together to treat the incoming patient. It consisted of:

Bruno Riou - Senior Anaesthetist
Daniel Eyraud - Anaesthetist Intensive Care
Dominique Hagnere - Male Nurse

There was an urgent need for a thoracic surgeon to deal with the thoracic injury – discovered by Martino just after 1.06 a.m. – which could have been the cause of the internal bleeding that had led to the low blood pressure – also detected by Martino soon after 1.06 a.m.

When Diana arrived at 2.06 a.m. the hospital medical team was still unaware that a thoracic surgeon was required.[a] At the inquest Lienhart was asked if Martino passed on "a message with information about the patient to Professor Riou". Lienhart replied: "Yes, indeed".[1650]

Even though Martino spoke directly with Riou at the hospital, he still failed to pass on the information regarding Diana's thoracic trauma.

---

[a] The thoracic surgeon was only called after the X-rays had been looked at – see below.

Early Treatment: 2.06 to 2.10 a.m.

Dr Bruno Riou was in charge from the outset.

After Diana's arrival at the hospital events moved quickly. The following occurred, in time order:

- X-rays were taken of Diana's chest and pelvic area[1651]
- femoral arterial line inserted to measure blood pressure[1652]
- Diana is given noradrenalin[a], a stronger replacement of the dopamine[1653]
- Diana receives transfusion of type 'O' negative blood[1654b]
- the X-rays reveal a major right-side haemothorax – bleeding in the thorax region[1655]
- decision is made to conduct a thoracotomy operation[1656c]
- Drs Dahman[d] and Pavie[e] are called[1657]
- blood pressure drops and slowing heart beat is detected[1658f]
- the noradrenalin dosage is increased[1659] and colloids (plasma) are administered[1660]
- drain is started to remove excess blood from the thorax.[1661]

Dr Bruno Riou told Paget:

> **She was transfused with supplies of 'O' negative blood held in the Recovery Room, as her blood group had not been established.**[1662] **(WFJ)**

One would think that the establishment of Princess Diana's blood group would have been a high priority as soon as the hospital became aware that she was to be arriving. A simple phone call to Buckingham Palace would have probably established this – or at least pointed them in the right direction to find out.

This could be a confirmation that Diana's identity wasn't disclosed to the hospital until approximately 1.55 a.m., as stated by Dr Eyraud:

> **We were warned of the arrival of the Princess of Wales some ten minutes before she was actually brought in.**[1663]

And it is a reminder that La Pitié Salpêtrière was not used to dealing with VIPs. If Diana had been sent to Val de Grâce – the main Paris hospital for

---

[a] A catecholamine and vasoconstrictor – it has the effect of narrowing the arteries and thus should increase blood pressure. As was the case in the ambulance, this would have had the effect of increasing the pressure on the source of the bleeding.

[b] This is administered through the line that had already been inserted by the SAMU: Riou: 15 Nov 07: 20.9

[c] Opening up the thorax.

[d] General surgeon.

[e] Cardio-Thoracic specialist.

[f] Readings were either not recorded or not revealed, or both.

VIPs – establishment of blood group would have probably been standard procedure.

The jury never got to hear this blood group evidence.

Cardiac Arrest: 2.10 to 2.15 a.m.

Dr Dahman, the general surgeon, and Dr Pavie, the cardio-thoracic surgeon, were called by 2.10 a.m.

While Dr Pavie – who was asleep at home[1664] – was waking up and preparing to attend the hospital, events were occurring quickly in the recovery room:

- Dr Dahman – who was already in the hospital – arrives[1665]
- Diana suffers a cardiac arrest – her heart stops beating[1666]
- Riou starts external heart massage[1667a]
- a second femoral veinous line is inserted to re-transfuse back in the already drained blood.[1668]

Effective Time of Death: 2.12 a.m.

Princess Diana's first and only cardiac arrest occurred after the arrival of Dr Dahman, but before he commenced the thoracotomy[b] operation.

Riou: the cardiac arrest occurred "after the arrival of Dr Dahman"[1669]

Riou: "the thorax was opened when the heart had just stopped"[1670]

Eyraud: "the Princess's heart stopped just prior to this [thoracotomy] being done"[1671]

Diana arrived at the hospital at 2.06 a.m. Dr Dahman was called at around 2.10.

Princess Diana effectively passed away when her heart stopped beating. If her heart had restarted after that point, the witnesses would have said.

No one did.

The evidence places Diana's time of death between 2.10 and 2.15 a.m.[1672] Dr Dahman completed the right-side thoracotomy before Dr Pavie arrived[1673] – and Pavie was woken at 2.10 and arrived 12 minutes later at 2.22.[1674]

Dr Dahman was in the hospital when he was called and there is no reason to suggest that he did not arrive quickly. He had already completed the operation before 2.22 a.m.

This evidence indicates that Diana, Princess of Wales passed away at approximately 2.12 a.m. on 31 August 1997.

---

[a] Although not stated this would presumably have initially been done mechanically – not by applying manual pressure to the chest. Later internal heart massage was carried out.

[b] Opening up of the thorax area.

This is about 1¾ hours earlier than the official time of her death: 4.00 a.m.[a] This could be because the official time of death is generally called at the point when resuscitation efforts finish.

However, Diana's effective time of death is more significant than the official time of death.

Within about 6 minutes of arriving at the hospital Diana was dead.

Hospital Treatment

The treatment of Princess Diana at La Pitié Salpêtrière Hospital between 2.12 a.m. and 4.00 a.m. – her official time of death – is covered in Chapter 10 of Part 2.

The doctors there – Bruno Riou, Dahman and Alain Pavie – did the best they could to bring Diana back to life, but there was really no hope because it was already too late when she was passed into their care.

---

[a] The details of death on the jury's inquest verdict read: "Diana, Princess of Wales died ... at around 4.00 a.m. on 31 August 1997....": 7 Apr 08: 7.2

80   Death By Ambulance

Within six minutes of arriving at the hospital Princess Diana was dead.

That places her time of death very close to the time Dr Jean-Marc Martino relinquished control to Dr Bruno Riou.

In other words, Martino was in control of Diana's care for 1 hour and 26 minutes and she died 6 minutes after he passed on control.

This puts the spotlight more closely on the mystery period of 5 minutes when the ambulance stopped near the hospital gates.

By the time the thoracotomy was commenced, Diana had already died.

There are four very specific and substantial areas of suspicion surrounding the actions of Drs Martino and Derossi:

1) failure to divulge thoracic trauma to the SAMU base
2) pumping of vaso-constricting catecholamines into Diana to increase her blood pressure above 70, despite the knowledge of thoracic trauma
3) huge delays in the tunnel and in the ambulance
4) five minute stoppage near the hospital.

Looking at the events now retrospectively, it seems that points 2, 3 and 4 – the catecholamines, the delays and the stoppage (and whatever it was that occurred within those periods) – were the factors that finally brought about the death of Princess Diana.

Had Diana's blood pressure been maintained at a level that kept her alive[a], had she arrived at the hospital substantially earlier, or had whatever occurred during the 5 minute stoppage not taken place, then the well-intentioned doctors at the hospital would have had a reasonable chance of saving her.

Once Diana was in the hospital the doctors acted very quickly – the opposite to the snail's pace efforts of Martino and Derossi – but it was already too late.

There are effectively two main ways of viewing the volumes of evidence relating to the medical treatment of Princess Diana between 12.23 a.m., the time of the crash, and 2.06 a.m., the time of her hospital arrival – 1 hour and 43 minutes later.

---

[a] Rather than trying to increase the blood pressure.

It was either:

1)   a disastrous series of unconnected errors and unusual events on the night, followed by a further series of unconnected instances of memory malfunctions among some of the most vital witnesses throughout the years that followed, and accompanied by two of the most inept and fruitless national police investigations ever carried out;

Or it was:

2)   a thoroughly coordinated and orchestrated operation that on the night was aimed at pretending that the Princess of Wales was given proper medical treatment, but instead was designed to ensure that she was delivered to the hospital in an unsurvivable condition. This was then followed by a huge inter-governmental cover-up on a scale that has seldom been seen in history.

Just following through on one aspect: are the following events unconnected?

a)   Martino's discovery of a combination of thoracic trauma and low blood pressure just after 1.06 a.m.

b)   Derossi's statement made twice to Lejay at 1.20 a.m.: "nothing to report for the thorax"

c)   Derossi's failure to pass on the discovery of thoracic trauma to the SAMU base at any time

d)   Lejay's failure to disclose to the hospital that Diana had thoracic trauma – he obviously didn't know himself

e)   The failure of the hospital to have a thoracic surgeon on hand when Diana arrived – this would have been her last hope of survival.

There are huge unexplained issues surrounding the pre-hospital medical treatment of Princess Diana – right from the inconsistent evidence of Dr Mailliez and the SAMU ambulance that travelled to the scene at 11½ kph, through to the five minute stoppage by that same ambulance while it was in sight of the La Pitié Hospital.

When Martino first arrived he described Princess Diana as "alert" with a Glasgow coma rating of 14, right frontal trauma and an injured arm – yet he left the SAMU base believing for 40 minutes that she only had an injured arm.

The SAMU base was never told by Derossi about the thoracic trauma.

But then, there are many significant events in this sorry story of Diana's medical treatment.

A picture emerges that the doctors involved directly in caring for Diana – Mailliez, Martino and Derossi – did not have the Princess' best interests in mind. Instead, particularly in the cases of Martino and Derossi, there is a sinister effort to delay Diana's arrival at the hospital – this, despite the knowledge that the hospital was the only place where she could have been saved.

By the time Diana made it to the hospital, after being in Martino and Derossi's care for 1 hour and 26 minutes, she was unconscious and her heart was only just beating. She suffered a cardiac arrest soon after arriving.

There is a paradox in the arguments put forward by the French medical witnesses regarding stabilising the patient: If the patient's condition is good, then they move them towards the hospital. If the patient's condition is bad, then they don't move them towards the hospital, instead waiting until the condition improves.

Yet hospitals are designed for people who are in bad condition.

Martino delayed Diana's removal to the ambulance to the maximum. But then, once she is in the ambulance – and he has the full knowledge of the thoracic trauma and low blood pressure combination, and therefore the urgency to reach a hospital – then the delays become unconscionable: Diana was precisely a full hour in the ambulance.

The comments made by Lejay – "Are you ready to roll?" (1.20 a.m.) and "Are you en route yet?" (1.29 a.m.) – reveal that he was expecting the ambulance to be on the move, even though he had no knowledge of the thoracic trauma.

Instead of waiting for Diana to stabilise, the evidence indicates that Martino and Derossi were waiting for her to die, while they pumped catecholamines into her to speed the process – knowing full well that they shouldn't have done that with a thoracic trauma. When they re-evaluated the situation just short of the hospital, they may have decided that, even after all they had done, she could still survive the night.

Orban witnessed a rocking ambulance. At that stage Martino and Derossi appear to have carried out an undisclosed action that ensured that – although Diana would be delivered to the hospital alive – she would not be in a position from which she could be revived.

For this entire operation to succeed, it required much more than the involvement of Drs Martino and Derossi. It is most unlikely that those men would have had any particular personal motive that led to their actions. They would have been working on the night on behalf of an intelligence agency and there is little doubt that their motive would have involved some form of reward, probably monetary.

Evidence relating to the role of the Elysée Palace and the British Embassy – covered in Part 2[a][b] – indicates that on the night the doctors were in contact

---

[a] Prior Knowledge section of Chapter 9D.

[b] There were three phone calls: Elysée Palace to the embassy's George Younes – 1.10 a.m.; Younes to Shannon – after 1.15 a.m.; Shannon to Moss – around 1.20 to 1.25 a.m. In essence they show that at 1.10 a.m. the British Embassy already knew that Diana was going to La Pitié – 10 minutes before Lejay was told.

with a person or persons outside the tunnel: a line of organisation with a connection to the French Government.

In addition, the wide-ranging cover-up that has developed since the crash, has drawn in organisations such as SAMU, even though they do not appear to have had any prior knowledge of the events.

The evidence presented at the inquest – Riou, Pavie, Lejay[a] – indicates that the French medical system has closed ranks since the crash, in order to defend the plainly unconscionable and sinister actions of Drs Martino and Derossi.

This fits with the overwhelming evidence which will later be presented regarding the actions of the French authorities in response to the crash.

By the time the inquest took place, Dr Martino had effectively disappeared – in the words of Scott Baker: "It took us a long time to find him."[1675] He was discovered in Germany after a search lasting several months.

Why was it not just a simple procedure of checking with SAMU and establishing where he had moved to?

I suggest that Dr Martino could not have carried out his actions on the night without an awareness, after the event, on the part of those in the French medical community. Princess Diana was held in high esteem by the French public – this is reflected in the large number of French eye-witnesses who have been willing over the years to give their evidence.

It may be that Dr Martino found it "too hot" to continue to pursue a medical career in Paris.

The bank accounts and mobile phone records of those involved – Mailliez, Martino and Derossi – should have been checked as part of the investigations.

They have not been.

When Scott Baker came to give his Summing Up to the jury he quickly skimmed through the evidence, drawing the barest outline – only 1,100 out of his over 80,000 words are dedicated to the pre-hospital medical evidence.[1676]

In doing this Baker avoided dealing with the critical evidence that has been covered in this book[b] – evidence that cannot be ignored if one's intention is to reveal a true picture of the events that occurred on that night.

---

[a] Covered in Part 2, Section Three: Medical Treatment.
[b] Covered in more thorough detail in Part 2, Section Three.

"With this type of injury, time is of the essence.... In the United States the delay in getting [Diana] to the hospital could constitute gross malpractice. There's no excuse for it."
- Dr Michael Baden, Chief Forensic Pathologist for New York State Police

"Given that [Diana] was still alive after nearly two hours, if they'd have gotten her [to the hospital] in an hour, they might have saved her."
- Dr John Ochsner, US Cardio-Vascular Surgeon

"If they had gotten [Diana] to the emergency room sooner, she would have had a far greater chance. You could never diagnose that kind of injury in the field, never.... Spending all that time on on-site treatment was absolutely the wrong approach for this patient."
- Dr David Wasserman, US Emergency Room Doctor

"We believe that you have a 'golden hour' to save someone's life…. As soon as you get to the casualty, you stabilise them, then you move them as fast as possible, often by helicopter, to a centre where you can perform surgery…. If [Diana] had had that done, most of us [cardiologists] think she probably would have lived."
- Dr Stephen Ramee, A Leading New Orleans Cardiologist

"[Diana's] death stunned me all the more as I was able to get a look at the particulars of the autopsy findings very soon after her death…. She died of internal bleeding. The injury which caused the bleeding was to a vein which doesn't bleed particularly quickly – in fact, it bleeds rather slowly…. If Princess Diana had been brought to hospital within 10 minutes of the accident … she could have survived."
- Prof Christiaan Barnard, Prominent South African Heart Specialist

81   Securing British Control

The British Government moved quickly to control events at La Pitié Salpêtrière Hospital.

Within nine minutes of Princess Diana's arrival at the hospital the British Consul-General turned up[a] and proceeded to set up an "incident room".[1677] (WFJ) His location just happened to be next door to the second floor room Diana's body was shifted into at around 7 a.m.[1678] (WFJ)

Speaking about the period of around two hours before the princess officially died, Moss told Paget: "We kept in regular touch with to [sic] the FCO, Balmoral, number 10 Downing Street and the local authorities".[1679] (WFJ)

Then around 30 minutes after Diana's official time of death, at around 3.30 a.m.[b] Lieutenant Colonel Malcolm Ross, the Comptroller of the Lord Chamberlain's Office, made a crucial phone call to the president of Kenyons in London.[c] (WFJ)

Gérard Jauze, the PFG[d] Branch Director in Paris, told Paget that "the director of the Paris agencies of PFG, M. Hervé Racine, was contacted by the British subsidiary of PFG, who are called Kenyons[e]."[1680] (WFJ)

According to Operation Paget the call to Racine was made at around 5 a.m. Paris time.[1681] (WFJ)

The purpose of this call to Racine was to pass on what had been conveyed in the earlier call from Ross – a request for PFG to conduct the French end of

---

[a] Moss arrived at 2.15 a.m. (22 Nov 07: 12.15) – seven minutes before the cardio-thoracic surgeon, who arrived at 2.22.

[b] UK time.

[c] This is addressed in Part 4, section on Malcolm Ross in the Early Royal Control chapter.

[d] PFG are the French funeral directors employed to handle the repatriation of Princess Diana and Dodi Fayed.

[e] Kenyons were Funeral Directors for the Royal Family until the early 1990s: Alan Puxley, Witness Statement, 16 June 2004, reproduced in *The Documents* book, p462 (UK Edition).

the same-day repatriation of Princess Diana and Dodi Fayed's bodies. Via Kenyons, PFG were also asked to arrange the Paris embalming of Diana, with a specific request for it to be carried out by a female embalmer.[a] (WFJ)

The timing of these calls – 3.30 and 4 a.m. in the UK and waking people up – is a reflection of an early requirement for the royal family to take control of the post-crash situation. There was a move from Balmoral[b] to get the French side of events moving quickly – enabling a same-day repatriation of Diana's body and ensuring an embalming took place before any transfer of that body.

How these events transpired is addressed later.

---

[a] This is addressed in Part 4, section on Pre-Embalming Events in the French Embalming chapter.
[b] Where the Queen was on holiday.

82   A Suspicious Death

Soon after Princess Diana's official death the doctor in charge, Bruno Riou, completed the death certificate.

He was interviewed by British police officers in 2006:

> **DS Grater showed Professor Riou a copy of ... [a blank] 'Certificat de Décès'. Professor Riou confirmed that he had completed a form similar to this one for the Princess of Wales at the time of her death.... Professor Riou explained that he would probably have ticked 'OUI' [YES] box for 'Obstacle Medico-Legal (voir 2 au verso[a])', which translates as 'Medico-Legal issue'.... By ticking the 'YES' box, it means that a Legal Physician must examine the body prior to allowing it to be released for burial or cremation.**[1682] **(WFJ)**

This completed death certificate has never surfaced in any police investigation and it was not presented at the inquest.

Why?

---

[a] This translates as "see 2 overleaf" – see blank JM/12 form below.

[TN: Printed form - relevant parts only translated]

JM/12

DEATH CERTIFICATE

In accordance with the decree of 24 December 1996

DEPARTMENT:

To be completed by the Doctor

DISTRICT:

Post Code:

SURNAME:

Forenames:

Date of birth: Sex:

Address:

The undersigned doctor of medicine certifies that the death of the person named opposite

on at hrs is real and constant (see 1 overleaf)

Medical legal obstacle (see 2 overleaf) YES NO

FOR TOWN HALL USE ONLY

The serial number of death in the Register entered opposite must be reproduced overleaf

SERIAL NO OF DEATH:

At on

Signature (legible surname) and doctor's stamp (mandatory)

Figure 22

Blank death certificate form – known as JM/12 in the police files. The reverse side appears below. Bruno Riou stated that he completed this form in relation to the death of Princess Diana on 31 August 1997. The jury did not get to see this blank form. (TN = Translator's Note).

HOW THEY MURDERED PRINCESS DIANA

[TN: Printed form – relevant parts only translated]

NOTES FOR COMPLETING THE ADMINISTRATION SECTION

IMPORTANT

1. The date and time of death must be given - where applicable, approximately. Do not quote the date of the report. However, in the event of a death that presents a medical legal obstacle, these details will be confirmed subsequently in the forensic expert's report.
2. Medical legal obstacle: suicide or suspicious death, the origin of which appears to be related to an offence. In this case, the body is at the disposal of the judicial authorities. The following funeral arrangements are suspended until authorisation is given by the judicial authority:
   - Handing over of the body (article R363-10 of the Local Authority Code)
   - Embalming (article 365-8 of the Local Authority Code)
   - Transportation of the body to the home of the deceased or to a medical establishment prior to its placing in the coffin (article R363-6 of the Local Authority Code)
   - Admission to a funeral parlour prior to placing in the coffin (articles R361-37 and R361-38 of the Local Authority Code)
   - Taking samples with a view to investigating the cause of death (article R363-11 of the Local Authority Code)
   - Closing the coffin (article 363-18 of the Local Authority Code)
   - Burial (as a result)
   - Cremation (article R361-42 of the Local Authority Code).

The same funeral arrangements are suspended when there is a claim linked to the cause of death (accident at work, occupational illness, or as a result of injuries for a person receiving a war pension).

Figure 23

> Reverse side of JM/12 "Death Certificate" form shown above.

The death certificate form's instructions say: "Medical legal obstacle: suicide or suspicious death, the origin of which appears to be related to an offence".

Diana's death could not possibly have been a suicide, so ticking "YES" means the death is believed to be "suspicious" and "an offence" appears to have been committed.

In other words, at the time of completing Princess Diana's death certificate Professor Bruno Riou believed that the circumstances of her death were suspicious.

The inquest jury did not hear this.

Why?

Why did Riou tick "YES" for medical legal obstacle?

A SUSPICIOUS DEATH

At the time, the circumstances of Diana's death must have been all too clear to Riou, who was involved right from the first phone call to the hospital from Dr Lejay at 1.25 a.m. He may have even been aware that the crash had occurred just before 12.30 a.m. There was communication between ambulance doctor Martino and Riou at the time of Diana's arrival.[1683]

There are a critical set of factors that on the night would have raised serious questions in the mind of Riou:

-     the thoracic trauma that was externally evident but was not communicated to the hospital ahead of arrival
-     the inordinate delay in getting to hospital given the combination of thoracic trauma and low blood pressure – i.e. it would have been known in the ambulance that Diana's life could not be saved outside of a hospital
-     Diana had arrived unconscious and stopped breathing 6 minutes after that arrival – yet the crash had occurred 1 hour and 43 minutes earlier.[a]

Earlier it was shown that Diana's ambulance was seen rocking during a five minute stoppage near the hospital.

What if the rocking ambulance – which has never been explained[b] – was because Princess Diana was still alive and physically put up a struggle against her "treatment"?

What if, instead of increasing the dopamine outside the hospital, Martino had administered a substance that sped up Diana's deteriorating situation?

I am not suggesting that Riou was aware of the circumstances of the 5 minute stoppage, or even aware that it actually happened.

He didn't need to be.

Riou was definitely aware of the earlier three factors – the combination of external thoracic trauma with low blood pressure; the huge delay in arrival; the death occurring 6 minutes after arrival.

This should have been enough to raise the question of suspicion in the mind of an experienced doctor, as Riou was.[c]

Based on the circumstances Professor Bruno Riou was confronted with, he did the only decent thing that was in his power to do – he ticked "YES" in the medical legal obstacle box on Diana's death certificate.

---

[a] At the hospital press conference held at 5.55 a.m. Riou said: "Tonight the Princess of Wales was the victim of a high-speed car accident. The Paris ambulance service took charge and tried at once to resuscitate her. But when she arrived here, she was haemorrhaging very badly from the thorax – and then her heart stopped.": Diana: The Night She Died, Channel 5 Documentary, 2003. (WFJ)

[b] The rocking ambulance evidence was not even mentioned at the inquest, outside of the reading of Orban's statement.

[c] In 1997, Riou had 12 years experience as a doctor: 15 Nov 07: 2.2.

Riou's subsequent evidence on the reason he ticked "YES" is illogical – he has said that "the 'YES' box is normally always ticked when the death is not natural ... for example suicide, car crash etc": thus requiring "a Legal Physician [to] examine the body".[1684]

This statement runs directly counter to:

a)   what it states on the reverse of the form – see earlier

b)   the evidence of Monteil and Steiner that body examinations are not relevant for car crash passengers[1685]

c)   common sense, which tells us that it would be ridiculous for body examinations to be conducted on dead passengers in all car crashes.

I suggest that Riou knows that this statement is false and has been pressured – by the French authorities – to lie, as a part of the wide-ranging cover-up that has occurred in France since 31 August 1997.

83   Autopsy in Paris

After Dr Riou had noted that the death of Princess Diana was suspicious the public prosecutor's office had to decide on whether an autopsy would be ordered.

Deputy Public Prosecutor Maud Coujard told Paget:

> **The decision to make during the night was whether to carry out post mortems on the Princess of Wales and Mr Al Fayed.... We ... proceeded the way we normally do in relation to road traffic accidents and only ordered the autopsy of the driver, Henri Paul. Nevertheless the Public Prosecutor or I ... decided to request that an experienced forensic pathologist proceed with an external physical examination of the bodies of the Princess of Wales and Dodi Al Fayed. Professor Lecomte accepted this task, which she conducted, to my knowledge, early the next morning.[1686] (WFJ)**

Coujard stated that Dominique Lecomte was instructed to carry out an "external physical examination" of both bodies – Diana and Dodi.

It is common sense that the authorities would request it for both – had they just ordered it for Diana then questions would have been asked: Why Diana and not Dodi? But the evidence is clear that the suspicion from Riou revolved around the death of Diana – he had no dealings with Dodi, who died on impact.

Other evidence shows that Lecomte conducted autopsies – not just external examinations – on both bodies.

Diana's autopsy took place at La Pitié Hospital at 5.30 a.m.[1687] (WFJ)

Professor Lecomte's "forensic report" of Diana's examination clearly states:

> **From my examination, I conclude that death was due to ... a rupture of the pericardium and a wound to the left pulmonary vein, upon which surgery was performed.[a] (WFJ)**

On 31 August 1997, after conducting Diana's examination, Lecomte stated in writing that she had determined the cause of death "from my examination". It is impossible to conclude that a person has a ruptured pericardium and a wounded left pulmonary vein by an external examination.

---

[a] This document – which was not shown to the jury – is reproduced in Part 4, the Autopsy In Paris chapter.

And Lecomte does not claim in that document that the examination was external – she calls it a "forensic report" and stated that her job was to "examine the body". (WFJ) [a]

Examinations are generally not carried out on the bodies of passengers in a car crash:[b]

- "usually, there is no post mortem[c] for the passengers because it is completely irrelevant"[1688] – Eva Steiner, inquest expert on French law

- "it is not usual to carry out a post mortem on the passengers because in most cases it is not relevant"[1689] (WFJ) Martine Monteil, Brigade Criminelle Chief.[d]

An examination of passengers in a car crash was not normal procedure, so why then were body examinations called for in this particular case?

The reverse side of the death certificate completed by Riou[e] states that when there is a medical legal obstacle "the body is at the disposal of the judicial authorities".

After Riou completed this form, following the death of Princess Diana, a copy of it would have been immediately faxed or delivered to the "judicial authorities" – i.e. the Public Prosecutor's office, or Maud Coujard.

From that point on, conducting a body examination of Princess Diana would have been a foregone conclusion. Coujard and Bestard were presented with an official death certificate completed by the officiating doctor stating that he had concerns that the circumstances of the death of Diana, Princess of Wales were suspicious.

Even though the body examination took place 1½ hours after any attempted life-saving activity had finished[a], both Riou and Pavie stayed

---

[a] A more detailed analysis of other evidence revealing an autopsy was conducted is in Part 4, the Autopsy In Paris chapter.

[b] There are also indications in Coujard's evidence that she may have been aware that what occurred was not normal practice. When Coujard says in her statement – not heard by the jury – that it was normal to order an autopsy of the driver, she then adds "nevertheless" she or Bestard "decided to request that an experienced forensic pathologist proceed with an external physical examination" of Diana and Dodi's bodies. In her statement Coujard is cagey about disclosing who actually authorised this procedure: "the Public Prosecutor or I, without being any more precise". Paget Report, p535 (WFJ). At the inquest Coujard stated: "I was not the one who made the decision – it is the Public Prosecutor": 20 Nov 07: 15.1.

[c] Post-Mortem: Oxford definition: "an examination of a dead body to establish the cause of death". The Lecomte examination reports for both Diana and Dodi both conclude with a cause of death based on the results of the examination.

[d] Monteil goes on to say: "In the event, it was the Public Prosecutor's Department that decided to examine the bodies". She doesn't distinguish between the words "post mortem" and "examine". This is supported by the Oxford definition of a post mortem: "an examination of a dead body to establish the cause of death".

[e] Blank form reproduced previous chapter.

around and spoke with Lecomte ahead of the examination.[1690] It may be that they communicated genuine concerns to Lecomte regarding Diana's treatment in the ambulance. Riou – who is a specialist in anaesthetics and resuscitation[1691] – or Pavie, may have been suspicious enough to specifically suggest samples to be taken.[b]

On the night:

1)   Riou ticked "YES" in the medical legal obstacle box on Diana's death certificate

2)   Coujard received that death certificate – probably within minutes, by fax

3)   Coujard consulted Bestard, telling him of the situation

4)   Bestard decided that Lecomte needed to conduct a body examination to determine cause of death

5)   Coujard formally requested Lecomte to conduct the examination

6)   Riou and Pavie spoke with Lecomte after her arrival at the hospital, but before she conducted the examination

7)   Lecomte carried out the examination in the presence of an unidentified police photographer – who took photos[c] – and Jean-Claude Mulès.[1692]

Most of the evidence of what occurred was withheld from the Baker inquest jury. It is particularly significant that: a) the completed JM/12 death certificate cannot be "found"; b) the jury never got to hear about the existence of the JM/12 form – blank or completed; and c) the jury never got to hear what Riou had to say on this subject.

This evidence – that Riou may have believed Diana's death was suspicious – is supported by the terminology used on the three key known

---

[a] Diana's official time of death was 4 a.m. and the examination commenced at 5.30.

[b] It may be significant that Lecomte appeared to deny that any contact with the doctors took place: "Question: Do you know what the doctors did to the body beforehand? Answer: No, when I arrived I made an external examination. I did not take any samples." If suggestions had been put to Lecomte during this conversation that Diana's death was suspicious, this could give rise to a situation where she would deny the conversation ever took place – which is what has happened. There would not appear to be any benefit in Lecomte denying the conversation if it had only been about the surgical actions taken by the doctors. Source: Dominique Lecomte, Witness Statement, Operation Paget, Paris, 9 March 2005, reproduced in The Documents book, p141.

[c] The fact photos were taken was confirmed in statements made by Martine Monteil, Jean-Claude Mulès and Richard Shepherd – all of these statements were withheld from the jury. This evidence is in Part 4, Autopsy in Paris chapter.

541

body examination documents: the Lecomte examination reports for Diana and Dodi and the police report for Dodi.

The heading on Lecomte's report for Diana[a] reads: "FORENSIC REPORT". (WFJ) Dodi's report heading[b] reads: "FORENSIC MEDICAL REPORT". (WFJ) In his report Mulès describes Dodi's examination as "forensic observations".[cd]

All three key known reports describe these examinations as "forensic" – not "external". The Oxford dictionary definition for "forensic" reads: "relating to the use of scientific methods to investigate crime".

The examination of Princess Diana's body was conducted as a result of concerns raised by Professor Bruno Riou[e], early on 31 August 1997, that a crime had been committed.[f]

This evidence is also supported during the cross-examination of Maud Coujard at the inquest. Coujard confirmed that the Diana and Dodi examinations' results "meant that actually there were not any barriers to their burial".[1693] When questioned further by Ian Burnett, Coujard confirmed that after the results of the examinations came in and the consequent issuing of burial certificates, "there was [now] no forensic reason to retain the bodies" of Princess Diana and Dodi Fayed.[1694]

There may have been an additional reason for the conduct of the Lecomte examination of Princess Diana.

When the subject of body examinations came up at the inquest, Maud Coujard immediately added an unsolicited "sophistication":

In August, we knew that the Princess of Wales had undergone extended medical examinations.[1695]

This could point to a concern about pregnancy – mainly because it's difficult to imagine any other topic that could link these three factors: the death of the princess; extended medical examinations; and a post-death body examination.[g]

Pregnancy would not have been a concern to the French, but it may have been an issue for sections of the British Establishment. Evidence on the

---

[a] Reproduced in Part 4, Figure 1.

[b] Shown in *The Documents* book, p397 (UK edit).

[c] Reproduced as Figure 4 in Part 4. Also viewable on the inquest website: INQ0041592.

[d] The police report for Diana's body examination has never surfaced.

[e] When he completed form JM/12.

[f] A similar examination was conducted on Dodi Fayed's body so as not to draw specific attention to the fact an examination had been conducted on the body of Princess Diana.

[g] Diana's final visit to her GP, Dr Wheeler, was to address a problem with breakthrough bleeding: Dr Peter Wheeler, Witness Statement, 28 June 2006, included in Part 4, Autopsy in Paris chapter. (WFJ)

embalming[a] shows that the British were involved in the decisions that were being made in the La Pitié Salpêtrière Hospital following the death of Princess Diana.

If the British were involved with the embalming then why wouldn't they have been involved with the body examination?

The conduct by Lecomte of a body examination would have been an opportunity to carry out sampling of blood and urine, which could have been tested at the hospital to establish – or dismiss – pregnancy.[b] Pavie said to British police in March 2005 – in the context of the medical treatment at the hospital – "She had practically none of her own blood left, because of the many drips."[1696] (WFJ)

In light of this evidence – that Diana may not have had her own blood in her body after she died – a sample of urine may have been more accurate as a test for pregnancy. Later evidence will show that in the context of the embalming in Paris and the post-mortem in London, urine takes on increased significance.

Where Are the Documents?

Why has there been a major suppression of documentation surrounding these body examinations?

Why is it that after nine years of investigation there are still documents that the author of this book has not seen – the official request by the Public Prosecutor's Department for the conduct of the examinations; the police report of Princess Diana's examination; the completed JM/12 death certificate; the death certificate kept by the FCO? [c]

Why is it that the jury were not shown any of those documents and also were prevented from seeing the other documents reproduced earlier or in Part

---

[a] See later.

[b] The police report for Dodi's Paris examination – reproduced in Part 4 – shows that blood and urine samples were taken from the body of Dodi Fayed. It could be significant, in the light of that evidence, that the police report on Diana's examination is missing.

[c] Paget's interview of Riou: "DS Grater showed Professor Riou a copy of a document obtained via the Foreign and Commonwealth Office (FCO).... Professor Riou confirmed that this is the form on which he recorded the Princess of Wales' death and her time of death immediately after she was deceased. He also confirmed his signature. He explained that this is the form used for certification of death at the hospital and for hospital administration purposes." That form – which is separate to the JM/12 document – was also not shown to the inquest jury. Source: Prof Bruno Riou, Witness Statement, 7 March 2006, reproduced in The Documents book, p375 (UK Edition).

4: Lecomte's examination report for Diana; the blank JM/12 death certificate form; Mulès' September 5 correction report[a]? And also Lecomte's examination report for Dodi?[b]

Why is it that out of a total of at least 9 documents relating to the body examinations, the jury only saw one – the police report of Dodi Fayed's examination?

1 out of 9. Why?

Why is it that out of the players who were involved in the examinations – Lecomte, Coujard, anonymous police photographer, Riou[c], Bestard, Monteil, Mulès[d] – the evidence of only one, Coujard, was heard at the inquest?

1 out of 7.[e] Why?[f]

This chapter deals with a French examination of the body of Britain's Princess Diana. Why did the British inquest get to hear so little about such a major operation?

The answer to all of these questions is that it was not in the interests of the British authorities for evidence to be seen by the jury indicating that early on 31 August 1997 the officiating doctor had serious concerns that the death of Princess Diana occurred under suspicious circumstances.

Additionally it was not in the interests of the British authorities to see evidence indicating that an opportunity was possibly taken to conduct a pregnancy test on samples from the body of Princess Diana.

If the examination of /Diana's body by Professor Lecomte was just a "normal" external examination, why was it that the jury were not provided with most of the evidence relating to it?

Autopsy in Paris

As with every aspect of this case so far, no one event should be seen as a stand-alone, but must be viewed in the context of the surrounding events.

The examination conducted by Lecomte at 5.30 a.m. must be looked at along with the embalming that took place in Paris later that day and

---

[a] This is a report raised by Mulès to "correct" his police report of Dodi's examination – it is reproduced and addressed in the Autopsy in Paris chapter in Part 4.

[b] Reproduced in *The Documents* book, p397.

[c] Riou was cross-examined at the inquest, but not about the body examination or the JM/12 form.

[d] Mulès was cross-examined at the inquest, but not about the body examinations.

[e] At least 7 – this list does not include the anonymous "team" that Monteil stated she sent to the Diana examination: Martine Monteil, Witness Statement, 15 November 2006, reproduced in The Documents book, p57 (UK Edition) (WFJ).

[f] If the jury only hears the evidence of one person, this prevents them from being able to compare testimony and see possible conflicts between witness accounts.

eventually should also be seen in the context of the final post-mortem, conducted by Robert Chapman in London at 8.21 p.m.[a] that evening.

It is only when these events are viewed as a complete package that one can understand the full significance of each individual event that took place.

This will become clearer as the amazing story revealed in this book continues to unfold....

Meanwhile events were moving quickly back at the crash scene.

---

[a] London time.

84   Techniques in the Tunnel

The French employed some strange techniques in their investigation of the Alma Tunnel during the early hours of that Sunday morning.

Investigating in the Dark

Prefect of police Philippe Massoni – who was standing in the tunnel from about 12.50 a.m. – stated that he "told the Logistics Directorate to send powerful lighting to the scene".[1697] This indicates that Massoni was aware that the tunnel lights were inadequate.

Did Massoni happen to notice that the "powerful lighting" didn't arrive?

In all of the post-crash photo evidence – including the police's own shots – there is not one picture including any lighting other than the fixed tunnel lights or headlights of vehicles. Also, the evidence of the investigators was:

-       the lights of the emergency vehicles "enabled us to see these second marks of tyres"[1698] – Thierry Brunet, BCA police sergeant
-       "we had just the light of these vehicles"[1699] – Brunet
-       "the lighting was not so great"[1700] – Thierry Clotteaux, BCA police sergeant
-       "because it was night-time [the single tyre mark] was not very visible – [the investigators] couldn't see it"[1701] – Hubert Pourceau, BCA police deputy sergeant

One does not need to be a crash investigator to realise that when an investigation is conducted at night then there is a requirement for adequate lighting, in order to see the detail of the crash scene – tyre markings, debris etc.

Yet this is clearly not what occurred. The initial investigation was carried out in a tunnel that provided only very basic lighting – at best – and with no torches.

This evidence raises the question: Why did Massoni specifically mention in his 2006 statement that he called for powerful lighting?

Was he trying to create an illusion that there was powerful lighting, when there wasn't?

It is regrettable that no lawyers followed up on this, to ask why the tunnel investigation was carried out under such ridiculous conditions.

Tyre Marks

There were two sets of tyre marks at the crash scene:
1) a single 19 metre mark that started just inside the tunnel entrance
2) a double 32 metre parallel set of tyre marks that commenced about 10 metres after the single mark finished – these double marks led straight to the point of impact, the 13th pillar.[a]

The inquest heard:

> **The French investigators reached the surprising conclusion that the pair of curved tyre marks had not come from the Mercedes.**[1702]

MPS QC Richard Horwell describes this conclusion as surprising. It is also surprising that Horwell stated "I do not want to take too long on this"[1703] and Nicholas Hilliard[b] said "we don't need to go into" their reasons for reaching that conclusion.[1704]

Why wouldn't the lawyers – Horwell, police; Hilliard, inquest – reveal the reasoning and detail of the French calculations?

We have a pair of tyre marks that run straight into the 13th pillar, yet the French concluded that they did not relate to the Mercedes.

Why?

An understanding of what occurred in the French investigation is critical to the case. If there was evidence of a French cover-up, then what were they covering up?

The fact that both of these lawyers only alluded to this issue – it was not addressed by any other lawyers – indicates that there was a concerted effort, probably directed by Baker, to ensure that the detail of the erroneous French reasoning was withheld from the jury.[c]

Spotting the Debris

The French investigators failed to collect all the crash debris.

There are several reasons for this failure.

First, they did not have their own light source and the Alma Tunnel lighting is not adequate for the conduct of a thorough crash investigation.

Second, Brunet said that they "waited for the emergency services to evacuate the victims". He added that "these very safety vehicles had already

---

[a] The tyre marks can be viewed on the plan just before the earlier Overtaking the Mercedes chapter or alternatively in the inquest evidence: INQ-PLAN-0007.
[b] Inquest lawyer.
[c] There was also no mention of this issue in the Paget Report.

drove on the marks or the evidence which we could have".[1705] Diana's ambulance did not leave the scene until 1.41 a.m. – 48 minutes after the arrival of Brunet and Clotteaux – and other emergency vehicles left later than that. This means there was a lengthy period in which debris evidence was being compromised – driven and walked over.

Third, Jean-Claude Mulès, who headed the investigation, had a very strange method for collecting debris:

> **What we do is what we call a scanning of all the road from the car ... and I scanned all the parts of the road to find any type of debris.**[1706]

Searching for debris by car, rather than walking with powerful torches, could compromise efforts to secure all debris.

Fourth, Brunet, who was senior to Clotteaux, admitted to the inquest that he was "not an expert".[1707]

Brunet stated that the debris "we did not circle was not significant"[1708] and Clotteaux said: "we circled everything which had to be circled".[1709] And Mulès claimed that "it was not necessary to pick up the debris that was elsewhere" – i.e. away from the tyre marks.[1710]

Mulès added: "I could not pick up all of the debris that was in the tunnel".[1711]

These three investigators did not pick up all the debris they saw, but instead made decisions in the tunnel (under poor lighting) about what was relevant.

Mulès and Brunet agreed that "old debris" was not collected,[1712] but Clotteaux said "I have no knowledge about that".[1713]

When Brunet was asked if it was possible to tell "at the scene how old it is", he replied: "I cannot answer. I do not know."[1714]

When it was put to Clotteaux that "you did not know whether any other vehicle had been involved", he replied "Yes, you are right".[1715] However, when Croxford put to Clotteaux: "You understood ... that there was a possibility that another vehicle had been involved", he responded "Yes, I did".[1716]

So yes, he wasn't aware of another vehicle being involved, and later, yes, he was aware.

Brunet testified that "we had debris of various colours",[1717] but when asked later about this (twice) by Hilliard, he said "The white ones and the red ones were similar".[1718]

Mulès confirmed that part of his role was to "personally [walk] through the tunnel" to identify debris,[1719] but moments later describes himself "scanning ... all the road from the car in the one way and also in the opposite way of the tunnel ... to find any type of debris".[1720]

Hubert Pourceau, another BCA investigator, stated that when he arrived at 8 a.m. the road cleaning crew "were cleaning up the oil that was on the road and the debris", then when confronted on that, immediately changed his account to say that the debris "had [already] been swept off".[1721]

Neither of Pourceau's scenarios – cleaning up or sweeping away – is acceptable when it comes to the collection of debris from a crash scene that is under investigation.

The French evidence is inconsistent and conflicting and the tunnel investigation appears to have been conducted in a very sloppy fashion. There is every reason to conclude that not all the debris was collected, and this is certainly supported by witness evidence from journalist Andrei Chtorkh.

Chtorkh arrived at the scene at 6.30 a.m. and saw "several pieces of glass littering the ground". He added:

> **These were tiny pieces of glass and then I picked up the largest of these pieces, which measures about 2 centimetres by 1.**

He later handed in one of these pieces to the police.[1722]

Chtorkh located the debris at "15 metres from the entrance at the Concorde end"[1723] – this fits with the information on the tunnel plans.[a]

If the item of debris that Chtorkh handed in had not related to the crash, then we would have heard about it before now. A major concern though is that Chtorkh didn't just see this one piece of glass, but "pieces", plural.

Paget investigator Anthony Read also stated that reconstructions of the Fiat and Mercedes' lights "appear to show that there are significant pieces of debris missing".[1724]

Ian Croxford QC pointed out failures in Read's investigation:

-       failure to raise the issue of the missing debris with the French, despite accusing them in his report – Read replied: "I cannot answer you that, I am afraid. There was a lot to do. It was one of many things. It was not asked" and "it must have been an omission"[1725]

-       Read was unable to reference a quote from Mulès that he included in his report – he told the inquest: "I know it is [in my report] and I do not know where it was that I found that comment" that not all the debris was collected.[1726]

At best, Read is a sloppy investigator and this point was amply shown earlier in his shameful involvement in misleading the jury regarding the French testing of paparazzi motorcycles.[bc]

---

[a] See INQ-PLAN-0007. This plan was also reproduced earlier.

[b] See earlier chapter on Were the Motorbikes Paparazzi?

[c] Read also changed his evidence to state that the Fiat Uno didn't veer out of the right lane when the evidence shows that it must have – see Part 1, section on Which Lane? in the White Fiat Uno chapter.

85   Removing the Evidence

At 4.55 a.m. the Mercedes S280 was removed from the Alma Tunnel[1727] and then the cleansing of the crash scene commenced.

First Cleansing

The scene was cleansed just 4½ hours after the crash.

Head of Operation Paget John Stevens told Henri Paul's parents that "the road services had cleaned everything up after the accident at around 5 a.m."[1728] This is supported by journalist Samuel Goldschmidt who stated that after the removal of the Mercedes "the tunnel was going to be cleaned [and] at 5.25 [a.m.] … it was re-opened to traffic."[1729a]

First Reopening

Within 30 minutes of the first cleaning the lanes were open.

French police lieutenant Bruno Bouaziz said that "the road was re-opened to traffic at 0525 hours [5.25 a.m.]."[1730]

Newsweek Paris correspondent Christopher Dickey visited the tunnel at around 7 a.m.:

> **I wanted to see the scene. I was sure it would be closed, but it was completely open. I was astonished. This was Diana. She was dead. This was a big thing. I was sure the police would close the tunnel for several days, but it was completely open at 7 a.m.[1731] (WFJ)**

Second Cleansing

An hour later the westbound lanes were closed again and the site was re-cleansed.

Hubert Pourceau visited the tunnel at 8 a.m.[1732] He "noticed that cleaning services were present and there was still some oil on the carriageway where the Mercedes had come to a halt." He stated that "the opposite carriageway" was still open – just the westbound side was closed and cleaned.[1733] (WFJ)

---

[a] A photo of the truck cleansing the tunnel with detergent is shown on the cover of Part 3.

Pourceau added that the westbound "carriageway was re-opened when he left the scene at around 10 a.m. to 10.30 a.m." [1734] (WFJ)

Removing The Evidence

There is a definite chain of events – cleaning, all lanes reopened, closure of westbound lanes, cleaning, reopening of westbound lanes.

What is most shocking about this evidence is that within 5 hours of the crash the scene had been cleaned, and within 8 hours it had been cleaned twice.

There was a major effort on the part of the French authorities to very quickly remove all traces of the crash.

This is not normal practice for a crash investigation intent on gleaning as much evidence as possible from the scene.

86 Time to Settle Up

Early on Sunday morning the first edition of London's *Daily Mirror* contained the article – titled: "Queen 'to strip Harrods of its Royal Crest'".[a] The author Andrew Golden stated:[b]

> **The Royal Family may withdraw their seal of approval from Harrods ... as a result of Diana's affair with owner's son, Dodi Fayed. The top people's store, with its long and proud tradition of Royal patronage may be about to lose the Prince of Wales Royal crest.... The Royal Family are furious about the frolics of Di, 36, and Dodi, 41, which they believe have further undermined the Monarchy. Prince Philip, in particular, has ... made no secret as to how he feels about his daughter-in-law's latest man, referring to Dodi as an 'oily bedhopper'. At Balmoral next week, the Queen will preside over a meeting of the Way Ahead Group, where the Windsors sit down with their senior advisers to discuss policy matters. MI6 has prepared a special report on the Egyptian-born Fayeds, which will be presented to the meeting. The delicate subject of Harrods and its Royal warrants is also expected to be discussed and the Fayeds can expect little sympathy from Philip. A friend of the Royals said yesterday 'Prince Philip has let rip several times recently about the Fayeds – at a dinner party during a country shoot and while on a visit to close friends in Germany. He has been banging on about his contempt for Dodi and how he is undesirable as a future stepfather to William and Harry. Diana has been told in no uncertain terms about the consequences should she continue the relationship with the Fayed boy.... Now the Royal Family may decide it is time to settle up.[1735]**

Andrew Golden should have been heard from at the inquest, but that never happened.

---

[a] This paper was withdrawn from circulation on Sunday morning, following the crash.

[b] Reproduced earlier in the Special WAG Meeting chapter.

87   James Andanson: Was He There?

At 5.48 a.m. – just 23 minutes after the Alma Tunnel was reopened to traffic – high-flying paparazzo James Andanson exited the motorway at La Folie-B/Paris heading for Paris' Orly airport.[1736]

After arriving he purchased an airline ticket to Corsica at precisely 6.23[1737] and was airborne on the flight by 7.20 a.m.[1738]

Andanson would later use this trip as an alibi for the crash.

But was this a genuine alibi?

Or was James Andanson driving his white Fiat Uno in the Alma Tunnel at 12.23 a.m. on 31 August 1997?

Who Did Witnesses See?

Three witnesses – Souad Moufakkir, Georges and Sabine Dauzonne – gave descriptions of the white Fiat Uno driver and a dog in the back of the car.

In Souad's only detailed description of the driver she stated:

> **He was Mediterranean, short – because his head was only just above the steering wheel. His skin was tanned and his hair was very dark brown and wiry. He was in his mid-30s. In the back seat was a huge Alsatian [dog].[1739] (WFJ)**

Georges Dauzonne provided a description to the French police in September 1997:

> **The driver ... was a male, of European appearance, with white skin, possibly 40 to 50 years of age, with short brown hair, and he may have been tall.[1740] (WFJ)**
> **A large dog was on the rear seat.... It must have been an Alsatian or a black Labrador. It was wearing an orange muzzle or 'bandana'.[1741] (WFJ)**

And Sabine also told the police within three weeks of the crash:

The driver was European-looking, fair-skinned but a bit Mediterranean, I think his eyes must be dark, his hair was dark brown and short, he must be between 35 and 45.[1742] **(WFJ)**

In the boot of the car ... there was a fairly big dog with a long nose. It might have been a German shepherd. I remember one colour detail, a muzzle going round its face but not down to its nose or just a bandanna around its neck. Anyway this was brightly coloured, red or orange.[1743] **(WFJ)**

Under cross-examination Elisabeth Andanson admitted that their family dog – which was "a Labrador, sand colour like a Golden Retriever"[1744] – had worn a red bandanna at some undisclosed stage.[1745]

Figure 24

Profile photo of James Andanson driving. This image should have been included as an identification photo for the witnesses and jury, but wasn't.

Witness Descriptions				Andanson
Feature	**Souad**	**Georges**	**Sabine**	**Andanson**
Age	Mid 30s	40 to 50	35 to 45	51
Skin Colour	NA	White	Fair	White
Appearance	Mediterranean; Tanned	European	European Mediterranean	Tanned
Hair	Wiry	Short	Short	Short; Thinning
Hair Colour	Dark Brown	Brown	Dark Brown	Dark Brown
Height	Short	Maybe Tall	NA	1.75m[a]; Medium
Weight	NA	NA	Medium[b]	Medium
Description of Dog				**Andanson's Dog**
Type	Alsatian; German Shepherd[c]	Alsatian; Black Labrador.	German Shepherd Profile/[d]	Golden Labrador
Size	Huge	Large	Fairly big	2 years; Large
Colour	Dark Brown; Black Spots[e]	Black	NA	Brown
Details	NA	Muzzle or bandanna: Red[f] or orange	Muzzle or bandanna: Red or Orange; Long Nose	Red Bandanna

[a] 5 ft. 9 ins. From Andanson's passport: 7 Feb 08: 21.18.
[b] Stated to Hello! Magazine in January 1998: Fiat Uno Witnesses, Hello! magazine, January 17 1998, www.public-interest.co.uk/diana/dianafuwit.htm (WFJ)
[c] At the inquest: 6 Nov 07: 72.14.
[d] At inquest: 29 Oct 07: 59.2
[e] At the inquest: 6 Nov 07: 72.17.
[f] At inquest: 29 Oct 07: 21.14

Andanson: "I Was There"

Around Christmas 1997 James Andanson told the Dard family that he was in the Alma Tunnel at the time of the crash.

This conversation took place four months after the crash, about two months after Andanson had sold the Uno[1746] and a month before he received warning from *France Soir* that the French police were going to be interviewing him.[1747]

Andanson was primarily visiting the well-known French author Frédéric Dard, who later died.[a] Other family members were present during the conversation.

Dard's wife Françoise told Paget:

> |Andanson| followed |Diana and Dodi| by motorbike and witnessed
> the crash of which he took photographs. This is in no way an
> interpretation on my part – it is what he told me.[1748] (WFJ)

Their daughter Joséphine testified:

> |Andanson| said that he was there and he said that he had
> photographs.[1749]

Françoise told the inquest that "these photographs were kept in a safe"[1750] and Joséphine revealed Andanson's motive in relaying his story to her father, the author. She told Paget:

> James Andanson wanted to work with her father on a book about the
> death of the Princess of Wales. He said that he had some pictures of
> the incident and wanted her father's assistance with producing the
> text.... When questioned further, James Andanson apparently chose
> not to speak any more, preferring to make an appointment for a later
> date.[1751] (WFJ)

If Andanson was the driver of the Uno in the Alma Tunnel, he would not necessarily trust the disclosure of that fact to anyone. If he was working on behalf of an intelligence agency like MI6, he would have received clear instructions not to divulge his part in the plot to anyone else. That could explain why Andanson would include erroneous information like the use of his motorbike.

If Andanson did play a role in the assassination of Diana, he may have been promised access to the photos that were taken during the journey – as part of his reward.

If he had access to the journey photos, he may have sensed an opportunity for a very successful book, which would have included the previously unpublished crash-related photos.

This dream would have collapsed in a heap a month later, when the French police were forced by circumstance[a] to seriously interview him as a suspect

---

[a] Dard died on 6 June 2000.

regarding his possible involvement in the crash. There is no record of Andanson making claims regarding the crash after he publicly became a suspect as the driver of the Fiat Uno. Joséphine stated that the claims were made in his second to last meeting with the Dards[1752] (WFJ) and it appears that it was not a topic of discussion in his final meeting.

The story he told the Dards provided enough information for Frédéric Dard to have understood that James Andanson had access to the photos, but without implicating himself as part of any plot surrounding the crash.

In 1998 the Dards should have been interviewed by the French police and Andanson should have been challenged with the Dards' evidence of the conversation. If the police weren't aware of the Dards before, they would have been after Francis Gillery produced his 1998 documentary on James Andanson.[1753]

Why weren't the Dards interviewed at that stage – when Frédéric Dard and James Andanson were both still alive?

Instead, the first police interview was in October 2006,[1754] just two months before the Paget Report was published. By then, Frédéric Dard and James Andanson were both dead, and the evidence relied on the nine year old recall of Frédéric's wife and daughter, who both admitted that they didn't hear the full conversation.[1755]

Changing Alibis

Brigade Criminelle Lieutenant Eric Gigou made the initial police contact with James Andanson on 11 February 1998.[1756] Andanson told Gigou that "he had been in St Tropez on the night of the crash".[1757]

When Jean-Claude Mulès spoke with him the next day, Andanson stated that "he had been at home in Lignières".[1758]

Two different alibis in two days.

When Gigou is confronted with this at the inquest he dismisses it with: "What he told me was not official because it was on the phone".[1759]

This approach is typical of the French attitude to the investigation.

In his official French statement Andanson said:

> **On Saturday 30th August 1997 I was at Le Manoir[b] in the company of my wife and my daughter, Kimberley. Before leaving at 4 o'clock in the morning by car, to get to Orly and catch a plane at 7.20 a.m. for Corsica (Bonifacio), I went to bed at 10.30 p.m. I listened to the news on Europe No 1, as every day. I took my vehicle at about 3.45 a.m. and**

---

[a] In short, Al Fayed investigators located Andanson's white Fiat Uno in an auto yard: 4 Feb 08: 87.22.
[b] Andanson's family home.

took the motorway at Bourges, exit number 7. There I took my ticket, which I paid for at the Survilliers tollgate with my credit card.... It came to 102 francs. I took my plane to Bonifacio.[1760]

Andanson stated that he was at home in bed during the crash – this was approximately 280 km south of the Alma Tunnel. His earliest supporting documentation was an exit tollway ticket at Paris at 5.48 a.m. on 31 August 1997 – 5 hours and 25 minutes after the crash.

Elisabeth Andanson also told Paget:

I can tell you that we slept together. I remember getting up for James' departure at 4 a.m. and having said goodbye to him when he left.[1761] (WFJ)

Andanson claims that he was home on 30 August "in the company of my wife and my daughter". His wife Elisabeth's evidence is that she was not at home for a substantial period of the day – more than nine hours.

She has testified that she was visiting James' boss, Hubert Henrotte, 280 km away in Paris.[a] Elisabeth stated at the inquest that the meeting took place "in the early afternoon, at around 2/2.30."[1762] And in February 1998, she told the French police: "I remember perfectly coming back from Paris on 30.08.97 at 9.00 p.m. at the latest...." [1763]

Elisabeth said that the Paris to Lignières trip took about 2½ hours each way. This would indicate that she left home sometime before noon. Elisabeth therefore would have been away from home for a period at least nine hours on 30 August 1997.

It means that Andanson's wife is unable to vouch for her husband's movements during the afternoon and evening of Saturday August 30.

There are three possibilities:
1) Andanson was home and had forgotten that Elisabeth wasn't
2) Andanson was home but is lying about Elisabeth being there
3) Andanson was not at home.

James' daughter, Kimberley, who was aged nine in 1997, has never been interviewed and was not called at the inquest. Elisabeth stated in 2006 that she and Kimberley returned from the south of France on 24 or 25 August, "when Kimberley went back to school and I took her back myself".[1764]

Elisabeth's wording indicates that this was to a boarding school. In her evidence – statements and inquest – Elisabeth made no mention of Kimberley's presence at home that weekend.

James Jnr., who is not mentioned in his father's statement, was home that weekend though.

In his February 1998 statement James Jnr said "I think I remember that [my father] telephoned us, my mother and me, at about 4.30 a.m. or 5.00 a.m. on 31.8.97." [1765] This was a phone call James Andanson made to advise his

---

[a] Henrotte confirmed this meeting took place: 21 Feb 08: 14.13.

family of the death of Princess Diana. James Jnr. states the call was to "us, my mother and me", and makes no mention of the presence of his sister.

James Jnr told the French police in February 1998: Referring to the weekend of 30-31 August 1997: "I do not remember where my father was, but one thing is certain, he was not at home."[1766]

James Andanson stated that: "On Saturday 30th August 1997 I was at Le Manoir in the company of <u>my wife and my daughter</u>, Kimberley" – clearly his wife was not there for a large part of the day, there is no supporting evidence that his daughter was there, but there is evidence that his son <u>was</u> there.

Why does Andanson mention the presence of his wife – not there for nine hours – and daughter – never corroborated – but not his son – who was there.

James Jnr testified to the police that his father was not at home that weekend – he said that is "one thing [that] is certain".

Was Andanson in the Tunnel?

Judge Baker told his jury in his Summing Up:

> **No longer could it be suggested that Mr Andanson was behind the wheel of his Fiat Uno. The evidence does not begin to provide any support for that.[1767]**

But is that true? Or did Scott Baker simply ignore – or even disallow – the full evidence regarding James Andanson's involvement?

What is the evidence that James Andanson was not in the Alma Tunnel? It basically relies on the alibi from his wife, Elisabeth, who said that on the night James was in bed beside her. Evidence in Part 1[a] reveals that Elisabeth Andanson is an unreliable witness. In this light, particularly to be considered is James Jnr's early evidence that his father was not at home on that weekend.

The early witness descriptions of the Fiat Uno driver fit James Andanson – the jury only heard parts of these.

Although I believe it is impossible, on the available information, to prove absolutely that James Andanson was the driver of the Fiat Uno in the tunnel, the weight of evidence[b] points strongly in that direction:

The coroner, in his Summing Up, repeatedly said that James Andanson was not there,[c] but this assertion was not based on the evidence presented.

The difficulties for the jury were:

1) They didn't get to hear, or have access to, some of the most important and earliest witness statement evidence

---

[a] Chapter 5C.
[b] Covered more fully in Part 1 Chapter 5C.
[c] See also 1 Apr 08: 33.25 and 1 Apr 08: 39.19.

2) The inquest Fiat Uno evidence was spread over two months, with other subjects being dealt with in between

The coroner removed any reference to the Fiat Uno in the final verdicts available to the jury. If they had believed that the Uno driver was culpable, they would have had to return an Open Verdict.

88   Early Royal Decisions

Much of the early decisions following the death of Princess Diana were made from Balmoral – even though Diana was no longer a royal.

Royal Structure

On the morning of the crash, 31 August 1997, the key royal – family and household – figures were in various locations throughout the UK.
See diagram later in this chapter.[ab1768]

Royal Decisions

Early in the morning critical decisions were being made at Balmoral:[c]
-      a decision to repatriate Diana's body on that day
-      a decision for Charles to travel to Paris, accompanied by Diana's sisters, to carry out that repatriation
-      a decision to cover Diana's coffin with the royal standard
-      a decision to deploy royalty protection officers to the Fulham Mortuary[d]
-      a decision to falsely state the burial of Diana would be at Windsor Castle – this led to the royal coroner illegally taking jurisdiction of Diana's body
-      a decision to ensure that Diana's dead body was returned to royal land – at St James' Palace – as soon as possible.

---

[a] Locations are shown directly under the name of the individual.
[b] The evidence of only two of these key people was heard at the inquest: Fellowes and Mather. Another six – the Queen, Janvrin, Ogilvy, Ross, Harding, Ridley – have also never been interviewed by any of the police investigations. Burton gave a police statement which was not read out at the inquest.
[c] The detailed evidence regarding these decisions is in Part 4, Chapters 3 and 4. The evidence is also addressed earlier and later in this book.
[d] This is covered in Part 4, the Police Presence section of the UK Post-Mortems chapter.

HOW THEY MURDERED PRINCESS DIANA

The key people who were entrusted with ensuring that these decisions were carried out – Malcolm Ross, Anthony Mather, John Burton, Prince Charles, Peter Harding, David Ogilvy – were all directly or indirectly answerable to Queen Elizabeth.

In the hours following the death of Princess Diana, the Queen of England was not in a state of inactive, paralysed shock – as has tended to be portrayed by both the media and entertainment industries over the years.

The question is: Why did the Queen move so quickly and definitely to reinstate Diana as a royal, and thereby ensure her control over the dead Diana's body?

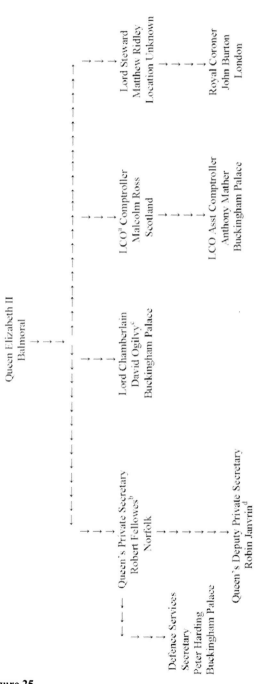

Figure 25

89   Royal Rush

As the morning progressed more people were learning about the tragedy that had unfolded: there had been a fatal crash in Paris' Alma Tunnel killing Dodi Fayed and the driver and now news was spreading that Diana, Princess of Wales had also died.

PM Tony Blair's press secretary Alistair Campbell received a call at 4 a.m.[a] from Robert Fellowes, the Queen's private secretary and Diana's brother-in-law.

Campbell wrote in his diary that he "got a flavour of the royal Establishment's approach" when Fellowes said:

> **'You know about Diana, do you? She's dead.' I said yes…. It was all very matter-of-fact and practical.**[1769]

Meanwhile plans for the Paris embalming and same-day rapid repatriation rolled on.

At around 5.30 a.m. PFG president Hervé Racine – who had earlier been woken by a call from London from Kenyons' president – phoned Michel Chapillon, the PFG French director, who was on holiday at the time.[1770] (WFJ)

Chapillon then set about notifying those in PFG who needed to be informed about the plans for embalming and/or repatriation. At 6.30 he rang Patrick Launay, PFG's repatriation director, who was on call that weekend. Launay told Paget: "[Chapillon] told me to be on standby".[1771] (WFJ)

At 7 a.m. Chapillon phoned Jean-Claude Plumet, PFG Director of Paris Agencies. He asked Plumet "to go into his office to deal with arrangements required for the Princess of Wales".[1772] (WFJ)

At the same time – 6 a.m. in the UK – the Queen's Lord Chamberlain's Office Comptroller Malcolm Ross, who was in Scotland, called his assistant Anthony Mather in London.[1773] Mather told Paget that "as a result of [Ross' phone call] I went straight to Buckingham Palace".[1774] (WFJ)

Mather stated:

> **There was never a separate plan for the funeral arrangements of Diana, Princess of Wales, as she was not at the time of her death a member of the Royal Family.**[1775] (WFJ)

---

[a] 5 a.m. Paris time.

He was told by Ross to immediately employ Operation Overstudy for the repatriation.[1776] (WFJ) Ross also told Mather that UK embalmers would be needed in Paris early – early enough to conduct an embalming ahead of the repatriation.

Before leaving home Mather phoned Levertons, the royal funeral directors. He got the resident manager, Daniel Tassell, and informed him that "there had been a death in Paris and it was not the Queen Mother".[1777] (WFJ)

At 6.30 Tassell phoned Keith Leverton and passed on this message: To "telephone Mather immediately at his home, not at Buckingham Palace".[1778] (WFJ)

When Leverton called, Mather informed him about the deaths. Leverton told Paget:

> **[Mather] instructed that we utilise Operation Overstudy to return her body to the United Kingdom. He said ... she would eventually be [buried] at St Georges Chapel, Windsor.... There was nothing else discussed or instructed during this conversation.[1779]**

Leverton said "nothing else ... [was] instructed".

Why does he say this?

His actions reveal that to be false – instead he was told by Mather that Diana would need to be embalmed that day in Paris by his people.

At 7.45 Keith Leverton phoned his brother Clive who was staying at his "mother-in-law's in Cheltenham".[1780] They then immediately contacted two embalmers.

Embalmer David Green was "away in Hampshire" when he received a call from Keith, who told him about Diana's death and to "return to our office in Camden immediately".[1781] (WFJ)

Meanwhile Clive contacted the second embalmer, Bill Fry.[1782] (WFJ)

Clive Leverton later told the inquest:

> **We had to get out to Paris quickly – we were under pressure getting our staff assembled.[1783]**

There was pressure because Levertons had been instructed to do an embalming of Diana – they were not told that the French had also received a similar instruction. David Green stated that he "learnt that [Diana] had received some embalming treatment by the French upon our arrival at the Salpêtrière Hospital".[1784] (WFJ)

Mather authorised the despatch of the two UK embalmers to Paris as a back-up plan. If the French embalming – which will be shown to have been illegal – had been prevented from taking place, then the British embalmers had the equipment with them to carry out a quick embalming prior to repatriating Diana.

This evidence reveals how keen the royals were to ensure an embalming of Diana took place before her body arrived back in the UK.

Why?

90 Fraud at the IML

Events were also moving rapidly in France.

Professor Dominique Lecomte concluded her hospital autopsy of Princess Diana at around 6.20 a.m. – 5.20 in London – and left La Pitié heading to the nearby IML.

Earlier in the morning both Henri Paul and Dodi Fayed's bodies had been transferred to the IML. Henri's was officially received at 3.40 a.m.[1785] (WFJ)

At 6.45 Lecomte commenced Dodi's autopsy – as authorised by the Public Prosecutor's Office[a] – and completed it around 7.15.[1786]

Professor Lecomte's most significant work that day was still to come – the autopsy of the Mercedes S280 driver, Henri Paul.

Two-Body Autopsy

The autopsy of Henri Paul commenced at 8.20 and concluded about 10 a.m.[1787]

Its most outstanding and fraudulent feature was that it was not just an autopsy on Henri Paul, but instead there were two bodies in the room – and both were autopsied as "Henri Paul".

One of the bodies was Henri Paul, but the other had a completely different identity.

The evidence to support this – two bodies in the room – is both strong and wide-ranging.

The inquest's own expert toxicologist, Robert Forrest, himself suggested that the samples extracted during this autopsy were not "good-quality samples of known provenance" and one couldn't be certain they came from "the right patient".[1788]

Were the samples that were later tested for alcohol[b] extracted from Henri Paul's body?

The evidence that there were two bodies in the IML autopsy room on Sunday morning 31 August 1997 includes:
- There were two sets of measurements recorded.

---

[a] See earlier Autopsy in Paris chapter.
[b] And used to indicate Henri Paul was drunk behind the wheel (see later).

On page 3 of Lecomte's official autopsy report – written up in 1 September 1997, the day following the autopsy – she has shown under the heading "External Examination of the Body" the words: "height 1m72, weight 73kg".[1789]

On page 12 of the report, the body map shows the weight as "76kg".[1790a]

The police report for the autopsy shows Henri Paul's height as "1m67" and his weight was "76kg".[1791]

The correct measurements at his time of death were height 1m67 and weight 76kg.

Lecomte appears to have inadvertently used details relating to the second body when she completed her main autopsy report the following day.

- There were two autopsy sample forms – Documents 12A and 13A – with completely different sample quantities recorded on each form.

Both documents appear below.

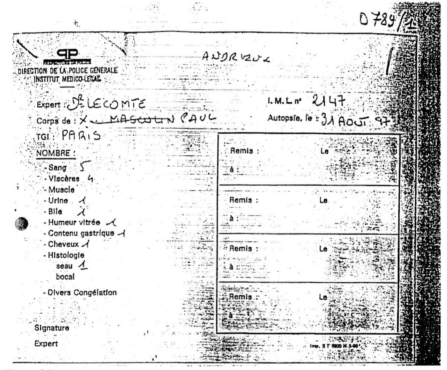

Figure 26

Autopsy sample document, numbered at the inquest as "13A".

---

[a] The body map was not shown to the inquest jury, but it is reproduced in The Documents book p70 (UK Edition).

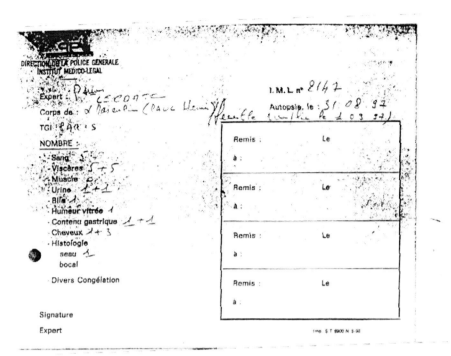

Figure 27

Autopsy sample document, numbered at the inquest variously as "12A", "13" or "UK 485".

Both documents 12A and 13A claim to be a record for the 31 August 1997 autopsy of Henri Paul, IML body number 2147.

Yet there are major differences between the forms – e.g. the sample quantities are quite different – Form 12A appears to record two lots of samples taken.

These forms are analysed in detail in Part 3.[a]

- The term "X Masculin" or "XM" ("unknown male") was used to describe the body on forms and on the label for one of the blood samples extracted.

On form 13A the "X Masculin" has been clearly replaced with "Paul". On 12A the "X Masculin" remains the prominent identification, with "Paul Henri" only showing in brackets.

Why do the forms say "X Masculin" on them when the identity of the body was known at the time of the autopsy?

---

[a] Autopsy Documentation section of 1st Autopsy chapter.

The first blood sample tested had "XM" on its label instead of "Henri Paul". This is shown in the Paget Report on page 298. This information was doctored – apparently to deceive the jury – on the form presented to the inquest (INQ0004440): "XM" was removed and there was a note that read: "Labelling possibly incorrect".

Both of these documents have been reproduced, adjacent to each other, in Part 3.[a]

- One body was described as coming from the fridge, the other wasn't.

Jean-Claude Mulès – who was present at this autopsy – told Paget:

Normally when a body arrived at the IML it was ... measured, weighed and tagged. It would then be placed in a refrigerator to await examination by the pathologist. In this case, however, because it was a Sunday and autopsies are not normally performed on a Sunday, the only bodies not in the fridges were those of Henri Paul and Dodi Al Fayed.[1792] (WFJ)

In support of this, the inquest was told that "Commander Mulès ... reports that the body of the late Henri Paul was never placed in the refrigerator unit at IML".[1793]

However Dominique Lecomte reported "performing an autopsy on ... a body which had been removed from the refrigerator".[1794]

- Some photos show the ID tag on the wrist only, while other photos show it on the ankle only.

Richard Shepherd stated:

There was, in fact, only one [ID] label. In the first of the three [photo] films, it could be seen attached to one of [Henri's] wrists.... But in the second and third of the films, it is seen attached to his ankle.[1795]

None of the 40 autopsy photos[1796] have ever been released and even the jury were prevented from viewing them. Duncan MacLeod[b] stated that "the jury for obvious reasons won't" see the photos[1797] but if Baker was serious about giving the jury the opportunity to discover precisely what happened in this autopsy, then they should have been provided with the evidential photos taken during it.

Why are photos taken during an autopsy if they cannot be used later as evidence in an inquest? What is the point in taking photos if the very people who are expected to draw conclusions on the veracity of the autopsy results are not allowed to view them?

At the inquest Mulès was not challenged on the label inconsistencies as revealed by the photos. When one considers that he was the only witness present who was heard from, this is not a minor oversight.

---

[a] Figures 5 and 6 in the section on Label Descriptions in the 1st Autopsy chapter.
[b] MPS lawyer.

- During cross-examination Mulès inadvertently used the term "bodies" (plural) in reference to the autopsy of Henri Paul.

He told the inquest:

The autopsy |of Henri| had been totally completed. The only operations which had to remain were ... for the <u>bodies</u> to become visible.[1798]

- Lecomte has recorded two separate and conflicting versions of the blood sample source – the heart and the chest cavity.

Lecomte failed to disclose the sample source in her September 1 autopsy report. Then nine days later she stated in an additional report that "the blood was taken from the left haemothorax area".[1799]

The following year in another report for the French investigation Lecomte[a] wrote that the source was "cardiac".[1800] (WFJ)

- There is photo evidence of two sample bottles containing blood taken prior to the opening of Henri Paul's chest.

Richard Shepherd told the inquest:

I believe |from seeing the photos| ... there are two small glass bottles containing blood before the chest of Mr Henri Paul was opened.[1801]

- Gilbert Pépin – the toxicologist who tested the samples – described two completely different sample labels for Blood Sample 2[b] – on different documents.

The first document was raised by Dr Pépin and was filed in the French investigation dossier at D826.[c] (WFJ)

The record of the sample label on that document reads:

PAUL Henri
I.M.L. no. 2147
31 August 1997
Mme Professor LECOMTE

This differs considerably from the evidence the inquest heard – taken from Pépin's 9 September 1997 report:[1802]

Henri Paul
Institute Medico-Legal number 2147
31st August 1997
Professor Lecomte

---

[a] A joint report with toxicologist Gilbert Pépin.
[b] The detail identifying sample numbers is in Part 3, section on Sample Labelling in Chapter 1.
[c] Reproduced in Part 3, Figure 7.

All 4 items of information are shown differently on each label. The main consistency is that both labels are devoid of a sample source.[a]

- The finding of an elevated carbon monoxide level that is not supported by evidence relating to Henri Paul.

Carbon monoxide measured 20.7% in this autopsy.[1803]

After viewing the CCTV footage, the experts at the inquest agreed that Henri Paul showed no signs at the Ritz Hotel of having a carbon monoxide level of 20.7%.

Expert toxicologist Professor Robert Forrest stated:

The probability that [Henri] has a carboxyhaemoglobin[b] concentration of that order of magnitude [20.7%] [is] very, very unlikely.[1804]

Another expert toxicologist Professor John Oliver stated:

[Carbon monoxide of 20.7%] would have been very obvious ... from the way [Henri] was behaving.... He would never have come down the [Ritz] stairs ... without stumbling.[1805]

Both the CCTV and witnesses revealed that Henri was walking and behaving normally in the period at the hotel prior to departure.[c]

- Elevated BAC[d] levels that do not reflect the evidence relating to Henri Paul.[e]

- There were drugs found present in the samples that Henri Paul wasn't taking at the time of his death, yet drugs that he could have been taking were not found.[f]

There are two drugs – Prozac and Zentel – that were clearly detected in the blood but were not being used by Henri in the lead-up to the crash.

And there are two other drugs – Noctamide and Aotal – which had probably been dispensed to Henri in July 1997, but were not detected in the blood or hair.[g]

There was also evidence of very recent use of Aotal by Henri, in the form of an empty packet in his office rubbish bin.[1806]

---

[a] See above point regarding Lecomte's conflicting evidence on the blood sample source.

[b] Carbon monoxide.

[c] See the earlier Was Henri Drunk? chapter.

[d] Blood alcohol concentration.

[e] See earlier Was Henri Drunk? chapter.

[f] Toxicology and blood alcohol test results are dealt with thoroughly in Part 3, Chapters 3 (Alcohol) and 6 (Drugs).

[g] The detailed evidence is covered in Part 3, chapter on Drugs.

Wrong Samples Tested

Some of the above factors indicate the samples tested came from the wrong body – i.e. not Henri Paul's.

These include:

- the high reading of carbon monoxide
- the elevated BAC level
- the variation between drug results when compared to evidence of what Henri Paul was actually taking at the time
- "XM" showing on the label of Sample 1.

Fraud at the IML

The realisation that there were two bodies in the autopsy room at the time of Henri Paul's autopsy completely changes one's perspective of what occurred. A huge puzzle of conflict and error with no accompanying logic evolves into a far clearer picture of the actual events that transpired. What were previously unanswerable questions – e.g. why were there two autopsy sample documents with a similar name at the top? – are provided with solutions that make sense and add to the knowledge of the case. Gaps that existed in the jigsaw start disappearing.

The main player – Professor Dominique Lecomte – is an expert in her field, appointed by the Supreme Court of France. Lecomte is a forensic scientist who has been the Head of the IML, Paris' Institute of Forensic Medicine, since 1988. She also is Professor of Forensic Medicine at the University of Paris.[1807]

Yet somehow, when entrusted with what may have been the most important autopsy of her career, Lecomte managed to perform that procedure so poorly that Judge Stéphan felt he had to do something he had never done before – attempt to replace Lecomte's autopsy by calling for a second one.[1808a]

It is very significant that the inquest jury never got to hear any evidence from Dominique Lecomte – in person or read out – despite the fact that Operation Paget had taken a statement from her in 2005.[b]

The British police failed to interview any other member of the IML staff. Even though Yves Andrieu[c] was interviewed by a French investigation in February 2007,[d] that statement was not read out at the Baker inquest.

In fact no evidence from any IML staff was heard at the inquest.

---

[a] The second autopsy is addressed later.
[b] Reproduced in The Documents book, p139.
[c] IML identifier present at Henri Paul's autopsy.
[d] Reproduced in The Documents book, p230.

HOW THEY MURDERED PRINCESS DIANA

Why?

91　Preparing to Embalm

Following the hospital autopsy Princess Diana's body was not transferred to the mortuary.

She remained lifeless in the autopsy room for about 40 minutes and then the inexplicable happened.

Choosing the Wrong Room

At 7 a.m. Diana was moved within the hospital to an upstairs ward – Room No. 1.006, a room with "three beds, but was used solely for her".[1809] (WFJ)

Dr Bruno Riou explained to Paget what occurred:

> **The body of a person deceased on this ward would then normally have been taken to the Hospital Morgue ... but the hospital administration decided that this building was too far away.[1810] (WFJ)**

Riou added that she was not taken to the morgue "because of the media interest and the fact the Princess of Wales was a VIP".[1811] (WFJ)

The move occurred very close to sunrise in Paris, which on that morning was at 7.06 a.m.[1812] (WFJ).

Just after this – "between 0700 and 0800"[a] – British ambassador Michael Jay departed the hospital and headed back to the embassy.[1813]

Jay later told Paget:

> **I left Keith Moss at the Hospital with instructions to ensure that no one entered the room where the Princess' body lay without his agreement and without being accompanied by him or by another member of the Embassy staff.[1814]**

Ambassador Jay was aware of the circumstances – that Princess Diana's body had been moved to the first floor room adjacent to Moss – and made no move to remedy a foreseeable crisis: a warming room[b] which could threaten the condition of the body.

---

[a] 7 to 8 a.m.

[b] There was no air-conditioning – see below.

Why?

Was Jay involved in the decision to move Princess Diana to this room?

Warming the Body

Instead of making moves to cool Diana's body – e.g. transferring her to the hospital morgue – it was allowed to warm up.

This new 1st floor room was devoid of air conditioning[1815] and on what was to become a hot Paris summer's day – the temperature that day climbed to 30.3 degrees Celsius[1816a] – the atmosphere inside the room would become predictably warm.

Keith Moss, the British consul general who was there, confirmed this:

> **As the day progressed – and bearing in mind this is Paris in August – the ... outside temperature began to increase and with it, therefore, the risk of the temperature in the room in which the Princess's body had been placed increasing as well.**[1817]

And other witnesses reveal this is indeed what happened – the temperature rose.

British Vice Consul Stephen Donnelly said that Moss called around 8.20 and told him that "it was extremely hot" in the room.[1818]

Despite Moss' early awareness – by 8.20 a.m. – of the increasing heat, there is no evidence of any attempt to move Princess Diana's body to a cooler location.

Why wasn't she moved?

Diana's driver Colin Tebbutt entered around 12 noon and later stated:

> **The hospital room was getting hotter ... it was just so hot.**[1819] **(WFJ)**

In addition to the summer heat, there were several other factors that contributed to the increasing temperature in the room and its potential to have an effect on the body:

- the room had no built-in air conditioning
- the hospital had no dry ice – Donnelly stated that Moss informed him around 8.20 that "the hospital had told him that they did not have any" dry ice[1820]
- the overhead lighting in the room – Michael Gibbins[b] testified that Tebbutt had phoned him and said "the room ... was hot and there was overhead lighting"[1821]
- the use of blankets instead of sheets over the windows to block media intrusion – Tebbutt: "I could have used sheets, but we only were given blankets, which I suppose increased the heat unfortunately".[1822]

---

[a] 86.5 degrees Fahrenheit.

[b] Diana's private secretary, who was in London.

Needless to say, had Diana's body been transferred to the hospital mortuary, as was the normal procedure, then none of these problems could have arisen.

Instead the room where Princess Diana's body was held was extremely hot, over a period from after 8.00 a.m. through to about lunchtime.

Organising the Embalmer

In the meantime the royal instructions regarding Diana's embalming and same-day repatriation were being passed down the PFG line.

At around 7.45 a.m. Jean-Claude Plumet phoned Jean Monceau, a director and embalmer in BJL, a subsidiary of PFG. He requested Monceau – who was at home – to arrange for the embalming of Diana at La Pitié Hospital and told him it needed to be carried out by a female.[1823] (WFJ)

About half an hour later Monceau phoned Sophie Hauffman, who was organising the planning for embalmings that day, and asked her to find a suitable female operator to carry out the embalming of Princess Diana.[a] (WFJ)

BJL embalmer Huguette Amarger stated that she received a call at home at about 9 a.m. She told Paget:

> **My company called me ... about 9 a.m. It was the person dealing with planning who called me.... I was told "Don't leave home, your services are going to be required, listen to the radio".[1824]**

---

[a] This is a very complex issue regarding these early calls to BJL and within BJL – the full evidence is covered in detail in Part 4, sections on Phone Calls and Dry Ice in the French Embalming chapter.

92   Phantom Dry Ice

Princess Diana had been moved into the warming first floor room[a] and at some point after sunrise her body started to deteriorate.

During the 8.20 a.m. call[b] Keith Moss told Stephen Donnelly that "he had asked the hospital to provide [dry] ice to put around the body, but … the hospital had told him that they did not have any." Donnelly said that Moss "asked me to try to find some [dry] ice."[1825]

Donnelly then told Paget what happened next:

> **On reflection, I decided to call PFG.... I was surprised to be put through to a man who introduced himself [as] the president of the company… This call … would have been made around 9 a.m.... It was as if he had been expecting my call. I explained the problem of the heat at the hospital and that there was no ice. I told him which hospital and I asked him if he could help. I do not recall his exact words, but he informed me that he could help and that he would deal with it.[1826]**

Donnelly was speaking with Alain Caltiau, who was Assistant General Manager[c] of PFG and "came into the office … to deal with the telephone calls".[1827] (WFJ)

Jean Monceau stated that he "left home at around 0900hrs [9.00 a.m.] and … got to [the] hospital at around 0930 to 0940hrs." [1828] (WFJ)

The inquest heard an elaborate account from Monceau, describing the application of dry ice to Princess Diana after his arrival at the hospital.[1829]

There is however substantial evidence that indicates dry ice was never applied to Princess Diana's body – and Monceau's account is fabricated.

There are several points:

---

[a] Diana had previously been in a section of the hospital that was below ground level – "the floor – one below ground": Prof Bruno Riou, Witness Statement, 7 March 2006, reproduced in The Documents book, p375 (UK Edition) (WFJ).

[b] See previous chapter.

[c] Caltiau was the most senior PFG employee present on the day. Patrick Launay said that he "was the company representative at all levels, as well as being Mr Chapillon's superior": Patrick Launay, Witness Statement, 21 March 2006, reproduced in The Documents book, p512 (UK Edition) (WFJ).

1) Monceau stated that the dry ice was applied by a BJL employee, Michel Lebreton.[1830] Lebreton has never been interviewed by any police investigation and was not heard from at the inquest.

2) At the inquest Monceau stated that Lebreton was not in Diana's room when he arrived: "I know he was not there when I got there."[1831]

In his 2005 statement he said the opposite: "Michel Lebreton, the dry ice operative, was already in the room. He was alone."[1832]

3) The inquest heard three times that it was Monceau's account that he and Lebreton were alone in the room with Diana's body when the dry ice was administered:

a) Lebreton "was alone" when Monceau arrived[1833]

b) "I am alone with Michel Lebreton in the room"[1834]

c) "only Mr Lebreton was with you"[1835a]

No other witnesses have described being alone in the room at any time.[b]

Huguette Amarger – who later did the embalming – stated:

> **I was never alone in the room. There were always some French policemen and authorities who came to gather their thoughts.... The head of the French police officers ... asked that only women stayed with me, and ... my assistant ... had arrived in the meantime.... He was [then] the only man in the room, with two policewomen.[1836]**

It is common sense that Princess Diana's body was under constant police guard, possibly from as early as her 2.06 a.m. arrival at La Pitié Hospital.[c]

Yet Monceau has asked us to believe that this police guard was dispensed with whilst he and Lebreton administered the dry ice.

Why would there be a police guard throughout the embalming, but not during the application of dry ice?

4) Outside of Monceau, there is absolutely no evidence that dry ice was applied to Diana's body.

It is not just that there is no evidence of the administration of the dry ice itself, but there are no references to it whatsoever – nothing about any

---

[a] Ian Burnett, confirmed by Monceau.

[b] The closest anyone gets to saying this is Plumet who gave this account: "[Plumet] states that he looked into the room where the Princess of Wales' body was; she was on a bed and had been dressed. The embalming had taken place, and no one else was in the room." Plumet describes looking into the room, but not entering it. If he had entered it, he may have been closely followed by police who were guarding the room from the outside. Source: Jean-Claude Plumet, Witness Statement, 11 November 2005, reproduced in The Documents book, p473 (UK Edition) (WFJ).

[c] Keith Moss also said in his statement: "Teams of police officers permanently guarded the corridor.": Keith Moss, Witness Statement, 22 October 2004, reproduced in *The Documents* book, p651 (UK Edition) (WFJ).

preparation before administration, nothing about any aftermath of the presentation, no evidence from anyone that Lebreton was even present, and no mention of discussion of any intention to apply dry ice or anything about it at all.

It is very convenient that Monceau has stated there was no one else present in the room when he and Lebreton administered the dry ice – convenient, because it "fits" with there being no witnesses.

Moss and Tebbutt should have been asked about this at the inquest, but weren't.

5) Monceau gave evidence that dry ice shouldn't be used "to prepare a body to make it presentable",[1837] yet he claims to have supervised the application of dry ice to Diana's body.

6) Monceau was asked by Burnett: "Did you in fact come to the conclusion that the dry ice should be removed?" Monceau replied:

Well, my idea was to explain what would happen if we were to just use dry ice to present the body. Obviously I thought that had to be removed if we were to apply another treatment[a] to the body, but it was not removed at that very moment.[1838]

Monceau's reply raises three issues:

a) Monceau has indicated here that he applied the dry ice in order to show those who needed to see – presumably Moss and other authority figures present – how ineffective dry ice was in the situation.

This is an amazing comment and there is absolutely no evidence of Monceau showing Diana's body – after dry ice had been administered – to any people.

b) Monceau's inquest account was that dry ice "burns the skin".[1839] When this is viewed in the light of his account that the dry ice "was not removed at that very moment", Monceau has admitted to deliberately carrying out a post-death action that would have damaged the body of Princess Diana.[b]

c) Monceau states: "Obviously I thought [the dry ice] had to be removed … but it was not removed at that very moment."

This conflicts directly with his statement:

[Lebreton] had started putting on the dry ice, but as soon as I saw the physical condition of the body, I told Michel Lebreton to remove the dry ice.... We therefore removed the dry ice together.[1840] (WFJ)

To Paget the dry ice was removed even before it had been fully applied. At the inquest the dry ice is fully applied and not removed until later.

---

[a] i.e. embalming.
[b] When dry ice is applied, a cloth bag is used to prevent burning, but Monceau failed to mention that in his evidence – instead claiming that dry ice "burns the skin".

There is no evidence from any witness – other than Monceau – that dry ice was removed from Diana's body at any point.

7)   Tebbutt said in his statement: "I also noticed three hospital funeral directors[a], two male and one female, were present when I was in the room."[1841] (WFJ)

Other evidence shows that these three people must have been Monceau, Amarger and Josselin Charrier.[b] If Lebreton had been there, then Tebbutt would have seen four people.

8)   Monceau said that the first thing he did after arriving at the hospital was to report to Philippe Massoni, Prefect of Police, to inform him that he "had been called to apply dry ice to the body of Princess of Wales".[1842cd] (WFJ)

This was put to Massoni and he denied it outright: "Not at all".[1843]

9)   The general evidence is that Diana's body was in a state of deterioration prior to the embalming being carried out.[e] Had dry ice been applied then the condition of the body would have been stabilised.

Despite Stephen Donnelly being told at 9 a.m. that Alain Caltiau "would deal with it", there is no credible evidence of this request for dry ice being followed up.

Caltiau should have been interviewed by the police or the inquest. This has never happened.

Why?

---

[a] Tebbutt calls the embalmers "funeral directors".

[b] Charrier assisted Amarger throughout the embalming – see later.

[c] This – about the dry ice – was in Monceau's police statement, but he said he didn't remember it at the inquest: 20 Nov 07: 68.3.

[d] Later in his inquest cross-examination, Monceau appeared to inadvertently forget about this meeting with Massoni: "actually, when I arrived at the hospital, I was just walked to the room by a nurse".

[e] See next chapter.

93 "The Princess is Melting"

BJL's chief embalmer Jean Monceau arrived at the hospital around 9.35 a.m. and found that "the heat in the room ... [was] high"[1844] (WFJ) – but failed to apply any dry ice.

For over 3 hours – from 9 a.m., when PFG was made aware of the need for dry ice, until about 12.30 p.m. – no action was taken by PFG or BJL to cool the body of Princess Diana.

As time passed the condition of the body was allowed to deteriorate.

After 11.30 a.m. Colin Tebbutt walked into the room. He later told the police:

> **I was informed that the body would start to deteriorate quite rapidly. This was also the opinion of the nursing staff, as it was just so hot.... The information that I had been given was that the Princess was melting.**[1845]

This was supported by Michael Gibbins[a] who told Paget that Tebbutt called him from the hospital:

> **Colin [Tebbutt] told me that he had been into a room to see the Princess's body and that there was damage to one side of her face.**[1846] **(WFJ)**

Paul Burrell also viewed Diana's body around the same time as Tebbutt. In his 2003 book he states: "What I witnessed ... was indescribable, and it is not appropriate to explain further."[1847] (WFJ)

---

[a] Diana's private secretary who was in London.

94　An Illegal Embalming

Embalmer Jean Monceau did nothing to prevent the decomposition of Princess Diana's body until three hours after he arrived at the hospital.

Huguette Amarger arrived at about 10.45 a.m.[1848] and the embalming finally commenced – under Monceau's orders – around 12,30 p.m.[a]

Monceau later claimed that the inordinate delay was to seek legal authorisation for the embalming.

Monceau's Lies

Did Jean Monceau himself believe that he acted within the law, when he instructed Amarger to conduct the embalming?

Monceau was asked by Paget "if it was [his] decision and [his] decision alone to proceed with the embalming". He volunteered in his answer:

> **I did not do anything illegal or wrong or inappropriate that day.[1849] (WFJ)**

This statement had no connection to the question.

Later he was asked by Richard Horwell[b] at the inquest: "Do you consider that you did anything illegal or wrong on that day?" – Monceau replied:

> **Yes, because what I did wrong was that I did the thing that I did.[1850]**

That wasn't the answer Horwell wanted, so he asked again: "Did you at the time ... think that you were doing anything wrong or illegal?" Answer: "No, not at all."[1851]

Monceau has two conflicting accounts – in his statement: not illegal; at the inquest: illegal, then next answer, not illegal.

Did he think what he did was illegal?

Unfortunately for Monceau, under cross-examination he backed up his first account – that what he did was illegal – with an explanation:

---

[a] Full evidence regarding the timing of embalming events is in Part 4, Pre-Embalming Events section of the French Embalming chapter.

[b] Police QC.

I would have waited until the next Monday.[a] I would have waited until I would have received all the necessary official authorisations.[1852]

Monceau went ahead with the embalming with the full knowledge that he didn't have "all the necessary official authorisations".

In other words, Monceau knew at the time that what he did was illegal, and he has lied twice – once in his statement and once at the inquest – when he said that it wasn't illegal.

Why did he act illegally?

Other evidence shows that Monceau wasn't making the decisions – he was acting on instructions from unidentified persons outside of the known players. Monceau has possibly been paid well – probably by a British authority – to supervise the embalming and provide false evidence to the police and the inquest.

In his statement – not heard by the jury[b] – Monceau did provide a defence for his illegal actions:

> **On that day I had verbal agreements, but under those exceptional circumstances this was enough to proceed with embalming on the understanding that everything would be regularised. It was not my place to refuse – even the Prefect of Police was present at the hospital.[1853] (WFJ)**

There are several problems with this:

1)   Monceau states that "the Prefect of Police was present". The prefect of police – Philippe Massoni – was not present at the hospital before or during the embalming.[c]

Massoni told police that he did not have "any recollection of being involved in the decision to embalm".[1854]

When asked if he recalled a conversation with Monceau, Massoni said "Not at all."[1855]

Outside of Monceau there is no evidence of Massoni being at La Pitié at this time and the question is: What would Massoni be doing at the hospital, when his priority presumably would have been setting up a major police investigation into the crash?

2)   Monceau said: "I had verbal agreements" or authorisations. He is referring to authorisations from Keith Moss, Martine Monteil, Jean-Claude Plumet and Gérard Jauze.[d]

---

[a] If Monceau had gotten cold feet and not carried out this embalming, a backup plan was already in place: headed to the Paris hospital were two British embalmers – see earlier Royal Rush chapter.

[b] Most of the witness evidence regarding the legality – or more correctly, illegality – of the embalming, was not heard at the inquest.

[c] Massoni was only at the hospital late in the afternoon, for the visit of Prince Charles.

[d] See below.

Monceau actually had authorisation from none of these people.
Monceau met with Moss who said to Paget:

**Monceau told him "about the decomposition of the body and said that
the remains would be in a real mess and that he was there to make it
as presentable as possible for the family."[1856a]**

Moss makes no mention of authorising the embalming – instead it is
Monceau telling Moss he is there to make the body presentable.[b]

Monceau told Paget that Martine Monteil told him "that everything would
be in order and the authorisations would be given." He added: "She left me
her mobile phone number".[1857] (WFJ)

Brigade Criminelle boss Monteil has stated:

**I do not have any recollection of a conversation with Monsieur
Monceau.[1858] (WFJ)**

Monceau says: "I met ... Mr Plumet and Mr Jauze ... [at] around 1130hrs
[11.30 a.m.]. I told them about my intention to request authorisation to carry
out embalming".[1859] (WFJ)

Plumet says he "does not remember seeing or speaking with Mr Monceau
at the hospital".[1860] Jauze was also asked by Paget and he said: "I do not
remember the conversation". He stated that he was not at the hospital at 11.30
a.m.[1861c]

3)   Monceau stated that "everything would be regularised". There is no
evidence that ever occurred. Instead, at the conclusion of Monceau's 2005
statement[d] it reads:

**During my statement you have shown me the following documents:
OD137 (folder 24) – full copy of the _'Acte de Décès'_ [Record of Death]
OD137 (folder 24) - authorisation to close the coffin
OD137 (folder 24) – mortuary pass
I can inform you that you are missing:
- the Death Certificate, which you could obtain from the Town Hall of
the 13th arrondissement.
- the request for authorisation to embalm together with the
declaration by the embalmer that you can obtain from the registrar of**

---

[a] The family being Charles and sisters Sarah and Jane who were to visit the hospital
later in the day.
[b] This is a complex issue which is covered thoroughly in Part 4, section on Monceau-
Moss Conversation in Chapter 2.
[c] Other evidence in Part 4 reveals that Plumet and Jauze did not arrive at the hospital
until about 4.50 p.m. – over four hours after the embalming commenced. See Timing
of Events section of Chapter 2.
[d] Not heard by the jury.

deaths in the Town Hall of the 13th arrondissement or from the Office of Mortuary Operations at the Prefecture of Police.
- the authority for embalming treatment (which also summonses the police, which you can obtain from the Registrar of Deaths at the Town Hall of the 13th arrondissement or at the Office of Mortuary Operations at the Prefecture of Police.
- an official report of embalming[a] which you can obtain from the police station of the 13th arrondissement where the duty officer of the Judicial Police would have been on the day in question. [1862] (WFJ)

The point here is that out of the above 7 documents listed by Monceau, only one – the death certificate[b] – was available to the inquest jury.

Why is this?

Monceau has listed 4 missing documents: 1) the request for authorisation to embalm; 2) the embalmer's declaration; 3) the embalming authority; 4) the embalming report.

If this embalming documentation exists:

a)   why didn't the British police obtain copies of it after taking Monceau's statement in 2005?
b)   why were there not copies of it at the inquest?
c)   why did the jury not even get to hear that this documentation should have existed?

The most likely answer to these three questions is that the embalming documentation doesn't actually exist.

Why is it that when Monceau's short defence for his actions is analysed, virtually every aspect of it is found to be predicated on false evidence? Massoni was not present; there never was any verbal authorisation; and it appears that the embalming documentation never was "regularised".

Breaking French Law

French law requires authorisation from the mayor or the Prefect of police, or their representative.

To obtain that authorisation, there are three requirements:

1)   Authorisation in the last will of the deceased. Failing that, written authorisation from a family member. Failing that, written authorisation from a person who "has been nominated [by the family] to take over".
2)   "A statement describing the procedure of embalming", in writing.[a]

---

[a] In a direct contradiction of this, Monceau had stated earlier in the same statement: "You have asked me if I made out an embalming certificate. No, that does not exist, but at the bottom of the form requesting authorisation to embalm, signed by the family or a representative, I make a statement. This is done before the embalming and even before the request at the town hall.": Jean Monceau, Witness Statement, 18 Oct 05, reproduced in The Documents book, p418. (WFJ)

[b] Shown in Figure 19 of Part 2.

3)   "A medical certificate establishing ... that the death is not suspicious".

The official authorisation document is then presented to the police officer present at the embalming.[1863] (Part WFJ)

To simplify this: six things were required ahead of time to legalise the embalming process:

-    authorisation from Diana's will or her family or someone representing her family

-    a description of the embalming procedure

-    a medical certificate showing the death was not suspicious

-    the above three items needed to be shown to the mayor or the Prefect or one of their representatives

-    authorisation from the mayor, Prefect or representative

-    presentation of the authorisation to the police present at the embalming.

What occurred, point by point, in the case of the embalming of Diana, Princess of Wales?

1)   Family authorisation.

There is absolutely no evidence of any attempt to get hold of a copy of Diana's will to find out what her "will" might be regarding a potential embalming.

Failing that, there is then absolutely no evidence of an attempt by anyone – Moss, Monceau, Tebbutt, Gibbins – to make contact with any member of Diana's family.[b]

Because there was no attempt to contact the family, it becomes evident that there was then no person appointed to represent her family and give the authorisation.

Point 1 was not fulfilled.

2)   Embalming statement.

Eva Steiner, the inquest's expert on French law, said: "Reading the documents I have been provided with, this condition has been fulfilled."[1864]

Steiner has qualified this with "the documents I have been provided with" – as though she may be aware there are other documents she might not have been provided with.

---

[a] Although the law does not specifically use the term "in writing" it is clear from the nature of what is required – "the location and time of the operation, as well as the name and address" of the embalmer – that it is referring to a written document.

[b] Prince Charles was not a member of Diana's family – they were divorced on 28 August 1996.

We are not told which documents Steiner had been given – if it was the embalming statement then she would have said.[a] She may have only had Monceau's police statement of what occurred.[b]

Earlier evidence has shown – and this is revealed in more detail in Part 4[c] – that Monceau is a very unreliable witness.

The legal reality is that even if Monceau had told the truth in his statement, there was still no written document presented to the Prefect's representative outlining the embalming procedure.[d]

So the second requirement still would not have been fulfilled anyway – contrary to Steiner's account.

Point 2 was not fulfilled.

3) Medical Certificate.

Steiner's police statement: "This … was done in this case, Dr Lecomte concluding that the death was not suspicious".[1865] (WFJ)

The medical certificate was produced by Lecomte.[e]

Point 3 was fulfilled.

4) and 5) Visit to Prefect's representative and subsequent authorisation.

At the inquest Steiner confirmed that Monteil's conversation with Monceau "was adequate authorisation on behalf of the Mayor or the Prefect".[1866]

What the jury didn't hear was Monteil's statement evidence: "I do not have any recollection of a conversation with Monsieur Monceau, the embalmer".[1867] (WFJ)

There are 3 points:

a)   Monteil has denied this conversation ever took place

b)   it is common sense that Monteil would not be standing around the hospital, when she was in charge of the Brigade Criminelle investigation

c)   there is an accumulation of evidence that Jean Monceau has lied about the events of that day.[f]

It is most unlikely that this conversation between Monceau and Monteil ever actually took place.

---

[a] The general evidence is that the embalming statement does not exist, and never did.

[b] As was pointed out at the conclusion of Monceau's statement – see earlier – Paget had no embalming documentation at all. There has never been any evidence to suggest that they obtained any documents subsequent to that.

[c] Chapter on French Embalming.

[d] The law is that the three items being discussed are presented to the Prefect's representative (in lieu of the mayor or Prefect) for his/her authorisation.

[e] Just three hours later this same pathologist, Dominique Lecomte, would be in control of the fraudulently conducted autopsy of the driver, Henri Paul – see earlier Fraud at the IML chapter.

[f] This is particularly revealed in Part 4, chapter on French Embalming.

The evidence is that the Prefect representative's authorisation was not given. Points 4 and 5 were not fulfilled.

6)   Presentation to police.

Steiner is an expert on French law, yet she neglected to mention – in her statement or at the inquest – that it was a requirement for the authorisation to be shown to the police present.

It is obvious that point 6 was not fulfilled because there never was any written authorisation – point 5 – as required by the law.

Out of 6 steps – all of which were required for a legal embalming to take place – only one was actually fulfilled.

1 out of 6.

In other words, the embalming of Princess Diana was carried out illegally under French law.

How is it then that the inquest's expert in French law, Eva Steiner, was able to tell the jury that the embalming was legal?

The short answer is: she didn't.[a]

There are several points:

1)   Under oath at the inquest Steiner never actually said the embalming was legal.

Baker told the jury in his Summing Up; "In Dr Steiner's view everything was done to comply with French law."[1868]

But the Lord Justice failed to tell the jury that Steiner had reservations.

Inquest lawyer, Jonathon Hough, asked the critical question twice:

"Do you think ... [Monceau] acted legally ...?" Steiner: "I think he did. I think he did. I cannot – well, it is difficult for me...."[1869] And Steiner moves on to question Princess Diana's status – the procedure is different for a royal than a commoner: "this is not for me to decide, whether or not she was considered as a private or a public citizen".[1870]

Hough – not content with this answer: "If there was some failure to comply technically with the French legal provisions, do you think that M Monceau did his best in the circumstances to comply?"[1871]

Now the question has changed. Hough has accepted that Monceau may not have followed the law, so "do you think that M Monceau did his best"?

Steiner: "I think he did. I mean, these are exceptional circumstances."[1872]

Steiner's view was that Monceau "did his best" considering the "exceptional circumstances".

---

[a] In contrast, in Steiner's police statement she indicated the embalming was legal – "At this stage the authorisation to embalm could legally proceed" (WFJ) – but the jury did not hear that. Source: Eva Steiner, Witness Statement, 29 September 2006, reproduced in The Documents book, p466 (UK Edition).

That is quite different to Baker's "everything was done to comply with French law".[a]

Steiner's account to the inquest – "this is not for me to decide, whether or not she was considered as a private or a public citizen" – contrasts starkly with her statement account, defending the embalming decision: "here ... in circumstances where a member of the British Royal family was involved".[1873] (WFJ)

So at the inquest "not for me to decide" if she was a royal; in her 2006 statement, categorical: "a member of the British Royal family".

It is ridiculous that one of the inquest's legal experts is unsure of the status of the person whose death is being investigated. The rest of the civilised world knew the status of Princess Diana: she had clearly been stripped of her royal status by the Queen in August of 1996 – 12 months before the crash.[b]

Steiner has lied on two occasions – in her statement, where she said Diana was a royal; and secondly at the inquest, where she indicated that Diana's status was not known.

2)   Steiner qualified her comments – at the inquest she said: "reading the documents I have been provided with" regarding the embalming statement.

3)   In answers Steiner diverted attention away from the main issue. When she was asked whether Moss' authorisation would have been valid, Steiner said: "Everything to do with private matters such as death, births, adoption, are dealt with the Consulate [Moss]. I mean, the Ambassador [Jay] has nothing to do with that."

The reality is that issue was nothing to do with Moss v Jay. The issue was whether consul-general Moss, as the British representative in Paris – it could just as easily have been ambassador Jay – had the right to authorise the embalming, on behalf of Diana or her family.[c]

4)   It has already been shown that Steiner was prepared to lie to the jury.[d] Monceau failed to attain 5 out of 6 requirements for legality. When Steiner's evidence is closely analysed[e] it can be seen that the jury was misled, and she was an active participant in achieving that. For example, Steiner, a legal expert, must have been aware that documents would have been required for a

---

[a] Baker goes on to tell the jury: "Be that as it may, you may think that everyone concerned acted in good faith and did their best in unusually trying circumstances.": 31 Mar 08:87.4. The reality is that Baker has misrepresented the position of Dr Eva Steiner, his own expert.

[b] The significance of the status of Princess Diana is thoroughly addressed in the Royal Control chapter of Part 4.

[c] This issue is addressed in Part 4, section on Notification of Family in the French Embalming chapter.

[d] Regarding Diana's status – see above.

[e] Addressed thoroughly in Part 4, section on Was the Embalming Legal? in Chapter 2.

legal authorisation – yet there is no documentation for four of the steps. It would have been impossible for the Prefect's representative – allegedly, Monteil – to have legally authorised this embalming without seeing the form completed by a representative of the family. Steiner must have realised that, yet the transcript shows her leaving the jury with the impression that what occurred was okay.

Effectively, by the time Baker in his Summing Up had stated that "Steiner's view [was] everything was done to comply with French law", the jury had been completely misled – between the combined efforts of Baker, Hough and Steiner.

The inquest employed a French legal expert, Eva Steiner, and the jury were told that she had prepared "independent reports on French legal matters for the purposes of ... these inquests".[a]1874

When it comes to the topic of embalming[b], and you scrutinise what actually occurred on 31 August 1997, then compare that to what was told to the inquest – only one out of 13 witnesses were cross-examined[c], and that was Jean Monceau, a compulsive liar. Add Eva Steiner to the mix[d] – a comprehensively illegal embalming is made to appear legal – and one can see that what was shown to the jury was smoke and mirrors: they never heard what really occurred on the day and they had a judge summing up to them that it was all within the law.

Nothing could have been further from the truth.

In her inquest evidence Steiner brought up the issue of "whether or not [Diana] was considered as a private or a public citizen". The embalming evidence shows that in death, Princess Diana was treated far worse than a private citizen – a private citizen would have been treated with a legal embalming: six out of six.

Diana, Princess of Wales was accorded one out of six – and even the "one" was a medical statement from a dodgy practitioner.[e]

---

[a] Technically there were two inquests – one for Diana, one for Dodi – but practically it was conducted as a single inquest.

[b] Embalming was the main issue addressed by Eva Steiner.

[c] See French Evidence Table in Chapter 2 of Part 4.

[d] Evidence regarding Henri Paul's autopsies was scrutinised by several experts. This did not occur with the evidence of the embalming of the princess – there was just the one "independent" expert, Eva Steiner. There was no peer-based scrutiny of her evidence.

[e] Professor Dominique Lecomte.

95 "Extremely Badly Done"

Huguette Amarger performed the embalming of Princess Diana, commencing at around 12.30 and concluding about an hour later.[a]

There is evidence that the quality of the work done was very poor.

Fulham Mortuary manager Robert Thompson saw Princess Diana's body after it arrived back in the UK – about seven hours after the Paris embalming.

He described to Paget what he saw:

> **As soon as the coffin was opened I could see that the Princess had been embalmed and that it had been done particularly badly.... During my profession within the mortuary business I experienced many embalmed bodies. In the case of Diana, Princess of Wales ... it seemed as though it had been done in a hurry.[1875] (WFJ)**

In an earlier 2001 affidavit Thompson had said: "The embalming had been done extremely badly."[1876] (WFJ)

This was one of the most significant embalmings ever undertaken by BJL, so why did they do such a poor job?

There were three BJL embalmers present at the hospital on that day – Jean Monceau, Huguette Amarger and Josselin Charrier.[1877]

Jean Monceau said in his statement:

> **In my case, [I had embalmed] roughly 13,000 bodies. Josselin Charrier has done rather less because he worked in the provinces and it will be less still for Mrs Amarger as she was newer to the profession.[1878] (WFJ)**

On the day, Monceau – the senior embalmer present – handed over the embalming of Princess Diana to a far less experienced embalmer.

If this wasn't because the British had asked for a female,[b] then why was it?

---

[a] The timing of the embalming is a complex issue – it is covered in the Timing section of the French Embalming chapter in Part 4.

[b] See earlier Securing British Control chapter.

Why was Huguette Amarger, a person who "was newer to the profession", chosen to carry out one of the most significant embalmings BJL had ever been called on to do?

This was a question that the jury should have heard asked. They didn't.

They also never heard: a) that Amarger "was newer to the profession" and b) that Monceau stated that Charrier "did the embalming with Mrs Amarger, whilst I took care of the liaison".[1879] (WFJ)

The jury were never in a position where they could compare the level of experience between Amarger and Monceau – but then they wouldn't have thought it was relevant because they heard Monceau state on live videolink[a] under oath, that the embalming was carried out by "Mrs Amarger, Josselin Charrier and myself, Jean Monceau".[1880]

This was a lie that conflicted with his own statement that he was doing "liaison" while the embalming occurred. Amarger also stated that Charrier "was the only man in the room" during the embalming.[1881]

Amarger told Paget:

> **There was a panic on ... my boss told me to be quick because Prince Charles was arriving.**[1882]

Yet at the inquest Monceau stated that by the time he spoke to Moss – 12 noon and pre-embalming – he had been "told that the Prince was expected at about 5 o'clock, at Villacoublay, the airport".[1883bc]

At that stage it was still over 5 hours before Charles was due to arrive at the hospital. Given that a full embalming only takes three hours, [1884] (WFJ) why then did Monceau tell Amarger to be quick?

Amarger says she was only told "Prince Charles was arriving in the afternoon"[1885] – even though Monceau himself had a specific time: after 5 p.m.

It was known before 9 a.m. that an embalming had to be carried out – at the request of the "British".[d]

Amarger arrived at the hospital before 11 a.m., but Monceau stated[a] that he believed Charles wasn't coming until 5 p.m. Monceau therefore had a window of approximately 6 hours to carry out the embalming.

---

[a] Between Paris and London.

[b] Charles and Diana's sisters arrived at the hospital at 5.40 p.m.: Louise Jury, The Tragedy: Prince Paid His Last Respects ... Then the Coffin Lid Was Closed, The Independent, 1 September 1997.

[c] Levertons were told by 11 a.m. French time that Diana's body would be landing back at RAF Northolt at 8 p.m. French time: Keith Leverton, Witness Statement, 27 October 2004, reproduced in The Documents book, p499 (UK Edition).

[d] Amarger stated: "I learned that the British wanted it to be a woman to take care of giving the treatment.": 8 Mar 05 Statement read out 22 Nov 07: 91.17.

Yet Monceau rushed Amarger, to the point where she went ahead with the embalming even though there was no documentation to support it. In other words, the embalming was illegal – not authorised[b] – but it appears Amarger agreed to do it anyway, because of a "panic" created by Monceau.

It is possible that if Monceau had not rushed Amarger she may have refused to do the embalming without the required paperwork.

Amarger also told Paget:

> **Before I could start my work, I was put out by seeing the Scotland Yard police officers putting black sticky tape over the blinds lowered over the windows. There was therefore only a very little light and I was going to be hampered in my work.**[1886]

The embalming was conducted in an ordinary hospital ward under difficult circumstances: "there was a panic" and "there was … only a very little light".

These two factors – the panic and the poor lighting – may have placed Amarger (who was much less experienced than Monceau) under increased pressure and could have affected the quality of the embalming.

Why did the Paris embalming seem "as though it had been done in a hurry"?

Because it was.

Why was it "done extremely badly"?

Because it was carried out under panic conditions in a dimly-lit room by an inexperienced embalmer.

---

[a] Stated to the police – he withheld the timing from Amarger.

[b] See previous chapter.

96   Was Diana Pregnant?

Why were senior royals so keen to ensure Princess Diana was embalmed before she was returned to London? [a]

Was it because an embalming carried out before any UK post-mortem would help cover up a possible pregnancy?

Removing Urine

There was one aspect of this Paris embalming that was successfully carried out – it was the complete removal of the urine.

On 8 March 2005 French police officer Isabelle Deffez recorded Huguette Amarger's Paget statement. [b] (WFJ)

Four months later, on July 19, Paget officer Philip Easton – who was present – made an official statement where he pointed out Deffez omitted Amarger saying that "urine was also suctioned into [a] container for disposal". [1887] (WFJ)

This complete removal of urine was confirmed during the UK post-mortem – the pathologist's report read :"the bladder was empty". [1888] (WFJ)

Why did Deffez[c] leave out the removal of urine from Diana's body during the embalming? It's not just that it was left out once, but it was left out twice: Easton stated:

> **DI Scotchbrook and I … asked whether [the organ content suctioning] included urine. Mrs Amarger confirmed that urine was also suctioned....[1889] (WFJ)**

Deffez omitted both the question and the answer relating to urine. Why?

---

[a] Instructions to embalm in Paris were given to both French and British embalmers. See earlier Royal Rush chapter.

[b] The statement was made in Paris in French. Paget officers "[Jane] Scotchbrook and [Philip Easton] asked Mrs Amarger a number of questions, which Capitaine Deffez recorded, along with the answers given". Philip Easton, Witness Statement, 19 July 2005, page 1. (WFJ)

[c] In 1997 Deffez was a Brigade Criminelle lieutenant.

Easton's evidence indicates that the Amarger interview was not electronically recorded – he says the urine comment was "still fresh in my memory"[1890] (WFJ) – and I suggest that is astounding for a 21st century 1st world police force (French or British).[a]

The relevance of urine is that it can be tested to establish whether a person is pregnant.[b] It is normal practice in the modern embalming process to remove urine and other fluids because they start to decompose after death. Embalming.net describes a process of "suctioning fluids out of the internal organs in the abdomen and thoracic cavity".[1891] (WFJ)

This is a process that would have been known to the British authorities who requested the embalming.

Deffez's omission was possibly an attempt to cover up the deliberate removal of urine from Diana's body to hide evidence of pregnancy.[c]

The final act in this chain of events was the withholding from the inquest jury of all relevant evidence:

- virtually all references in Amarger's statement regarding the embalming procedure[d]
- the addition to Amarger's statement submitted by Easton, stating that the urine was suctioned
- the UK post-mortem report of pathologist Robert Chapman.[ef]

Pregnancy Perception

The issue is not only whether Princess Diana was pregnant – it was about whether there was a perception that she could be pregnant, or even could become pregnant.

---

[a] The interview took place at the Brigade Criminelle Headquarters in Paris.

[b] Part 2 included a 2000 report from Janusz Knepil, showing that pregnancy testing on urine contaminated by embalming fluid could produce an incorrect result. In 1997 that information would not necessarily have been known to the people making the decisions on the handling of Diana's body. See Part 2, Pregnancy chapter, under "Embalming and Post-Mortem".

[c] There is additional evidence regarding this in Part 4, section on Procedure in the French Embalming chapter.

[d] The jury heard much of Amarger's statement, but the lawyer broke off when it came to her evidence on the embalming procedure: 22 Nov 07: 94.20.

[e] How is it that the jury who are investigating the circumstances and nature of the death of a person, Princess Diana, aren't provided access to, or a reading of the post-mortem conducted on the body of that person?

[f] Redacted copies of the post-mortem reports and statements are in The Documents book – they were redacted in 2010 by the author due to privacy concerns. More detailed excerpts are included in Part 4 (published 2011) – which addresses the Embalmings and Post-Mortems – where necessary to reveal what occurred during the post-crash cover-up by authorities.

Even a perception could lead to a decision to embalm in order to remove the possibility – the risk factor.

Pregnancy factors are addressed in Part 2, the chapter entitled Pregnancy.[a]

Possible or perceived pregnancy is not just a possible motive for embalming – it is also a possible motive for murder, particularly in the light of Diana's fast-developing romance with Dodi Fayed, a Muslim.

Pre-Post Mortem Embalming

An embalming has a major effect on the ability to conduct a normal post-mortem – the blood will be contaminated or replaced, the contents of organs are removed.

Professor Robert Chapman, who conducted Diana's UK post-mortem, said an embalming "will make toxicology difficult or indeed sometimes impossible".[1892]

UK embalmer David Green told Paget that "any incisions, fluids removed or added could destroy evidence as to the cause of death".[1893] (WFJ)

And René Deguisne – Monceau's boss at BJL – told British police: "We would simply not have carried out that [embalming] treatment ... [had we known] that an autopsy was going to be carried out".[1894] (WFJ)

Monceau was asked by police officers if he "had known that the Princess of Wales was going to undergo an autopsy ... would [he] have done anything different?"

His reply was: "No, because the embalming does not affect the autopsy."[1895] (WFJ)

This is another blatant lie from Monceau.

The evidence is the embalming does affect the autopsy – the opposite of what Monceau is saying.

In this particular case the bladder was drained during the embalming – this meant that no urine sample could be taken during the London post-mortem[b].

---

[a] It is the author's intention to write another chapter in Part 7 regarding possible pregnancy – this would include additional evidence that has come to light since the publication of Part 2.
[b] Post-mortem or autopsy.

97   Operation Royal Clockwork

On the other side of the Channel, British embalmers were hurriedly readying themselves – on royal orders – to rush across to Paris to conduct a quick embalming on the same body Amarger was embalming – also on royal orders.

Plans to bring about the speedy same-day repatriation were also rapidly developing.

At 8.30 a.m.[a] LCO[b] Assistant Comptroller Anthony Mather arrived at Buckingham Palace. He said the Lord Chamberlain – David Ogilvy – was already there.[1896] (WFJ)

Mather told Paget:

> **I established a telephone link between the Palace and Balmoral where the Queen, and the Prince of Wales were in residence.**

And he organised "an RAF BAe 146 [that] was sent to Aberdeen from RAF Northolt to collect the Prince of Wales".[1897] (WFJ)

Ogilvy arranged for the despatch of the Royal Standard to Levertons' office in Camden[1898] (WFJ) – this was later deployed to cover Diana's coffin.

At 10 a.m.[c] a meeting was held at Levertons' office in Camden – attending were Clive and Keith Leverton and duty manager, Daniel Tassell.[1899] The royal standard arrived.[1900] (WFJ) Mather phoned from the Palace – he informed Levertons they would need to be at RAF Northolt with the embalmers and equipment by 1 p.m., ready to board the special flight to Paris. Mather also told the royal funeral directors that the return flight carrying Prince Charles with Diana's body would be landing at Northolt at 7 p.m.[1901] (WFJ)

Half an hour later Robert Thompson, the manager of Fulham Mortuary – the location for the Diana and Dodi London post-mortems – arrived at work. Thompson described what he saw:

---

[a] 9.30 in Paris.
[b] Lord Chamberlain's Office.
[c] 11 a.m. in Paris.

There were a lot of people hanging around in the car park and in particular several men in dark suits who ... I assumed were police officers from Royalty Protection.[1902] **(WFJ)**

Detective Superintendent Jeffrey Rees[a] confirmed at the inquest that there were "in plain clothes, a number of royalty protection department officers ... most of whom ... had flown down from Balmoral".[1903]

This is further evidence of early control of events from the royals at Balmoral.

While early plans were being made for Diana's embalming in the Paris hospital, the employment of Operation Overstudy, Charles' mission to Paris, and Burton's illegal jurisdiction over Diana's body,[b] preparations were in place for a team of Royalty Protection officers to be despatched from Balmoral, headed to the Fulham Mortuary.

All with clockwork precision – to ensure that by midnight, just 24 hours after the crash, the dead Princess Diana would be embalmed, autopsied and "safely" ensconced on royal land.[c]

---

[a] Headed the early UK investigation – see next chapter.
[b] See later Illegal Jurisdiction chapter.
[c] Before midnight Diana was delivered to St James' Palace – see later Midnight Embalming at the Palace chapter.

98 Choosing the Wrong Man

As word of Princess Diana's death reached senior personnel at Scotland Yard, a decision was made on Sunday morning to open a UK-based investigation – and appoint the right person to head it.

It was decided by Commissioner Paul Condon that the investigation would be run by the Organised Crime Group (OCG).

On the day of the crash David Veness[a] appointed Detective Superintendent Jeffrey Rees[b] to the role of senior investigating officer (SIO) of the British police investigation into the deaths of Princess Diana and Dodi Fayed.

There are major concerns regarding the selection process.

Rees was chosen for this role, even though he wasn't available, there was a known major conflict of interest, he couldn't speak French and there was at least one other more suitable SIO available in London.

Helicopter Him Home

OCG DCI Peter Heard told Paget that "Jeffrey Rees was spending that weekend away with his family".[1904] (WFJ) Harrods security chief John Macnamara met Rees later that evening and said that he "was on holiday" when he was chosen.[1905] (WFJ)

Rees stated at the inquest that he "was in Rutland".[1906]

Coroner Michael Burgess[c] told Paget that Rees had been "flown in by helicopter from Leicester"[1907] (WFJ) – Leicester is next door to Rutland.

The question is: Why would the police interrupt a family break and helicopter their man back to London when there was at least one other more suitable SIO[d] already available in London?

---

[a] MPS Assistant Commissioner Specialist Operations.
[b] Acting Head of the OCG.
[c] Burgess conducted Dodi's London post-mortem.
[d] See below.

Conflict of Interest

At the time of the Paris crash Jeffrey Rees had already been appointed head of an investigation into an allegation by Tiny Rowland that "Mohamed Al Fayed, or persons employed by him, had stolen property from safe deposit boxes at Harrods Limited".[1908]

David Veness was "aware that [Rees] was in charge of the safety deposit box inquiry" at the time he appointed him as SIO of the investigation into the Diana and Dodi deaths.[1909]

This was a clear conflict of interest.

Surrey Coroner's Officer Keith Brown attended the Fulham post-mortems. He later told Paget:

> **Rees explained that he was somewhat surprised to have been requested to be the senior officer in charge from the MPS as he either was, or had been, investigating Mohamed Al Fayed in a separate matter.[1910] (WFJ)**

On 31 August 1997 Jeffrey Rees was appointed to head an investigation – into the Paris crash – that involved Mohamed Al Fayed,[a] when Rees was already head of a current investigation – the Harrods safety deposit box case – that also involved Mohamed Al Fayed.

In January 1998 Rees wrote up a report detailing this conflict of interest. He stated:

> **I formally raise and put on record my concerns about what might be perceived as a conflict of interest in the two investigations.[1911]**

Despite this, Rees was not removed from the Paris investigation.

Why?

Overlooking the Obvious

Rees was appointed to head an investigation of a crash in Paris – yet he didn't speak French.

He was forced to admit this at the inquest.[1912]

And there was at least one other SIO in London who could speak French, was available and didn't have any conflict of interest.

John Macnamara, has stated that he spoke with Rees at Fulham Mortuary on 31 August 1997:

> **"Rees told me that a most experienced Detective Superintendent, Geoffrey Hunt, was on call ... [but] David Veness insisted that [Rees]**

---

[a] Mohamed's son died in the crash and the driver, Henri Paul, who also died, was an Al Fayed employee.

should attend personally [and] sent a helicopter" to collect him.[1913] **(WFJ)**

Geoff Hunt was an SIO and was available in London on the day and had relevant experience – he had "been in charge of several complex inquiries, including murders abroad".[1914] (WFJ)

And Hunt was "a fluent French speaker" according to his biography with Community Service Development (CSD) Global Group, an organisation he worked for after leaving the MPS.

At the inquest, Scott Baker prevented the jury from hearing the accounts from both Keith Brown and John Macnamara.[a]

Choosing the Wrong Man

Jeffrey Rees was not selected for being the right man for the job – because he wasn't: he wasn't available, couldn't talk the language and had a major conflict of interest.

This indicates that Rees was selected for some other reason.

It has already been shown[b] this was a UK government-orchestrated assassination. This in turn means that there was a requirement to follow it with a police cover-up – not a proper, thorough investigation.

That then called for the appointment of an officer who would be comfortable going along with and coordinating that cover-up – a person who was corrupt or could be corrupted.

That man was Detective Superintendent Jeffrey Rees.

---

[a] Macnamara was cross-examined but not asked about this subject.
[b] In this book and in more detail in the Diana Inquest volumes.

99 Illegal Repatriation

While David Veness was interrupting Jeffrey Rees' family holiday, Levertons were full-steam ahead in their mission to repatriate and embalm Princess Diana.

"Pressures and Time Constraints"

The team – Clive Leverton and embalmers David Green and Bill Fry – assembled at Camden and departed from RAF Northolt after 1 p.m.[1915] Keith Leverton remained in London to handle the UK side and receive further instructions from Anthony Mather.[1916] (WFJ)

The team carried with them Diana's coffin, the royal standard and their embalming equipment.[1917] (WFJ) David Green stated:

I took with me a large case containing all the items required for embalming.[1918] (WFJ)

They were met at Paris' Villacoublay airport by PFG's Patrick Launay.[1919] (WFJ) He escorted them to the Pitié Hospital and they arrived at about 3.40 p.m. Paris time.[1920]

Upon his arrival in the ward, Green recounted: "I spoke to two of the French embalmers in broken English and they told me that they had done some embalming…. They handed me two Phials of samples of the fluid they had used".[1921] (WFJ)

Green later told British police:

Had I been told to start any embalming and to carry out a complete job it would not have been possible because of the time limitation.[1922] (WFJ)

This "time limitation" had been set by the royals and the orders were coming through the Lord Chamberlain's Office, via Anthony Mather.

Clive Leverton told Paget:

There were pressures and time constraints placed upon us.[1923] (WFJ)

Green stated:

We were required to return her quickly.[1924] (WFJ)

There were two factors driving the rush.

They needed time to do the embalming – it turned out that was no longer required – the French had done it.[a] And they had been told a same-day repatriation was required – that Charles would be arriving and was expecting to take the body home.

Green said: "Clive and I knew that the Prince of Wales, and the Princesses' two sisters were en route".[1925] (WFJ)

Missing Documents

The repatriation was so rushed it was illegal.

Kenyon's Alan Puxley,[b] who is very experienced,[c] has outlined what documents are required during a repatriation:
- a death certificate
- an embalming certificate
- a transportation declaration regarding the suitability of the coffin
- "the deceased Passport, or a Laisse Passer, which is a Mortuary passport"
- "a Freedom from Infection certificate known as a F.F.I."
- "Consular or Mortuary Certificate"
- "a funeral directors certificate"
- an airwaybill
- "a Coroners order for burial".[1926] (WFJ)

In addition PFG's Patrick Launay mentioned the need for:
- the burial certificate
- police authority for transportation.[1927] (WFJ)

Operation Paget officers showed the following documents to Launay:
- death certificate
- mortuary pass
- "record of the placing of the body in the coffin".[1928] (WFJ)

Clive Leverton – in evidence not heard by the jury – has stated:

Our staff or myself received none of this paperwork at the time of the repatriation ... nor any since.[1929] (WFJ)

Leverton gives two completely different explanations for not having any documentation:

---

[a] The evidence indicates the British were told to prepare for an embalming as a precaution – just in case the French got cold feet or failed to accomplish it. This is addressed in Part 4, section on Use of British Embalmers in Chapter 4.

[b] Vice-President Operations at Kenyon International.

[c] Puxley said: "For 25 years I was General Manager at Will Case and Partners ... who are registered funeral directors". He also stated that he had worked at Kenyons since 2001. (WFJ) Alan Puxley, Witness Statement, 16 June 2004, reproduced in The Documents book, pp456-7 (UK Edition).

1) "I presumed someone else was dealing [with it]"[1930] (WFJ)
2) "the requirement for all concerned to carry out a professional and very fast repatriation".[1931] (WFJ)

The first explanation – "someone else was dealing" – appears to presume that there was paperwork, but Levertons just didn't get to see any.

The second – professionalism and speed – raises a very important question: How do you achieve a "professional" repatriation without any documentation?

Effectively, in the repatriation of Diana, Princess of Wales, there are 7 out of 12 documents missing: embalming certificate; coffin transportation declaration; FFI; Consular certificate; funeral directors certificate; air waybill; coroner's burial order.

Only one document out of the 12 was seen by the jury investigating the death – the death certificate.

Why is it that this documentation would exist for a normal citizen, but it doesn't exist for Princess Diana? [a]

Clive stated:

This paperwork would normally be required ... to enable repatriation to be allowed.[1932] (WFJ)

Clive Leverton was never asked about this missing documentation at the inquest.

Why?

The evidence points to the royals being obsessed with taking control of Diana's body as quickly as possible and this approach led to a complete failure to abide by the law in their conduct of the repatriation.

---

[a] There was also a lack of documentation for the embalming – see earlier An Illegal Embalming chapter.

100 Retrieved by the Ex-Husband

The RAF BAe 146 organised by Mather was sent up to Aberdeen and Charles boarded it at 2.22 p.m. along with Sandy Henney his press secretary.[1933] The flight had to divert to pick up Diana's two sisters waiting in Oxfordshire at RAF Brize Norton.[1934]

They landed at Villacoublay airport at 5 p.m. and were met by ambassador Michael Jay and his wife Sylvia. The group travelled to the hospital by car – on the way Charles commented to Jay that "often tragedies happen in August".[1935]

After arriving at the hospital at 5.40 p.m. – precisely two hours after the British embalmers – they met staff and dignitaries and viewed Diana's body.

The convoy of cars carrying Princess Diana – covered with the Royal Standard – and the entourage left the hospital at 6.15 p.m. and departed from Villacoublay just after 7 p.m.

Why the Ex-Husband?

Was it logical that Charles would be the one who would repatriate the dead Diana?

The Charles dash across the Channel was the public face, on the day, of the early royal control of Princess Diana's body. The trip was widely reported in the press – the media were present at the hospital and also for the 7 p.m.[a] landing at RAF Northolt.

Media coverage was very positive – one *Associated Press* report described "Prince Charles … escorting the body of his 'English rose'".[1936]

Was this how Princess Diana would have wanted it?

---

[a] UK time.

The history of Diana's 16 years of mistreatment at the hands of the royal family is well documented in many books[a] and it is not something I can address in this book.

Diana herself has described her marital relationship with Charles, following the birth of Harry in 1984 – just three years after their wedding:

> **Then suddenly as Harry was born it just went bang, our marriage, the whole thing went down the drain.... Something inside me closed off. By then I knew he had gone back to his lady [Camilla] but somehow we'd managed to have Harry.[1937]**

Princess Diana recorded those words in 1991[b], well before the late-1992 separation and subsequent divorce in 1996.

An analysis of the Diana-Charles relationship[c] reveals that the marriage had effectively broken down by 1985, but a public face was maintained to avoid the sensitivity of a royal separation or divorce.

By late 1995 – a year before the official divorce – the relationship had sunk so far that Diana believed Charles intended to remove her in a car crash. Diana wrote:

> **This particular phase of my life is the most dangerous – my husband is planning 'an accident' in my car, brake failure and serious head injury.... I have been battered, bruised and abused mentally by a system for 15 years[d] now.... I am strong inside and maybe that is a problem for my enemies.**
>
> **Thank you Charles, for putting me through such hell and for giving me the opportunity to learn from the cruel things you have done to me.[1938]**

Effectively what occurred was that Diana's body was repatriated from France by the very person she believed could have planned the crash – her ex-husband Charles.

Charles was a person Diana had indicated was an enemy, who had put her "through such hell".

Charles would have been the last person Diana would have wanted to "rescue" her from the French hospital.

---

[a] I point readers to books such as: *Diana: Her True Story – In Her Own Words* by Andrew Morton; *Charles at Fifty* by Anthony Holden and *Princess Diana: The Lamb to the Slaughter* by Joy Jones Daymon.

[b] They were published in 1992.

[c] As has been done by other authors – see footnote above.

[d] The courtship started in 1980 and the note was written in 1995. The abuse started during the courtship, but the inexperienced 19 year old Diana believed that things would improve after the wedding.

Omission from Inquest

Sarah McCorquodale was a key witness to the rushed Charles trip to Paris – she was the only person from that royal flight to appear at the inquest.[a]

Yet, when the subject arose during Sarah's cross-examination the inquest lawyer Ian Burnett completely bypassed it. He said:

> **I don't need to ask you any questions at all about what happened in Paris and events surrounding those hours or indeed those one or two days.**[1939]

And no other lawyers took this subject up with Sarah.
Why?

---

[a] No evidence at all – cross-examination or statement – was heard from Prince Charles or Jane Fellowes, or anyone else who may have been on that critical flight to Paris.

101 Panic in Paris

At around 3.00 p.m. (Paris time) Jeffrey Rees in Rutland received a call from Leicester Police. Rees then called royal coroner John Burton who wrote in his notes from the day:

> **Inspector Rees ... is informed there are problems in France in releasing bodies.**[1940]

Rees also notified the coroner for Dodi, Michael Burgess, and by 3.30 p.m. John Macnamara had received a call from Burgess. Macnamara told Paget:

> **[Burgess] told me that unfortunately the repatriation of Dodi's body from Paris would be delayed. He said that he had just received a phone call from someone at Scotland Yard. That person told him that the deaths were regarded as suspicious and were not the result of a straightforward traffic accident.**[1941] **(WFJ)**

Burgess told Macnamara that "unfortunately he had not taken the [Yard] person's name".[1942] (WFJ) Macnamara – who had previously worked at Scotland Yard – proceeded to try and verify the information from Burgess. He phoned MPS Commander Michael Messinger who said that he "had not telephoned Mr Burgess and was personally unaware of any such call".[1943] (WFJ)

Macnamara then phoned Ritz president Frank Klein in Paris. Klein later confirmed to Paget that Macnamara had called him to relay what Burgess had said. At the time Klein was at the IML and he noticed that "Dodi Al Fayed's body was already in the car in preparation for the journey to Issy-les-Moulineaux Heliport." He went over to Dominique Lecomte and passed on what Macnamara had said.[1944] (WFJ)

Klein then described Lecomte's reaction:

> **She seemed startled ... [and] immediately instructed that Dodi Al Fayed's body would not leave the country. Frank Klein stated that she then left him in a hurry, saying she was going to contact the authorities.**[1945] **(WFJ)**

Other witnesses support Klein's account.

Claude Roulet, who was standing with Klein, said that "Lecomte ... immediately instructed that Dodi Al Fayed's body was not to leave France".[1946] (WFJ)

Two PFG employees were also at the IML. Jean-Claude Plumet said that "Lecomte ... told everyone to stop".[1947] (WFJ) Gérard Jauze was with him and told police: "She said something to the effect of 'you're not leaving', addressing the funeral directors".[1948] (WFJ)

As Lecomte had conveyed, she proceeded to "contact the authorities". Who did Lecomte call?

She told Klein that she phoned "various judicial authorities". He believed it was "the French Director of Judicial Police, Patrick Riou and the French Minister of the Interior" M. Chevènement.[1949] (WFJ)

Jauze was waiting for Dodi's release and stated that a "plain-clothes police officer kept walking back and forth and told them that Professor Lecomte was speaking with the Public Prosecutor about this".[1950] (WFJ)

After about half an hour – at around 4.35 p.m. – Lecomte announced that the body could be released and subsequently Dodi's body left the IML, heading to London.

Klein testified that Lecomte then said: "Mr Klein and Mr Roulet, you have to go now to see Patrick Riou".[1951]

At 5.40 p.m. the two men met with Riou, head of the Judicial Police. Police Capitaine German Nouvion recorded the conversation:

> **[Klein and Roulet] informed us that they have today received information from London stating that the French National Police would have intelligence according to which the death of Mr Dodi Al Fayed would be suspicious.... [Riou] informed them that in the current stage of the investigation no information to this effect had been uncovered by the investigators.**[1952] **(WFJ)**

Panic in Paris

Why did Lecomte hold up the body transfer?

John Burton told Paget:

> **Michael Burgess ... informed me that the French authorities were apparently delaying the release of the body of Mr Dodi Al Fayed, as they were concerned that an investigation was to be carried out in England.**[1953] **(WFJ)**

Evidence in Part 3[a] indicates that this knowledge of French concerns about a British investigation arose as a result of Klein's 4 p.m. conversation with Lecomte at the IML. Klein's account of what he told Lecomte was that information had been received "from Michael Burgess saying that the death of Dodi Al Fayed was suspicious and not the result of a straightforward traffic accident".[1954] (WFJ)

To Lecomte this was information indicating "an investigation was to be carried out in England".

---

[a] Hold-Up in Body Transfer section, in Chapter 16.

Hearing this would have caused major concern to her because earlier in the day she had carried out a fraudulent autopsy on Princess Diana's driver Henri Paul.[a]

The French were in the midst of a major cover-up – not a proper investigation. Therefore knowledge of a possible British investigation could have been very troubling.

The following includes speculation, but is based on the known evidence.

When Chevènement was given the "news" that the British believed the crash was not an accident, he would have been as alarmed as Lecomte, and could have made immediate contact with his counterpart in the UK – Home Secretary, Jack Straw.

Maybe checks would have been made with Scotland Yard – specifically police Commissioner Paul Condon – and there is little doubt that at a high governmental level the French concerns would have been dissipated by English assurances that there was never going to be a proper investigation carried out in the UK. That message could have been passed to Chevènement, down to Riou and finally to Lecomte, who then lifted the embargo on the body transfer.

Michael Burgess was not subjected to cross-examination at the inquest – since his statement also was not read out, the jury heard no evidence from him whatsoever.[b]

Why?

---

[a] See earlier Fraud at the IML chapter.
[b] Michael Burgess was awarded an OBE in 2009 – a year after the conclusion of the Diana inquest.

102 Search and Remove: The Photos

The French failed to carry out a proper investigation of the crash, but they were far more proactive when it came to tracking down any photos associated with the events.

Seizing The Photos

The police seized the cameras and film from the paparazzi at the time of their arrest in the Alma Tunnel – 12.40 a.m.

Paget reported:

> **The negatives of photographs taken by the [paparazzi] arrested at the scene ... were provided to Operation Paget.**[1955] **(WFJ)**

Prior to those arrests, three of the paparazzi – Benhamou, Chassery and Odekerken – had already left the tunnel, with their film.

The French authorities were however determined to secure any photos relating to the events.

Later in the day the police raided Paris photo agencies Sygma and Sipa.

Maud Coujard told the inquest that she supervised these two raids which were conducted at 6 p.m. – Sygma – and 8 p.m. – Sipa.[1956] She declared:

> **I know that there were other searches [of other agencies] conducted by other magistrates.**[1957]

23 photos were taken from Sygma[1958] and 12 from Sipa.[1959]

Coujard was asked if the agency raids were "because of the concern about photographs". She avoided the question, instead replying:

> **Well, I am not the one that made that decision – it is the Public Prosecutor who had asked me to proceed to those two searches.**[1960]

The French quest for photos did not stop at the agencies. They also searched "the home of [paparazzo] David Odekerken's mother"[1961]; paparazzo Serge Benhamou's home and the home of his parents.[1962]

Journalist Mark Selle was arrested trying to sell photos taken by Fabrice Chassery.[1963] Laurent Sola was also arrested and negatives he possessed of Chassery's photos were seized by police.[1964]

Destruction of Photographic Evidence

French police did not just search and remove photos – there is also evidence within the Paget Report that they destroyed them "in line with French procedures":

> **Operation Paget officers were shown ... [photo] images of the removal of the Princess of Wales from the vehicle and her subsequent medical treatment before being placed in the SAMU ambulance.... Operation Paget was told by the French authorities that these photographs were destroyed on 26 May 2005 in line with French procedures.[1965] (WFJ)**

If there was nothing to cover up, then why destroy the photos? No explanation has ever been provided.

Expanding the Photo Search

Just after 1 a.m. on August 31 London-based Sipa-connected royalty photographer Lionel Cherrualt received a call from Mark Saunders, a British photographer in Florida.[1966]

Saunders told him that "he knew of a photographer who had been in the tunnel and that he would be able to get pictures of the crash scene for me".[1967]

Within a couple of hours Princess Diana had died and Cherrualt heard nothing more from Saunders.[1968]

Then at around 3.15 a.m. the next morning (September 1) Cherrualt's home was burgled, while he and his family lay sleeping.

Among the items stolen was computer equipment containing royal photos.[1969]

Cherrualt was visited on September 4 by an MPS crime prevention officer, William Kemp.

Cherrualt later told Paget:

> **[Kemp] said, 'I am assuming you are not recording this conversation. I have examined your report. I have to tell you that you were not burgled but targeted.' I said, 'By that do [you] mean the grey men.' He replied 'MI5, Flying Squad or hired local hoodlums.' He also said 'Not to worry your lives were not in any danger.'[1970]**

Cherrualt confirmed this at the inquest.[1971]

A burglary suspect was arrested but no charges have ever been laid.[1972]

Darryn Lyons, head of Big Pictures in London, received photos electronically from the crash scene on the night.[1973]

Lyons later told Paget:

> **In the days following the crash we heard strange clicking noises when we used the office phones. I did not know what was causing these noises but the thought crossed my mind that our phones could be**

bugged.... I remember an incident [on September 4] where my staff and I left the office late one evening at around 10.30 p.m. We went to a local Indian restaurant called the Taj Mahal. When we returned to the office after midnight it was in darkness. I thought this was strange as the lights were still on in the offices of our immediate neighbours. I entered and heard a ticking noise and believe I saw a shadow of a person at the back of the office. I immediately called the police.... From memory nothing was found.... The [electricity] company ... said that it was impossible for it to happen as we were on a grid system. The police arrived and searched the building with torches. Nothing was found, there was no sign of forced entry and nothing had been taken. I have no explanation as to why the lights were switched off or how the lighting was eventually restored.[1974]

103   Illegal Jurisdiction

The royal flight carrying Princess Diana's coffin shrouded in the royal standard, Prince Charles and Diana's sisters Jane and Sarah, touched down at RAF Northolt on time – 7 p.m. local.

Waiting on the tarmac was an official party that included PM Tony Blair and the Queen's Lord Chamberlain, David Ogilvy.

Just 13 minutes after arriving – at 7.13 p.m. – Prince Charles reboarded the flight to head back to Aberdeen and Balmoral.

Sarah and Jane accompanied Diana's body in the cortège which headed to the Fulham Mortuary. The route and the footbridges down the A40 were lined with people and flowers were tossed over the cars. Vehicles on both sides of the motorway stopped to honour the passing princess.

Royal coroner John Burton was waiting at Fulham Mortuary. It was he who would preside over her UK post-mortem.

But was that legal?

Was it legal that Diana – now a non-royal – would be subject to a post-mortem by the royal coroner?

Finding the Right Coroner

For John Burton to be eligible to conduct the post-mortem on Princess Diana he had to claim legal jurisdiction over her body.

Her Majesty's Coroners Eastern District of London website specifically addresses what happens when a body is "brought into the jurisdiction from abroad":

> **If a body is repatriated to this country it is generally accepted that the Coroner within whose jurisdiction the body will finally lay must be notified. The Coroner will then decide if an inquest is necessary.**[1975a]

Legal jurisdiction falls to the coroner of the intended burial location – where "the body will finally lay".

---

[a] This is supported by Home Office Circular 89/1983.

After Diana's sisters Sarah and Jane arrived with her body at Fulham Mortuary, they went straight into a meeting with Burton.

Anthony Mather escorted them from the airport to the mortuary. He stated what happened:

I took them to the office area where Dr Burton spoke to them concerning his role and the post mortem examination.[1976] **(WFJ)**

Burton told Paget:

I explained to them that as the coroner of the Royal Household I had taken jurisdiction over Diana Princess of Wales and was obliged to hold an inquest and order that a post mortem be carried out.[1977] **(WFJ)**

Burton then added:

I believed at this time that Diana Princess of Wales was to be <u>buried at Windsor Castle</u> so I transferred jurisdiction ... to myself as coroner for the Royal Household in writing. This made sense and was expedient.[1978] **(WFJ)**

After seeing Sarah and Jane, Burton said he believed Diana would be buried at Windsor and then proceeded to claim jurisdiction.

He completed a formal jurisdiction transfer request:

The body of Diana Princess of Wales was returned to Northolt from France.
The death had been notified to me as Coroner of the Queen's Household. It was thought that the funeral might be held at Windsor. This conformed with Home Office Circular 79/1983.
In order to direct a post mortem examination before the body arrived within that jurisdiction, this is a request in writing in accord via section 14 of the Coroners Act 1988, from West London to the Queen's Household.

[signed in handwriting]
John Burton

Figure 28

Undated document raised by John Burton, transferring jurisdiction for the body of Princess Diana to himself, as royal coroner. This action was based on Burton's belief that Diana's "funeral might be held at Windsor" Castle. This document is incomplete or not grammatically correct – it reads: "this is a request in writing in accord via section 14 of the Coroners Act 1988, from West London to the Queen's Household" – the critical missing words are "to transfer jurisdiction", which should appear before "from West London". This document has been reproduced from the 8 January 2007 inquest pre-hearing held by Elizabeth Butler-Sloss – it was not shown to the inquest jury.

In Burton's notes from the day he wrote about the jurisdiction decision following the meeting with Sarah and Jane:

> **See family of Diana. <u>Now to be funeral at Althorpe</u>. Body to lie in St James. Body in my jurisdiction – physically – so give Burial order.**[1979]

This reveals that following the family meeting – and before the post-mortem – Burton was aware Princess Diana would be buried at Althorp. Yet he went ahead and formalised transfer to his jurisdiction – the Queen's Household – based on the false premise "that the funeral might be held at Windsor".

Based on British law, this was an illegal action.

Burton knew the body would be buried at Althorp – instead of transferring jurisdiction to the coroner at Northamptonshire[a] he transferred it to himself, as royal coroner.

The fact that he falsely used the expectation of a Windsor burial as the basis for this decision shows that he was fully aware of what he was doing.

Prior to the commencement of the post-mortem Burton claimed illegal jurisdiction over Princess Diana's body.

Why?

---

[a] The location of Althorp.

104   Changing Her Status

Royal coroner John Burton's illegal seizure of jurisdiction was one of the final acts in securing royal control over Princess Diana's body.

Not a Royal

Prince Philip's private secretary stated at the inquest:

> **The Princess was no longer a member of the Royal Family after the divorce in August 1996.**[1980]

This was supported by the LCO Assistant Comptroller Anthony Mather in his police statement – not heard by the jury:

> **Diana, Princess of Wales ... was not at the time of her death a member of the Royal Family.**[1981] **(WFJ)**

Yet following her death Princess Diana was quickly turned back into a royal.

A Dead Royal

Five events that occurred within 25 hours of Diana's death reveal that the Queen quickly welcomed the dead Diana back into the royal fold.

First, within a few hours of her death Levertons,[a] the royal funeral directors, had been ordered to take care of the embalming and repatriation of Diana's body.

Second, the appearance of the royal standard to cover Diana's coffin.

Third, using the royal coroner to claim jurisdiction and conduct the post-mortem.

---

[a] In their statements, Keith and Clive Leverton both said: "We are the funeral directors who have since 1991 been asked by the Lord Chamberlains office to care for members the Royal Family in the event of one of them passing away." See The Documents book, Clive p488; Keith p497. (WFJ)

Fourth, Prince Charles' visit to Paris to repatriate Diana's body

Fifth, delivery of Diana's body to St James' Palace, where she was embalmed for the second time.[a]

Changing Her Status

By the time Diana's body rested at St James' Palace – on royal territory – her royal makeover was complete.

The evidence reveals that this was all about control – the illegal jurisdiction claim by Burton enabled the Queen to obtain control over Diana's body.

This in turn enabled the royal coroner – who answered to Balmoral – to oversee and control the London post-mortem that began straight after the meeting between Burton and Diana's sisters.

But this was to be no ordinary post-mortem....

---

[a] See later.

105　Fraud at Fulham

After arriving at Fulham Mortuary, the second post-mortem[a] of Diana, Princess of Wales commenced at 8.21 p.m.

It was conducted by forensic pathologist Professor Robert Chapman, under the direction of the royal coroner, John Burton.

Missing Chain of Custody

Despite the significance of this post-mortem, there are several basic deficiencies in the recording methods employed by the Fulham Mortuary and Chapman.

Princess Diana's body was never assigned a body number.

This is the best possible start, if one was interested in covering up post-mortem related documents – if there is no body number then there is no central reference point to put at the top of documents related to the body.

And that is exactly what occurred – there is a general lack of reference numbers or reference codes on the key mortuary documents relating to Princess Diana's post-mortem.[b]

The jury were not shown any of these documents, so they would not have been in a position to see that Diana, Princess of Wales was not allocated a Fulham Mortuary body number.

Samples taken during the post-mortem were only referenced by the pathologist's initials, e.g. RC/2.[1982] (WFJ)

Other deficiencies were:[c]

---

[a] The first had been conducted earlier in the day in Paris by Professor Dominique Lecomte – see earlier Autopsy in Paris chapter.

[b] The post-mortem documents – all withheld from the jury – are shown in Chapter 7 of The Documents book. Some sensitive material has been redacted by the author. Where relevant to the case, parts of the redacted material have been shown in Part 4, Chapter 5.

[c] These are all addressed in detail in Part 4, UK Post-Mortems chapter.

- there were no unique identifying numbers or names on the sample labels received by the toxicologist[1983] (WFJ)
- although the toxicologist received samples in sealed police bags there were apparently no associated seal reference numbers on the bags[1984] (WFJ)
- no source was shown on the blood sample label[1985] or in the post-mortem report[1986] (WFJ)
- the pathologist's official post-mortem report was undated[1987] (WFJ)
- there was a sample – vitreous humour – later recorded as taken,[1988] (WFJ) that did not appear in the official Exhibits report written up during the post-mortem[1989a] (WFJ)
- there were eight samples of major organs taken for which no records were made by the pathologist, or anyone else[1990]
- there are no photos of any of the sample bottles or labels.

The result of these serious deficiencies means that in the case of Princess Diana the chain of custody that is required to protect the integrity of the samples is virtually non-existent – I believe worse than that of Henri Paul's.[b]

Robert Chapman is a very experienced forensic pathologist. So, why is it that he conducted this post-mortem of Princess Diana – possibly the most significant of his career – in such a negligent fashion?

Why is it that again we are studying a subject about which the 2008 inquest jury heard only paltry levels of evidence?

Blinding the Jury

The documentary evidence reproduced in Part 4[c] and in the UK Post-Mortems chapter of *The Documents* book reveals that 21 important documents – copies of which were held by Scott Baker – were withheld from the eyes of the jury.

The only people the jury heard from were Robert Chapman, Jeffrey Rees and Philip Stoneham – the pathologist and two police officers.

Nothing was heard from John Burton (royal coroner),[d] Michael Burgess (Dodi's coroner), Robert Thompson (mortuary manager), Keith Brown (coroner's officer), Harry Brown (coroner's officer), Nigel Munns (senior mortuary officer), Richard Wall (police), Dennis Sharp (police), Michael Walker (police), Neal Williams (police photographer) and Mark Taylor

---

[a] See Figure 20 in Part 4.
[b] The chain of custody for Henri Paul is addressed in Part 3, Chain of Custody chapter.
[c] UK Post-Mortems chapter.
[d] Burton died before the inquest commenced, but his police statement was withheld from the jury.

(assistant police photographer) – no statements read out and no cross-examination from any of these people.

Why was the inquest jury also prevented from seeing the post-mortem and toxicology reports of the people whose deaths they were supposed to be investigating – Princess Diana and Dodi Fayed?

What is the point in holding a post-mortem – which is to determine cause of death – if the inquest jury – who are also determining cause of death – are not allowed to view the reports from it?

Why was all this evidence withheld?

It appears to be because the evidence reveals information Baker did not want the jury to be aware of – particularly the discovery that Princess Diana's samples were tampered with.

Manipulation of Samples

The toxicology testing was carried out on samples that did not come from the body of Princess Diana:

-    Diana's body had been embalmed, but there was no embalming fluid detected in the tested samples

The toxicologist Dr Susan Paterson included a special note in her Paget statement:

> **There was no evidence to show that the blood had been contaminated with embalming fluid.[1991] (WFJ)**

-    Diana had consumed alcohol,[a] but there was no alcohol in the tested samples

Fulham Mortuary manager Robert Thompson declared to Paget:

> **When [Diana's] stomach was opened I smelt what I believe was alcohol.[1992] (WFJ)**

But Susan Paterson stated:

> **Ethanol[b] was not detected in either the preserved blood or vitreous humor.[1993] (WFJ)**

-    there was no vitreous humour sample taken during the post-mortem, yet a vitreous humour sample was tested

-    the Property Register reveals that the samples were "retained by Dr Chapman" with no record of them going to the toxicologist[c] (WFJ)

-    the Biological Samples report reveals that in late 2006 Operation Paget had the samples from Diana[1994a] (WFJ)

---

[a] This is addressed in Part 4, Alcohol section of UK Post-Mortems chapter.

[b] Alcohol.

[c] The Property Register is reproduced in The Documents book, from p665. The section of the register relating to Diana's samples are also shown in Part 4, Figure 28.

- the stomach contents sample recorded in the Biological Samples report is twice the size of the sample officially tested by the toxicologist

The MPS Biological Samples report reveals Diana's stomach contents sample held by the police was 429 grams.[1995] (WFJ) Paterson stated in her report that the sample size remaining was "approximately 200 mL".[1996b] (WFJ)

- the sample labels received by Paterson[1997] (WFJ) – for both blood and liver – read differently to the descriptions in the post-mortem documentation[1998c] (WFJ)

- the stomach contents sample label received by Dr Alexander Allan[d1999] (WFJ) reads differently to the sample received by Paterson[2000e] (WFJ)

- there are no police seal numbers or unique reference numbers quoted in the official post-mortem and toxicology reports, but there were seal numbers in the police Property Register and also quoted on the samples officially taken by the police [f]

- the samples held at the Imperial College (and toxicology tested by Paterson) have never been subjected to DNA testing.

The public perception is that Princess Diana's post-mortem samples were tested and the results were made public in the Paget Report[g] and at the inquest.[h]

There are two main problems with this public perception:

1) the toxicology results were based on tested samples that appear to have come from a body other than Princess Diana's [i]

---

[a] There is no evidence of the tested samples being removed from the Imperial College (where they were tested by Paterson). This is supported by the 2004 letter from Paget to Susan Paterson – see Part 4, Figure 26.

[b] This disparity is addressed in detail in Part 4, section on Sample Movements in Chapter 5.

[c] This is addressed in detail in Part 4, section on Sample Movements in Chapter 5.

[d] A forensic scientist who did work for the MPS.

[e] This is addressed in detail in Part 4, section on Sample Movements in Chapter 5.

[f] This is addressed in detail in Part 4, section on Sample Identification in Chapter 5.

[g] The Paget Report covered Paterson's toxicology results – including selective excerpts from her report – on pages 642-3.

[h] The results were briefly addressed during the cross-examination of Robert Chapman on 26 November 2007: Dodi at 12.4 and Diana at 23.1.

[i] There is additional evidence to support this in Part 4, section on Possible Scenario in Chapter 5.

2)   the full results were not provided – neither the Paget Report nor the inquest revealed that there was no evidence of embalming fluid in the tested samples.

Post-Mortem Fraud

No one can accuse the authorities of not doing a post-mortem – in other words, "no stone left unturned"[a] – but any information from the post-mortem has been effectively neutralised because:

a)   the jury investigating the death were not allowed to see the post-mortem report

b)   the jury were not allowed to see the toxicology report

c)   the toxicology report was apparently dealing with samples from another body anyway.

Diana's samples may have been switched out of knowledge or fear of what the samples might have revealed – possible pregnancy or possibly a harmful substance administered in the ambulance.

The toxicology report reveals that the samples were devoid of embalming fluid – but the jury did not hear that.

There are two actions that should be carried out:

1)   The samples held by Operation Paget and LGC Forensics should be subjected to extensive toxicological testing.

2)   The samples held at the Imperial College should be subjected to DNA testing.[b]

Only then can the truth of what has occurred be more fully established.

---

[a] There were actually many stones left unturned, but we are talking about the public perception here.

[b] When the authorities wanted to conduct a DNA test to verify the blood on the Mercedes carpet, they did it with RC/1 – the hair sample retained by the police – and did not use the samples that were held at the Imperial College. Had they used any of the Imperial College samples, there would have been no match – but instead many red faces. Source: Roy Green, Witness Statement, 23 November 2006, reproduced in Part 4, pp594-5. This is also addressed in more detail in Part 4, Sample Movements section of Chapter 5.

106 Midnight Embalming at the Palace

Princess Diana's post-mortem concluded at 11.20 p.m.

But the final invasive act on her body was yet to occur.

Keith Leverton testified to Paget:

> **We waited inside the [Fulham Mortuary] building until the body was released. I then learnt from Mather that Diana, Princess of Wales was to be taken to St James', a Royal Palace, as soon as possible....**
>
> **The Lord Chamberlains office had their own plans [which] … involved the requirement for embalming....[2001] (WFJ)**

At the conclusion of the late-night post-mortem Diana was in a "safe" environment – a London mortuary. The body was in a situation where it could be refrigerated overnight. Mather could have left instructions for the body to remain at Fulham Mortuary – Mather, Clive, Keith and Green could have all gone home, had a good night's sleep, and continued in the morning.

But that is not what we see happening.

Instead we see Mather obsessed with making sure Diana made it to St James' Palace that night.[a]

Why? Why not leave Diana in Fulham Mortuary overnight?

There are three relevant differences between Fulham Mortuary and St James' Palace:

- Fulham Mortuary provides body refrigeration facilities, St James' Palace doesn't
- Fulham Mortuary provides embalming facilities, St James' Palace doesn't
- St James' Palace was royal territory, Fulham Mortuary wasn't.

---

[a] Mather was very familiar with St James' Palace – he said at the inquest: "75 per cent of my time is in St James' Palace and 25 per cent was in Buckingham Palace": 22 Nov 07: 83.19.

Anthony Mather appears to have received instructions that Diana had to be returned to royal property that night. He apparently had to stay around to make sure that occurred.

This embalming was conducted in the Chapel Royal, a building with no facilities for that – in the words of Clive Leverton: "carrying it out at the chapel was not ideally suited";[2002] (WFJ) and at the inquest: "it was a very difficult situation, it was in the Chapel Royal".[2003a]

The evidence indicates Diana was returned to royal land at St James' Palace that night to help provide early credibility to the illegal claim by John Burton – royal coroner – for jurisdiction over the body.[b]

This is further evidence of a highly coordinated royal operation – each person playing their role, but all these people answerable to the Queen.[c]

David Green – who carried out the embalming – has stated that "it took about five hours to carry out the work to my satisfaction".[2004] (WFJ)

Princess Diana officially died at 4 a.m. on 31 August 1997. Within 25 hours – by 4 a.m. UK time, the following day – Diana's body had been subjected to two post-mortems – one in France, one in the UK – and two embalmings.

---

[a] Levertons may have been very surprised: in the middle of the night, they were forced to whisk Diana away from an ideal situation at Fulham Mortuary – refrigeration, embalming facilities – to a chapel at St James' Palace that was far from ideal, and had no appropriate facilities.
[b] This act didn't give Burton legal jurisdiction, but the fact that Diana was now on royal land may have helped create the perception that the inquest should be conducted by the royal coroner.
[c] See Royal Structure diagram in earlier Early Royal Decisions chapter.

107   Testing the Wrong Samples

The following morning – Monday September 1st – focus shifted back to Paris and the analysis of the Mercedes driver's blood samples.

Professor Ivan Ricordel, the police toxicologist received a blood sample from the previous day's autopsy.

He recorded the label details – instead of showing the name, it read "XM" which means, unknown male.[2005] (WFJ)

At the inquest this label was read out to the jury, but because the document prepared for the inquest had been fraudulently compiled, there was nothing showing for the name – the "XM" was missing.[2006] Instead there was a note at the bottom that read: "Labelling possibly incorrect".[a]

Ricordel tested this sample – Blood Sample 1[b] – twice: at 9.44 a.m. and then again at 9.52. The respective results were 1.8718 and 1.8750. This was reported as 1.87 g/L.[2007]

Then at 11.38 a.m. Paris toxicologist Dr Gilbert Pépin received a fax from the Public Prosecutor.

Pépin told Paget:

> **I was consulted for a second assessment after Professor Ricordel, to carry out just a control blood alcohol test on the blood of Henri Paul.[2008] (WFJ)**

Pépin quickly arranged to pick up Blood Sample 2 from the IML and conducted a test at 1.19 p.m.[2009] (WFJ)

He achieved a result of 1.74 g/L.[2010]

Unauthorised Tests

Two hours later Pépin started conducting unauthorised testing on the same blood sample.

---

[a] The fraudulent document can be viewed on the website: INQ0004440. It has also been reproduced in Part 3, Figure 5.

[b] The listing of blood samples is in Part 3, the Blood Sample Labels Table section of Chapter 1.

Operation Paget reported:

Attached to [Pépin's report] ... were six 'Millenium Spectrum Review' reports showing a date of 1 September 1997 – timed between 15.37 [3.37 p.m.] and 15.45.... These charts referred to cotinine, caffeine, fluoxetine and fluoxetine metabolite and lidocaine.[2011] (WFJ)

Paget stated there were six test reports, but only listed five substances. It is very likely that the sixth substance – not disclosed by Paget – was carbon monoxide.[a]

At that point Pépin had only been requested to test for blood alcohol – see above.

When answering an unrelated question, Pépin told Paget:

If an expert carries out tests for which he was not assigned, he could be struck off.[2012] (WFJ)

This has not occurred in the case of Dr Gilbert Pépin – and he has not been held to account. Pépin has never provided a credible explanation for conducting these unauthorised tests.[b]

The jury were also not told about the unauthorised tests.

Tell the World He Was Drunk

In the afternoon the Public Prosecutor's office publicised the high BAC result to the world's media. London's *Evening Standard* was the first British paper to report on it, in their final edition for the day under the headline: "Di's Driver 'Was Drunk'".[2013c]

Following this, on Monday September 2 one of the world's leading forensic pathologists travelled to Paris – at Mohamed Al Fayed's request – with the intention of conducting an independent autopsy of Henri Paul.[2014]

This was refused by the French investigation,[2015] now headed by examining magistrate, Hervé Stéphan.

The next day, September 3, Henri Paul's apartment was searched by the police. They found "a bottle of champagne and a quarter-full bottle of Martini".[2016]

At this point Stéphan officially requested Pépin to "carry out a complete analysis of the samples ... for the purpose of revealing the presence of any toxins as well as ... medicinal products."[2017]

Then the next morning Stéphan ordered Dr Jean-Pierre Campana to conduct a second autopsy on the body of Henri Paul, directing it to

---

[a] There are major problems related to the carbon monoxide level in these samples – see earlier Fraud at the IML chapter.

[b] A full analysis of the evidence is in Part 3, Unauthorised Testing section of Chapter 7C.

[c] A reproduction of the first part of the article appears in the 2013 book Alan Power Exposed, Figure 10.

commence later that day at 5 p.m.[2018] Stéphan later told Paget that he "decided to do something that [he] had never done before" – he would personally attend this second autopsy at the IML.[2019] (WFJ)

Evidence indicates that the unexpected presence of leading pathologist Peter Vanezis in Paris and asking for an independent autopsy was putting additional pressure on what was a corrupt French investigation.

108   Second Autopsy

The samples tested from the first autopsy had been taken from the second body – not Henri Paul's. It is likely that the September 1 "unauthorised" testing by Pépin for substances[a] may have been to establish if there would be any surprises in this body – anything that could cause problems for the investigation.

As it turned out, there was – carbon monoxide tested at 20.7%,[b] far too high to be even falsely attributed to Henri Paul.

Carbon monoxide dissipates over time.[2020]

This second autopsy appears to have been called for two possible reasons. First: the hope of securing a more acceptable carbon monoxide level.[c] And second: to create an external perception that all was being done to be thorough and seek the truth.

After all, not just one autopsy was done on the driver, but there were two, using different pathologists.

Professor Robert Forrest, the inquest's expert toxicologist, maintained that the second autopsy was to collect "a small amount of tissue from the thigh and the exploration of Scarpa's Triangle".[2021]

But the jury did not get to hear that Stéphan's written appointment of Pépin as toxicologist for this autopsy shows that it was much more:

> **"Samples of blood and tissues" were to be taken "for the purpose of carrying out a full toxicological analysis".[2022] (WFJ)**

Coroner Baker advised his jury in the Summing Up:

> **You may want to consider whether, if there is any doubt about the results from 31st August [1st autopsy], it is not safer to concentrate on 4th September [2nd autopsy].[2023]**

But is this true? Was it safe for the jury to rely on the second autopsy?

---

[a] Mentioned in the previous chapter.
[b] See earlier chapter Fraud at the IML.
[c] The carbon monoxide level achieved in the second autopsy was 12.8%. The issues around this are addressed in Part 3, Chapter 7B.

Was It Safe?

There are several major problems with this September 4 autopsy:[a]
-    there was a significant delay of four days before it was carried out
Independent experts stated that this delay was "quite abnormal" and was not "according to the usual rules of procedure".[2024] (WFJ)
Robert Forrest himself also wrote in a report:

When the [blood] samples are obtained ... several days after death, then a degree of caution always has to be used in interpreting the results.... As time passes ... the possibility of interferences in the sample that will interfere with the analyses ... does increase.[2025] (WFJ)

-    interested parties were prevented from attending or being represented
This autopsy was carried out without notifying Henri Paul's parents[2026] (WFJ) and also not informing Peter Vanezis until after it had occurred.[2027]
-    the body was never properly identified
Stéphan stated:

I was taken to see a body which I was informed was that of Henri Paul. I requested the officers from the Forensic Science and Identification Service to photograph the body and face.[2028]

No one who knew Henri Paul was ever asked to identify his body before either autopsy. The photos Stéphan referred to have never been seen by anyone who knew Henri Paul.
-    there is no photo evidence of the autopsy being carried out despite a photographer being present[b]
-    Lieutenant Daniel Bourgois' photos taken the following day show no femoral incisions
Stéphan stated in his report:

Dr Campana then took a blood sample from the right femoral artery and after that from the left femoral artery.[2029]

Bourgois wrote in his report:

On 5 September 1997, at the request of Mr Stéphan, Examining Magistrate ... I went to the Paris Institut of Forensic Science, accompanied by Police Constable Vinsonneau, during the visit by the Examining Magistrate. I am submitting the attached two copies of the photographs taken on that occasion, together with a plan of the premises.[c][2030] (WFJ)

---

[a] There is a more complete analysis of the problems in Part 3, Chapter 2.
[b] This is addressed in Part 3, section on Photo Evidence in Chapter 2.
[c] I am not aware of why a plan of the premises would have been appropriate – this may be just a bureaucratic procedure.

These photos were viewed by inquest expert Richard Shepherd. He stated to Paget that there was an "absence of any sign of dissection of ... the femoral region" in the photos.[2031] (WFJ)

- the blood samples were incorrectly labelled "sang cardiaque" – which means cardiac or heart blood[2032]

Four witnesses – Stéphan, Christian Le Jalle,[2033] (WFJ) Campana[2034] and Pépin[2035] (WFJ) – stated that the blood samples came from the femoral area – not the heart.

- ToxLab[a] records reveal that there are "two entirely independent entries with different codes purporting to be the same left femoral blood sample"[2036]
- Professor Richard Shepherd saw a sample handed over that had a label which read significantly different to what Paget and Professor Roy Green described

Shepherd wrote in a report to Paget that he witnessed a blood sample handed over to the British police in March 2005 from the Campana autopsy – the label read:

> **"'Henri PAUL 912147' dated '04/09/1997' and inscribed 'fluoridated cardiac blood Dr Campana'".[2037][b] (WFJ)**

Roy Green – who carried out the UK DNA testing – described a label that read:

> **"IML: 972147; Nom: Paul Henry; Date: 4/09/1997; Sang Cardiaque; Médecin: Campana".[2038]**

Paget confirmed that this was the sample they received in March 2005 – they gave the identical description as Green confirmed at the inquest.[2039] (WFJ)

When one considers this was the one sample handed to the British to conduct their own DNA testing – which they employed Green to do – it becomes very significant that there are two completely different sample descriptions for what is ostensibly the same sample.

Why is this?

Deceiving the Jury

None of the people present at this second autopsy were heard from at the inquest – no cross-examinations and also no statements read out.

At the inquest there was a major emphasis on the issues surrounding the August 31 autopsy which was shown to be seriously deficient.[c]

---

[a] Toxlab is Dr Pépin's company. Pépin was present during the autopsy and was handed the left femoral sample for testing at Toxlab: 30 Jan 08: 92.3.

[b] A photo of this sample appears at Figure 11 in Part 3. Also viewable on the website: INQ0004627.

[c] See earlier Fraud at the IML chapter.

However, when it came to the September 4 autopsy, the evidence relating to the problems was not addressed or was quickly glossed over. Yet the flaws surrounding this 2nd autopsy are extremely serious and substantial.[a]

This strategy resulted in the jury being presented with a clear picture: The 1st autopsy was severely flawed, but the 2nd autopsy – although it had a couple of minor problems – was performed under much better conditions and its test results should be relied on.

Although this picture was clear, it was completely erroneous.

The jury never got to hear about most of the problems relating to that 2nd autopsy – throughout this relatively short chapter, "WFJ"[b] appeared 10 times.

Having this evidence withheld, the jury were put in the impossible situation of making assessments of what happened from incomplete accounts. They were presented with a distorted picture of what occurred, but would have been under the impression that they were hearing all of the evidence. This became particularly relevant after Baker told the jury in his Summing Up to "consider whether ... it is not safer to concentrate on 4th September".

Why is this? Why is it that the Baker inquest jury only got to hear half of the story of what occurred at the September 4 autopsy? Why is it that none of the witnesses to the second autopsy were heard from at the inquest – not Stéphan, Stéphan's clerk, Campana, Pépin, Le Jalle or Boulet?[c]

The entire proposition that Princess Diana died as a result of an accident and not a staged crash has been founded right from 1 September 1997 – when the Paris Public Prosecutor went public with the first autopsy's astounding results – on the understanding that Henri Paul was driving drunk behind the wheel of the Mercedes S280. In turn, this allegation completely stands on the integrity of the autopsy results – there is effectively no other credible evidence whatsoever that indicates in any way that Henri Paul was drunk.

Because the autopsy evidence is so critical to the case, at the inquest it became imperative to the Establishment that the jury would be shown evidence that would lead to them believing that the 2nd autopsy results were bona fide and supported the belief that Henri Paul was drunk.

Conversely, if both the 1st and 2nd autopsies could be shown to be a sham, then the allegation that Henri Paul was drunk would have completely disintegrated before the jury's eyes. This could have led to the understanding that the autopsies of Henri Paul formed a critical part of a French cover-up of the events.

---

[a] The flaws are fully addressed in Part 3, chapter on 2nd Autopsy.
[b] WFJ = Withheld From Jury.
[c] Police Constable Christophe Boulet – he was the photographer present on September 4.

In turn that knowledge could have had a significant impact on the jury's assessment of what actually had occurred in the Alma Tunnel – otherwise, why would there have been a cover-up if there was nothing to cover up?

109 Planting "Evidence"

The September 3 search of Henri Paul's apartment had uncovered two bottles of alcohol – unopened champagne and an opened bottle of Martini, both in the fridge. [2040]

That was evidently considered inadequate by the investigation, because six days later – on the 9th – they conducted a second search.

This later search was more fruitful.

The police uncovered:

In the fridge
- Two small bottles of beer, unopened
- One bottle of champagne, unopened

In the lobby:
- Various aperitifs – Crème de Cassis, Ricard, Suze, Port, partially drunk to various degrees
- Beer, red wine, champagne, unopened

On lobby table:
- Various aperitifs – Martini Bianco, Vodka, Pinot, Suze, unopened
- Fortified wine, unopened bottle

In kitchen cupboard:
- Various aperitifs – Ricard, Bourbon 4 Roses, Martini Bianco, opened. [2041] (WFJ)

Two bottles were found on September 3, then six days later, there were 18 bottles.

Why this huge difference?

Lieutenant Marc Monot was involved in the initial operation – in his statement at the time he said that it was "a detailed search". [2042]

When Monot was confronted with what the second search had yielded, he said that was because it occurred "following the analysis of blood that had been undertaken in the meantime". [2043]

But clearly the first search occurred two days after the autopsy results were known, on September 1.

Henri's friend Claude Garrec was present during the second search. He later stated:

> **The police "wrote down the names of alcoholic drinks they claimed they had found, but were not there."[2044] (WFJ)**

The French police have never provided a credible explanation for why they conducted the second search and why there was such a big variation in the alcohol found.

110   Phantom Uno Search

Georges and Sabine Dauzonne got a close look at the white Fiat Uno and its driver straight after it emerged from the Alma Tunnel, post-crash.

Avoiding the Witness

Georges contacted the French police the next day, September 1. He told the inquest what happened:

> **On Monday morning, I called the [police] commissariat.... They said, "We have had a lot of calls, sir. No, it does not seem to be very relevant for us". So that is all.[2045]**

Then on September 12 the French investigation positively identified tail-light fragments from the tunnel belonging to a Fiat Uno manufactured between May 1983 and September 1989.[2046] (WFJ)

Five days later, on the 17th, the French police went public – they told the media they were now looking for the driver of a second car, a white Fiat Uno that had contact with the Mercedes S280.

This led to Dauzonne again contacting the police:

> **I was getting home on the 17th or 18th September, and my daughter called me, "You know, they were talking about the paint of a white Fiat Uno on Princess Diana's car". I said, "What?", and that is why I called the police again. I said, "Listen, I called you two or three weeks before". I explained that nobody wanted to take my testimony and now I am back here. They said, "Yes, we will be looking for you. We heard someone called for a Fiat Uno. We did not know it was you, but come over right now", which I did. As a matter of fact, I went right away.[2047]**

Georges Dauzonne was finally interviewed by the police on the 18th and his wife Sabine the following day.[a]

---

[a] The evidence of what they saw has been covered earlier in the Fiat Uno Post-Crash chapter.

Why didn't the police contact Georges Dauzonne on September 12 – as soon as they became aware they were looking for a white Fiat Uno?

Phantom Search

On September 18 the *Mirror* reported:

Detectives are now prepared to interview the owner of every Fiat Uno in France to trace the missing driver.[2048ab] **(WFJ)**

On Thursday October 9 – exactly three weeks later – Glasgow's *Daily Record* stated that "French police have made a massive breakthrough". The paper reported that "the search for a Fiat Uno ... has been narrowed to just 300 cars". And this: "Investigators had feared they would have to trace all 100,000 Unos in France."[2049] (WFJ) On the same day *The Mirror* reported: "There are more than 100,000 Unos in France, but only 300 made between 1983 and 1989 feature the same [tail]light."[2050] (WFJ)

On Wednesday November 5, *The Independent* reported:

French police plan to interview 40,000 owners of Fiat Unos.... The car owners, starting with those in the Paris area, will be invited to come to a police station to account for their movements on 31 August.[2051] **(WFJ)**

On the same day *The Buffalo News* quoted the police source: "If we don't find anything in the Paris region, we will widen the search to include more of France".[2052] (WFJ) On November 6 *The New York Times* stated:

In a countrywide search ... French police began questioning the owners of 40,000 French-registered Fiat Unos this week.

That paper went on to say: "The police have been looking for the Fiat ... concentrating first on cars registered in the western suburbs of Paris." Next, *The New York Times* quoted two specific cases of people interviewed by the police:

-       "Julien Fernandez, a Fiat driver for *Paris-Match* magazine, in suburban Asnieres-sur-Seine on Tuesday" November 4 – "He was on vacation in Spain" at the time of the crash

-       "Edwige Pelmard, 30, another Fiat driver" – "She was asleep at the time".[2053] (WFJ)

On November 7 and 8 several US newspapers reported that "the costly inquiry ... is angering some French judges, lawyers and police". On the 8th the *Los Angeles Times* quoted Paris judge Jean-Claude Bouvier:

---

[a] At that time there were around 100,000 Fiat Unos in France.
[b] The paper quoted a French police source who said: "We shall start our search in Paris, but we're quite prepared to spread the net".

This was an accident – not a terrorist attack. I have never seen such a deployment of people and a lavishing of resources on what, after all, was an incident involving a car.[2054] (WFJ)

The *New York Times* said on 1 January 1998:

French authorities began questioning drivers of more than 3,000 Fiat Uno cars registered in the Paris region in early November but have not found the mystery vehicle, according to investigators. They have never explained whether the search has been broadened to include thousands of other white Fiats registered elsewhere in France.[2055] (WFJ)

On the same day *BBC News* reported:

Police have so far traced only about 10% of the 40,000 or so Unos which answer the description.[2056] (WFJ)

On Saturday 17 January 1998 *Hello!* magazine stated that since the crash the "police have questioned thousands of Fiat Uno owners in the Paris area, but have admitted that the task is like looking for a needle in a haystack." (WFJ)

The above chronology of reports is a summary of worldwide media coverage of the French police search for the white Fiat Uno. These articles are based on information leaked to the press by police sources, throughout the period of the search.

When Brigade Criminelle Lieutenant Eric Gigou was asked about the press reports of the search, he stated to the inquest:

If you call for all the owners of the white Fiat Unos in two areas, which are Hauts de Seine [Department 92] and Yvelines [Department 78], then you cannot keep this information being secret.[2057]

The above media summary repeatedly shows that there never was any public knowledge that just two departments – 78 and 92 – were the subject of the search.

The summary reveals several developments over the period:
1) 17 September 1997: French police announce that they are looking for a Fiat Uno, but there are 100,000 in France
2) October 9: French police announce the search has narrowed down to just 300 Fiat Unos – based on tail-light evidence[a]
3) November 4: French police announce the commencement of the interviewing of 40,000 Fiat Uno owners in the Paris region

---

[a] There has never been an explanation for why this narrowing of the search to 300 vehicles was apparently abandoned – by early November the French had again widened the search to 40,000 Unos.

4) November 7: French judges, lawyers and police express anger over the increasing cost of the investigation

5) 1 January 1998: BBC reports that about 4,000 Unos have been traced.

There is a major factor missing in the police announcements and media reporting from the period of the search: There is no suggestion in any announcement, leak or report that this investigation was limited to just two departments – Haute de Seine (92) and Yvelines (78).

The first public information indicating such a limitation on the search appeared on page 704 of the Paget Report, published on 14 December 2006 – over 8 years after the conclusion of the search.

The Paget Report stated that these "geographical parameters were set to make the task manageable". The report then went on to falsely claim: "These parameters were based on the evidence of ... Georges and Sabine Dauzonne".[2058ab] (WFJ)

At the inquest, this line was slightly changed – the reason for choosing to only search 78 and 92 was no longer related to making the task manageable – it was now completely based on both the Dauzonnes evidence,[2059] a false premise.[c]

There are two completely different stories that have been publicised regarding the white Fiat Uno search:

1) Police announcements and media reports during the search itself, October 1997 to January 1998: It was set up to be a thorough search of 40,000 Fiat Unos in the Paris area, with extension to the remainder of France if need be. By January 1998 this had fizzled down to a search of about 4,000 Fiat Unos with no substantive results.

2) Official statements from 2006 onwards – in the Paget Report and later at the inquest: It was a thorough search that was geographically limited from the outset to two departments – 92 and 78. 4,668 Unos were checked[2060d] and there were no substantive results.

Which is true? They can't both be true. Or, are neither of these scenarios true?

There is a third possibility that has received no publicity: that is that there never was any search on the scale that the police have stated.

Even if the police investigation only checked 4,668 Fiat Unos in a 3 month period, that is still a huge operation. Where then is the evidence of an operation on that scale occurring?

---

[a] The explanation of why this is false is in Part 3, section on White Fiat Uno Search in Chapter 14.

[b] The Dauzonne evidence is revealed in detail in Part 1, Chapters 4C and 5B.

[c] The explanation of why this is false is in Part 3, section on White Fiat Uno Search in Chapter 14.

[d] All those registered in departments 78 and 92.

There would be documentary evidence of the thousands of visits, interviews or searches conducted. Police generally keep detailed records of operations such as this. There would be detailed articles in newspapers reflecting a major event on this scale.

If, as was suggested in media reports, people were to be invited to check in at police stations, how were the invitations made? Was the media used, or was it a letter box drop? Was it carried out one area at a time?

At the inquest we were told that there was a "huge spreadsheet".[2061]

When this was put to Gigou, he evaded the question:

Hough asked: "Is this right, that a huge spreadsheet was drawn up and numerous interviews were conducted over an operation lasting many months?" Gigou replied:

> **We had, if I remember well, the reference of the painting of this car, and if I remember well, it was – the reference and the code were 'bianco' ... plus figures or letters following – for that sort of match. Then we also looked at the years when these Fiat Unos were put on the market.[2062]**

Gigou was never made to answer the question.

If there is a huge spreadsheet, why wasn't it – or evidence of it – shown to the jury?

There is evidence of just three Unos being located in this major operation:[a]

1)   Le Van Thanh.

Le Van was treated as a possible suspect at the inquest.[b]

Before the Le Van interviews were conducted, four police turned up to view his Uno.[2063] Does this mean that four police attended each of 4,668 Uno inspections?

Le Van's Uno was repainted – from white to red – around the time of the crash.[2064] It is possible that a neighbour or work colleague had noticed that repainting had occurred and could have notified the local police.

Le Van's Uno was a four door,[2065] whereas the Uno seen by Georges and Sabine was a two door.[2066] (WFJ)

2)   Julien Fernandez, an employee of *Paris-Match* magazine, who lived in Asnieres-sur-Seine – part of department 92 – but too far to the north to have taken the Alma Tunnel on the way home.

---

[a] James Andanson's Uno was located by Mohamed Al Fayed's investigators – not part of this police operation: 4 Feb 08: 87.22.

[b] The evidence relating to him is addressed in Part 1, Le Van Thanh section of Chapter 5C; also Chapters 4C, 5, 5B and other sections in 5C.

Because of the paparazzi presence, there was a specific interest in linking media industry employees to the crash. Fernandez's name could have come up during a search of Paris-based media industry owners of Fiat Unos.

3) "Edwige Pelmard, 30, female. There was no specific comment made in the *New York Times* report about how Pelmard's name came up. Pelmard is a woman and the Dauzonnes both said the driver was a male.

It really doesn't make a lot of sense that the French police would carry out a large scale search for an Uno that their bosses must have known could not turn up the offending car – particularly while there are sections of the judiciary speaking out about the excessive cost of the investigation.

The lack of evidence indicates there was no large scale search for the white Fiat Uno – there is nothing credible showing such a search ever took place. I believe the police have maintained the line that such a search occurred to satisfy public expectations.

Martine Monteil, Head of Brigade Criminelle, told Paget in 2006:

> **Investigations were carried out in respect of approximately 113,000 [Fiat Uno] vehicles, 5,000 of which were examined, with checks on the owners. No effort was spared.**[2067] **(WFJ)**

This claim is from the same person who has falsely stated that "almost a thousand witnesses were interviewed" by the French investigation.[2068] (WFJ)

Monteil appears to have come up with the figure of 113,000 which may have been the number of Unos in France. There is no evidence that "investigations were carried out" on those vehicles, as Monteil has claimed.

Monteil has stated that 5,000 Unos "were examined" – this figure appears to relate to the 4,668 Unos which were located in departments 92 and 78. Again, there is no substantive evidence that what Monteil has stated has occurred.

The Fiat Uno that evidence indicates was involved in the crash belonged to James Andanson. That vehicle was discovered by the Al Fayed investigation team – not the French police.[2069]

111   Suppressing Evidence

Following the French revelation on September 17 – that the police were searching for a second car and its driver – MPS Commissioner Paul Condon received a phone call from Diana's lawyer, Lord Victor Mishcon.

Receiving Evidence

Mishcon had held onto a note he had made following an October 1995 meeting in which Princess Diana had predicted she could die in a targeted car crash.[a] He arranged a meeting with Condon for the following day.

At the meeting – which was also attended by David Veness (who took notes) – Mishcon handed over his typed up notes from the 1995 meeting with Diana.

This note became known as the Mishcon Note.

Mishcon died before the inquest but did give a statement to Operation Paget. He told them:

> He "met with
> … Condon and … Veness at New Scotland Yard in order to bring the note to their attention. He read out the note … and emphasised that he was acting in a private capacity rather than on behalf of his firm or the Royal Family."[2070] (WFJ)

Sandra Davis, a lawyer working for Mishcon at the time, told the inquest:

> [Mishcon] was concerned to take the note … because he thought that it was important that the police knew that he had made it and that she had said what she had said.[2071]

Commissioner Condon's reaction to receiving this evidence[b] was to lock it away in his office safe.

---

[a] See earlier She Feared For Her Life chapter.
[b] A copy of the Mishcon Note was reproduced earlier in the She Feared For Her Life chapter.

Suppressing Evidence

Condon told Paget:

> **It was ... agreed [in the meeting] that if at any time ... the circumstances of [Diana's] death were to be regarded as suspicious, the [Mishcon] note and the Princess of Wales' concerns would be revisited....**
> **Lord Condon stated that his belief at the time of the meeting was that the car crash in Paris was a tragic accident and since that meeting nothing had been brought to his attention that would alter that view.**[2072] **(WFJ)**

The Mishcon Note was evidence of a person claiming they would be murdered in an orchestrated car crash – and within two years that person did die in a car crash.

Despite being police commissioner, Condon appeared to miss the point that the Mishcon Note was evidence in itself of a possible criminal case – it was therefore illegal for the police to suppress the note and fail to investigate it.

Why did Condon miss this vital point?

Instead of investigating the note, it remained locked away in the safe for over two years until Condon retired. In January 2000 he handed the note over to his successor, John Stevens. Stevens then continued to keep it in the safe for a further nearly four years.

All up the Mishcon note was suppressed by Scotland Yard for over six years.

Forced to Come Clean

Then on 20 October 2003 Diana's butler Paul Burrell published what became known as the Burrell Note. It was an October 1995 note in Princess Diana's handwriting that predicted she could be targeted in a car crash organised by her then husband, Prince Charles.[a]

The publication of this fresh note placed Scotland Yard – at that time run by John Stevens – in a predicament.

Within days Mishcon was trying to contact Stevens. Stevens initially apparently tried to avoid making contact with him – Mansfield to Stevens at the inquest:

> **[Mishcon] rings on 27th October.... You are not available. He rings on the 29th, you are not available. He then sees you on the 30th.**[2073]

But it was worse than that for Stevens.

---

[a] See earlier She Feared For Her Life chapter.

People other than Mishcon were aware of Princess Diana's claims at the 1995 meeting and also were aware of the Mishcon Note and the fact the police were holding it.

There were other people present at the meeting:[a] Patrick Jephson, Diana's private secretary; Maggie Rae and Sandra Davis, both lawyers from Mishcon de Reya.

Davis testified at the inquest:

> **Some of the partners at Mishcon's knew that Lord Mishcon had made a foray to the police with a note that he had kept in the safe; his safe.[2074]**

A corroborating document – as the Burrell Note was – put the MPS commissioner in a difficult position. If he failed to investigate then there were several senior lawyers who were aware that there was not just one note, the Burrell Note (now public), but a corroborating note, the Mishcon Note.

Stevens' first reaction was to seek legal advice.

He told the inquest that he did that on October 23[2075] – four days before Mishcon made his first attempt to contact him.

> **We had a meeting with our senior solicitors, took legal advice, obviously opened the note and I handed that note – I got Mr Veness up and handed that note to our solicitors' department for legal advice.[2076]**

It's possible Stevens stalled the meeting with Mishcon – waiting on the legal advice. The evidence was that Mishcon called twice, on October 27 and 29 and was told Stevens was unavailable.

Finally they met on October 30.

A decision was made to disclose the Mishcon Note to the royal coroner of the day, Michael Burgess.

Even then, it still took these sluggish police eight weeks to deliver the Mishcon Note to Burgess. It finally arrived three days before Christmas, on December 22.[2077]

The publication of the Burrell Note had appeared to force the hand of the British authorities.

Events starting moving after Burrell went public.

Within three months Michael Burgess opened the inquests into the deaths of Princess Diana and Dodi Fayed, on 6 January 2004.

---

[a] Listed in the Mishcon Note.

HOW THEY MURDERED PRINCESS DIANA

112 Fabricating Documents

David Veness took notes during the September 18 meeting with Victor Mishcon.[2078] They are reproduced on the following pages.

A meeting took place at New Scotland
Yard at 11.30am THURSDAY 18.9.97.
Presents: LORD MISCHON
CORMISSIONER
ACSO'

A note of a meeting of 30.10.95 between
LM and HRH. was read out by LORD M.
who emphasised that he was doing so
in his personal capacity and not on
behalf of his firm or the family.

The Commr. stated that he appreciated
being informed of what that transpired at
that meeting and regarded it as highly
proper that LORD M. should have
brought this matter to his prompt
attention.

It was the Commr view on the
facts of the accident as so far
ascertained that this occurrence
was purely the result of a tragic
set of circumstances but if and
it appeared that there were some
suspicious factors his possession
of this memorandum would at once
be referred to with contact at a
confidential level being made
with LORD M. and/or his firm.

(MR JULIUS) Paul Gordon
Commissioner
18.9.97
12.15 Pm

It was agreed that meanwhile this matter should be treated with the utmost confidence since to any leakage could do immeasurable harm and cause needless pain.

The Commr. authorised Lord M. when reporting to members of the family to tell them that if anyone of them wished to see him on this matter or on anything related to it he would be pleased to see them.

The Commr. said that the copy memorandum with which he had been supplied would be held with the utmost security in his office.

It was agreed that knowledge of the memorandum or its contents should if possible be limited to those who were already apprised of them, including members of the immediate family (ie D. Paul's sister + brother)

Paul Condon
Commissioner
18-9-97
12-35 Pm

D Veness

Figure 29 | Notes of meeting between Victor Mishcon, Paul Condon and David Veness at Scotland Yard on 18 September 1997. This document was doctored by the police – the whole of page 2 was added after the death of Victor Mishcon in 2006. Inquest copies are on the website: INQ0006336 & INQ0006337.

A close analysis of the above notes and associated evidence reveals that the document appears to have been doctored.

There are serious doubts about the veracity of the second page.

The first page was written up by Veness and signed by the three parties – Condon, Veness, Mishcon – on 18 September 1997, but the second page does not appear to have been created until around 2007, prior to the commencement of the London inquest.

There are several points:

1)   Victor Mishcon's signature on page 2 differs from his signature on page 1 – on page 2 there is a line drawn under his signature, but that line is missing on page 1.[a]

2)   The two pages appear to have been written up on different original pads. Page 1 has four folio holes down the left hand side – those are missing from page 2.

3)   The two pages appear to have been copied at different times and possibly using different equipment. On page 1 the lines are narrower and the handwritten words are smaller than they are on page 2.[b]

4)   Generally with a signed multi-page document the pages are numbered, often detailing "1 of 2"; "2 of 2" – there is no numbering at all on this document.

5)   Often multi-page documents are initialled by the parties on each page, with full signatures only appearing on the final page. In this case, not only are full signatures on both pages but also Paul Condon has dated and timed his signature on both pages. It is likely that when Condon dated and timed his signature on page 1 that was the sole page of the document.

6)   Condon appears to have initially put the wrong time on page 2 – probably "13.35" – and appears to have then written over it to match page 1, "12.35".[c]

7)   Condon's signature is slightly different on page 2. The "u" in "Paul" is not defined at all on page 2 – whereas there is a slightly defined "u" in the "Paul" on page 1.[d]

---

[a] Each page shows three signatures – David Veness, Paul Condon and Victor Mishcon. Mishcon's signature appears at the bottom right of both pages.
[b] This could be due to setting a different zoom ratio or copying on a different machine, or both.
[c] There is a possibility Condon misread the time from page 1 when he completed page 2 – and then had to change it. The writing of the time on page 1 is very small. People's eyesight often deteriorates as they age – by 2007 Condon was aged 60.
[d] A person's signature can change slightly over the years. It will be shown below that it is possible page 2 was written up in 2007, 10 years after page 1.

8) The Paget Report includes a description of this September 18 note. It states:

A note of that [September 18] meeting was produced.... It details the then Commissioner's view that the facts so far ascertained showed [Diana's] death was the result of a tragic set of circumstances. The note concluded that if it ever appeared there were some suspicious factors to the crash in Paris, the Commissioner would make contact at a confidential level with Lord Mishcon or his firm. Lord Mishcon agreed with this course of action.[2079] (WFJ)

Paget records that the note concluded with the statement that Mishcon would be contacted if suspicious factors emerged.

The point being that this sentence of the September 18 note appears at the bottom of page 1. Paget stated that this was the conclusion of the note. That then indicates that when the Paget Report was compiled in 2006 there was only one page in the note.

9) Sarah McCorquodale[a] stated that Diana's "sisters and brother ... have not seen [the Mishcon note] ... or knew of its existence" until after the Paget Report was published in 2006.[2080] Sarah was supported by Diana's brother-in-law, Robert Fellowes, who said: "I have never seen the [Mishcon] note".[2081]

Yet page 2 of the September 18 note states that "members of [Diana's] immediate family (i.e. DPOW's[b] sisters and brother) ... were already apprised of" the contents of the Mishcon Note.

There is a major conflict.

There is no mention of Diana's family on page 1 but there are three mentions[c] on page 2: a) the one noted above; b) the mention of "immeasurable harm and ... needless pain" is an implied reference to the effect of the Mishcon Note on Diana's children; c) the description of Condon telling Mishcon to tell Diana's family that "he would be pleased to see them" in connection with the Mishcon Note.

There is no reason to suspect Sarah or Fellowes of lying on this issue.[d]

10) The content and nature of the two pages differ markedly from each other.

a) Page 1 is not a record of agreement.[a]

---

[a] Diana's sister.

[b] Diana, Princess of Wales.

[c] Two specific mentions and one inference.

[d] This highlights the failure of Scott Baker to conduct a thorough inquest – Diana's sister, Jane, and brother, Charles, should have been asked about this, but weren't. No evidence from Charles or Jane was heard at the inquest.

There are just three paragraphs: i) Mishcon reads out the Mishcon Note and outlines his personal capacity; ii) Condon thanks Mishcon for letting him know so promptly; iii) Condon states that the crash was an accident, but if suspicious factors emerged he makes a commitment to immediately contact Mishcon.

The signing by the parties at the foot of page 1 is not an agreement – it instead is an acknowledgement that the meeting content has been accurately recorded by David Veness.

b)   Parts of page 2 record an agreement between the parties.[b]

There are four paragraphs: i) an agreement to avoid leakage of the Mishcon Note; ii) Condon tells Mishcon he would be pleased to talk to Diana's family members; iii) Condon commits to keeping the Mishcon Note secure; iv) an agreement to limit knowledge of the Mishcon Note to those who already know about it – including Diana's siblings.[c]

The signatures at the foot of page 2 indicate an acknowledgement of accuracy in Veness' write-up but there is also now an implied acceptance of the two agreements contained on that page – not to leak to avoid harm and pain, presumably to Diana's children; not to tell anyone else about the Mishcon Note.

The content of page 2 was used at the inquest to support the suppression of the Mishcon Note by the police.[d]

Taken together, the above points indicate that page 2 of the September 18 document was created separately sometime between late 2006 and early 2008 – i.e. after the publication of the Paget Report on 14 December 2006 and prior to David Veness' cross-examination on 15 January 2008.

Victor Mishcon had died on 27 January 2006. In turn this indicates Mishcon's signature was forged onto page 2 either by the police or on behalf of the police.[e] In the process a line appeared underneath Mishcon's signature – this line is missing from his signature on page 1.[f]

---

[a] Condon and Veness claimed at the inquest that there was an agreement made between Mishcon and themselves. This is addressed in Part 6, section on Flawed Police Testimony in Chapter 2.

[b] Condon and Veness claimed at the inquest that there was an agreement made between Mishcon and themselves. This is addressed in Part 6, section on Flawed Police Testimony in Chapter 2.

[c] Sandra Davis – a colleague of Mishcon's – stated that Mishcon told people at his law firm that he had taken the note to the police (see previous chapter).

[d] This is addressed in Part 6, section on Flawed Police Testimony in Chapter 2.

[e] There is no evidence to suggest anyone other than the British police had possession of this document.

[f] A comparison of the Mishcon signatures – without the line – on pages 1 and 2 indicates they are similar but not identical.

The original September 18 document should have been tabled at the inquest. That never occurred.

It is possible that a forensic analysis of both original pages could increase understanding regarding the actions of the police.

The fabrication of page 2 indicates the police may have intended to lead people who read that page – for example, the inquest jury – to believe a falsified picture of what occurred during the September 18 meeting.

113   Forces We Don't Know

Diana's butler, Paul Burrell, met with the Queen on 19 December 1997 – just 3½ months after the crash.

He stated in his 2003 book:

> **Looking over her half-rimmed spectacles, she said: 'Be careful, Paul. No one has been as close to a member of my family as you have. There _are_ powers at work in this country about which we have no knowledge,' and she fixed me with a stare where her eyes made clear the 'Do you understand?'** [2082]

Roberto Devorik said that Burrell related the Queen's remarks during a luncheon at Elsa Bowker's house "sometime after [his] conversation with the Queen". [2083]

Devorik told Paget:

> **[Burrell] … told us about an audience he had with the Queen. Lady Bowker asked him if he had asked the Queen if they killed her. He said that the Queen had replied to him something like 'We shouldn't awake forces we don't know'.** [2084]

There are significant conflicts between these two accounts – they are addressed thoroughly in Part 5.[a]

One of the main differences is that Burrell is indicating a belief by the Queen – "there are powers at work" – whereas Devorik's is a statement apparently aimed at discouraging action – "we shouldn't awake forces".[b]

---

[a] "Dark Forces" section of the Royals chapter.

[b] Paul Burrell is a particularly unreliable witness – he even admitted that he "didn't tell the whole truth" at the inquest: 13 Feb 08 Transcript of Meeting in a New York Hotel read out 6 Mar 08: 6.2. Devorik's account of the Queen's statement restores some credibility to Burrell – it removes the possibility that he could have completely made this statement by the Queen up, for publicity or other purposes. In other words, Devorik's evidence – even though it conflicts with Burrell's – shows that the Queen did say something significant to Burrell.

Devorik's account also directly connects the Queen's statement to the Paris crash. He says: "Bowker asked [Burrell] if he had asked the Queen if they killed her" and Burrell gave the Queen's reply.

Burrell's reaction at the inquest to Devorik's account of the Queen's statement is: "No, that's not true." Then he adds: "I wouldn't ask a question such as that to Her Majesty".[2085a]

The question Burrell is referring to is: "Lady Bowker asked [Burrell] if he had asked the Queen if they killed her."

Devorik doesn't say that Burrell said he asked the Queen that specific question. Devorik says: "<u>Lady Bowker asked [Burrell]</u> if he had asked the Queen".

Devorik then says: "He said that the Queen had replied...."

Putting oneself in the position of Burrell, who had just recently lost his boss – Princess Diana – who he was close to, there has to be a possibility that Burrell did ask the Queen a question about the crash. He could have asked something like: "Do you think Princess Diana was murdered?" [b]

At that time Burrell admits to having concerns along those lines. The inquest lawyer, Jonathon Hough, said to Devorik:

> **[Burrell] raised some concerns about the circumstances of the crash.**[2086]

That is what the Devorik statement shows,[2087] and that is confirmed by Burrell at the inquest[2088] – his concerns were: "that the French had not found the white car";[2089] "that the cameras on the tunnel were always working, but hadn't done so at the time of the crash";[2090] "the length of time it took for the ambulance to reach hospital".[2091c]

Devorik elaborated on his account at the inquest:

> **[Burrell] asked to the Queen her point of view.... The sense was: we shouldn't disturb the forces we don't know.... I said to him, "What does it mean?" "That's what it means", he answers me, not to ask more questions.**[2092]

This response – "not to ask more questions" – indicates that Burrell was uncomfortable about what the Queen said.

---

[a] With Burnett's help, this was Burrell's key argument – that he wouldn't have put a question like Bowker's to the Queen – "I wouldn't ask a question such as that to Her Majesty": 16 Jan 08:146.14; "I wouldn't be so presumptuous": 147.6; "I did not ... ask her a question of that nature": 147.7; "I would not ask Her Majesty the Queen such a personal, intimate question of her daughter-in-law": 147.21.

[b] Burrell also could have made a comment about the crash – maybe saying he had concerns – that the Queen replied to.

[c] There is a possibility that Burrell's concerns had increased after hearing the Queen's comment – and that is when he met with Devorik and Bowker.

HOW THEY MURDERED PRINCESS DIANA

The Queen's statement – "we shouldn't awake forces we don't know"[a] – is significant, for several reasons:

- it indicates the Queen could be aware that Diana was murdered
- it indicates a desire by the Queen to cover it up
- it appears intended to discourage Burrell from attempting to establish what actually happened.[b]

Why would the Queen say something like this? [c]

I suggest it indicates one of two possibilities:

1)   that the Queen was not involved in the assassinations, but knows who was and does not want them to be held accountable for it – in other words, the Queen wants it covered up

2)   the Queen herself was involved in the assassinations and she is discouraging Burrell from seeking the truth.[de]

---

[a] As recalled by Devorik.

[b] In this sense, it could be viewed as a warning to Burrell to just leave the issue of Diana's death alone.

[c] Devorik is not saying these are the exact words, but it was words to that effect. Those words are from his earliest recall, which was the August 2005 statement, over 7½ years after the lunch. Devorik's inquest testimony wasn't until another almost 2½ years later, in January 2008. I suggest that it is most unlikely that Devorik would have remembered the precise words, and he admits this several times – "something like" (statement); "precisely exactly the words I could not put in my mouth as I could on that day, but the sense was" (17 Jan 08: 192.12); "something [of] the sort" (twice) (192.15; 193.4); "I think the words were like" (193.3) – but the general sentiment of a statement of this significance directly attributed to a person of the Queen's stature would not be difficult to remember. It is the sentiment that is important, not the exact words.

[d] It's interesting that in the initial November 2002 interview, when Burrell first went public with this, he said: "It was not a threat, it was sound advice." The question is: Why would anyone introduce the possibility of this statement being a threat, unless they believed the Queen either had knowledge or was herself involved? Source: Robert Jobson, Queen and the Dark Forces, *Evening Standard*, 6 November 2002 (WFJ).

[e] In his book Burrell says that the Queen's statement occurred "as the meeting neared its end". It is possible that the Queen could have been displeased with the comment or question from Burrell that triggered her statement, and terminated the meeting. Source: *A Royal Duty*, p318 (WFJ).

114   Diana's "Best Friend"

What was the true nature of the relationship between Princess Diana and Rosa Monckton?[a]

Diana's "Best Friend"

The public perception – which is generally moulded by the media – is that Monckton was Diana's best friend, or at the least, a very close friend. This is the image that the British newspapers and magazines have – particularly since Diana's death – consistently portrayed:

-    "Rosa Monckton: long-time friend in whom Diana confided" – BBC News, 31 August 1997 [2093]

-    "Rosa Monckton, one of the Princess's closest friends" – Sunday Telegraph, 24 November 2002

-    "[Rosa Monckton] was a rock to her friend Princess Diana" – ES[b] Magazine, 10 November 2006 [2094]

-    "Diana's best friend, Rosa Monckton" – The Telegraph, 27 August 2007 [2095]

-    "Rosa Monckton: Diana's most loyal ally" – The Times, 28 August 2007 [2096]

-    "Rosa Monckton is ... famous for being best friends with ... Princess Diana" – You Magazine[c], 21 October 2007 [2097]

-    "Diana was a true friend, weeps [Diana's] closest confidante Rosa [Monckton]"[d] – Daily Mail, 14 December 2007 [2098]

-    "one of [Diana's] closest friends, Rosa Monckton" – The Telegraph, 16 December 2007 [2099]

---

[a] See earlier chapter: Rosa Monckton: Friend or Foe?
[b] Evening Standard.
[c] Daily Mail magazine.
[d] This was a headline referring to a statement made by Monckton during her cross-examination by Michael Mansfield – "we were proper true friends": 14 Dec 07: 6.15.

-     Rosa Monckton, best friend of ... Diana" – Daily Mail, 29 April 2011.[2100]

Deceiving the British Public

Is this media and public perception – that Monckton and Diana were best friends – true?

Monckton told the inquest that she was the one Diana rushed to after she received upsetting letters from Prince Philip.

Monckton testified:

> **All of [the letter showings] were in London, either in my flat or in Kensington Palace, or if ... we could not meet up, [Diana] would fax them to me and then we would talk about it on the telephone and I would draft the replies and get them back to her.[2101]**
> **I ... showed [the letters] to my husband[a] after having consulted Diana and he helped draft a lot of the replies with me.[2102]**

Unfortunately for Monckton Diana's close friend Lucia Flecha de Lima had four years earlier related what occurred to royal journalist Richard Kay. Following that November 2003 interview, Kay wrote:

> **The de Limas allowed [Diana] to use their home as a sanctuary.... It was there that she took the now infamous [1992] letters from Prince Philip[b] ... and there that [Diana] and Lucia would pour [sic] over her responses.**
> **Later, Lucia attempted to return the Philip letters to Diana.... "But Diana wanted me to keep them so, in the end, we compromised. I had copies made, which I kept in the [Brazilian Embassy] diplomatic pouch".[2103] (WFJ)**

At the inquest Monckton had dishonestly usurped Lucia's role of helping with the letters – in an apparent attempt to strengthen her "best friend" status.[c]

Other evidence points to this "best friend" perception not only being untrue, but being the opposite of the truth:[d]

-     Rosa's brother Anthony is a known MI6 officer [a]

---

[a] Other evidence indicates that Monckton's husband Dominic Lawson was an MI6 agent – see Chapter 1. No evidence was heard from Lawson at the inquest.

[b] There were five letters from Philip and five replies from Diana – commencing with Philip's initial letter on June 18 and concluding with Diana's final reply on 30 September 1992. See following footnote.

[c] The full evidence on what occurred around the Philip letters is addressed in Part 5, Philip-Diana Letters section in the Rosa Monckton chapter. Any reader who is particularly interested in this subject should read that section – it is a very interesting story.

[d] The evidence covered here should be viewed with the knowledge that MI6 is an extremely secretive organisation and information about the status and activities of agents and officers is hidden from public knowledge.

- Monckton's husband Dominic Lawson is a known MI6 agent [b]
- the timing of Monckton's initial meeting with Diana fits with a period when Buckingham Palace was concerned that Diana was cooperating with Andrew Morton on the compilation of a book that could have been damaging to the royal family [c]
- there is a significant degree of conflicting evidence on the circumstances that led to the initial meeting between Diana and Monckton [d]
- Monckton has provided a false account of Diana seeking her advice on an upcoming holiday with Mohamed Al Fayed, before the offer of the holiday was even made [e]
- Monckton organised to borrow a boat[f] from "friends" to go on a cruise with Diana[g] less than 18 days after British intelligence would have become aware of Diana accepting the Mohamed holiday offer and also making a very public address stating she was on a personal crusade against landmines [h]
- Diana was assassinated in Paris just 11 days after the conclusion of her boating holiday with Monckton[i]
- there is credible evidence indicating Diana was aware of Monckton's MI6 connections and didn't trust her [j]
- there are substantial areas of conflict in most of the key points of Rosa Monckton's evidence at the inquest – including: a) conflict with the accounts of other witnesses; b) conflict with other accounts Monckton has given; and c) conflict within her own inquest evidence [kl]
- Monckton is the only "friend" who rang Diana during her final week: "I rang [Diana's] mobile telephone"[2104] – all nine others, who have related

---

[a] See Chapter 1.

[b] See Chapter 1.

[c] See Chapter 1.

[d] See Part 5, Meeting Diana section of Rosa Monckton chapter.

[e] See Chapter 8.

[f] Monckton has never supplied a name for this boat and wasn't asked for it at the inquest.

[g] It may not be a coincidence that MI6 officer, Sherard Cowper-Coles – who was the Head of the Hong Kong Department at the time was in Hong Kong at the same time as Rosa Monckton, for the handover.

[h] See Chapter 10.

[i] The assassination was August 31 and the cruise finished August 20 – see Chapter 10.

[j] See Chapter 9.

[k] Meaning, at one point during the inquest cross-examination she said something under oath which she contradicts at another point in her inquest testimony.

[l] The evidence is presented in detail in Part 5, the Rosa Monckton chapter.

how the call occurred, say that Diana rang them. They are: Frank Gelli: "Diana called ... from the ... yacht";[2105] (WFJ) Annabel Goldsmith: "Diana rang me";[2106] Sarah McCorquodale: "[Diana] rang me";[2107] Rita Rogers: "[Diana] called me";[2108] Richard Kay: "[Diana] rang me";[2109] Susan Kassem: "the Princess of Wales contacted [Kassem]";[2110] (WFJ) Elsa Bowker: "[Diana] called me";[2111] (WFJ) Richard Attenborough: "[Diana] rang me on a mobile";[2112] (WFJ) Roberto Devorik: "Diana called from a mobile".[2113] [a]

- at the inquest Monckton provided false evidence claiming that she assisted Diana with the replies to Philip's 1992 letters – when the truth is that Lucia Flecha de Lima fulfilled that role [b]

- when Monckton was asked to read the closing excerpt of a letter from Diana to Philip, she misread "from, Diana"[c] and instead read "yours, Diana"[2114] – all nine letters, to various people, reproduced at the inquest closed with "from, Diana" [d]

- there is evidence of Monckton colluding with Philip – a person who Diana feared[e] – to protect his reputation, at the expense of Diana's interests.[fg]

Monckton said to Mansfield at the inquest: "We were proper true friends"[2115], but the evidence indicates otherwise.

Working Against Diana

Why has Monckton promoted her friendship with Diana to a level that was never achieved?

The evidence points to Monckton being connected to MI6, and – although it is primarily circumstantial because of the secrecy of MI6 – it also points to Monckton working for MI6 against Princess Diana.

This is not to suggest that Monckton was directly involved in Diana's assassination – it is probable that Monckton was as shocked as the next

---

[a] See also Part 5, Final Phone Call section of Chapter 1C.
[b] See above and Part 5, Philip-Diana Letters section in the Rosa Monckton chapter.
[c] Princess Diana's letter to Prince Philip, dated 12 July 1992 – viewable as Figure 7 in Part 5; also INQ0058942 on website.
[d] See Part 5, Philip-Diana Letters section in the Rosa Monckton chapter.
[e] See Chapter 5.
[f] See Part 5, Philip-Diana Letters section in the Rosa Monckton chapter. The evidence of this collusion is in connection with Prince Philip's press release of 23 November 2002 (INQ0058969) and Monckton's *Mail on Sunday* interview published the following day: Andrew Alderson, Diana's Friends Confirm Duke's Account of His Letters, Mail on Sunday, 24 November 2002.
[g] Rosa Monckton doesn't receive a mention in Diana's bodyguard, Ken Wharfe's book, even though he didn't resign until late 1993, over 18 months after Monckton and Diana met.

person when she first heard about the crash in the Alma Tunnel.[a] Monckton's role against Diana would have been to seek information and intelligence on her intentions – regarding moving to the US, her anti-landmine campaign, her feelings about the Establishment and the royal family and by August 1997, her relationship with Dodi Fayed.

MI6 operates on a "need to know" basis – and it is unlikely that Monckton would have needed to know that Diana was going to be eliminated.

Monckton went to great lengths at the inquest – particularly regarding the Philip letters evidence – to claim that she was very close to Diana. The automatic effect of that belief is that it discounts the relevance of other evidence that came out, that she had a connection to MI6. And it makes it very unlikely that any jury member would have been taking the MI6 connection any further – to asking themselves if Monckton was actually employed as an MI6 agent.

The establishing of Rosa Monckton being the best friend of Princess Diana is one of the major myths that have emerged since the 1997 Paris crash, with the main witness who could either confirm or deny it – Diana herself – dead and buried.

There is no question that there was some sort of a friendship – Diana was godmother to Monckton's daughter, Diana arranged for the burial of Monckton's stillborn baby in her Kensington Palace yard[b] – but the evidence shows the level of it has been grossly exaggerated.

The fact that there was a relationship between Rosa Monckton and Princess Diana does not mean that Monckton was not an MI6 agent. It is standard procedure for an MI6 agent to come across as normal as possible[c] and it would have been essential for Monckton to befriend Diana in order to obtain useful intelligence from her. The Monckton-Diana friendship has been made to look very close and completely normal – but the evidence in this chapter and in Part 5[d] has revealed otherwise.

On top of lying at the inquest, Rosa Monckton was generally an evasive witness – an analysis of her cross-examinations reveals she replied to questions with "I have no idea" 7 times, she couldn't remember something 40 times and couldn't recall information or events on 11 occasions. That makes

---

[a] There are several MI6 agents who were involved, but who would have been unaware of the intention to assassinate – e.g. Henri Paul and Claude Roulet.
[b] Since her death, Monckton has been involved in Diana's memorial fund – this has helped promote her standing as an ally of Diana.
[c] That is part of the culture of secrecy and deceit – see Part 5, MI6 Culture section of Chapter 1A.
[d] Rosa Monckton chapter.

58 times all up that Rosa Monckton failed to provide information that was requested of her at the inquest.

Evidently Monckton had something to hide from the inquest – I believe this book has helped shed light on what that might have been.

There has been a massive effort to cover up the true nature of the relationship between Princess Diana and Rosa Monckton. The now generally accepted view is that Monckton was Diana's "best friend" – the build-up of evidence reveals something quite different: that Rosa Monckton acted against Princess Diana as an agent collecting information on behalf of MI6.

115   An Assassin Dies

Key evidence of the white Fiat Uno's role in the crash was destroyed in 1999 and 2003.

Destroying More Evidence

In a 2006 interview Paris Deputy Public Prosecutor, Sylvie Petit-Leclair, revealed that the right front door of the Mercedes S280 had been "destroyed in a fire on May 26, 1999".[2116] (WFJ)

Petit-Leclair also stated:

> **The destruction of the right front wing was ordered by a judge [and was] carried out on June 17, 2003.**[2117] **(WFJ)**

It is no coincidence that these two parts of the Mercedes – the right front wing and door – happen to be the parts used to forensically link a white Fiat Uno to the crash.[2118]

Within a year of fire destroying the Mercedes door, the Fiat Uno driver died in another mysterious fire in the area of Loulette Forest, near Millau.

"You Could Not Miss the Hole"

On Thursday 4 May 2000 James Andanson drove south in his BMW to around 400 km from his home. He left the road and proceeded to drive cross-country about 300 to 400 metres into "the middle of the wood", near a military area.[2119]

At 9.34 p.m. the fire brigade received a call from "an infantry sergeant who had seen [a] fire whilst he was on patrol".[2120]

Christophe Pelat was one of the first fire officers on the scene. He later stated that on arriving they found a "badly-burnt car and inside a badly-burnt body".[2121]

The body was later identified as James Andanson.

Pelat told UK author and film-maker David Cohen that there was "a hole in Andanson's skull". He said he had "no idea how it got there but you could not miss the hole".[2122]

No gun was found at the scene.

French authorities determined that this was death by suicide.[2123]

It is not the purpose of this book to establish whether Andanson suicided or was murdered. In the final analysis – from the point of view of the Paris crash – if Andanson was proven to have been murdered, then it could be as a result of his alleged involvement in the crash, or it could have been related to his knowledge about the death of the French Prime Minister Pierre Bérégovoy.[a] Likewise, if he was proven to have suicided, it could be a result of domestic issues, or it could be because he was weighed down over his role in the death of Princess Diana.

Searching for Photos

At 12.30 a.m. on 16 June 2000, 43 days after Andanson's death, the Sipa offices in Paris were burgled.

The French investigation of this failed to result in any charges,[2124] even though the intruders stayed for about three hours.[2125] A nightwatchman was shot in the foot[2126] and staff were held hostage, bound and locked up in toilets.[2127] The stolen property included computers and disks,[2128] and items belonging to James Andanson.[2129]

During the inquest inadequacies in the French investigation of the burglary were exposed.[b]

---

[a] Bérégovoy allegedly committed suicide using a policeman's gun, in May 1993. His death was discussed at the inquest: Cross-examination of Christophe Lafaille, 7 Feb 08: 15.8 , 57.1 & 89.25.

[b] See cross-examinations of Madame Natacha Foucquet and Goksin Sipahioglu on 7 March 2008.

116 Royal Resistance: The Four Coroners

When John Burton, the royal coroner, illegally seized for himself jurisdiction over Diana's dead body, he effectively gained control for the Queen, his principal. This was control not only of the post-mortem conducted that night, but also of any future inquest.

It was clearly in the Queen's interests to acquire this control – it has since been shown that evidence points to royal involvement in the plan to assassinate Princess Diana. Control of the inquest would ensure the path taken would not be one that could uncover the full truth of what occurred.

"A Waste of Time and Money"

UK law requires an inquest when a British citizen dies unnaturally overseas.[a]

Robert Thompson, Fulham Mortuary manager, stated in a 2001 affidavit:

> **I remember on one occasion Dr Burton walked into the [Fulham Mortuary] staff room whilst we were discussing Princess Diana and he said something along the lines of, "I have a good mind to hold the bloody thing (i.e. the inquest) and not tell anyone".... I am not sure why Dr Burton is continuing as Coroner in this case. He is aged 71 and the normal retiring age is 70.... As far as I know, he is solely staying on as Coroner for the Royal Household to conduct the inquest into Princess Diana. Unusually, he frequently carries the file relating to Princess Diana's post mortem with him. The usual practice is for the file to be kept in his office.[2130] (WFJ)**

Thompson was not heard from at the inquest.

---

[a] Coroners Act 1988 s8 (1): "When a coroner is informed that the body ... is lying within his district and ... has died ... an unnatural death ... then ... the coroner shall as soon as practicable hold an inquest into the death...." (WFJ)

In April 2001, 3½ years after the crash, London's *Daily Telegraph* conducted an interview with John Burton. He told the paper:

> **An inquest into Diana and Dodi's deaths would be "a waste of everyone's time and money. Nobody can be forced to give evidence as a witness and it would serve no purpose. The aim of an inquest is to identify the cause of death, but in this case all the evidence was collected in France and any inquest would just be a forum for different people's views."[2131] (WFJ)**

The *Telegraph* wrote:

> **The coroner who is due to hold the inquest into the death of Diana, Princess of Wales is campaigning for a change in the law so that the inquiry never takes place.**
>
> **Dr John Burton, the coroner for the Royal Household, believes that any inquest into the Princess's death, and that of her companion, Dodi Fayed, would be costly and pointless. He told the *Telegraph* that he has been lobbying Jack Straw, the Home Secretary, for a change in the law that requires an inquest in every case where a body is returned to Britain after a death abroad.[2132] (WFJ)**

John Burton had very little appetite to conduct an inquest into the deaths – even to the point of trying to have the law changed. And he also, aged 71, was hanging on to the role of royal coroner for as long as he could.

By March 2002, 11 months after the *Telegraph* article, Burton was forced to resign as royal coroner due to ill health. He died from prostate cancer on 8 December 2004.

Burgess, Butler-Sloss, Baker

Michael Burgess, Burton's deputy, took over as royal coroner, but he too failed to hold the required inquest.

But events did take over.

In October 2003 Paul Burrell, Diana's butler, published a handwritten copy of the note Diana wrote expressing fear of a plot to remove her in a car crash.[a]

This was a circuit-breaker.

It led to the disclosure by the police of the Mishcon Note and Burgess was forced to open the inquest in January 2004. At that point he called for the holding of a Scotland Yard investigation into the crash and John Stevens, police commissioner at that time, was appointed to head it.

Burgess then adjourned the inquest until the completion of the police investigation.

---

[a] Reproduced earlier in She Feared For Her Life chapter.

These happenings helped to further delay the inquest. The police inquiry, called Operation Paget, took nearly three years and produced its report, the Paget Report, in December 2006.

In the meantime Burgess had resigned as coroner of the case in July 2006, citing a heavy workload. He retained his role as royal coroner. It is likely that he actually resigned because it was becoming known that it was illegal for the inquest to be conducted by the royal coroner, because the royals had earlier taken illegal jurisdiction over Diana's body.[2133]

Elizabeth Butler-Sloss took over as coroner in September 2006 but she resigned just seven months later in April 2007, citing inexperience with juries – despite the fact that she had 50 years of experience in the British legal system.

It was becoming evident that the case was too-hot-to-handle. The inquest into the deaths of Princess Diana and Dodi Fayed was going to require a judge who was very corrupt.

Enter Lord Justice Scott Baker.

Baker took over as coroner for the case in June 2007 and he conducted the inquest, which commenced four months later, in October.

One of his first moves after becoming coroner was to remove Scotland Yard's Paget Report from the inquest website.

Then early in his Opening Remarks to the inquest jury on 2 October 2007 he stated:

The conclusions of the ... Paget Report are neither here nor there.[2134]

After all the toing and froing, including a three year MPS investigation that was deemed "neither here nor there", the British Establishment had effectively delayed the inquest by 10 years. It opened precisely 10 years 1 month and 2 days after the crash.

And by that time a substantial section of the British and worldwide public had "moved on" and had lost interest in the case.

117 Paget Pantomime

In 1999 the French concluded a two year investigation into the deaths of Princess Diana and Dodi Fayed.

Why then did Royal Coroner Michael Burgess in 2004 order a second police investigation ahead of the inquest?

The Paget Report reveals the answer:

> It was "to help [Burgess] decide whether [the Al Fayed claims of conspiracy] would fall within the scope of the investigation carried out at the inquests".[2135] (WFJ)

The scope of an inquest investigation is laid down by law – it is, as outlined by Scott Baker to his jury, to answer the following questions:

> Who the deceased were, when they came by their deaths, where they came by their deaths and how they came by their deaths.[2136]

On the same morning – the first morning of the inquest – Baker also told the jury:

> The conclusions of the ... Paget Report are neither here nor there if you take a different view.[2137 ab]

---

[a] A different view than what was concluded in the Paget Report.

[b] There is an implicit message here to those members of the jury who agreed with the Paget Report findings. By qualifying the "neither here nor there" with "if you take a different view", Baker appears to be suggesting that the Paget Report conclusion is relevant at the inquest for those in the jury who agreed with it. Baker is saying he wanted to distance the inquest from the Paget Report – but only for those who didn't agree with it. In other words, for those jury members who did agree with the Paget Report, he does not seek for them to change their opinions. A balanced approach would have been for Baker to tell the whole jury the Paget was neither here nor there – not just the ones who didn't agree with it. This approach by Baker raises the possibility that he had already decided the crash was an accident – Paget finding – before the inquest started. He therefore leaves those who agree with him alone and instead speaks directly to those jury members who "take a different view". One could

The Operation Paget investigation commenced in January 2004 and was completed in December 2006 – close to three years.

It was set up to investigate Mohamed Al Fayed's allegations and to then let Burgess know whether those allegations would "fall within the scope of" the inquest – i.e. who died, when, where and how.

Mohamed's claims – detailed at length in the Paget Report – revolve around an alleged conspiracy to murder Princess Diana and his son, Dodi.

The question Burgess was asking Stevens to answer was: Does Mohamed's allegation of conspiracy to murder fall within the inquest questions – the who, when, where and how of the deaths?

Operation Paget took three years to answer this.

This is not a particularly difficult question to answer.

The conspiracy allegation – as described in the Paget Report, based on a July 2003 letter from Mohamed's lawyer[a] – is:

> **Murder [as] the result of a conspiracy by the 'Establishment' and particularly HRH Prince Philip, who used the 'Security Services' to carry it out.[2138] (WFJ)**

One does not need a section of the police force to understand that an allegation that a murder was carried out by an organisation – the security services – on behalf of a person – Prince Philip – is directly connected to the question: How did Diana and Dodi come by their deaths?

And that question – the "how" of the deaths – is one of the four key questions that faced the inquest, by law.

If the purpose of Paget was to establish if Mohamed's conspiracy allegation fell within the scope of the inquest investigation – as stated by Burgess – then it appears to have been a waste of time, effort and tax-payer pounds.

Given that it was Burgess who called for the setup of the Paget investigation, we should be able to rely on his reason for doing so.

Stevens actually came up with a different reason in his Paget Report Overview:

> **The primary purpose of the [Paget] investigation has been to assess whether there is any credible evidence to support an allegation of conspiracy to murder.[2139] (WFJ)**

And in the conclusion to that Overview, Stevens writes:

---

argue that Baker felt that those were the people he needed to win over – throughout the inquest – to the accident theory.

[a] This letter has never been made available.

I do not believe that any evidence currently exists that can substantiate the allegation of conspiracy to murder that has been made. [2140] **(WFJ)**

In other words, the conspiracy allegation is unfounded and wrong.

That is the conclusion of Scotland Yard's three year investigation – the result of three years of intense investigation by some of the best detectives in the land.

All it actually achieved was to reach the same conclusion as the French investigation – the crash was an accident caused by a driver who had been drinking and was also speeding.

Why then hold an inquest?

Well, the inquest was required by law.[a] The authorities – Burton, Burgess, Condon – knew that all along.

So the inquest had to happen. Right from when Diana and Dodi died overseas from unnatural causes, there had to be an inquest.

The real question is not: Why have an inquest? The real question is: Why have the Paget investigation?

Burgess said it was to establish if the conspiracy fell within the scope of the inquest investigation.

But everyone, even the general public, already knew that it did – without holding another three year police investigation.

Why then was the Paget investigation held?

The answer lies in understanding two key points:

-    that the Paget investigation was very deeply flawed[b]
-    that Stevens was already compromised – by his involvement in the Mishcon Note suppression[c] – before he was appointed to head Paget.[d]

This is the crux of the issue.

The evidence indicates that by 6 January 2004[e] Michael Burgess must have been aware that the MPS had illegally suppressed the Mishcon Note for six years.

This knowledge should have rung loud warning bells to Burgess – warning bells indicating that the MPS was not an appropriate organisation to investigate the deaths of Diana and Dodi. The point here is that Stevens was already compromised and Stevens headed the MPS – so even if Burgess had

---

[a] See previous chapter.

[b] The detail of the many flaws is covered in the 2007 book *Cover-Up of a Royal Murder: Hundreds of Errors in the Paget Report*. It is not the purpose of this current book to explain the flaws.

[c] See earlier Suppressing Evidence chapter.

[d] Another point – not as directly relevant – is that there already was a police investigation completed by the French in 1999.

[e] The date Burgess opened the inquest and appointed Stevens to head the police investigation.

appointed Stevens' deputy to head the investigation, the deputy would still have been answerable to Stevens.

Royal Coroner Michael Burgess' appointment of the MPS, and Stevens specifically, to run the Paget investigation was flawed.

Operation Paget was a flawed investigation even before it commenced operations.

Top Money...

Twelve months after his appointment John Stevens resigned from his role as Commissioner of Police – but he stayed on as Head of Operation Paget.

This enabled Stevens to reduce his responsibility – he was no longer Commissioner – but significantly increased his income – he could renegotiate his price under contract.

And this is what he did.

In 2007 London's *Mail on Sunday* uncovered what occurred, under Freedom of Information:

> Britain's former top policeman Lord Stevens was paid £1,000 a day for taking charge of the inquiry into the death of Diana, Princess of Wales....
>
> He was being paid double what he would have earned in his former role as Met Police Commissioner.
>
> The payments, for his part-time role in charge of Operation Paget, are among a number of lucrative deals that Porsche-driving Lord Stevens has secured since he retired two years ago....
>
> While he was at the Yard from 2000 to 2005, Lord Stevens was paid £150,000 a year, the daily equivalent of approximately £420 – less than half the fees for his two-and-a-half years' work on the Diana probe.
>
> The FOI reply from the Met's Directorate of Professional Standards – which took almost a year to be answered – discloses that between February 28, 2005, and September 30, 2007, his company Stevens Consultancy raked in £276,125 for Operation Paget. He was also reimbursed £26,550 for accommodation costs away from home – mainly in London hotels. And he received £13,599 for travel costs plus £97.51 for meals, making a total of £316,000....
>
> Richard Barnes, a Tory member of the Metropolitan Police Authority, last night described the Operation Paget fee as 'ludicrous'.
>
> Scotland Yard would not add to its FOI statement and was unable to say why it took almost a year to provide a reply.[2141] (WFJ)

John Stevens' generous remuneration at tax-payer's expense did not stop after the publication of the Paget Report.

Stevens revealed that he was still employed on Paget even at the inquest. He stated that he had attended for "much of the proceedings" adding that "is still part of my responsibility to Paget".[2142]

... For a Corrupt Outcome

Stevens was provided with the dossier from the two year French investigation.

In the end, after three years of investigating, Stevens parroted the French conclusion – Diana and Dodi died as a result of being passengers in a car driven by a driver influenced by drink who was also speeding.

This conclusion was based on what were clearly two fraudulent autopsies on the Mercedes driver, Henri Paul.

The police ignored the evidence that revealed the fraud, ignored the clear evidence from the Ritz witnesses and CCTV footage that Henri Paul was sober and ignored the witness accounts of powerful motorbikes seen pursuing the Mercedes.

They also failed to interview hundreds of important witnesses that would have helped immensely in revealing a truer picture of what occurred. These included witnesses in the tunnel, witnesses near the tunnel, witnesses along the route, witnesses regarding the white Fiat Uno, paparazzi, key MI6 personnel in London, key royals in the family and household, ambulance personnel, Ritz Hotel witnesses, important French officials and police officers, witnesses regarding Henri Paul's activities, witnesses of the Henri Paul autopsies and witnesses of Diana's UK post-mortem.

Paget almost completely ignored the issue of Princess Diana's anti-landmine campaign, even though the evidence of the case clearly indicates that could have been a motive for her assassination.

There is really no area of the investigation that Operation Paget investigated thoroughly. And in the end the product of the investigation, the 832 page Paget Report, was deeply flawed and riddled with error.

The book *Cover-Up of a Royal Murder: Hundreds of Errors in the Paget Report* exposes the multitudinous flaws and deceptions in the report.

118 Judicial Corruption

After waiting ten long years, the conduct of the six month 2007-8 inquest into the deaths of Princess Diana and Dodi Fayed was really the final insult to anyone who was seeking justice in this case.

Lord Justice Scott Baker stopped at nothing in his efforts to manipulate the final outcome – the jury's verdict.[a]

Baker did not act alone.

He was assisted by the work of some of the lawyers present – at times, inquest lawyers Ian Burnett[b] Nicholas Hilliard[c] and Jonathon Hough,[d] but more particularly those acting on behalf of the metropolitan police, Richard Horwell[e] and Duncan MacLeod.[a] Those two men lied repeatedly throughout

---

[a] Baker's efforts are documented in the six volumes of the *Diana Inquest* series, listed near the beginning of this book.

[b] Examples of Burnett's work: He misled the jury over evidence from Rita Rogers – see Part 1, Unidentified Red Car section of Chapter 4A; he lied about the reason one of the Philip letters wasn't shown – see Part 5, Philip-Diana Letters section of Chapter 1C.

[c] Examples of Hilliard's work: He altered a statement made by Robert Forrest – see Part 3, Results Analysis section of Chapter 3B; he altered a statement made by Peter Vanezis – see Part 3, Results Analysis section of Chapter 3B.

[d] Examples of Hough's work: He altered Frank Klein's evidence regarding Henri Paul's links to intelligence agencies – see Part 1, MI6 section of Chapter 1; he altered Gisèle Paul's evidence about Henri's tips – see Part 1, Unexplained Cash section of Chapter 1; he misrepresented the evidence of Rene Deguisne – see Part 4, Role of Rene Deguisne section in Chapter 2; he falsified evidence about requirements for embalming – see Part 4, Was It Required By Law? section of Chapter 2; he misrepresented Paul Burrell's evidence – see Part 5, "Dark Forces" section of Chapter 3.

[e] Examples of Horwell's work: He changed evidence from Claude Roulet – see Part 1, MI6 section of Chapter 1; he misrepresented evidence regarding Andanson's white Fiat Uno – see Part 1, History to 1997 and Condition in 1997-8 sections of Chapter 5B; he misrepresented the Andanson-Angeli relationship – see Part 1, Other Claims section of Chapter 5C; he misrepresented the reason Barry Mannakee was removed

the inquest, whenever they appeared to feel it was necessary to swing the jury's thinking towards their position.[b]

Baker told the jury that the "conspiracy theories ... have been examined in the minutest detail through the evidence of over 250 witnesses".[2143] In total, 177 witnesses were cross-examined.[c] But Baker failed to point out that there were over 250 other important witnesses who were not cross-examined.[d] The jury needed to hear from a wide cross-section of witnesses to be able to form a properly balanced view of what occurred.

That never happened.

There are witnesses who have been shown in the *Diana Inquest* books to have lied in their evidence – some of them repeatedly with no apparent accountability. These people include, in no particular order:[efg]

Michael Burgess;[h] John Burton;[i] Paul Condon;[a] John Stevens;[b] David Veness;[c] Claude Roulet;[d] Trevor Rees-Jones;[e] Kez Wingfield;[f] Paul Burrell;[g]

---

from Princess Diana's protection – see Part 2, Barry Mannakee section of Chapter 7; he lied about the source of Diana's landmine dossier information – see Part 5, Allegations Against MI6 section in Chapter 1A; he lied about the nature of the contents of Diana's landmine dossier – see Part 5, Allegations Against MI6 section in Chapter 1A; he lied about the break-ins to John Stevens' office – see Part 6, Break-Ins section of Chapter 3.

[a] Examples of MacLeod's work: He altered statements made by Atholl Johnston – see Part 3, Results Analysis section of Chapter 3B; he altered Dr Dominique Mélo's evidence – see Part 3, Drugs Prescribed section of Chapter 5; he misrepresented the status of LGC – see Part 3, British Testing section of Chapter 9; he altered Claude Garrec's evidence – see Part 3, Did Henri Drink and Drive? section of Chapter 5. A more comprehensive listing of MacLeod's deceptions and misrepresentations can be found in Part 5, Footnotes in Bar Vendôme section of Chapter 1B.

[b] See previous two footnotes.

[c] All witnesses heard at the inquest are listed in Part 1, The Witnesses near the front of the book.

[d] The Witnesses Not Heard are listed near the front of each of the *Diana Inquest* books. Most are near the front of Part 1 but others that cropped up throughout the investigation are added in the later volumes.

[e] This list includes examples of lies drawn from all witness evidence – most but not all is from the testimony at the inquest.

[f] This is not a complete list of those who lied in their evidence – this list covers most of those who have been proven to have lied.

[g] The listings of lies in the following footnotes are not exhaustive – it includes the lies that are provable from the available evidence.

[h] Burgess lied about the legal requirement for a post-mortem – see Part 4, Was It Legally Required? section of Chapter 5.

[i] Burton lied about the legal requirement for a post-mortem – see Part 4, Was It Legally Required? section of Chapter 5; he lied about his knowledge of Diana's burial location – see Part 4, Royal Coroner section of Chapter 3.

JUDICIAL CORRUPTION

Patrick Jephson;[h] Alberto Repossi;[i] David Meynell;[j] Dr Jean-Marc Martino;[k] Dr Arnaud Derossi;[a] Dr Frédéric Mailliez;[b] Gilbert Pépin;[c] Dominique

---

[a] Condon lied about the content of the post-crash meeting with Victor Mishcon – see Part 6, Paul Condon section of Chapter 2; he lied about his knowledge of the presence of Mishcon's signature on his police statement – see Part 6, Role of Victor Mishcon section in Chapter 2; he lied about the reasons for suppressing the Mishcon Note – see Part 6, Flawed Police Testimony section of Chapter 2.

[b] Stevens lied about the purpose in seeking legal advice regarding the Mishcon Note – see Part 6, Post Burrell Note Events section in Chapter 2; he lied about a statement made by Henri's parents – see Part 6, Analysis section of Chapter 3; he lied about the reasons for suppressing the Mishcon Note – see Part 6, Flawed Police Testimony section of Chapter 2.

[c] Veness lied about contact with Victor Mishcon following the publication of the Burrell Note – see Part 6, Analysis section of Chapter 3; he lied about the content of the post-crash meeting with Victor Mishcon – see Part 6, David Veness section of Chapter 2; he lied about the use of the term SIO – see Part 6, Was This An Investigation? section in Chapter 1; he lied about the reasons for suppressing the Mishcon Note – see Part 6, Flawed Police Testimony section of Chapter 2.

[d] Roulet lied about the time he left the Ritz Hotel – see Part 1, Roulet Meeting section of Chapter 2C; he lied about meeting Henri Paul at La Bourgogne – see Part 1, Roulet Meeting section of Chapter 2C; he lied about the content of his meeting with Patrick Riou and Frank Klein – see Part 3, Hold-Up in Body Transfer section of Chapter 16.

[e] Rees-Jones lied about the origin of the decoy plan – see Part 1, Telling the Bodyguards section of Chapter 3C; he lied about his awareness that Henri had consumed alcohol – see Part 1, Bodyguards section of Chapter 3B.

[f] Wingfield lied about the origin of the decoy plan – see Part 1, Telling the Bodyguards section of Chapter 3C; he lied about his awareness that Henri had consumed alcohol – see Part 1, Bodyguards section of Chapter 3B.

[g] Burrell lied about the circumstances of Diana's break-up with Hasnat Khan – see Part 2, Hasnat Khan Break-Up section of Chapter 1; he lied regarding a secret he shared with Diana – see Part 2, Burrell's Secret section of Chapter 3.

[h] Jephson lied about his reaction to Diana's fears for her life – see Part 6, Reliable Sources section of Chapter 2.

[i] Repossi lied about events during Dodi's visit to his Paris store – see Part 2, Repossi Paris Store Visit section of Chapter 2.

[j] Meynell lied regarding the content of a meeting with Diana in 1994 – see Part 2, Police Issues section of Chapter 8; he lied about electronic sweeping of Diana's apartment – see Part 2, Police Issues section of Chapter 8.

[k] Martino fabricated evidence of a cardiac arrest he claimed Diana had when being moved from the Mercedes – see Part 2, "Cardiac Arrest" section of Chapter 9C; he lied about the time taken transferring Diana to the ambulance – see Part 2, Transfer Into the Ambulance section of Chapter 9C; he lied about the circumstances around the departure of the ambulance from the tunnel – see Part 2, Delay In the Tunnel section of Chapter 9D.

HOW THEY MURDERED PRINCESS DIANA

Lecomte;[d] Hervé Stéphan ;[e] Christian Le Jalle;[f] Robert Forrest;[g] Véronique Dumestre-Toulet;[h] Jean-Claude Mulès;[i] Jeffrey Rees;[j] Jean Monceau;[k] Eva Steiner;[l] Clive Leverton;[m] Keith Leverton;[n] Rene Deguisne;[a] Michael Jay;[b]

---

[a] Derossi lied about the nature of his role – see Part 2, Role of Dr Derossi section in Chapter 9D.

[b] Mailliez lied about Diana's situation in the Mercedes – see Part 2, Dr Mailliez section of Chapter 9A.

[c] Pépin lied about the blood samples taken from Toxlab by the French police – see Part 3, French Testing section of Chapter 9; he lied about sampling from the 1st autopsy – see Part 3, Label Descriptions section of Chapter 1; he lied about the samples Toxlab had – see Part 3, British Testing section of Chapter 9.

[d] Lecomte lied about the nature of her statements around sampling – see Part 3, Quantity Taken section of Chapter 1; she lied about the sample source in the 1st autopsy – see Part 3, Blood Sample Source section of Chapter 1.

[e] Stephan lied about the presence of Bourgois at the 2nd autopsy – see Part 3, Sample Labels section of Chapter 2.

[f] Le Jalle lied about the presence of Bourgois at the 2nd autopsy – see Part 3, Sample Labels section of Chapter 2.

[g] Forrest lied about the validity of the 1st autopsy – see Part 3, Conclusions section of Chapter 3A.

[h] Dumestre-Toulet lied regarding her signature on a sample receipt form – see Part 3, Timing Issues of Chapter 4.

[i] Mulès lied about errors in the 1st autopsy – see Part 3, Chapter 1.

[j] Rees lied about being named by John Burton – see Part 3, Hold-Up in Body Transfer section of Chapter 16; he lied about the 4.15 p.m. meeting at Scotland Yard – see Part 3, Rees Movements section of Chapter 16 and Part 4, Scotland Yard Meeting section in Chapter 5; he lied about the presence of coroners at post-mortems – see Part 4. Coroner's Role section of Chapter 5; he lied about the content of a conversation with John Macnamara at the Fulham Mortuary – see Part 6, Jeffrey Rees section of Chapter 1; he lied about the use of the term SIO – see Part 6, Was This An Investigation? section in Chapter 1.

[k] Monceau lied about conversations to get embalming authorisation – see Part 4, Timing of Events section of Chapter 2; he lied about an accounting document for an order from PFG for dry ice – see Part 4, Non-Existent Documentation section of Chapter 2; he lied about the legality of the embalming – see Part 4, Was the Embalming Legal? section of Chapter 2; he lied about the requirement for a burial certificate prior to embalming – see Part 4, Was the Embalming Legal? section of Chapter 2.

[l] Steiner lied when she indicated the embalming was legal under French law – see Part 4, Was the Embalming Legal? section of Chapter 2; she lied about Diana's status at the time of her death – see Part 4, Was the Embalming Legal? section of Chapter 2.

[m] Clive lied about where the time pressure was coming from – see Part 4, Speed of Repatriation section of Chapter 3; he lied about not receiving any embalming instructions – see Part 4, Use of British Embalmers section of Chapter 4.

[n] Keith lied about not receiving any embalming instructions – see Part 4, Use of British Embalmers section of Chapter 4.

Robert Fellowes;[c] Anthony Mather;[d] Michael Gibbins;[e] Jean-Claude Plumet;[f] Robert Chapman;[g] MI6 witnesses – Richard Dearlove,[h] Miss X,[i] Mr E Richard Fletcher,[j] Mr 4 Eugene Curley;[k] Lucia Flecha de Lima;[l] Rosa Monckton;[m] Keith Moss[n] and Miles Hunt-Davis.[o]

---

[a] Deguisne lied about there being no records from 1997 – see Part 4, Non-Existent Documentation section of Chapter 2.

[b] Jay lied about the timing of his awareness of the embalming – see Part 4, Michael Jay section of Chapter 2; he lied about being in the decision-making process for the Charles visit – see Part 4, Repatriation by Charles section of Chapter 3; he lied about the circumstances and timing of Sherard Cowper-Coles' arrival at the embassy – see Part 5, Sherard Cowper-Coles section of Chapter 1B; he lied about MI6 staff not being deployed during August 30 and 31 – see Part 5, Sherard Cowper-Coles section of Chapter 1B; he lied about the timing of his notification about the crash – see Part 5, Phone Calls section of Chapter 2.

[c] Fellowes lied about being on holiday for the week after Diana's death – see Part 4, Robert Fellowes section of Chapter 3; he lied about the nature of discussion topics at the WAG meetings – see Part 5, Way Ahead Group section of Chapter 3.

[d] Mather lied about the timing of events on 31 August 1997 – see Part 4, Anthony Mather section of Chapter 3.

[e] Gibbins lied when he denied prior knowledge of key events – see Part 4, Communication With Gibbins section of Chapter 3.

[f] Plumet lied about the involvement of a Commissaire regarding the repatriation paperwork – see Part 4, Police Authority section of Chapter 4.

[g] Chapman lied about the extent of the embalming – see Part 4, Effect of Embalming section in Chapter 5.

[h] Dearlove lied about the relevance of MI6 capabilities to the case – see Part 5, The Increment section of Chapter 1; he lied about the MI6 role in security for royal visits overseas – see Part 5, Links to Intelligence Agencies section of Chapter 3.

[i] X lied about assassination proposals in her time at MI6 – see Part 5, Does MI6 Murder People? section of Chapter 1A.

[j] Fletcher lied over his awareness of assassination plots – see Part 5, Does MI6 Murder People? section of Chapter 1A.

[k] Curley lied about the timing of his departure from Paris – see Part 5, Sherard Cowper-Coles section of Chapter 1B; he lied about still being head of MI6 France at the time of the crash – see Part 5, Sherard Cowper-Coles section of Chapter 1B.

[l] Flecha de Lima lied to protect Rosa Monckton – see Part 5, Rosa Monckton chapter.

[m] Monckton lied when she denied talking about the Philip letters – see Part 5, Philip-Diana Letters section of Chapter 1C; she lied about her level of knowledge of the importance of the Philip letters – see Part 5, Philip-Diana Letters section of Chapter 1C.

[n] Moss lied about not viewing Diana's body – see Part 4, Monceau-Moss Conversation section of Chapter 2.

[o] Hunt-Davis lied about the nature of discussion topics at the WAG meetings – see Part 5, Way Ahead Group section of Chapter 3.

In addition to these issues, hundreds of critical documents were withheld from the jury's eyes and ears. These included very basic items like the post-mortem and toxicology reports relating to the bodies of the people whose deaths were being investigated – Princess Diana and Dodi Fayed. Hundreds of the most important withheld documents – including those reports – have been reproduced in the 2010 book *Diana Inquest: The Documents the Jury Never Saw*.

Blame for withholding all this important information falls squarely in the lap of the corrupt judge, Lord Justice Scott Baker.

But he did even more to prevent his own inquest from arriving at a just conclusion.

Many key witness statements were taken by the French police in the hours, days and weeks following the Paris crash. The jury were not allowed to have access to most of those, but instead were expected to rely on a witness' recall in the stand of events that had occurred over ten years earlier. When the jury realised the importance of these statements, they made a special request to Scott Baker on 11 December 2007. Baker announced to the court that the jury had said that "they would like to be able to see witness statements".[2144] His reply to the jury was:

No, you cannot have the statements.[2145]

Baker had legal argument to support his decision, but it is clear that it neither passes the common sense nor the justice test.

There can be no comparison between a witness' account taken soon after an event and one taken ten years later.

This is very basic.

The jury were forced to arrive at a verdict, in one of the most important cases of the 20th century, with one hand tied behind their backs – only half of the witnesses were heard; much of the evidence that was heard relied on witness recall of events that occurred over ten years earlier; witnesses were allowed to lie under oath, often repeatedly, with no apparent expectation that they could be held to account; hundreds of evidential documents were withheld.

Then, as if to add insult to injury, Baker's 2½ days spent on his 80,000-word Summing Up was riddled with lies, omissions and manipulation of key areas of evidence. These instances – and there are many – have been covered in detail in the six volumes of the *Diana Inquest* series of books.

But there is more.

During his Summing Up, on 31 March 2008, Baker announced to the jury that he was withdrawing murder as a possible verdict. He told them:

It is not open to you to find that Diana and Dodi were unlawfully killed in a staged accident.

Incredibly he added that "sufficient evidence [to support a murder finding] simply does not exist".[2146]

This meant that if they found for murder they would have to return an open verdict.

Clearly when a jury are told by a judge that murder is not an option, that then puts substantial pressure on them to return an alternative verdict – one that the judge has allowed and finds acceptable.

By the time the Summing Up was concluded and the jury commenced their deliberations, they had been provided with a substantially distorted view of what actually took place.

So it is really quite amazing that they were able to return a verdict that was different to what Baker was apparently hoping for. Baker may have been expecting a rubber-stamp of the French and British police conclusions – an accident caused by a driver who had been drinking and was speeding.

The jury actually found that the deaths were brought about by "unlawful killing, grossly negligent driving of the following vehicles and of the Mercedes".[2147]

The driver of the Mercedes was known – that was Henri Paul. But the drivers of the "following vehicles" were unidentified – and were clearly not paparazzi.

It is another major blot on the record of the British and French authorities that, since that verdict was announced on 7 April 2008, not a finger has been lifted in any attempt to establish the identities of the riders of the pursuing motorbikes. Given that they have already been found guilty by a jury of the unlawful killing of Princess Diana and Dodi Fayed, the next natural step would be to renew efforts to establish their identities.

Had the victims not been Princess Diana and Dodi Fayed, then that is what would have happened.

But instead, all we have heard since the conclusion of the British inquest is a deathly silence from the British authorities.

Why?

119   How They Murdered Princess Diana

The death of Princess Diana on 31 August 1997 was one of the most shocking events of the latter part of the 20th century.

Even more shocking though is the full knowledge of the circumstances of her death – assassination at the hands of the British Secret Intelligence Service under the directions of senior members of the royal family, headed by Queen Elizabeth II.

Princess Diana's life was stolen by MI6 and the royals, and her death was stolen by the Queen, Scotland Yard and the British judiciary.

Diana was abused throughout her marriage – seriously mistreated by senior royals, including her husband Prince Charles. But after being assassinated, her body was mistreated – with multiple embalmings and post-mortems – principally under the direction of the Queen. Then the investigation of her death was hijacked by corrupt senior officials in the French and British police, including MPS commissioners Paul Condon and John Stevens. The final injustice was carried out at the hands of Lord Justice Scott Baker, who pretended to conduct a thorough investigation, but instead presided over one of the most corrupt and mismanaged inquests in British history.

Along the way some critical witnesses have died in a timely fashion – James Andanson, driver of the white Fiat Uno, died in the midst of planning a book on the crash including photos of the final journey; Gary Hunter, who saw cars fleeing the scene post-crash at high speed, died close to the commencement of the Paget investigation; Victor Mishcon, who recorded Diana's fear of death in an orchestrated car crash, died before the commencement of the British inquest into the deaths.

Senior members of the royal family were stunned when Princess Diana went public in 1992 with accounts of their cruel abuse of her. Within months the Queen made sure that Diana was officially separated from her son, Prince

Charles. Then there was more upset when in November 1995 Diana went on nationwide TV talking about her mistreatment and her marriage. Within a month the Queen had instructed Diana and Charles to divorce – and the marriage ended in August 1996.

The Queen went further – she proceeded to separate Diana from the royal family and removed her HRH title. This had the effect of putting Diana outside of the Queen's legal reach – so if Diana was to continue to misbehave then the Queen was no longer in a position to punish her, legally.

Princess Diana did continue to "misbehave". Throughout late 1996 and into 1997 she compiled a dossier as part of her campaign to eradicate landmines – and she made high-profile visits to heavily mined areas in Angola and Bosnia.

These actions upset the leadership of Britain, France and the US – the three most prolific weapons-trading nations in the western world.

Then in the middle of 1997 Diana again riled the Queen. This time she accepted an offer to holiday with Mohamed Al Fayed – viewed by the Establishment as a pariah – at his villa in the South of France.

That would not have been a problem – but this was a family holiday and Diana would be accompanied by her two sons, the Queen's grandchildren, Princes William and Harry.

Over the following weeks a romance developed between Mohamed's son, Dodi, and the princess.

The Queen called a special meeting of the royal Way Ahead Group, chaired by herself. It was around this time that a decision was made by senior royals to eliminate Princess Diana – with the acquiescence and knowledge of the leaders of the UK, France and USA: Tony Blair, Jacques Chirac and Bill Clinton.

Diana, Princess of Wales was a "loose cannon", had caused too much trouble and now had to go.

MI6 was handed the job. Senior personnel were drafted into France and Sherard Cowper-Coles, who later was promoted to ambassador to Saudi Arabia, headed the Paris operation. The assassination was carried out in the Alma Tunnel in Paris on 31 August 1997 – MI6 received assistance from the CIA and the French intelligence agencies, the DST and DGSE.

Assassination was not enough.

Diana's punishment continued into death, when she was subjected to two post-mortems and two embalmings in Paris and London.

What then followed was one of the largest and most comprehensive cover-ups in history. Orchestrated through France's Brigade Criminelle and Britain's Organised Crime Group, top police officers pretended over a period of ten years to carry out a thorough investigation of the death. Instead, their purpose was to ensure the truth of the deaths of Princess Diana and Dodi Fayed, who died with her, would forever be covered up.

This huge cover-up operation culminated in the much-delayed London inquest into the deaths, which commenced in October 2007, headed by coroner Lord Justice Scott Baker.

This six month inquest has been exposed as one of the most corrupt investigations in British judicial history.

The central issue of this case is the number of elephants in the room – there is not just one elephant. In fact there are so many elephants in this room that eventually the room must collapse and the entire house may come crashing down.

These "elephants in the room" – major issues that were either ignored or covered up in the official investigations – are:

- Princess Diana was no longer a member of the royal family – so why did she suddenly become royal immediately after dying?
- Ritz CCTV and witness evidence reveal that Henri Paul, the Mercedes driver, was sober on the night
- the two autopsies and sample testing on Henri Paul were clearly fraudulent
- there has never been any credible explanation for the elevated carbon monoxide level in the blood tested
- Dominique Lecomte and Gilbert Pépin – the two people responsible for Henri's autopsies and toxicology testing – both refused to appear at the inquest and the jury also heard no statement evidence from them
- it took a second search by French police of Henri's apartment before large quantities of alcohol were "uncovered"
- failure of the investigations to establish the source of funds in Henri's overflowing bank accounts
- the pursuing motorbikes – seen by many witnesses – were clearly not paparazzi
- there is no CCTV footage of the final journey despite there being traffic cameras along the route
- London lawyer, Gary Hunter, witnessed vehicles fleeing the scene at speed
- the crash occurred at a time when there was no back-up car, even though it was required practice to have one – every other Diana-Dodi trip in Paris that weekend had involved a back-up car
- Henri Paul drove the Mercedes S280 even though he didn't have a chauffeur's licence and had never previously driven Ritz clients
- the French thoroughly cleansed the scene twice within hours of the crash – before the crash site investigation was complete
- the French allowed and ordered the destruction of the parts of the Mercedes that had contact with the white Fiat Uno

- it took one hour 43 minutes to get Diana to hospital even though it was medically evident she had an internal injury that required hospital treatment
- the actions of the ambulance doctors, Jean-Marc Martino and Arnaud Derossi, were not caring – instead they hastened Diana's death
- no credible explanation has been given for why the ambulance stopped for five minutes within sight of the hospital gates
- there were people in Diana's ambulance who were not identified to the inquest jury
- the Val de Grâce was the hospital for VIPs – yet Diana was taken to a hospital where the required cardio-thoracic specialist was at home asleep
- Dr Bruno Riou ticked the "suspicious death" box on Diana's death certificate
- the British Embassy's pre-crash occurrence log of incoming and outgoing phone calls was not looked at by any of the investigations
- Diana predicted her own death by orchestrated car crash in both the Mishcon and Burrell notes
- senior British police officers suppressed the Mishcon Note – a vital piece of evidence in the case – for six years
- the police testimony was that they were waiting for evidence before investigating the Mishcon Note – but the note itself was the evidence
- letters written by Prince Philip abusing Diana were seen by Simone Simmons and Paul Burrell
- Dodi Fayed did purchase an engagement ring from Repossi's on Saturday, 30 August 1997
- Diana and Dodi had clear plans to live together in Julie Andrews' former Malibu home, with a part-time residence in Paris
- Diana was viewed as a "loose cannon" who members of the Establishment thought the country would be better off without
- Grahame Harding found a signal from a surveillance device during a search of Kensington Palace
- Princess Diana was embalmed twice – once, illegally, in Paris and once in London
- Diana's body was kept in a hot room ahead of the French embalming – it should have been transferred to the hospital morgue
- post-mortems were conducted on both Diana and Dodi in Paris and London – post-mortems aren't normally carried out on passengers in a car crash
- the jury were prevented from seeing the post-mortem and toxicology reports for Diana and Dodi, the people whose deaths they were investigating

HOW THEY MURDERED PRINCESS DIANA

- Diana's UK post-mortem samples were switched with another female's before testing
- MI6 does have a long history of involvement in assassination plots
- the inquest spent several days on the Milosevic plot, that revolved around a document that has been destroyed, but ignored the Gaddafi plot – "this is not an issue in these inquests"[2148] – even though it was a fully-fledged MI6 operation
- MI6 witnesses are required to put the national interest ahead of telling the truth
- professional weeders go through MI6 files removing unwanted records
- the Way Ahead Group – which dealt with major issues facing the royal family – held a special meeting in the month before the death of Diana
- Jeffrey Rees was appointed to head the Operation Paris investigation even though he had a major conflict of interest and was not available
- Paul Condon was commissioner yet has never been asked about the appointment of Jeffrey Rees as the early head of the crash investigation
- the Paget Report is one of the most severely flawed documents ever produced by Scotland Yard
- dozens of witnesses committed perjury at the London inquest – yet none have been held to account
- the jury found for unlawful killing by the following vehicles – yet the authorities have not lifted a finger to establish the identities of those following motorbike riders.

Any one of the above 44 issues is a problem, but taken together they reveal that Princess Diana was assassinated in Paris on 31 August 1997 and the British and French authorities have orchestrated a huge cover-up rather than a proper investigation.

One of the key aspects of the Establishment's handling of Diana's death has been the timing – the incredible delay of ten years between death and the commencement of the inquest.

The authorities know that if there is a long enough delay – and ten years is enough – then people will lose interest and will no longer be seeking the truth.

Even in the case of someone as iconic as Princess Diana.

It is the coroner, Lord Justice Scott Baker, who played the final despicable role in this saga of evil. Baker incessantly lied, manipulated evidence, and deceived his own jury – particularly during his final Summing Up.

Why did Baker do this?

Clearly he was a critical person in the cover-up, but there is no evidence that he had a personal reason to deceive his own jury.

It is likely that Baker was leaned on to run the inquest.

HOW THEY MURDERED PRINCESS DIANA

This was no ordinary inquest – it was an inquest where the desired conclusion was predetermined.[a] Murder was not an acceptable verdict – and Baker ensured it was removed just before the jury went out to deliberate.

As it turned out, despite Baker's best efforts of deception and manipulation, the jury still returned with the unlawful killing verdict.

There has been no justice in the case of the deaths of Princess Diana and Dodi Fayed.

What there has been is an inter-governmental pretence that the deaths were being investigated – but in actual fact what has occurred is one of the largest and most extensive, coordinated cover-ups in British police and judicial history.

People say: "Let Diana rest in peace".

Princess Diana cannot rest in peace whilst her killers walk free and the people who ordered this assassination and the ensuing massive cover-up live in peace – and are not brought to account.[b]

The question I leave the reader with is this:

Why are there – after 17 years and three major official investigations – still so many elephants in this overcrowded room?

---

[a] UK judges are required during their swearing in to take two oaths – the oath of allegiance and the judicial oath. The oath of allegiance states: "I will be faithful and bear true allegiance to Her Majesty Queen Elizabeth the Second". The judicial oath states: "I will well and truly serve our Sovereign Lady Queen Elizabeth the Second".: http://www.judiciary.gov.uk/about-the-judiciary/oaths/ It is logical to conclude that if a judge had to choose between serving the Queen's interests and achieving a just outcome, the allegiance to the Queen would prevail.

[b] There were a large number of people who had a role – large or small – in the assassination of Princess Diana and the subsequent cover-up. Some ask: "How could so many people keep quiet?" Yet this happens. In the Lance Armstrong case – the biggest fraud ever in sporting history – many people held their silence for a period of over ten years. The 1989 UK Hillsborough tragedy – 96 spectators died watching an FA Cup semi-final – is also relevant. It developed into a case of police corruption on a massive scale – including deliberate falsification of over 100 witness statements. In late 2012 the High Court granted a second inquest and that is occurring at the time of writing, in 2014 – this is 25 years after the deaths occurred. In this current case – the death of Diana – a key motivation for silence could have involved an underlying expectation by members of the Establishment to protect the Monarchy, at any cost. In that environment the truth plays second fiddle to the overriding need to maintain the current system. People can also be paid to keep their silence, others may be intimidated, others may have been killed. Money or fear are big motivators and can lead people to do things that they would otherwise deem to be unconscionable.

Evidence, Maps, Diagrams & Photos

Bibliography

Books

Andersen, C., (1998). *The Day Diana Died.* New York: William Morrow & Co Inc.

Arbiter, D., (2014), *On Duty with the Queen*, UK, Blink Publishing

Barnard, C., (2001), *50 Ways to a Healthy Heart*, Australia, Harper Collins

Blair, T., (2010), *A Journey: My Political Life*, USA, Alfred A. Knopf

Bloch, J., & Fitzgerald, P., (1983), *British Intelligence and Covert Action*, London, Junction Books Ltd

Botham, N. (2004). *The Murder of Princess Diana.* Kensington Publishing Corp.

Burrell, P., (2003), *A Royal Duty*, Australia: Penguin Books

——,(2004), *A Royal Duty*, London, Penguin Books

——, (2006), *The Way We Were: Remembering Diana*, London, Harper

Cohen, D., (2004), *Diana: Death of a Goddess*, Arrow Books

Collins Publishers

Campbell, A., (2007), *The Blair Years*, London, UK: Hutchinson

——, (2011), *The Alastair Campbell Diaries: Volume 2: Power and the People: 1997-1999*, Hutchinson

Cowper-Coles, S., (2012), *Ever The Diplomat: Confessions of a Foreign Office Mandarin*

Delorm, R., Fox, B., & Taylor, N. (1998). *Diana & Dodi: A Love Story.* Los Angeles, USA: Tallfellow Press.

Dorril, S., (2001), *MI6: Fifty Years of Special Operations*, UK, Fourth Estate

Foreign & Commonwealth Office, (1996), *The Diplomatic Service List 1996*, London, Her Majesty's Stationery Office

——, (1997), *The Diplomatic Service List 1997*, London, Her Majesty's Stationery Office

——, (1998), *The Diplomatic Service List 1998*, London, Her Majesty's Stationery Office

——, (1999), *The Diplomatic Service List 1999*, London, Her Majesty's Stationery Office

——, (2000), *The Diplomatic Service List 2000*, London, Her Majesty's Stationery Office

————, (2002), *The Diplomatic Service List 2002*, London, Her Majesty's Stationery Office

Holden, A., (1998), *Charles at Fifty*, Random House

Hounam, P. & McAdam, D., Who Killed Diana?, 1999

Morgan, J., (2007), *Cover-Up of a Royal Murder: Hundreds of Errors in the Paget Report*, USA: Amazon

————, (2009), *Diana Inquest: The Untold Story*, USA, Amazon

————, (2009), *Diana Inquest: How & Why Did Diana Die?*, USA, Amazon

————, (2010), *Diana Inquest: The French Cover-Up*, UK, Lightning Source

————, Editor, (2010), *Diana Inquest: The Documents the Jury Never Saw*, UK, Lightning Source

————, (2011), *Diana Inquest: The British Cover-Up*, UK, Lightning Source

————, (2012), *Diana Inquest: Who Killed Princess Diana?*, Australia, Lightning Source

————, (2012), *Paris-London Connection: The Assassination of Princess Diana*, Australia, Shining Bright

————, (2013), *Diana Inquest: Corruption At Scotland Yard*, Australia, Shining Bright

————, (2013), *Alan Power Exposed: Hundreds of Errors in 'The Princess Diana Conspiracy'*, Australia, Shining Bright

Morton, A., (1997), *Diana: Her True Story – In Her Own Words*, Australia: Harper Collins

————, (2004), *Diana: In Pursuit of Love*, Michael O'Mara Books

Norton-Taylor, R., (1990), *In Defence of the Realm?: The Case For Accountable Security Services*, London, The Civil Liberties Trust

Rees-Jones, T., & Johnston, M. (2000). *The Bodyguard's Story: Diana, The Crash and the Sole Survivor.* New York, USA: Warner Books Inc.

Sancton, T., & MacLeod, S. (1998). *Death of a Princess: An Investigation.* London, UK: Weidenfeld & Nicolson.

Simmons, S., (2005), *Diana: The Last Word*, London, Orion Books

Thomas, G., (1999), *Gideon's Spies: The Secret History of the Mossad*, Pan Books

Tomlinson, R., (2001), *The Big Breach*, Edinburgh, Cutting Edge

West, N., (1990), *The Friends: Britain's Post-War Secret Intelligence Operations*, Coronet Books

Wharfe, K., with Jobson, R., (2002), *Diana: Closely Guarded Secret*, London, UK, Michael O'Mara Books Limited

Websites

British Monarchy   www.royal.gov.uk
Cavity Embalming   www.embalming.net
Coroners Eastern District of London   www.walthamforest.gov.uk
Diana Conspiracy   www.dianaconspiracy.com
Diplomatic Service Interviews   www.chu.cam.ac.uk/archives
Famous Speech Transcripts   http://thespeechsite.com
Federal Climate Complex: Temperatures
                    http://www7.ncdc.noaa.gov/CDO/cdodata.cmd
Freedom of Information   www.foiacentre.com
Judiciary of England and Wales   www.judiciary.gov.uk
Map Distances   http://distancecalculator.himmera.com
MI6 Officer List   www.cryptome.org
MPS Paget Report   www.met.police.uk/news/operation_paget_report.htm
MPS SAS Soldier N Investigation
http://princessdianadeaththeevidence.weebly.com/scotland-yard-report.html
National Archives   http://yourarchives.nationalarchives.gov.uk
Official Inquest at National Archives
http://webarchive.nationalarchives.gov.uk/20080521144222/http://www.scott
baker-inquests.gov.uk/
Onassis Foundation   www.onassis.gr/en/
Police Oracle   http://www.policeoracle.com/news
POLSA Canada   www.polsa.ca
Public Interest   www.public-interest.co.uk/diana
Queensland Health   http://www.health.qld.gov.au
Ricard   www.ricardpastis.com
Royal Albert Hall   www.royalalberthall.com
South of France   www.south-of-france.com
Sunrise and Sunset Times   www.timeanddate.com
Treasury Solicitor   www.tsol.gov.uk/about_us.htm
We The People   www.wethepeople.la
Wikipedia   http://en.wikipedia.org/wiki/
Yachts   www.sailingpoint.com/yachting
                                               www.greeceyachts.com
                                       www.charterworld.com/index.html
                                               www.superyachts.com

Media Websites

BBC: www.bbc.co.uk/news
Connolly, Kevin, Paris Despatch, BBC News, 1 January 1998
Government Backs Diana in Landmines Row, BBC Politics 97, 25 June 1997
Long Line of Princely Gaffes, BBC News, March 1 2002
Princess Diana Sparks Landmines Row, BBC News, 15 January 1997
Reynolds, Paul, Royal Family's Changing Guard, BBC News, 31 August 1998
What Were You Doing When ...?, BBC News, 31 August 1997

CNN: http://edition.cnn.com
Larry King Live, CNN, 28 May 04

Newspapers & Periodicals

Alderson, Andrew, Coroner Seeks New Law to Forgo Diana Inquest, *Daily Telegraph*, April 1 2001
Allen, Peter & Arnold, Harry, Diana 1961-1997 – Investigation: Find the
Ansari, Massoud & Alderson, Andrew, Why Surgeon Could Not Marry Princess Diana, *The Telegraph*, 16 December 2007
Fiat Uno, *The Mirror*, 18 September 1997
Associated Press, Nightmare Ending to a British Fairy Tale Death of a Princess, *Cincinnati Post*, 1 September 1997
Bain, Charlie, Did Diana Do Down Tories?; Non Says Princess. Oui Says Her Interviewer, *The Mirror*, 28 August 1997
Barak, Daphne, Building Up Confidantes, *Sunday Times*, 19 March 1995
Breakfast at Rosa's, *ES Magazine*, 10 November 2006
Britain Revokes Wedding Invite To Syria Envoy, *Wall Street Journal*, 28 April 2011
Buckley, Nick, Diana and, in the Aegean, Diana is Cruising Again, *Mail on Sunday*, 17 August 1997
Burrell: I Lied to Di Inquest, *The Sun*, 18 February 2008
Camilla's Car Flew at Me Like a Missile, *The Mirror*, 13 June 1997
Chaytor, Rod, Diana Exclusive: Car Parts Destroyed, *Daily Mirror*, 8 May 2006
Clinton Backs Diana on Mine Ban, *Daily Mail*, 19 August 1997
Cojean, Annick, The Princess With A Big Heart, Le Monde, 27 August 1997
Collins, Laura, How Rupert Lost His Babykins to Big Willie, *Daily Mail*, 19 August 2006
Dahlburg, John-Thor, Investigators of Diana's Death Begin Examining Fiats, *Los Angeles Times*, 8 November 1997
Dassanayake, Dion, "With Love From Diana" Last Letter Written By Queen of Hearts, *Daily Express*, 21 April 2014
Di and Dodi Crash Horror, *The People*, 31 August 1997

BIBLIOGRAPHY

Diana Anguish As Tories Slam Her Over Landmines, *Daily Mirror*, 26 June 1997

Diana Crusades Against Blasts from the Past, *Seattle Post-Intelligencer*, 17 January 1997

Diana Eludes Media Again, *The Record*, 19 August 1997

Diana Plays It Cool, *The News Letter*, 21 August 1997

Diana Shaken Up In 5-Car Crash, *The Mirror*, 23 March 1996

Diana: The Last Days; Part 8: Princess In Disguise, *Daily Record*, 24 August 1998

Diana 'Walks into Minefield' Tories Savage Princess of Wales over Reported Political Comments, *The News Letter* (Belfast), 28 August 1997

Diana Was A True Friend, Weeps [Diana's] Closest Confidante Rosa, *Daily Mail*, 14 December 2007

Dovkants, Keith & Laville, Sandra, Di's Driver "Was Drunk", *Evening Standard*, Final Edition, 1 September 1997

Dowdney, Mark, Di Cops Narrow Hunt for Death Smash Fiat Uno – Net Closes, *Daily Record*, 9 October 1997

————, The Truth – Piece by Piece, *The Mirror*, 9 October 1997

Duckworth, Lorna, "Diana, You Are Not Much of a Princess", *Mail on Sunday*, 16 June 1996

Evans, M., Diana's Life Could Have Been Saved Says Doctor, *Daily Express*, 19 June 2007

Fiat Uno Witnesses, *Hello! Magazine*, 17 January 1998

Fisk, Robert, 'Abu Henry' and the Mysterious Silence, *The Independent*, 30 June 2007

Garner, Clare, House of Windsor Joins the PR Circus, *The Independent*, 23 February 1998

Golden, Andrew, Queen to Strip Harrods of Its Royal Crest, *Sunday Mirror*, 31 August 1997

Green, Michelle, Ping-Pong Princes, *People Magazine*, 6 September 1993

Hardcastle, Ephraim, So Apart from Tony Blair and Gordon Brown, Who Are the Other Notable Royal Wedding Absentees?, *Daily Mail*, 29 April 2011

Hastings, Chris, Queen Sacked Us Over Diana Interview, Says BBC, *Daily Telegraph*, 29 January 2006

Heap, Peter, The Truth Behind the MI6 Facade, *The Guardian*, 2 October 2003

Hitchen, Alexander, I Saw Fiat Driver Kill Di, *The People*, 18 January 2004

Hussell, Lesley, Diana 1961-1997: Mirror Investigates: The Fiction and the Facts, *The Mirror*, 11 September 1997

Kay, Richard, Diana In Car Crash Drama, *Daily Mail*, 23 March 1996

————, The Real Truth About Diana, *Daily Mail*, 29 November 2003

————, The Words I Never Said, By Diana, Daily Mail, 28 August 1997

Kay, Richard & Cobain, Ian, Will He Phone Me?, *Daily Mail*, 20 August 1997

Kempster, Doug & Wingett, Fiona, Is Diana's Baby Clock Ticking?, *Sunday Mirror*, 20 July 1997

Kerr, Jane, Abolish Them: Two Thirds of Our Readers Want Rid of the Royal Family, *The Mirror*, 11 April 2001

————, Paul Burrell Revelations, *Daily Mirror*, 11 November 2002

Klein, Edward, The Trouble with Andrew, *Vanity Fair*, August 2011

Lawson, Dominic, A Crucial Personal Detail ... and the Truth About Diana's Death, *Daily Mail*, 4 June 2006

Leake, Christopher, Exposed: The Diana Inquiry Cop Who Was On £1,000 A Day, *Daily Mail*, 23 December 2007

Lichfield, John, Car Search in Diana Inquiry, *The Independent*, 5 November 1997

Luckhurst, T., & Thompson, T., The Delay That Cost Diana Her Life, *The Scotsman*, September 29 1997

Maier, Timothy, The Bugging of the APEC in Seattle, *Insight Magazine*, 29 September 1997

Montgomery, David, Chauffeur Tells of Faults with Diana Death Car, *The Scotsman*, 28 July 1998

Morrisroe, C., Diana's Last Secret: She Asked Me to Marry Her & Dodi, Says Priest, *The People*, 15 October 2000

O'Neill, Sean, Special Branch Absorbed into Counter-Terror Unit, *The Times*, 3 October 2006

Palmer, Richard, Diana is Still Loved ... But Her Palace Postcards are Banned, *Daily Express*, May 8 2007

Pierce, Andrew, Diana Was Not Pregnant, Says Mortuary Manager, *The Times*, 19 August 2006

Posner, G., Al Fayed's Rage, *Talk Magazine*, September 1999

Princess Diana: Ex-wife of soldier who claimed SAS murdered royal now in hiding, *Sunday Mirror*, 13 October 2013

Princess Diana Sparks Frenzy Of Sightings, *Daily Gazette*, 19 August 1997

Pritchard, Louise, A Harlot, a Trollop and a Whore...., *Mail on Sunday*, 10 November 2002

Revamping the Royals, *The Economist*, 12 March 1998

Roberts, Laura, MI6 Chief Sir John Sawers Says Secrecy is Vital to Keep UK Safe, *The Telegraph*, 28 October 2010

Robinson, Eugene, Elizabeth II Offers to Pay Taxes: Queen Trimming Family's Costs, *Washington Post*, 27 November 1992

Rosa Monckton, *You Magazine*, 21 October 2007

Royal Family Gathers to Chart Its Future: Way Ahead Group Talks About Church Links, Rules for Succession, *The Spectator* (Toronto), 17 September 1996

Royal Family Rethinks Future Role for Survival, *The Washington Times*, 1 September 1996

Search Launched For Car in Crash that Killed Diana, *The Buffalo News*, 5 November 1997

Sengupta, Kim, Conservatives In Crisis: Senior Detective Takes Charge of Inquiry, *The Independent*, 24 November 1999

Simpson, Aislinn, Camilla: "I Won't Attend Princess Diana Service", The Telegraph, 27 August 2007

The Face: Rosa Monckton, *The Times*, 28 August 2007

The Media Swarm Greek Isles, In Search Of Diana, *Philadelphia Inquirer*, 18 August 1997

"This Is Diana Being Totally Irresponsible", *Sunday Mirror*, 13 July 1997

Thomas, Gordon, Diana's Secret Tapes, *Canada Free Press*, 4 October 2006

Travis, Alan, Support for Royal Family Falls to New Low, *The Guardian*, 12 June 2000

Twomey, John, Soldier's claim SAS hit squad 'did kill Princess Diana' is 'utterly convincing', *Daily Express*, 5 September 2013

Van Gelder, Lawrence, Chronicle, *The New York Times*, 19 August 1997

Walker, Tom, & Ivanovic, Milorad, Vengeful Serbs Betray Top MI6 Man, *Sunday Times*, 16 August 2004

Weathers, Helen, My Down's Daughter Changed My Life, *Daily Mail*, 14 November 2007

White, Stephen, Diana 1961-1997: Last Goodbye: My Life Is Bliss, Bye Bye, *The Mirror*, 8 September 1997

Whitney, Craig, French Police Detain 3 More Photographers, *New York Times*, September 5 1997

————, Police Hunt for a Fiat Tied to Diana, *The New York Times*, 6 November 1997

————, French Police Press the Search for a Fiat in Diana Crash, *The New York Times*, 1 January 1998

Whitney, Craig and Ibrahim, Youssef, Diana's Driver: Unsettling Piece in the Puzzle, *New York Times*, 23 September 1997

Press Releases

Buckingham Palace, Divorce: Status and Role of the Princess of Wales, PR Newswire Europe Ltd, www.prnewswire.co.uk/cgi/news

Press Office Downing Street, Change of Her Majesty's Ambassador to the Republic of Finland, 26 January 2006

Media Documentaries, Interviews and Transcripts

Allied Stars and Associated Rediffusion Productions, *Unlawful Killing*, Documentary Film, 2011

BBC, The Panorama Interview, 20 November 1995, www.bbc.co.uk/politics97/diana/panorama

Channel 5, *Diana: The Night She Died*, Psychology News, 2003

Gifts of Speech – Princess Diana Landmine Address: 12 June 1997: http://gos.sbc.edu/d/diana.html

Hallmark Entertainment, *Diana: Queen of Hearts*, TV Documentary, 1998

ITV Documentary, *Diana – The Secrets Behind the Crash*, June 3, 1998

ITV, *Diana: Her True Story*, Documentary, 1998

Sherard Cowper-Coles interview conducted by Malcolm McBain on Friday 4 March 2011 in Cowper-Coles' office at BAE Systems, London

YouTube video of Princess Diana Angola address in January 1997: https://www.youtube.com/watch?v=rU0APrqxUxc

Documents from Operation Paget Investigation File

Allan, Alexander, Witness Statement, 12 December 2006

Burgess, Michael, Witness Statement, 16 August 2004

Burton, John, Witness Statement, 16 June 2004

————, Witness Statement, 29 August 2004

Chapman, Robert, Witness Statement, 10 September 1997

Cole, Michael, Witness Statement, 6 July 2006

Coujard, Maud, Witness Statement, 15 Nov 06

Deguisne, René, Witness Statement, 9 May 2005

Derossi, Dr Arnaud, Witness Statement, 12 March 1998

Easton, Philip, Phone Call to Dr Pépin, 20 September 2005

————, Witness Statement, 19 July 2005

Flecha de Lima, Lucia, Witness Statement, 1 September 2004

Gourmélon, Xavier, Witness Statement, 5 February 1998

Green, David, Witness Statement, 13 July 2004

————, Witness Statement, 17 September 2004

Jauze, Gérard, Witness Statement, 21 March 2006

Jay, Michael, Witness Statement, 13 December 2005

Launay, Patrick, Witness Statement, 21 March 2006

Le Jalle, Christian, Witness Statement No 203/97, 4 September 1997

Lecomte, Dominique, Forensic Report; Princess Diana, 31 August 1997

————, Witness Statement, 31 May 2006

Lejay, Dr Marc, Witness Statement, 6 October 2005

Leverton, Clive, Witness Statement, 13 July 2004

Leverton, Keith, Witness Statement, 27 October 2004

Macnamara, John, Witness Statement, 3 July 2006
Mailliez, Dr Frédéric, Witness Statement: 31 August 1997
Major Incident Property Register, Diana Princess of Wales
Martino, Dr Jean-Marc, Witness Statement, 12 March 1998
————, Witness Statement, 12 May 2005
Mather, Anthony, Witness Statement, 23 August 2005
Monceau, Jean, Witness Statement, 18 October 2005
Monteil, Martine. Witness Statement, 15 November 2006
Moss, Keith, Witness Statement, 22 October 2004
Mulès, Jean-Claude, Police Interview, 19 July 2006
Patterson, Susan, Witness Statement, 28 September 2004
Pavie, Alain, Witness Statement, 9 March 2005
Plumet, Jean-Claude, Witness Statement, 4 November 2005
Puxley, Alan, Witness Statement, 16 June 2004
Riou, Prof Bruno, Police Interview, 7 March 2006
Steiner, Eva, Witness Statement, 29 September 2006
Tebbutt, Colin, Witness Statement, 5 July 2004
Thompson, Robert, Witness Statement, 9 November 2004

Witness Affidavits

Chall, Trixi, Statutory Declaration, Beaulieu-Sur-Mer, France, 3 August 2011
Thompson, Robert, Affidavit, 13 June 2001
Tomlinson, Richard, 12 May 99 Affidavit to the French Investigation

Expert Reports

Kelly, Haydn, Mr, *Gait Analysis Report*, London Medical Centre, 4 September 2007

Other Documents

Guidelines on Special Branch Work in the United Kingdom, Home Office, Communication Directorate, March 2004
Lord Justice Scott Baker, Ruling on Verdicts, After 20 Mar 08

Reference Works

Medical Dictionary on MedTerms website: www.medterms.com
Merriam-Webster: www.mereriam-webster.com
Soanes, C., & Hawker, S., (2005), Editors, *Compact Oxford English Dictionary of Current English*, UK, Oxford University Press

Legislation

UK: Coroners Act 1988

Index

INDEX

703

INDEX

INDEX

Author Information

John Morgan was born in Rotorua, New Zealand in 1957, and has lived in Australia for the last 26 years. He and his wife currently reside in Redcliffe, on the shores of Moreton Bay, near Brisbane.

John is an investigative writer with a diploma in journalism from the Australian College of Journalism. He completed his first book titled *Flying Free* in 2005 – about life inside a fundamentalist cult.

In his earlier life John was an accountant for various organisations in Auckland and Sydney. Later during the 1990s, he became a retailer operating a shop on Sydney's northern beaches. Since the 1980s John travelled widely throughout the Pacific, Asia and the Middle East.

He retired in 2003 at the age of 46, after being diagnosed with a severe neurological illness called multiple system atrophy. After a year or two of coming to terms with that devastating turn of events, he eventually found that the forced retirement created an opportunity to fulfil a lifelong ambition to write.

Following the death of Diana, Princess of Wales in 1997, John developed an interest in the events that had led to the Paris crash. Since 2005 he carried out extensive full-time research into those events and studied the official British police report after it was published in late 2006. John subsequently completed a book on that subject in September 2007 – it was titled *Cover-Up of a Royal Murder: Hundreds of Errors in the Paget Report*.

Throughout 2008 John Morgan continued his investigations into the crash and closely followed the British inquest into the deaths of Princess Diana and Dodi Fayed. That research resulted in the six evidence-based volumes of the highly acclaimed *Diana Inquest* series – written and published between 2009 and 2013.

After publicising the second volume of that series, in late 2009 John received a large volume of unpublished documentation from within the official British police Paget investigation. As a result of that in 2010 he was able to compile a dedicated volume entitled: *Diana Inquest: The Documents the Jury Never Saw*.

During 2012 John completed a page-turning summary of the shocking story of Diana's death, *Paris-London Connection: The Assassination of Princess Diana*.

John's health has continued to deteriorate but he maintains a strong determination to publicise the truth about the 1997 deaths and push for some belated justice in the case. It is this determination that has enabled him to complete this current major work *How They Murdered Princess Diana: The Shocking Truth.*

Notes

1 Andrew Morton, Diana: In Pursuit of Love, 2004, pages 31-32
2 Andrew Morton, Diana: In Pursuit of Love, 2004, page 35 and Andrew Morton, Diana: Her True Story – In Her Own Words, 1997, pages 14-15
3 Andrew Morton, Diana: Her True Story – In Her Own Words, 1997, page 17 and Andrew Morton, Diana: In Pursuit of Love, 2004, pages 37,159
4 Andrew Morton, Diana: In Pursuit of Love, 2004, page 49
5 Andrew Morton, Diana: Her True Story – In Her Own Words, 1997, page 17
6 Anthony Holden, Charles at Fifty, 1998, page 273 and Jonathon Dimbleby, The Prince of Wales: A Biography, 1994, page 489
7 Andrew Morton, Diana: Her True Story – In Her Own Words, 1997, page 251
8 Lydia Denworth and others, Argentine Adventure, Time, December 11 1995
9 Paul Burrell, A Royal Duty, 2003, pages 220-1
10 Paul Burrell, A Royal Duty, 2003, page 222
11 Dickie Arbiter, On Duty with the Queen, 2014, pp173-4
12 The Operation Paget Inquiry Report into the Allegation of Conspiracy to Murder Diana, Princess of Wales and Emad El-Din Mohamed Abdel Moneim Fayed, December 14 2006, page 300
13 The Operation Paget Inquiry Report into the Allegation of Conspiracy to Murder Diana, Princess of Wales and Emad El-Din Mohamed Abdel Moneim Fayed, December 14 2006, page 318
14 Andrew Morton, Diana: In Pursuit of Love, 2004, pages 31-32
15 Richard Kay, The Real Truth About Diana, Daily Mail, 29 November 2003
16 Lucia Flecha de Lima, Witness Statement, 1 September 2004, reproduced in Diana Inquest: The Documents the Jury Never Saw, 2010, p29 (UK Edition)
17 Andrew Morton, Diana: In Pursuit of Love, 2004, page 32
18 Andrew Morton, Diana: In Pursuit of Love, 2004, page 35 and Andrew Morton, Diana: Her True Story – In Her Own Words, 1997, pages 14-15
19 Andrew Morton, Diana: In Pursuit of Love, 2004, page 49
20 Inquest Transcripts: 13 Dec 07: 150.21
21 Tom Walker & Milorad Ivanovic, Vengeful Serbs Betray Top MI6 Man, Sunday Times, 16 August 2004
22 Foreign & Commonwealth Office, The Diplomatic Service List 2002, p100
23 Andrew Morton, Diana: In Pursuit of Love, 2004, page 37
24 Paul Burrell, A Royal Duty, 2003, page 157
25 24 Jan 08: 104.14 to 105.2
26 18 Dec 07: 90.2
27 Andrew Morton, Diana: In Pursuit of Love, 2004, p76
28 Richard Kay, The Real Truth About Diana, Daily Mail, 29 November 2003
29 INQ0058917

[30] 12 Feb 08: 4.11
[31] 12 Feb 08: 4.8
[32] Anthony Holden, Charles at Fifty, 1998, page 273 and Jonathon Dimbleby, The Prince of Wales: A Biography, 1994, page 489
[33] Michelle Green, Ping-Pong Princes, People, 6 September 1993
[34] Richard Kay, The Real Truth About Diana, Daily Mail, 29 November 2003
[35] Lucia Flecha de Lima, Witness Statement, 1 September 2004, reproduced in Diana Inquest: The Documents the Jury Never Saw, 2010, pp31-32 (UK Edition)
[36] Lucia – 18 Dec 07: 93.21; Rosa – 13 Dec 07: 135.2.
[37] Michelle Green, Ping-Pong Princes, People Magazine, 6 September 1993
[38] Ken Wharfe with Robert Jobson, Diana: Closely Guarded Secret, 2002, page 222
[39] Michelle Green, Ping-Pong Princes, People Magazine, 6 September 1993
[40] Michelle Green, Ping-Pong Princes, People Magazine, 6 September 1993
[41] Ken Wharfe with Robert Jobson, Diana: Closely Guarded Secret, 2002, page 224
[42] Ken Wharfe with Robert Jobson, Diana: Closely Guarded Secret, 2002, page 208
[43] Ken Wharfe with Robert Jobson, Diana: Closely Guarded Secret, 2002, page 214
[44] Michelle Green, Ping-Pong Princes, People Magazine, 6 September 1993
[45] Ken Wharfe with Robert Jobson, Diana: Closely Guarded Secret, 2002, page 214
[46] Michelle Green, Ping-Pong Princes, People Magazine, 6 September 1993
[47] Ken Wharfe with Robert Jobson, Diana: Closely Guarded Secret, 2002, page 214
[48] Daphne Barak, Building Up Confidantes, Sunday Times, 19 March 1995
[49] Ken Wharfe with Robert Jobson, Diana: Closely Guarded Secret, 2002, pp230-5.
[50] Grahame Harding, Police Statement, 4 July 2006 – Paget Report, pp119-120.
[51] From 7 Jan 08: 52.6
[52] 7 Jan 08: 73.19
[53] David Meynell, Meeting with HRH Princess of Wales 10.45 a.m. on 18 October 1994. Internal MPS document, 18 October 1994 reproduced in full in Diana Inquest: How & Why Did Diana Die, pp381-3
[54] 16 Jan 08: 160.13
[55] 4 Mar 08: 62.21
[56] 4 Mar 08: 62.4
[57] 4 Mar 08: 63.21
[58] 16 Jan 08: 166.2
[59] 4 Mar 08: 56.20
[60] 4 Mar 08: 64.20
[61] 4 Mar 08: 66.13
[62] 4 Mar 08: 67.1
[63] 7 Jan 08: 103.15
[64] 24 Jan 08: 148.25
[65] 4 Mar 08: 68.23
[66] 4 Mar 08: 69.10
[67] 4 Mar 08: 70.4
[68] 4 Mar 08: 68.7
[69] 4 Mar 08: 68.7

[70] 4 Mar 08: 94.13
[71] 4 Mar 08: 78.6
[72] 4 Mar 08: 56.20
[73] 4 Mar 08: 79.9
[74] 16 Jan 08: 166.2
[75] 17 Jan 08: 12.16
[76] 17 Jan 08: 6.8
[77] 4 Mar 08: 79.23
[78] 17 Jan 08: 6.24
[79] 17 Jan 08: 27.17
[80] 17 Jan 08: 13.3
[81] 17 Jan 08: 25.1
[82] 17 Jan 08: 24.11
[83] 4 Mar 08: 49.8
[84] 17 Jan 08: 26.14
[85] 4 Mar 08: 55.6
[86] 17 Jan 08: 16.25
[87] 17 Jan 08: 17.4
[88] Letter from JoAnn Grube, NSA Deputy Director Policy, dated 5 November 1998 – read out to inquest: 13 Mar 08: 79.20.
[89] 13 Mar 08: 80.5
[90] 13 Mar 08: 80.10
[91] 13 Mar 08: 80.20
[92] 20 Feb 08: 57.14
[93] 26 Feb 08: 56.11
[94] 20 Dec 07: 17.5
[95] 10 Jan 08: 69.25
[96] 12 Dec 07: 26.13
[97] Confirmed to Ian Burnett – 13 Dec 07: 145.3
[98] 18 Dec 07: 105.7
[99] 3 Mar 08: 95.10
[100] 7 Jan 08: 18.12
[101] 7 Jan 08: 56.15
[102] 15 Jan 08: 27.7
[103] 21 Nov 07: 40.12
[104] Confirmed to Ian Burnett – 28 Jan 08: 101.11
[105] 24 Jan 08: 66.16
[106] 24 Jan 08: 170.13
[107] 14 Jan 08: 92.14
[108] 14 Jan 08: 92.10
[109] 14 Jan 08: 92.19
[110] 7 Jan 08: 84.19
[111] 9 Jan 08: 111.22
[112] Paget Report, p132
[113] Paget Report, p129
[114] Paget Report, p130

[115] 3 Mar 08: 84.24

[116] 17 Jan 08: 174.8

[117] 17 Jan 08: 174.20

[118] 10 Jan 08: 44.12

[119] 15 Jan 08: 6.17

[120] 15 Jan 08: 39.17 – confirmed to Mansfield

[121] 3 Mar 08: 84.12

[122] 9 Jan 08: 111.21

[123] 12 Dec 07: 26.6

[124] 18 Feb 08: 2.21

[125] 14 Feb 08: 92.15

[126] 19 Feb 08: 38.4

[127] Paul Burrell, A Royal Duty, 2003, pages 322-3 and Inquest Evidence Reference INQ0010117.

[128] 28 Jan 08: 70.5

[129] 15 Jan 08: 203.6. See also: 14 Jan 08: 97.21

[130] The Panorama Interview, BBC, 20 November 1995, www.bbc.co.uk/politics97/diana/panorama

[131] 12 Dec 07: 62.8

[132] 17 Jan 08: 173.7

[133] Louise Pritchard, A Harlot, a Trollop and a Whore…., Mail on Sunday, November 10 2002

[134] Jane Kerr, Paul Burrell Revelations, Daily Mirror, 11 November 2002

[135] 28 Jan 08: 76.15

[136] 28 Jan 08: 78.8

[137] 28 Jan 08: 78.20

[138] Unlawful Killing, Allied Stars and Associated Rediffusion Productions, Documentary, 2011

[139] 13 Dec 07: 76.17

[140] 13 Dec 07: 77.3

[141] 13 Dec 07: 76.25

[142] 13 Dec 07: 97.1

[143] 13 Dec 07: 78.10

[144] 13 Dec 07: 78.20

[145] 18 Dec 07: 166.4

[146] 3 Mar 08: 87.2

[147] Alistair Campbell, The Blair Years, 2007, page 152; Inquest Transcripts – 15 Jan 08: 26.11

[148] 17 Jan 08: 174.20

[149] 17 Jan 08: 178.12

[150] 18 Feb 08: 2.21

[151] Gordon Thomas, Diana's Secret Tapes, Canada Free Press, 4 October 2006

[152] Simone Simmons with Ingrid Seward, Diana: The Last Word, 2005, page 179

[153] 24 Sep 04 Statement read out 3 Mar 08: 83.8

[154] 15 Jan 08: 209.4

[155] 24 Jan 08: 152.8

[156] Simone Simmons with Ingrid Seward, Diana: The Last Word, 2005, page 179

[157] 17 Jan 08: 222.16

[158] 17 Jan 08: 224.19

[159] 31 Mar 08: 132.18

[160] Anthony Holden, Charles at Fifty, 1998, page 323

[161] Chris Hastings, Queen Sacked Us Over Diana Interview, Says BBC, Daily Telegraph, 29 January 2006; Anthony Holden, Charles at Fifty, 1998, page 321

[162] Andrew Morton, Diana: Her True Story – In Her Own Words, 1997, page 261

[163] Andrew Morton, Diana: Her True Story – In Her Own Words, 1997, page 251; Anthony Holden, Charles at Fifty, 1998, page 324; Paul Burrell, A Royal Duty, 2003, pages 220-2

[164] Richard Kay, Diana In Car Crash Drama, Daily Mail, 23 March 1996

[165] Diana Shaken Up In 5-Car Crash, The Mirror, 23 March 1996

[166] Buckingham Palace, Divorce: Status and Role of the Princess of Wales, PR Newswire Europe Ltd, www.prnewswire.co.uk/cgi/news

[167] 13 Dec 07: 82.6

[168] Anthony Mather, Witness Statement, 23 August 2005, reproduced in Diana Inquest: The Documents the Jury Never Saw, 2010, p663 (UK Edition)

[169] Keith Moss, Witness Statement, 22 October 2004, reproduced in Diana Inquest: The Documents the Jury Never Saw, 2010, p653 (UK Edition)

[170] Tony Blair, A Journey: My Political Life, 2010, p144

[171] Anthony Mather, Witness Statement, 23 August 2005, reproduced in Diana Inquest: The Documents the Jury Never Saw, 2010, pp661,663 (UK Edition)

[172] John Burton, Witness Statement, 16 June 2004, reproduced in Diana Inquest: The Documents the Jury Never Saw, 2010, p557 (UK Edition)

[173] 17 Jan 08: 174.17

[174] 12 Dec 07: 62.8

[175] 17 Jan 08: 174.20

[176] 12 Dec 07: 38.3

[177] 17 Jan 08: 166.5, part confirmed to Hough

[178] 28 Jan 08: 99.19

[179] 3 Mar 08: 86.6

[180] Simone Simmons, Diana: The Last Word, 2005, page 180

[181] Simone Simmons, Diana: The Last Word, 2005, page 184

[182] 10 Jan 08: 53.15

[183] You Tube video: https://www.youtube.com/watch?v=rU0APrqxUxc

[184] Anthony Holden, Charles at Fifty, 1998, page 340

[185] Simone Simmons with Ingrid Seward, Diana: The Last Word, 2005, page 189

[186] Simone Simmons with Ingrid Seward, Diana: The Last Word, 2005, pages 178-180

[187] 10 Jan 08: 58.23

[188] 12 Dec 07: 33.25

[189] 12 Dec 07: 81.17

[190] 12 Dec 07: 73.13

[191] 12 Dec 07: 75.9

[192] 12 Dec 07: 75.21

[193] Alistair Campbell, The Blair Years, 2007, pages 145-6

[194] 12 Dec 07: 73.15

[195] Princess Diana Sparks Landmines Row, BBC News, 15 January 1997

[196] 20 Dec 07: 30.20

[197] 12 Dec 07: 68.21

[198] 12 Dec 07: 77.20

[199] 12 Dec 07: 79.10

[200] 12 Dec 07: 81.7

[201] 12 Dec 07: 74.5

[202] 12 Dec 07: 53.5

[203] Simone Simmons with Ingrid Seward, Diana: The Last Word, 2005, page 180

[204] Gordon Thomas, Diana's Secret Tapes, Canada Free Press, 4 October 2006

[205] Gordon Thomas, Diana's Secret Tapes, Canada Free Press, 4 October 2006

[206] 16 Jan 08: 27.11

[207] Simone Simmons with Ingrid Seward, Diana: The Last Word, 2005, pages 188-9 –
read out at inquest: 10 Jan 08: 52.8

[208] 10 Jan 08: 74.14

[209] 10 Jan 08: 74.22

[210] 10 Jan 08: 54.13

[211] 10 Jan 08: 79.17

[212] 10 Jan 08: 55.18

[213] 10 Jan 08: 54.5

[214] Gifts of Speech: http://gos.sbc.edu/d/diana.html

[215] Michael Cole, Witness Statement, 6 July 2006, p4

[216] 13 Dec 07: 132.9

[217] Dominic Lawson, A Crucial Personal Detail ... and the Truth About Diana's
Death, Daily Mail, 4 June 2006

[218] 10 Jan 08: 105.15

[219] 18 Feb 08: 189.1

[220] Long Line of Princely Gaffes, BBC News, March 1 2002

[221] Andrew Golden, Queen "To Strip Harrods of Its Royal Crest", Sunday Mirror, 31
August 1997

[222] 13 Dec 07: 113.4

[223] 13 Dec 07: 114.17

[224] 13 Dec 07: 150.24

[225] 13 Dec 07: 181.20

[226] 13 Dec 07: 151.18

[227] 18 Dec 07: 131.9

[228] 18 Dec 07: 131.11

[229] 10 Jan 08: 72.21

[230] 10 Jan 08: 73.1

[231] 10 Jan 08: 84.24

[232] 10 Jan 08: 85.1
[233] 10 Jan 08: 73.2
[234] Simone Simmons with Ingrid Seward, Diana: The Last Word, 2005, page 170
[235] Simone Simmons with Ingrid Seward, Diana: The Last Word, 2005, page 196
[236] Simone Simmons with Ingrid Seward, Diana: The Last Word, 2005, page 196
[237] 18 Dec 07: 131.10
[238] 18 Dec 07: 130.22
[239] 18 Dec 07: 130.23
[240] 18 Dec 07: 132.2
[241] 13 Dec 07: 150.24
[242] 10 Jan 08: 73.4
[243] 13 Dec 07: 130.9
[244] 13 Dec 07: 133.7
[245] 13 Dec 07: 133.10
[246] 13 Dec 07: 138.21
[247] 13 Dec 07: 138.24
[248] 13 Dec 07: 139.4
[249] 13 Dec 07: 144.6
[250] 13 Dec 07: 144.7
[251] 13 Dec 07: 144.10
[252] 13 Dec 07: 144.16
[253] Lucia Flecha de Lima, Witness Statement, 1 September 2004, reproduced in Diana Inquest: The Documents the Jury Never Saw, 2010, p29 (UK Edition)
[254] Lucia Flecha de Lima, Witness Statement, 1 September 2004, reproduced in Diana Inquest: The Documents the Jury Never Saw, 2010, p29 (UK Edition)
[255] Diana Anguish As Tories Slam Her Over Landmines, Daily Mirror, 26 June 1997
[256] 13 Dec 07: 138.25
[257] 13 Dec 07: 139.18
[258] Tony Blair, A Journey: My Political Life, 2010, pp139-140
[259] Alastair Campbell, The Alastair Campbell Diaries: Volume 2: Power and the People: 1997-1999, 2011, page 83
[260] Tony Blair, A Journey: My Political Life, 2010, p139
[261] 12 Feb 08: 99.2
[262] 12 Feb 08: 99.8
[263] 31 Jan 08: 183.24
[264] 31 Jan 08: 115.14
[265] 31 Jan 08: 184.6
[266] 12 Feb 08: 98.15
[267] 17 Jan 08: 39.3
[268] 17 Jan 08: 39.10
[269] 31 Jan 08: 117.7
[270] 13 Mar 08: 56.8
[271] 12 Feb 08: 43.3
[272] 12 Feb 08: 43.6
[273] 12 Feb 08: 99.15
[274] 12 Feb 08: 44.13

[275] 13 Dec 07: 79.17

[276] 13 Dec 07: 80.20

[277] "This Is Diana Being Totally Irresponsible", *Sunday Mirror*, 13 July 1997

[278] Christopher Andersen, The Day Diana Died, 1998, page 80

[279] Christopher Andersen, The Day Diana Died, 1998, page 80

[280] 9 Jan 08: 113.4

[281] 9 Jan 08: 132.3

[282] 9 Jan 08: 132.15

[283] Words as reported in the *Chicago Tribune*.

[284] 20 Dec 07: 10.11

[285] 17 Jan 08: 227.23

[286] 18 Feb 08: 185.18

[287] 20 Dec 07: 29.24

[288] Read out: 18 Feb 08: 190.2

[289] 12 Dec 07: 11.22

[290] 10 Jan 08: 108.7

[291] 14 Jan 08: 25.19

[292] 10 Jan 08: from 110.5

[293] Read out: 12 Feb 08: 104.12. Doug Kempster and Fiona Wingett, Is Diana's Baby Clock Ticking?, Sunday Mirror, 20 July 1997

[294] 12 Feb 08: 4.8

[295] 12 Feb 08: 113.8

[296] 12 Feb 08: 5.11

[297] 12 Feb 08: 115.13

[298] Doug Kempster and Fiona Wingett, Is Diana's Baby Clock Ticking?, Sunday Mirror, 20 July 1997

[299] 13 Dec 07: 59.2

[300] 13 Dec 07: 59.14

[301] 13 Dec 07: 62.19

[302] 13 Dec 07: 75.8

[303] 12 Feb 08: 4.16

[304] 12 Feb 08: 101.9

[305] 13 Dec 07: 62.19

[306] 13 Dec 07: 101.2

[307] Royal Family Rethinks Future Role for Survival, The Washington Times, 1 September 1996

[308] Royal Family Gathers to Chart Its Future: Way Ahead Group Talks About Church Links, Rules for Succession, The Spectator (Toronto), 17 September 1996

[309] Clare Garner, House of Windsor Joins the PR Circus, The Independent, 23 February 1998

[310] Revamping the Royals, The Economist, 12 March 1998

[311] Paul Reynolds, Royal Family's Changing Guard, BBC News, 31 August 1998

[312] Alan Travis, Support for Royal Family Falls to New Low, The Guardian, 12 June 2000

[313] Jane Kerr, Abolish Them: Two Thirds of Our Readers Want Rid of the Royal Family, The Mirror, 11 April 2001

[314] Laura Collins, How Rupert Lost His Babykins to Big Willie, Daily Mail, 19 August 2006

[315] Edward Klein, The Trouble with Andrew, Vanity Fair, August 2011

[316] Britain Revokes Wedding Invite To Syria Envoy, Wall Street Journal, 28 April 2011

[317] 13 Dec 07: 60.12

[318] 13 Dec 07: 60.18

[319] 13 Dec 07: 101.12

[320] 13 Dec 07: 100.13; 13 Dec 07: 101.12

[321] 13 Dec 07: 75.3

[322] 13 Dec 07: 75.8

[323] 13 Dec 07: 75.15

[324] 13 Dec 07: 61.21

[325] 13 Dec 07: 62.15

[326] 12 Feb 08: 4.8

[327] 12 Feb 08: 99.8

[328] 12 Feb 08: 6.17

[329] 31 Mar 08: 125.18

[330] 13 Dec 07: 69.13

[331] Andrew Golden, Queen to Strip Harrods of Its Royal Crest, Sunday Mirror, 31 August 1997

[332] Andrew Golden, Queen to Strip Harrods of Its Royal Crest, Sunday Mirror, 31 August 1997

[333] 13 Dec 07: 60.2

[334] 13 Dec 07: 69.13

[335] 12 Feb 08: 5.9

[336] 12 Feb 08: 5.11

[337] 12 Feb 08: 5.18

[338] 18 Mar 08: 152.9

[339] 12 Feb 08: 114.25

[340] 12 Feb 08: 5.18

[341] Treasury Solicitor's website – www.tsol.gov.uk/about_us.htm

[342] 12 Feb 08: 114.25

[343] 12 Feb 08: 115.3

[344] 12 Feb 08: 115.9

[345] 12 Feb 08: 5.18

[346] 13 Dec 07: 61.15

[347] 12 Feb 08: 113.8

[348] 12 Feb 08: 6.16

[349] 12 Feb 08: 99.8

[350] 31 Jan 08: 184.2

[351] 31 Jan 08: 184.10

[352] 31 Jan 08: 115.14

[353] 31 Jan 08: 115.16

[354] Lucia Flecha de Lima, Witness Statement, 1 September 2004, reproduced in Diana Inquest: The Documents the Jury Never Saw, 2010, p29 (UK Edition)

[355] 18 Dec 07: 98.14

[356] 13 Dec 07: 132.18

[357] 24 Sep 04 statement read out 3 Mar 08: 88.24

[358] "This Is Diana Being Totally Irresponsible", *Sunday Mirror*, 13 July 1997

[359] 27 Jul 97 letter to Dodi read out 18 Feb 08: 195.6. Handwritten copy available on the inquest website: dd3 through to dd6

[360] 24 Sep 04 statement read out 3 Mar 08: 87.8

[361] 14 Jan 08: 52.16

[362] 6 Jul 04 statement read out 18 Dec 07: 169.21

[363] 28 Jan 08: 184.8

[364] 14 Jan 08: 47.19

[365] Burrell: I Lied to Di Inquest, The Sun, 18 February 2008, page 1

[366] Paul Burrell, The Way We Were, 2006, page 156

[367] 14 Jan 08: 47.14

[368] Paul Burrell, The Way We Were, 2006, pages 156-7

[369] 14 Jan 08: 47.15

[370] Paul Burrell, The Way We Were, 2006, page 156

[371] 14 Jan 08: 47.12

[372] Paul Burrell, The Way We Were, 2006, page 157

[373] 14 Dec 07: 5.2

[374] 13 Dec 07: 136.24

[375] 1 Apr 08: 4.13

[376] 5 Dec 07: 170.20

[377] 10 Jan 08: 17.15

[378] Read out 10 Jan 08: 31.15

[379] 5 Aug 97 letter to Dodi read out 18 Feb 08: 196.6. Handwritten copy available on the inquest website: dd8 to dd9

[380] 6 Aug 97 letter to Dodi read out 14 Dec 07: 20.7. Typed copy available on the inquest website: INQ0058899

[381] Andrew Morton, Diana: Her True Story – In Her Own Words, 1997, page 270

[382] Paul Burrell, A Royal Duty, 2003, page 280

[383] Letter reproduced: Dion Dassanayake, "With Love From Diana" Last Letter Written By Queen of Hearts,, Daily Express, 21 April 2014

[384] Rene Delorm, Barry Fox & Nadine Taylor, Diana & Dodi: A Love Story, 1998, pages 94-101

[385] 17 Jan 08: 240.19

[386] 17 Jan 08: 229.23

[387] 17 Jan 08: 229.9

[388] Read out 14 Dec 07: 23.8

[389] Rene Delorm, Barry Fox & Nadine Taylor, Diana & Dodi: A Love Story, 1998, pages 102-107

[390] 19 Feb 08: 31.12

[391] 18 Feb 08: 191.5

[392] 17 Jan 08: 208.19

[393] 28 Jan 08: 110.14

[394] 9 Jan 08: 113.4

[395] 10 Jan 08: 68.12

[396] 14 Jan 08: 62.9

[397] 13 Dec 07: 141.9

[398] 18 Mar 08: 98.25

[399] 18 Mar 08: 95.18

[400] 18 Mar 08: 99.7

[401] 18 Mar 08: 97.1

[402] 19 Feb 08: 36.4

[403] 19 Feb 08: 37.1

[404] 18 Mar 08: 97.20

[405] 18 Mar 08: 101.6

[406] 19 Feb 08: 51.6

[407] 10 Jan 08: 115.21

[408] 10 Jan 08: 22.4

[409] 18 Feb 08: 191.5

[410] 16 Jan 08: 139.9

[411] 16 Jan 08: 139.19

[412] 31 Mar 08: 97.15

[413] 19 Feb 08: 36.9

[414] 19 Feb 08: 37.1

[415] 19 Feb 08: 37.10

[416] 19 Feb 08: 51.6

[417] 13 Dec 07: 182.21

[418] 13 Dec 07: 139.1

[419] 13 Dec 07: 139.8

[420] 13 Dec 07: 139.19

[421] 13 Dec 07: 139.12

[422] 13 Dec 07: 139.15

[423] 13 Dec 07: 139.18

[424] Paul Burrell, A Royal Duty, 2003, pxi

[425] Paul Burrell, A Royal Duty, 2003, pxi

[426] Nick Buckley, Diana and, in the Aegean, Diana is Cruising Again, Mail on Sunday, 17 August 1997

[427] Lawrence Van Gelder, Chronicle, The New York Times, 19 August 1997

[428] Richard Kay & Ian Cobain, Will He Phone Me?, Daily Mail, 20 August 1997

[429] Diana Plays It Cool, The News Letter, 21 August 1997

[430] Stephen White, Diana 1961-1997: Last Goodbye: My Life Is Bliss, Bye Bye, The Mirror, 8 September 1997

[431] Diana: The Last Days; Part 8: Princess In Disguise, Daily Record, 24 August 1998

[432] www.sailingpoint.com/yachting; www.greeceyachts.com

[433] Sunrise and Marala: www.charterworld.com/index.html; Sea Sedan (renamed Huntress) www.superyachts.com

[434] Princess Diana Sparks Frenzy Of Sightings, Daily Gazette, 19 August 1997

[435] Diana Eludes Media Again, The Record, 19 August 1997

[436] The Media Swarm Greek Isles, In Search Of Diana, Philadelphia Inquirer, 18 August 1997

[437] Diana Plays It Cool, The News Letter, 21 August 1997

[438] 13 Dec 07: 131.18

[439] 13 Dec 07: 132.1

[440] The Operation Paget Inquiry Report into the Allegation of Conspiracy to Murder Diana, Princess of Wales and Emad El-Din Mohamed Abdel Moneim Fayed, December 14 2006, page 616

[441] The Operation Paget Inquiry Report into the Allegation of Conspiracy to Murder Diana, Princess of Wales and Emad El-Din Mohamed Abdel Moneim Fayed, December 14 2006, page 616

[442] 13 Feb 08: 90.4

[443] Rene Delorm, Barry Fox & Nadine Taylor, Diana & Dodi: A Love Story, 1998, pages 55-56

[444] 11 Feb 08: 95.25

[445] 11 Feb 08: 128.16

[446] Michael Jay, Witness Statement, 13 December 2005, reproduced in Diana Inquest: The Documents the Jury Never Saw, 2010, pp632-3 (UK Edition)

[447] Foreign & Commonwealth Office, The Diplomatic Service List 1997, p32

[448] Foreign & Commonwealth Office, The Diplomatic Service List 1997, p32

[449] Foreign & Commonwealth Office, The Diplomatic Service List 1997, p161

[450] Foreign & Commonwealth Office, The Diplomatic Service List 1998, p167

[451] 29 Feb 08: 40.7

[452] 29 Feb 08: 42.20

[453] 29 Feb 08: 42.2

[454] Foreign & Commonwealth Office, The Diplomatic Service List 1997, p161; Foreign & Commonwealth Office, The Diplomatic Service List 1998, p167

[455] Foreign & Commonwealth Office, The Diplomatic Service List 1998, p34

[456] Foreign & Commonwealth Office, The Diplomatic Service List 1998, piii

[457] 29 Feb 08: 42.6

[458] 29 Feb 08: 42.9

[459] 29 Feb 08: 42.13

[460] Michael Jay, Witness Statement, 13 December 2005, reproduced in Diana Inquest: The Documents the Jury Never Saw, 2010, p640 (UK Edition)

[461] 11 Feb 08: 93.11

[462] 29 Feb 08: 42.2

[463] Foreign & Commonwealth Office, The Diplomatic Service List 1998, p167

[464] 29 Feb 08: 43.11

[465] Michael Jay, Witness Statement, 13 December 2005, reproduced in Diana Inquest: The Documents the Jury Never Saw, 2010, p634 (UK Edition)

[466] Michael Jay, Witness Statement, 13 December 2005, reproduced in Diana Inquest: The Documents the Jury Never Saw, 2010, p634 (UK Edition)

[467] Michael Jay, Witness Statement, 13 December 2005, reproduced in Diana Inquest: The Documents the Jury Never Saw, 2010, p634 (UK Edition)

[468] Michael Jay, Witness Statement, 13 December 2005, reproduced in Diana Inquest: The Documents the Jury Never Saw, 2010, pp630-1 (UK Edition)

[469] Michael Jay, Witness Statement, 13 December 2005, reproduced in Diana Inquest: The Documents the Jury Never Saw, 2010, p640 (UK Edition)

[470] Foreign & Commonwealth Office, The Diplomatic Service List 1998, p34

[471] 11 Feb 08: 93.11

[472] 11 Feb 08: 117.14

[473] Michael Jay, Witness Statement, 13 December 2005, reproduced in Diana Inquest: The Documents the Jury Never Saw, 2010, p637 (UK Edition)

[474] Michael Jay, Witness Statement, 13 December 2005, reproduced in Diana Inquest: The Documents the Jury Never Saw, 2010, p636 (UK Edition)

[475] Michael Jay, Witness Statement, 13 December 2005, reproduced in Diana Inquest: The Documents the Jury Never Saw, 2010, p637 (UK Edition)

[476] 29 Feb 08: 40.18

[477] Foreign & Commonwealth Office, The Diplomatic Service List 1997, p157

[478] Foreign & Commonwealth Office, The Diplomatic Service List 1997, p8

[479] Interview with Sherard Cowper-Coles conducted by Malcolm McBain on Friday 4 March 2011 in Cowper-Coles' office at BAE Systems, London

[480] Michael Jay, Witness Statement, 13 December 2005, reproduced in Diana Inquest: The Documents the Jury Never Saw, 2010, pp632, 639 (UK Edition)

[481] Sherard Cowper-Coles, Ever The Diplomat: Confessions of a Foreign Office Mandarin, 2012, p182

[482] Sherard Cowper-Coles, Ever The Diplomat: Confessions of a Foreign Office Mandarin, 2012, p181

[483] Sherard Cowper-Coles, Ever The Diplomat: Confessions of a Foreign Office Mandarin, 2012, p182

[484] 17 Dec 07: 109.8

[485] Michael Jay, Witness Statement, 13 December 2005, reproduced in Diana Inquest: The Documents the Jury Never Saw, 2010, p635 (UK Edition)

[486] Michael Jay, Witness Statement, 13 December 2005, reproduced in Diana Inquest: The Documents the Jury Never Saw, 2010, p637 (UK Edition)

[487] Keith Moss, Witness Statement, 22 October 2004, reproduced in Diana Inquest: The Documents the Jury Never Saw, 2010, p651 (UK Edition)

[488] Clinton Backs Diana on Mine Ban, Daily Mail, 19 August 1997

[489] Clare Morrisroe, Diana's Last Secret: She Asked Me to Marry Her & Dodi, Says Priest, The People, 15 October 2000

[490] 22 Sep 04 Statement read out 22 Jan 08: 148.13

[491] 6 Jan 05 Statement read out 20 Dec 07: 65.15

[492] 18 Dec 07: 55.5

[493] Trixi Chall, Statutory Declaration, 3 August 2011. The full declaration is at: http://princessdianadeaththeevidence.weebly.com/the-witnesses.html

[494] 20 Oct 05 Statement read out: 6 Dec 07: 11.13

[495] 5 Dec 07: 48.14

[496] 6 Dec 07: 11.16

[497] 20 Oct 05 Statement read out: 6 Dec 07: 11.13

[498] 5 Dec 07: 47.1

[499] 5 Dec 07: 47.6

[500] 5 Dec 07: 11.18; 5 Dec 07: 7.7; 5 Dec 07: 6.15

[501] 5 Dec 07: 15.17; 5 Dec 07: 48.16;The Operation Paget Inquiry Report into the Allegation of Conspiracy to Murder Diana, Princess of Wales and Emad El-Din Mohamed Abdel Moneim Fayed, December 14 2006, page 42

[502] 5 Dec 07: 47.22

[503] 5 Dec 07: 22.1; 5 Dec 07: 49.2

[504] Clare Morrisroe, Diana's Last Secret: She Asked Me to Marry Her& Dodi, Says Priest, The People, 15 October 2000

[505] 12 Dec 07: 20.9

[506] 19 Feb 08: 44.22

[507] 19 Feb 08: 44.15

[508] 13 Mar 08: 70.16

[509] 11 Feb 08: 21.4

[510] Gordon Thomas, Gideon's Spies: The Secret History of the Mossad, 1999, page 18

[511] Annick Cojean, The Princess With A Big Heart, Le Monde, 27 August 1997 translated and reproduced: www.dianaforever.com/lemonade.htm

[512] Annick Cojean, The Princess With A Big Heart, Le Monde, 27 August 1997 translated and reproduced: www.dianaforever.com/lemonade.htm

[513] Diana 'Walks into Minefield' Tories Savage Princess of Wales over Reported Political Comments, The News Letter (Belfast), 28 August 1997

[514] Diana 'Walks into Minefield' Tories Savage Princess of Wales over Reported Political Comments, The News Letter (Belfast), 28 August 1997

[515] Charlie Bain, Did Diana Do Down Tories?; Non Says Princess. Oui Says Her Interviewer, The Mirror, 28 August 1997

[516] Richard Kay, The Words I Never Said, By Diana, Daily Mail, 28 August 1997

[517] Richard Kay, The Words I Never Said, By Diana, Daily Mail, 28 August 1997

[518] Richard Kay, The Words I Never Said, By Diana, Daily Mail, 28 August 1997

[519] Richard Tomlinson, 12 May 99 Affidavit to the French Investigation

[520] The Operation Paget Inquiry Report into the Allegation of Conspiracy to Murder Diana, Princess of Wales and Emad El-Din Mohamed Abdel Moneim Fayed, December 14 2006, page 767

[521] 21 Feb 08: 34.12

[522] 21 Feb 08: 87.7

[523] 6 Feb 08: 4.8

[524] 21 Feb 08: 19.21

[525] 11 Mar 08: 152.21

[526] 21 Feb 08: 19.21

[527] 21 Feb 08: 19.24

[528] 11 Mar 08: 153.4

[529] 7 Feb 08: 18.16

[530] 7 Feb 08: 19.3

[531] 5 Feb 08: 29.4

[532] 6 Feb 08: 14.9

[533] Diana: The Night She Died, Channel 5 Documentary, 2003; Noel Botham, The Murder of Princess Diana, 2004, page 263

[534] 21 Feb 08: 7.9

[535] James Andanson letter to Hubert Henrotte, 30 August 1997, p1: INQ0009206

[536] INQ0009103

[537] The Operation Paget Inquiry Report into the Allegation of Conspiracy to Murder Diana, Princess of Wales and Emad El-Din Mohamed Abdel Moneim Fayed, December 14 2006, pages 693-4

[538] 21 Feb 08: 25.1

[539] 21 Feb 08: 14.2

[540] 21 Feb 08: 46.16

[541] 21 Feb 08: 46.20

[542] INQ0009103

[543] 21 Feb 08: 46.24

[544] 21 Feb 08: 13.7; 21.11

[545] 21 Feb 08: 13.23

[546] 21 Feb 08: 14.3

[547] INQ0009103; INQ0009106

[548] 21 Feb 08: 12.17

[549] 5 Feb 08: 32.5

[550] 5 Feb 08: 32.11

[551] 21 Feb 08: 56.4

[552] 21 Feb 08: 56.15

[553] 21 Feb 08: 81.17

[554] 21 Feb 08: 81.20

[555] 21 Feb 08: 72.6; 21 Feb 08: 82.6

[556] 5 Feb 08: 33.6

[557] 21 Feb 08: 43.24

[558] INQ0009106

[559] 21 Feb 08: 60.14

[560] 21 Feb 08: 40.24

[561] 5 Feb 08: 35.12

[562] 5 Feb 08: 35.5

[563] 21 Feb 08: 60.10

[564] 29 Nov 07: 132.22

[565] 5 Dec 07: 33.11

[566] 3 Dec 07: 77.18

[567] The Operation Paget Inquiry Report into the Allegation of Conspiracy to Murder Diana, Princess of Wales and Emad El-Din Mohamed Abdel Moneim Fayed, December 14 2006, page 160

[568] The Operation Paget Inquiry Report into the Allegation of Conspiracy to Murder Diana, Princess of Wales and Emad El-Din Mohamed Abdel Moneim Fayed, December 14 2006, page 159

[569] The Operation Paget Inquiry Report into the Allegation of Conspiracy to Murder Diana, Princess of Wales and Emad El-Din Mohamed Abdel Moneim Fayed, December 14 2006, page 191
[570] 31 Jan 08: 131.2
[571] 16 Sep 97 Statement read out 17 Mar 08: 121.19
[572] 17 Sep 97 Statement read out 13 Mar 08: 52.5
[573] 4 Sep 97 Statement read out 13 Mar 08: 59.13
[574] 13 Mar 08: 88.25
[575] Laura Roberts, MI6 Chief Sir John Sawers Says Secrecy is Vital to Keep UK Safe, The Telegraph, 28 October 2010
[576] 5 Feb 08: 80.10
[577] Paget Report, pp178-181
[578] Paget Report, pp178-181
[579] The Operation Paget Inquiry Report into the Allegation of Conspiracy to Murder Diana, Princess of Wales and Emad El-Din Mohamed Abdel Moneim Fayed, December 14 2006, page 182
[580] The Operation Paget Inquiry Report into the Allegation of Conspiracy to Murder Diana, Princess of Wales and Emad El-Din Mohamed Abdel Moneim Fayed, December 14 2006, page 181
[581] 5 Feb 08: 72.22
[582] 28 Jan 08: 89.19
[583] ITV Documentary, Diana – The Secrets Behind the Crash, June 3 1998
[584] 5 Feb 08: 4.19
[585] 5 Feb 08: 82.12
[586] 5 Feb 08: 83.12
[587] 5 Feb 08: 83.16
[588] 5 Feb 08: 82.5
[589] 5 Feb 08: 84.20
[590] The Operation Paget Inquiry Report into the Allegation of Conspiracy to Murder Diana, Princess of Wales and Emad El-Din Mohamed Abdel Moneim Fayed, December 14 2006, page 184
[591] 4 Feb 08: 13.18
[592] 4 Feb 08: 13.5
[593] 29 Nov 07: 110.2
[594] The Operation Paget Inquiry Report into the Allegation of Conspiracy to Murder Diana, Princess of Wales and Emad El-Din Mohamed Abdel Moneim Fayed, December 14 2006, page 184
[595] The Operation Paget Inquiry Report into the Allegation of Conspiracy to Murder Diana, Princess of Wales and Emad El-Din Mohamed Abdel Moneim Fayed, December 14 2006, page 183
[596] 31 Jan 08: 153.25
[597] 5 Feb 08: 101.18
[598] Paget Report, p181
[599] 5 Feb 08: 93.10

[600] 5 Feb 08: 75.7

[601] 5 Feb 08: 103.24

[602] Paget Report, p180

[603] The Operation Paget Inquiry Report into the Allegation of Conspiracy to Murder Diana, Princess of Wales and Emad El-Din Mohamed Abdel Moneim Fayed, December 14 2006, page 183

[604] 31 Jan 08: 153.14

[605] 27 Mar 08 description of letter from Stuart Benson to the inquest read out 31 Mar 08: 8.20

[606] 1 Apr 08: 88.20

[607] 29 Feb 08: 47.10

[608] 29 Feb 08: 48.5

[609] 29 Feb 08: 56.10

[610] 29 Feb 08: 47.25

[611] The Operation Paget Inquiry Report into the Allegation of Conspiracy to Murder Diana, Princess of Wales and Emad El-Din Mohamed Abdel Moneim Fayed, December 14 2006, page 767

[612] 29 Feb 08: 61.21

[613] 29 Feb 08: 62.1

[614] 29 Feb 08: 62.19

[615] 29 Feb 08: 62.10

[616] 29 Nov 07: 105.7

[617] 31 Jan 08: 138.17

[618] 4 Feb 08: 56.22

[619] 13 Feb 08: 34.2

[620] 4 Feb 08: 26.1

[621] 4 Feb 08: 14.1

[622] 31 Jan 08: 155.16

[623] 4 Feb 08: 26.1

[624] 5 Dec 07: 38.11

[625] 31 Mar 08: 65.18

[626] 31 Jan 08: 155.16

[627] Jean-François Clair, Deputy Head of DST: 23 Jun 05 letter read out 13 Mar 08: 76.20

[628] 1 Apr 08: 87.22

[629] 31 Mar 08: 64.19

[630] 31 Jan 08: 130.6

[631] 16 Sep 97 Statement read out 17 Mar 08: 120.22

[632] 16 Sep 97 Statement read out 17 Mar 08: 121.10

[633] 28 Aug 97 Certificate read out 19 Feb 08: 9.12

[634] 16 Sep 97 Statement read out 17 Mar 08: 126.3

[635] 31 Jan 08: 160.19

[636] Christopher Andersen, The Day Diana Died, 1998, page 147

[637] Christopher Andersen, The Day Diana Died, 1998, page 147

[638] The Operation Paget Inquiry Report into the Allegation of Conspiracy to Murder Diana, Princess of Wales and Emad El-Din Mohamed Abdel Moneim Fayed, December 14 2006, page 195

[639] 29 Nov 07: 103.25

[640] Noel Botham, The Murder of Princess Diana, 2004, pages 166-7

[641] The Operation Paget Inquiry Report into the Allegation of Conspiracy to Murder Diana, Princess of Wales and Emad El-Din Mohamed Abdel Moneim Fayed, December 14 2006, page 163

[642] 29 Nov 07: 131.12

[643] 5 Dec 07: 196.18

[644] The Operation Paget Inquiry Report into the Allegation of Conspiracy to Murder Diana, Princess of Wales and Emad El-Din Mohamed Abdel Moneim Fayed, December 14 2006, pages 162-3

[645] The Operation Paget Inquiry Report into the Allegation of Conspiracy to Murder Diana, Princess of Wales and Emad El-Din Mohamed Abdel Moneim Fayed, December 14 2006, page 193

[646] The Operation Paget Inquiry Report into the Allegation of Conspiracy to Murder Diana, Princess of Wales and Emad El-Din Mohamed Abdel Moneim Fayed, December 14 2006, page 193

[647] Rene Delorm, Barry Fox & Nadine Taylor, Diana & Dodi: A Love Story, 1998, pages 154

[648] Trevor Rees-Jones & Moira Johnston, The Bodyguard's Story, 2000, page 90

[649] 4 Sep 97 statement read out 13 Mar 08: 16.22

[650] 1 Apr 08: 84.12

[651] Trevor Rees-Jones & Moira Johnston, The Bodyguard's Story, 2000, pages 89-90

[652] The Operation Paget Inquiry Report into the Allegation of Conspiracy to Murder Diana, Princess of Wales and Emad El-Din Mohamed Abdel Moneim Fayed, December 14 2006, page 614

[653] The Operation Paget Inquiry Report into the Allegation of Conspiracy to Murder Diana, Princess of Wales and Emad El-Din Mohamed Abdel Moneim Fayed, December 14 2006, page 615

[654] 23 Jan 08: 69.17

[655] 4 Sep 97 statement read out 11 Mar 08: 97.2

[656] Rene Delorm, Diana & Dodi: A Love Story, 1998, page 154

[657] 14 Nov 06 statement read out 21 Nov 07: 57.22

[658] 31 Aug 97 Diary read out 11 Feb 08: 105.20

[659] 11 Feb 08: 153.9

[660] 11 Feb 08: 91.14

[661] The Operation Paget Inquiry Report into the Allegation of Conspiracy to Murder Diana, Princess of Wales and Emad El-Din Mohamed Abdel Moneim Fayed, December 14 2006, page 616

[662] 11 Feb 08: 93.2

[663] Michael Jay, Witness Statement, 13 December 2005, reproduced in Diana Inquest: The Documents the Jury Never Saw, 2010, p632 (UK Edition)

[664] Michael Jay, Witness Statement, 13 December 2005, reproduced in Diana Inquest: The Documents the Jury Never Saw, 2010, pp632-3 (UK Edition)

[665] 31 Aug 97 Diary read out 11 Feb 08: 105.20

[666] The Operation Paget Inquiry Report into the Allegation of Conspiracy to Murder Diana, Princess of Wales and Emad El-Din Mohamed Abdel Moneim Fayed, December 14 2006, page 620

[667] The Operation Paget Inquiry Report into the Allegation of Conspiracy to Murder Diana, Princess of Wales and Emad El-Din Mohamed Abdel Moneim Fayed, December 14 2006, page 607

[668] The Operation Paget Inquiry Report into the Allegation of Conspiracy to Murder Diana, Princess of Wales and Emad El-Din Mohamed Abdel Moneim Fayed, December 14 2006, pages 607 to 613

[669] The Operation Paget Inquiry Report into the Allegation of Conspiracy to Murder Diana, Princess of Wales and Emad El-Din Mohamed Abdel Moneim Fayed, December 14 2006, page 611

[670] The Operation Paget Inquiry Report into the Allegation of Conspiracy to Murder Diana, Princess of Wales and Emad El-Din Mohamed Abdel Moneim Fayed, December 14 2006, page 766

[671] The Operation Paget Inquiry Report into the Allegation of Conspiracy to Murder Diana, Princess of Wales and Emad El-Din Mohamed Abdel Moneim Fayed, December 14 2006, page 804

[672] The Operation Paget Inquiry Report into the Allegation of Conspiracy to Murder Diana, Princess of Wales and Emad El-Din Mohamed Abdel Moneim Fayed, December 14 2006, page 620

[673] The Operation Paget Inquiry Report into the Allegation of Conspiracy to Murder Diana, Princess of Wales and Emad El-Din Mohamed Abdel Moneim Fayed, December 14 2006, page 210

[674] Michael Jay, Witness Statement, 13 December 2005, reproduced in Diana Inquest: The Documents the Jury Never Saw, 2010, p632 (UK Edition)

[675] Trevor Rees-Jones & Moira Johnston, The Bodyguard's Story, 2000, pages 89-90

[676] The Operation Paget Inquiry Report into the Allegation of Conspiracy to Murder Diana, Princess of Wales and Emad El-Din Mohamed Abdel Moneim Fayed, December 14 2006, page 615

[677] Trevor Rees-Jones & Moira Johnston, The Bodyguard's Story, 2000, pages 90-91

[678] 2 Sep 97 Statement read out 29 Jan 08: 175.17

[679] 2 Sep 97 Statement read out 29 Jan 08: 175.22

[680] 2 Sep 97 Statement read out 18 Dec 07: 145.9

[681] 1998 Diana & Dodi: A Love Story read out 5 Dec 07: 201.6

[682] Nov 05 Statement read out: 19 Dec 07: 25.18

[683] 3 Dec 07: 42.14

[684] 29 Jan 08: 30.14

[685] 18 Dec 07: 150.15

[686] 19 Dec 07: 20.25

[687] 4 Sep 97 statement read out 13 Mar 08: 17.25

[688] 17 Jan 08: 232.4

[689] 17 Jan 08: 235.20

[690] Thomas Sancton and Scott MacLeod, Death of a Princess: An Investigation, 1998, page 123
[691] 18 Feb 08: 58.9
[692] 5 Dec 07: 91.15
[693] 20 Oct 05 Statement read out: 6 Dec 07: 11.13
[694] 10 Dec 07: 21.17; Paget Report, p65
[695] 10 Dec 07: 22.3
[696] Timeline Repossi Visits, PDF on inquest website.
[697] At inquest: 10 Dec 07: from 11.15
[698] Mora: 5 Dec 07: 17.22 and Repossi: 10 Dec 07: 22.1.
[699] Gobbo: 11 Dec 07: 70.12
[700] The Operation Paget Inquiry Report into the Allegation of Conspiracy to Murder Diana, Princess of Wales and Emad El-Din Mohamed Abdel Moneim Fayed, December 14 2006, page 65
[701] The Operation Paget Inquiry Report into the Allegation of Conspiracy to Murder Diana, Princess of Wales and Emad El-Din Mohamed Abdel Moneim Fayed, December 14 2006, page 66
[702] The Operation Paget Inquiry Report into the Allegation of Conspiracy to Murder Diana, Princess of Wales and Emad El-Din Mohamed Abdel Moneim Fayed, December 14 2006, page 66
[703] The Operation Paget Inquiry Report into the Allegation of Conspiracy to Murder Diana, Princess of Wales and Emad El-Din Mohamed Abdel Moneim Fayed, December 14 2006, page 58
[704] The Operation Paget Inquiry Report into the Allegation of Conspiracy to Murder Diana, Princess of Wales and Emad El-Din Mohamed Abdel Moneim Fayed, December 14 2006, page 58
[705] 5 Dec 07: 123.7; The Operation Paget Inquiry Report into the Allegation of Conspiracy to Murder Diana, Princess of Wales and Emad El-Din Mohamed Abdel Moneim Fayed, December 14 2006, page 59
[706] The Operation Paget Inquiry Report into the Allegation of Conspiracy to Murder Diana, Princess of Wales and Emad El-Din Mohamed Abdel Moneim Fayed, December 14 2006, page 60
[707] The Operation Paget Inquiry Report into the Allegation of Conspiracy to Murder Diana, Princess of Wales and Emad El-Din Mohamed Abdel Moneim Fayed, December 14 2006, page 62
[708] The Operation Paget Inquiry Report into the Allegation of Conspiracy to Murder Diana, Princess of Wales and Emad El-Din Mohamed Abdel Moneim Fayed, December 14 2006, pages 63-64
[709] 5 Dec 07: 63.20
[710] 5 Dec 07: 64.19
[711] 6 Dec 07: 7.25; The Operation Paget Inquiry Report into the Allegation of Conspiracy to Murder Diana, Princess of Wales and Emad El-Din Mohamed Abdel Moneim Fayed, December 14 2006, page 59

[712] The Operation Paget Inquiry Report into the Allegation of Conspiracy to Murder Diana, Princess of Wales and Emad El-Din Mohamed Abdel Moneim Fayed, December 14 2006, page 60
[713] The Operation Paget Inquiry Report into the Allegation of Conspiracy to Murder Diana, Princess of Wales and Emad El-Din Mohamed Abdel Moneim Fayed, December 14 2006, page 64
[714] 5 Dec 07: 76.17
[715] 11 Dec 07: 86.23
[716] The Operation Paget Inquiry Report into the Allegation of Conspiracy to Murder Diana, Princess of Wales and Emad El-Din Mohamed Abdel Moneim Fayed, December 14 2006, page 62
[717] 5 Dec 07: 64.19
[718] 11 Dec 07: 85.24
[719] 5 Dec 07: 67.14
[720] 5 Dec 07: 68.4
[721] 5 Dec 07: 81.1
[722] The Operation Paget Inquiry Report into the Allegation of Conspiracy to Murder Diana, Princess of Wales and Emad El-Din Mohamed Abdel Moneim Fayed, December 14 2006, page 58
[723] 5 Dec 07: 123.7; The Operation Paget Inquiry Report into the Allegation of Conspiracy to Murder Diana, Princess of Wales and Emad El-Din Mohamed Abdel Moneim Fayed, December 14 2006, page 59
[724] The Operation Paget Inquiry Report into the Allegation of Conspiracy to Murder Diana, Princess of Wales and Emad El-Din Mohamed Abdel Moneim Fayed, December 14 2006, page 60
[725] The Operation Paget Inquiry Report into the Allegation of Conspiracy to Murder Diana, Princess of Wales and Emad El-Din Mohamed Abdel Moneim Fayed, December 14 2006, page 62
[726] The Operation Paget Inquiry Report into the Allegation of Conspiracy to Murder Diana, Princess of Wales and Emad El-Din Mohamed Abdel Moneim Fayed, December 14 2006, page 64
[727] 5 Dec 07: 67.5
[728] 5 Dec 07: 72.13
[729] The Operation Paget Inquiry Report into the Allegation of Conspiracy to Murder Diana, Princess of Wales and Emad El-Din Mohamed Abdel Moneim Fayed, December 14 2006, page 64
[730] 5 Dec 07: 72.15
[731] The Operation Paget Inquiry Report into the Allegation of Conspiracy to Murder Diana, Princess of Wales and Emad El-Din Mohamed Abdel Moneim Fayed, December 14 2006, page 72
[732] 5 Dec 07: 86.2
[733] 5 Dec 07: 85.14
[734] 10 Dec 07: 92.10
[735] 11 Dec 07: 82.3
[736] 5 Dec 07: 89.15

[737] The Operation Paget Inquiry Report into the Allegation of Conspiracy to Murder Diana, Princess of Wales and Emad El-Din Mohamed Abdel Moneim Fayed, December 14 2006, page 63
[738] The Operation Paget Inquiry Report into the Allegation of Conspiracy to Murder Diana, Princess of Wales and Emad El-Din Mohamed Abdel Moneim Fayed, December 14 2006, page 72
[739] 5 Dec 07: 123.12
[740] 6 Dec 07: 23.19
[741] 6 Dec 07: 23.22
[742] 5 Dec 07: 48.14
[743] 5 Dec 07: 121.2
[744] The Operation Paget Inquiry Report into the Allegation of Conspiracy to Murder Diana, Princess of Wales and Emad El-Din Mohamed Abdel Moneim Fayed, December 14 2006, page 65
[745] 10 Dec 07: 25.1
[746] 10 Dec 07: 17.14
[747] 10 Dec 07: 20.25
[748] 29 Feb 08: 53.15
[749] The Operation Paget Inquiry Report into the Allegation of Conspiracy to Murder Diana, Princess of Wales and Emad El-Din Mohamed Abdel Moneim Fayed, December 14 2006, page 767
[750] 29 Feb 08: 54.2
[751] The Operation Paget Inquiry Report into the Allegation of Conspiracy to Murder Diana, Princess of Wales and Emad El-Din Mohamed Abdel Moneim Fayed, December 14 2006, page 767
[752] 29 Feb 08: 56.9
[753] The Operation Paget Inquiry Report into the Allegation of Conspiracy to Murder Diana, Princess of Wales and Emad El-Din Mohamed Abdel Moneim Fayed, December 14 2006, page 816
[754] 29 Feb 08: 53.8
[755] 12 May 99 Affidavit by Richard Tomlinson to Judge Hervé Stephan
[756] 29 Feb 08: 61.16
[757] 29 Feb 08: 65.9
[758] 29 Feb 08: 36.5
[759] Foreign & Commonwealth Office, The Diplomatic Service List 1998, p154
[760] Press Office Downing Street, Change of Her Majesty's Ambassador to the Republic of Finland, 26 January 2006: www.gov-news.org/gov/uk/news
[761] Foreign & Commonwealth Office, The Diplomatic Service List 1998, p162
[762] 29 Feb 08: 37.17
[763] Foreign & Commonwealth Office, The Diplomatic Service List 1998, p272
[764] 29 Feb 08: 40.11
[765] 29 Feb 08: 40.22
[766] 29 Feb 08: 41.1
[767] 29 Feb 08: 41.5

[768] 29 Feb 08: 38.6
[769] 29 Feb 08: 35.24
[770] 29 Feb 08: 36.19
[771] 29 Feb 08: 38.7
[772] 29 Feb 08: 36.1
[773] 29 Feb 08: 36.8
[774] 29 Feb 08: 38.11
[775] The Operation Paget Inquiry Report into the Allegation of Conspiracy to Murder Diana, Princess of Wales and Emad El-Din Mohamed Abdel Moneim Fayed, December 14 2006, page 767
[776] 29 Feb 08: 53.24
[777] 29 Feb 08: 36.5
[778] 29 Feb 08: 37.18
[779] 29 Feb 08: 41.5
[780] 4 Sep 97 Statement read out 13 Mar 08: 19.7
[781] 23 Jan 08: 72.21
[782] 23 Jan 08: 73.25
[783] 5 Dec 07: 180.8
[784] 5 Dec 07: 186.13
[785] 23 Sep 97 Statement read out 17 Oct 07: 10.21
[786] 3 Dec 07: 17.5
[787] 3 Dec 07: 18.22
[788] The Operation Paget Inquiry Report into the Allegation of Conspiracy to Murder Diana, Princess of Wales and Emad El-Din Mohamed Abdel Moneim Fayed, December 14 2006, page 211
[789] 4 Dec 07: 72.21
[790] Trevor Rees-Jones & Moira Johnston, The Bodyguard's Story, 2000, page 91
[791] Trevor Rees-Jones & Moira Johnston, The Bodyguard's Story, 2000, page 94
[792] The Operation Paget Inquiry Report into the Allegation of Conspiracy to Murder Diana, Princess of Wales and Emad El-Din Mohamed Abdel Moneim Fayed, December 14 2006, page 212
[793] The Operation Paget Inquiry Report into the Allegation of Conspiracy to Murder Diana, Princess of Wales and Emad El-Din Mohamed Abdel Moneim Fayed, December 14 2006, page 213
[794] 29 Jan 08: 36.24
[795] The Operation Paget Inquiry Report into the Allegation of Conspiracy to Murder Diana, Princess of Wales and Emad El-Din Mohamed Abdel Moneim Fayed, December 14 2006, page 213
[796] Trevor Rees-Jones & Moira Johnston, The Bodyguard's Story, 2000, page 95
[797] The Operation Paget Inquiry Report into the Allegation of Conspiracy to Murder Diana, Princess of Wales and Emad El-Din Mohamed Abdel Moneim Fayed, December 14 2006, page 209
[798] The Operation Paget Inquiry Report into the Allegation of Conspiracy to Murder Diana, Princess of Wales and Emad El-Din Mohamed Abdel Moneim Fayed, December 14 2006, page 212
[799] 3 Oct 97 Statement read out 7 Mar 08: 102.22

[800] 3 Dec 07: 52.1

[801] 3 Dec 07: 78.17

[802] 4 Dec 07: 4.18

[803] The Operation Paget Inquiry Report into the Allegation of Conspiracy to Murder Diana, Princess of Wales and Emad El-Din Mohamed Abdel Moneim Fayed, December 14 2006, page 210

[804] 5 Dec 07: 143.14

[805] 3 Dec 07: 17.12

[806] 3 Dec 07: 17.15

[807] 5 Dec 07: 94.17

[808] The Operation Paget Inquiry Report into the Allegation of Conspiracy to Murder Diana, Princess of Wales and Emad El-Din Mohamed Abdel Moneim Fayed, December 14 2006, page 210

[809] The Operation Paget Inquiry Report into the Allegation of Conspiracy to Murder Diana, Princess of Wales and Emad El-Din Mohamed Abdel Moneim Fayed, December 14 2006, page 211

[810] 5 Dec 07: 93.11

[811] 5 Dec 07: 93.16

[812] The Operation Paget Inquiry Report into the Allegation of Conspiracy to Murder Diana, Princess of Wales and Emad El-Din Mohamed Abdel Moneim Fayed, December 14 2006, page 209

[813] 5 Dec 07: 92.8

[814] 20 Oct 05 Statement read out 6 Dec 07: 33.4

[815] The Operation Paget Inquiry Report into the Allegation of Conspiracy to Murder Diana, Princess of Wales and Emad El-Din Mohamed Abdel Moneim Fayed, December 14 2006, page 201

[816] 5 Dec 07: 144.18

[817] 17 Mar 08: 28.19

[818] 17 Mar 08: 21.19

[819] 5 Dec 07: 142.23

[820] 5 Dec 07: 146.19

[821] 5 Dec 07: 142.10

[822] The Operation Paget Inquiry Report into the Allegation of Conspiracy to Murder Diana, Princess of Wales and Emad El-Din Mohamed Abdel Moneim Fayed, December 14 2006, page 209

[823] The Operation Paget Inquiry Report into the Allegation of Conspiracy to Murder Diana, Princess of Wales and Emad El-Din Mohamed Abdel Moneim Fayed, December 14 2006, pages 244-5

[824] 3 Sep 97 Statement read out 29 Oct 07: 67.17

[825] 3 Dec 07: 18.3

[826] 3 Oct 97 Statement read out 7 Mar 08: 103.14

[827] 4 Dec 07: 73.4

[828] 4 Dec 07: 72.23

[829] 4 Dec 07: 73.4

[830] 4 Dec 07: 90.18
[831] 29 Jan 08: 183.21
[832] 29 Jan 08: 38.5
[833] 29 Jan 08: 183.21
[834] 29 Jan 08: 34.2
[835] 31 Aug 97 statement read out 11 Mar 08: 138.17
[836] The Operation Paget Inquiry Report into the Allegation of Conspiracy to Murder Diana, Princess of Wales and Emad El-Din Mohamed Abdel Moneim Fayed, December 14 2006, page 212
[837] 4 Dec 07: 90.15
[838] 31 Aug 97 statement read out 11 Mar 08: 138.17
[839] 3 Dec 07: 16.1
[840] 4 Dec 07: 90.18
[841] 3 Dec 07: 53.3
[842] The Operation Paget Inquiry Report into the Allegation of Conspiracy to Murder Diana, Princess of Wales and Emad El-Din Mohamed Abdel Moneim Fayed, December 14 2006, page 193
[843] The Operation Paget Inquiry Report into the Allegation of Conspiracy to Murder Diana, Princess of Wales and Emad El-Din Mohamed Abdel Moneim Fayed, December 14 2006, page 193
[844] 4 Dec 07: 69.2
[845] 4 Dec 07: 69.15
[846] 4 Dec 07: 85.13
[847] The Operation Paget Inquiry Report into the Allegation of Conspiracy to Murder Diana, Princess of Wales and Emad El-Din Mohamed Abdel Moneim Fayed, December 14 2006, page 193
[848] The Operation Paget Inquiry Report into the Allegation of Conspiracy to Murder Diana, Princess of Wales and Emad El-Din Mohamed Abdel Moneim Fayed, December 14 2006, page 201
[849] 29 Nov 07: 137.3
[850] 3 Oct 97 Statement read out 7 Mar 08: 99.11
[851] 3 Oct 97 Statement read out 7 Mar 08: 100.5
[852] 3 Oct 97 Statement read out 7 Mar 08: 102.17
[853] 3 Oct 97 Statement read out 7 Mar 08: 103.6
[854] The Operation Paget Inquiry Report into the Allegation of Conspiracy to Murder Diana, Princess of Wales and Emad El-Din Mohamed Abdel Moneim Fayed, December 14 2006, page 206
[855] 4 Dec 07: 60.2
[856] The Operation Paget Inquiry Report into the Allegation of Conspiracy to Murder Diana, Princess of Wales and Emad El-Din Mohamed Abdel Moneim Fayed, December 14 2006, page 195
[857] 26 Nov 07: 118.23
[858] The Operation Paget Inquiry Report into the Allegation of Conspiracy to Murder Diana, Princess of Wales and Emad El-Din Mohamed Abdel Moneim Fayed, December 14 2006, page 201
[859] 5 Dec 07: 140.1

[860] 5 Dec 07: 139.4
[861] 5 Dec 07: 140.4
[862] 5 Dec 07: 140.20
[863] 6 Dec 07: 33.12
[864] 5 Dec 07: 92.10
[865] 7 Mar 08: 90.9
[866] 4 Sep 97 Statement read out 13 Mar 08: 59.23
[867] 29 Nov 07: 166.16
[868] 7 Mar 08: from 90.21
[869] 1 Apr 08: 87.5
[870] 17 Mar 08: 14.19
[871] 17 Mar 08: 23.8
[872] 17 Mar 08: 23.23
[873] The Operation Paget Inquiry Report into the Allegation of Conspiracy to Murder Diana, Princess of Wales and Emad El-Din Mohamed Abdel Moneim Fayed, December 14 2006, page 201
[874] 12 Mar 08: 143.1 and 159.7
[875] The Operation Paget Inquiry Report into the Allegation of Conspiracy to Murder Diana, Princess of Wales and Emad El-Din Mohamed Abdel Moneim Fayed, December 14 2006, page 201
[876] 1 Apr 08: 86.25
[877] 17 Mar 08: 21.19
[878] 5 Dec 07: 139.7
[879] 5 Dec 07: 140.1
[880] 5 Dec 07: 140.20
[881] Christopher Andersen, The Day Diana Died, 1998, page 147
[882] 4 Feb 08: 32.18
[883] Craig Whitney & Youssef Ibrahim, Diana's Driver: Unsettling Piece in the Puzzle, New York Times, September 23 1997
[884] The Operation Paget Inquiry Report into the Allegation of Conspiracy to Murder Diana, Princess of Wales and Emad El-Din Mohamed Abdel Moneim Fayed, December 14 2006, page 203
[885] 31 Jan 08: 145.16
[886] 31 Jan 08: 145.10
[887] 17 Sep 97 statement read out 13 Mar 08: 53.4
[888] 22 Jan 08: 72.3
[889] 17 Sep 97 Statement read out 13 Mar 08: 53.19
[890] 4 Mar 08: 109.8
[891] The Operation Paget Inquiry Report into the Allegation of Conspiracy to Murder Diana, Princess of Wales and Emad El-Din Mohamed Abdel Moneim Fayed, December 14 2006, page 202
[892] 13 Mar 08: 91.1
[893] Inquest Timeline Summary of Key Events

[894] The Operation Paget Inquiry Report into the Allegation of Conspiracy to Murder Diana, Princess of Wales and Emad El-Din Mohamed Abdel Moneim Fayed, December 14 2006, page 200

[895] 13 Mar 08: 91.3

[896] The Operation Paget Inquiry Report into the Allegation of Conspiracy to Murder Diana, Princess of Wales and Emad El-Din Mohamed Abdel Moneim Fayed, December 14 2006, page 207

[897] The Operation Paget Inquiry Report into the Allegation of Conspiracy to Murder Diana, Princess of Wales and Emad El-Din Mohamed Abdel Moneim Fayed, December 14 2006, page 216

[898] The Operation Paget Inquiry Report into the Allegation of Conspiracy to Murder Diana, Princess of Wales and Emad El-Din Mohamed Abdel Moneim Fayed, December 14 2006, page 208

[899] The Operation Paget Inquiry Report into the Allegation of Conspiracy to Murder Diana, Princess of Wales and Emad El-Din Mohamed Abdel Moneim Fayed, December 14 2006, page 208

[900] The Operation Paget Inquiry Report into the Allegation of Conspiracy to Murder Diana, Princess of Wales and Emad El-Din Mohamed Abdel Moneim Fayed, December 14 2006, page 209

[901] 3 Dec 07: 53.19

[902] The Operation Paget Inquiry Report into the Allegation of Conspiracy to Murder Diana, Princess of Wales and Emad El-Din Mohamed Abdel Moneim Fayed, December 14 2006, page 208

[903] 3 Dec 07: 78.17

[904] 3 Dec 07: 52.11

[905] The Operation Paget Inquiry Report into the Allegation of Conspiracy to Murder Diana, Princess of Wales and Emad El-Din Mohamed Abdel Moneim Fayed, December 14 2006, page 215

[906] The Operation Paget Inquiry Report into the Allegation of Conspiracy to Murder Diana, Princess of Wales and Emad El-Din Mohamed Abdel Moneim Fayed, December 14 2006, page 208

[907] 6 Dec 07: 2.19

[908] 1 Apr 08: 43.7

[909] 1 Apr 08: 84.19

[910] The Operation Paget Inquiry Report into the Allegation of Conspiracy to Murder Diana, Princess of Wales and Emad El-Din Mohamed Abdel Moneim Fayed, December 14 2006, page 362

[911] 1 Apr 08: 43.6

[912] 31 Aug 97 Statement read out 11 Mar 08: 77.17

[913] 3 Dec 07: 53.3

[914] Trevor Rees-Jones & Moira Johnston, The Bodyguard's Story: Diana, The Crash and the Sole Survivor, 2000, page 97

[915] 4 Dec 07: 29.13

[916] 4 Dec 07: 29.21

[917] The Operation Paget Inquiry Report into the Allegation of Conspiracy to Murder Diana, Princess of Wales and Emad El-Din Mohamed Abdel Moneim Fayed, December 14 2006, page 209
[918] 31 Aug 97 Statement read out 11 Mar 08: 78.1
[919] The Operation Paget Inquiry Report into the Allegation of Conspiracy to Murder Diana, Princess of Wales and Emad El-Din Mohamed Abdel Moneim Fayed, December 14 2006, page 222
[920] The Operation Paget Inquiry Report into the Allegation of Conspiracy to Murder Diana, Princess of Wales and Emad El-Din Mohamed Abdel Moneim Fayed, December 14 2006, page 222
[921] The Operation Paget Inquiry Report into the Allegation of Conspiracy to Murder Diana, Princess of Wales and Emad El-Din Mohamed Abdel Moneim Fayed, December 14 2006, page 223
[922] 10 Sep 97 Statement read out 4 Dec 07: 10.8
[923] Inquest Timeline Summary of Key Events
[924] 1 Apr 08: 90.21
[925] 1 Apr 08: 91.9
[926] 31 Mar 08: 54.14
[927] 31 Mar 08: 54.10; 1 Apr 08: 91.15; 1 Apr 08: 92.23
[928] 31 Mar 08: 54.10
[929] 23 Jan 08: 95.22; 29 Jan 08: 68.2
[930] 2 Sep 97 Statement read out 29 Jan 08: 57.23
[931] 2 Sep 97 Statement read out 29 Jan 08: 57.25
[932] 2 Sep 97 Statement read out 29 Jan 08: 58.14
[933] 29 Jan 08: 163.3
[934] 3 Jul 98 Statement read out: 29 Jan 08: 206.3
[935] 3 Jul 98 Statement read out: 29 Jan 08: 206.14
[936] The Operation Paget Inquiry Report into the Allegation of Conspiracy to Murder Diana, Princess of Wales and Emad El-Din Mohamed Abdel Moneim Fayed, December 14 2006, page 233
[937] *The Bodyguard's Story* read out 24 Jan 08: 37.21
[938] 29 Jan 08: 124.12
[939] 15 Feb 05 Statement read out 29 Jan 08: 113.22
[940] 15 Feb 05 Statement read out 29 Jan 08: 138.10
[941] 15 Feb 05 Statement read out 29 Jan 08: 112.23
[942] 15 Feb 05 Statement read out 29 Jan 08: 138.2
[943] 29 Jan 08: 109.8
[944] Trevor Rees-Jones & Moira Johnston, The Bodyguard's Story: Diana, The Crash and the Sole Survivor, 2000, pages 200-6
[945] 19 Sep 97 Statement read out 24 Jan 08: 33.11
[946] 19 Sep 97 Statement read out 24 Jan 08: 33.17
[947] 2 Oct 97 Statement read out 23 Jan 08: 79.11
[948] 21 Dec 04 Statement read out 23 Jan 08: 119.6
[949] 21 Dec 04 Statement read out 23 Jan 08: 122.24

[950] 21 Dec 04 Statement read out 23 Jan 08: 124.12
[951] 2 Oct 97 Statement read out 23 Jan 08: 79.14
[952] 21 Dec 04 Statement read out 23 Jan 08: 122.22
[953] 21 Dec 04 Statement read out 23 Jan 08: 124.17
[954] 23 Jan 08: 80.2
[955] 24 Jan 08: 34.10
[956] 23 Jan 08: 127.4
[957] 29 Jan 08: 70.15
[958] 29 Jan 08: 163.3
[959] 14 Feb 08: 110.6
[960] 23 Jan 08: 143.24
[961] The Operation Paget Inquiry Report into the Allegation of Conspiracy to Murder Diana, Princess of Wales and Emad El-Din Mohamed Abdel Moneim Fayed, December 14 2006, page 163
[962] 29 Nov 07: 131.12
[963] 5 Dec 07: 98.3
[964] 3 Dec 07: 31.18
[965] 4 Dec 07: 81.19
[966] 3 Dec 07: 65 19
[967] 4 Dec 07: 63.17
[968] 3 Dec 07: 65.21
[969] The Operation Paget Inquiry Report into the Allegation of Conspiracy to Murder Diana, Princess of Wales and Emad El-Din Mohamed Abdel Moneim Fayed, December 14 2006, page 678
[970] 4 Dec 07: 96.19
[971] 1 Apr 08: 92.16
[972] 1 Apr 08: 99.4
[973] 5 Dec 07: 98.8
[974] The Operation Paget Inquiry Report into the Allegation of Conspiracy to Murder Diana, Princess of Wales and Emad El-Din Mohamed Abdel Moneim Fayed, December 14 2006, page 221
[975] The Operation Paget Inquiry Report into the Allegation of Conspiracy to Murder Diana, Princess of Wales and Emad El-Din Mohamed Abdel Moneim Fayed, December 14 2006, page 346
[976] Craig Whitney & Youssef Ibrahim, Diana's Driver: Unsettling Piece in the Puzzle, New York Times, September 23 1997
[977] 10 Sep 97 Statement read out 3 Dec 07: 74.11
[978] 4 Dec 07: 14.7
[979] 11 Dec 07: 52.12
[980] 11 Dec 07: 103.21
[981] 29 Jan 08: 45.1
[982] Inquest Evidence, INQ0011280, 23 Jan 08
[983] The Operation Paget Inquiry Report into the Allegation of Conspiracy to Murder Diana, Princess of Wales and Emad El-Din Mohamed Abdel Moneim Fayed, December 14 2006, page 220
[984] 29 Jan 08: 45.1

[985] 10 Sep 97 Statement read out 4 Dec 07: 10.8

[986] Trevor Rees-Jones & Moira Johnston, The Bodyguard's Story: Diana, The Crash and the Sole Survivor, 2000, page 203

[987] 29 Jan 08: 45.6

[988] INQ0001693; also viewable in Part 1, section on Bodyguards in Henri Paul Movements chapter.

[989] Trevor Rees-Jones: 23 Jan 08: 78.2:

[990] 29 Jan 08: 45.9

[991] 29 Jan 08: 46.19

[992] April 06 Statement read out 17 Jan 08: 128.1

[993] 23 Jan 08: 85.23

[994] 31 Jan 08: 3.22

[995] Haydn Kelly, Gait Analysis Report, 4 September 2007, pages 12 to 13

[996] 29 Nov 07: 127.16

[997] 4 Dec 07: 75.5

[998] 7 Feb 08: 39.3

[999] 28 Feb 06 Statement read out 11 Mar 08: 144.9

[1000] 6 Oct 97 Statement read out 13 Mar 08: 28.17

[1001] 30 Sep 97 Statement read out 11 Mar 08: 32.4

[1002] 14 Oct 97 Statement read out 12 Mar 08: 39.20

[1003] 17 Oct 97 Statement read out 10 Mar 08: 50.25

[1004] 4 Sep 97 Statement read out 11 Mar 08: 101.19

[1005] 28 Feb 06 Statement read out 11 Mar 08: 144.9

[1006] 4 Sep 97 Statement read out 13 Mar 08: 20.21

[1007] 6 Oct 97 Statement read out 13 Mar 08: 28.17

[1008] 16 Oct 97 Statement read out 29 Oct 07: 103.5

[1009] 30 Sep 97 Statement read out 11 Mar 08: 31.20

[1010] 18 Sep 97 Statement read out 11 Mar 08: 206.13

[1011] 4 Dec 07: 20.17

[1012] 11 Mar 08: 4.17

[1013] 11 Mar 08: 4.17

[1014] 10 Oct 97 Statement read out 10 Mar 08: 122.2

[1015] 31 Aug 97 Statement read out 12 Mar 08: 64.19

[1016] 4 Sep 97 Statement read out 11 Mar 08: 102.15

[1017] 30 Sep 97 Statement read out 11 Mar 08: 33.6

[1018] The Operation Paget Inquiry Report into the Allegation of Conspiracy to Murder Diana, Princess of Wales and Emad El-Din Mohamed Abdel Moneim Fayed, December 14 2006, page 207

[1019] 10 Sep 97 Statement read out 6 Dec 07: 3.5

[1020] 5 Dec 07: 96.24

[1021] 6 Dec 07: 2.11

[1022] The Operation Paget Inquiry Report into the Allegation of Conspiracy to Murder Diana, Princess of Wales and Emad El-Din Mohamed Abdel Moneim Fayed, December 14 2006, page 207

[1023] 29 Jan 08: 58.4

[1024] The Operation Paget Inquiry Report into the Allegation of Conspiracy to Murder Diana, Princess of Wales and Emad El-Din Mohamed Abdel Moneim Fayed, December 14 2006, page 247

[1025] 3 Sep 97 Statement read out 4 Dec 07: 76.25

[1026] 28 Mar 06 Statement read out 4 Dec 07: 97.22

[1027] The Operation Paget Inquiry Report into the Allegation of Conspiracy to Murder Diana, Princess of Wales and Emad El-Din Mohamed Abdel Moneim Fayed, December 14 2006, page 248

[1028] The Operation Paget Inquiry Report into the Allegation of Conspiracy to Murder Diana, Princess of Wales and Emad El-Din Mohamed Abdel Moneim Fayed, December 14 2006, page 248

[1029] 4 Dec 07: 23.18

[1030] The Operation Paget Inquiry Report into the Allegation of Conspiracy to Murder Diana, Princess of Wales and Emad El-Din Mohamed Abdel Moneim Fayed, December 14 2006, page 248

[1031] 4 Dec 07: 60.17

[1032] The Operation Paget Inquiry Report into the Allegation of Conspiracy to Murder Diana, Princess of Wales and Emad El-Din Mohamed Abdel Moneim Fayed, December 14 2006, page 250

[1033] The Operation Paget Inquiry Report into the Allegation of Conspiracy to Murder Diana, Princess of Wales and Emad El-Din Mohamed Abdel Moneim Fayed, December 14 2006, page 250

[1034] The Operation Paget Inquiry Report into the Allegation of Conspiracy to Murder Diana, Princess of Wales and Emad El-Din Mohamed Abdel Moneim Fayed, December 14 2006, page 248

[1035] 1 Apr 08: 93.18

[1036] The Operation Paget Inquiry Report into the Allegation of Conspiracy to Murder Diana, Princess of Wales and Emad El-Din Mohamed Abdel Moneim Fayed, December 14 2006, page 250

[1037] The Operation Paget Inquiry Report into the Allegation of Conspiracy to Murder Diana, Princess of Wales and Emad El-Din Mohamed Abdel Moneim Fayed, December 14 2006, page 249

[1038] 4 Dec 07: 21.7; 18 Mar 08: 38.15

[1039] 5 Dec 07: 98.11

[1040] 4 Dec 07: 84.13

[1041] 3 Dec 07: 24.13

[1042] 23 Jan 08: 70.21

[1043] The Operation Paget Inquiry Report into the Allegation of Conspiracy to Murder Diana, Princess of Wales and Emad El-Din Mohamed Abdel Moneim Fayed, December 14 2006, page 193

[1044] The Operation Paget Inquiry Report into the Allegation of Conspiracy to Murder Diana, Princess of Wales and Emad El-Din Mohamed Abdel Moneim Fayed, December 14 2006, page 254

[1045] 18 Mar 08: 41.1

[1046] 18 Mar 08: 40.22

[1047] 4 Sep 97 Statement read out 10 Mar 08: 26.3

[1048] 4 Oct 07: 58.4

[1049] The Operation Paget Inquiry Report into the Allegation of Conspiracy to Murder Diana, Princess of Wales and Emad El-Din Mohamed Abdel Moneim Fayed, December 14 2006, page 254

[1050] 29 Apr 98 Statement read out 10 Mar 08: 156.19

[1051] 17 Oct 97 Statement read out 10 Mar 08: 48.12

[1052] 18 Mar 08: 39.19

[1053] 18 Mar 08: 41.11

[1054] 18 Mar 08: 46.5, 46.24

[1055] 11 Mar 08: from 5.15

[1056] 3 Sep 97 Statement read out 10 Mar 08: 145.16

[1057] 3 Sep 97 Statement read out 10 Mar 08: 148.7

[1058] 3 Sep 97 Statement read out 10 Mar 08: 146.19

[1059] 12 Mar 08: 16.13

[1060] 3 Sep 97 Statement read out 10 Mar 08: 146.24

[1061] 12 Mar 08: 17.22

[1062] 3 Sep 97 Statement read out 10 Mar 08: 146.4

[1063] 3 Sep 97 Statement read out 10 Mar 08: from145.4

[1064] 3 Sep 97 Statement read out 10 Mar 08: from146.9

[1065] 10 Oct 97 Statement read out 10 Mar 08: 122.24

[1066] The Facts, Diana Conspiracy, page 5, www.dianaconspiracy.com/index.html and The Upcoming Witness Summit: Who's Real and Who's Fake, www.wethepeople.la/witness.htm

[1067] 17 Oct 97 Statement read out 10 Mar 08: 52.18

[1068] 31 Aug 97 Statement read out 11 Mar 08: 14.2

[1069] 1 Sep 97 Statement read out 11 Mar 08: 20.20

[1070] 1 Sep 97 Letter to French police read out 1 Nov 07: 42.18

[1071] 24 Sep 97 Statement read out 1 Nov 07: 46.18

[1072] Undated Anthony Scrivener QC Interview read out 1 Nov 07: 59.12

[1073] 11 Oct 07: 57.13

[1074] 1 Nov 07: 51.4

[1075] 1 Nov 07: 42.21

[1076] 23 Jan 08: 46.9

[1077] 23 Jan 08: 46.12

[1078] 24 Sep 97 Statement read out 1 Nov 07: 46.17

[1079] 27 April 98 Statement read out 1 Nov 07: 53.24

[1080] 29 Oct 07: 110.22

[1081] 29 Oct 07: 111.6

[1082] 1 Nov 07: 41.7

[1083] 24 Sep 97 Statement read out 1 Nov 07: 47.4

[1084] 24 Sep 97 Statement read out 1 Nov 07: 47.24

[1085] 10 Oct 07: 7.24

[1086] 29 Oct 07: 111.4

[1087] 1 Sep 97 Statement read out 11 Mar 08: 20.8
[1088] The Operation Paget Inquiry Report into the Allegation of Conspiracy to Murder Diana, Princess of Wales and Emad El-Din Mohamed Abdel Moneim Fayed, December 14 2006, page 436
[1089] 11 Oct 07: 6.9
[1090] The Operation Paget Inquiry Report into the Allegation of Conspiracy to Murder Diana, Princess of Wales and Emad El-Din Mohamed Abdel Moneim Fayed, December 14 2006, page 436
[1091] The Operation Paget Inquiry Report into the Allegation of Conspiracy to Murder Diana, Princess of Wales and Emad El-Din Mohamed Abdel Moneim Fayed, December 14 2006, page 437
[1092] The Operation Paget Inquiry Report into the Allegation of Conspiracy to Murder Diana, Princess of Wales and Emad El-Din Mohamed Abdel Moneim Fayed, December 14 2006, page 437
[1093] The Operation Paget Inquiry Report into the Allegation of Conspiracy to Murder Diana, Princess of Wales and Emad El-Din Mohamed Abdel Moneim Fayed, December 14 2006, page 437
[1094] The Operation Paget Inquiry Report into the Allegation of Conspiracy to Murder Diana, Princess of Wales and Emad El-Din Mohamed Abdel Moneim Fayed, December 14 2006, page 436
[1095] The Operation Paget Inquiry Report into the Allegation of Conspiracy to Murder Diana, Princess of Wales and Emad El-Din Mohamed Abdel Moneim Fayed, December 14 2006, page 437
[1096] The Operation Paget Inquiry Report into the Allegation of Conspiracy to Murder Diana, Princess of Wales and Emad El-Din Mohamed Abdel Moneim Fayed, December 14 2006, page 436
[1097] The Operation Paget Inquiry Report into the Allegation of Conspiracy to Murder Diana, Princess of Wales and Emad El-Din Mohamed Abdel Moneim Fayed, December 14 2006, page 437
[1098] 31 Aug 97 Statement read out 12 Mar 08: 124.4
[1099] 1 Sep 97 Statement read out 15 Oct 07: 106.21
[1100] Trevor Rees-Jones & Moira Johnston, The Bodyguard's Story, 2000, page 114
[1101] 29 Nov 07: 170.15
[1102] The Operation Paget Inquiry Report into the Allegation of Conspiracy to Murder Diana, Princess of Wales and Emad El-Din Mohamed Abdel Moneim Fayed, December 14 2006, page 455
[1103] 24 Oct 07: 8.6
[1104] The Operation Paget Inquiry Report into the Allegation of Conspiracy to Murder Diana, Princess of Wales and Emad El-Din Mohamed Abdel Moneim Fayed, December 14 2006, page 439
[1105] 17 Oct 07: 99.3
[1106] 17 Oct 07: 100.15
[1107] 24 Oct 07: 23.13
[1108] 24 Oct 07: 26.1
[1109] 24 Oct 07: 14.8
[1110] 24 Oct 07: 14.15

[1111] 24 Oct 07: 26.1

[1112] The Operation Paget Inquiry Report into the Allegation of Conspiracy to Murder Diana, Princess of Wales and Emad El-Din Mohamed Abdel Moneim Fayed, December 14 2006, page 450

[1113] 1 Apr 08: 121.16

[1114] 1 Apr 08: 122.10

[1115] 24 Oct 07: 23.7

[1116] 1 Apr 08: 122.18

[1117] 1 Apr 08: 122.17

[1118] 1 Apr 08: 122.20

[1119] 31 Aug 97, 2.30 a.m. Statement read out 12 Mar 08: 77.20

[1120] 12 Sep 97 Statement read out 12 Mar 08: 93.23

[1121] 31 Aug 1997 2.30 a.m. Statement read out 12 Mar 08: 79.18

[1122] 31 Aug 1997 6.00 a.m. Statement read out 12 Mar 08: 83.1

[1123] Inquest Evidence, INQ0002350, 17 Oct 07

[1124] 24 Oct 07: from 43.24

[1125] 1 Apr 08: 35.14

[1126] 1 Nov 07 43.8

[1127] 1 Nov 07 43.8

[1128] 7 Nov 07: 4.22

[1129] 7 Nov 07: 103.22

[1130] 11 Mar 08: 57.20

[1131] 11 Mar 08: 57.5

[1132] 11 Mar 08: 57.9

[1133] Rat: 31 Aug 97 Statement read out 11 Mar 08: 14.6; Darmon: 29 Oct 07: 112.7

[1134] 5 Feb 08: 45.5

[1135] 5 Feb 08: 45.8

[1136] 5 Feb 08: 47.13

[1137] 2 Apr 08: 35.13

[1138] 1 Apr 08: 99.5

[1139] 2 Apr 08: 33.1

[1140] 2 Apr 08: 35.9

[1141] 1 Apr 08: 37.7

[1142] John Twomey, Soldier's claim SAS hit squad 'did kill Princess Diana' is 'utterly convincing', Daily Express, 5 September 2013

[1143] Princess Diana: Ex-wife of soldier who claimed SAS murdered royal now in hiding, Sunday Mirror, 13 October 2013

[1144] Princess Diana: Ex-wife of soldier who claimed SAS murdered royal now in hiding, Sunday Mirror, 13 October 2013

[1145] Stephen Dorril, MI6: Fifty Years of Special Operations, 2001, page 639

[1146] Richard Norton-Taylor, In Defence of the Realm?: The Case For Accountable Security Services, 1990, pp64, 91-2

[1147] Jonathan Bloch & Patrick Fitzgerald, British Intelligence and Covert Action, 1983, pp40,44-5

[1148] Richard Norton-Taylor, In Defence of the Realm?: The Case For Accountable Security Services, 1990, p64

[1149] 12 May 99 Affidavit by Richard Tomlinson to Judge Hervé Stephan

[1150] 12 May 99 Affidavit by Richard Tomlinson to Judge Hervé Stephan

[1151] 13 Feb 08: 52.12

[1152] Richard Tomlinson, The Big Breach, 2001, page 74

[1153] 20 Feb 08: 116.11

[1154] 20 Feb 08: 120.15

[1155] 20 Feb 08: 124.24

[1156] 20 Feb 08: 125.4

[1157] 20 Feb 08: 116.11

[1158] 20 Feb 08: 120.15

[1159] 20 Feb 08: 124.24

[1160] 20 Feb 08: 116.16

[1161] 20 Feb 08: 125.19

[1162] 20 Feb 08: 127.2

[1163] 20 Feb 08: 116.19

[1164] 20 Feb 08: 117.1

[1165] 20 Feb 08: 125.23

[1166] 20 Feb 08: 120.19

[1167] 20 Feb 08: 120.15

[1168] 20 Feb 08: 126.2

[1169] 20 Feb 08: 121.17

[1170] 20 Feb 08: 127.2

[1171] 24 Oct 07: 23.7

[1172] 24 Oct 07: 25.9

[1173] The Operation Paget Inquiry Report into the Allegation of Conspiracy to Murder Diana, Princess of Wales and Emad El-Din Mohamed Abdel Moneim Fayed, December 14 2006, page 483

[1174] 31 Aug 1997 6.00 a.m. Statement read out 12 Mar 08: 81.25

[1175] 2 Apr 08: 23.21

[1176] 17 Oct 07: 97.13

[1177] 14/15 Sep 97 ABC News Interview read out 17 Oct 07: 131.1

[1178] The Operation Paget Inquiry Report into the Allegation of Conspiracy to Murder Diana, Princess of Wales and Emad El-Din Mohamed Abdel Moneim Fayed, December 14 2006, page 439

[1179] 1 Apr 08: 116.9

[1180] The Operation Paget Inquiry Report into the Allegation of Conspiracy to Murder Diana, Princess of Wales and Emad El-Din Mohamed Abdel Moneim Fayed, December 14 2006, page 455

[1181] 14 Oct 97 Statement read out 11 Oct 07: 23.10

[1182] 24 Oct 97 Statement: read out 11 Oct 07: 27.6

[1183] Alexander Hitchen, I Saw Fiat Driver Kill Di, The People, January 18 2004

[1184] Thomas Sancton and Scott MacLeod, Death of a Princess: An Investigation, 1998, page 186

[1185] 24 Oct 07: 47.1

[1186] The Operation Paget Inquiry Report into the Allegation of Conspiracy to Murder Diana, Princess of Wales and Emad El-Din Mohamed Abdel Moneim Fayed, December 14 2006, page 455

[1187] The Operation Paget Inquiry Report into the Allegation of Conspiracy to Murder Diana, Princess of Wales and Emad El-Din Mohamed Abdel Moneim Fayed, December 14 2006, page 452

[1188] 6 Nov 07: 73.22

[1189] ITV Documentary, Diana – The Secrets Behind the Crash, June 3 1998, Transcript

[1190] 13 Feb 08: 52.3

[1191] 20 Feb 08: 121.22

[1192] 26 Feb 08: 72.2

[1193] 26 Feb 08: 172.11

[1194] 26 Feb 08: 195.25

[1195] 20 Feb 08: 121.22

[1196] 20 Feb 08: 121.25

[1197] 20 Feb 08: 122.3

[1198] 20 Feb 08: 122.4

[1199] 20 Feb 08: 122.19

[1200] 20 Feb 08: 122.6

[1201] 20 Feb 08: 122.2

[1202] 20 Feb 08: 122.15

[1203] 26 Feb 08: 70.21

[1204] 26 Feb 08: 71.4

[1205] 26 Feb 08: 71.15

[1206] 26 Feb 08: 172.11

[1207] 26 Feb 08: 171.22

[1208] 26 Feb 08: 195.20

[1209] Richard Tomlinson, 12 May 99 Affidavit to the French Investigation

[1210] SAS Website: www.sasequip.com – this website has been removed from the internet: see footnote.

[1211] Wikipedia, Strobe Light, History

[1212] Lord Justice Scott Baker, Ruling on Verdicts, After 20 Mar 08, p10

[1213] 31 Mar 08: 40.16, 52.8, 63.19, 63.24; 1 Apr 08: 118.11; 2 Apr 08: 32.1

[1214] Princess Diana: Ex-wife of soldier who claimed SAS murdered royal now in hiding, Sunday Mirror, 13 October 2013

[1215] 11 Jun 98 CBS Interview read out 23 Oct 07: 84.24

[1216] The Operation Paget Inquiry Report into the Allegation of Conspiracy to Murder Diana, Princess of Wales and Emad El-Din Mohamed Abdel Moneim Fayed, December 14 2006, page 453

[1217] The Operation Paget Inquiry Report into the Allegation of Conspiracy to Murder Diana, Princess of Wales and Emad El-Din Mohamed Abdel Moneim Fayed, December 14 2006, page 455

[1218] Thomas Sancton and Scott MacLeod, Death of a Princess: An Investigation, 1998, page 186

[1219] Thomas Sancton and Scott MacLeod, Death of a Princess: An Investigation, 1998, page 186

[1220] The Operation Paget Inquiry Report into the Allegation of Conspiracy to Murder Diana, Princess of Wales and Emad El-Din Mohamed Abdel Moneim Fayed, December 14 2006, page 475

[1221] 23 Sep 97 Statement read out 22 Oct 07: 24.15

[1222] 23 Sep 97 Statement read out 22 Oct 07: 31.1

[1223] 22 Oct 07: 106.9

[1224] 27 Apr 98 Statement read out 1 Nov 07: 52.2

[1225] 23 Sep 97 Statement read out 11 Oct 07: 132.14

[1226] 29 Oct 07: from 120.20

[1227] 11 Oct 07: 136.15

[1228] 22 Oct 07: 49.7

[1229] 22 Oct 07: 51.23

[1230] 22 Oct 07: 64.6

[1231] 22 Oct 07: 50.16

[1232] 22 Oct 07: 44.16

[1233] 22 Oct 07: 51.8

[1234] 22 Oct 07: 54.13

[1235] 24 Oct 07: 43.24

[1236] 24 Oct 07: 45.16

[1237] 24 Oct 07: 44.24

[1238] The Diana Forum, page 8, www.wethepeople.la/diforum2.htm recording of Brian Anderson interview June 11 1998

[1239] Eye-witness Reports, Public Interest, www.public-interest.co.uk/diana/dianaewa.htm and Princess Diana Dead After Paris Car Crash, CNN, www.public-interest.co.uk/diana/dipress.htm

[1240] Eye-witness Reports, Public Interest, www.public-interest.co.uk/diana/dianaewa.htm and Princess Diana Dead After Paris Car Crash, CNN, www.public-interest.co.uk/diana/dipress.htm

[1241] 22 Oct 07: 72.16

[1242] The Operation Paget Inquiry Report into the Allegation of Conspiracy to Murder Diana, Princess of Wales and Emad El-Din Mohamed Abdel Moneim Fayed, December 14 2006, page 450

[1243] The Operation Paget Inquiry Report into the Allegation of Conspiracy to Murder Diana, Princess of Wales and Emad El-Din Mohamed Abdel Moneim Fayed, December 14 2006, page 450

[1244] 21 Nov 07: 85.7

[1245] 1 Sep 97 Statement read out 22 Oct 07: 25.18

[1246] The Operation Paget Inquiry Report into the Allegation of Conspiracy to Murder Diana, Princess of Wales and Emad El-Din Mohamed Abdel Moneim Fayed, December 14 2006, page 473

[1247] Thomas Sancton and Scott MacLeod, Death of a Princess: An Investigation, 1998, page 186

[1248] 24 Oct 07: 84.19

[1249] The Operation Paget Inquiry Report into the Allegation of Conspiracy to Murder Diana, Princess of Wales and Emad El-Din Mohamed Abdel Moneim Fayed, December 14 2006, page 455

[1250] 11 Mar 08: 74.23

[1251] 22 Oct 97 Statement read out 17 Oct 07: 24.9

[1252] Thomas Sancton and Scott MacLeod, Death of a Princess: An Investigation, 1998, pages 226-7

[1253] The Operation Paget Inquiry Report into the Allegation of Conspiracy to Murder Diana, Princess of Wales and Emad El-Din Mohamed Abdel Moneim Fayed, December 14 2006, page 502

[1254] The Operation Paget Inquiry Report into the Allegation of Conspiracy to Murder Diana, Princess of Wales and Emad El-Din Mohamed Abdel Moneim Fayed, December 14 2006, page 495

[1255] 6 Nov 07: 80.8

[1256] Alexander Hitchen, I Saw Fiat Driver Kill Di, The People, January 18 2004

[1257] The Operation Paget Inquiry Report into the Allegation of Conspiracy to Murder Diana, Princess of Wales and Emad El-Din Mohamed Abdel Moneim Fayed, December 14 2006, page 486

[1258] Thomas Sancton and Scott MacLeod, Death of a Princess: An Investigation, 1998, page 241

[1259] Fiat Uno Witnesses, Hello magazine, January 17 1998, www.public-interest.co.uk/diana/dianafuwit.htm

[1260] The Operation Paget Inquiry Report into the Allegation of Conspiracy to Murder Diana, Princess of Wales and Emad El-Din Mohamed Abdel Moneim Fayed, December 14 2006, page 477

[1261] 1 Apr 08: 32.25

[1262] Alastair Campbell, The Blair Years: The Alastair Campbell Diaries, 2007, page 232

[1263] 1 Sep 97 Statement read out 11 Mar 08: 22.18

[1264] 31 Aug 97 Statement read out 10 Mar 08: 106.21

[1265] 4 Sep 97 Statement read out 11 Mar 08: 109.5

[1266] 26 Sep 97 Statement read out 28 Nov 07: 51.3

[1267] 31 Aug 97 Statement read out 28 Nov 07: 43.9

[1268] 19 Nov 07: 77.4

[1269] 6 Mar 98 Statement read out: 23 Jan 08: 46.22

[1270] 16 Jun 98 Statement read out 12 Nov 07: 96.14

[1271] 29 Sep 97 Statement read out 12 Nov 07: 104.7

[1272] 25 Oct 07: 77.7

[1273] 26 Sep 97 Statement read out 28 Nov 07: 51.3

[1274] 28 Nov 07: 11.19

[1275] Diana Was Unconscious, Moaning at Crash Scene, Reuters, http://www.public-interest.co.uk/diana/dianadiunc.htm

[1276] 13 Nov 07: 23.5

[1277] Christopher Andersen, The Day Diana Died, 1998, pages 206-7

[1278] 13 Nov 07: 23.1

[1279] 2 Apr 08: 40.19

[1280] Christopher Andersen, The Day Diana Died, 1998, pages 206-7

[1281] 13 Nov 07: 15.22

[1282] Master Chronology of Events Surrounding the Crash, www.wethepeople.la/chron.htm and The Upcoming Witness Summit: Who's Real and Who's Fake, www.wethepeople.la/witness.htm

[1283] 13 Nov 07: 12.23

[1284] The Operation Paget Inquiry Report into the Allegation of Conspiracy to Murder Diana, Princess of Wales and Emad El-Din Mohamed Abdel Moneim Fayed, December 14 2006, page 512

[1285] Thomas Sancton and Scott MacLeod, Death of a Princess: An Investigation, 1998, page 16

[1286] Thomas Sancton and Scott MacLeod, Death of a Princess: An Investigation, 1998, pages 16-17

[1287] Master Chronology of Events Surrounding the Crash, www.wethepeople.la/chron.htm

[1288] Master Chronology of Events Surrounding the Crash, www.wethepeople.la/chron.htm

[1289] Thomas Sancton and Scott MacLeod, Death of a Princess: An Investigation, 1998, page 17

[1290] Peter Hounam & Derek McAdam, Who Killed Diana?, 1999, page 140

[1291] Andrew Pierce, Diana Was Not Pregnant, Says Mortuary Manager, The Times, 19 August 2006

[1292] 13 Nov 07: 25. 3

[1293] 13 Nov 07: 25. 10

[1294] 31 Aug 1997 6.00 a.m. Statement read out 12 Mar 08: 85.3

[1295] Thomas Sancton and Scott MacLeod, Death of a Princess: An Investigation, 1998, page 17

[1296] Thomas Sancton and Scott MacLeod, Death of a Princess: An Investigation, 1998, page 17

[1297] 13 Nov 07: 29.11

[1298] 13 Nov 07: 41.20

[1299] The Operation Paget Inquiry Report into the Allegation of Conspiracy to Murder Diana, Princess of Wales and Emad El-Din Mohamed Abdel Moneim Fayed, December 14 2006, page 590

[1300] 13 Nov 07: 71.13

[1301] Christopher Andersen, The Day Diana Died, 1998, page 203

[1302] 13 Nov 07: 71.9

[1303] 28 Nov 07: 12.17

[1304] 28 Nov 07: 13.1

[1305] 13 Nov 07: 71.2

[1306] 13 Nov 07: 23.18

[1307] The Operation Paget Inquiry Report into the Allegation of Conspiracy to Murder Diana, Princess of Wales and Emad El-Din Mohamed Abdel Moneim Fayed, December 14 2006, page 512

[1308] Diana Was Unconscious, Moaning at Crash Scene, Reuters, http://www.public-interest.co.uk/diana/dianadiunc.htm

[1309] Diana Was Unconscious, Moaning at Crash Scene, Reuters, http://www.public-interest.co.uk/diana/dianadiunc.htm

[1310] Christopher Andersen, The Day Diana Died, 1998, page 205

[1311] Christopher Andersen, The Day Diana Died, 1998, page 207

[1312] Larry King Live, CNN, 28 May 04

[1313] 13 Nov 07: 16.14

[1314] Larry King Live, CNN, 28 May 04

[1315] 13 Nov 07: 12.13

[1316] Tim Luckhurst & Tanya Thompson, The Delay That Cost Diana Her Life, The Scotsman, September 29 1997 and The Upcoming Witness Summit: Who's Real and Who's Fake, www.wethepeople.la/witness.htm

[1317] 31 Aug 97 10.30 a.m. Statement read out 10 Mar 08: 106.6

[1318] Christopher Andersen, The Day Diana Died, 1998, page 205

[1319] 16 Jun 98 Statement read out 12 Nov 07: 97.12

[1320] 16 Jun 98 Statement read out 12 Nov 07: 97.16

[1321] 13 Nov 07: 14.6

[1322] The Operation Paget Inquiry Report into the Allegation of Conspiracy to Murder Diana, Princess of Wales and Emad El-Din Mohamed Abdel Moneim Fayed, December 14 2006, page 512

[1323] 13 Nov 07: 6.5

[1324] 13 Nov 07: 6.15

[1325] 13 Nov 07: 19.19

[1326] 13 Nov 07: 6.22

[1327] 13 Nov 07: 7.2

[1328] 13 Nov 07: 4.22

[1329] 28 Nov 07: 11.19

[1330] 28 Nov 07: 19.25

[1331] 13 Nov 07: 52.24

[1332] 28 Nov 07: 19.6

[1333] Christopher Andersen, The Day Diana Died, 1998, page 207

[1334] Tim Luckhurst & Tanya Thompson, The Delay That Cost Diana Her Life, The Scotsman, September 29 1997

[1335] 13 Nov 07: 52.11

[1336] 13 Nov 07: 53.5

[1337] 14 Nov 07: 8.25

[1338] 14 Nov 07: 9.13

[1339] 14 Nov 07: 14.9

[1340] The Operation Paget Inquiry Report into the Allegation of Conspiracy to Murder Diana, Princess of Wales and Emad El-Din Mohamed Abdel Moneim Fayed, December 14 2006, page 513

[1341] 14 Nov 07: 8.22

[1342] 14 Nov 07: 8.13

[1343] Christopher Andersen, The Day Diana Died, 1998, pages 206-7

[1344] 14 Nov 07: 7.2

[1345] 14 Nov 07: 9.24

[1346] 26 Sep 97 Statement read out 28 Nov 07: 51.3

[1347] 2 Apr 08: 40.20

[1348] 13 Nov 07: 49.21

[1349] 14 Nov 07: 9.21

[1350] 13 Nov 07: 48.22

[1351] 13 Nov 07: 59.10

[1352] 13 Nov 07: 62.25

[1353] 13 Nov 07: 57.17

[1354] 13 Nov 07: 22.4

[1355] 13 Nov 07: 49.15

[1356] 13 Nov 07: 53.15

[1357] 14 Nov 07: 9.19

[1358] 26 Sep 97 Statement read out 28 Nov 07: 51.3

[1359] 11 Dec 07: 6.10

[1360] 13 Nov 07: from 68.12. This transcript is also in Part 2, section on Journey to the Crash Scene in Chapter 9B

[1361] 12 Mar 98 Statement read out 14 Nov 07: 21.3

[1362] 24 Jan 08: 115.8

[1363] INQ0004774

[1364] 29 Nov 07: 34.7

[1365] 11 Dec 07: 6.10

[1366] 13 Nov 07: 69.22

[1367] 24 Jan 08: 115.8

[1368] 12 Mar 98 Statement read out 14 Nov 07: 21.14

[1369] E.g. Francois Levistre: 15 Oct 07: 82.14

[1370] 24 Jan 08: 111.18

[1371] 24 Jan 08: 109.13

[1372] 19 Nov 07: 9.10

[1373] 24 Jan 08: 117.22

[1374] 19 Nov 07: 6.2

[1375] 19 Nov 07: 5.11

[1376] 19 Nov 07: 5.17

[1377] 19 Nov 07: 22.10

[1378] Tim Luckhurst & Tanya Thompson, The Delay That Cost Diana Her Life, The Scotsman, September 29 1997

[1379] 13 Nov 07: 44.10

[1380] 19 Nov 07: 9.21

[1381] INQ0004774. Also viewable in Part 2, Communication Blackout section of Chapter 9C

[1382] 19 Nov 07: 89.23

[1383] 15 Nov 07: 32.22

[1384] 24 Jan 08: 116.14

[1385] 11 Dec 07: 7.8

[1386] 11 Dec 07: 7.13

[1387] 13 Nov 07: 59.10

[1388] The Operation Paget Inquiry Report into the Allegation of Conspiracy to Murder Diana, Princess of Wales and Emad El-Din Mohamed Abdel Moneim Fayed, December 14 2006, page 513

[1389] The Operation Paget Inquiry Report into the Allegation of Conspiracy to Murder Diana, Princess of Wales and Emad El-Din Mohamed Abdel Moneim Fayed, December 14 2006, page 513

[1390] 24 Jan 08: 117.1

[1391] 11 Dec 07: 8.8

[1392] 29 Nov 07: 9.14

[1393] 29 Nov 07: 40.21

[1394] 11 Dec 07: 8.8

[1395] 11 Dec 07: 8.8

[1396] 21 Nov 07: 10.17

[1397] 9 Jan 08: 83.19

[1398] 24 Sep 04 Statement read out 3 Mar 08: 92.12

[1399] Dickie Arbiter, On Duty with the Queen, 2014, p184

[1400] 26 Nov 07: 76.13

[1401] 5 Dec 07: 168.10

[1402] 18 Dec 07: 40.6

[1403] 10 Jan 08: 29.25

[1404] 26 Nov 07, 23.3

[1405] 23 Jan 08: 152.15

[1406] The Operation Paget Inquiry Report into the Allegation of Conspiracy to Murder Diana, Princess of Wales and Emad El-Din Mohamed Abdel Moneim Fayed, December 14 2006, page 421

[1407] The Operation Paget Inquiry Report into the Allegation of Conspiracy to Murder Diana, Princess of Wales and Emad El-Din Mohamed Abdel Moneim Fayed, December 14 2006, page 421

[1408] 13 Nov 07: 54.5

[1409] 14 Nov 07: 8.3

[1410] The Operation Paget Inquiry Report into the Allegation of Conspiracy to Murder Diana, Princess of Wales and Emad El-Din Mohamed Abdel Moneim Fayed, December 14 2006, page 421

[1411] The Operation Paget Inquiry Report into the Allegation of Conspiracy to Murder Diana, Princess of Wales and Emad El-Din Mohamed Abdel Moneim Fayed, December 14 2006, page 421

[1412] 7 Nov 07: 99.12

[1413] 27 Nov 07: 81.7

[1414] 4 Feb 08: 9.24

[1415] 10 Oct 97 Statement read out 10 Mar 08: 128.4

[1416] 14 Nov 06 Statement read out 21 Nov 07: 56.5

[1417] 14 Nov 06 Statement read out 21 Nov 07: 56.5

[1418] The Operation Paget Inquiry Report into the Allegation of Conspiracy to Murder Diana, Princess of Wales and Emad El-Din Mohamed Abdel Moneim Fayed, December 14 2006, page 572

[1419] Abdelatif Redjil: 12 Nov 07: 97.12.

[1420] 31 Aug 97 Statement description read out 12 Nov 07: 121.6

[1421] 13 Nov 07: 58.4

[1422] 20 Nov 07: 9.7

[1423] 20 Nov 07: 8.15

[1424] 21 Nov 07: 58.17

[1425] Michael Jay, Witness Statement, 13 December 2005, reproduced in Diana Inquest: The Documents the Jury Never Saw, 2010, pp631-3 (UK Edition)

[1426] Keith Moss, Witness Statement, 22 October 2004, reproduced in Diana Inquest: The Documents the Jury Never Saw, 2010, pp648-9 (UK Edition)

[1427] Keith Moss, Witness Statement, 22 October 2004, reproduced in Diana Inquest: The Documents the Jury Never Saw, 2010, pp648-9 (UK Edition)

[1428] Tony Blair, A Journey: My Political Life, 2010, pp138-141

[1429] 22 Nov 07: 10.20

[1430] 22 Nov 07: 10.19

[1431] 22 Nov 07: 10.19

[1432] 22 Nov 07: 11.7

[1433] 14 Nov 06 Statement read out 21 Nov 07: 58.17

[1434] 20 Nov 07: 8.5

[1435] 20 Nov 07: 6.12

[1436] 20 Nov 07: 9.22

[1437] 16 Nov 06 Statement read out 21 Nov 07: 52.6

[1438] 14 Nov 06 Statement read out 21 Nov 07: 57.15

[1439] Martine Monteil, Witness Statement, 15 November 2006, reproduced in Diana Inquest: The Documents the Jury Never Saw, 2010, p56 (UK Edition)

[1440] 5 Feb 08: 63.16

[1441] 13 Dec 07: 39.6

[1442] 6 Nov 07: 10.23

[1443] 6 Nov 07: 27.22

[1444] The Operation Paget Inquiry Report into the Allegation of Conspiracy to Murder Diana, Princess of Wales and Emad El-Din Mohamed Abdel Moneim Fayed, December 14 2006, page 573

[1445] The Operation Paget Inquiry Report into the Allegation of Conspiracy to Murder Diana, Princess of Wales and Emad El-Din Mohamed Abdel Moneim Fayed, December 14 2006, pages 571-2

[1446] 20 Nov 07: 12.4

[1447] 20 Nov 07: 12.11

[1448] 20 Nov 07: 12.19

[1449] 16 Nov 06 Statement read out 21 Nov 07: 51.18

[1450] 6 Nov 07: 28.11

[1451] 5 Feb 08: 62.25

[1452] 20 Nov 07: 45.21

[1453] 20 Nov 07: 46.5

[1454] 6 Nov 07: 27.22

[1455] 16 Nov 06 Statement read out 21 Nov 07: 51.18

[1456] 20 Nov 07: 12.2

[1457] 20 Nov 07: 57.5

[1458] 20 Nov 07: 12.5

[1459] 20 Nov 07: 11.6 and 45.14

[1460] Martine Monteil, Witness Statement, 15 November 2006, reproduced in Diana Inquest: The Documents the Jury Never Saw, 2010, p56 (UK Edition)

[1461] 16 Nov 06 Statement read out 21 Nov 07: 51.18

[1462] 20 Nov 07: 11.6

[1463] 20 Nov 07: 11.6

[1464] 20 Nov 07: 11.8

[1465] 20 Nov 07: 12.21

[1466] Martine Monteil, Witness Statement, 15 November 2006, reproduced in Diana Inquest: The Documents the Jury Never Saw, 2010, p56 (UK Edition)

[1467] 20 Nov 07: 11.12

[1468] 20 Nov 07: 45.21

[1469] 20 Nov 07: 46.4

[1470] Martine Monteil, Witness Statement, 15 November 2006, reproduced in Diana Inquest: The Documents the Jury Never Saw, 2010, p55 (UK Edition)

[1471] 6 Nov 07: 10.23

[1472] The Operation Paget Inquiry Report into the Allegation of Conspiracy to Murder Diana, Princess of Wales and Emad El-Din Mohamed Abdel Moneim Fayed, December 14 2006, page 572

[1473] 24 Jan 08: 121.14

[1474] 13 Nov 07: 44.7

[1475] 12 Mar 98 Statement read out 14 Nov 07: 22.6

[1476] 14 Nov 07: 14.24

[1477] 12 Mar 98 Statement read out 24 Jan 08: 137.13

[1478] 11 Dec 07: 16.1

[1479] 19 Nov 07: 133.21

[1480] 19 Nov 07: 91.11

[1481] 19 Nov 07: 134.23

[1482] 19 Nov 07: 134.23

[1483] 19 Nov 07: 10.15

[1484] 19 Nov 07: 10.17

[1485] 24 Jan 08: 123.11

[1486] 13 Nov 07: 54.22

[1487] 14 Nov 07: 11.16

[1488] 11 Dec 07: 16.1

[1489] 24 Jan 08: 123.11

[1490] 19 Nov 07: 10.13

[1491] 24 Jan 08: 123.25

[1492] The Operation Paget Inquiry Report into the Allegation of Conspiracy to Murder Diana, Princess of Wales and Emad El-Din Mohamed Abdel Moneim Fayed, December 14 2006, page 514

[1493] 15 Nov 07: 90.15

[1494] 24 Jan 08: 123.25

[1495] 24 Jan 08: 143.5

[1496] 12 Mar 98 Statement read out 24 Jan 08: 137.13

[1497] 24 Jan 08: 143.9

[1498] 11 Dec 07: 31.24

[1499] 11 Dec 07: 32.17

[1500] 11 Dec 07: 33.1

[1501] 12 Mar 98 Statement read out 14 Nov 07: 22.9

[1502] 15 Nov 07: 4.22

[1503] 19 Nov 07: 131.15

[1504] 14 Nov 07: 14.14

[1505] 24 Jan 08: 122.10

[1506] 19 Nov 07: 7.5

[1507] 19 Nov 07: 22.15

[1508] 11 Dec 07: 32.8

[1509] 19 Nov 07: 130.5

[1510] 19 Nov 07: 129.4

[1511] 29 Nov 07: 2.1

[1512] 29 Nov 07: 16.10

[1513] 19 Nov 07: 135.24

[1514] 24 Jan 08:111.9

[1515] 11 Dec 07: 23.19

[1516] 11 Dec 07: 13.7

[1517] 11 Dec 07: 12.12

[1518] 11 Dec 07: 12.18

[1519] 11 Dec 07:8.8

[1520] 29 Nov 07: 29.12

[1521] INQ0053176 – also shown in Part 2 at end of Chapter 9B.

[1522] The Operation Paget Inquiry Report into the Allegation of Conspiracy to Murder Diana, Princess of Wales and Emad El-Din Mohamed Abdel Moneim Fayed, December 14 2006, page 514

[1523] 11 Dec 07: 40.1

[1524] 24 Jan 08:114.3

[1525] Jean-Marc Martino, Witness Statement, 22 May 2005, reproduced in Diana Inquest: The Documents the Jury Never Saw, 2010, p305 (UK Edition)

[1526] 24 Jan 08: 140.13

[1527] 19 Nov 07: 5.11

[1528] 11 Dec 07: 13.13
[1529] 11 Dec 07: 13.20
[1530] 11 Dec 07: 13.20
[1531] 11 Dec 07: 13.23
[1532] 11 Dec 07: 14.5
[1533] 11 Dec 07: 14.9
[1534] 11 Dec 07: 14.9
[1535] 29 Nov 07: 15.25
[1536] 11 Dec 07: 14.16
[1537] 11 Dec 07: 14.19
[1538] 11 Dec 07: 14.22
[1539] 11 Dec 07: 35.15
[1540] 11 Dec 07: 14.25
[1541] 11 Dec 07: 15.1
[1542] 29 Nov 07: 17.24
[1543] 29 Nov 07: 18.9
[1544] 11 Dec 07: 14.1
[1545] 24 Jan 08:124.16
[1546] 24 Jan 08: 125.23
[1547] 24 Jan 08:124.24
[1548] 24 Jan 08:126.6
[1549] 29 Nov 07: 32.5
[1550] 29 Nov 07: 32.10
[1551] 24 Jan 08: 134.11
[1552] 11 Dec 07: 27.20
[1553] Until 29.21
[1554] 19 Nov 07: 42.16
[1555] 11 Dec 07: 34.21
[1556] 29 Nov 07: 2.9
[1557] 19 Nov 07: 11.25
[1558] 19 Nov 07: 102.20
[1559] 29 Nov 07: 18.3
[1560] 11 Dec 07: 20.4
[1561] 11 Dec 07: 20.11
[1562] 29 Nov 07: 18.9
[1563] 11 Dec 07: 19.23
[1564] 11 Dec 07: 20.1
[1565] 24 Jan 08: 139.24
[1566] 24 Jan 08: 135.13
[1567] 24 Jan 08: 137.16
[1568] 24 Jan 08: 135.20
[1569] 24 Jan 08: 141.10
[1570] 24 Jan 08: 141.15
[1571] 19 Nov 07: 9.7

[1572] 11 Dec 07: 25.6
[1573] 11 Dec 07: 13.23
[1574] 29 Nov 07: 11.24
[1575] 29 Nov 07: 15.14
[1576] 29 Nov 07: 17.15
[1577] 11 Dec 07: 18.17
[1578] 11 Dec 07: 29.15
[1579] 29 Nov 07: 24.21
[1580] 29 Nov 07: 24.22
[1581] 29 Nov 07: 24.24
[1582] 29 Nov 07: 25.1
[1583] 29 Nov 07: 25.2
[1584] 29 Nov 07: 25.3
[1585] 19 Nov 07: 36.7
[1586] 15 Nov 07: 7.25
[1587] 15 Nov 07: 8.7
[1588] 15 Nov 07: 37.23
[1589] 15 Nov 07: 38.6
[1590] 29 Nov 07: 26.23
[1591] 29 Nov 07: 26.24
[1592] 29 Nov 07: 26.23
[1593] 15 Nov 07: 37.24
[1594] 29 Nov 07: 26.24
[1595] The Operation Paget Inquiry Report into the Allegation of Conspiracy to Murder Diana, Princess of Wales and Emad El-Din Mohamed Abdel Moneim Fayed, December 14 2006, page 518
[1596] 15 Nov 07: 37.25
[1597] Di and Dodi Crash Horror, The People, August 31 1997
[1598] 11 Dec 07: 17.4
[1599] 11 Dec 07: 15.17
[1600] 19 Nov 07: 32.8
[1601] 19 Nov 07: 32.12
[1602] 19 Nov 07: 35.3
[1603] 19 Nov 07: 33.13
[1604] The Operation Paget Inquiry Report into the Allegation of Conspiracy to Murder Diana, Princess of Wales and Emad El-Din Mohamed Abdel Moneim Fayed, December 14 2006, page 515 and Inquest Transcripts: 19 Nov 07:1.22
[1605] 12 Mar 98 Statement read out 14 Nov 07: 22.25
[1606] 29 Nov 07: 22.9
[1607] 29 Nov 07: 22.12
[1608] 29 Nov 07: 26.1
[1609] 24 Jan 08: 144.24
[1610] 24 Jan 08: 145.4
[1611] 12 Mar 98 Statement read out 14 Nov 07: 23.5
[1612] Thomas Sancton and Scott MacLeod, Death of a Princess: An Investigation, 1998, page 30

[1613] 12 Mar 98 Statement read out 14 Nov 07: 23.7

[1614] 28 Feb 06 Statement read out 11 Mar 08: 150.4

[1615] The Operation Paget Inquiry Report into the Allegation of Conspiracy to Murder Diana, Princess of Wales and Emad El-Din Mohamed Abdel Moneim Fayed, December 14 2006, page 515

[1616] 19 Nov 07: 13.20

[1617] 19 Nov 07: 138.3

[1618] 12 Mar 98 Statement read out 14 Nov 07: 23.15

[1619] 24 Jan 08: 131.8

[1620] 24 Jan 08: 131.8

[1621] 24 Jan 08: 144.12

[1622] The Operation Paget Inquiry Report into the Allegation of Conspiracy to Murder Diana, Princess of Wales and Emad El-Din Mohamed Abdel Moneim Fayed, December 14 2006, page 515

[1623] The Operation Paget Inquiry Report into the Allegation of Conspiracy to Murder Diana, Princess of Wales and Emad El-Din Mohamed Abdel Moneim Fayed, December 14 2006, page 515

[1624] 24 Jan 08: 144.7

[1625] 2 Apr 08:44.23

[1626] 29 Nov 07: 39.24

[1627] 24 Jan 08: 144.15

[1628] The Operation Paget Inquiry Report into the Allegation of Conspiracy to Murder Diana, Princess of Wales and Emad El-Din Mohamed Abdel Moneim Fayed, December 14 2006, page 515

[1629] The Operation Paget Inquiry Report into the Allegation of Conspiracy to Murder Diana, Princess of Wales and Emad El-Din Mohamed Abdel Moneim Fayed, December 14 2006, page 515

[1630] 23 Sep 97 Statement read out 17 Oct 07: 13.7

[1631] 23 Sep 97 Statement read out 17 Oct 07: 13.3

[1632] 28 Feb 06 Statement read out 11 Mar 08: 150.22

[1633] 28 Feb 06 Statement read out 11 Mar 08: 150.17

[1634] 24 Jan 08: 130.16

[1635] The Operation Paget Inquiry Report into the Allegation of Conspiracy to Murder Diana, Princess of Wales and Emad El-Din Mohamed Abdel Moneim Fayed, December 14 2006, page 516

[1636] 11 Dec 07: 38.14

[1637] 24 Jan 08: 145.4

[1638] The Operation Paget Inquiry Report into the Allegation of Conspiracy to Murder Diana, Princess of Wales and Emad El-Din Mohamed Abdel Moneim Fayed, December 14 2006, page 516

[1639] The Operation Paget Inquiry Report into the Allegation of Conspiracy to Murder Diana, Princess of Wales and Emad El-Din Mohamed Abdel Moneim Fayed, December 14 2006, page 516

[1640] 13 Nov 07: 64.11

[1641] 13 Nov 07: 59.10

[1642] 11 Dec 07: 3.6

[1643] 12 Mar 98 Statement read out 14 Nov 07: 23.15

[1644] 23 Sep 97 Statement read out 17 Oct 07: 13.7

[1645] The Operation Paget Inquiry Report into the Allegation of Conspiracy to Murder Diana, Princess of Wales and Emad El-Din Mohamed Abdel Moneim Fayed, December 14 2006, page 515

[1646] The Operation Paget Inquiry Report into the Allegation of Conspiracy to Murder Diana, Princess of Wales and Emad El-Din Mohamed Abdel Moneim Fayed, December 14 2006, page 515

[1647] The Operation Paget Inquiry Report into the Allegation of Conspiracy to Murder Diana, Princess of Wales and Emad El-Din Mohamed Abdel Moneim Fayed, December 14 2006, page 520

[1648] 11 Mar 98 Statement read out 14 Nov 07: 26.5

[1649] 15 Nov 07: 9.20

[1650] 10 Nov 07: 14.6

[1651] 15 Nov 07: 11.20

[1652] 15 Nov 07: 12.3

[1653] 15 Nov 07: 13.24

[1654] 15 Nov 07: 20.9

[1655] 15 Nov 07: 16.15

[1656] 15 Nov 07: 18.24

[1657] 15 Nov 07: 16.7

[1658] 15 Nov 07: 13.3

[1659] 15 Nov 07: 13.22

[1660] 15 Nov 07: 15.1

[1661] 15 Nov 07: 15.7

[1662] The Operation Paget Inquiry Report into the Allegation of Conspiracy to Murder Diana, Princess of Wales and Emad El-Din Mohamed Abdel Moneim Fayed, December 14 2006, page 520

[1663] 11 Mar 98 Statement read out 14 Nov 2007: 25.23

[1664] 15 Nov 07: 61.4

[1665] 15 Nov 07: 16.7

[1666] 15 Nov 07: 17.14

[1667] 15 Nov 07: 17.21

[1668] 15 Nov 07: 17.25

[1669] 15 Nov 07: 17.14

[1670] 15 Nov 07: 21.12

[1671] 11 Mar 98 Statement read out 14 Nov 07: 27.9

[1672] 15 Nov 07: 17.18

[1673] 15 Nov 07: 21.22

[1674] 15 Nov 07: 62.19

[1675] 2 Apr 08: 43.9

[1676] 2 Apr 08: from 40.4

[1677] Keith Moss, Witness Statement, 22 October 2004, reproduced in Diana Inquest: The Documents the Jury Never Saw, 2010, p649 (UK Edition)

[1678] Keith Moss, Witness Statement, 22 October 2004, reproduced in Diana Inquest: The Documents the Jury Never Saw, 2010, p651 (UK Edition)

[1679] Keith Moss, Witness Statement, 22 October 2004, reproduced in Diana Inquest: The Documents the Jury Never Saw, 2010, p650 (UK Edition)

[1680] Gérard Jauze, Witness Statement, 21 March 2006, reproduced in Diana Inquest: The Documents the Jury Never Saw, 2010, p477 (UK Edition)

[1681] The Operation Paget Inquiry Report into the Allegation of Conspiracy to Murder Diana, Princess of Wales and Emad El-Din Mohamed Abdel Moneim Fayed, December 14 2006, page 563

[1682] Prof Bruno Riou, Witness Statement, 7 March 2006, reproduced in Diana Inquest: The Documents the Jury Never Saw, 2010, pp375-6 (UK Edition)

[1683] 10 Nov 07: 14.6

[1684] Prof Bruno Riou, Witness Statement, 7 March 2006, reproduced in Diana Inquest: The Documents the Jury Never Saw, 2010, p376 (UK Edition)

[1685] Eva Steiner: 21 Nov 07: 79.21; Martine Monteil, Witness Statement, 15 November 2006, reproduced in Diana Inquest: The Documents the Jury Never Saw, 2010, p58 (UK Edition)

[1686] The Operation Paget Inquiry Report into the Allegation of Conspiracy to Murder Diana, Princess of Wales and Emad El-Din Mohamed Abdel Moneim Fayed, December 14 2006, page 535

[1687] Dominique Lecomte, Witness Statement, 31 May 2006, reproduced in Diana Inquest: The Documents the Jury Never Saw, 2010, p151 (UK Edition)

[1688] 21 Nov 07: 79.21

[1689] Martine Monteil, Witness Statement, 15 November 2006, reproduced in Diana Inquest: The Documents the Jury Never Saw, 2010, p58 (UK Edition)

[1690] Alain Pavie, Witness Statement, 9 March 2005, reproduced in Diana Inquest: The Documents the Jury Never Saw, 2010, p389 (UK Edition)

[1691] 15 Nov 07: 2.2

[1692] 5 Feb 08: 8.20

[1693] 20 Nov 07: 15.23

[1694] 20 Nov 07: 16.3

[1695] 20 Nov 07: 15.1

[1696] Alain Pavie, Witness Statement, 9 March 2005, reproduced in Diana Inquest: The Documents the Jury Never Saw, 2010, p387 (UK Edition)

[1697] 14 Nov 06 Statement read out 21 Nov 07: 57.7

[1698] 6 Nov 07: 18.21

[1699] 6 Nov 07: 22.11

[1700] 6 Nov 07: 50.17

[1701] 6 Nov 07: 40.12

[1702] 12 Nov 07: 76.24

[1703] 12 Nov 07: 76.23

[1704] 8 Nov 07: 102.22

[1705] 6 Nov 07:11.12

[1706] 5 Feb 08: 65.8

[1707] 6 Nov 07: 23.11

[1708] 6 Nov 07: 20.16

[1709] 6 Nov 07: 52.2

[1710] 5 Feb 08: 4.2

[1711] 5 Feb 08: 4.1

[1712] 6 Nov 07: 21.1

[1713] 6 Nov 07: 52.20

[1714] 6 Nov 07: 21.9

[1715] 6 Nov 07: 52.10

[1716] 6 Nov 07: 53.16

[1717] 6 Nov 07: 27.12

[1718] 6 Nov 07: 30.12

[1719] 5 Feb 08: 64.2

[1720] 5 Feb 08: 65.11

[1721] 6 Nov 07: 34.6

[1722] 26 Sep 97 Statement read out 11 Oct 07: 127.23

[1723] 11 Oct 07: 128.7

[1724] 8 Nov 07: 71.3

[1725] 8 Nov 07: 3.25

[1726] 8 Nov 07: 11.10

[1727] Samuel Goldschmidt: 23 Sep 97 Statement read out 11 Oct 07: 144.8

[1728] 4 Feb 08: 45.23

[1729] 23 Sep 97 Statement read out 11 Oct 07: 144.8

[1730] 31 Aug 97 Statement read out 12 Nov 07: 120.5

[1731] Diana: The Night She Died, Channel 5 Documentary, 2003

[1732] 6 Nov 07: 33.12

[1733] The Operation Paget Inquiry Report into the Allegation of Conspiracy to Murder Diana, Princess of Wales and Emad El-Din Mohamed Abdel Moneim Fayed, December 14 2006, page 574

[1734] The Operation Paget Inquiry Report into the Allegation of Conspiracy to Murder Diana, Princess of Wales and Emad El-Din Mohamed Abdel Moneim Fayed, December 14 2006, page 574

[1735] Andrew Golden, Queen 'To Strip Harrods of its Royal Crest', Daily Mirror, 31 August 1997 – Article read out 12 Feb 08: 105.23

[1736] 4 Feb 08: 96.13

[1737] 5 Feb 08: 32.21

[1738] James Andanson: 12 Feb 98 Statement read out 5 Feb 08: 25.17

[1739] Alexander Hitchen, I Saw Fiat Driver Kill Di, The People, January 18 2004

[1740] The Operation Paget Inquiry Report into the Allegation of Conspiracy to Murder Diana, Princess of Wales and Emad El-Din Mohamed Abdel Moneim Fayed, December 14 2006, page 704

[1741] The Operation Paget Inquiry Report into the Allegation of Conspiracy to Murder Diana, Princess of Wales and Emad El-Din Mohamed Abdel Moneim Fayed, December 14 2006, page 477

[1742] The Operation Paget Inquiry Report into the Allegation of Conspiracy to Murder Diana, Princess of Wales and Emad El-Din Mohamed Abdel Moneim Fayed, December 14 2006, page 705

[1743] The Operation Paget Inquiry Report into the Allegation of Conspiracy to Murder Diana, Princess of Wales and Emad El-Din Mohamed Abdel Moneim Fayed, December 14 2006, page 477

[1744] 21 Feb 08: 37.3

[1745] 21 Feb 08: 79.15

[1746] 7 Feb 08: 4.18

[1747] 21 Feb 08: 73.7

[1748] The Operation Paget Inquiry Report into the Allegation of Conspiracy to Murder Diana, Princess of Wales and Emad El-Din Mohamed Abdel Moneim Fayed, December 14 2006, page 702

[1749] 6 Feb 08: 38.10

[1750] 6 Feb 08: 10.24

[1751] The Operation Paget Inquiry Report into the Allegation of Conspiracy to Murder Diana, Princess of Wales and Emad El-Din Mohamed Abdel Moneim Fayed, December 14 2006, page 703

[1752] The Operation Paget Inquiry Report into the Allegation of Conspiracy to Murder Diana, Princess of Wales and Emad El-Din Mohamed Abdel Moneim Fayed, December 14 2006, page 703

[1753] 6 Feb 08: 17.21

[1754] 6 Feb 08: 1.25

[1755] Françoise – 6 Feb 08: 8.15; Joséphine – 6 Feb 08: 30.7

[1756] 4 Feb 08: 89.24

[1757] 4 Feb 08: 92.14

[1758] 4 Feb 08: 92.14

[1759] 4 Feb 08: 92.18

[1760] 12 Feb 98 Statement read out 5 Feb 08: 25.17

[1761] The Operation Paget Inquiry Report into the Allegation of Conspiracy to Murder Diana, Princess of Wales and Emad El-Din Mohamed Abdel Moneim Fayed, December 14 2006, page 696

[1762] 21 Feb 08: 42.10

[1763] The Operation Paget Inquiry Report into the Allegation of Conspiracy to Murder Diana, Princess of Wales and Emad El-Din Mohamed Abdel Moneim Fayed, December 14 2006, page 696

[1764] The Operation Paget Inquiry Report into the Allegation of Conspiracy to Murder Diana, Princess of Wales and Emad El-Din Mohamed Abdel Moneim Fayed, December 14 2006, page 696

[1765] The Operation Paget Inquiry Report into the Allegation of Conspiracy to Murder Diana, Princess of Wales and Emad El-Din Mohamed Abdel Moneim Fayed, December 14 2006, page 697

[1766] The Operation Paget Inquiry Report into the Allegation of Conspiracy to Murder Diana, Princess of Wales and Emad El-Din Mohamed Abdel Moneim Fayed, December 14 2006, page 697

[1767] 31 Mar 08: 51.21

[1768] Location details are based on the general evidence included in this book. Structure details from: The Role of the Private Secretary, The Lord Chamberlain, The Lord Chamberlain's Office, The Official Website of the British Monarchy, www.royal.gov.uk/TheRoyalHousehold/RoyalHouseholddepartments; Private Secretary to the Sovereign, Wikipedia, http://en.wikipedia.org/wiki

[1769] Alastair Campbell, The Alastair Campbell Diaries: Volume 2: Power and the People: 1997-1999, 2011, page 125

[1770] Jean-Claude Plumet, Witness Statement, 4 November 2005, reproduced in Diana Inquest: The Documents the Jury Never Saw, 2010, p469 (UK Edition)

[1771] Patrick Launay, Witness Statement, 21 March 2006, reproduced in Diana Inquest: The Documents the Jury Never Saw, 2010, p510 (UK Edition)

[1772] Jean-Claude Plumet, Witness Statement, 4 November 2005, reproduced in Diana Inquest: The Documents the Jury Never Saw, 2010, p469 (UK Edition)

[1773] 22 Nov 07: 85.18

[1774] Anthony Mather, Witness Statement, 23 August 2005, reproduced in Diana Inquest: The Documents the Jury Never Saw, 2010, p662 (UK Edition)

[1775] Anthony Mather, Witness Statement, 23 August 2005, reproduced in Diana Inquest: The Documents the Jury Never Saw, 2010, p663 (UK Edition)

[1776] Anthony Mather, Witness Statement, 23 August 2005, reproduced in Diana Inquest: The Documents the Jury Never Saw, 2010, p663 (UK Edition)

[1777] Keith Leverton, Witness Statement, 27 October 2004, reproduced in Diana Inquest: The Documents the Jury Never Saw, 2010, p498 (UK Edition)

[1778] Keith Leverton, Witness Statement, 27 October 2004, reproduced in Diana Inquest: The Documents the Jury Never Saw, 2010, p498 (UK Edition)

[1779] Keith Leverton, Witness Statement, 27 October 2004, reproduced in Diana Inquest: The Documents the Jury Never Saw, 2010, p498 (UK Edition)

[1780] 22 Nov 07: 71.16

[1781] David Green, Witness Statement, 13 July 2004, reproduced in Diana Inquest: The Documents the Jury Never Saw, 2010, p502 (UK Edition)

[1782] Keith Leverton, Witness Statement, 27 October 2004, reproduced in Diana Inquest: The Documents the Jury Never Saw, 2010, p499 (UK Edition)

[1783] 22 Nov 07: 79.3

[1784] David Green, Witness Statement, 17 September 2004, reproduced in Diana Inquest: The Documents the Jury Never Saw, 2010, p506 (UK Edition)

[1785] Receipt of Cadaver at the Medico-Legal Institute, reproduced in Diana Inquest: The Documents the Jury Never Saw, 2010, p63 (UK Edition)

[1786] Brigade Criminelle report, reproduced in Part 4, Autopsy in Paris chapter. Also viewable on inquest website: INQ0041592

[1787] INQ0041596

[1788] 21 Jan 08: 18.1

[1789] INQ0001653

[1790] 21 Jan 08: 23.22

[1791] 5 Feb 08: 15.2

[1792] The Operation Paget Inquiry Report into the Allegation of Conspiracy to Murder Diana, Princess of Wales and Emad El-Din Mohamed Abdel Moneim Fayed, December 14 2006, page 284

[1793] 22 Jan 08: 4.14

[1794] 22 Jan 08: 4.3

[1795] 22 Jan 08: 137.24

[1796] 22 Jan 08: 114.16

[1797] 31 Jan 08: 37.5

[1798] 5 Feb 08: 48.15

[1799] 21 Jan 08: 36.5

[1800] The Operation Paget Inquiry Report into the Allegation of Conspiracy to Murder Diana, Princess of Wales and Emad El-Din Mohamed Abdel Moneim Fayed, December 14 2006, page 319

[1801] 22 Jan 08: 117.19

[1802] 21 Jan 08: 64.10

[1803] 21 Jan 08: 111.15

[1804] 22 Jan 08: 26.23

[1805] 30 Jan 08: 189.21

[1806] 21 Jan 08: 16.19

[1807] INQ0001652.

[1808] 22 Jan 08: 52.3

[1809] Prof Bruno Riou, Witness Statement, 7 March 2006, reproduced in Diana Inquest: The Documents the Jury Never Saw, 2010, pp374-5 (UK Edition)

[1810] Prof Bruno Riou, Witness Statement, 7 March 2006, reproduced in Diana Inquest: The Documents the Jury Never Saw, 2010, pp374-5 (UK Edition)

[1811] Prof Bruno Riou, Witness Statement, 7 March 2006, reproduced in Diana Inquest: The Documents the Jury Never Saw, 2010, p375 (UK Edition)

[1812] Sunrise and Sunset for France – Paris – August 1997, www.timeanddate.com

[1813] Michael Jay, Witness Statement, 13 December 2005, reproduced in Diana Inquest: The Documents the Jury Never Saw, 2010, p635 (UK Edition)

[1814] Michael Jay, Witness Statement, 13 December 2005, reproduced in Diana Inquest: The Documents the Jury Never Saw, 2010, pp635-6 (UK Edition).

[1815] 22 Nov 07: 19.19

[1816] Federal Climate Complex: Global Surface Summary of Day Data: Paris – Orly – Station No:071490, Maximum Temperature 31 August 1997, NNDC Climate Data Online, NOAA Satellite and Information Service, http://www7.ncdc.noaa.gov/CDO/cdodata.cmd

[1817] 22 Nov 07: 19.23

[1818] 22 Sep 05 Statement read out 17 Dec 07: 121.22

[1819] Colin Tebbutt, Witness Statement, 5 July 2004, reproduced in Diana Inquest: The Documents the Jury Never Saw, 2010, pp439-441 (UK Edition)

[1820] 22 Sep 05 Statement read out 17 Dec 07: 121.22

[1821] 21 Nov 07: 8.19

[1822] 26 Nov 07: 91.20

[1823] René Deguisne, Witness Statement, 9 May 2005, reproduced in Diana Inquest: The Documents the Jury Never Saw, 2010, p451 (UK Edition)

[1824] 8 Mar 05 Statement read out 22 Nov 07: 90.23

[1825] 22 Sep 05 Statement read out 17 Dec 07: 121.22

[1826] 22 Sep 05 Statement read out 17 Dec 07: 122.4

[1827] Gérard Jauze, Witness Statement, 21 March 2006, reproduced in Diana Inquest: The Documents the Jury Never Saw, 2010, pp476-478,485 (UK Edition)

[1828] Jean Monceau, Witness Statement, 18 October 2005, reproduced in Diana Inquest: The Documents the Jury Never Saw, 2010, pp409-410 (UK Edition)

[1829] 20 Nov 07: from 68.16

[1830] 20 Nov 07: 69.12

[1831] 20 Nov 07: 69.1

[1832] Jean Monceau, Witness Statement, 18 October 2005, reproduced in Diana Inquest: The Documents the Jury Never Saw, 2010, p410 (UK Edition)

[1833] 20 Nov 07: 69.21

[1834] 20 Nov 07: 72.3

[1835] 20 Nov 07: 72.8

[1836] 8 Mar 05 Statement read out 22 Nov 07: 93.21

[1837] 20 Nov 07: 64.18

[1838] 20 Nov 07: 70.17

[1839] 20 Nov 07: 64.15

[1840] Jean Monceau, Witness Statement, 18 October 2005, reproduced in Diana Inquest: The Documents the Jury Never Saw, 2010, p410 (UK Edition)

[1841] Colin Tebbutt, Witness Statement, 5 July 2004, reproduced in Diana Inquest: The Documents the Jury Never Saw, 2010, p439 (UK Edition)

[1842] Jean Monceau, Witness Statement, 18 October 2005, reproduced in Diana Inquest: The Documents the Jury Never Saw, 2010, p410 (UK Edition)

[1843] 14 Nov 06 Statement read out 21 Nov 07: 60.18

[1844] Jean Monceau, Witness Statement, 18 October 2005, reproduced in Diana Inquest: The Documents the Jury Never Saw, 2010, p412 (UK Edition)

[1845] Colin Tebbutt, Witness Statement, 5 July 2004, reproduced in Diana Inquest: The Documents the Jury Never Saw, 2010, p441 (UK Edition)

[1846] The Operation Paget Inquiry Report into the Allegation of Conspiracy to Murder Diana, Princess of Wales and Emad El-Din Mohamed Abdel Moneim Fayed, December 14 2006, page 544

[1847] Paul Burrell, A Royal Duty, 2003, p288

[1848] 8 Mar 05 Statement read out 22 Nov 07: 91.12

[1849] Jean Monceau, Witness Statement, 18 October 2005, reproduced in Diana Inquest: The Documents the Jury Never Saw, 2010, p416 (UK Edition)

[1850] 20 Nov 07: 87.2

[1851] 20 Nov 07: 87.13

[1852] 20 Nov 07: 87.10

[1853] Jean Monceau, Witness Statement, 18 October 2005, reproduced in Diana Inquest: The Documents the Jury Never Saw, 2010, p415 (UK Edition)

[1854] 14 Nov 06 Statement read out 21 Nov 07: 60.2

[1855] 14 Nov 06 Statement read out 21 Nov 07: 60.18

[1856] 22 Nov 07: 63.16

[1857] Jean Monceau, Witness Statement, 18 October 2005, reproduced in Diana Inquest: The Documents the Jury Never Saw, 2010, p413 (UK Edition)

[1858] Martine Monteil, Witness Statement, 15 November 2006, reproduced in Diana Inquest: The Documents the Jury Never Saw, 2010, p58 (UK Edition)

[1859] Jean Monceau, Witness Statement, 18 October 2005, reproduced in Diana Inquest: The Documents the Jury Never Saw, 2010, p411 (UK Edition)

[1860] Jean-Claude Plumet, Witness Statement, 4 November 2005, reproduced in Diana Inquest: The Documents the Jury Never Saw, 2010, p474 (UK Edition)

[1861] Gérard Jauze, Witness Statement, 21 March 2006, reproduced in Diana Inquest: The Documents the Jury Never Saw, 2010, p484 (UK Edition)

[1862] Jean Monceau, Witness Statement, 18 October 2005, reproduced in Diana Inquest: The Documents the Jury Never Saw, 2010, p419 (UK Edition)

[1863] General Codes of Territorial Collectivities (CGCT): "Civil Code: Funeral Operations: Embalming: Article R2213-2": Included in email from Jean Monceau to Philip Easton (Paget), 19 September 2005, reproduced in Diana Inquest: The Documents the Jury Never Saw, 2010, pp421-3 (UK Edition); Eva Steiner: 21 Nov 07: from 68.14; Eva Steiner, Witness Statement, 29 September 2006, reproduced in Diana Inquest: The Documents the Jury Never Saw, 2010, pp463-6 (UK Edition)

[1864] 21 Nov 07: 71.2

[1865] Eva Steiner, Witness Statement, 29 September 2006, reproduced in Diana Inquest: The Documents the Jury Never Saw, 2010, p466 (UK Edition)

[1866] 21 Nov 07: 74.4

[1867] Martine Monteil, Witness Statement, 15 November 2006, reproduced in Diana Inquest: The Documents the Jury Never Saw, 2010, p58 (UK Edition)

[1868] 31 Mar 08: 87.3

[1869] 21 Nov 07: 74.21

[1870] 21 Nov 07: 75.10

[1871] 21 Nov 07: 75.16

[1872] 21 Nov 07: 75.19

[1873] Eva Steiner, Witness Statement, 29 September 2006, reproduced in Diana Inquest: The Documents the Jury Never Saw, 2010, p466 (UK Edition)

[1874] 21 Nov 07: 64.25

[1875] Robert Thompson, Witness Statement, 9 November 2004, page 6

[1876] Robert Thompson, Affidavit, 13 June 2001, page 3

[1877] 20 Nov 07: 78.4

[1878] Jean Monceau, Witness Statement, 18 October 2005, reproduced in Diana Inquest: The Documents the Jury Never Saw, 2010, p416 (UK Edition)

[1879] Jean Monceau, Witness Statement, 18 October 2005, reproduced in Diana Inquest: The Documents the Jury Never Saw, 2010, p413 (UK Edition)

[1880] 20 Nov 07: 78.4

[1881] 8 Mar 05 Statement read out 22 Nov 07: 94.14

[1882] 8 Mar 05 Statement read out 22 Nov 07: 93.7

[1883] 20 Nov 07: 74.23

[1884] David Green, Witness Statement, 17 September 2004, reproduced in Diana Inquest: The Documents the Jury Never Saw, 2010, p503 (UK Edition)

[1885] 8 Mar 05 Statement read out 22 Nov 07: 93.7

[1886] 8 Mar 05 Statement read out 22 Nov 07: 94.2

[1887] Philip Easton, Witness Statement, 19 July 2005, page 1

[1888] Robert Chapman, Witness Statement – Internal Examination, 10 September 1997, pages 11-14

[1889] Philip Easton, Witness Statement, 19 July 2005, page 1

[1890] Philip Easton, Witness Statement, 19 July 2005, page 1

[1891] Cavity Embalming, www.embalming.net

[1892] 26 Nov 07: 27.9

[1893] David Green, Witness Statement, 13 July 2004, reproduced in Diana Inquest: The Documents the Jury Never Saw, 2010, pp504-5 (UK Edition)

[1894] René Deguisne, Witness Statement, 9 May 2005, reproduced in Diana Inquest: The Documents the Jury Never Saw, 2010, p453 (UK Edition)

[1895] Jean Monceau, Witness Statement, 18 October 2005, reproduced in Diana Inquest: The Documents the Jury Never Saw, 2010, p418 (UK Edition)

[1896] Anthony Mather, Witness Statement, 23 August 2005, reproduced in Diana Inquest: The Documents the Jury Never Saw, 2010, p662 (UK Edition)

[1897] Anthony Mather, Witness Statement, 23 August 2005, reproduced in Diana Inquest: The Documents the Jury Never Saw, 2010, p662 (UK Edition)

[1898] John Burton, Witness Statement, 16 June 2004, reproduced in Diana Inquest: The Documents the Jury Never Saw, 2010, p561 (UK Edition)

[1899] 22 Nov 07: 72.10

[1900] Keith Leverton, Witness Statement, 27 October 2004, reproduced in Diana Inquest: The Documents the Jury Never Saw, 2010, p499 (UK Edition)

[1901] Keith Leverton, Witness Statement, 27 October 2004, reproduced in Diana Inquest: The Documents the Jury Never Saw, 2010, p499 (UK Edition)

[1902] Robert Thompson, Witness Statement, 9 November 2004, reproduced in Diana Inquest: The Documents the Jury Never Saw, 2010, pp601-2 (UK Edition)

[1903] 17 Dec 07: 34.19

[1904] The Operation Paget Inquiry Report into the Allegation of Conspiracy to Murder Diana, Princess of Wales and Emad El-Din Mohamed Abdel Moneim Fayed, December 14 2006, page 626

[1905] John Macnamara, Witness Statement, 3 July 2006, reproduced in Diana Inquest: The Documents the Jury Never Saw, 2010, p520 (UK edition)

[1906] 17 Dec 07: 87.12

[1907] Michael Burgess, Witness Statement, 16 August 2004, reproduced in Diana Inquest: The Documents the Jury Never Saw, 2010, pp536-7 (UK Edition)

[1908] 22 Jan 98 Report read out 17 Dec 07: 44.12

[1909] 15 Jan 08: 51.3

[1910] The Operation Paget Inquiry Report into the Allegation of Conspiracy to Murder Diana, Princess of Wales and Emad El-Din Mohamed Abdel Moneim Fayed, December 14 2006, page 629

[1911] 22 Jan 98 Report read out 17 Dec 07: 50.6

[1912] 17 Dec 07: 78.18

[1913] John Macnamara, Witness Statement, 3 July 2006, reproduced in Diana Inquest: The Documents the Jury Never Saw, 2010, p520 (UK edition)

[1914] Kim Sengupta, Conservatives In Crisis: Senior Detective Takes Charge of Inquiry, The Independent, 24 November 1999

[1915] 22 Nov 07: 73.11

[1916] Keith Leverton, Witness Statement, 27 October 2004, reproduced in Diana Inquest: The Documents the Jury Never Saw, 2010, pp497-500 (UK Edition)

[1917] Keith Leverton, Witness Statement, 27 October 2004, reproduced in Diana Inquest: The Documents the Jury Never Saw, 2010, p499 (UK Edition)

[1918] David Green, Witness Statement, 13 July 2004, reproduced in Diana Inquest: The Documents the Jury Never Saw, 2010, p502 (UK Edition)

[1919] Patrick Launay, Witness Statement, 21 March 2006, reproduced in Diana Inquest: The Documents the Jury Never Saw, 2010, p511 (UK Edition)

[1920] 22 Nov 07: 74.6

[1921] David Green, Witness Statement, 13 July 2004, reproduced in Diana Inquest: The Documents the Jury Never Saw, 2010, pp503-4 (UK Edition)

[1922] David Green, Witness Statement, 13 July 2004, reproduced in Diana Inquest: The Documents the Jury Never Saw, 2010, pp=503 (UK Edition)

[1923] Clive Leverton, Witness Statement, 13 July 2004, reproduced in Diana Inquest: The Documents the Jury Never Saw, 2010, p490 (UK Edition)

[1924] David Green, Witness Statement, 17 September 2004, reproduced in Diana Inquest: The Documents the Jury Never Saw, 2010, p504 (UK Edition)

[1925] David Green, Witness Statement, 13 July 2004, reproduced in Diana Inquest: The Documents the Jury Never Saw, 2010, pp=503 (UK Edition)

[1926] Alan Puxley, Witness Statement, 16 June 2004, reproduced in Diana Inquest: The Documents the Jury Never Saw, 2010, pp458-9 (UK Edition)

[1927] Patrick Launay, Witness Statement, 21 March 2006, reproduced in Diana Inquest: The Documents the Jury Never Saw, 2010, pp514-5 (UK Edition)

[1928] Patrick Launay, Witness Statement, 21 March 2006, reproduced in Diana Inquest: The Documents the Jury Never Saw, 2010, p515 (UK Edition)

[1929] Clive Leverton, Witness Statement, 13 July 2004, reproduced in Diana Inquest: The Documents the Jury Never Saw, 2010, pp489-490 (UK Edition)

[1930] Clive Leverton, Witness Statement, 13 July 2004, reproduced in Diana Inquest: The Documents the Jury Never Saw, 2010, pp492-3 (UK Edition)

[1931] Clive Leverton, Witness Statement, 13 July 2004, reproduced in Diana Inquest: The Documents the Jury Never Saw, 2010, p493 (UK Edition)

[1932] Clive Leverton, Witness Statement, 13 July 2004, reproduced in Diana Inquest: The Documents the Jury Never Saw, 2010, pp489-490 (UK Edition)

[1933] Colin Tebbutt, Witness Statement, 5 July 2004, reproduced in Diana Inquest: The Documents the Jury Never Saw, 2010, pp444-5 (UK Edition)

[1934] Dickie Arbiter, On Duty with the Queen, 2014, p162

[1935] Michael Jay, 31 Aug 97 Diary read out 11 Feb 08: 106.10

[1936] Associated Press, Nightmare Ending to a British Fairy Tale Death of a Princess, Cincinnati Post, 1 September 1997

[1937] Andrew Morton, Diana: Her True Story – In Her Own Words, 1997, pages 54-55

[1938] Paul Burrell, A Royal Duty, 2003, pages 322-3 and Inquest Evidence Reference INQ0010117.

[1939] 28 Jan 08: 111.14

[1940] INQ0033876 – Expanded Handwritten Jottings re 31 August 1997

[1941] John Macnamara, Witness Statement, 3 July 2006, reproduced in Diana Inquest: The Documents the Jury Never Saw, 2010, p519 (UK edition)

[1942] John Macnamara, Witness Statement, 3 July 2006, reproduced in Diana Inquest: The Documents the Jury Never Saw, 2010, p519 (UK edition)

[1943] John Macnamara, Witness Statement, 3 July 2006, reproduced in Diana Inquest: The Documents the Jury Never Saw, 2010, pp519-520 (UK edition)

[1944] The Operation Paget Inquiry Report into the Allegation of Conspiracy to Murder Diana, Princess of Wales and Emad El-Din Mohamed Abdel Moneim Fayed, December 14 2006, page 646

[1945] The Operation Paget Inquiry Report into the Allegation of Conspiracy to Murder Diana, Princess of Wales and Emad El-Din Mohamed Abdel Moneim Fayed, December 14 2006, page 646

[1946] The Operation Paget Inquiry Report into the Allegation of Conspiracy to Murder Diana, Princess of Wales and Emad El-Din Mohamed Abdel Moneim Fayed, December 14 2006, page 646

[1947] The Operation Paget Inquiry Report into the Allegation of Conspiracy to Murder Diana, Princess of Wales and Emad El-Din Mohamed Abdel Moneim Fayed, December 14 2006, page 648

[1948] Gerard Jauze, Witness Statement, 21 March 2006, reproduced in Diana Inquest: The Documents the Jury Never Saw, 2010, p480 (UK edition)

[1949] The Operation Paget Inquiry Report into the Allegation of Conspiracy to Murder Diana, Princess of Wales and Emad El-Din Mohamed Abdel Moneim Fayed, December 14 2006, page 646

[1950] The Operation Paget Inquiry Report into the Allegation of Conspiracy to Murder Diana, Princess of Wales and Emad El-Din Mohamed Abdel Moneim Fayed, December 14 2006, page 649

[1951] 29 Nov 07: 154.17

[1952] The Operation Paget Inquiry Report into the Allegation of Conspiracy to Murder Diana, Princess of Wales and Emad El-Din Mohamed Abdel Moneim Fayed, December 14 2006, pages 647-8

[1953] John Burton, Witness Statement, 16 June 2004, reproduced in Diana Inquest: The Documents the Jury Never Saw, 2010, p559 (UK edition)

[1954] The Operation Paget Inquiry Report into the Allegation of Conspiracy to Murder Diana, Princess of Wales and Emad El-Din Mohamed Abdel Moneim Fayed, December 14 2006, page 646

[1955] The Operation Paget Inquiry Report into the Allegation of Conspiracy to Murder Diana, Princess of Wales and Emad El-Din Mohamed Abdel Moneim Fayed, December 14 2006, page 405

[1956] 20 Nov 07: 18.24

[1957] 20 Nov 07: 21.21

[1958] 20 Nov 07: 20.16

[1959] 20 Nov 07: 21.10

[1960] 20 Nov 07: 18.24

[1961] 6 Mar 08: 50.3

[1962] 27 Nov 07: 60.24

[1963] 6 Mar 08: 36.25

[1964] 27 Nov 07: 65.7

[1965] The Operation Paget Inquiry Report into the Allegation of Conspiracy to Murder Diana, Princess of Wales and Emad El-Din Mohamed Abdel Moneim Fayed, December 14 2006, page 404

[1966] The Operation Paget Inquiry Report into the Allegation of Conspiracy to Murder Diana, Princess of Wales and Emad El-Din Mohamed Abdel Moneim Fayed, December 14 2006, page 786

[1967] 3 Mar 08: 8.12

[1968] 3 Mar 08: 8.24

[1969] 3 Mar 08: 19.6

[1970] The Operation Paget Inquiry Report into the Allegation of Conspiracy to Murder Diana, Princess of Wales and Emad El-Din Mohamed Abdel Moneim Fayed, December 14 2006, page 788

[1971] 3 Mar 08: 23.18

[1972] 3 Mar 08: 46.9; The Operation Paget Inquiry Report into the Allegation of Conspiracy to Murder Diana, Princess of Wales and Emad El-Din Mohamed Abdel Moneim Fayed, December 14 2006, page 785

[1973] 4 Mar 08: 2.14; The Operation Paget Inquiry Report into the Allegation of Conspiracy to Murder Diana, Princess of Wales and Emad El-Din Mohamed Abdel Moneim Fayed, December 14 2006, page 791

[1974] The Operation Paget Inquiry Report into the Allegation of Conspiracy to Murder Diana, Princess of Wales and Emad El-Din Mohamed Abdel Moneim Fayed, December 14 2006, page 792

[1975] Coroners Office, Her Majesty's Coroners Eastern District of London, www.walthamforest.gov.uk

[1976] Anthony Mather, Witness Statement, 23 August 2005, reproduced in Diana Inquest: The Documents the Jury Never Saw, 2010, p662 (UK Edition)

[1977] John Burton, Witness Statement, 16 June 2004, reproduced in Diana Inquest: The Documents the Jury Never Saw, 2010, p561 (UK Edition)

[1978] John Burton, Witness Statement, 16 June 2004, reproduced in Diana Inquest: The Documents the Jury Never Saw, 2010, p561 (UK Edition)

[1979] INQ0033875. Also reproduced in Part 4, section on Royal Coroner in Early Royal Control chapter.

[1980] 13 Dec 07: 82.6

[1981] Anthony Mather, Witness Statement, 23 August 2005, reproduced in Diana Inquest: The Documents the Jury Never Saw, 2010, pp661,663 (UK Edition)

[1982] Dr Robert Chapman, Witness Statement, 10 September 1997, reproduced in Diana Inquest: The Documents the Jury Never Saw, 2010, p575 (UK Edition)

[1983] Dr Susan Patterson, Witness Statement, 28 September 2004, reproduced in Diana Inquest: The Documents the Jury Never Saw, 2010, pp614-5 (UK Edition)

[1984] Dr Susan Patterson, Witness Statement, 28 September 2004, reproduced in Diana Inquest: The Documents the Jury Never Saw, 2010, pp614-5 (UK Edition)

[1985] Dr Susan Patterson, Witness Statement, 28 September 2004, reproduced in Diana Inquest: The Documents the Jury Never Saw, 2010, pp614-5 (UK Edition)

[1986] Dr Robert Chapman, Witness Statement, 10 September 1997, reproduced in Diana Inquest: The Documents the Jury Never Saw, 2010, p575 (UK Edition)

[1987] Diana – Princess of Wales, Post-Mortem Report, reproduced in Diana Inquest: The Documents the Jury Never Saw, 2010, p573 (UK Edition)

[1988] Dr Robert Chapman, Witness Statement, 10 September 1997, reproduced in Diana Inquest: The Documents the Jury Never Saw, 2010, p575 (UK Edition)

[1989] Figure 20, Diana Inquest: The British Cover-Up, 2011, p554

[1990] Robert Chapman, Witness Statement, 24 February 2005, pp7-9, reproduced in Diana Inquest: The British Cover-Up, pp561-2; Dr Robert Chapman, Witness Statement, 24 February 2005, reproduced in Diana Inquest: The Documents the Jury Never Saw, 2010, p588 (UK Edition)

[1991] Dr Susan Paterson, Witness Statement, 28 September 2004, reproduced in Diana Inquest: The Documents the Jury Never Saw, 2010, p616 (UK Edition)

[1992] The Operation Paget Inquiry Report into the Allegation of Conspiracy to Murder Diana, Princess of Wales and Emad El-Din Mohamed Abdel Moneim Fayed, December 14 2006, page 641

[1993] Dr Susan Paterson, Witness Statement, 28 September 2004, reproduced in Diana Inquest: The Documents the Jury Never Saw, 2010, pp614-5 (UK Edition)

[1994] Figure 27, Diana Inquest: The British Cover-Up, 2011, p598

[1995] Figure 27, Diana Inquest: The British Cover-Up, 2011, p598

[1996] Dr Susan Paterson, Witness Statement, 28 September 2004, reproduced in Diana Inquest: The Documents the Jury Never Saw, 2010, p616 (UK Edition)

[1997] Dr Susan Paterson, Witness Statement, 28 September 2004, reproduced in Diana Inquest: The Documents the Jury Never Saw, 2010, p615 (UK Edition)

[1998] Figure 20, Diana Inquest: The British Cover-Up, 2011, p554

[1999] Dr Alexander Allan, Witness Statement, 12 December 2006, reproduced in Diana Inquest: The British Cover-Up, 2011, p601

[2000] Dr Susan Paterson, Witness Statement, 28 September 2004, reproduced in Diana Inquest: The Documents the Jury Never Saw, 2010, p614 (UK Edition)

[2001] Keith Leverton, Witness Statement, 27 October 2004, reproduced in Diana Inquest: The Documents the Jury Never Saw, 2010, p500 (UK Edition)

[2002] Clive Leverton, Witness Statement, 13 July 2004, reproduced in Diana Inquest: The Documents the Jury Never Saw, 2010, p493 (UK Edition)

[2003] 22 Nov 07: 77.21

[2004] David Green, Witness Statement, 13 July 2004, reproduced in Diana Inquest: The Documents the Jury Never Saw, 2010, p504 (UK Edition)

[2005] The Operation Paget Inquiry Report into the Allegation of Conspiracy to Murder Diana, Princess of Wales and Emad El-Din Mohamed Abdel Moneim Fayed, December 14 2006, pages 298. 299

[2006] 22 Jan 08: 10.9

[2007] 21 Jan 08: 58.10 to 59.4

[2008] The Operation Paget Inquiry Report into the Allegation of Conspiracy to Murder Diana, Princess of Wales and Emad El-Din Mohamed Abdel Moneim Fayed, December 14 2006, page 300

[2009] The Operation Paget Inquiry Report into the Allegation of Conspiracy to Murder Diana, Princess of Wales and Emad El-Din Mohamed Abdel Moneim Fayed, December 14 2006, page 302

[2010] 21 Jan 08: 65.9

[2011] The Operation Paget Inquiry Report into the Allegation of Conspiracy to Murder Diana, Princess of Wales and Emad El-Din Mohamed Abdel Moneim Fayed, December 14 2006, page 303

[2012] The Operation Paget Inquiry Report into the Allegation of Conspiracy to Murder Diana, Princess of Wales and Emad El-Din Mohamed Abdel Moneim Fayed, December 14 2006, page 304

[2013] Keith Dovkants & Sandra Laville, Di's Driver "Was Drunk", Evening Standard, Final Edition, 1 September 1997

[2014] 30 Jan 08: 18.23

[2015] 30 Jan 08: 20.10

[2016] 4 Feb 08: 53.14

[2017] INQ0004451

[2018] The Operation Paget Inquiry Report into the Allegation of Conspiracy to Murder Diana, Princess of Wales and Emad El-Din Mohamed Abdel Moneim Fayed, December 14 2006, page 288

[2019] The Operation Paget Inquiry Report into the Allegation of Conspiracy to Murder Diana, Princess of Wales and Emad El-Din Mohamed Abdel Moneim Fayed, December 14 2006, page 287

[2020] 30 Jan 08: 53.14

[2021] 22 Jan 08: 52.3

[2022] The Operation Paget Inquiry Report into the Allegation of Conspiracy to Murder Diana, Princess of Wales and Emad El-Din Mohamed Abdel Moneim Fayed, December 14 2006, page 288

[2023] 1 Apr 08: 59.24

[2024] The Operation Paget Inquiry Report into the Allegation of Conspiracy to Murder Diana, Princess of Wales and Emad El-Din Mohamed Abdel Moneim Fayed, December 14 2006, page 337

[2025] The Operation Paget Inquiry Report into the Allegation of Conspiracy to Murder Diana, Princess of Wales and Emad El-Din Mohamed Abdel Moneim Fayed, December 14 2006, page 326

[2026] The Operation Paget Inquiry Report into the Allegation of Conspiracy to Murder Diana, Princess of Wales and Emad El-Din Mohamed Abdel Moneim Fayed, December 14 2006, page 567

[2027] 30 Jan 08: 23.9

[2028] Report read out 21 Jan 08: 71.15

[2029] 21 Jan 08: 71.20

[2030] The Operation Paget Inquiry Report into the Allegation of Conspiracy to Murder Diana, Princess of Wales and Emad El-Din Mohamed Abdel Moneim Fayed, December 14 2006, page 292

[2031] The Operation Paget Inquiry Report into the Allegation of Conspiracy to Murder Diana, Princess of Wales and Emad El-Din Mohamed Abdel Moneim Fayed, December 14 2006, page 293

[2032] 6 Mar 08: 96.23

[2033] Christian Le Jalle, Witness Statement No 203/97, 4 September 1997, reproduced in Diana Inquest: The Documents the Jury Never Saw, 2010, p88 (UK Edition)

[2034] 21 Jan 08: 85.23

[2035] The Operation Paget Inquiry Report into the Allegation of Conspiracy to Murder Diana, Princess of Wales and Emad El-Din Mohamed Abdel Moneim Fayed, December 14 2006, page 291

[2036] 30 Jan 08: 105.24

[2037] The Operation Paget Inquiry Report into the Allegation of Conspiracy to Murder Diana, Princess of Wales and Emad El-Din Mohamed Abdel Moneim Fayed, December 14 2006, page 294

[2038] 6 Mar 08: 96.8

[2039] The Operation Paget Inquiry Report into the Allegation of Conspiracy to Murder Diana, Princess of Wales and Emad El-Din Mohamed Abdel Moneim Fayed, December 14 2006, page 354

[2040] 4 Feb 08: 53.14

[2041] The Operation Paget Inquiry Report into the Allegation of Conspiracy to Murder Diana, Princess of Wales and Emad El-Din Mohamed Abdel Moneim Fayed, December 14 2006, page 169

[2042] 4 Feb 08: 69.24

[2043] 4 Feb 08: 55.11

[2044] Noel Botham, The Murder of Princess Diana, 2004, pages 176-7

[2045] 29 Oct 07: 27.21

[2046] Thomas Sancton and Scott MacLeod, Death of a Princess: An Investigation, 1998, page 195

[2047] 29 Oct 07: 28.7

[2048] Peter Allen & Harry Arnold, Diana 1961-1997 – Investigation: Find the Fiat Uno, The Mirror, 18 September 1997

[2049] Mark Dowdney, Di Cops Narrow Hunt for Death Smash Fiat Uno – Net Closes, Daily Record, 9 October 1997

[2050] Mark Dowdney, The Truth – Piece by Piece, The Mirror, 9 October 1997

[2051] John Lichfield, Car Search in Diana Inquiry, The Independent, 5 November 1997

[2052] Search Launched For Car in Crash that Killed Diana, The Buffalo News, 5 November 1997

[2053] Craig Whitney, Police Hunt for a Fiat Tied to Diana, The New York Times, 6 November 1997

[2054] John-Thor Dahlburg, Investigators of Diana's Death Begin Examining Fiats, Los Angeles Times, 8 November 1997

[2055] Craig Whitney, French Police Press the Search for a Fiat in Diana Crash, The New York Times, 1 January 1998

[2056] Kevin Connolly, Paris Despatch, BBC News, 1 January 1998

[2057] 4 Feb 08: 87.8

[2058] The Operation Paget Inquiry Report into the Allegation of Conspiracy to Murder Diana, Princess of Wales and Emad El-Din Mohamed Abdel Moneim Fayed, December 14 2006, page 704

[2059] 4 Feb 08: 85.6

[2060] The Operation Paget Inquiry Report into the Allegation of Conspiracy to Murder Diana, Princess of Wales and Emad El-Din Mohamed Abdel Moneim Fayed, December 14 2006, page 704; 4 Feb 08: 85.25

[2061] 4 Feb 08: 86.7

[2062] 4 Feb 08: 86.7

[2063] 18 Mar 08: 103.11

[2064] 18 Mar 08: 105.5

[2065] Photo of car in Figure 15, Part 1; also INQ0019913

[2066] Georges: The Operation Paget Inquiry Report into the Allegation of Conspiracy to Murder Diana, Princess of Wales and Emad El-Din Mohamed Abdel Moneim Fayed, December 14 2006, page 704; Sabine: The Operation Paget Inquiry Report into the Allegation of Conspiracy to Murder Diana, Princess of Wales and Emad El-Din Mohamed Abdel Moneim Fayed, December 14 2006, page 705

[2067] Martine Monteil, Witness Statement, 15 November 2006, page 3.

[2068] Martine Monteil, Witness Statement, 15 November 2006, page 3

[2069] 4 Feb 08: 87.22

[2070] The Operation Paget Inquiry Report into the Allegation of Conspiracy to Murder Diana, Princess of Wales and Emad El-Din Mohamed Abdel Moneim Fayed, December 14 2006, page 97

[2071] 15 Jan 08: 42.5

[2072] The Operation Paget Inquiry Report into the Allegation of Conspiracy to Murder Diana, Princess of Wales and Emad El-Din Mohamed Abdel Moneim Fayed, December 14 2006, page 98

[2073] 14 Feb 08: 42.9

[2074] 15 Jan 08: 42.2

[2075] 14 Feb 08: 33.2

[2076] 14 Feb 08: 11.23

[2077] 14 Feb 08: 43.21

[2078] 16 Jan 08: 176.4

[2079] The Operation Paget Inquiry Report into the Allegation of Conspiracy to Murder Diana, Princess of Wales and Emad El-Din Mohamed Abdel Moneim Fayed, December 14 2006, page 97

[2080] 28 Jan 08: 188.8
[2081] 12 Feb 08: 122.14
[2082] Paul Burrell, A Royal Duty, 2003, p318
[2083] 16 Jan 08: 143.23
[2084] 17 Jan 08: 195.19
[2085] 16 Jan 08: 146.14
[2086] 17 Jan 08: 192.2
[2087] 17 Jan 08: 192.1
[2088] 16 Jan 08: from 144.23
[2089] 16 Jan 08: 144.23
[2090] 16 Jan 08: 145.8
[2091] 16 Jan 08: 145.20
[2092] 17 Jan 08: 192.11
[2093] What Were You Doing When ...?, BBC News, 31 August 1997. This article is dated 30 August 1997, but it was clearly written after the crash.
[2094] Breakfast at Rosa's, ES Magazine, 10 November 2006
[2095] Aislinn Simpson, Camilla: "I Won't Attend Princess Diana Service", The Telegraph, 27 August 2007
[2096] The Face: Rosa Monckton, The Times, 28 August 2007
[2097] Rosa Monckton, You Magazine, 21 October 2007
[2098] Diana Was A True Friend, Weeps [Diana's] Closest Confidante Rosa, Daily Mail, 14 December 2007
[2099] Massoud Ansari & Andrew Alderson, Why Surgeon Could Not Marry Princess Diana, The Telegraph, 16 December 2007
[2100] Ephraim Hardcastle, So Apart from Tony Blair and Gordon Brown, Who Are the Other Notable Royal Wedding Absentees?, Daily Mail, 29 April 2011
[2101] 13 Dec 07: 118.13
[2102] 13 Dec 07: 119.9
[2103] Richard Kay, The Real Truth About Diana, Daily Mail, 29 November 2003
[2104] 13 Dec 07: 146.11
[2105] Quote in the third person from People interview: Clare Morrisroe, Diana's Last Secret: She Asked Me to Marry Her & Dodi, Says Priest, The People, 15 October 2000
[2106] 17 Dec 07: 9.11
[2107] 28 Jan 08: 108.9
[2108] 1998 Book Excerpt read out 17 Jan 08: 237.23
[2109] 20 Dec 07: 27.14
[2110] The Operation Paget Inquiry Report into the Allegation of Conspiracy to Murder Diana, Princess of Wales and Emad El-Din Mohamed Abdel Moneim Fayed, December 14 2006, page 29
[2111] Diana: Her True Story, Independent Television News, Documentary, 1998
[2112] Diana: Queen of Hearts, TV Documentary, Hallmark Entertainment, 1998
[2113] 18 Jan 08: 189.8
[2114] 13 Dec 07: 126.14
[2115] 14 Dec 07: 6.15
[2116] Rod Chaytor, Diana Exclusive: Car Parts Destroyed, Daily Mirror, 8 May 2006

[2117] Rod Chaytor, Diana Exclusive: Car Parts Destroyed, Daily Mirror, 8 May 2006

[2118] 7 Nov 07: 120.1

[2119] 7 Feb 08: 97.6

[2120] 7 Feb 08: 95.16

[2121] David Cohen, Diana: Death of a Goddess, 2004, p366

[2122] David Cohen, Diana: Death of a Goddess, 2004, p366

[2123] 7 Feb 08: 129.10

[2124] 7 Mar 08: 36.8

[2125] 7 Mar 08: 31.10 & 42.21

[2126] 7 Mar 08: 44.4

[2127] 7 Mar 08: 31.10

[2128] INQ0053605

[2129] 7 Mar 08: 40.5

[2130] Robert Thompson, Affidavit, 13 June 2001, reproduced in Diana Inquest: The Documents the Jury Never Saw, 2010, p598 (UK Edition)

[2131] Andrew Alderson, Coroner Seeks New Law to Forgo Diana Inquest, Daily Telegraph, April 1 2001

[2132] Andrew Alderson, Coroner Seeks New Law to Forgo Diana Inquest, Daily Telegraph, April 1 2001

[2133] Royal Coroner Resigns Diana Inquest After FOIA Revelation Shows He Had No Jurisdiction, FOIA Centre, 24 July 2006: www.foiacentre.com/news-diana-060724.html
Also reproduced in Appendix 1 of Part 4.

[2134] 2 Oct 07: 18.4

[2135] The Operation Paget Inquiry Report into the Allegation of Conspiracy to Murder Diana, Princess of Wales and Emad El-Din Mohamed Abdel Moneim Fayed: Overview, December 14 2006, page 1

[2136] 2 Oct 07: 9.19

[2137] 2 Oct 07: 18.4

[2138] The Operation Paget Inquiry Report into the Allegation of Conspiracy to Murder Diana, Princess of Wales and Emad El-Din Mohamed Abdel Moneim Fayed: Overview, December 14 2006, page 3

[2139] The Operation Paget Inquiry Report into the Allegation of Conspiracy to Murder Diana, Princess of Wales and Emad El-Din Mohamed Abdel Moneim Fayed: Overview, December 14 2006, page 2

[2140] The Operation Paget Inquiry Report into the Allegation of Conspiracy to Murder Diana, Princess of Wales and Emad El-Din Mohamed Abdel Moneim Fayed: Overview, December 14 2006, page 9

[2141] Christopher Leake, Exposed: The Diana Inquiry Cop Who Was On £1,000 A Day, Daily Mail, 23 December 2007

[2142] 14 Feb 08: 45.14

[2143] 31 Mar 08: 9.19

[2144] 11 Dec 07: 54.11

[2145] 11 Dec 07: 66.7

2146 31 Mar 08: 13.25
2147 7 Apr 08: 5.5
2148 26 Feb 08: 152.1

CPSIA information can be obtained
at www.ICGtesting.com
Printed in the USA
LVOW08s1146030817
543646LV00022B/990/P